Subnational Capital Markets in Developing Countries

From Theory to Practice

Subnational Capital Markets in Developing Countries

From Theory to Practice

Editors
Mila Freire and John Petersen
with Marcela Huertas and Miguel Valadez

LIBRARY ST. MARY'S COLLEGE

A copublication of the World Bank and Oxford University Press

ISBN 0-8213-5464-7

Library of Congress Cataloging-in-Publication Data

Subnational capital markets in developing countries: from theory to practice /
edited by Mila Freire and John Petersen.
    p. cm.
    Includes bibliographical references and index.
    ISBN 0-8213-5464-7
Debts, Public—Developing countries. 2. Capital market—Developing countries.
3. Subnational governments—Developing countries. I. Freire, Mila. II. Petersen, John E. III. World Bank.
HJ8899.S857 2003
332'.041'091724–dc22
                                                                        2003061373

Contents

Boxes

Figures

Tables

Preface

This book examines institutional aspects of subnational capital markets and presents case studies of subnational borrowing, showing what has worked, what has not, and why. As decentralization continues and urbanization spreads, local authorities need to provide more services with fewer resources from the central government. Subnational borrowing, leveraging on reliable cash flows and prudent fiscal management, can be an alternative for funding some investments, especially when the useful life of the service is long (such as schools, roads, and public utilities).

Worries that fiscal decentralization may contribute to structural deficits and fiscal imbalances are common, especially in countries where the main policy priority is to control aggregate public sector borrowing. When traditions of fiscal responsibility are weak, accountability systems are immature, and administrative discipline is poorly developed, there is a risk that lower-level governments may abuse their borrowing authority, contributing to aggregate fiscal imbalance with adverse macroeconomic consequences.

However, many analysts argue that, with an adequate legal framework and sound macroeconomic fundamentals in place, local government access to capital markets is compatible with fiscal stability and promotes development of an important segment of the financial market. Necessary conditions include effective supervisory authorities; judicially enforceable contracts; tax decentralization; civic norms that promote fiscal prudence; availability of skilled staff; and adequate accounting, disclosure, and reporting standards.

Increasing numbers of local governments are borrowing from banks and issuing bonds, although in these turbulent times the path has been neither steady nor smooth. During the 1990s 120 subnational governments in Latin America engaged in market borrowing, 150 in Eastern and Central Europe, 11 in East Asia, and nearly 500 in Africa. Domestic bond markets started to blossom in

Poland, Russia, South Africa, and Zimbabwe. However, by the late 1990s the international market for subnational debt entered a period of sustained slump. Domestic bond markets, though not immune to the troubled economic conditions and ongoing structural changes, have continued to rise in importance. The participation of subnational governments in these domestic markets—where success will be critical to reenergizing international access—is the focus of this study.

This book draws from the findings of the Global Program on Subnational Capital Markets launched in 1998 by the World Bank with the sponsorship of the governments of Austria, Finland, Japan, Spain, Sweden, and Switzerland. Led by Augusto de La Torre, Mila Freire, and Marcela Huertas under the supervision of Danny Leipziger and Guillermo Perry, the program examined the experiences of subnational governments in accessing domestic and international capital markets. The objective was a mixture of fact finding and analysis of how countries deal with subnational borrowing and how they reconcile it with budgetary and fiscal balance.

The two-year program significantly advanced knowledge in this area. Among the outputs were regional studies for Latin America, Central Europe, East Asia, and Sub-Saharan Africa, undertaken in collaboration with major universities, rating agencies, investment banks, and development banks. The findings were disseminated through seminars and workshops, international conferences, and training materials. The program brought to light the challenges of allowing subnational governments access to debt financing and the need for a regulatory framework that protects all interested parties: local governments, central governments, and bond issuers.

This book also draws on a variety of other sources and studies, consolidating that work and deriving lessons about how to improve efforts to promote credit market access. It pools information on the issuing of subnational debt and its characteristics, analyzes the role of macroeconomic conditions and market development in the success or failure of such borrowing, and offers policy guidelines for ongoing efforts. The goal is to assist the World Bank and its clients to work as strategic partners in developing and strengthening capital markets as sources of funds for local governments in emerging economies.

The book provides a framework for analysis based on a systematic study of subnational governments as borrowers and the array of credit markets in which they may operate. Complementing the framework is a set of case studies that document the recent experience of 18 countries in developing markets for subnational borrowers.

Mila Freire
Regional Advisor
Latin America and the
  Caribbean Region
World Bank

John Petersen
Professor
School of Public Policy
George Mason University

Acknowledgments

The book was prepared by John Petersen and Mila Freire, lead editors, with the collaboration of Marcela Huertas and Miguel Valadez. John Petersen was lead author, with chapter contributions from Asad Alam, Michael D'Angelis, Colleen Butcher, Benjamin Darche, John Dunn, Samir El Daher, Peter D. Ellis, Giovanni Giovanelli, Mathew Glasser, Steven Hochman, Robert Kehew, Kremena Ionkova, João C. Oliveira, David Rosen, Pryianka Sood, Stepan Titov, Rodrigo Trelles Zabala, Miguel Valadez, and Roland White. Useful insights and materials were obtained from many, including Barbara Boone (Moody's Investor Services), Jane Eddy (Standard & Poor's), and Gersan Zurita (Fitch Ratings).

Also very valuable were inputs prepared for the earlier work on subnational borrowing by AB Asesores, with the assistance of Marcela Huertas, on the Latin American case studies; Benjamin Darche on the European and Central Asian case studies; SRIC Corporation, Research Triangle Institute on the East Asian studies, and Enrique Asturizaga; and Remy Prud'homme on the African case studies. The initial project was encouraged and approved by Frannie A. Leautier, Vice President of the World Bank Institute, and funded by the President's Contingency Fund under the leadership of Mr. James D. Wolfensohn. The work was conducted under the supervision of Danny Leipziger, Director of the World Bank's Latin America and the Caribbean Region's Finance, Private Sector, and Infrastructure Department. Eleoterio Codato, Anwar Shah, and Clemente del Valle served as internal reviewers. Useful comments were received from Anjali Kumar and Victor Vergara and from external reviewers. The book was edited by Meta de Coquereaumont of Communications Development Inc., and Mary Fisk, Office of the Publisher, served as production editor.

Abbreviations and Acronyms

AMC	Ahmedabad Municipal Corporation
ARD/GFG	Municipal bond consulting firm
Arg$	Argentina currency unit
AVK	Securities and Finance Ltd./Corporation
BANOBRAS	Banco Nacional de Obras y Servicios Públicos
BAPEPAM	The Securities Regulatory Body in Indonesia
BAPPENAS	Indonesia's National Planning Agency
BAPRO	Banco de la Provincia de Buenos Aires
BGN	Bulgarian Currency Unit Leva
BIS	Bank of International Settlement
BNA	Banco de la Nación Argentina
BNDES	Brazil's Federal Development Bank
BNP	Bond Dealing Corporation [Argentina]
BOCON	Bonos de Consolidación
BPP	Banks Privatization Program
BSF	Bond Service Fund
CAPMAC	Capital Markets Assurance Company
CARE	Indian Credit Rating Agency
CEF	Brazil's Federal Housing and Savings Bank (Caixa Economica Federal)
CIP	Communal Investment Program
COA	Central Office of Audit
CLF	Consolidated Loan Fund
CMC	Chennai Municipal Corporation
CMIP	Consolidated Municipal Infrastructure Programme
CPSCL	Caisse de Prêts et Soutien aux Collectivités Locales
CRISIL	Credit Rating Information Service of India, Limited
CRR	Cash Reserve Ratio
CSFB	Credit Suisse First Boston
CSN	Brazilian company

CZK	Czech local currency
DAK	Indonesia government grant
DAU	Indonesia government equalization grant
DBP	Development Bank of the Philippines
DBSA	Development Bank of Southern Africa
DFLA	Development Fund for Local Authorities
DS	Debt Service
DTC	Depository of Notes in Argentina
EBRD	European Bank for Reconstruction and Development
ECCI	East Coast Constructions and Industries Private, Limited
EMU	European Monetary Union
ESAP	Economic Structural Adjustment Program
ESR	Environmental and Social Report
EU	European Union
EUR	Euro currency unit
FCL	Fiscal Coordination Law
FDI	Foreign direct investment
FEC	Communal Infrastructure Fund
FI	Financial Institution
FINDETER	Financiera de Desarrollo Territorial
GAAP	Generally Accepted Accounting Principles
GDP	Gross domestic product
GFIs	Government Financial Institutions
GoH	Government of Hungary
GOI	Government of India
GoTN	Government of Tamil Nadu
GRP	Gross regional product
GSIS	A pension fund
HCMC	Ho Chi Min City
HDFC	Housing Development Finance Corporation
HIGC	Philippines Government Guarantee
HUDCO	Housing and Urban Development Corporation
HUF	Hungarian currency unit
IADB	Inter-American Development Bank

ICICI	Industrial Credit and Investment Corporation of India, Limited
ICMS	Value-added tax in Brazil
ICRA	Indian Credit Rating Agency
IDP	Integrated Development Plan
IFI	Type of foreign debt [Russia]
IGT	Intergovernmental Transfer
IL&FS	Infrastructure Leasing and Financial Services Limited
IMF	International Monetary Fund
INCA	Infrastructure Corporation of Africa
IPTU	Brazil property tax
IRA	Internal Revenue Allotment [Philippines]
ISS	Brazil services tax
JBIC	Japanese bank
LALF	South African Loan Portfolio
LBP	Land Bank of the Philippines
LECOP	Argentinian money bonds
LGCF	Local Government Credit Fund
LGLA	Local Government Loans Institution
LGLB	Local Government Loans Board
LGU	Local Government Unit
LGUGC	Local Government Unit Guaranty Corporation
LIBID	Interest rate
LIBOR	London Interbank Offered Rate
Lpcd	Litres Per Capita Daily
LWUA	Local Water Utilities Administration
MBIA	Bond Insurance Company
MBS	Mortgage Backed Securities
MCMC Act	Indian Act
MDF	Municipal Development Fund
MFM Bill	Municipal Finance Management Bill
MLG	Ministry of Local Government
MoF	Ministry of Finance
MOHA	Ministry of Home Affairs
MUDF	Municipal Urban Development Fund

MUFIS	Czech Local Government Fund
NAFTA	North American Free Trade Agreement
NGO	Nongovernmental organization
NPA	Non-Performing Assets
NSE	National Stock Exchange
O&M	Operate and Monitor
OECD	Organisation for Economic Co-operation and Development
OMBs	Open Market Bonds
OTC	Over the Counter
OTP	National Savings Bank [Hungary]
PDAM	Local water utility
PDF	Provincial Development Fund
PNB	Philippines National Bank
POSB	Post Office Savings Bank
PPP	Public Private Partnership
PRI	Panchayati Raj Institutions
PSE	Public Sector Enterprise
RBI	Reserve Bank of India
RDA	Regional Development Authority Funds [Indonesia]
RDI	Government Loan
RSC levies	Regional Services Council levies
RTI/SCRI	Consulting Firm
S&P	Standard & Poor's
SEBI	Securities and Exchange Board of India
SLA	Subsidiary Loan Agreement
SLR	Statutory Liquidity Ratio
SOE	State Owned Enterprise
SSA	Sub-Saharan Africa
STP	Sewerage Treatment Plant
TE	Total Expenditures
TD	Tunisian currency unit (Dinars)
TNUDF	Tamil Nadu Urban Development Fund
TNUDP	Tamil Nadu Urban Development Project

TNUIFSL	Tamil Nadu Urban Infrastructure Financial Services, Limited
TR	Total Revenues
UBS	United Bank of Switzerland
UDI	Unidades de Inversión [México]
ULB	Urban Local Body
UNCHS	United Nations Centre for Human Settlements
UNDP	United Nations Development Program
UPAP	Urban Policy Action Plan
USAID	United States Agency for International Development
USD	United States Currency Unit
VAT	Value-added tax
ZAR	Zimbabwe currency unit

Executive Summary

Raising capital for investment in infrastructure facilities is a universal concern in developing and transitioning economies. These long-lived facilities are crucial for building healthier, better-served populations and for creating competitive economies. Properly planned, operated, and maintained, such investments provide benefits for many years. However, in these countries long-term capital is scarce and has many claimants.

The challenge to raise funds comes at a time of transition and uncertainty. Devolutionary changes in the scheme of governance and dispersal of fiscal decisionmaking are pushing down responsibility for meeting capital needs and for subsequently operating facilities to a vast array of provinces, cities, and villages. Concurrently, there is increasing pressure to make government at all levels more accountable to citizens and more attuned to the demands of the marketplace. This sensitivity to market behavior in the face of limited resources includes the drive to make more activities self-supporting, to curtail the provision of free service, and to shed services that the private sector can provide better.

A critical issue in this transfer of responsibility and fiscal resources from the center to subnational governments is how to increase the access of subnational governments to financial markets, broadly defined as the banking system and the securities markets. The word *markets* implies a system with a variety of borrowers and lenders and with credit allocation based on pricing decisions that balance supply and demand. It also implies an array of alternatives for accessing capital funds. Accordingly, the development of financial markets is an important objective for developing economies. As economies develop and financial markets mature, markets are expected to evolve to bring together subnational needs for investment capital and the supply of funds. Will that happen?

This book explores markets for subnational government debt and the successes and failures that emerging and transitioning economies have experienced in promoting the development of such markets over the past decade. It assesses these experiences and extracts lessons to inform future efforts to establish and strengthen local government access to credit and improve the chances for success.

The book has six parts. The first five parts establish an analytical framework for studying the way subnational government credit markets function, the kinds of credit instruments and security arrangements available, and the main participants in the market. From this analysis, much of which deals with the technical design of transactions and the attributes of debt instruments, come a number of findings that form the basis for policy guidelines. Part six is a series of country-based studies that review the experiences of building markets for local government debt. These studies show that a large variety of economic and institutional settings influence the nature and extent of local government borrowing, from large-scale borrowing in international markets to building more effective state-sponsored intermediaries.

The Analytical Framework

The analytical framework examines the components of the supply of and demand for subnational debt, noting several perspectives from which to assess the feasibility and desirability of introducing local government securities to credit markets.

Part 1. Political, Legal, and Financial Framework

Credit needs and market structures vary greatly and depend on the political, fiscal, financial, and legal settings in which they are embedded. Chapters 2 and 3 examine the tensions and difficulties caused by the devolution of fiscal systems and the risks associated with the decentralization of borrowing decisions. They discuss the needs for a hard budget constraint, managerial capacity, and transparency and ways to achieve them to promote effective markets. A description of the levels of financial market development and the frictions in creating new financial markets and greater competition among credit providers sets the scene for later chapters. Also explored are legal systems and their ability to support the operation of markets and to understand the contracts they must enforce.

Part 2. Borrowing Instruments and Restrictions on Their Use

Borrowing is at heart an economic activity played out in financial markets. It is technical, with its own nomenclature and methods of analysis that revolve around balancing risk and rewards. Chapter 4 discusses the characteristics of potential subnational borrowers and what qualifies them as candidates. It walks through the wide variety of subnational government structures and conditions, noting that many localities are too poor and too small to have the need or the resources to borrow in markets. In many other cases both the need and resources are there, but inexperienced and immature governments require help to become creditworthy borrowers, a subject that reemerges later. The discussion concludes that, while needs and capacities differ, it is best not to prejudge by overly restrictive classification systems. Where possible and with appropriate help, market access can help instill fiscal discipline and responsible behavior.

Chapters 5, 6, and 7 lay the foundations for the kinds of borrowing that may be undertaken by subnational governments and explore the nature of the resources that can be pledged to repay indebtedness. They examine the variety of borrowing instruments, their technical design (maturity, interest payment schemes), and the methods by which they are offered to the market. Markets with sufficient competition and transparency should be allowed a good deal of flexibility in setting the parameters of individual transactions within a general framework of widely shared rules. The corollary is that the more developed a market is, the more it can be relied on to enforce the "rules" for subnational borrowing.

Chapter 7 also turns to authorization and approval of subnational debt and the limitations that may be placed on its use and magnitude. The chapter examines the legal and market issues related to the various types of security that may be pledged. A review of the wide variety of restrictions and possible pledges argues for avoiding ill-designed, overly restrictive cures that can cause more harm than good.

To ensure that transparent procedures and overarching prudential restrictions are as useful as possible, there should be regularized rules that leave room for market-based determinations. Furthermore, notions of security must reflect the needs of financial markets, including sure and speedy remedies when transactions go awry. While comprehensive borrowing laws are a desirable end result, their construction should be incremental, occurring as borrowing needs arise and loan contracts are drafted. While not everything needs to be in place before markets can operate, participants should be mindful of elements that are still a work in progress.

Part 3. Characteristics of Financial Market Regulation and Disclosure

Chapters 8 and 9 consider the structure, operation, and regulation of the domestic financial markets in which subnational governments seek to borrow. Domestic credit markets are often small, have few participants, and are easily overwhelmed by the demands of the sovereign and the banking system. A recurring theme is the difficulty that markets have in matching governments' long-term borrowing needs with the limited investible funds and the short time horizons of investors. However, the types of investors that may be interested in purchasing subnational government debt are growing in rank and importance.

Also examined are the links between domestic financial markets and international markets. The emerging bond markets, recently viewed as a promising alternative source of funds, languished after the world monetary crises of the late 1990s and subsequent economic slowdown. Those markets, while sidelined, continue to have enormous potential capacity. However, until the international monetary system demonstrates greater stability and financial markets improve, the ability to tap that capacity is constrained by strong aversion to the risk found in emerging market credits.

Part 4. Evaluating, Monitoring, and Assisting Subnational Governments

The operation of financial markets depends on assessments of the creditworthiness of market participants. Only in that way can risks be judged and offset by adequate rewards. As chapter 10 details, a major concern in emerging markets is assessing the operations and financial conditions of subnational government borrowers as a basis for assessing risk to investors. The archetype of such assessment, or credit analysis, is the opinions of rating agencies. Their practices and the influence of their opinions are examined in chapter 8. Relying on credit ratings presents major issues for small and emerging financial markets where skills, resources, and markets for opinions are limited. Still, the value of the rating process in enforcing disciplined behavior can be great. The chapter also briefly examines the use of private credit enhancements, in particular, the use of bond insurance. Because of the uncertainties in emerging markets, the dominant private sector firms have shown little interest; however, some important homegrown applications have been found in emerging markets.

Chapter 11 discusses how surveillance and analysis of credits by markets can complement and benefit from the monitoring of subnational governments by higher level governments. The information produced in a good monitoring scheme is useful to market and government officials at all levels. In addition to illuminating how well governments are performing, such information is critical for enforcing prudential regulations. In practice, however, periodic financial reporting is a weak spot, often because it is not considered essential. Efforts to regularize and harmonize reporting and improve its content are indispensable to market development.

A related area is what the national government does when faced with local financial emergencies. Devising techniques that allow intervention to protect vital services, while seeing that weak budgeting and risky behavior by subnational governments are punished, is a difficult but necessary part of enforcing a hard budget constraint. A clear process for handling such circumstances and restoring local financial health reduces risk to markets but softens the budget constraint. Similarly, passing too much of the risk to the creditor can stifle market growth. Finding the right balance is the issue.

Chapter 12 focuses on how to assist subnational governments in gaining access to credit markets. The process faces a number of pitfalls and limitations, not only among prospective borrowers but in the markets themselves. The design of credit assistance programs must deal with the fact that there are strong twin traditions of curtailing subnational government access to private credit markets and of meeting capital needs through national government grants and concessionary lending programs. The long-term loan capital available for these programs typically is provided by multilateral and bilateral donor organizations through on-lending programs administered by central government agencies and guaranteed by the sovereign. While such competition makes private market development more costly and difficult, subnational governments will need to find a route if they are to meet large and growing needs for capital and to lessen obvious dependencies. Credit assistance to subnational governments covers a wide variety of possible aids, ranging from technical assistance and credit enhancements to specialized intermediaries and direct lending programs. Depending on the creditworthiness and managerial capacity of the subnational government and the nature and depth of the financial markets, each technique has its advantages and drawbacks. A promising technique is the use of a financial intermediary that combines the borrowing of smaller governments into larger issues that afford economies of scale while exposing the underlying borrowers to market-oriented requirements. Another is the use of credit enhancements to offer assurance to lenders while schooling borrowers in ways to improve their credit stature.

A major challenge in programs that directly extend credit is the need to avoid making subnational borrowers captives of such programs and to encourage borrowing in domestic markets where possible. Part of the solution is to integrate grant and lending programs in ways that not only encourage but also reward governments for achieving credit market access. Chapter 11 reflects on ways to extend the maturity of debt in markets that are unwilling or unable to lend for the long term.

Part 5. Policy Guidelines

Chapter 13 provides policy guidance based on experience, both good and bad, with subnational credit markets:

- While there may be no one "right way" of developing subnational credit markets (due to the enormous variety of circumstances and structures), there are ways of achieving that end where it is both desired and possible.
- Subnational borrowing appears to have clear positive effects on credit markets. While accessing credit markets imposes burdens and risks, exposure of subnational governments to the market's appraisal of transactions, demands for information, and requirements for budgetary discipline is beneficial and is an important component of responsible self-governance. While not all political and economic systems are capable of supporting a market for subnational debt, emulating the required behavior and laying the foundations for a market flowering when conditions permit are worthwhile activities.
- Weak, unstable, and corrupt central governments undermine the ability of subnational governments to achieve good credit ratings and the ability of financial markets to function fairly and efficiently. Instability in international financial markets renders them an unreliable, "fair-weather" source of funds, at least in the near term. Thus building viable domestic financial markets is an immediate task—one to which subnational governments may contribute if they are fiscally stable.
- Subnational governments could be given broader powers, the more open and competitive the financial markets they are to enter and the more stable their fiscal circumstances. Regulatory schemes for subnational borrowing need to have prudential limits that are clearly stated, well-monitored, and enforceable. Good information systems are key components of success.

- In line with the development of markets, subnational governments need a clearly stated range of types of security they can pledge. Intergovernmental transfers and shared taxes often predominate as sources of funds. Especially in fiscal systems that want subnational self-determination as well as the economies of central collection of revenues, the ability to use and pledge these funds is vital to providing adequate security to investors. Where all subnational revenues are consumed by expenditures for vital services, subnational governments should not be borrowing.

- Information and subnational accountability are key factors in the effective operation of markets. Assessment of risk, crucial for determining the cost of capital, requires reliable, complete, and timely information. Subnational governments need to develop the capacity to report and manage their affairs in plain view. Without the discipline of the hard budget constraint, markets have little reason to distinguish among credits, and the rationale for market allocation of resources is lost.

- Credit assistance should be used surgically, with supporting efforts to build subnational skills to make financial decisions. Credit assistance should help subnational governments tap into private credit markets. The integration of grants and concessional lending, with access to conventional markets essential to avoid undermining conventional markets. For small borrowers and shallow markets, either bank-centered or specialized lending intermediaries hold promise as ways to take advantage of economies of scale while preserving market-driven behavior and constraints.

Part 6. Country Case Studies

Part 6 consists of 18 country studies on subnational borrowing. The studies vary in approach, but the shared objective is to examine recent experience with subnational borrowing and to assess what has worked and what has not and the reasons for the successes and failures. The studies illustrate the wide range of government and market settings.

Latin America and the Caribbean

Latin America has the highest volume of subnational borrowing in private markets of developing regions, but with borrowing highly concentrated among large provinces and major cities. Much of the credit has been used to fund accumulated operating deficits. Through the years, huge central government bailouts were engineered to avoid the collapse of the debtor governments. Accumulated debt reached such great proportions in Argentina and Brazil, as it had in Mexico before them, that its continued financing has been a major source of economic destabilization.

Argentina and Brazil both had some early success in the sale of subnational debt in the emerging international bond markets. However, recent defaults have largely closed these markets to them. The excesses by a few large borrowers have precluded many smaller ones from enjoying market access, as national governments tightened the regulatory leash. A legacy of bad debt behavior continues to plague the weakened domestic markets.

In contrast to Argentina and Brazil, Colombia essentially used a market-based mechanism to impose limits on local borrowing, allowing it to continue in a controlled environment. Colombia made a significant shift—though with restrictions—toward decentralization in the 1990s. Initially, borrowing restrictions were lax because of legislated mandates to increase central transfers, and subnational borrowing doubled relative to GDP. The transfers contributed to growing fiscal deficits of the central government. In 2001 the central government implemented new laws to streamline the intergovernmental transfer regime and free up extra revenues to address imbalances. The new laws require approval from the Ministry of Finance for additional debt and link borrowing controls to the fiscal health of local governments. Thus strong central control curbed an earlier acceleration in subnational borrowing. Surprisingly, continuing deficiencies in the regulatory framework have not led to widespread fiscal difficulties, though decentralization and mandated spending have continued to strain fiscal balances.

Mexico, meanwhile, has taken a bold initiative to resurrect its previously troubled subnational borrowing by requiring that bank loans and bond issues be rated by internationally recognized rating agencies. All these countries have large vertical imbalances, with subnational governments highly dependent on central government collection and transfer of revenues. However, even among the wreckage of the Argentine system, some positive lessons have emerged on the use of trustees and the structuring of loans to lessen the risk of devaluation.

Sub-Saharan Africa

Sub-Saharan Africa exhibits great contrasts in subnational government borrowing, with major challenges for the future. Both South Africa and Zimbabwe have had relatively sophisticated financial systems and active municipal bond markets.

In South Africa prior to 1994 municipal borrowing was largely limited to relatively well-off, historically "white" municipalities and was effectively underwritten by central government. From the late 1990s to the present the central government has undertaken a large number of structural, institutional, and policy reforms in subnational government. The ongoing change and uncertainty this introduced into the municipal sector, coupled with ongoing problems of budgetary and financial management in many subnational governments, have created a climate in which municipal lending has stagnated. Notwithstanding the success of certain private sector initiatives targeted at improving access to the markets (in particular, the Infrastructure Finance Corporation of South Africa), private sector lending to municipalities has declined while public sector lending has expanded. As of mid-2003, with crucial aspects of the legal and regulatory framework governing municipal finances and municipal borrowing still to be enacted, the future of the private municipal debt market—both direct bond financing and intermediated debt—remains unclear. This lack of clarity exists despite the sophistication and liquidity of South Africa's capital markets and significant potential demand from subnational governments that badly need funds for investment in local infrastructure.

Zimbabwe illustrates a situation in which a small municipal credit market was created and sustained artificially for many years by central government policies that favored—even compelled—institutional investment in subnational lending and, accordingly, entrenched moral hazard, with predictable results. The policy issues surrounding this market and attempts to reform it have been dwarfed by the impact of the larger political and economic crisis that has consumed Zimbabwe for the last few years. Until this nationwide crisis is resolved, it is most unlikely that borrowing will become an effective, accessible form of financing for subnational authorities in Zimbabwe or that any initiative to modernize subnational borrowing practices will have a reasonable chance of success.

Middle East and North Africa

North Africa, as represented in the Tunisia and Morocco case studies, presents a different approach to the issues of subnational credit markets. Both countries have continued in a highly centralized political system where subnational financial markets and subnational governments are only slowly gathering new powers. With limited banking systems and nascent financial markets, the focus has been on onlending activities, financed by donor loan programs. Meanwhile, most major infrastructure spending remains a central government responsibility, and subnational capital needs tend to be for small projects. The institutional framework needed to make subnational credit market access a reality remains to be developed. The next stage of development has been to propose the use of financial intermediaries that would access markets on behalf of smaller subnational governments. In this case, the specialized lending institution would play a twin development role: instilling more fiscal discipline and accountability in subnational governments while providing a new investment outlet for markets.

Asia

Asian nations that are emerging from highly centralized government structures reflect very different stages of economic development.

China, Indonesia, the Republic of Korea, and the Philippines have diverse experiences with subnational borrowing.

The People's Republic of China presents something of an enigma: a highly centralized state that is loosely organized, with extreme variations in subnational fiscal capacity and high levels of investment by companies owned by subnational governments that themselves cannot borrow. Although China is a unitary state, it has devolved a great deal of spending responsibility to its subnational units, which are both legion in number and, at the provincial level, as large in population as many countries. While the subnational governments are precluded from borrowing directly using their own credits, they effectively borrow through special-purpose vehicles, which are wholly owned companies that have their own revenues and often supply infrastructure needs on a quasi-commercial basis. Rationalizing the activities of these "off–balance sheet" borrowers, which often have to rely on borrowing from state-owned banks, is a major challenge the country faces as it carefully enters into a regime of financial markets—and the world's financial markets.

Before the financial crisis of 1997 Indonesia had embarked on a plan to offer local water utility and housing bonds in its small but relatively active domestic bond market. Following the East Asia financial crisis, the government structure has undergone radical reform, and a rapid and pervasive devolution of government power is under way. Indonesia's difficult economic conditions, a beleaguered banking system, and political turbulence have delayed resumption of efforts to steer subnational governments toward credit markets. While access is being contemplated, many subnational governments have defaulted on outstanding loans from the national development fund, and all subnational borrowing has ceased. Resolution of defaults and restoration of domestic financial markets are needed before subnational borrowing resumes. How that borrowing should be accomplished within the new political framework is a topic of considerable debate.

In the Republic of Korea there has been considerable borrowing by subnational governments, largely steered, if not controlled, by the central government. Subnational governments that conform to a national planning framework are permitted to borrow on favorable terms from national entities. Korea also has employed a form of "forced lending" that requires participation in loans by private firms that undertake certain nationally franchised activities. Borrowing in private financial markets is growing, however, including bond sales. The Korean bond market was badly shaken by the Asian crisis of the late 1990s and has taken time to recover its footing. As it does, subnational borrowers are likely to play an increasing role.

In the Philippines a small but active municipal bond market operates alongside a subnational credit system dominated by two government-owned banks and two municipal development funds. Recovering from a period of massive defaults that followed the Marcos regime, subnational governments have proved the most creditworthy borrowers in the Philippine economy, thanks to the large and steady transfers from the central government and the ability of state-owned institutions to intercept the transfers. A specialized bond insurance company was formed to increase subnational government access to private capital markets, and all recent municipal bond issues have used its coverage to enhance creditworthiness. Meanwhile, government financial institutions, while still benefiting from mandates that subnational governments use them as depositories, see their dominance challenged.

South Asia

India's federal system has undergone decentralization over the past decade, giving constitutional recognition to subnational governments. The federal relationship between the center and the states has been under stress, with significant vertical imbalances, and subnational governments often find themselves without resources. Nonetheless, there has been progress toward a more market-oriented subnational government borrowing regime. A municipal bond market has emerged, and concessionary development fund loans have been revamped to reflect market conditions and discipline. Tamil Nadu has converted its development fund from a state-administered loan fund to a public-private fund. Acting as an intermediary, this hybrid fund raises capital in domestic financial markets and complements its lending activities with technical assistance.

Europe and Central Asia

The transitional economies of Europe and Central Asia have addressed subnational government credit market access in a variety of ways, with several false starts and changes along the way.

Bulgaria's experience is representative of the more slowly evolving situations of fiscal decentralization found in South-Central Europe (the Balkans). The case study focuses on borrowing undertaken by the city of Sophia, which successfully executed loans in the euro-market and managed to maintain a credible budget under trying circumstances. Other transitional countries, with fewer resources and slower to set aside the old systems, are likely to follow models of bank lending and euro-market access by specialized intermediaries.

The Czech Republic, Hungary, and Poland followed more conservative paths in developing markets for subnational debt and avoided large-scale credit problems at the subnational government level. In each country a few major cities have successfully followed the sovereign government into international bond markets, and a few have entered domestic debt markets. After initial flurries of activity, however, most subnational government credit needs have been met by a combination of bank loans and development funds. Moreover, subnational capital demands have been reduced through tightened legal limitations on borrowing and the availability of receipts from the sale of privatized assets. Growth in subnational government borrowing in credit markets also has been retarded by weak economies, the uncertainties created by the unsteady devolution of fiscal powers to subnational governments, and the reluctance of these governments to borrow. Recently, many of their capital needs have been met by concessional loans and grants. European Union structural funds will make borrowing easier for subnational governments as the inhibiting factors mentioned above lose potency.

There have been several bond sales in these three countries' domestic markets, but the domestic bond markets have been slow to grow. This is due in large part to high interest rates, the small number of long-term investors, and the difficulties of attracting investors to small, soft-currency investments. The markets are generally illiquid, have few participants, and are preoccupied with financing sovereign debt. However, with these countries' pending accession to the European Union, domestic financial markets have begun to reflect the convergence and the broader European securities markets. The amply funded and far-reaching grant and loan activities of the European Bank for Reconstruction and Development now strongly influence the development of subnational government credit as several transitioning countries set their sights on meeting standards required to enter the European Union. While domestic bond markets will serve needs at the margin, the focus appears to be on bank lending and accessing the Eurobond market. As part of the process, it is likely that a role will emerge for specialized lending institutions ("bond banks") that can access euro credit markets to meet the needs of smaller borrowers.

The Russian Federation has had the most dramatic (and chaotic) experience with subnational borrowing, reflecting the fragmentation that occurred after the dissolution of the Soviet Union. In the mid-1990s, Russian regions and major cities issued large amounts of debt in both domestic and international financial markets. Massive defaults of subnational debt followed the 1998 financial crisis, as payments of shared taxes and grants from the central government evaporated and the national government was forced into default and devaluation. However, the two major cities of Moscow and St. Petersburg managed to avoid defaulting on their debts and have continued to enjoy some limited access to much shrunken markets. The case study describes St. Petersburg's struggle to preserve its creditworthiness in the midst of the turbulent conditions at the turn of the twenty-first century.

Chapter 1

Introduction

The decentralization[1] of governments throughout the world has brought new prerogatives and responsibilities to subnational governments as service providers to their local constituents. Part of a larger move toward greater democratization of government, reliance on markets, private provision of many activities formerly carried out by governments,[2] and globalization of commerce and finance, decentralization also has encompassed a desire to use private capital markets as allocators of credit.

In developing countries the twin tasks of building more dispersed and democratic governments and opening economies to freer markets and greater private ownership have been attempted in tandem—and have proved a difficult undertaking. A reduction in barriers to the movement of capital and goods has been a nearly universal objective.[3] However, implementation of the required reforms has meant tough competition for domestic industries and increasing constraints on the fiscal and monetary policies of national governments. In the face of economic slowdowns and unstable financial markets, many emerging and developing economies have found privatization and the opening up of their economies to be painful and unpopular. The steep price and uncertain benefits of joining global markets have their critics.[4]

Subnational governments, for their part, are being required to do more things, to do them more efficiently, and to be more self-reliant in raising resources.[5] At the same time devolution and hard-pressed budgets have constrained the ability of central governments to provide for the needs of subnational governments. After years of neglect and with expectations rising, the needs for infrastructure are particularly daunting. The enormous funding requirements cannot be met either practically or equitably without long-term investment. International lending and grant-giving institutions, another traditional source of funds, are also limited in their resources and restricted by rules and customary practice to dealing only through sovereign governments.

Nevertheless, the increased need of subnational governments to mobilize private capital to meet their infrastructure requirements is seen as a positive development in prompting the movement toward greater democratization and decentralization. The day-to-day scrutiny of government operations by credit markets helps to reinforce transparency and encourage efficiency and prudence. However, the markets' rewards are not without risks. Efficient functioning of markets requires rules of procedure for both buyers and sellers and an overarching societal agreement on what is for sale and what is not.

Realizing the Promise of Access to Financial Markets

This book examines the experience of subnational governments in accessing the credit marketplace, seeking lessons about how to realize the promises of credit market access while avoiding the pitfalls. The focus is on countries that are either "developing," in the sense that they are attempting to attain more modern and productive economies, or "transitioning," in the sense that they are moving from a highly centralized and large government sector to a more decentralized and market-based one.[6] Countries often have characteristics of both groups. The commonality is that they are relatively poor in the material sense, have a large central government sector, and have underdeveloped financial markets.

Countries differ, however, in the role that subnational governments have in financial markets and in the nature of their financial markets. Whatever the goals of greater autonomy and capacity at the subnational level, subnational governments vary greatly in political power and decisionmaking authority, in part reflecting differences among unitary states, hierarchical federal states, and governance systems that recognize separate spheres for each level. These differences are embedded in constitutions and legal systems that condition the degree to which subnational governments are free to act and to control the resources with which to act.

Some systems have been devolved at least on paper for many years (as in several Latin America countries), while others are starting from scratch (such as the transitioning countries of Eastern and Central Europe and several Asian counties). Institutional structure and history are important: many of the harsher lessons about balancing subnational debt finance[7] with national macroeconomic stability have to do with the misadventures of poorly designed governmental systems and long-standing problems of fiscal mismatches, political corruption, and mismanagement.

The nature of credit markets also varies. Few developing countries have active securities markets. Where the markets do exist, subnational governments have rarely been participants. Significant domestic markets for subnational debt have begun to emerge in some countries, but the passage has been neither easy nor swift. In a few areas, such as South America, some subnational governments have been active borrowers, but results have been uneven. In most other parts of the world, such as South and Southeast Asia, development at the subnational level has been slower. In the transitioning countries of Eastern and Central Europe, which have had substantial government restructuring and credit market development, subnational borrowing from private sources has risen slowly.[8]

Several larger and better-known subnational governments have borrowed in foreign markets, an avenue that appeared promising until the twin crises of foreign currency collapse and global economic slowdown that occurred in the late 1990s. While restoration of world capital markets will help governments meet their financing needs, the more immediate issue for the vast majority of subnational governments in developing countries is how to raise funds in domestic capital markets.

Presenting Governments with Market-Based Alternatives

Several vantage points are possible when surveying subnational government access to financial markets. One is that of the "macro-level" policymaker determining how best to fit a municipal borrowing component into domestic and international credit markets, given a host of other policy constraints and objectives. A second is that of the prospective subnational government borrower, intent on achieving as much flexibility as possible in financing decisions and on securing capital on the best possible terms. A third is that of the lender or investor who needs information to assess relative rewards and risks (including remedies in case of trouble) and assurances that the rules of the game will not be violated or changed arbitrarily.

While these three views are not always consistent, the ultimate objective is the same: to improve subnational governments' access to private credit markets in ways that are consistent with the overall fiscal health of government and the viability of the domestic financial markets. However attractive the rhetoric, achieving the objective requires making choices and taking risks.[9] Without being prescriptive about a best approach in all cases, this book starts from the premise that subnational control and decisionmaking are desirable outcomes that should be cultivated and encouraged. While acknowledging the need for rules, the book also argues for maximizing competition among private sector financial options at the subnational government level, where possible and prudent. This reflects a belief that presenting governments with market-based alternatives is invariably better than any single "my way or no way" of doing things. The book further calls for a liberal view of the risks that subnational governments should be allowed to run; this liberal view entails a presumption that these governments assume the risks at their own peril but that they do so in capital markets that are fair and reasonably efficient.[10]

The terms *credit market* and *capital market* are used broadly. In many emerging economies the banking system is the leading provider of credit—and the banking system too is likely to be undergoing transformation. The reliance on banks may be either a substitute for or a precursor to a functioning domestic securities market in subnational government obligations.

Where possible, a securities market should be seen as a desirable means of obtaining long-term capital. Appealing to the rapidly growing numbers of nonbank institutional investors, securities markets were developing rapidly until repeated crises struck emerging bond and equities markets in the late 1990s. Activities in these markets slowed abruptly in reaction to unsettled conditions in global financial markets, a series of currency crises, and the general slowing of the world economy. The arguments in favor of securities markets do not deny the critical importance of the banking system as the bulwark of the financial system. To develop and thrive, markets for longer term debt require strong banking systems on which they can depend for a reliable system of payments. In many countries, the practical outcome may be to promote competition among institutions that lend to subnational governments or even to find ways to reproduce the benefits of competition. Immature capital markets should not deter efforts to create structures that can reproduce such benefits.

Setting Out the Analytical Framework

Thus the analytical framework for this study rests on the principle that a subnational government securities market is desirable and that subnational borrowing will be dictated largely by the operation of the market, working within a framework of rules necessary to keep it a free and efficient allocator among competing uses. Many conditions need to be met, but four are key:

- Subnational governments borrow of their own volition and rely on their own resources for security and repayment of debt.
- Capital markets are free of excessive restrictions—with an arm's-length relationship between government and markets and banks—and allocate resources on the basis of risk and reward.
- The market has full access to the information required to assess the financial condition of borrowers and to determine risk and reward.
- Subnational borrowing is subject to appropriate oversight by the central government before it is made available. The central government plays a supportive role, intervening only when well-established rules of borrowing are flouted or subnational government mismanagement threatens fiscal crisis.

The ability—and desire—of governments and financial markets to achieve these conditions depend on several related policy and technical issues. A variety of government structures, schemes of devolution, and problems of macroeconomic stability influence decisions about the nature and feasibility of subnational government borrowing (chapter 2), as do a country's legal systems and financial market structures (chapter 3). Thus it is important to understand the political, economic, and legal environments in which subnational government borrowing occurs.

In analyzing options and possibilities for markets in subnational obligations, some key questions need to be asked. On the borrowers' side, important issues are credit capacity, borrowing powers, and regulation within the government sector (chapters 4–7). What types of debt security are available? What debt instruments are to be used? What types of subsovereign governments are good candidates to borrow? How is subnational debt to be authorized? What limitations should be placed on borrowing? What is the role of monitoring and oversight? What are the remedies in case of fiscal problems?

On the investors' side, regulation, investor needs, and the operation of financial markets are important concerns (chapters 8 to 12). What is the financial market structure? Who are the potential investors, and what are their investment objectives and constraints? What is the regulatory framework of the marketplace? What is the role of disclosure, and how is it accomplished? What is the role of credit analysis and credit ratings? How can the private sector mitigate risks? How should credit assistance be provided to comport with the market?

These questions represent economists' familiar separation between the demand for loanable funds by the subnational government sector and the supply of funds by private suppliers of credit. This separation is conceptually useful, but in practice matters are more complicated. The links between subnational governments and credit markets, even in countries with only a nascent financial sector, are diffuse and complex. Few actors are interested in only one financial relationship, such as borrowing, and the relationships are often more than financial. Nevertheless, the point of departure is that subnational governments are increasingly important economic actors, and the stage on which decisions are made is increasingly that of the market. All these issues are explored in the first part of the book.

The second part is a series of case studies that discuss recent experiences in 18 developing and transitional countries. The case studies range from general reviews of subnational credit access on a countrywide basis to more detailed discussions of debt transactions and lending. The case studies present a rich variety of experiences, good and bad, with subnational government borrowing and offer lessons about which approaches have been successful and why. They also illustrate experiences that have been disappointing and attempt to explain why.

Notes

1. The terms *devolution, decentralization,* and *deconcentration* are frequently used synonymously to describe the process of giving more decisionmaking power to subnational governments. In practice, this process varies greatly, as does the degree to which fiscal powers are devolved. In many cases, decentralization has meant a dispersal of spending and taxing powers that remain tightly controlled by the central government. In other cases, localities have been given a full range of taxing and spending powers, including the power to borrow. The terms are used interchangeably unless otherwise noted.

2. The conflict between government control and the freeing of markets was a common theme throughout the twentieth century and is treated on a global scale in Yergin and Stanislaw (1999).

3. This is the often-cited "Washington Consensus" for liberalizing trade and international financial flows. It has been actively promoted by the International Monetary Fund, the World Bank, the World Trade Organization, and the U.S. Treasury.

4. See, among others, Stiglitz (2002).

5. This book often uses the terms *local, municipal, subnational,* and *subsovereign* interchangeably, unless dealing in a specific context. The terms

can also encompass states, regions, provinces, and other subnational governments, depending on context.

6. The terms *developing, emerging,* and *transitioning* (*transitioning* is typically applied to Eastern and Central European states that are changing from communist to democratic regimes) are used interchangeably.

7. *Debt, loans,* and *bonds* are used interchangeably to refer to subnational government debt finance, depending on context.

8. Noel (2000) notes that subnational debt markets have grown rapidly in Argentina and Brazil (representing as much as 5 percent of GDP), but they remain "embryonic" in most emerging and transitioning economies, including the relatively advanced states of Central Europe (p. 1). He foresees a clash between the rapidly rising needs for infrastructure finance and the limited development of the domestic markets.

9. Noel (2000) sees the movement as being from either a nonexistent or a monopoly market for subnational government debt to one of active competition among alternative sources of private capital (from a closed to an open system of financing investment needs). It is a movement filled with risks and tensions among key stakeholders: the national government, private investor institutions, and subnational governments. This is usually a simplification since there are competing interests within the sectors. The private sector has tensions among commercial banks, other financial institutions, and securities markets. The central government may have competing interests among agencies (the treasury and the central bank, for instance) and competition among the local governments themselves, which once were agents for the central government and now are striving to become more independent.

10. A source of continuing concern is that of the moral hazard that local governments present when they enter capital markets with an implied sovereign guarantee that the national government will be compelled to bail them out if things go wrong and they cannot pay their debts as promised. There are a large number of assumptions surrounding the implied existence of such guarantees and quite a bit of history as well. The assumption in this book is that sovereigns as part of the move toward devolution are reluctant to make such guarantees and are inclined to have their local governments face a "hard" budget constraint.

Part I

Political, Legal, and Financial Framework

John Petersen and Mila Freire

Chapter 2

Fiscal Devolution

Devolution—the granting of greater political and fiscal responsibility and power to subnational units of government and the performance of more government functions at the subnational level—has been in full swing worldwide for the last decade. A 1994 World Bank report noted that of the 75 developing countries with populations greater than 5 million, all but 12 were in the process of transferring fiscal power from the center to subnational governments (Dillinger 1994). In the once highly centralized communist states with virtually no subnational autonomy, devolution has been a universal phenomenon. In some countries subnational governments have long existed but frequently only as agents of the central or provincial government and with little real authority or financial autonomy. In other countries, a history of tension between competing "sovereigns" at the center and in the regions has left a legacy of imperfect and damaged intergovernmental relationships.

Principle of Subsidiarity

There are well-rehearsed economic and political arguments in favor of devolution that appeal to the efficiency and desirability of grassroots decisionmaking and accountability. To the economist the subnational government's greater knowledge of subnational needs strengthens the links between tax revenues and spending benefits that accrue to subnational taxpayers. Subnational authorities can respond more readily and effectively to local conditions, resulting in improved delivery of government services. Bringing expenditure assignments closer to revenue sources enhances accountability and transparency. Political arguments often adhere to the principle of subsidiarity, that is, in a democracy, the lowest level of government that can determine and effectively meet the needs of its constituency is the most appropriate structure of government.

The details of the extent and effectiveness of devolution are specific to each country. The process can be complex and filled with uncertainty. Making the transition from a highly centralized system of governance to a more localized one is a serious task, subject to interruptions and miscalculations along the way.[1] In the end, the degree of devolution depends on the degree of *de jure* fiscal autonomy and *de facto* willingness and ability to tap resources. Countries vary greatly in both respects.

Borrowing and Devolution from the Subnational Perspective

Subnational access to credit markets usually derives from devolution. Borrowing becomes a critical issue of local initiative only when there is a move toward localized delivery of services requiring capital investments that will not be met by central government resources. Devolution is of great practical consequence for credit markets and for how subnational governments access those markets. If effective, devolution places decisionmaking at the subnational level and erodes what has often been the de facto monopoly of the central government over subnational capital financing decisions, including the use of credit.

With decentralization of finances and financial decisionmaking, investors and lenders care how well subnational governments are managed because they have money at risk, and their scrutiny drives greater transparency and efficiency at the subnational level. However, subnational governments first must have the ability to raise and use resources and to make binding commitments that are politically and legally sustainable. For many countries, this constitutes a huge change in perspective and in the balance of political power.

Measuring Fiscal Decentralization

While the idea of devolving spending, revenue-raising, and borrowing decisions from central to local and regional governments seems conceptually clear, the process has proven cumbersome, contentious, complex, and confusing.[2] The shifting down of spending responsibilities often has not been accompanied by a corresponding shifting down of resources, so that subnational governments have been faced with both mandated spending requirements over which they have little influence and weak and constrained revenue systems.

Most devolutions have involved large shared-tax and fiscal transfer programs that are not tied to specific spending programs. Furthermore, such financial management practices as public deposit management, investments, and borrowing procedures have been slow to adjust to the new devolutionary regime, restricting the financial decisionmaking ability of subnational governments and their day to day management and planning (see box 2.1). In India, for example, State Finance Commissions are responsible for implementing the devolution of financial resources to subnational governments. They regularly review the finances of subnational bodies (panchayats and municipalities) and make recommendations on the sharing and assignment of state government revenues and grants in aid (see the India case study, chapter 24).

Quantifying the amount of subnational autonomy in a fiscal system is difficult. Internationally statistics on government finance leave large gaps in understanding the nature of local revenue and expenditure systems and the degree of autonomy that subnational governments have to make "devolved" fiscal decisions (Ebel and Yilmaz 2001). For example, systems with substantial dictated expenditures or programs of large fiscal transfers and tax sharing that are subject to discretionary change at the center do not qualify as devolution, nor do categorical grants from the central government that are restricted to specific uses. Fiscal autonomy is also effectively lessened when subnational governments cannot control either the rate or base of local taxes.

The upshot of devolution in many developing and transitional countries is that subnational governments are undergoing structural change and typically have restricted power to borrow and limited own-source resources for securing debt. Understandably, would-be lenders, unfamiliar with the ways of subnational government and aware of the intergovernmental tumult, have been cautious in their lending.

Budget Constraints and Local Control

Apart from a subnational government's ability to raise taxes, levy charges, and commit resources as it sees fit, effective devolution requires a "hard budget" constraint at the subnational level. A hard budget constraint means that the subnational government must live within its resources and cannot depend on the central government to cover its deficits or repay its debts. A hard budget is possible, as long as certain basic services are provided and the risks are acknowledged and "paid for." Assumption of the risks by those who have decided to take them is an important and often delicate point in governance. Freedom to fail is one of the liberties and consequences that accompany greater subnational government freedom and responsibility in decisionmaking.

Fiscal discipline is achieved only if those taking risks and failing are made to pay the price. Activities and borrowers deemed unsuitable for paying a price for mistakes may be effectively precluded from the markets ei-

---

Box 2.1. Devolving Responsibility for Elementary School Teachers' Salaries in Romania

In 2000 the Romanian government passed to municipal governments the responsibility for paying public elementary school teachers' salaries; however, the salaries were set uniformly at the national level. The central government transferred revenues to the municipalities to pay the salaries, dedicating a portion of the national value added tax (VAT) for that purpose.

With the new spending requirements, local government budgets increased substantially and their composition changed. The discretionary portion of local budgets plummeted, while the portion going to employee wages rose. The new payments significantly increased overall transfers to localities, especially earmarked revenues.

The change also affects the borrowing status of Romanian municipalities. By law, the increase in current operating revenues from permanent sources increased the amount that a local government could borrow based on total current revenues. However, the new exposure of local government budgets to paying the salaries of a large and influential employee group and the uncertain reliability of future shared revenues from the VAT probably reduced the amount investors are willing to invest. By impairing the future fiscal flexibility of localities and their ability to pledge funds for debt payment, the change may have made borrowing more difficult. The episode indicates the limitations of legally imposed ceilings and the importance of market perceptions in deciding what is prudent behavior.

Source: Petersen 2002.

---

ther by fiat or by the unwillingness of investors to invest. Both developed and emerging credit markets are full of examples where certain activities and facilities are held as essential to the public sector and cannot be used as collateral to secure borrowings. Markets in developed economies have found ways to achieve sufficient security.

There has been considerable concern, particularly among central governments, about the destabilizing impact of fiscal decentralization, especially of excessive subnational borrowing. They worry that decentralization will permit, if not encourage, subnational governments to spend too much, forcing central governments to run deficits of their own as they bail out the local excesses. This kind of destabilizing behavior arises primarily in one of two largely unrelated circumstances. One is the case of federal system countries with weak fiscal coordinating power by a central government that will not or cannot impose a hard budget constraint on the subnational governments.[3] Another is the case of subnational governments that are the putative borrowers from an entity such as a national development fund but the borrowing decisions are effectively made by the central government, with the localities merely "signing on the dotted line," or where the localities were placed in a position of substantial moral hazard because of the nature of the program design (see the Indonesia case study, chapter 25).

Another part of the devolutionary equation is the need for local control of resources that can be used to secure debt. Two problems are common. First, subnational revenue systems are often inadequate, and meeting expenditures mandated by the central government exhausts the budgetary resources. As a practical matter, even if subnational governments have potentially viable revenue sources and can muster the political will, the inability to raise taxes and spend funds as they wish can be a severe constraint on the ability to borrow. Second, even where localities have substantial physical assets, they are legally precluded from using them to secure credit. This inability to pledge physical assets has been a constraint in many countries where bank lending, in particular, is secured by asset pledges.

Impact of Devolution on Subnational Finances

The impact of devolution on the ability to borrow has to do with how resources are assigned to governments and how resources are balanced against spending responsibilities. Several factors affect the resources available to subnational governments for meeting both operating needs and debt commitments. Among them are the following:

- The overall size of transfers and their size relative to a subnational government's overall operating revenues.
- The extent of earmarking of transfers (as opposed to being generally usable or available for debt service).

- The revenue sources legally available to subnational governments, the revenue potential of those sources, and the ability of subnational governments to use revenues for general rather than specific purposes.
- The flexibility subnational governments have in setting rates or charges and defining tax and charge bases.
- The overall political and institutional risk to which revenue and fiscal transfer systems are subject, that is, the potential for producing changes that can disrupt subnational finances.

On the spending side, a related set of factors affects subnational government creditworthiness and credit access:

- The degree of discretionary spending, the size and type of mandated spending, and the impacts of mandates on the future flexibility of subnational budgets.
- How specific expenditure types are funded, such as those earmarked from specific revenue sources.
- The degree of flexibility a subnational government has in adjusting its budget over the economic cycle or in response to changes in local conditions.
- Demographic and economic factors that determine the demand for services and the ability of localities to control or plan for them.

The more that subnational governments are expected to be self-reliant in financing their activities, the more these factors count. Conversely, to the extent that subnational government borrowing is formally guaranteed by the central government (or that credit markets expect a national government bailout of subnational government debt in the event of difficulty), the less fiscal devolution has taken place; accordingly, the less important local fiscal affairs and demonstrated discipline are to private sector lenders.

Devolution, Borrowing, and Macroeconomic Stability

The subnational government's desire to pursue fiscal autonomy is one side of the devolution coin. The other is the central government's need to maintain macroeconomic and fiscal balance, which implies maintaining subnational debt under limits.

Central government concerns over control of the macroeconomic balance stem from its need to manage the national economy and currency and so the need to have centralized monetary and fiscal policies. Decentralization of a large share of public expenditures, even when subnational governments are constrained by taxation and borrowing limits, can adversely affect aggregate demand and international competitiveness, undermining national stabilization policy.[4] Similarly, public debt at local levels that becomes effectively "monetized" can interfere with monetary policy and, by extension, hamper the central bank's effectiveness in carrying out national policy.

In theory, decentralization should establish a virtuous cycle of behavior by subnational governments that helps to maintain macroeconomic stability. Bringing expenditure assignments closer to revenue sources should enhance accountability and transparency in government actions. Underpinning the downward shift in responsibility is greater reliance on the benefit principle; taxpayers should pay for the public services they receive and get the services they pay for, linking taxes to the benefits provided. Taxpayers are made aware of the cost of goods and services that they consume and, as consumers, they should be more concerned about efficiency and better able to do something about it.

If poorly conceived and executed, however, decentralization can imperil macroeconomic stability. Given the greater difficulty in coordinating government actions when subnational governments enjoy greater policymaking autonomy, the challenge is to design a system of multilevel public finances that allows the efficient provision of local services while it maintains fiscal discipline nationally and subnationally (De Mello 2000). Much of the concern is rooted in the unwillingness of the central government to let go and in the web of political relationships between the central government and its subsovereign governments. Lack of discipline and transparency may induce subnational governments to spend beyond their means, leading to higher borrowing costs because of the risk premium associated with a higher probability of default.

Avoiding these problems requires that subnational governments exercise fiscal discipline and that their fiscal position be effectively monitored. Thus, decentralization should include either firm rules or strong incentives for prudence in debt and expenditure management. While these notions are conceptually straightforward, decentralization in practice is the product of political decisionmaking, and the required changes create winners and losers. Not surprisingly, decentralization in many countries has been plagued by confusion and compromise that undermine both the transparency of fiscal relationships and the fiscal discipline of the newly empowered subnational governments.

Decentralization of Responsibilities and Revenues

The literature on decentralization suggests rational guidelines for the allocation of responsibilities across government levels, assuming the managerial and technical capacity needed to carry them out. While the functions to be sorted out are many, as are the questions of local or regional points of service delivery and places of tax collection, a brief summation of principles is possible. Looking first at expenditures:

- The central level should retain expenditures that can strongly influence aggregate demand, that involve income redistribution, and that have large economies of scale or public-good characteristics on a national scale; examples include national defense, interstate communications, foreign policy, and research and development. Subnational governments generally assume responsibility for local activities such as local infrastructure and services.
- Sharing responsibilities should be considered in the case where the activity is national in scope but implementation is more effective at the subnational level, as in the case of education or health.

On the revenue side of the ledger:

- Base income taxation should be kept at the central government level to facilitate efficient collection and to preserve the government's macroeconomic stabilization and redistribution functions.
- Overlapping tax bases between the center and subnational levels are common in partial assignments of income tax, where subnational governments can piggyback on the national income tax by applying surcharges.
- To minimize unwanted tax-induced incentives, the central government should retain mobile tax bases such as the corporate income tax. A homogeneous tax system across all subnational governments is important to discourage enterprises from moving to areas with lower corporate taxes and eliminating tax competition among regions that could erode the tax base.
- The central level should receive the most unevenly distributed and fortuitous tax bases (such as natural resources) so that redistributive policies are possible and gross power differentials are not promoted inadvertently.
- Single-stage and excise taxes, such as the property tax, utility fees, and betterment tax, can be effectively assigned to the subnational lev-

el because the base is immobile and there is a close link between the tax and the benefiting user.[5] However, these guiding principles can collide with reality. In many cases, levels of government have traditional scopes of competency unrelated to their ability to raise revenues, requiring the transfer of funds from one level to another in an effort to balance resources and needs.

Intergovernmental Transfers

Transfers from the center reflect the disparity between decentralized revenues and the responsibilities associated with providing certain services at a subnational level.[6] While many services can be decentralized, revenue sources at the subnational level are generally inadequate to fund the services. Intergovernmental transfers, whether as a proportion of a set of central collected taxes or as grants, help fill that gap.

There is a vast body of literature on intergovernmental transfers (see, for example, Bird and Vaillancourt 1998). A critical issue is the impact of transfers during times of fiscal or other economic difficulty. The central government may need additional revenues, but the share of them appropriated to subnational governments is fixed. Grants from the central government tend to be more discretionary than shared revenues, a feature that may create revenue uncertainty for subnational governments in volatile economic times. Thus, an inherent tension exists between the predictability that is helpful to stabilizing subnational government finances and the rigidity that may destabilize the national fiscal balance.

Transfers can be important to credit market development, since they constitute a large share of available revenue and may act as security on subnational government loans and bonds. Transfers also can be limiting. In Hungary tight fiscal policies have constrained budgetary transfers from the central government, impairing the ability of subnational governments to meet the levels and standards of service required of them. Competing claims for scarce budgetary resources have led, in particular, to large funding gaps for local infrastructure investments (see the Hungary case study, chapter 29).

Subnational Borrowing as a Destabilizing Element

Major financial crises in Latin America in the late 1990s and in 2002 were in part a product of excessive subnational borrowing and central government assumption of subnational debt. This experience highlights the negative impact of subnational debt on the national aggregate debt exposure. It also underscores the difficulty that central governments can have in monitoring the exposure of subnational governments.

In theory, competitive capital markets establish interest rates for government debt according to differences in perceived risk and in the tax and regulatory benefits that holding such debt may afford. Interest rates (risk premia) reflect the borrower's creditworthiness when the risk is assumed by the subnational government and not absorbed by the central government through explicit or implicit promises of bailouts or guarantees. However, even where the central government backs subnational debt, market forces may induce greater fiscal discipline at the subnational level once the debt is traded on the open market. Greater fiscal discipline can improve resource allocation, eliminate waste, and benefit the local population directly by increasing resources. Two key assumptions are that capital markets are competitive and that bondholders or the governments themselves suffer the consequences. Without the threat of "pain," discipline fails on both sides of the market.

Problems in Subnational Debt Markets

Fiscal discipline by subnational governments depends in large measure on their relationship with the center. How much autonomy do they have, and will the central government step in—and, if so, when—to avoid financial calamity? Relationships between central and subnational governments can give rise to the problems of adverse selection and moral hazard.

Adverse selection arises when asymmetric information or misaligned incentives lead to decisions that would have been avoided with more information or a different set of incentives. Subnational governments have an incentive to hide negative information about their finances from potential investors. Information asymmetries, common in all markets, must be mitigated through legislation, regulation, and institutional development. Where well enforced, securities and tax fraud laws can be powerful antidotes.

Moral hazard refers to the creation of incentives that distort behavior because parties are not held accountable for the risks involved in their actions. A local jurisdiction with borrowing privileges needs to maintain fiscal discipline to retain an adequate credit rating and satisfy creditor scrutiny. However, where an explicit or implicit central government promise exists to bail out subnational government, the costs of default are transferred to the center and neither the borrower nor the lender faces the consequences of the borrower's failures. With the penalties removed, the costs of inadequate discipline disappear, so that over-lending and over-spending are "rational behaviors" for both borrower and lender. Perceived permissive behavior at the center inverts the incentive system, making it "profitable" for subnational governments not to live up to their obligations.

Worries about moral hazard stem from ambiguities in the relationships among the sovereign government, subnational governments, and potential creditors. Often, national governments have relaxed the subnational budget constraint by permitting or even encouraging excessive spending. Creditors base their investment decisions on the financial viability of the subnational government to which they lend. Because of the unstable flow of revenues and less knowledge about the creditworthiness of the subnational government, creditors often seek a sovereign guarantee. Private sector lenders and multinational institutions and bilateral lenders alike often require that subnational loans carry sovereign guarantees. Private lenders are understandably circumspect about the moral hazard such behavior entails. They are unwilling to extend nonguaranteed loans in competition against the risk-free borrowing that subnational governments effectively enjoy (or risk-free lending that subnational government creditors enjoy) with a sovereign guarantee.

Setting a Precedent

If past interventions by the central government have set precedents for future interventions, the cycle is difficult to break. Moral hazard challenges confront countries from the start of decentralization. In the early stages, when subnational authorities are not fully in control of local expenditures, the central government is expected to fill expenditure holes, as has happened frequently in transitioning countries. As a result, the subnational authority is not held fully accountable for its expenditures. This type of moral hazard should decline once the system of revenue sharing and grants is established and subnational governments are made accountable for the services assigned to them. However, the sequencing of assigning responsibilities and resources and applying appropriate restraints is often defective.

A central government that has a history of bailing out subnational governments sends an implicit message that it will intervene in the future. Changing this perception can be difficult, since the causes are often deeply ingrained in the political and financial systems. In theory, intervention can be designed so that the subnational government bears the costs if it defaults and needs help from the central government. However, convincing creditors that subnational governments need to be creditworthy to have access to credit markets requires a consistent and sustained policy of letting subnational governments default without bailing them out. In weak and unstable regimes the disruption caused by such failures may not be politically sustainable.

Why have central governments felt the need to intervene in subnational defaults? The answers are rooted in both politics and economics. Defaults where the creditor has effective remedies can lead to lost jobs and reduced services as subnational governments are forced to pay up. Where creditors are not able to enforce claims, private lenders may simply stop lending to those they hold responsible, including the central government. Creditors may threaten a downgrading of sovereign debt if subsovereign debt does not receive central backing.[7] Very large or systemic defaults may undercut the strength of financial institutions and cause them to close or rely on a state bailout of their own.

This pressure to tie subsovereign obligations to the central authority reinforces historical perceptions of the dependency of subnational authorities on the central government. The main prescription, besides disavowing any such implicit central guarantee, is to enforce local reliance on own-source and discretionary revenues. This, in conjunction with effective market regulation and stable central government policies on expenditure assignments and transfers, should mitigate the moral hazard problems of subnational borrowing., However, while a competitive financial market structure should be used to enforce and help instill fiscal discipline, a myriad of other conditions needs to be met as well. Effectiveness of market discipline depends on the extent of local accountability, which is in turn a function of transparency, available resources relative to expenditure assignments, fiscal management, and the political environment.

Transparency and Financial Management

Transparency—easy access to accurate and timely information about a government's finances—is often the major obstacle to financial market development. The few subnational governments that have accessed international financial markets have had to radically revise and upgrade their financial reporting practices (see box 2.2). Having little or no information on fiscal activity impedes reform. In the context of subnational government borrowing, transparency relates to budgeting, accounting, and auditing:

- *Budgeting*. In many countries subnational government budgets do not distinguish between current and capital expenditures or between ordinary revenues and loan receipts, or they provide inaccurate num-

---

Box 2.2. Rio and the International Marketplace

In the late 1990s Rio de Janeiro's municipal administration, in preparation for an international bond sale, gained a clear understanding of the need for transparency and adequate information disclosure. It was the first and only municipality in Brazil to retain internationally recognized auditors to examine its books. Even though the city's financial reporting was among the more comprehensive for Latin American subnational authorities, it still suffered from serious gaps. The city did not produce a balance sheet and, therefore, lacked a reliable view of its net asset position. In addition, it prepared financial statements in accordance with Brazilian legislation, which at times diverged significantly from international accounting standards. For the launch of its first issue of securities in the international market, Rio dramatically improved its reporting system, even providing regular and updated information on the Internet.

Source: Chapter 15, case study on Brazil.

---

bers for capital expenditures. The design of the fiscal transfer system may create incentives that foster misreporting of the overall financial picture. As a practical matter, it may be impossible to determine whether borrowing is used for investment or for financing a subnational government's short-term deficit. This lack of information undermines borrowing rules and impedes the ability to monitor for problems and compliance.

- *Accounting.* Deficient accounting rules and practices defeat transparency. Without a well-defined, uniformly applied set of accounting standards, it is impossible to judge a jurisdiction's financial health. Consequently, the absence of accurate reporting and clear applications of definitions undermines the establishment of effective parameters for borrowing, managing local assets and finances, and monitoring financial behavior.
- *Auditing.* Independent, third-party auditing of accounts can help ensure accuracy and legitimacy. Unfortunately, the list of possible auditing candidates in many developing countries is small, and consistent

auditing standards may not have been developed. Furthermore, few incentives exist to promote professional discipline and minimal checks of auditing practices.

Controlling Subnational Government Borrowing

Macroeconomic stability requires reducing the moral hazard that allows subnational governments to borrow too much and investors to lend to them unwisely. Needed is a hard local budget constraint requiring that the future resources to pay the debt be prudently calculated and the door to the national treasury be resolutely closed to bailouts. To accomplish this, some key ideas need to prevail:

- Rules for grants must be clear, and an effective monitoring system must be established for grants targeted to particular uses. Grants for capital purposes should be integrated with "market-based" loans to the extent feasible.
- Central government lending to subnational governments should be curbed where possible and subject to the fiscal capacity of subnational governments. Subnational governments without access to private capital can be "taught" debt management through borrowing from the central government. However, the possibility of graduating to private capital markets must exist, and the lending programs should not undercut the operation of private credit markets.
- Explicit limits on any sovereign guarantees should be set and the use of such guarantees should be avoided. Develop a prudent, rule-driven framework for subnational borrowing, setting forth clearly the appropriate limitations and procedures to follow.
- Any "implied" sovereign guarantee should be explicitly disavowed and procedures for dealing with defaulting or bankrupt subsovereign governments and with creditor rights and processes should be in place

Regimes for Coordination and Control

Controls on subnational fiscal relationships can be cooperative, rule-based, or direct central government regulation (Ter-Minassian and Craig 1997, chapter 7). The choice depends on the political heritage of the country and its form of government, the confidence that can be placed in the efficacy of market discipline, and success in imposing a hard budget constraint.

The cooperative model involves negotiation between national and sub-national levels to establish limits on indebtedness that place subnational governments firmly in line with macroeconomic objectives and key fiscal parameters. This approach maintains overall deficit targets and growth guidelines for revenue streams at the central government level. The main drawback is that cooperation may not be politically possible or may be lop-sided, with the center unilaterally "forcing down" decisions or the subnational government refusing to cooperate without major concessions. In the absence of a strong center to enforce discipline, the approach requires shared fiscal discipline and a conservative borrowing mentality. Weak fiscal management or weak central government leadership will derail the stability of the system.

A rules-based approach strengthens central control by embedding the framework for subnational borrowing within legislation. By establishing the rules upfront, it avoids the quarrelling between levels of government typical of the cooperative system. Uniform accounting standards are required to eliminate subnational governments' circumvention of the rules. This entails the creation of a financial information system that provides data on the expenditures and financial operations of all levels of government. Enforcement can come through the market or administrative oversight, with professionals attesting to observance of the rules and held culpable if they break them.

Direct central government control may involve setting annual limits on borrowing, reviewing debt proposals, or formally sanctioning specific debt transactions. Central controls allow debt policy to be readily linked with overall macroeconomic policy, but the process has several shortcomings. When there are many subnational borrowers, approvals can be time consuming. There are also issues of competency and corruption. Officials approving the transactions may have little knowledge or interest, and layers of approval always open the door to political discretion and corruption. Central government approval, especially in the context of donor-funded on-lending programs, can be viewed as tantamount to a guarantee. However, in domestic private markets, central review and approval need not imply a guarantee, and borrowing governments can still face a hard budget constraint. Nonetheless, if the central government approves all subnational borrowing, it may be politically difficult not to bail out subnational governments that default.[8]

The regime of subnational borrowing controls needs to be examined in the context of the overall argument in favor of devolution of political decisionmaking. Direct administrative control may be the most comfortable and conservative approach from the center's point of view, but it means a diminution in the fiscal powers and prowess of the subnational governments. It likely means less access to credit markets, a continuing subordination of local self-sufficiency, and continuing, if not greater, reliance on central resources. Eventually, the rules on subnational borrowing will reflect the stage of market and political development of each country, the rigor in employing strict budgetary constraints at the subnational level, independence from political cycles, and the strength of accountability mechanisms. The next chapters review how these components of subnational market development fit together.

Notes

1. A point not to be overlooked is that political and fiscal devolution calls for a substantial element of sacrifice on the part of national politicians that give away power and resources (and patronage) to lower levels of government in the process. As a result, for devolutionary movements to be effective, local political powers need to be persuasive and potent on the national level.

2. Perhaps unappreciated is the difficulty national governments have in reorganizing themselves to operate on a more local basis. In many countries, holding a central government job has been a reward for the brightest and best, and devolution has meant a step down in occupational status and a new constituency to serve. Familiar political and administrative power structures have been capsized in the process.

3. Argentina and Brazil have traditions of high levels of local and regional autonomy. For largely political reasons, the imposition of hard budget constraints proved impossible, and the national governments accumulated large debt burdens to cover the operating deficits of local governments (see chapters 14 and 15 for Argentina and Brazil case studies).

4. Subnational governments, if left unconstrained in their fiscal conduct, cause problems for the national government. For example, the imposition of local taxes on commerce and trade can adversely affect costs and revenues at the national level. Borrowing in foreign currency can lead to build-ups in foreign-denominated liabilities that create demand for foreign currency. Borrowing large amounts from banks can undercut creditworthiness if default looms. These problems are most evident in certain federa-

tions, such as Argentina, where the central government has weak control over subnational fiscal behavior.

5. See table 14.1 in chapter 14 on Argentina for an example of distribution of responsibilities that maps well to these guidelines.

6. Transfers can have other uses, including smoothing regional economic shocks and providing targeted boosts to a regional economy.

7. This alleged "threat" is something of a curiosity in the absence of a specific pledge by the sovereign to make good on local debts. On the contrary, among the major rating agencies, it is the act of bailing out failed borrowers in the absence of such a pledge that can lead to downgrading a rating. That is because once the bailout happens, the entire stock of local debt then becomes a potential contingent liability of the sovereign. The more likely causes of "implicit" sovereign guarantees are the weakness of the banking system if much of the debt defaults and the political power of other investors to force central actions to protect their investments.

8. Approval by the central government can mean different things, including not only implied "sponsorship" by the national authorities but also the kind of tax treatment a security will receive and its eligibility for investment by certain groups of investors. In Russia during the heyday of its "Wild West" municipal bond market, approval of local issues by the Federation's Ministry of Finance was needed to obtain tax exemption and to permit investment by institutions, even though the status of a state guarantee was unclear. In the absence of clear laws, would-be issuers would bargain with the central authorities for designation as an "approved" security, making it a political exercise (see Halligan 1996).

Chapter 3

Market Setting and Legal Framework

The financial operations of subnational governments are strongly affected by the financial market and the legal framework. The two are intimately linked. For markets to thrive, laws and regulations on their operation and structure should be in place and enforced. Financial markets, dealing in vast amounts of funds with numerous buyers and sellers, are by definition advanced marketplaces that are efficient and ultimately sustainable only to the degree that an equally vast variety of transactions is quickly and honestly handled. Borrowing rests on the premise that funds are lent with the expectation of their repayment and with compensation for their use. The debt instrument is a contract to that effect. The capacity of subnational governments to access credit markets, by bank loan or bond issue, depends on the perception of their debt contracts as a strong promise to pay so that funds can be secured on favorable terms.

Financial Market Structures and Subnational Finance

Credit market access for subnational governments is strongly tied to the character and stage of development of domestic financial markets.[1] While financial markets vary greatly, some generalizations seem to apply. In growing market systems, liberalization of capital markets and greater devolution have tended to go hand in hand, although not always at the same pace. These are difficult transformations, still under way.

Stages of Development

Domestic financial sectors are undeveloped in most emerging economies, with limited formal financial market activity and few institutions to supply credit and mobilize savings. The size and vigor of financial markets are typically considered a leading index of economic development. Most studies have concluded that economic progress is closely allied to the appearance of private sector financial institutions that can marshal resources, accommodate payments, pool risks, allocate credit and make equity investments, and monitor borrowers and ownership interests (World Bank 2002c). However, many important provisos arise. For example, to operate well financial markets require strong supporting institutions. To meet these conditions, these supporting institutions must often undergo reform themselves.

Most reformers agree on what the destination should look like, that is free markets working efficiently within an acceptable framework of social justice. Agreement on how to achieve the goal within the boundaries of acceptable short-term costs is more elusive. Some would have all reforms in place before trusting the market to be an efficient allocator. Others believe that experience is the best teacher and that a better course is making incremental reforms to meet needs as they arise.

Most emerging and transitioning economies are notable for the low level of bank deposits and lending relative to their gross domestic product (GDP). Bank lending to the private sector is limited as are investments by other financial institutions, so investment tends to be self-financed from firms' current savings. As an economy develops, there is greater use of external funds, first from banks and later from stock and bond markets; these, in turn, depend on the development of private nonbank financial institutions, including pension funds, insurance companies, mutual funds, and securities markets. The operation of banks and nonbank financial intermediaries depends on the regulatory framework, while the potential size and scope of the financial system depend on the size and vigor of the economy.

The Role of Banks and Securities Markets

Generally, two different "visions" have evolved on the role of the banking sector and nonbank financial institutions in the provision of capital. Banks, as suppliers of credit, have dominated most financial systems throughout the world and continue to do so in most developing countries, as well as in Western Europe. In the United States and several other developed countries, however, a broader model of a financial market system dominates, with strong securities markets for active trading of equities and debt among a variety of investors (see box 3.1)

Sometimes, the banking system spurs development of capital markets. In the Philippines, private banks have begun to purchase municipal bonds rather than lend funds to municipalities. Lending to municipalities is dominated by government-owned banks, with close political and financial ties to local politicians and captive deposits of subnational government funds (required by law). Nevertheless, financial and tax incentives and the reasonably developed underwriting infrastructure in the Philippines have created a nascent municipal bond market, actively assisted by international donors (see the Philippines case study, chapter 26).

Debate continues on the advantages and disadvantages of the banking system and securities market approaches for raising capital, but in most countries a mixture has been found to be useful, especially for long-term borrowing.[2] The more important issue appears to be competition: can subnational governments seek capital in credit markets with effective competition among several private sector providers? For small countries with concentrated banking systems and few nonbank institutional investors, the possibilities are remote for domestic financial markets to meet competitive norms.

Another set of concerns is the regulation and optimal structure of financial markets. In most developing and transitioning economies, banks dominate the financial sector, often growing out of a tradition of one or a few government-owned banks that monopolize credit provision. Financial liberalization and the emergence of securities markets as countries move toward greater private ownership and market-based economies tend to begin with the creation of a primitive "money market" (securities markets for short-term debt obligations), soon followed by an equity market and stock exchanges (Schuler, Sheets, and Weig 1998).

The sequence is appropriate. Money markets, frequently narrow in the number of buyers and sellers and focusing on a few frequently traded short-term obligations, have often been the exclusive domain of banks trading overnight funds. A strong banking system is a necessary component of a market-based system. Securities exchanges are important because they offer a mechanism for making longer term debt obligations liquid, but without an efficient banking system and payments mechanism, stock and bond markets are unlikely to survive. The question is whether the money market and the stock market will form the launching platform for a longer-term debt market and if that market will be accessible to subnational governments.

Another feature of many emerging and transitioning economies is the heavy reliance on the banking system to finance central government debt; this reliance can be an impediment to the development of markets for private debt and subsovereign debt (see box 3.2).[3] Sovereign debt, commonly at generous yields, tends to squeeze out available capital for "riskier" pri-

Box 3.1. Banks and Securities Markets: Are Both Needed for Development?

Research indicates that financial structure does not explain cross-country differences in long-term GDP growth, industrial production, use of external funds by firms, or firm growth. However, there is a correlation between the level of a country's wealth on the one hand and development of nonbank financial institutions and the relative size of the securities market on the other.

Financial structure tends to change with development, because banks and securities markets have different requirements for information and contract enforcement. The information that banks collect is private and gathered in their direct relationship with clients, which limits the reliance on outside support services such as accountants or rating agencies. A bank can control a borrower's conduct by threatening to withhold credit or to hold the borrower's deposits, but large financing needs may exceed the resources of individual banks or violate their prudential restrictions. Securities markets depend on bondholder and equity-owner protections, reliable and timely accounting and other information, and external analysis by credit rating agencies and investment funds, among others.

Borrowers will seek access to security markets to increase competition for their investments and to enjoy more options in type of financing. Security markets require both interested investors and a strong support system to protect investor rights and the functioning of markets.

Source: World Bank 2002c.

vate sector loans. It also has lessened the desire of investors to finance subsovereign debt, often viewed as junior in status and, in effect, subordinated to the sovereign debt.

Stock exchanges (often seen as the banner institution of capitalism) have been created in many emerging economies, often as by-products of

---

Box 3.2. Brazilian Banks' Excessive Concentration in Government Securities

Banks can be exposed to financial turmoil because of banking capital adequacy regulations that foster reliance on the banks' domestic sovereign government obligations. For example, Standard and Poor's downgraded Brazilian Banks in mid-2002, not for weak private loan portfolios but for excessive concentration in central government obligations. These are domestically favored under capital adequacy norms that view them as the most secure uses of capital. They are weighted as "zero risk" under the conventions of the prevailing capital adequacy system and do not require a capital allocation from a regulatory point of view.

However, in the sterner world of international finance, a declining currency and a shaky central government can lead to a downgrading of the banks for reasons that are diametrically opposed to the capital adequacy norm. In Brazil's case there was an across the board downgrading of banks even though the domestic private loan portfolios were judged to be secure because of the weakness of the central government (which sets the upper end of the scale in terms of the sovereign risk limit) and the heavy concentration of the banks in central government bonds, along with the rapid depreciation of the Brazilian real.

Source: Standard & Poor's Research, *Brazilian Banks in Time of Turbulence* (July 24, 2002).

---

converting government-owned industries into private concerns. An objective has been to stimulate increased private capital formation and to create new sources of investment funds. Credit financing per se and the listing of debt obligations on exchanges have not usually been central features of the new financial systems. Furthermore, in many domestic markets, high inflation rates, unstable economies, bank domination of credit, and evolving legal systems have combined to discourage the use of credit market instruments by private entities.

Both the bank-dominated and market-dominated models have their advocates. Here, the presumption is that as other financial institutions grow in importance, there will be a natural push to develop debt markets as an outlet for their funds and to meet needs for asset-liability matching, diversification, and liquidity. Accordingly, the following chapters pay considerable attention to the creation and operation of bond markets and the groups of "passive" investors that may supply credit by that means.

Experience in Developed Economies

Developed countries have used a variety of borrowing methods, institutions, and debt instruments to finance long-term subnational infrastructure needs, but two forms predominate: government-sponsored financing institutions and bond markets. Specialized lending institutions have been the preferred approach in Western Europe, while direct access to bond markets has been the preferred approach in the United States. Political history and financial circumstance have generally guided the choice of model.

In Europe the unitary state structure, strong state-owned banking systems, and the limited and subordinated role of subnational governments led to the late development of subnational capital financing responsibilities. State-owned banks specializing in extending credit to subnational governments emerged in the early twentieth century in a number of countries. In Austria, Belgium, Germany, Finland, France, Italy, the Netherlands, Spain, and Sweden, these institutions often were financed by special deposits that provided low-cost funds for lending to subnational governments.[4] Sometimes localities formed cooperative financial institutions (as in Finland, the Netherlands, and Sweden) to finance their borrowing needs. For the most part, these institutions amounted to state-sponsored credit monopolies.[5] They became increasingly market-oriented as deregulation enabled them to raise funds by borrowing in capital markets.

In the late 1980s, with the move toward privatization, state-owned specialized banks became candidates for private capitalization. An outstanding example is the transformation of the Credit Locale de France into a private stock company in 1987. No longer a depository institution, Credit Locale became a major bond issuer in the domestic and international markets. Its merger with the Belgian Credit Communal de Belgique led to the formation of Dexia in 1996, a full-service, "relationship" banking institution that makes loans and underwrites subnational government bond issues through its affiliates. Dexia has bought shares in the specialized subnational lending institutions of Austria, Italy, and Spain. It has about a 40 percent share of the French local government loan market and a 90 percent share of the Belgian market. Dexia seeks long-term relationships with its subnational clients and provides management and planning services in addition to banking services. This model is similar to that of the traditional European bank, which often has close operational relationships with its corporate clients.

The U.S. experience is different. Its federal system has prevented heavy central involvement at the subnational level. State and local governments are responsible for most public works spending and have their own strong revenue systems. With a fragmented banking system and a highly developed capital market, this structure of broad local responsibilities and substantial fiscal capacity encouraged direct borrowing from bond markets, helped by the exemption of interest on state and local bonds from federal and state income taxes.

The U.S. municipal bond market is by far the largest in the world, with some 14,000 new bond and note issues sold each year.[6] As of late 2002 approximately $2 trillion in U.S. municipal bonds was outstanding, an amount equal to all the corporate, financial institution, and government bonds outstanding in emerging markets (IMF 2002, p. 49). Size, wealth, a long tradition of federalism and subnational government autonomy, and strong institutional development combine to make the U.S. experience with subnational direct borrowing in the bond markets unique. Nonetheless, other countries, including those in Europe, have permitted or actively promoted the direct use of bond markets by major subnational issuers.

However, as noted, there is some specialized intermediation activity in U.S. municipal bond markets as well. In 12 states small governments can use bond banks, and many other states have special revolving funds for environmental purposes that were created using special capital grants from the federal government in the early 1980s.[7] In addition to tax exemption of interest income, the U. S. tax code contains provisions for the treatment of bank investments in subnational government obligations that favor borrowing by small governments.[8] Emerging and transitioning economies are applying elements of both the European banking-based and U.S. capital market-based models. In addition, most have looked to donor-assisted loan funds as the principal sources of capital. Operated by national or state government entities, municipal development funds are the sole source of long-term funds in many countries, with interest rates and terms much better than would be otherwise obtainable in domestic capital markets—where these markets exist.

Municipal development funds usually have multiple objectives and may provide training, technical assistance, and grants in addition to loans. The funds have had mixed success. In Brazil state-level municipal funds have had impressive results in working with municipalities (on concessionary terms, however, effectively precluding competition from private market sources). A major issue is how to wean the funds from donor dependence and reshape them to promote more private sector involvement in subnational finance. One fund, the Tamil Nadu Municipal Development Fund in India, has been converted into public-private joint ownership with private sector management. It has sold bonds on the Indian capital market and increasingly acts as an intermediary (see the India case study, chapter 24). Multinational organizations, leery of creating a culture of dependency in credit programs, are seeking ways to leverage more private capital into financing infrastructure.[9]

An Array of Options

Subnational governments have an extensive array of potential domestic sources of credit, from direct loans from agencies of the central government and various state-sponsored specialized loan funds to private capital markets (figure 3.1). What options are actually available to subnational governments depends on various limitations and controls, including laws and regulations, private sector capacity, and market-imposed limitations. For example, subnational governments may be precluded by law or practice from borrowing in the private sector, or they may have nominal access but little interest in their securities.

Most developing and transitioning countries are still emerging from a time when the central government was the exclusive provider of capital funds or took primary responsibility for capital projects. This was the case for the unitary states that emerged from the former communist states and for highly centralized countries elsewhere. Much of the story of improving access to credit markets for these countries is one of moving from a central government monopoly in the provision of credit or in responsibility for capital projects.

The options among sources of funds are not mutually exclusive. Even in relatively undeveloped economies several sources may operate simultaneously. In addition, financial structures are undergoing change. There has been a worldwide move toward privatization of bank ownership. A subnational government that has relied on a government-owned bank for capital might have to find a new source of funds, although in some cases the cred-

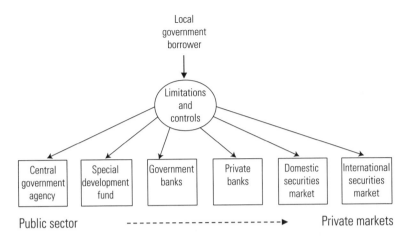

Figure 3.1. Market Structures and Sources of Capital for Local Government Borrowing

it and depository activities of subnational governments are sequestered and retained by government-owned institutions.

Access by subnational governments to international securities markets is still a rare occurrence. Few subnational governments have managed to attract foreign investors; national governments, concerned about the implications for monetary and exchange rate policies, have banned access to international securities markets or have supervised it carefully. For example, after the devaluation of the ruble in 1998 and widespread defaults, the Russian national government forbade new lending in the international markets by subnational authorities (see the Russian Federation case study, chapter 31).

Barriers to the Market

The financial operations of most subnational governments are still highly regulated by the center, effectively precluding or severely limiting private sector interest in their debt. A common restriction is that subnational governments must keep their deposits with the central government treasury or in a government-owned bank (see the South Africa case study, chapter 18). Moreover, the traditional insulation of subnational government from private sector financial institutions has led to mutual ignorance, if not distrust.

Subnational governments may find that accessing private capital sources is uneconomic or politically difficult to justify. This can occur where the central government or its lending institutions provide direct funds on terms that are much better than those of the private credit markets. A major source of such concessionary loan funds has been donor-based on-lending programs, which offer low rates of interest, generous grace periods, and longer term loans than the private sector can. Even where there is a long wait for the low-cost funds and waiting costs are high, local leaders are reluctant to borrow from higher-cost private sources.

Concessional lending has had mixed results, at best. There have been concerns about the long-term efficiency of channeling capital into low-return public projects and about the incentives that are created for governments in order to qualify for such borrowing. Hence, a special concern in meeting the capital financing needs of subnational governments is to wean them away from concessionary finance and to make them both better able and more willing to compete for funds in commercial markets. Of course, private sources of capital must be willing and able to make such loans. Bringing subnational governments and capital markets to the requisite levels of willingness and ability to receive and make loans and to issue and invest in securities is, as outlined in the following chapters, a great challenge.

The Role of Subnational Government Borrowing in Developing Financial Markets

Subnational obligations ought to be viewed in the context of credit market development. Their contribution to that development, while seldom acknowledged, can be substantial. Even with the tide of devolution, the notion that subnational governments would seek resources from private sources was novel and has taken some getting used to by private market participants.

While the options for credit access differ by country, the transition from central government monopoly to private market competition has tended to move from exclusive reliance on the central government to increasing reliance on the banking system and then finally to access to securities markets (figure 3.2). These sources are not mutually exclusive, and they may be tapped in tandem, with larger borrowers that are better able to compete moving toward the use of the securities markets as they develop. Business firms have followed much the same trajectory. As is the case with private firms, the evolution in credit markets often stops with the banking system, which dominates the financial landscape in many countries. However, in economies that are intent on developing securities markets, subnational governments will eventually either directly enter the securities market or be greatly influenced by it, accessing it indirectly through intermediaries.

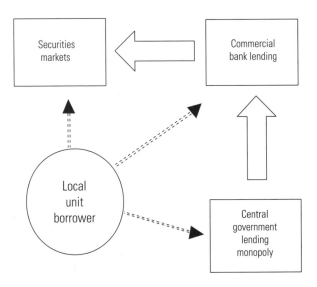

Figure 3.2. Stages of Development in Credit Market Access

The move toward privatization in most developing and emerging economies has left subnational governments in a quandary. The presumption has been that financial markets were a private sector phenomenon and that governments had little to offer in the way of resources or security. Where government activities in the sector were profitable, they were viewed as belonging in the private sector and the solution was to privatize them.

While that thinking continues in many countries, a more balanced appraisal sees the subnational government as a supplier of vital services and critical infrastructure for an improved society and thus as a strong stimulus for the development of capital markets. Good models are provided by Canada, the United States, and a growing number of Western European countries whose subnational governments and their enterprises are often the major providers of public services, using their own resources and making their own investment decisions. Since most such governments are well-run and benefit from their monopoly positions as potential borrowers, investors operating in well-regulated financial systems see the obligations of these governments as safe outlets for their funds.[10] In many emerging economies subnational government obligations can attain a level of creditworthiness that makes them attractive investments for the private sector and for banks, although banks are limited in their ability to provide the long-term financing needed for infrastructure. Additionally, in some emerging economies subnational governments have already entered securities markets, providing new investment outlets.

The Legal Setting

Underdeveloped legal systems and weak and corrupt judiciaries can make it difficult for subnational governments to convince wary private investors to invest in their obligations. Increasing subnational borrowings in domestic financial markets often requires adjusting regulations on borrowing authority and the issuance, registration, and servicing of debt, as in Morocco, for example. Market distortions that lead to a preference for one instrument over another (loans rather than bonds, for example) need to be removed. The regulatory and supervisory framework for subnational borrowing needs to be strengthened, especially prudential regulations and bankruptcy laws (see the Morocco case study, chapter 20).

Institutions and large individual investors are interested in knowing that the obligations in which they invest are valid obligations that create enforceable claims against the obligors, based on underlying contracts. Contracts and their enforceability vary according to the legal system under which they are drafted and the transparency, competence, and honesty of the judicial system that enforces them. These attributes of legality and enforceability of contracts, basic to the fair and efficient operation of capital markets, are often undeveloped and weak in developing and transitioning economies.

Differences in Legal Systems

Legal traditions have had a profound influence on fundamental concepts of ownership and creditor rights and consequently on the development of financial markets. There are wide differences in how quickly and how well laws pertaining to investor and creditor rights are enforced. These rights are not inherent in the securities but are determined by law. This can have a profound effect on the ability of countries to establish effective securities markets for debt and equity capital.[11] Laws governing financial markets and securities strongly influence the accessibility and cost of capital for subnational governments.

Security—what the lender can look to for assurance that a loan will be repaid or, if not, what asset it will be able to seize—is a fundamental concept in private capital markets. Numerous complications can arise. Some legal systems are weak in describing creditors' legal rights: the priority of creditors' claims may be unclear, the legal presumption may run to the party that has physical possession and use of the asset, no matter the liens against it. Laws governing secured transactions may be in conflict or may predate modern commerce and financial relationships and instruments. Thus laws may limit who can lend, what types of collateral may be pledged, and how the collateral is to be identified and physically kept. However, even where the ability to use collateral as security is clear, there may be no central registry to keep track of liens against collateral. The ability to collateralize a right to revenues (and assign them, as in the case of tax collections) may be ambiguous or nonexistent (World Bank 2002c).

The local financial obligations of some Czech municipalities are guaranteed by national institutions, but most are not explicitly guaranteed and it is unclear how creditors would recover their money in case of default. The Czech Bankruptcy and Composition Act does not cover municipalities, an omission believed to contribute to the reluctance of the banking system to finance municipalities. Municipalities, for their part, have been granting loans and guarantees to businesses to support local development activities. Although these financial activities require the approval of municipal assemblies, the procedures to be followed are not clear. The lack of debt monitoring and supervisory mechanisms softens local budget constraints and creates moral hazard incentives, contributing to higher fiscal risk (see Czech Republic case study, chapter 28).

In addition to the complexities of pledging properties and gaining rights to revenues, a lender's willingness to accept pledges depends on enforcement and the ease with which claims can be settled. When the ability to enforce pledges surely and quickly is in doubt, loans are not forthcoming or are forthcoming only at higher rates. While enforcement problems are acute for loans to private parties in the case of moveable property, they are exacerbated in loans to the public sector by restrictions on pledges of public property and the difficulties in enforcing such pledges against the sovereign or its subdivisions.

A practical problem is the independence of the judiciary and its competence to understand financial issues and adjudicate impartially. Modern securities markets depend on concepts that may exceed the mastery of traditional judges. They also depend heavily on the integrity of a system of laws rather than on traditional or political relationships. An "absentee creditor" many miles removed from the scene who relies on a written contract is unlikely to obtain justice in settings with a corrupt or weak judiciary.

Implications of the Legal System for Subnational Borrowing

Subnational government borrowing is part of a larger legal fabric that sets the roles and responsibilities of public and private sector entities in the operation of a subnational government credit market. Several policy issues that have a substantial impact on subnational government borrowing can be covered only tangentially in this book. Examples are policies and practices on ownership of public property and property rights associated with such ownership, the structure of intergovernmental revenue sharing, the adequacy and reliability of the accounting standards, regulation of the banking system and other financial sectors, and judicial enforcement.[12]

Nonetheless, an imperfect legal system and evolving fiscal situation are not necessarily impediments to the initial development of a subnational government credit market. Many countries have had imperfect legal structures when they began pilot projects in market-based subnational government borrowing. Some now have developed substantial subnational government credit markets. Many of the risks can be diminished through provisions in the loan contracts, even before a fully developed legal framework is in place. In fact, the practical problems of developing "pioneer" transactions have exposed gaps in law and practices and prompted solutions.

Both policy reforms and market practices are likely to be implemented incrementally. A successful subnational government credit market must be built both from the top down, by building a legal and policy framework to support efficient credit market operations, and from the bottom up, by accumulating practical experience in banks and other lenders in making loans and in subnational governments in borrowing to finance high priority investments and making timely debt service payments. Both tracks should move forward simultaneously.

Legal Framework—Planning Ahead

Several emerging and transitioning countries have confronted the reality of large-scale subnational government borrowing and been obliged to construct a legal framework after the fact to accommodate the interests of stakeholders on both sides of the market. Developing subnational markets can benefit from examining the difficulties in countries where subnational borrowing got out of hand. From Brazil to Russia excessive borrowing by some subnational governments in the absence of an adequate legal framework has exacerbated national economic crises. The promise of soundly based subnational borrowing is large, but the risks in badly prepared borrowing are also large. All parties (subnational governments, banks, and potential investors) share an interest in fully understanding the policy issues surrounding credit market development and in having an appropriate legal framework in place before substantial borrowing occurs.

Notes

1. The term *financial market* is used generically and encompasses both bank and non-bank institutions and other potential providers of capital, including various governmental entities that may lend to subnational governments. Although governments themselves are not participants in the equity markets, their companies and projects can be from time to time, and since stock exchanges frequently deal in both equities and debt, their existence and activity are of interest here. The term *credit* is also used generically to describe debt obligations and not just bank loans.

2. The crux of the matter is finding a financial structure that suits the needs of investors and potential borrowers. To finance infrastructure, local governments need access to long-term capital. On the investors' side, there are institutions and individuals that prefer long-term investments to offset their long-term liabilities. Banks, on the other hand, are constrained by the mismatch between their short-term liabilities (deposits) and the long-term assets that loans for infrastructure represent. Another desirable attribute of the securities market is the need for disclosure and the collateral benefits of wide scale information about the financial conduct of governments.

3. To the extent that a market for debt securities existed at all, it was dominated by central government or central bank obligations. Frequently, the debt market existed primarily if not exclusively to finance central government deficits. Regulation of investments and bank assets is tilted toward providing a ready market for the national government debt. The extension of credit to private entities often has taken a back seat in banking operations.

4. Except for Finland, the Netherlands, and Sweden, all the specialized banks have been privatized. For a discussion of national experiences with specialized municipal lending institutions, see Peterson 1998.

5. Japan, as a unitary state with close fiscal linkages between the central and local governments, has followed a similar pattern. About 75 percent of its local government financing needs are met by specialized central government-owned entities. Low-cost funds are available from the Fiscal Investment and Loan Program, financed indirectly by Post Office savings accounts. The other 25 percent is made up of direct borrowings from private sector institutions or bond issues. Subnational borrowings need the ap-

proval of the central government. See Mihajek, p. 297. Lending to local governments is treated as part of the counter-cyclical policy in Japan and terms are made easier at times when the national government is seeking to stimulate the economy.

6. The term *municipal bond* is used generically to mean the obligations of subnational governments.

7. State revolving funds were set up as loan funds to replace the federal direct grant program for water pollution control. Some revolving funds employ interest rate subsidies. Some also leverage borrowed funds on top of the capitalization supplied by the federal government and the 80 percent match required of the states.

8. Section 265 of the tax code permits commercial banks to partially write off the cost of capital for holdings on bonds that are sold by issuers that borrow less than 10 million dollars in a given year. The upshot is that interest rates on these bonds are usually 15 to 25 basis points lower than those on similar bonds sold by larger governmental units.

9. Chapter 12 addresses these issues of design in greater detail. The World Bank has recently emphasized the need to move municipal development funds toward "market" behavior; see, for example, World Bank 2001, p. 49.

10. These well-deserved reputations were not built overnight or without disappointments along the way. The United States, in particular, had a long and lurid history of defaults in the nineteenth century that gave rise to restrictions (imposed by the states upon themselves) and hard-nosed market practices (imposed by lenders). These reforms ultimately laid the foundation for subnational bond markets viewed as being the safest next to that of sovereign bond markets. Bank regulation of investment requirements and required documentation, the large size and sophistication of the market, and the strength of the underlying revenue systems all contributed to the development of the quality of the market.

11. Several studies have examined the impact of the legal system on the development of the financial markets. The general conclusion is that of the four "families" of law, countries employing the French civil law tradition have the weakest protection for investors (and creditors) whereas those that follow the common law (British) tradition have the strongest. The other two families of laws, the German and Scandinavian, fall in between. Furthermore, enforcement is often slow and subject to corruption. Regions (such as South America and parts of Africa and Europe) that follow the French civil law frequently provide an unattractive legal environment for

investors, often with high concentrations of financial markets and ownership of assets (see Burke and Perry 1998, chapter 4).

12. Additionally, laws relating to public procurement, tariff setting, and own-source revenues can have a substantial impact on the development of a subnational credit market. Stability and clarity in the generic laws and the ability to specify and monitor conduct in the loan contract are key ingredients to limited obligation "project" financing.

Part II

Borrowing Instruments and Restrictions on Their Use

John Petersen and Miguel Valadez

Chapter 4

Subnational Governments as Borrowers

Subnational debt can be the obligation of a local, regional, provincial, or state government or of projects they sponsor through subsidies, partnerships, or concessions with the private sector. Subnational governments enter into many types of legal and financial relationships, which can differ markedly among countries. In many places these relationships are evolving, and even where they are established, they continue to be dynamic. Thus, policymakers and analysts must be prepared to examine a variety of factors and risk exposures when dealing with the debt transactions of subnational governments.

Subnational government borrowers have much in common with other borrowers such as public utilities and private firms. But there are also some special features relating to the powers, structure, and operation of subnational governments. For example, most subnational governments deal exclusively in domestic currency for revenues and expenditures. Thus, except for certain types of facilities (electric power, ports, airports, telecommunications), they have little access to foreign currency payments. For some services, governments have powers approaching monopoly status that may be enforced by regulation. Additionally, governments are site-specific and unable to change the geographic locus of business or the fundamental nature of the services they provide. They rarely go out of business.[1]

Debt Classification

A fundamental distinction in classifying debt is whether the subnational government is the borrower, relying primarily on its taxing power and other general governmental revenues to back the loan, or whether the government is just a party to the loan, as when the obligation is limited to a particular revenue source of an enterprise to which the general governmental credit is not pledged (a limited or nonguaranteed obligation). This distinction is reasonably clear in the United States, where a revenue-generating project or enterprise that is financed with a limited obligation is referred to as a *revenue bond*.

Elsewhere, the distinctions between general and limited pledges can be blurry, as in the case of projects financed with a mixture of public and private funds, service and off-take contracts, profit-sharing arrangements, or concessions with guarantees of use. Confusion is especially likely in countries where various government commercial and industrial activities are being privatized. The credit structure may be especially complex, with a blend of risk factors involving both the public and private sectors, in "project finance" cases, where the private sector is not only a direct investor in a project but also an equity provider and actively engaged in operation and management.

The following discussion and accompanying figures describe three prototypical financing and credit structures involving subnational governments. For ease of exposition, the borrowing is assumed to involve a project, as is typically the case, although it could as well be used for other purposes, including relending, to meet emergency needs or to fund accumulated deficits.

General Government Obligation

With a general government obligation the government uses its general revenues to make debt service payments and owns and operates the project itself (figure 4.1). In most countries this would be the likely structure for capital expenditures for public safety, public education, health and welfare, and similar activities that are not revenue producing. The government issues the debt in its own name and pledges its general revenues. However, neither the financed project nor its earnings are specifically tied to repayment of the debt. In an important variant on this theme, the subnational government receives intergovernmental assistance, such as shared taxes or grants, that is pledged as part of the security.

Government Limited Obligation (revenue obligation)

In a government limited obligation, the debt is secured primarily or exclusively on the earnings of a project enterprise that produces revenues through charges and fees that are used to defray much or all of the costs of operation and debt service (figure 4.2). General revenues of the government are typi-

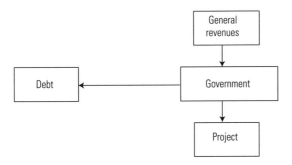

Figure 4.1. General Government Obligation

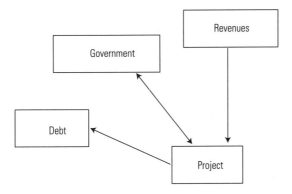

Figure 4.2. Government Limited Obligation

cally not pledged directly, and there may even be a prohibition against their use. Common subnational enterprises are public utilities, such as water and sewer, electric distribution, local toll facilities, public markets, harvest processing facilities, and local ports and terminals. The debt is issued either by the project itself, which may be a limited-purpose special district, or on behalf of the project by the general government sponsor.

Project Financings (public-private undertakings)

In public-private undertakings, typically in utility-type projects, the government contracts with the private sector, through concessions or partnership agreements, to build, own, or operate the project (figure 4.3). The government may contribute in various ways to the financing, including equity

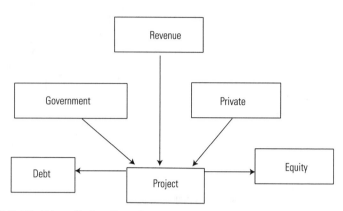

Figure 4.3. Public-Private Project Financing

interests, subsidies, and guarantees related to the demand for outputs or for supplying needed inputs. The private sector, or international lending entities, also may contribute debt, equity, and various enhancements to the financial mix. The contract sets outs the obligations of the respective parties and the returns to each. The debt is typically issued in the name of the project and may be non-recourse, looking only to project earnings, ownership, or assets for security.

Classifying Potential Subnational Borrowers

Many subnational governments already have access to credit through government-sponsored lending programs, bank lending, or sales of bonds in domestic or international capital markets. However, many more do not, and many factors influence whether and how they will gain access.

Classification Based on Fiscal Capacity and Financial Acumen

The fiscal capacity and financial acumen of subnational jurisdictions, which relate to the ability and willingness to pay, are fundamental considerations in determining which units are candidates for borrowing. Although these are not always correlated with size, private creditors generally prefer larger jurisdictions because of their greater sophistication, ability to draw on more resources, and ability to spread the fixed costs of debt transactions over larger volumes of borrowing. In most countries three groups of jurisdictions can be identified in terms of the likelihood for the issuance of subsovereign debt in private markets:[2]

- Those that already have access to capital markets because of their size, financial and managerial resources, and political clout. This group includes the largest and best known subnational governments with large economies and political muscle.
- Those with limited or no access to capital markets but that can generate adequate revenues to meet their responsibilities and otherwise are capable of borrowing private capital. This group consists of subnational governments that are large and capable of attracting private interest without direct central government help and those that are too small or that lack the managerial capability to attract private lending but that could gain access with assistance. One approach is to combine the needs and resources of individual governments and borrow as part of this larger group.
- Those that cannot generate sufficient revenue to provide the current services they require or to build and operate the needed infrastructure. Jurisdictions in this group, which for all practical purposes are "financial wards" of higher levels of government, do not have access to capital markets and most likely should not.

Jurisdictions in the first two groups have the potential to use private credit resources under a regime in which central government assistance to municipal market development, if any, is accommodative and indirect, focused on laws and regulations that create an enabling environment for subnational government borrowing in credit markets. Subnational governments in the third group, the very small and poor, neither can nor should borrow in private credit markets.

As handy as the above triage of candidates for borrowing might appear to be, it is one that defies drawing strict lines of demarcation in practice. Advocates of light-handed intervention and believers in market solutions say that the market itself will define, better than government regulation, which jurisdictions fall into which category. Others argue that markets assume a symmetry of skill and information between buyer and seller that is not met in the case of subnational governments, especially those that are smaller and unsophisticated. Left untended, the unwary can wander into the credit market with unfortunate results.

Like any classification scheme, this one is situational and dynamic. Some governments that are too small and too poor to gain access to credit markets using their general revenue funds may latch on to a project financing scheme that is creditworthy. Even subnational governments with otherwise insufficient own-source revenues might qualify for private credit if they can pledge a share of their intergovernmental transfers to secure the debt.

Policies to Improve the Creditworthiness of Subnational Governments

Government policies on intergovernmental finance and technical and credit assistance to small and unsophisticated jurisdictions affect how markets assess creditworthiness. It is likely that countries with weakly financed and poorly managed subnational governments will have to forgo direct entry into private credit markets or will need to devise policies to help subnational governments advance up the creditworthiness ladder.

To promote subnational government access to private markets, the Philippines has used a four-quadrant strategy that considers two primary dimensions: a subnational government's wealth and the revenue-generating potential of the proposed improvement (figure 4.4). For the smallest and poorest subnational governments that need to finance non-revenue-producing facilities, grants are the preferred means of assistance (lower-left quadrant). For subnational governments with adequate wealth and self-supporting projects, access to bond markets was the preferred financing mechanism for larger projects, with commercial bank lending at commercial rates with no grants or subsidies for smaller but commercially viable projects (upper-right quadrant). Because bank lending to subnational governments has been dominated by government financial institutions, an added dimension of the approach is to move from government financial

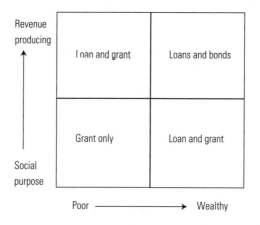

Figure 4.4. Matrix of Subnational Government Financing Capacity

institution lending (the loan and grant quadrant) to private credit sources (the loans and bonds quadrant).[3] Government financial institutions were to facilitate the move to private capital as governments grew stronger and projects became self-financing (see the Philippines case study, chapter 26).

Distinctions among Subnational Jurisdictions

Approaches like these based on existing creditworthiness are useful for analytic purposes, such as describing potential demand for credit and the likely size and viability of a subnational government securities market. However, should such distinctions be codified into law or regulation to identify which subnational governments can access credit markets? In developed economies credit markets effectively classify borrowers and reflect their credit assessments in the prices (interest rates) charged for borrowing, based on perceived differences in economic vitality, managerial efficiencies, financial condition, political sway, and the viability of individual projects.

While detailed regulatory prescriptions are best avoided, senior levels of government have a legitimate interest in the financial market behavior of subnational governments, as chapter 2 describes. Even in mature markets, most national governments and some state governments employ regulatory classification systems to guard against imprudent behavior (see box 4.1). These classifications differentiate among jurisdictions in allowable maximum outstanding debt or, more typically, the maximum debt outstanding in relation to some revenue source, such as a property tax. In the United States most state governments differentiate among subnational governments through legal classifications that can include differential borrowing authority. However, in subsovereign financial systems being put into place for the first time or being radically redesigned, classifications may be overused, poorly designed, or unenforceable. The strongest argument against rigid regulatory classification is that upward mobility in classifications of financial strength and managerial maturity should be encouraged. Classifying a jurisdiction in a way that encourages it to depend on external assistance and avoid responsible borrowing on its own is exactly the opposite effect that government intends to have. Artificially limiting market access runs counter to the basic policy goal of pursuing greater private sector investment.

Subnational Borrowers by Type of Entity

Subnational debt also may be incurred by municipal enterprises and quasi-municipal entities created by agreement of existing municipalities or by

Box 4.1. Defining and Controlling Public Debt

How public debt is defined can determine the boundaries of subnational government borrowing. EU legislation, which limits public indebtedness under the deficit and debt limits of the Maastricht Treaty, defines public debt as the debt of the central, regional, and local governments, including social security funds but excluding the debt of public enterprises. The limitation thus is expressed in terms of the institutional units producing non-market services as their main activity rather than in terms of ownership of the facility. A concern has been how to coordinate debt at the subsovereign level with that at the sovereign level.

Subnational governments have an incentive to place as much of their debt as possible on a self-supporting, commercial basis to avoid macro-level curbs on borrowing. Evidently, however, the EU definitions also include certain contingent obligations that subnational governments might enter into in support of commercial debt, such as obligations to purchase a commodity or service (an off-take guarantee) and pledges to make up project operating deficits or debt service deficiencies from general funds.

The curbs on general obligation tax-supported debt embodied in the EU limits are akin to the individual state-based limitations of tax-supported debt that arose in the United States. In the United States the restrictions on general debt hastened the rise of the non-recourse revenue-bond obligation that is used for enterprise activities and other forms of non-recourse obligations such as the moral obligation bond. These limited obligations, many of which are de facto supported by taxes and fees raised by the general government, once represented only a small fraction of municipal borrowing. They now typically make up 60 to 70 percent of all bonds sold in the United States.

One application of special districts is in the use of business improvement districts. These special taxing units levy a tax in addition to the normal taxes and have the powers and personnel to address the special needs of downtown areas, especially distressed areas, including extraordinary sanitation and public safety needs. The concept has caught on in parts of Europe and may be spreading to developing economies as well.

Source: Petersen and Crihfield 2000.

national or regional legislation. These special-purpose arrangements are of four types:

- Separate restricted funds, accounting arrangements, or special-purpose entities within a municipality, the revenues and expenditures of which are restricted to specific purposes and are separated from the general fund. These entities typically derive their power from the municipalities, although they may have considerable independence.
- Entities created by agreement among municipalities to accomplish a special purpose, such as to provide fire protection across a broad area. Their revenues and expenditures can be separated from those of the organizing municipalities. Their powers can derive solely from the municipalities ("joint powers") or through state or national legislation that limits or extends such combining powers.
- Quasi-municipal entities created by state or national legislation to provide municipal services (such as water development, disease control, or transport services) where needs do not necessarily relate to municipal boundaries. Their powers would be described in authorizing legislation.
- Public-private arrangements, such as project financing, where governments and private sector entities share in the ownership of projects that usually are built and operated by the private sector partner. These arrangements have been heavily advocated by reformers as a way to re-capitalize projects and make enterprises, particularly public utilities, more efficient.

In theory, such special-purpose subnational governmental entities might issue limited obligation debt based on their own revenue sources and the ability to borrow against them. In practice, however, issues are more complicated.

As might be expected, there are two sides to the special-purpose, special-entity borrowing coin. Establishing such entities can allow services to be delivered by an appropriate entity with targeted taxes, fees, and charges. That characteristic is appealing to those that favor an application of the benefit principle and rational pricing of services. Moreover, since geographic areas of traditional general governments have typically inherited a political and economic logic that may be long out of date, the case for promoting special service districts along the lines of economic service areas is often compelling. On the negative side is the possibility of a proliferation and fragmentation of local government and of diffusion of local revenue sources. There are also questions of the nature of the relationship between the governmental parents and their special-purpose children, a relationship that may rely on subsidies and guarantees, stated or implied, and the exposures that accompany them.

These issues are illustrated in the case of the People's Republic of China. The People's Republic of China presents something of an enigma: a highly centralized state that is loosely organized, with extreme variations in subnational fiscal capacity and high levels of investment by companies owned by subnational governments that themselves cannot borrow. Although China is a unitary state, it has devolved a great deal of spending responsibility to its subnational units, which are both legion in number and, at the provincial level, as large in population as many countries. While the subnational governments are precluded from borrowing directly using their own credits, they effectively borrow through special-purpose vehicles, which are wholly owned companies that have their own revenues and often supply infrastructure needs on a quasi-commercial basis. Rationalizing the activities of these "off–balance sheet" borrowers, which frequently have to rely on borrowing from state-owned banks, is a major challenge the country faces as it carefully enters into a regime of financial markets—and the world's financial markets (see box 4.2).

The practical implication of this discussion is that subnational government borrowing powers should remain flexible enough to address both common and special infrastructure problems. An example is the special taxing and fee district, which may permit a unit of government to gear its taxing and charging powers to the particular needs of subdivisions, as is the case in the United States. However, care needs to be taken to ensure that the legal and operational arrangements are clearly stated and that dealings are both correct and transparent.

Cooperation among Subnational Governments

For many projects, financing and operation are more efficient when the scale is larger than an individual subnational government. In many cases the desire to provide more local self-determination has led to the establishment of many small governments that are assigned service responsibilities that exceed their fiscal and managerial capabilities and encompass service areas that exceed their geographic boundaries (see box 4.3). Cooperation is imperative if services are to be prepared in a rational way and capable of being financed by users on a local basis.

Box 4.2. China: Off-Budget Finance and the Transmuted Bond

Under the series of changes in the intergovernmental fiscal system that have occurred in China over the past two decades, Chinese localities found it increasingly attractive to hive off many activities into the off-budget category and have them carried on by government-owned entities. Given the austerity in many subnational governments and the changing mechanics of tax-sharing, the local government-owned companies had the appeal of raising their own revenues, being kept away from the formal budget calculations, and being able to pursue activities either not allowed or not financeable by the subnational government itself. While information is incomplete, it appears that such off-budget activity is about equal to that carried on by the regional and local governments on their formal budgets and may represent as much as 20 percent of Chinese GDP.

One appeal of the off-budget financing is the ban against subnational borrowing from nongovernmental sources on the local government's own credit. However, the special-purpose entities that they create and own can borrow. This is especially important in financing infrastructure and has resulted in a phenomenon known as the "transmuted bond." To access credit, a Chinese subnational government will create an economic entity, which has a close, if legally murky, relationship to the parent, to accomplish the financing through the sale of "corporate" bonds. In some cases, such as Quinyang district of Chengdu City, bonds are sold locally to retail investors, although the usual purchasers are banks and investment funds.

The debt of these special purpose vehicles, whose proceeds frequently are re-lent to the government and repaid by governmental funds, is widely understood to be a contingent obligation of the parent government. Because this transmuted debt is not subject to an orderly process of approval (and financial oversight and reporting), and in view of the prohibition against government guarantees, this debt is seen as constituting a substantial risk for both the financial system and for the underlying government debtors.

Source: China case study, chapter 22.

Many countries have achieved this goal through associations of subnational governments. Subnational governments often have legal authority to "collaborate or associate to perform public works"[4] through contractual relationships among participating subnational governments. Even with such legal authority, cooperative projects still need a legal contractual framework to permit subnational governments to work together in a way that enables the jointly created entity to access financing and avoid the inefficiency of separate financing of each government's share of the cost of a joint project.[5]

Box 4.3. Restructuring Subnational Government: From Few to Many (But How Many?)

The path to the democratization of the formerly communist Eastern and Central Europe states has not been easy. Restructuring unitary systems of government to foster more self-governance has led to a proliferation of subnational governments. In Hungary the number of subnational governments doubled after the 1990 reorganization, and the same pattern was seen in the Czech Republic, the Slovak Republic, and Ukraine. Meanwhile, the new units were given extensive service responsibilities unmatched by expanded local revenue-raising powers.

In large part, the difficulty has been in deciding which governing model to follow. After the fall of communism, territorial fragmentation was greatest in the state systems that followed the Napoleonic (or Southern European) system. The central government maintained a strong local presence through the prefecture system of administration and an array of national services reaching down to the local level. A key responsibility of subnational governments was to represent local interests to the central government, which retained the major sources of revenues, doled out grants, and imposed national standards.

An associated difficulty in devolution schemes has been the disregard of the optimal size of government needed to deliver local

---

services efficiently. Traditional concepts of "community" often led to high levels of government fragmentation. The idea, again, was representing the locality to the center, as opposed to exercising true self-sufficiency.

In the countries following the Northern European model (and Western federated systems), there was greater effort to achieve the optimal subnational government size needed to match assigned service responsibilities and revenues. The central government does not have a presence at the local level, and localities have more responsibility for delivering local services and for deciding what those services should be and how much to spend on them.

Reconciling the two conflicting views of the proper role of subnational governments has been a big source of tension. Efforts by central authorities to promote regional cooperation have often been resisted by new subnational governments that jealously guard their new autonomy and local resources.

Source: Davey and Gabor 1998.

Notes

1. This is not to say it cannot happen. In Poland, the old state's administrative districts (the Voidvoidships) were replaced by a new structure of counties, the Poviat. In other countries, there have been massive reorganizations and amalgamations. However, a new name on the government building is not the same thing as its being abandoned: somebody else picks up the duties and the liabilities.

2. Later, there will be a discussion of concessionary finance and technical assistance. At this stage, the concern is with identifying the likely "potential market" for private sector capital access and under what conditions.

3. It should be noted that sale of bonds by local governments in the Philippines is restricted by law to finance "self-supporting" projects.

4. Fed. LLSG, Article 16, Bosnia and Herzegovina.

5. In Latvia, the Law on Self-Government determines the right of local governments to "cooperate." However, the legislation does not state that institutions commonly established by self-governments can be juridical persons with their own budget. Thus, there is a question whether the "joint entity" can borrow, which means that each participant has to borrow on its own. This results in an inefficient structure for jointly financed projects.

Chapter 5

The Nature and Design of Debt

Types of debt are defined by the kind of security given by the borrower. Creditors want to know not only where the money is expected to come from but also what their remedies and security are in the event of default. Knowing the security on debt is important: uncertainty about remedy and security can create risks that build inefficiencies into the market. If the remedies and security are not deemed adequate, markets may set risk premiums so high that credit is unaffordable to many jurisdictions.

What remedies should be available to creditors by law? This question is critical. Any framework for subsovereign borrowing needs to spell out what powers a jurisdiction has to pledge assets and revenue streams and to exercise its powers to set taxes, tariffs, and other levies. It is also desirable to spell out how such security can be affected by default or other financial emergency.

General Obligations, Special Pledges, and Limited Obligations

In most emerging market economies general purpose subsovereign debt has had some form of sovereign government backing. In many cases the subsovereign governments were merely administrative units of the central government under a unitary government concept. In other cases the only long-term funds available were supplied by international lending entities that typically required a sovereign guarantee. However, this is changing. Devolution has meant that national governments are encouraging subnational governments to borrow on their own credit.

Precisely what constitutes the credit of a subnational government, without an explicit or implicit guarantee by the national government, is often unclear. Expressions such as "general obligation" or "balance sheet" debt often mask an unresolved question of ultimate security: what remedies are available to an investor if a subnational government fails to pay on time and in full?

Aside from the subnational government's good faith and the prospect of national government assistance if things get difficult, subsovereign general obligations have often been backed by the ability of creditors to seize financial and physical assets. For a number of reasons, this physical collateral system is not a sound approach to securing credits. Subnational governments with physical assets that are unrelated to their municipal service responsibilities, such as a commercial enterprise, might be better off to divest themselves of the asset to avoid diverting scarce city management capacity to manage a potentially private activity.

In addition to the problems in enforcing a claim on pledged public property are problems with title—does the locality actually own the property? The legal nature of the public domain continues to be unclear in many emerging and transitioning countries. Municipal assets that are used directly or indirectly to provide vital services should not be (and more often are not permitted to be) risked as collateral. The pledging of physical collateral can divert the government's attention from making sure its general revenues are sound enough to support borrowing. Despite these drawbacks, there can be times and places where a subnational government owns non-vital property that is "alienable" and useful in bolstering its creditworthiness.

The meaning of the general obligation pledge is also subject to variation. The term *full faith and credit* originated in the United States and is generally understood to mean more than a general, unsecured promise.[1] Debt not backed by specific revenue flows should be backed by a pledge of all general revenues as a source of debt service payment. The subnational government could be specifically obligated to use any and all of its general resources, including an increase in taxes and fees, to meet debt service obligations. Stronger and more specific remedies for creditors are likely to improve investor confidence in subsovereign debt in emerging market economies.

Several kinds of limited security can be pledged to secure subsovereign debt:

- Physical or monetary assets.
- The right to operate a facility or provide a service.

- Selected revenues, such as those from tariffs, fares, or rentals; particular taxes or special levies; and grants or shared taxes (intergovernmental transfers).
- Power to set specific tax rates, utility tariffs, and other levies.
- Executive agreement to budget for and recommend payment of future debt service, without an explicit binding pledge that those appropriations will be made.[2]
- Assignment of the payment of future intergovernmental transfers.
- Pledge by a higher level government to exact certain penalties against defaulting lower level government borrowers.[3]

Pledging Assets, Operating Rights, and Revenue Streams

A common pledge backing debt in developed markets is one that is restricted to a particular revenue stream or enumerated subnational government assets or one giving the creditor the right to step in and perform the activity and receive the revenues in the event of default. However, carving out specific revenues and giving the creditors rights to assets and operational powers both raise a host of operational and policy issues.[4] Local officials may be hesitant to pledge assets because their loss in the event of a default would be dramatic. There may be assets or revenue streams that are so vital to maintaining basic governance that they should be protected from a debt service pledge. Examples include:

- Intergovernmental transfers or local dedicated taxes that are intended to provide services to selected segments of the population.
- Transfers or taxes that are earmarked for mandated purposes.
- Physical facilities deemed essential to the public health, safety, and welfare, such as water supply, fire equipment, and hospitals.

Subnational governments have a limited number of pledgeable assets, especially non-vital properties. To the extent that governments are forced to pledge these assets to support debt, their future ability to secure loans is diminished and their financial flexibility is reduced.

As a practical matter, private sector lenders are of two minds about asset pledges. Lenders are anxious to have as much collateral as possible to apply leverage to reluctant debtors. Lenders may be willing to take marketable assets, such as vacant land, office buildings, parking lots, or sports facilities, but they are not likely to foreclose on indispensable physical assets or on essential service facilities, such as water or wastewater treatment plants, town halls, city streets, or fire stations. If the legal system provides adequate assurance, lenders are more likely to secure local debts by pledges of actual or potential revenue streams that are sufficient to cover the debt service.

Because of the practical and political problems of tying up essential facilities, a prohibition on pledging properties considered essential to public health and safety could be included in authorizing legislation with little impact on a market's development of other useful security devices. Minimum essential services can be defined by law, with the borrowers deciding what fits the definition. These might include services necessary for human health and safety, such as water, sewer, and refuse collection. Use of the assets relating to these services could be pledged, but the law should require minimum essential services to be continued at all times. These restrictions would not be barriers to borrowing, since lenders are not interested in repossessing pipes in the ground. They want revenue streams.

A pledge of revenues from public utilities is appropriate for financing related to the same utilities but not if the pledge is used to secure unrelated financing. Part of the concern is simple economics. When a jurisdiction subsidizes general expenditures at the expense of utility charges, resources are misallocated. The service that does the subsidizing tends to be under-allocated, and the service that gets the subsidies tends to be under-priced and thus over-allocated. Nevertheless, in cases where the demand for or the supply of the burdened service is relatively price inelastic, using revenues from that service is tempting since the costs of collection are low and the certainty of collections is high.[5]

Pledging to Set Tax Rates, Tariffs, and Other Levies

Where tariffs, rates, or charges can be increased or decreased at the discretion of the subnational authorities, a rate covenant to set and maintain the charges at adequate levels to meet operating costs and pay debt service is a useful financing tool. However, subnational governments in emerging and transitioning economies usually have quite limited revenue-raising powers, a legacy of unitary states with a center monopoly on decisions and revenue raising.[6]

Even subnational governments with considerable power to set rates and establish levies can experience ambiguity about their ability to pledge to set tariffs, tax rates, or other charges at a level sufficient to service a debt because of questions about whether such covenants unlawfully bind future administrations (see box 5.1). Without such a forward-looking and binding contract ability, a pledge is probably worthless.

In many emerging market economies the primary cause of debt service default and payment arrears is failure to increase the rates and charges that were to be the source of revenues for debt payment. Subnational jurisdictions would benefit from clear legal authority to covenant future tariff or tax

---

Box 5.1. Importance of the Rate-Setting Pledge

South Africa offers an interesting example of the importance of the rate-setting pledge in a revenue bond and of the potential problems when its application is uncertain. Several South African cities are attempting to implement privatization plans that involve nonrecourse revenue bonds. Debt service payments on the bonds would rely exclusively on the water tariffs of the privately operated water treatment plants. The tariffs are likely to need to be increased over time to meet rising operating costs and offset unforeseen expenditures. However, national legislation gives a national minister the discretion to set water tariff rates, in effect overriding local control and contracts. Should that happen, the private concessionaires want the local communities to make up any shortfall in revenues by raising property taxes.

Having such a clause in the contract would improve the creditworthiness of the bonds, but it raises other problems. First, if water rates are not raised, then taxes must be, eroding the general tax base of the municipality. Second, the water ratepayers and the property taxpayers are not the same people. The great majority of water users own little if any taxable property, and they greatly outnumber the better-off property taxpayers. This opens up the potential that local elected officials might even welcome a reneging on water rate increases by national officials, since it would shift the burden of the debt to the wealthier—and less numerous—constituents that pay the property taxes.

Source: Petersen and Crihfield 2000.

increases to secure debt. Jurisdictions may choose whether to use this mechanism, but they should have the legal authority to make such a covenant.

Intergovernmental Revenue Intercepts

In many countries, subnational governments can assign to creditors their interest in specific revenue streams, such as shared taxes and grants, received from higher-level governments (box 5.2). Called *revenue intercepts*, these assignments are attractive to creditors because of the promise of predictable revenue streams for paying debt service. Intercepts can be designed to ensure that adequate funds are available to meet debt service payments before they come due (an ex ante intercept) or to be tapped only in the event of a default (an ex post intercept). Another variant is to have a bank "stand-by" credit facility to advance money should funds not be on hand to meet debt service payments, with that loan then repaid out of future intercept receipts.

Some have argued that the pre-assignment of revenues to pay debt service tempts subnational governments not to budget for or pay debt service and induces intercept-protected creditors not to adequately assess the underlying worth of the investment being financed or the subnational government's financial performance. If these problems are thought to be compelling, charging borrowers that routinely use the intercept to pay debt service bills a large penalty or an administrative fee would ensure that the subnational government is always better off collecting its own revenues and paying its own bills.

Enterprise or "Self-Supporting" Limited Obligation Financing

A common use for special pledges of revenues and assets is for a self-supporting enterprise that generates its own means of repayment, without relying on recourse to general revenues.[7]

This limited obligation involves the pledge only of revenues from a specified system or project for repayment. This implies the creation of a special fund to receive the revenues that will be expended to meet costs associated with the enterprise, including debt payment. This concept focuses credit concerns on the viability of a particular project or system, rather than on the viability of the subnational government. It legally isolates certain self-sustaining activities and projects from the general affairs and financial backing of the sponsoring government. Even poor or unsound general purpose jurisdictions can have viable enterprises.[8]

Box 5.2. Intergovernmental Transfer Payments as Collateral

In many emerging market economies subnational governments are highly dependent on transfers from the central government for a major portion of revenues. While these transfers can be volatile, transfer intercepts are attractive for covering debt service payments.

As a general rule, if intergovernmental payments are used for pledging, the historic or expected level of transfers should cover the debt service payments by a fraction greater than one. In the Philippines cities receive about half of all revenues and the provinces about three-quarters through intergovernmental transfers from the national government. The smaller and more rural the subnational government, the higher the proportion of transfers to total revenues. In the Philippines, government-owned banks (the de facto required depositories for subnational governments) have gotten deeds of assignment of transfer payments to cover bank loans. As aid is received, the banks have a right of offset against any loan amounts owed the banks prior to dispersal for other purposes.

Mexico recently enacted legislation that permits states and cities to sell debt secured by a master trust that holds federal tax participation payments. Payments are made to the trust, which in turn pays out principal and interest to bondholders. Aguascalientes was the first Mexican city to issue bonds under the trust in December 2001. The bonds were sold in the domestic peso market.

Intercepts can have a powerful impact on subnational borrowers, especially small and remote governments. The assignment to bondholders of state payments to local school districts (which typically make up over 50 percent of revenues for the districts) is common in the United States. It is the basis for the high credit ratings enjoyed by local school districts covered by such programs. As a result of this widespread appreciation of the impact of state assistance and other small-borrower preferences, local schools are among the lowest cost borrowers in the U.S. municipal bond market.

Source: Authors.

Enterprise financing has several advantages:

- It establishes a relationship between the cost and the price of services, promoting more efficient operations. The cost-price relationship need not be absolute and can be modified, but it has the advantage of making any subsidy transparent.
- If the utility has run a surplus to subsidize other governmental functions, then the added "tax" burden on utility users becomes evident.
- Replacing general revenues that have subsidized enterprise operations with dedicated revenue structures will free up general revenues for other purposes.[9]
- Management and operation of revenue-producing facilities tend to be more efficient and the facilities better maintained since they need to be in shape to produce revenues. This can be encouraged by contractual provisions protecting income and value, paired with creditors' active interest in assets and their operation.
- When there are legitimate reasons to use general revenues as well as specific revenues, it may be better to use general revenues to reduce the amount of debt incurred. For example, this can be done by making a municipal "equity" investment in the asset up front, and borrowing to build or acquire the rest of the asset, pledging only revenues produced by the asset, or even a part of the asset's operations, to meet debt service requirements. This practice is common for many municipal utility operations in Western Europe.

Limited obligation, self-supporting financing also has several disadvantages:

- The expressions *asset stripping* or *security dilution* convey the concern of existing creditors of subnational governments that have relied on a utility to generate subsidies for the general fund when those revenues are instead peeled off and pledged to a utility-specific purpose.[10] Where prior lenders have looked to the overall revenues as a source of repayments, a subsequent sequestering or stripping away of revenue streams weakens the credits and creditworthiness of the jurisdiction.
- Limited obligations may impede redistribution of infrastructure and services among population groups (for example, from better-off groups to poor ones) by keeping potentially redistributable revenues

for the benefit of an already privileged area. Preferential and redistributive policies typically require financing from general funds.

- Enterprise financing is a contract between the public sector acting on behalf of the enterprise and the investor, who typically requires restrictions that reduce the financing options of borrowers in the future.[11] For example, borrowers must meet certain conditions before issuing more debt secured on the enterprise earnings (additional bonds test), must conform to certain requirements about reserves and insurance, and must abide by a rate covenant.

To improve creditworthiness and expand revenue sources, some subnational governments have used utility surpluses to subsidize the general budget.[12] However, transparency implies that utility surpluses used for cross-subsidization should be identified in a specific tax or surcharge that reflects the added cost of cross-subsidies. Without this transparency, it is not possible to see whether the utility is operating at an economic optimum in getting the most delivered service per unit of input. Having reached that optimum, the redistribution becomes a clear added cost for some and a benefit for others.

In addition to the traditional "natural monopolies," such as public utilities provided by subnational governments, other candidates for complete or partial financing through revenue bonds are more commercially oriented revenue-producing activities, such as transportation terminals, public markets, farm processing plants, industrial estates, tourism facilities (including hotels), and toll roads and bridges. Critical to their suitability to revenue bond financing are the reliability and growth of revenues, the technology used, the facilities' adequacy, and construction costs and future operating costs. Determining risks in these technical and economic factors requires engineering studies and market demand studies to obtain objective estimates of the net revenues available to pay debt service (see the section on grant and loan integration in chapter 12). Especially for new, free-standing projects with no operations experience, failing to do engineering and feasibility studies or not having them performed objectively by skilled professionals can lead to severe problems for the sponsoring subnational government, especially if that government pledges its own credit as part of the security (box 5.3).

Special District Financing

Special district financing is a variant of enterprise financing. A special district is created to provide infrastructure and services to a subset of the pop-

Box 5.3. Importance of Feasibility Reports: The San Pedro Sula, Honduras, Sports Complex

Projects that are intended to be self-supporting should generate sufficient revenues to pay for their operation and to meet capital costs. In many cases projects are monopolies—because they are essential in a technical sense (water and electricity), exclusive in location (toll roads and bridges), or subject to a high degree of market control through government regulation (solid waste and parking facilities). Other projects, such as sport or cultural venues, are not essential, are subject to competition, and face greater market demand risks. In all cases facilities may be subject to construction and technological risk, such as cost overruns, startup delays, or failure to produce output of the expected amount or quality.

Assessing these factors and associated risks is the role of the engineering and marketing studies conducted to establish a project's feasibility. Emerging market economies often lack the technical skills needed for engineering and market demand studies and the independence needed for objective analysis.

The difficulties of separating project promotion from technical analysis—and the unfortunate consequences of not doing so— are reflected in the fate of the sports complex built in the municipality of San Pedro Sula, Honduras. Expected to largely pay for itself, the complex was built to host the Central American Games. To partially meet expected costs of $25 million, some $15 million in bonds were sold, which were expected to be offset by a variety of revenues. The project ended up costing $36 million, and net project revenues fell far below expectations. The city made a general obligation pledge in addition to the project revenues, and it is now in serious financial difficulty.

The issuance of the bonds was not the problem. It was the lack of analysis that permitted the city to take on large and unknown risks. Among other problems, the feasibility study failed to do the following:

- Analyze the market for "special-seat" sales, although these were expected to generate nearly 80 percent of the operating revenues.
- Identify the assumptions used in the construction estimates.
- Examine alternatives, such as upgrading an existing stadium.
- Consider using the private sector and more equity in the construction project.
- Identify the various risks or contingencies if the complex's revenues were not realized.

In short, there was never a credible assessment of the project's economic prospects nor of the impact on the guaranteeing municipality's finances.

Source: Kehew 2002.

ulation or geographic area that demands special types or levels of service.[13] Special districts have been used to provide urban services (such as water, sewer, and roads), to areas that are developing rapidly or that have special needs (such as downtown areas). They are common in Western Europe and the United States and are beginning to appear in developing countries. As noted in chapter 4, the proliferation of subnational governments makes the need for cooperative ventures in project financing especially important among small governments.

If there are special benefits that can be ascribed to a particular area, the special district provides a mechanism for recovering the costs associated with the benefits. Special districts can transcend political boundaries or unite jurisdictions into a single financing unit to provide a regional service. Some types of new developments such as public utilities and transportation, storm drainage, and parks increase the attractiveness of an area and enhance property values, as well as other indices of economic activity and worth. If the costs of the capital improvements are borne by the public sector, the public sector should have some way to capture its investment. A special district can do that by adjusting its taxes or charges to pay for capital improvements that benefit specific properties.[14]

A successful special tax relies on good and timely measurement of values and an efficient collection system. In the United States, for example, some special taxing districts are administered by private for-profit organizations that undertake the calculations and do the tax billings as agents for the governments. The entire revenue-raising mechanism is meant to support obtaining credit and is specified in the loan or bond agreement. This improves the administration of taxes, and the integrity and efficiency of the system becomes, in effect, a matter of contract with bondholders. In Western Europe the special district or special authority covering all or parts of more than one political jurisdiction has facilitated the subsequent privatization of services, such as water utilities in France and the United Kingdom.

Notes

1. In the United States the term *full faith and power* means the application of the general taxing power to the repayment of the debt. That power in its traditional and strongest formulation has meant the imposing of taxes "unlimited as to rate or amount" sufficient to repay the debt. As a practical matter general obligation defaults are almost unheard of and are promptly cured by a mandamus from a court to levy taxes and the intervention of state governments to make sure that happens. States in the United States are usually very sensitive to the risk of getting a bad reputation because of the failure of a local government to pay its debts. Default by a general government means the loss of local governing powers, sometimes with the appointment of a control board or a receiver to take over operations until the debt is resolved.

2. This type of security is known in the United States as *appropriation* or *moral obligation debt*. It recognizes that the debt is not a full faith and credit binding obligation but rather is subject to the will of successive legislatures. Its origins are lease rental debt that holds that the obligation runs only from fiscal year to fiscal year and is subject to legislative reconsideration each year.

3. This is a seldom applied but potentially useful approach. The senior level does not commit to pay the creditor directly; rather, it agrees that it will withhold payments from the locality. It in effect avoids a contingent claim by the private party on the funds.

4. The Argentina case study, chapter 14, discusses two pledges that were used in tandem: intergovernmental transfers from a specific asset (hydrocarbon).

5. There are other cases to be made for taxing utility consumption. In many cases, the consumption can be used as a proxy for income. In others, the ability to piggyback on the billing process lowers collection costs. Last, the ability to shut off utility services provides a powerful means of enforcement. In many countries, however, shutting off utilities to non-payers is either illegal or extremely unpopular. This is particularly the case where utilities have been provided for free or heavily subsidized.

6. Problems of local revenue raising are particularly acute in transitioning economies. In the communist system taxes were buried within the state-owned corporate system and were frequently negotiated and changed by administrative fiat. Since the taxes were at the corporate level, citizens were unaware of the burden and have often resented the adoption of visible, explicit taxes (see Estirn 2002).

7. This is the traditional notion of the enterprise revenue bond. Many variations have been designed by states in the United States to circumvent restrictions on tax-supported debt. This approach encourages the allocation of the full costs of services to the beneficiaries, which is desirable economically because it leads to efficient allocation of scarce resources.

8. During the Great Depression of the 1930s in the United States, some states defaulted on their general obligation securities but continued to pay on revenue bonds supported by the motor fuel tax. People and businesses would forgo paying property taxes (on which states relied heavily) while continuing to use automobiles and purchase fuel. States subsequently shifted their tax systems to rely more on the sales tax.

9. In some places, such as in South Africa, the subsidy runs from the utility to the general fund, rather than the other way.

10. However, most economists would applaud this elimination of the cross-subsidy on efficiency grounds.

11. For example, there may be requirements that the borrower not pledge the same asset to another lender, except under stated conditions, that the revenues provide certain coverage of the debt service (rate covenant), and that revenues be retained for use on the facility and to benefit bondholders (closed loop). Negotiation of these restrictions and the associated tests is an integral part of the borrowing transaction.

12. Subsidies can be hard to detect. Where the utility is part of the government, the allocation of costs can be highly judgmental. A government

may allocate many of its administrative and other costs to the utility or it may receive utility services below cost or for free.

13. A district may be "dependent" and overseen by the governing body of the municipality or "independent" with an autonomous elected or appointed board. In many areas storeowners or homeowners form associations to manage the district and levy charges. The key is the ability to levy taxes and charges and to seize properties that do not pay.

14. In its most common form in the United States and a few places in Europe, the tax district uses property taxes (percentage of taxable property value) or assessments (fixed dollar levies). However, the district can use other bases to charge for the benefit or service, including square footage (or meters) or front footage (or meters), number of vehicular trips (for roads), impervious surface (for drainage), lumens of light (for lighting), residential bedrooms (for educational facilities), square footage of space (for parking), and so forth. The key is that there be a logical connection between the improvement and the form of charge that is used.

Chapter 6

Debt Instruments and Methods of Sale

Debt instruments are the legal embodiment of a credit transaction, setting out the terms and conditions of the loan, including how the principal is to be repaid, how long a debt will be outstanding, and how interest is figured and paid. Method of sale considerations involve the procedures by which debt is offered to the final investors and the debt obligations exchanged for the bond proceeds.

The general parameters of what instruments should look like and how sales are conducted are often covered in a nation's securities laws. As a rule, the precise details of these matters are determined by the market. Financial markets are fluid, and what might be attractive one day can be unattractive the next. Inflexibility is costly. However, in new markets both the borrowers and lenders are often unaccustomed to the process and perhaps unwary of the risks.

A major concern at the national level is to avoid creating regulations that interfere with the flexibility of lenders and borrowers in structuring debt in ways that best suit both parties. This chapter examines several of the alternatives that may be used in the design (often referred to as *structuring*) of subnational government debt transactions. It describes debt structure and illustrates the range of instruments available to suit the profiles of issuers and investors.

Maturity or Term of Debt

The *maturity* of a debt instrument refers to the period from the time the funds are borrowed to the time the principal is due to be repaid. The maturity should be matched to the economic life of the asset that the debt is financing. Ideally, the amortization of the liability on one side of the balance sheet is matched by the depreciation of the asset financed on the other side. Thus infrastructure assets, such as water systems, roads, or municipal buildings, which typically have lives of 15 to 30 years, should be financed with long-term bonds of similar duration. Matching asset life to debt term is also sound public policy because then facilities can be paid for by those who use them.

In many emerging market economies, however, private investors are unable or unwilling to extend loans beyond a few years. Even if longer term capital is available, the upward sloping yield curve—the longer the term of the debt, the higher the interest rate payable—may cause borrowers to prefer shorter-term debt. Investors want extra compensation for the lack of liquidity of long-term lending and the increasing uncertainty about economic conditions, price levels, and interest rates far into the future. However, this is not always the case. Short-term interest rates may be temporarily driven up by liquidity shortages and efforts to defend the currency. If expectations are that the prevailing level of interest rates is unsustainably high, and if rates are expected to fall, then the yield curve may be inverted, with short-term rates higher than long-term rates. In such cases, some borrowers may borrow on a short-term basis, if they believe long-term rates will fall. Others may choose to lock in the relatively lower long-term rates.

There is also a tradeoff between the lower rates typical of short-term debt and refinancing risk. If the debt is shorter in maturity than the life of the asset, the borrower is exposed to refinancing risk—new debt may have to be raised during the life of the asset at a higher rate than the original loan. If the borrower's credit risk has worsened, it may not be possible to refinance. Refinancing can, of course, work in favor of the borrower, if, for example, interest rates fall or the borrower's credit improves. In the case of general obligation bonds, this could happen as a result of the improved general creditworthiness of the subnational government. In the case of project finance, the construction and initial phases of operation are riskier than the later phases of a mature project, when it may be possible to refinance at lower rates. However, financiers are aware of this and rely on the later phases to provide some compensation for the additional risk taken at the outset. Thus they would probably reserve for themselves the right to refinance. All in all, maintaining an unhedged position is risky and usually not advisable with public funds.

Debt Service or Repayment Structures

There are several common cash flow profiles of debt, which describe the ways a borrower pays interest and principal over the life of the liability (figure 6.1). In addition, interest rates may be fixed or floating and bonds may pay interest on a variety of "coupon" dates.[1]

Loan Structure and Cash Flow Profiles

The debt service (that is, combined principal and interest) may be paid in approximately equal installments over the life of the debt, which is called

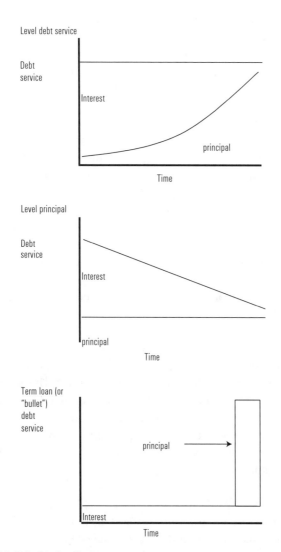

Figure 6.1. Debt Service Structures

level debt service. Another, more conservative approach is the *level principal structure*, in which the principal is repaid in equal increments and interest in declining increments, leading to a more rapid repayment of debt. This front-end-loaded structure frees up future borrowing capacity quickly and leads to progressively smaller debt service payments. Alternatively, the debt service schedule may be structured to increase over the life of the debt. A *term bond structure* typically has periodic interest payments but the principal falls due at the end. This back-end-loaded structure, sometimes called a *bullet loan*, is common in short-term securities and bank loans.

The variations on loan structures are practically limitless. Their shapes can be influenced by grace periods, deferrals of payment of the principal or interest or both for periods of time. Such structures are used when loans are to be paid from project earnings and there is a construction or start-up period before receipts start to flow. Original discount bonds, called *zeros* when they fully discount future interest payments, pay no or reduced interest. The investor realizes a return by buying the bond substantially below its principal value. Such bonds can be issued at discount or created synthetically by investment banks by stripping the coupon off a standard term or serial bond. Zeros are attractive to parties who want to secure a fixed amount of capital in the future without being exposed to reinvestment risk. Zero bonds are created synthetically when the coupon stream is stripped from a bond and sold to an investor who is interested primarily in an annuity flow.

Cash flow profiles can be engineered to match the cash flows generated by the activity being financed. Liabilities can be index linked, where revenue flows are expected to vary with an index, such as inflation or an input cost. Interest payments can go up or down, depending on the movement of the index. As noted, amortizing payments can be structured with an escalating profile, with lower debt service in the early years. This is common in commercial property finance, for example, where there is a "ramp-up" period when rentals are expected to escalate, and can be appropriate for certain municipal assets. Similarly, interest payments for initial periods can be deferred by using bond proceeds to pay interest costs in early periods (capitalized interest).

Fixed or Floating Interest Rates

Bank loans or municipal bonds may be made at fixed or floating rates of interest. In emerging market economies, the variable rate may be the only interest payment structure available for obligations beyond a short maturity.

Both have advantages and disadvantages. Floating rate debt implies continuous uncertainty about the cost of debt, but it can be appropriate where the matching revenues are expected to vary with changes in interest rates. However, this is not usually the case for municipalities. Financial flexibility and access to liquidity are important considerations for floating rate borrowers. If there is limited ability to change taxes or rates to respond to rising interest rates, then over-reliance on variable rate debt is worrisome. The rating company Standard and Poor's generally recommends that the combined short-term debt and variable rate debt not exceed 20 percent of total debt, but the share depends on the circumstances and degree of flexibility and matching of revenues with debt service.[2]

Cash Flow Concerns

There are several considerations in deciding on the cash flow of municipal bonds. Bonds may pay interest on a variety of "coupon" dates. Although semiannual payments are the most common in developed markets, structured loans can have varying coupon profiles (semiannual, quarterly, even monthly) to suit the cash flow requirements of the borrower and the capacities of the issuer. Most municipal bonds in emerging markets have had short maturities and many have had term bond or bullet maturity structures, meaning that most loans to subnational governments have been for construction and start-up costs. Implicit in the repayment structure has been the requirement that the borrower roll over the loan into a new one at maturity or come up with alternative means of long-term financing. This approach subjects issuers and lenders to great uncertainty about future debt service requirements and effectively holds borrowers hostage to future changes that may be forced on them when they come back to the market to renew the loan.

Legal Restrictions

A final area of policy regarding the structure of instruments concerns restrictions that may be placed on interest rates or on the maximum maturity of bonds. Interest rates may be capped by "usury rates" that set an absolute ceiling on rates. While this was once common practice in the United States, the restriction has disappeared for all practical purposes over the last 20 years. Limiting interest rates has the effect of rationing capital away from governments during periods of high interest rates. Such restrictions continue as a matter of contract in variable rate instruments, however, where a cap is specified or a borrower may purchase a rate cap contract from a commercial bank that will agree to pay the excess interest for a fee. The other common restriction is on maximum maturity of bonds, which is often specified in conjunction with the expected useful life of the improvement being financed. Again, these restrictions are seldom effective and the market itself provides the limitation on how far it will extend debt, especially at fixed interest rates.

Methods of Sale for Securities

Municipal securities can be sold to investors in a number of ways. Bonds can be auctioned competitively to the highest bidder or placed with the final investor, much as a direct loan is made from a bank. In most emerging markets the offering is made through negotiation, with the borrower selling its bonds through a financial services firm (such as an investment banking firm or, for larger issues, a combination of firms, called a *syndicate*). The firm underwrites the issue, agreeing either to buy all the bonds offered at a certain price or to act as an agent and make a "best effort" to sell the bonds, receiving a commission on the bonds sold.

Characteristics of Markets: Setting Interest Rates and Other Terms

A competitive sale environment requires an active market with a large number of issuers offering fairly standardized securities and a large number of investors interested in owning them. The large volume of activity results in a number of bankers following the market, making bids, and placing bonds to investors. It also means that there are other professionals who help to design the issues, prepare documents, and run the auctions.[3] The competitive auction, with several underwriters bidding on a bond issue, is common in the U.S. municipal bond market but a rarity in other markets. It may, however, become more prevalent as markets thicken in activity and experience develops.[4] A strong point in its favor is the transparency of the transaction, since barring collusion among bidders, the public auction clearly identifies how the bonds are priced.

Where bond markets are less homogeneous and sales are irregular, issuers typically rely on negotiations, hiring an underwriter to help prepare the issue and seek out possible investors. The negotiations can be made competitive by injecting elements of competition among firms into the underwriting selection process and subsequently by holding underwriters to the projected terms of the issue. To help achieve competition, the issuer may employ the services of a financial adviser knowledgeable about the design of transactions and the marketing of securities. The adviser usually helps the issuer select an underwriter and, among other tasks, helps to ensure that the issuer is being dealt with fairly by the underwriter (box 6.1).

The underwriting process has the advantage over the use of a best effort marketing arrangement of guaranteeing that sufficient funds will be borrowed. However, the investment banker undertakes the risk of reselling the issue and demands more remuneration when acting as an underwriter than when acting as a placement agent. To make a profit and to cover risk and expenses, the underwriter buys the bonds at a discount—for less than the value at which they are reoffered to the final investors. This price difference is known as the *spread*.

The mechanics of selling bonds and setting interest rates and other terms differ for various domestic securities markets. In countries with relatively small and inactive markets, the terms of the bond offering may be set well in advance of the sale date. The bonds then may be sold on a given day with a discount or premium to make returns competitive with then-prevailing conditions. Fixing terms before the sale date puts the underwriter at greater risk, so issuers pay an interest rate premium. Another approach is to commit to having the bonds underwritten at a certain mark-up or in relationship to some regularly published interest-rate index, usually that on government bonds. Finally, the terms can be determined by offering the bonds at a proposed structure and then changing the terms to meet the effective demand from investors in what amounts to an "informal" auction. The terms and their acceptability to the issuer remain open until the sales contract (the bond purchase agreement) with the underwriter is signed.

The bond instruments or other evidence of ownership then are delivered physically or electronically and money is exchanged for them (settlement). Depending on market conventions and the nature of the security, the issuer or the underwriter may have selected a paying agent or a trustee to receive funds from the issuer and to pay interest and principal. The trustee also oversees the bond contract between the issuer and ultimate buyers of the bonds, the investors, and looks after the interests of the investors, making sure that the terms of the bond contract are observed.

Importance of Impartiality and Transparency

Beyond the procedures set down by national enabling laws, the specifics of the bond offering are a matter of contract among the underwriter, the issuer, and the ultimate investor. Thus the issuer needs to obtain sound legal

Box 6.1. Selecting an Underwriter through Competitive Negotiation

The city of Krakow proposed a 15 million zloty bond issue in 1996. With the assistance of a financial adviser, the city sent a solicitation to a large number of investment banking and commercial banking firms, describing the project and needed funds, providing information about the city, and asking for proposals. The solicitation and selection process contained several elements designed to make the choice of firms transparent and competitive. The solicitation contained a tentative maturity structure for the issue and asked respondents to price the bonds (provide interest rates) and indicate their gross profit, assuming that the bonds had been sold on a given day. In addition, the respondents were asked to estimate an itemized list of costs and to indicate which costs would be met from their profits and which would be paid by the city. Firms were asked to critique the structure and suggest alternatives and to describe their experience and financial capacity.

A combination of factors was used in selecting the finalists, but the cost of borrowing was the most important. All costs, including future interest payments and fees paid by the city, were made comparable by using an all-in-cost internal rate of return calculation. Responses were analyzed by a committee, and individual firms were contacted to clear up any questions. Of the eight firms and syndicates that responded, the top three were invited to make presentations and to make their best and final offer. A syndicate was selected. The final offer committed the underwriting syndicate to price the proposed bonds on a par with Polish Treasury bonds of the same maturity, a highly aggressive bid.

Subsequently, Krakow received an investment grade credit rating from Standard & Poor's and sold bonds (Deutsche mark denominated) in the Euro market in late 1997. It was the first Polish city to do so.

Source: Petersen and Crihfield 2000.

and financial advice that is independent of that given by the underwriter and the final investor.

The transparency of the method of sale matters. The large amounts involved in bond sales and the ability of financial firms to make large profits on bond issues can be a temptation for corruption (see box 6.2).

Investments Related to Borrowing

An important element of subnational government borrowing is the types of investment that are permitted for the following.

- Proceeds of a borrowing that are awaiting application to the intended purpose.
- Funds held for paying debt service, including intercepted funds and reserve funds.

Box 6.2. Rigging a City's Bond Sale

Saõ Paulo was a heavy borrower in the Brazilian bond markets. As of January 2000 its outstanding debt was over 10 billion reais or nearly 1,600 reais per capita (equivalent then to about $800), some 20 times the average debt of Brazilian municipalities. The city's large appetite for borrowing was driven by more than its fiscal needs.

In early 2000, when the national government was negotiating an arrangement to allow the city to refinance its debt, a scandal broke out involving corruption in previous city bond sales. The mayor, who was formerly the city's finance officer, was accused of having rigged past bond sales. He sold bonds at a steep discount to a select group of underwriters and then participated with them in the profits when the marked-up bonds were reoffered on the open market. The mayor was removed from office by court order in March 2000.

Source: World Bank 2001.

In the case of bonds, such funds should be held in a custodial arrangement, segregated from other funds of the subnational governments, and invested with minimal credit risk exposure.[5] The funds must be available when needed for their intended purposes, and there should be no market risk associated with liquidation of the investments.

The legal framework for subnational governments is often silent on the parameters for investing bond-related funds, sometimes with unfortunate results.[6] Too much rigidity, as, for example, requiring that bond proceeds be held by the national treasury in non-interest-bearing accounts, can make bond issuance less attractive and more awkward to structure efficiently.[7] Regulation of allowable investments may be desirable, balancing flexibility and the need for prudent investment instruments in a changing environment.

Notes

1. A useful guide to concepts and terminologies used in designing and marketing subnational debt, along with many illustrations, is World Bank 2002c.

2. In the United States, where there is an upward sloping yield curve from short-term to long-term maturities, there has been a reward of 100 to 200 basis points for using variable-rate instead of fixed-rate debt. Debt typically can be called at the reset date, allowing flexibility to restructure debt.

3. Other professionals include financial advisers, legal counsel, auditing firms, and printers to produce the documents. There also may be banks to handle the investment of proceeds and to oversee payments under the debt contract (trustees and paying agents).

4. In Romania, for example, some cities are beginning to solicit bank loans on the basis of "bid sheets" that set forth the structure and terms that the city seeks and then asks for the respondent to fill in the interest rate. A motivating factor is the law on procurement, which generally forbids acquiring goods and services without a competitive bidding process.

5. In South Africa, municipalities may invest in a relatively short list of investments, including bank deposits and government securities (LGTA, Section 9).

6. In the 1998 Odessa bond issue in Ukraine, the proceeds of the borrowing were invested in the Ukrainian interbank market at negative arbitrage, many of the proceeds were unaccounted for, the projects were not completed, and the city defaulted on payment on the bonds.

7. In Romania local general governments must deposit funds in non-interest-bearing national treasury accounts, while enterprise funds can use private bank accounts.

Chapter 7

Restrictions on the Issuance and Use of Subsovereign Debt

Most national governments place restrictions on the use of debt by subnational governments, thereby substituting national policy for local flexibility and the regulating effect of markets on municipal borrowing. As chapter 3 shows, there are several regimes for regulating debt, but in most cases there is an overarching set of rules that governs subnational debt issuance. National regulations typically cover the authority of subnational governments to borrow and restrict the purpose of borrowing, the maturity, the amount of borrowing or debt outstanding, the use of proceeds, and the type of security given or recourse available to the lender. While the differences can be arbitrary, short-term debt is generally that due within one year or less, and long-term debt is anything due more than a year after it is incurred. Subnational government guarantees, which ought to be treated like any other debt, also may be subject to regulation.

Subnational Government Authority to Borrow

Subnational government autonomy is generally based on principles set forth in the national constitution,[1] although the laws on subnational government borrowing are often scattered across the legal landscape, reflecting the fact that defining such activities is frequently an afterthought. Determining a subnational government's legal authority to borrow and the associated legal parameters can require reconciling conflicting laws, regulations, and decrees. Explicit authorization and procedural requirements are essential, especially where these governments have had no experience with issuing financial obligations that are valid, binding, and enforceable.

Some people argue for a minimalist approach to subnational debt legislation that gives authority to the minister of finance or other central government authority to issue regulations, to be approved by the government, so that regulations can be adapted readily to experience and circumstance (Glasser 1998). This approach may provide some flexibility in an emerging market and in a changing environment. However, over the long term, all legal criteria and conditions for borrowing should be expressly contained within the legal framework, whether as law or regulation.

In Indonesia the implementation instructions for subnational government borrowing under Law 25 mandate that donors and external government lenders conclude direct agreements with subnational governments, but the agreements must be cosigned by the Ministry of Finance. External creditors do not have an explicit right to secure their debt with the general allocation grant intercept mechanism or the right to a sovereign guarantee, but these security structures can be negotiated with the Ministry of Finance—an opaque requirement that allows for considerable political interference in the approval process (see Indonesia case study, chapter 25).

Binding Nature of Debt

A frequent issue in developing credit markets is the concern that a commitment by a subnational government may not bind a subsequent government. Even if the problem is one of market perception rather than law, the lack of clarity about who exactly is bound and for how long can create uncertainty about the political commitment of succeeding governments to repay the debt (see box 7.1). For long-term finance to be available for subnational investment, capital markets must be confident that a financial obligation is binding on succeeding governments.

In Bulgaria the law prohibits a municipal council from contracting debt or extending short-term interest-free loans within six months of the expiration of its term of office (Municipal Budgets Act, Article 40 [4]). The intent is to prevent the issuance of debt for politically popular projects that may win over the electorate while encumbering the municipality with excessive debt that will be binding on the succeeding municipal council. While this requirement has little practical effect now, given the limited municipal borrowing activity, as the municipal credit market matures it could prevent a subnational government from taking advantage of commercial financing during a period of low market rates.

If long-term debt financing for subnational investment is to become widely available, capital markets must have confidence that succeeding leg-

---

Box 7.1. The Philippines: How Political Risks Can Inhibit Municipal Credit Markets

In the Philippine city of Cebu a newly elected mayor publicly questioned whether his administration would be bound to honor a debt incurred by the prior council. The mayor eventually withdrew his comments, and the city paid the debt on time and in full. However, the financial community lost confidence in the city, and as a result lenders have been inclined to limit loans and bond maturities for subnational governments in the Philippines to the current administration's term of office.

To counter this maturity limitation, some subnational governments have held voluntary referendums to demonstrate popular support for specific project debt financing and thereby overcome financial institutions' fears of the political risks associated with long-term lending.

Source: DeAngelis and Dunn 2002.

---

islative bodies will honor the financial obligations of their predecessors. This principle should be explicitly affirmed in any subnational debt legislation. The governing law should specify the binding nature of subnational obligations to repay duly authorized debt (see examples of France and Romania in box 7.2).

Authorizing and Approving Subnational Debt

Subnational government borrowing can be approved by the subnational government executive or governing body; the community at large through a referendum; or state, provincial, or national authorities. Each approval mechanism can be conditioned by a variety of considerations, including the financial capacity of the borrower to repay debt, the purpose of the borrowing, the form of borrowing, and its consistency with national economic policy. Most mechanisms also act as a curb on local officials' prerogatives by enforcing certain disciplines and limiting their authority to borrow.

Box 7.2. Examples of Language on the Binding Nature of Financial Obligations

France, Code Général des Collectivités Territoriales (Article L.1612-15)

- The only obligatory expenditures of subnational authorities are expenditures necessary to pay debts that come due and expenditures that have been expressly determined by law.

Romania: Local Public Finance Law, 1998 (Article 48)

- Local and judet councils and the General Council of the Municipality of Bucharest can approve the contracting of internal or external loans, for a long or a medium term, for public investments of local interest, as well as for refinancing the public debt, under the provisions of this chapter.
- Local and judet councils and the General Council of the Municipality of Bucharest may decide upon contracting loans by the vote of at least two thirds of their members.
- The local public debt incurred under the provisions of paragraph (1) represents a general obligation which needs to be reimbursed, according to the agreements concluded, from the sources available to the territorial administrative unit, with the exception of special purpose transfers from the state budget.

Source: DeAngelis and Dunn 2002.

Approval by the executive. Authorization often depends on the maturity and size of the borrowing. Authorization by the chief executive seems appropriate for relatively small amounts and for the short term, where the future financial health of the local jurisdiction is not at risk. Large amounts or long-term borrowing should require authorization by legislative act of the governing body. Longer term borrowing involves trading off future financial flexibility in exchange for investment capital today.

Approval by the legislature or the community. For large amounts of debt, a local governing body should determine the key borrowing issues: for what purpose and for how much? Experience suggests that without local governing body approval, the probability rises dramatically that debt will be repudiated or that the tax or tariff changes needed to meet debt service obligations will not be enacted. Furthermore, public debate on debt policies and plans helps keep the process open and visible (see box 7.3).

Legislative approval can range from simply approving the borrowing as part of the budget process to voting and authorizing a particular transac-

---

Box 7.3. The City of Cebu in the Philippines Considers a Deal

Subnational governments may lack the knowledge and procedures needed to fend for themselves as borrowers with expanded opportunities. The experience of the city of Cebu, Philippines, illustrates what can happen when politics and media influence local financing decisions. The city and its mayor were actively seeking financing for a ring road, a core element of a development plan. In mid-1998, two firms, one based in Hong Kong and one in Austria, proposed that the city enter into a $500 million loan and $75 million letter of credit to fund the ring road. The mayor liked the idea, and the firms, eager to facilitate the process, paid several councilmen from the mayor's party to travel to Europe to see, secretly it turned out, examples of what the firms had financed. The councilmen signed letters of intent to enter into an agreement in three months.

Subsequently, things began to get sticky. Political opponents asked whether this was a scam. The local representative of the investment firms was arrested on 32 counts of passing bad checks and after posting bail skipped town for Hong Kong. Local bank officials indicated that three signatures had been forged on documents shown in the transaction, evidently guaranteeing $150 million in city funds. The mayor established a committee to meet with the financiers, but the financiers refused to meet. By this time the Cebu scam saga was receiving daily press coverage in Cebu and Manila.

(Box continues on the following page.)

Box 7.3. (*continued*)

The mayor announced in late November that the financing consortium was embarrassed by the episode and would give the city a grant instead of a loan or at least contribute a few million pesos to the project. By the next day, however, the consortium changed its mind about any "grants instead of loans" and it was clear that the deal would collapse.

There are two perspectives on the ill-fated deal. One is that subnational governments lack the skills needed for such major decisions, so such decisions should be kept out of their reach. However, blandishments by project proponents who stand to gain (or by con artists who wish to defraud) are facts of life at all levels of government. A more positive perspective is that local party politics and news-hungry journalists are ready to shine bright lights on shady deals. A possible solution? Having local banks and bond dealers compete openly for the deal or help with the due diligence promotes disclosure and limits politically influenced decisionmaking.

Source: Petersen and Crihfield 2000.

---

tion and approving its terms. Special voting requirements may be employed. A "supermajority" vote by a subnational governing body has sometimes been used to demonstrate political support (see box 7.2). Such a supermajority vote can be required for certain types of subnational borrowing or for debt that is authorized just before an election, to avoid the perception of a politically motivated project.

Borrowing approval also can come from the community voting at large through a referendum. A popular vote may encourage citizen participation in decisionmaking and win community backing for the long haul, whatever the changes in the elected council. Voter approval for borrowing is not without problems, however. It adds time and expense and can turn financial decisions into political battles that may have little to do with the merits of the proposed financing. As with legislative approval, referendums may be limited to certain types of debt or special circumstances.

Approval and review by higher government level. National (or state) review and approval of subnational borrowing plans is not uncommon in emerging market economies and may be predicated on specific conditions. These could include the financial capacity to repay debt, as measured by credit analysis or a formula specified by law or regulation. Other relevant considerations include consistency of subnational borrowing with national economic policy (such as the timing of the borrowing) and the purpose and form of the borrowing. Such oversight can be used to prevent irresponsible borrowing at the local level, but it raises a number of issues. Reviews introduce delays, require oversight capacity at the national or state level, and provide an entry point for political rather than economic considerations. In general, advocates of market discipline argue that the marketplace, aided by appropriate disclosure rules, borrowing rules, and investor analysis, will do a better job of assessing financial capacity to repay debt.

There may be circumstances in which higher level review is appropriate. A state or national authority, while leaving the decisions to incur debt at the subnational level, might certify the procedures used in the borrowing process.[2] Certification can help build investor confidence and relieve individual investors of some of the due diligence that otherwise would be required. However, in most emerging market economies there may be little capacity at the higher levels of government to undertake this task for securities offerings. Imposing a procedural review that cannot be promptly executed slows the development of the market and opens a forum for political second-guessing and bickering.

Even where higher government approval is not routine, it might be desirable when a subnational government wishes to exceed its debt limit to have a central government entity authorize such an exception in certain narrow circumstances:

- The subnational government has a high degree of creditworthiness.
- The projects to be financed will clearly increase subnational revenues, and will be self-financing or will reduce subnational expenditures in future years and be effectively self-financing.
- The money is needed to respond to a natural disaster or civil calamity.

Additionally, some countries (for example, Ukraine) have tried to prevent "pyramid" schemes by prohibiting any refinancing of outstanding debt. Such prohibitions become problematic when a borrower experiences financial difficulties and a legitimate restructuring of debt would benefit all parties. Provisions could be made for exceptions in such cases, perhaps with special approval procedures.

Equal Treatment of all Forms of Debt

The legal framework for subnational debt should not differentiate based on the legal form of the debt. The authorization process, debt limitation, and allowable purposes for issuing debt should be uniform for loans and bonds. The decision of a subnational government about whether to use loans or bonds should be based on market factors rather than legal factors.[3] The Romanian Ministry of Finance adopted a regulation requiring its approval of subnational government bond issues (even though the Law on Local Public Finance did not require central government approval) but not of bank loans, thereby creating a legal environment favoring loans over bonds.[4] Ukraine has substantially different authorization procedures, amount limitations, and allowable purposes for bonds, loans, and guarantees.[5] In the Philippines loans may be taken for any purpose, but bonds may be sold only for "revenue-producing" facilities (see Philippine case study, chapter 26).

Details relating to the terms of subnational debt, such as maturity and interest rate limitations, are often not expressly set forth in the legal framework and so are open to interpretation. An area under intense scrutiny in many emerging market economies is the currency composition of the debt (see the South Africa case study, chapter 18). Except in unusual circumstances, subnational governments have limited ability to raise foreign currency funds themselves and are poorly positioned to hedge or speculate against currency fluctuations. Sofia, Bulgaria, used a U.S. dollar-denominated loan to fund the purchase of buses in 1994. During the term of the loan, the exchange rate rose from less than 30 lev to the dollar to more than 3,000 lev to the dollar. Subnational governments are often exposed to such risk through the on-lending programs of multilateral and bilateral lending programs. Subnational governments have sometimes been charged loan premiums for currency risk protection and in other cases have simply borne the risk directly, though often the risk has been mitigated by sovereign guarantees. Central government approval is often required for subnational government assumption of currency risk, which seems to be a sound policy.[6]

Restrictions on Short-Term Debt

Short-term financing can be a useful part of a subnational government's regular operations. It can be used to cover operations in anticipation of annual tax revenues or of nonrecurring revenue, such as from the sale of assets, receipt of a grant, or issuance of long-term debt. Operating expenses can be financed from borrowed funds or from a municipality's working capital, which usually is less expensive and more reliable, but not all subnational governments maintain adequate working capital funds. In that case subnational governments generally either match outflows with inflows or attempt to get advances from the national treasury, as in Romania.

Events can slow the receipt of revenues or cause unexpected surges in spending that lead to cash shortages. Ideally, governments would carry reserves to smooth fluctuations in working capital flows, but liquid reserves can be a source of political bickering and a temptation to politicians with other priorities. In some countries surplus funds are returned to the central government for redistribution or are held in non-interest-bearing national treasury accounts, yielding no benefits to subnational governments from investing surpluses.

Borrowing to meet short-term financing needs can provide opportunities for banks and subnational governments to develop working relationships and allow bankers to become familiar with the governments' financial affairs. Provided that the financing is repaid within the budget year and that carrying debt beyond the budget year is prohibited, there is no *a prioi* reason to limit such financing to capital spending.

Dangers of Misuse

A major concern is that short-term debt will be used to bridge an ever-growing gap between recurring revenues and recurring expenditures, reaching levels that compromise a subnational government's ability to deliver basic services. The "snowballing" of short-term debt as governments run chronic operating deficits has been a leading cause of financial emergencies, causing banks and other investors to lose confidence in a government's ability to run surpluses and repay its short-term debt. Allowed to accumulate too long, short-term debt can reach unsustainable levels, requiring a high proportion of revenues to be devoted to debt service at the expense of public services. Eventually, creditors may deny further credit extensions when they perceive that the floating debt has reached excessive levels (see box 7.4). This happened to New York City in the 1970s and more recently to subnational governments in Argentina, Brazil, and Mexico, contributing to financial crises.

Nature of Restrictions

Short-term borrowing should be restricted to financing intra-year cash flow budget deficits. The debt should be repaid within the budget year, with no

Box 7.4. Johannesburg Comes Up Short

South African municipalities may legally borrow to finance both routine and unusual short-term needs, but they are required by the national constitution to settle their short-term debts by the end of the fiscal year. The usual form of borrowing has been a bank overdraft, which creates an unsecured debt. In some cases, the overdrafts were not being settled as required by law at the end of the fiscal year. For Johannesburg, curing the snowballing short-term debt problem led to other problems for the nation's financial sector.

In 1997 Johannesburg found itself in a difficult position. It had accumulated a large amount of outstanding short-term debt to finance the start of a capital spending program that was to have been funded by the sale of long-term debt. Domestic markets closed to the city in late 1997. Ultimately, the Development Bank of Southern Africa (DBSA) stepped in and made a loan secured on a specific tax source.

However, the rescue had its repercussions. The South African commercial banks, which had refused to roll over the short-term loan, were disturbed that the DBSA had "peeled off" part of the general revenue base and had done the deal on terms that were only marginally better than they were offering.

Source: Authors.

refinancing beyond the end of the budget year. The volume of short-term borrowing also can be limited, with a ceiling set at some percentage of total budget revenues (see box 7.5 for some common formulas). Lithuania and Romania limit short-term debt to 5 percent of revenues.

A further protection against excessive debt accumulation is a requirement that short-term borrowing be paid off in full at least once a year, with appropriate safeguards against immediate re-borrowing. Because natural disasters or financial emergencies may make this difficult to enforce, some provision for national-level approval of exceptions might be needed.

Restrictions on Long-Term Debt

Long-term debt allows subnational governments to acquire or build capital improvements more quickly than they could on a pay-as-you-go basis. It allows more equitable payment schemes, since users can be made to pay for the capital cost of facilities as they are used over time. However, there are also costs and risks. Long-term debt limits a subnational government's future budget flexibility. Unwisely used, it can burden citizens with high taxes or service charges. Many countries permit long-term debt only for capital spending and not for operating deficits (sometimes called the "Golden Rule"). Some countries are even more restrictive, limiting bonds to "self-supporting" revenue-generating activities, as in the Philippines. Underlying these regulations is the conviction that governments should only borrow long term when the proceeds of the debt will contribute to some future capacity to repay.

Competing Prescriptions for Long-Term Debt Use

Long-term debt is clearly appropriate for capital investment when the term of the borrowing is related to the useful life of the capital asset being built or acquired. Less clear is whether multiyear debt should be allowed for other purposes in many developing countries, such as work-outs as part of a fiscal recovery package or extraordinary expenses related to the transition and restructuring of governments.

Typically, regulation of the purpose of long-term debt either allows subnational governments to borrow for any public purpose authorized by law—leaving it to the local jurisdiction to decide what is wise and appropriate and to the markets to decide whether the stated purpose is worth financing—or limits borrowing to specific public purposes. These might include:

- Building or acquiring a capital asset whose anticipated useful life will equal or exceed the term of the borrowing.
- Funding self-supporting revenue-generating projects.
- Funding accumulated operating deficits as part of a legal or administrative restructuring.
- Funding extraordinary needs, such as recovery from natural or human-caused disasters.

Each alternative has its advantages. Two factors favor a more liberal authorization policy. First, subnational government finance is an evolving art, and there should be room to adopt new forms and techniques of local finance. Second, if national policy favors decentralization (the operating premise of this book), then local managers should have decisionmaking flexibility. However, some restrictions may be appropriate for nascent subnational government debt markets. Specific limitations can provide clarity about what is permissible, which may reassure young capital markets, particularly where there is a perception that the public needs protection from politicians or managers who might try to use long-term debt for their own short-term gain.

Public Purpose Debt: Distinguishing between Public and Private Benefit

A frequent issue is the evolving standard for "public purpose" and the creation of legally defined boundaries distinguishing private and public benefit. The limited debt capacity of many subnational governments in emerging markets might best be devoted to projects that clearly serve a direct public purpose. Yet many subnational governments have inherited activities and facilities of a commercial nature, including ownership and operation of entrepreneurial businesses. Moreover, many reformers call for subnational governments to involve the private sector in the delivery of goods and services and the ownership of facilities. Such public-private engagements can rapidly turn to questions of how the subnational government can provide guarantees or even loans to make the facilities more attractive for private ownership or operation. In other words, both customary and new ways of "doing business" compound the difficulties of making brightline distinctions between public purpose and private benefit.

The governing law should distinguish between debt issued for a public purpose and debt issued for a publicly owned, but inherently private, entrepreneurial activity. In defining "public purpose," debt legislation should prohibit general obligation debt or subnational guarantees for the benefit of such private entrepreneurial activities. Sometimes a public purpose clause in the subnational debt legislation also explicitly prohibits the use of subnational borrowing authority to incur an obligation solely or primarily to benefit a private property owner or a business.[7] This can preclude issuing debt for the types of public-private projects being considered in many emerging market economies in which assets are to be transferred to the private sector or jointly operated by the public and private sectors.

Thus the standard for what constitutes a public purpose may be difficult to define in many contexts. Financing certain private entrepreneurial activities can be argued to have an indirect public benefit, such as increased employment, economic activity, or housing. This standard may be an appropriate issue for regulation, which should provide the necessary flexibility. The standard could initially be defined very conservatively and later expanded. Additionally, an argument could be made that, although the nature of the project is not directly related to a subnational unit's ability to pay the debt, creditors would rather be associated with a public purpose project that enjoys general political and popular support and enhances a subnational government's willingness to pay the debt associated with such a project.

Regulations concerning the public purpose need to be carefully phrased with provisions such as the following:

- The public purpose is paramount in the expenditure or loan, any private gain must be incidental to achieving that purpose, and such gain must be of a customary and appropriate degree.
- Financing that extends beyond the current budget year may be issued solely for investment or refinancing of debt issued for investment that serves a public purpose authorized in the municipal budget.
- The proceeds of a borrowing may be spent only on the investment for which the debt has been authorized, unless both the subnational governing body and the debt holders agree otherwise.

Restrictions on Amount of Debt

There is little agreement in practice on the amount of debt that a subnational government should be allowed to carry. A review of the case studies (chapters 14–31) shows that approaches occupy a spectrum: at one end is Hungary (chapter 29), with a Law on Local Self-Government that gives subnational governments unlimited borrowing authority; at the other end is the Republic of Korea (chapter 23), with very detailed borrowing criteria involving multiple measures of debt service and requiring higher level approval of individual issues. An International Monetary Fund publication (Ter-Minassian 1997) argues for rules-based control of subnational borrowing, with limits on the debt of individual jurisdictions that "mimic market discipline."[8] Such control could be framed in terms of a ratio between maximum annual debt service and a conservative projection of the revenues that would be available to pay debt service.[9]

The argument against such control is that there can be occasions when it is desirable for a local jurisdiction to temporarily exceed a given ratio as it invests for the future or spends down accumulated reserves. The argument favoring such control is that it protects the public from reckless borrowing by officials or elected representatives who may not be sensitive to the long-term risks.

Distinguishing General Fund and Limited Obligation Debt

For general fund debt an allowable ratio of outstanding debt or debt service to available resources for repayment can be set to provide reasonable protection without interfering with sound management. An escape clause could permit the debt limit to be exceeded for exceptional cases under emergency legislation or with special permission from higher level authorities (or local referendum, as in the United States). For self-financing or enterprise projects, where the pledge is clearly limited to project revenues, the debt limit need not apply. However, few emerging market economies make this legal distinction for limited obligation debt.

Some Practical Problems in Designing Limits

Limitations on subnational debt are widespread. Common debt limits are on the following:

- The amount of indebtedness issued, usually expressed as a ratio of actual or potential source of revenues, such as taxable property values.
- Annual debt service as a percentage of uncommitted annual revenue,most commonly 15 percent of recurring revenue.
- Short-term indebtedness, generally to mature within one fiscal period but often violated in practice.
- Long-term borrowing is restricted to capital investments and borrowing in foreign currency is prohibited.

Provisions are frequently open to differing interpretations, and enforcement can be uneven and fractious. Poland provides an example. In Poland, Regional Audit Agencies are charged with ensuring that cities comply with borrowing restrictions, but interpretations have been inconsistent. Although the borrowing law is silent on the agencies having oversight for project selection, cities and regions often have argued over the desirability of specific projects.

The main reason for ambiguity is that legal limitations on debt are not adequately detailed in regulations, leaving several questions about their application:

- Is it the debt service installments (principal and interest) payable in any single year that may not exceed the designated percentage or the total principal amount of the debt at the time of borrowing? While the intention would appear to be to limit debt service installments in any single year, the language often expressly refers to the "borrowing."
- If the test is based on annual debt service, exactly how is the formula calculated for future years? What assumptions are to be used for debt service when the interest rate is variable? What assumptions are used to predict future revenues?[10]
- If compliance in subsequent years is not tested at the time of issuance, what is the effect of violating the debt limitation in a future year? Is there any impact on the validity of the debt? What would prevent debt structures that defer a substantial portion of the principal repayment to later years?

If not clarified, these issues can cause substantial confusion, permit political skirmishing, and create barriers to the development of a credit market for subnational borrowing.

The annual debt service limitation should be tested at the time of issuance; if the debt service is within the limitation, it should not be subject to claims of violations of the limit in subsequent years. Each annual installment can be calculated as a percentage of the total current revenues of the budget in the year in which the debt is issued (or the prior year, if the data are more verifiable), assuming the interest rate at the time of issuance (providing it is based on an independent index, to prevent use of an artificially low rate to achieve compliance with a debt limitation.) This interpretation would be an incentive for "substantially equal annual debt service."

Many transition economies have restricted debt service to a percentage of budgeted revenues (table 7.1). Poland holds annual debt service to no more than 15 percent of budgeted revenues. Debt carried beyond the current year may not be greater than 60 percent of budgeted revenues.[11] The limit on annual debt service falls to 12 percent when total public debt (sovereign and subsovereign) hits 55 percent of GDP, and further borrowing is prohibited when the total hits 60 percent of GDP, the EU standard. Romania limits the annual debt service of subnational governments to 20 percent of total current recurring revenues, including the shared wage tax.[12] Lithuania holds borrowing to 10 percent of current revenues.

Table 7.1. Municipal Debt Limitations in Selected Eastern and Central European Countries

Country	Debt service ratio limit	Borrowing-to-revenue ratio limit	Other restrictions
Hungary	70 percent of own current revenues (local taxes, fees, interest revenues, environmental fines). Debt service includes potential liability under guarantee commitments.	None.	• Subnational governments with outstanding loans and expenses of more than 100 million forints must have external independent audits. • Loans cannot be secured with primary assets, general transfers from the state, shared personal income tax. • Debt-service restriction does not apply to short-term liquidity loans.
Lithuania	10 percent of total revenue, excluding earmarked grants.	Borrowing cannot exceed 10 percent of total "revenue" in approved budget (excluding earmarked grants); there is a sub-limit of 5 percent for short-term borrowing.	• Debt stock is limited to 20 percent (30 percent for Vilnius) of total revenue. • Short-term loans must be repaid within fiscal year. • There are no state guarantees. • The Ministry of Finance can impose lower borrowing ceiling for individual municipalities based on budget performance. • Long-term credit can be used only for investment and must be approved by a loan commission of the Ministry of Finance.
Poland	15 percent of total revenue (debt service includes potential liability under guarantee commitments).	None.	• Short-term loans must be repaid within fiscal year. • There is no state guarantee, unless explicitly stated. • Long-term credit is only for investment. • Carry-forward of unpaid principal on all debt to next budget year cannot exceed 60 percent of budgeted revenues.
Romania	20 percent of current revenues.	None.	• There is no state guarantee; debt registration documents must include a clause to this effect. • Debt incurred must be reported in the public debt register and reported annually. • Short-term cash balance loans are limited to 5 percent of total revenues. • External borrowing must be approved by a loan authorization commission.

Source: DeAngelis and Dunn 2002.

Central Government Review and Exceptions

Laws governing subnational debt sometimes provide for central government authority to review and approve requests to exceed the debt limit when the subnational government can demonstrate that its local revenue base would support a greater amount of debt. Exceptions might include:

- Additional financing for more creditworthy subnational governments.
- Financing of investments that have a positive net impact on cash flow either by generating increased revenues or by reducing operating expenses; examples are utility and energy conservation projects.
- Natural or civil calamity.

Considerations of Security and Collateral

Authorizing the use of various forms of security and collateral to secure subnational government obligations is an important part of the legal underpinnings of a subnational credit market. In view of the imperfect security provided by a general obligation pledge, subnational borrowing is often reinforced by additional, specific pledges of revenue, property, or a third-party guarantee. Some projects that have the potential to be "self-supporting" may not require the pledging of general credit.

Revenues

A subnational unit should be legally authorized to pledge to a creditor specified revenues over which it has spending discretion. The revenues should be identifiable and held apart from other funds. A creditor should have a first-priority secured position to such revenues, a critical element in the structure of a revenue-secured debt. Lack of experience with such pledges and with judicial recognition and enforcement creates uncertainty. It is clearly advantageous to have an express provision in the law for subnational governments to secure their loan repayments with identifiable future revenues and to ensure a creditor that it has a first-priority secured position to such revenues.

While a legally protected pledge is important, its absence has not precluded subnational borrowing when alternative arrangements have been available. Banks have loaned to subnational governments that deposit their funds (or some portion of them) with the bank. The possession of these deposits, backed up by a right of offset, reduces the risk that arises from not having a legally protected pledge.[13]

Physical Property

The ability to sell property is essential to the ability to pledge or mortgage property to secure a loan. However, the authority for subnational governments to use property as collateral is often clouded in legal uncertainties. Some countries have clear distinctions between subnational property in the "public domain," which is used to carry out mandated government functions, and property considered to be in the "private domain," which is unrelated to such essential government functions. Private domain property may be encumbered or otherwise disposed of, but public domain property is "inalienable."

The value of property as collateral also depends on the legal procedures to be followed by a creditor in case of a default. If it takes several years to foreclose on property, its value as collateral is substantially diminished. Often, procedures relating to subnational property have not been established or have not been used enough to create a reasonable expectation based on precedent.

Whatever the legal status of these issues, in many countries there appears to be a consensus that a subnational government may sell or otherwise encumber property that is not used in carrying out its mandated services.[14] Such practical understanding of the parameters of this authority seems to be based more on historical practice than on legal provisions. So even if the authority to use physical property as collateral is unclear, banks often lend on the basis of physical property as collateral since banks are familiar with this type of collateral. Additionally, bank regulatory requirements often establish preferred capital reserve requirements for loans secured with physical property. Property in the private domain that is owned by subnational governments may be sold or otherwise encumbered to secure debt.[15]

Intercepts

One of the most used and effective forms of security for subnational debt in emerging markets is an intercept provision. Intercepts give a lender a first claim on intergovernmental transfers due to the subnational government in the event of nonpayment. A number of countries specifically use legislatively authorized intercepts of intergovernmental transfers to enhance the ability of subnational governments to offer reliable security for their borrowing. Depending on the size and continuity of the transfers, intercepts can provide strong encouragement of credit market development without any implied central government guarantee or other cost to the national treasury. Thus intercepts merit particular consideration in the development of subnational borrowing policy and law.

Intergovernmental transfers are of several types. Some give subnational governments a specified portion of national tax revenues. Others are distributed not by formula but through annual appropriations by the national legislature or as a percentage of national revenue raised in each region or locality. Still others are provided as subsidies for specific projects (Bahl and Linn 1992). In the initial stages of credit market development, the share of the revenues derived from the central government pursuant to an established and reliable formula is often a preferred source of security for lenders. This form of security has opened the credit market to subnational governments that otherwise would not have access to it and lowered their interest costs.

Contractual intercept provisions must be carefully drafted to prevent abuse and overuse. Subnational governments can come to rely on the intercept rather than on the discipline of making timely debt payments. If the intercept law is too permissive, an ambitious mayor and council can tie up a disproportionate portion of a subnational government's main revenue sources for years to come, jeopardizing mandated service delivery.

In some countries problems arise because the central government and private lenders cooperate too closely in the administration of intercepts. The central government may make automatic payments to the commercial lender from a subnational government's allocation of a shared tax and then transfer only the residual funds to the subnational government, without any clear accounting for the intercept. To prevent this, the following assurances are important as part of applicable rules and regulations:

- That the subnational government not only enter into the intercept arrangement voluntarily but be in control of negotiating the specific terms and conditions.
- That there be clear conditions for when the intercept would be activated; the intercept should operate only in the case of defaults, not as a substitute for regular payments.
- That, at a minimum, the transferring government provide a clear accounting for any intercept funds diverted to a lender. Alternatively, intercepts can be administered through a special fiduciary arrangement established at the local level.

To discourage subnational governments from over-reliance on the intercept to cover delinquent debt payments, consideration can be given to limiting or imposing a financial penalty each time the intercept is used.[16] Also, to preclude any future question of an implied central government guarantee, the legislation might explicitly state that no central government guarantee is to be inferred for such credit without explicit central government authorization. The law could require that each subnational debt instrument contain a statement on its face that there is no express or implied central government guarantee and that the instrument does not represent any obligation of the central government (see boxes 7.5 and 7.6 for sample language).

Box 7. 5. Example of Language Denying Central Government Responsibility for Municipal Debt

Romania Local Public Finance Law 1998, Article 50

(1) The local public debt does not represent a debt or responsibility of the government, and it shall be reimbursed exclusively from the revenues though which the respective loan was guaranteed by the authorities of the local public administration.

(2) The documents registering the local public debt shall include a clause through which the respective territorial administrative unit places itself under the obligation to reimburse the debt, and to pay the interest and the commissions associated with that debt exclusively from the revenues of the respective local public authority; the government has no payment obligation whatsoever, and the credibility or taxation capacity of the government must not be used for guaranteeing the reimbursement of the debt contracted by the territorial administrative unit or of the payment of interest or commissions associated with that debt.

(3) The documents registering the local public debt which do not comply with the provisions under paragraph (2) shall not be considered as valid.

Source: As quoted in DeAngelis and Dunn 2002.

Box 7.6. Example of Language on Securing Debt with Own Revenues

Lithuania, Decree on Usage of Bank Credits by Local Authorities, 1998, Article 14

- When taking a loan, the municipality must guarantee its repayment only by the means of the municipality budget, and the municipality enterprise, only by the assets, which could serve as a source to recover the loan.

Romania, Local Public Finance Law, 1998, Article 49

(1) The due installments deriving from the contracted loans, the interest and commissions due by territorial administrative units, shall be provided in the local budget.
(2) The loans contracted by territorial administrative units can be guaranteed by the local public authority, from any revenue source, with the exception provided under article 48, paragraph 3. Any guarantee by revenues is valid and shall apply from the moment the guarantee is offered; the revenues representing the guarantee and which are collected by the local budget shall be subject to the respective guarantee agreement, which shall apply with priority against any other request of third parties addressed to the respective local public authority, irrespective of whether these third parties are aware of the guarantee agreement or not. The document through which the agreement of guaranteeing through revenues is concluded must be registered with the city hall or with the respective *judet* [county] council, and with the debtor.
(3) All loan agreements concluded according to the provisions of this law shall be considered as fully authorized and shall constitute obligations to be enforced on the respective local budgets.

Source: As quoted in DeAngelis and Dunn 2002.

Reserve Funds

A reserve fund, segregated from other funds of the subnational government and available only for debt payments should the government run into payment difficulty, enhances debt security. Governments should consider creating such a fund for securing debt. How that fund may be invested and by whom it shall be kept are important considerations.

Subnational Government Guarantees

In many emerging market economies subnational guarantees of municipally owned utility enterprises are a common financing device. Because these and other contingent obligations can present problems for controlling subnational debt, the guarantee should not be a mechanism for incurring debt indirectly that could not be incurred directly. Guarantees of third-party debt by subnational governments should be as follows:

- Authorized in the same manner as subnational debt.
- Restricted to projects in the public interest for which subnational debt could be issued.
- Limited to third parties created or controlled by the local government.[17]
- Counted toward the debt limitation in the same manner as direct debt or as a percentage of the amount until a payment is made on the guarantee, when the full amount would be allocated. The initial percentage could be based on some determination of the creditworthiness of the guaranteed party, although creating such credit distinctions may be too sophisticated a process in a new subnational market.

Notes

1. In Poland, for example, decentralization and self-governance are key constitutional principles (Constitution, Article 16.2). The Constitution of South Africa provides that the "executive and legal authority of a municipality is vested in its municipal council" (Section 151 [2]). Chapter 9 of the European Charter on Local Autonomy calls for local authorities to have access to capital markets to borrow the funds needed for capital investment.

2. In the United States, the bond counsel (a law firm specializing in municipal bond transactions) often drafts the needed resolutions and con-

tracts and provides opinions on whether the transaction conforms to applicable laws and regulations. Some states in the United States also have procedural checks. Texas local government issuers must obtain approval on procedures but not on use of proceeds or other substantive matters from the Office of the Attorney General before issuing debt. The office reviews the proposed bond issue's supporting documentation, certifies validity, and issues an opinion. The opinion is needed for the bonds to be legally binding and relieves individual purchasers of the need to inquire into the process by which the bonds were issued. Oregon requires that localities prepare bond documents following recommended guidelines. Many states require that prospective sales be reported to a central office and placed on an official calendar. North Carolina requires a filing and approval before sale, largely a procedural matter.

3. Certain forms of debt may nonetheless have additional legal requirements relating specifically to their form. For example, a publicly offered bond issue should be required to conform to standards of appropriate disclosure to investors.

4. This requirement has subsequently been repealed by the Ministry of Finance.

5. Law on Securities and the Stock Exchange, Law on Local Self-Government and the Budget Code.

6. In Romania a Government Debt Commission has been created to "approve" any local government debt issued in a foreign currency (Law on Local Public Finance, 1998). In the Philippines a Monetary Board "render[s] an opinion of the probable effects of the proposed operation on monetary aggregates, the price level, and the balance of payments" (Central Bank Act, Republic Act No. 7653, Sec. 123).

7. The Romanian Law on Local Public Finance allows only projects in the "public domain" to be financed with debt (Article 48 [1]). The Vietnamese Law on the State Budget authorizes a province or city to finance only infrastructure investments.

8. Teresa Ter-Minassian, editor, *Fiscal Federalism in Theory and Practice*, Washington DC, International Monetary Fund, 1997, pp. 171–172.

9. Although many government's debt ceilings are expressed in terms of the debt principal outstanding in relationship to either a measure of tax base or revenue flows, the best prescriptions are likely to use annual debt service in relationship to available revenues. Actually crafting such a restriction calls for considerable care in definitions. See Charles Smith, "Measuring and Forecasting Debt Capacity: The State of Oregon Experience,"

Government Finance Review (December 1998), pp. 52–54. As Smith points out, the legal limit is usually much higher than the effective market limit.

10. A debt limitation is most effective when it is an "issuance" test rather than a "continuing compliance" test that may be violated in subsequent years. Unfortunately, many such debt limitation provisions are written as requiring compliance in each year.

11. Law on Public Finances 1998, Articles 113 and 114.

12. Law on Local Public Finance 1998, Article 51).

13. In certain transitioning economies the formerly centrally owned banks have retained powers of offset on deposits that put them at the head of the line of creditors. In other countries the ability of the banks to exercise offset powers is limited, and depositors may elect to sever their relationships and withdraw funds. Where banks possess considerable powers to enforce security, they may stifle competition from the bond markets. They may assist the development of bond markets by acting as trustees on behalf of bondholders.

14. In Latvia local governments are expressly prohibited from guaranteeing a loan "with property that is necessary for the performance of governmental functions."

15. The requirement of a "public purpose" and the limitation on collateral to be in the "private domain" may effectively prevent the use of a financed project as collateral for the debt issued to finance the project.

16. In the Philippines local governments may pledge no more than 20 percent of "internal revenue allocations" (Local Government Code, Sections 287 and 324 [b]).

17. In Latvia, a local government cannot guarantee the debt unless it owns at least 50% of the borrower.(or an association that is at least 65% subnational-unit owned). Regulations of the Cabinet of Ministers on Self-Government Borrowings and Guarantees, 4/2/97.

Part III

Characteristics of Financial Market Regulation and Disclosure

John Petersen

Chapter 8

Financial Market Structure, Regulation, and Operations

Any examination of options for subsovereign borrowing must consider the supply side of the equation. To what extent does a market for subsovereign obligations exist, and how should would-be borrowers access it? Perhaps more relevant in most emerging market economies is the question of where subsovereign securities fit into an overall strategy to develop domestic financial markets. Promoting private capital markets has been a primary objective of financial market regulators and international donor and lending institutions that wish to encourage private ownership and functioning markets.

A financial market along the lines outlined in preceding chapters would have some level of effective competition in rates and terms and would involve private capital, even though government entities also might supply capital. The financial market would be primarily domestic, with borrowers and lenders (or issuers and investors) subject to domestic rules and dealing in local currency.

A key objective of many governments in recent years has been to create a municipal bond market for subnational securities. Most of the liberalization and subsequent growth of the domestic securities markets has focused on privatization and the desire to promote private sector equity ownership. It is in this setting of recasting the roles of the private and public sectors and capital markets that subnational borrowers must navigate.

Financial Market Structure

The topic of financial market structure and development far exceeds the scope of this book, but it is vitally important for judging the various linkages that subnational governments may forge with the capital markets. Most national debt markets are dominated by banks and by central government and state-owned enterprise debt. Early securities market growth in emerging and transitioning economies has focused on equity markets, and the few bond markets that exist are dominated by national governments and the commercial banking system, with private capital debt markets coming later and hesitantly. Corporate borrowing has traditionally been through the banking system, and there are few corporate bond issues. Nearly all bank lending to corporations is short term; long-term bank financing is almost nonexistent. Companies have relied on retained earnings or direct foreign investments to meet their long-term financing needs.

The ratio of the volume of listed securities of exchanges or transactions on the exchanges to the overall GDP is a rough indicator of the relative role of financial markets in the economy. A more precise measure of credit markets would look at listed securities in the debt market (including any exchange listings, as well as bonds in the over-the-counter market) in relation to GDP. The relative size of the banking sector can be measured by the three ratios of bank loans and investments to GDP, the size of securities markets to listed securities, and domestically held debt to GDP. Similar measures of other financial institutions and intermediaries provide indices of the development of domestic financial markets.[1]

Government's Role in Credit Market Development

Where subnational credit markets end up on their journey toward more openness and competition depends on policies, luck, and how a variety of competing interests are balanced. One commentator on the development of municipal credit argues that the development of subnational government borrowing should be tied to the methodical and sequential development of financial markets as a way of minimizing several risks inherent in the process (Noel 2000). In this view, there is a progression from state-controlled monopolies on lending, to oligopolies (often holdovers from the state-run system), to open, competitive markets, based on the following prerequisites:

- Reduced moral hazard.
- Greater market transparency.
- Strong financial market governance.
- A level playing field among investor groups.
- Subnational government capacity to manage and budget.

While basic laws need to be in place, in the end markets are developed by champions and risk-takers. The best lessons on market building are those that are taught by mistakes in an environment of accountability and discipline, where public resources and private fortunes are won or lost.

In many developing and transitioning economies, the private sector is a recent arrival on a scene that has been dominated by the state (box 8.1). The extent of central government involvement in the allocation of credit is not always immediately apparent. Government ownership of the banking system and other financial institutions (such as retirement funds and insurance companies) can be very influential in deciding which borrowers' needs are served and on what terms (box 8.2). For example, in laying out prudential rules and reserve requirements for financial institutions, governments can mandate or build in large incentives to invest in certain classes of obligations.

A common market support approach has been to require that reserves contain government bonds (both sovereign and subsovereign) or to set capital adequacy rules that favor these investments. These market development measures are often relaxed over time as a domestic market begins to emerge (Noel 2000).[2] Monetary policy requires that authorities have leverage over bank portfolios. In theory, open market operations can be carried on in any security. However, for subnational borrowers there is a continuing problem of adverse selection, as securities whose markets are directly manipulated by the monetary authorities are either supported or subverted for reasons unrelated to the subnational issuer.

Relationships Affecting Markets

The recurring turmoil in world financial markets has focused attention on the relationship between the finance industry, especially banking, and other industries. The extent of interlocking ownership, control of boards, and self-dealing between financial institutions and their nonbank affiliates has been at issue. Although subnational governments have been a relatively minor player in such concerns in Asia, in South America the relationship between municipal and provincial governments and the banking system has come under considerable scrutiny. Large cities and states in that region may own banks that serve as in-house providers of credit. While efforts have been made to privatize the banks or place them on an equal footing with private competitors, they still can come under political pressure to finance their governmental parent units. Financial institutions that may be called "banks" do not necessarily follow prudential practices, just as regulators do not necessarily regulate nor are laws enforced.

Box 8.1. Commercial Banking in Transitioning Economies

All banking systems in the transitioning economies of Central and Eastern Europe evolved from a single state-controlled bank that was responsible for both monetary policy and commercial banking. These monobanks routinely extended a high volume of credit to state-owned companies to direct production along the lines determined by central planners. The bank did not screen credit or base funding decisions on creditworthiness since credit allocation was a political decision, nor was loan payment enforced. The goal was to get capital funds out according to the plan. Planned economies hid inflation and guaranteed jobs for all, so the standard countercyclical activities of banks were not relevant. Loans to subnational governments were seen as just another production (local services) and employment policy of the state.

In the move from central planning to market planning, the protean monobanks were split into commercial bank and central bank activities, with commercial banking often set up along sectoral lines. New banks were allowed to form, and limited entry of foreign banks was allowed. At the outset, regulation by the central bank was often weak and subservient to political interests. Newly created commercial banks were also weak, with small depositors, unknown portfolios, and flaccid regulation. They also remained under state ownership and susceptible to political influence. Nonperforming loans were simply rolled over, and lax lending policies were used to keep state industries going. Inflationary pressure was created as the central bank printed more and more money, encouraging rapid disintermediation and abandonment of the currency.

Many small banks were established, but they were unsupervised and often closely tied to new private enterprises. Bank scandals erupted in Albania, Romania, and Russia, including Ponzi schemes that drew in thousands of gullible small depositors. Growth of bank loans has not kept pace with growth in the real sector. Private firms, while borrowing for working capital, rely more on retained earnings and direct foreign investment than in more mature systems. Commercial banks, attracted by the high yields and low risk, have tended to lend to each other and invest heavily in the national government's obligations.

Source: Berghof and Bolton 2002.

The ratio of the volume of listed securities of exchanges or transactions on the exchanges to the overall GDP is a rough indicator of the relative role of financial markets in the economy. A more precise measure of credit markets would look at listed securities in the debt market (including any exchange listings, as well as bonds in the over-the-counter market) in relation to GDP. The relative size of the banking sector can be measured by the ratio of bank loans and investments to GDP and the size of securities markets to listed securities and domestically held debt to GDP. Similar measures of other financial institutions and intermediaries provide indices to the development of the domestic financial markets.[2]

Box 8.2. The Bank for International Settlements' Reserve Requirements and Capital Rules

Prudential regulations can have a major impact on the market for various types of obligations. Many sovereign governments have effectively built in markets for their securities by requiring that financial institutions hold a certain amount of sovereign direct or guaranteed obligations as part of their reserves. Banks may be required to put up government debt as collateral if they wish to hold government accounts. For example, prior to the availability of deposit insurance for large denomination

(*Box continues on the following page.*)

Box 8.2. (*continued*)

accounts, the collateral requirement on public deposits was a powerful incentive for banks to hold U.S. municipal bonds.

One source of information on potential demand for subsovereign obligations (as well as an overall measure of perceived subsovereign risk) is seen in the weights that banks must apply to their assets to calculate their capital adequacy. Although these have varied internationally, they are increasingly coming into conformance with the Bank for International Settlements' (BIS) capital adequacy ratios (ratio of bank capital to performing loans; nonperforming loans carry special provisions). The BIS minimum is currently 8 percent. Virtually all countries have systems that meet or exceed the BIS standards.

Under the BIS regime, loans to the sovereign government of the same country as the bank are assigned a 0.0 sectoral risk weight (they are assumed to be domestically risk free) and those of private sector firms are assigned a 1.0. Recognizing that the relationship between the central government and subnational governments varies from country to country, the BIS allows the central bank to assign the appropriate risk weight. Thus the weightings provide the central bank's opinion of the risk of loans to the subnational governmental sector relative to loans to the sovereign and the private sectors.

In the United States the BIS credit factors range from 0.1 for general obligations to 1.0 for private activity (corporate) bonds. In foreign countries subnational government obligations with explicit central government guarantees have BIS ratios of 0.0 (which makes them tantamount to direct sovereign obligations), and those without such guarantees have ratios of up to 1.0 or even higher. Ratios can be changed to recognize overall changes in sectoral credit strength. This happened in South Africa, where the ratio was increased from 0.1 to 1.0 for subnational government securities when the national government announced that it would no longer guarantee municipal and provincial debt.

Prudential rules for other financial institutions such as insurance companies and pension systems have similar impacts on various types of security. To the degree that subnational securities have been lumped together with sovereign securities, they have often benefited from favorable treatment. However, to the extent they are seen as tantamount to corporate debt and loans, they can be disadvantaged.

The capital rules are being revised (Basel II), with an emphasis on the underlying creditworthiness of the obligor as well as on the character of the securities. This development may enhance the role of credit ratings in the determination of capital adequacy and give a boost to both information systems and credit analysis in domestic markets.

Market Development and Regulation

Since the 1980s, there has been a worldwide move to lessen direct regulation of financial markets and to open markets to greater domestic and international competition. This has involved all aspects of financial markets, from privatizing banking systems to creating stock exchanges to support the privatization of formerly state-owned enterprises. One result has been a greater number of domestic firms in the securities business and more openness to foreign firms doing business in domestic markets. The entrance of foreign firms has been important because they bring not only capital and competition but also experience in financing subsovereign obligations.

There also has been a move toward greater self-regulation by industry participants and away from regulation by administrative fiat and direct government involvement in investment decisions. Less regulation by ministerial fiat and less official involvement in individual transactions have made way for more general rules of fair dealing and capital adequacy and rules of the road for functioning markets. Thus the presence of more firms and a greater variety and number of financial instruments in the market means a need for more regulation and more sophisticated regulation. This changed regulatory mode depends on the operation of self-regulatory bodies rather than on central government agencies and is not without costs and risks.

Where do subnational governmental borrowers fit into the emerging securities market regulatory scheme? Since subnational government securities are still a rarity, the question is just beginning to be asked in most places. Emerging markets have seen a variety of regulatory schemes, including requirements designed to encourage sound business operations. In Chile publicly offered issues of corporate securities must be rated by a licensed rating agency. Indonesia's securities regulatory body, BAPEPAM, has similar requirements, which have been instrumental in creating the national rating agency, Perfindo. In Mexico the requirement that states and municipalities be rated by at least two credit rating agencies in order to borrow in commercial markets has created strong demand for ratings and helped build an active bond market.

The fundamental concept of regulation is to define the financial system and its rules of operation. That is easier said than done. Countries have different legal traditions that can influence the nature of a market's operation (box 8.3). Countries also have different traditions in regulating the banking system and other financial institutions, with the biggest debate between advocates of the "universal" banking systems and advocates of the separation of the banking system and the securities markets (as in the United States until recently.)[3]

Most emerging and transitioning economies come out of a bank-oriented financial system, often with government-owned or favored universal banks that have seen virtually every phase of domestic financial commerce as fair game. As financial markets broaden and mature, the regulatory boundaries between financial institutions need to be defined. For example, in addition to prudential regulation of traditional financial institutions such as banks, insurance companies, and pensions, there are new entities to regulate such as mutual funds, clearing and settlement operations, securities depositories, and markets in derivatives and asset-backed securities. Subnational governments that enter these markets are exposed to both the opportunities and risks that attend a dynamic marketplace and the ways it is regulated.

Financial market regulation has a variety of roles to play in emerging markets, and the end results may not always be in harmony. Among the competing objectives are the following:

Box 8.3. What Is a Security?

Defining a security is important from a legal perspective for establishing what an investor can look to in support of the obligation and from a securities regulation perspective for characterizing the nature of the transaction and the instrument involved. Efforts to regulate securities and to harmonize laws across countries have been hampered by different concepts of what constitutes a security.

For example, in the Spanish-speaking world and in the civil systems of Eastern and Central Europe the concept of a security has differed from that which evolved under English common law and exists in many English-speaking countries today. A security in Spanish-speaking countries is embodied in the concept of a *titulo valor*, which encompasses only a limited number of specific physical documents that have the right of ownership embodied in the document. Thus the only evidence of ownership for the security investor is the existence and possession of the document itself. The *titulo valor* instrument is like money, since it can be transferred physically without re-registration or even endorsement and is payable on presentation.

The *titulo valor* proved woefully inadequate as a concept for evidencing ownership given the nature of modern transactions. Not only does it pose physical safekeeping and transfer problems, but it does not fit the needs of new financial instrument constructs. New instruments necessarily rely on book entry and dematerialization, such as variable rate securities, derivatives, and investment contracts. New definitions of security now being enacted into law in Latin America rely on the economic basis of what constitutes the security, rather than on the strict definitions of what physical instruments qualify as *titulo valor.*

- *Market development*: Some regulations are intended to provide incentives to market development, especially as part of the effort to privatize government-owned institutions. Opening up markets, particularly to international capital flows and competition, is not without controversy. With proper regulation, however, the objective of encouraging competition and efficiency appears to be sound even if the means of achieving it are not entirely clear.

- *Market integrity*: Regulators want to foster lively, creative markets yet protect the integrity of the payments system and avoid excessive risk taking. This requires prudential measures to minimize systemic risk and protect the solvency of individual firms.
- *Fairness*: Regulators are keen to prevent fraud and manipulation and to protect investors and prevent monopoly power. Asymmetry of disclosure information (the issuers control it, the investors need it) can be an invitation to manipulation and fraud.
- *Efficiency*: Markets are allocators of capital resources. Realizing the benefits requires competition among players and fair price discovery mechanisms, but the participants must be limited to those that have adequate capital and experience and meet standards of behavior.

In most emerging market economies, subnational governments come to markets as largely untested small borrowers. Where they have adequate revenue bases, they can be viewed as potentially strong "credits" notwithstanding their small size. Even where banks have dominated direct lending, they benefit from the development of a securities market. The market provides banks with more liquidity as investors, even while promoting more competition among them by providing an alternative source of funds to direct bank loans. Furthermore, a more developed credit system allows banks other ways to earn fee incomes, such as acting as trustee and credit enhancer.

The Securities Marketplace

Domestic securities markets are in various stages of development, with different intensities of competition, technological development, and philosophies on regulation. Several measures of development are possible. One is the amount of trading in formal markets (exchanges) versus over-the-counter transactions. Over-the-counter transactions take place in electronic markets of dealer-to-dealer trades in securities that are not listed on the exchange or that can be traded off the exchange as well as on. Typically, registration and listing requirements are softer and less expensive than on formal exchanges.

Over-the-counter transactions give rise to several questions. How much off-market trading is reported, and how are such trades cleared, that is, how is the ownership of securities exchanged against payments of cash? How integrated are the markets? Is there a single market or are there segmented markets by types of instruments? The great advantages are ease of access for dealers and low cost for issuers. However, with few investors, over-the-counter markets in developing economies often languish from a lack of volume. Most investors buy to hold, and the liquidity provided by a deep and active market remains a goal rather than a reality.

In many transitioning economies, stock markets are a new development, often a by-product of the privatization of formerly state-owned enterprises. Many exchanges are small, with little activity and maybe a short lifespan (World Bank 2002c). To accelerate development of the exchange, regulators in emerging market economies have often required that all securities (equity and private debt) trade on the stock exchange. However, normal exchange listing requirements, typically modeled on those in developed countries, and the related registration fees can be burdensome, especially for new companies and small companies. One answer has been to create a separate bracket for smaller, higher risk companies, as in Japan. Another has been to allow the development of an over-the-counter dealer-to-dealer market or to restrict certain classes of offerings to sophisticated institutions and individuals. This approach provides trading liquidity to otherwise less liquid shares without exposing the general public to undue risk. New credits can be allowed to season before graduating to an exchange listing.

However, having a number of separate markets can lead to an undesirable diffusion of resources. Recently, the move has been toward fewer organized exchanges and screen-based, fully reported trading as opposed to the open-cry, single place market.[4] According to proponents of integrated markets, this leads to more self-policing. The more integrated and transparent a market's operation, the better defined are the market's participants and scope and the more likely that market competition, especially foreign competition, on the basis of price and quality of service, will discipline behavior without direct regulatory involvement.

Even advanced markets such as the United States must continue to work to achieve the correct mix of governmental oversight and market freedom that balance the goal of reasonable access to the markets by would-be issuers of debt with that of protecting the investing public. The boundaries of regulated activity can shift depending on evolving circumstances and events. Achieving an appropriate balance is even more difficult in developing countries, where an infrastructure of experience and legal mechanisms is not yet in place. Efforts to register and list new subnational government bond issues in a national stock exchange are discussed in box 8.4.

Box 8.4. After 60 Years, Municipal Bonds Return to Romania

In November 2001 two small Romanian cities, Predeal and Mangalia, issued municipal bonds, the first subnational government bond issuances in the country since 1941. The local currency-denominated issues were small (5 billion and 10 billion lei, or about $175,000 and $350,000) and short-term (maturities of two years). However, they were viewed by both the communities and the underwriting firms as a first step to opening up a fledgling capital market as an alternative to commercial bank lending. The proceeds of the bond issues were used for modest capital improvements, including a new sea wall for Mangalia and site improvements for Predeal's ski slope, the major business in the resort town.

Much effort went into designing the transactions and documentation, which all parties concerned saw as a pioneering effort. Eager for the exposure, both cities decided to list the stocks on the Bucharest Stock Exchange. This required Security Commission approval, but the commission's registration forms and disclosure requirements were designed for private companies and ill-suited for the municipalities. The commission staff and the applicants set about devising new standards and prospectus. The stock exchange, which acts as registrar and depository for securities issues, entered into contracts with the cities to receive regular reporting information, also a first.

By late November the new bonds were listed for trade, representing only the second and third listing of debt securities by the exchange. (The listing ceremony made the evening television news.) The national government is planning to list its own small-denomination note offerings on the exchange in hopes of cultivating more individual investments. Meanwhile, the Securities Commission is drafting new regulations to govern future bond municipal issuances.

Source: Petersen 2002.

Nature of Investors

In assessing the market environment, the nature of investors is an important consideration. Emerging market economies typically have few investors, and their appetite for long-term securities in locally denominated debt is often limited. Both institutional and individual investors look at the tradeoffs between risk and return. The tradeoffs can be very steep in the case of a domestic currency securities market in a developing economy. Many investors are reluctant to make long-term bets in currencies subject to large fluctuations.

National government securities, with large demand for funds and offering high returns, often sop up most of the supply of investible funds. Furthermore, capital requirements for banks and other financial institutions often reinforce the desirability of holding sovereign securities.[5] However, in many cases, these capital requirements, whether through oversight or intent, can give preferential treatment to subnational debt, which may be considered "governmental" for purposes of the calculations.[6]

The supply of long-term investible funds is especially limited. Because of the need to match assets against liabilities, banks are typically a poor source of such funding. When banks lend for even intermediate periods, the structure of the obligation is typically a variable interest rate, and the loan is often callable, should the need arise. Ideally, longer term funds would be forthcoming from institutions with long-term liabilities (pension funds and insurance companies) and individual investors with long-term savings. While several transitioning and developing countries have embarked on programs to promote these long-term investing institutions in the private sector, progress has been slow and the barriers daunting. There are several reasons.

First, any pool of domestic long-term capital is avidly sought by the national government and the banking system. Second, the institutional investors may be circumspect about making long-term investments in the local currency. Local currencies in small countries can be extremely volatile, with major uncertainties about future value, making them unappealing to investors with other options. Third, raising long-term funds is especially difficult if countries lack considerable liquidity (an active secondary market), as is often the case in emerging market economies.

Despite the difficulty, countries should try to promote longer term savings and to mobilize those savings for infrastructure investments. Banking laws and regulation of institutional investors should not discriminate against subnational issuers. In many emerging market economies long-term institutional investors with less need for liquidity, such as private pension systems and insurance companies, find themselves in a position similar to that of banks. The high yields on government securities, reserve requirements, and prudential requirements are impediments to investing in nonsovereign bonds, including those of subnational governments (Rosen 2002).

Tax Laws

Tax laws have a powerful effect on the development of credit markets and the motivation to participate in such markets. The distorting effects of tax laws on financial markets are well-known. Financial institutions and transactions, as highly visible components of the payments system, are relatively easy game for oft-frustrated tax collectors. A common measure is a flat rate withholding tax on interest income that is preemptive of any further payment due. Another is a turnover tax on transactions. Yet another measure is to grant tax exemptions on the interest received on long-term bank savings deposits and on foreign currency deposits held domestically. Depending on design and enforcement, all these tax strategies can stifle the development of bond markets.

Tax laws can favor the securities of subnational governments over other financial instruments. The exemption from federal income taxes is the major reason for the low interest rates on municipal bonds in the United States. Both Poland and the Philippines have extended limited tax exemption to subnational government bonds (see case studies, chapters 30 and 26). Most economists argue against tax exemptions for subnational debt on the grounds that exemptions distort the allocation of capital between the public and private sectors (Leigland 1998). Notwithstanding the shortcomings, such tax exemptions are common and can kick start market development. They have the advantage of being implemented through market activities—to enjoy the benefit a government has to initiate the borrowing and be prepared to repay the debt—and, if kept relatively simple, administrative costs are low.

International Markets

Large subnational borrowers and intermediaries that cater to them may have the option of borrowing in the "emerging-markets" tier of international financial markets. This source of funds had been growing rapidly until the series of financial crises and setbacks in the late 1990s. Since then international borrowing activity has receded rapidly. The hope remains, however, that when the broader international market recovers, subnational borrowers will again find it an attractive source of funds.

International financial markets are segmented between prime quality sovereign borrowers (public and private) that are able to borrow at the lowest rates and higher risk borrowers that have to pay higher rates of interest. The emerging market sector is part of this high-yield segment of the market (Rosen 2002).[7] Although the high-yield segment performed very well in the mid-1990s, it subsequently fell on hard times, making it difficult for emerging market borrowers of less than prime quality to sell bonds in the international markets. As a consequence subsovereign borrowers have been excluded from international debt transactions.

Domestic bond markets in emerging market economies appear to be expanding at least in part because international markets have become too difficult to access. However fleeting, the exposure that some subnational borrowers had in the international market provided useful lessons for both domestic and international markets. Chief among them were those related to market expectations for disclosure documentation and the importance of internationally accepted credit ratings. These two subjects are dealt with in chapter 9.

Notes

1. None of these measures is flawless. For example, there may be a large number of securities listings, but turnover may be low. Bank loans may be highly concentrated, with a high rate of nonperforming loans. Nonetheless, analysis indicates a positive correlation between the growth in financial markets and the pace of economic development (World Bank 2002c, chapter 5).

2. Noel (2000) sees the preferential treatment of government securities as leading to moral hazard in the financial system.

3. Until 1999, commercial banks in the United States were prohibited under the Glass Steagal Act from underwriting or dealing in corporate securities for resale. This prohibition was a product of reforms enacted in the 1930s after notorious abuses in the stock market. While it is too early to speculate, similar abuses in the late 1990s and early 2000s may lead to a revisiting of the recent reforms.

4. See, for example, "Survey: Financial Centers," *The Economist,* 9–15 May, 1998. The number of exchanges may be fewer but their physical location will be less important as trading occurs wherever a computer can be plugged in.

5. As noted, the capital adequacy requirements discussed above that are used internationally favor the investment of reserves in sovereign securities. Countries are not above using this, as well as domestic laws, to build in a captive market for their own securities. These often may be sold at below-market interest rates so that the market value is much less than the par value. However, the par value is what counts in meeting the legal requirements.

6. In the Philippines, the central bank reduced the risk weight assigned to local government obligations that are backed by an intercept of their internal revenue allotment and guaranteed by the Local Government Unit Guarantee Corporation from 100 percent to 50 percent, in effect making them more attractive investments for banks (see Tirona 2003 and the Philippine case study (chapter 26).

7. Interest rates are benchmarked to U.S. Treasury bond yields (usually the 10-year or 20-year maturity). Thus a prime borrower will enjoy a small "spread," that is, will trade at a hundred basis points above the U.S. Treasury security (seen as the safest and most liquid security). High-yield borrowers will trade at large spreads, which may amount to several hundred basis points above the Treasury bill rate.

Chapter 9

Disclosure and Financial Reporting

Information disclosure about issuers is a necessary condition for the effective operation of a securities market. Information—consistent, complete, timely, and comparable—is essential for judging the risks and rewards of investments. While information does not always answer all the questions (and bad information can give the wrong answers), an absence of information makes it difficult even to know what questions to ask.

Emerging and transitioning economies face particular difficulty with disclosure. Many countries are undergoing dramatic changes in their fiscal structure just as the structure and regulation of financial markets are changing as well. Direct guarantees by the sovereign are being replaced by newly minted local own-source revenue and transfer systems, as well as more specific pledges of assets and revenues. Some countries, such as South Africa, rely heavily on revenues pledged on commercial public utility operations. Other countries, for a variety of reasons, may choose to restrict long-term debt to self-supporting commercial operations.[1]

The ability of subnational governments to generate resources to support themselves or to generate surpluses for general revenue purposes depends on efficient technical and managerial operations. Even where governments rely primarily on transfer payments, information on trends in transfer payments compared with local expenses becomes vital to determining relative credit quality. Without uniform, regular, and reliable reporting, comparing and tracking the performance of subnational governments become impossible tasks, and market decisions are based more on faith than fact.

Regulating Disclosure

Disclosure can be required by the central government, by securities market regulation, or as a byproduct of market operations, through contracts and market practice and convention. Disclosures to securities markets originate with the borrowers themselves, the subnational governments. Borrowers may be assisted by the central or provincial government authorities in accumulating information, but the borrowing government is responsible for disclosures as the party financially responsible for timely and full payment of debt service. A closely related concept is that the party that controls decisions to honor obligations and thus has the relevant information is the one responsible for providing the information.[2]

In securities markets, disclosure is aimed at helping investors make informed investment decisions. An often overlooked but practical by-product of securities disclosure is that the performance, condition, and prospects of borrowers become publicly available information. These economic and financial factors are of material interest to many others in the market besides investors. Also, the concept of disclosure reaches beyond investor "protection" (that is, avoidance of fraudulent behavior) to encompass support for the rational allocation of resources on the ability to evaluate rewards versus risks, whatever their levels.[3]

Generally, formal disclosure requirements are met when the issuer sends published reports to the marketplace. In the bond markets, there are usually two phases in the process. First, the would-be borrower issues a document in conjunction with the initial sale that describes the transaction and provides pertinent information about itself, the security pledged, and the use of the bond proceeds, which is variously called an *official statement* or a *prospectus*. Second, after the sale, the borrower provides a stream of continuing information with respect to itself and the obligation, a process called *continuing disclosure*. The timing and scope of reporting information are important, and technology is changing the reporting process (see box 9.1). Another class of recipients of the information analyze it and convey their opinion to investors. The most important of these are the rating agencies, which, as is discussed in the next chapter, often act as a surrogate for disclosure to individual investors. Disclosure documents can be available from a central depository, using information received on a recurring or event-driven basis.[4]

The broad policy objective of developing a thriving securities market argues for balancing the need to protect investors with the need to ease access for certain classes of borrowers. Often, standards are lower for smaller issuers or for lower risk securities.[5] The content of disclosure statements can be dictated by the regulator's detailed list of required documents and schedules or by a flexible standard that relies on the issuer and its agents to provide information that investors need in reaching an investment decision. In practice, the two approaches are usually combined. Regulators provide a list of generic types of required information, leaving the particulars to the issuers. Since the scope and detail of meaningful disclosure can vary markedly, the trend has been to rely on market forces and self-regulatory bodies to specify the details of disclosure.

Box 9.1. Disclosure over the Internet

Electronic transmission of information over the Internet is changing the processes of bond sales and information disclosure in the securities markets. Although electronic transmission of data has been possible for many years, it was not until the use of the Internet became widespread that issuers were willing to move their bond sales to the Internet, taking bids in real time. An early experimenter was the city of Pittsburgh, which held its first Internet competitive bond auction in early 1997. That year, several large municipal bond issuers permitted bidders to file bids conventionally, in sealed envelopes, or over the Internet just prior to the close of auction.

In 1998 municipal issuers began to publish preliminary official statements over the Internet. Again Pittsburgh led the way. Investors could contact the city for a printed copy if they wished. While the city had previously printed 750 copies of the official statement at a cost of $15,000, once it began posting the statements on the Internet, it received only four requests for hard copies. Many issuers have started to post their budgets and financial statements on the Web.

The economies of posting bond disclosure over the Web are considerable for both bond sales and information disclosure. The access to a large number of investors and underwriters at low cost promotes improved disclosure. Just as exchanges in many emerging market economies are leap-frogging the stages of securities market development in many developed

(Box continues on the following page.)

Box 9.1. *(continued)*

countries, so too are new information technologies swiftly changing the flow of information in the markets.

In a related use of the Internet, subnational governments in Romania can access a Web site that provides a self-diagnostic program that allows them to compare their financial ratios with those of other governments. Administered by the Romanian Bankers Institute and funded by the U.S. Agency for International Development, the Web site also contains model loan and bond documents, a collection of state laws relating to local borrowing, and a listing of consultants and financial institutions interested in municipal finance.

Source: Authors.

Accounting Standards and Financial Disclosure

Uniform accounting standards for subnational government financial statements are critical to disclosure. In many countries accounting systems are under review with an eye toward improving their timeliness, transparency, and conceptual consistency.[6] International bodies are also working toward cross-country comparability. Strong accounting practices are central to improved financial management. The adoption of accounting standards has been expedited where the standards have been required for borrowers wishing to sell bonds or take out loans.[7]

Accounting standards vary greatly among countries and between the private and public sectors (see box 9.2). Most governments come from an orientation of controlling expenditures and revenues, stressing the legality of their actions and reporting on their conformance with legislation. This has led to the use of cash accounting techniques and has obscured the economic purpose or life of the expenditures. The biggest concerns with cash accounting techniques are their focus on short-term financial assets and liabilities and the ability to alter the results by accelerating receipts or delaying payments. It is not unheard of for governments to simply put the "bill in the drawer" or to delay making a payroll until the next fiscal year.[8] It is the case, however, that much credit analysis focuses on cash flows, particularly those flows related to the availability of cash to pay debt service in full and on time.[9]

When the government borrower is involved in an enterprise activity, it often uses accrual accounting techniques that conform to those used in the private sector. This has a sound economic rationale for determining the worth and period income performance of an activity. However, credit analysis typically requires conversion to a cash basis to ensure that adequate cash will be available when needed to meet debt service requirements.[10]

No accounting system is foolproof, and all are susceptible to misunderstanding and manipulation.[11] What matters most is whether the principles are being observed (that is, the accounts correctly kept in accordance with the chart of accounts and their definitions) and whether someone is systematically checking the books. An example of the importance of the consistent application of accounting principles in understanding what is going on is shown in box 9.3.

Another important issue is the frequency and independence of audits. Most subnational governments rely on audits performed by auditors from higher levels of government. The auditors typically check for compliance with program requirements rather than assess financial condition or assign costs to activities. Independent audits, which are sometimes required, may be difficult to implement because of a dearth of audit skills in the private sector or prohibitive costs for small borrowers (see Hungary case study, chapter 29). In some countries government financial records are not publicly available, and bank secrecy laws impede public disclosure of some portions of the financial statement. The very unavailability of such financial data is a warning flag that financial risk cannot be assessed and that political and legal risks are particularly important.

In addition to financial statements, appropriate disclosure may require information about the operations and characteristics of the service provided and the market served.[12] For example, investors in an enterprise-based security that looks to cash available after operating expenditures to repay debt want to know about the operating characteristics of the enterprise and the market it serves in order to judge how efficiently it is being operated and whether there are any concerns about such issues as the strength of demand, supplies, labor relations, environmental matters, and lawsuits. The list of items worthy of disclosure can be long, and the particulars will be dictated by the nature of the operation and the security pledged.[13] Thus, an

---

Box 9.2. Accounting for Accounting Differences

Differences in accounting and financial recordkeeping can make it hard to analyze the performance of governments and their enterprises. In some countries uniformity in these practices in the private sector arose from the tax systems and securities laws requirements. Because most subnational governments do not pay taxes on their activities and do not list their securities on stock exchanges, the pressure for prompt reporting and uniform accounting has been lacking.

Disclosure of information is meant to support analysis of the risk and reward relationship. Appraising "economic" risk—the risk that the borrower will be able to pay interest and principal as promised—depends on knowledge of its financial performance (operating statement) and condition (balance sheet). Since most problems involving "willingness to pay" are provoked by fiscal stress, strong financial reporting practices support assessment of this risk as well.

From a disclosure standpoint, the immediate objectives are getting financial data on a comparable basis; measuring the availability of dependable, recurring revenue streams to make debt service payments; and measuring liquid reserves available to continue meeting debt service requirements should the recurring revenues be interrupted. With proper reporting, other items, such as the strength and stability of the underlying economy, other indebtedness, and the mix and costs of inputs used by the borrower, also are disclosed or can be calculated from the financial statements and their footnotes.

Source: Authors.

---

important initial disclosure will be the intention or contractual commitment of the issuer to provide information on a recurring basis in the future.

Disclosure requirements do not mandate that every investor be able to read every document and understand every nuance of every deal. When disclosure requirements are particularly stringent, securities regulators may

Box 9.3 Why Did Czech Municipal Debt Grow So Fast?

It is not clear why the outstanding debt of municipalities in the Czech Republic grew so rapidly during the 1990s. There was no evident correspondence between the reported accounting flows of the revenues and expenditures of municipalities and their accumulation of debt. While the accounting reports indicated that the municipalities' fiscal balances were reasonably stable during the 1990s (that is, with rather small deficits alternating with small surpluses), the aggregate amount of municipal outstanding debt continued to rise rapidly.

This apparent discrepancy is thought to reflect a lack of uniformity in accounting practices that led to an inability to know what was actually going on. The evident inconsistency could have resulted from the following causes: differing interpretations by municipalities of accounting procedures and terminologies, including treating loan receipts as revenues; off-budget financial operations, including the treatment of grants from the state budget; and extrabudgetary funds that were inappropriately recorded as revenue by some municipalities. The Czech problem was not unique, as the accounting and financial reporting systems used by subnational governments during the transition often have been artifacts of the old unitary state system, which were not designed to measure their fiscal performance or condition.

Source: Czech Republic case study, chapter 28.

decide to promote reliance on private advisory and information services to examine disclosures and make informed judgments for which they are paid by investors. These opinions are published and become a "baseline" of the assessment process. An example of such services is provided by the credit rating agencies, which post ratings on issuers and issues and keep them under surveillance while the debt is outstanding. However, even if regulators are not doing the substantive reviews and forming opinions about the adequacy of disclosure, they need to institute meaningful safeguards to ensure that those who do (such as financial advisers, rating agencies, and other information providers) are professionally qualified, behave ethically, are not manipulating the market, and are free of conflicts of interest. Chapter 10 turns to the subject of credit analysis and credit ratings.

Notes

1. In the Philippines, bond issues by local governments are restricted to self-supporting projects. However, absent any definition of the term *self-supporting*, the restriction is not very effective.

2. A guarantee by a third party (such as the national government) has sometimes been seen as a reason to require less disclosure on the part of the actual borrower. That concept has been rejected in U.S. practice, where a guarantee (or insurance) does not obviate the need for full disclosure by the borrower. In South Africa and elsewhere the custom has been to relax requirements when the national government is the guarantor.

3. This is not just an academic distinction but goes to the heart of market regulation. If the primary purpose is to avoid fraud and investor loss, the emphasis should be on screening out high-risk securities that regulators feel might cause loss to the investors. This substitutes a bureaucratic decision for that of the marketplace. The other approach, and the one stressed in the U.S. philosophy, is to require full disclosure, and then to let the market decide on the appropriate rate of return to offset the level of risk, no matter what its magnitude.

4. In the United States this role is played in the municipal market by a limited number of officially sanctioned (but privately owned) repositories as well as a central repository operated by the Municipal Securities Rule-making Board.

5. Traditionally, government securities have belonged to this lower risk disclosure class, although that tradition has been eroded in the United States and elsewhere and the exceptions are less likely.

6. One team of investigators reviewing the Latin American markets stress the problem of financial information: "The first problem is the quality of municipal or subnational management and accounting, which is often poor and incomplete " (Freire, Huertas, and Darche 1998).

7. International Federation of Accounting (IFAC) *Guideline for Governmental Financial Reporting*. The IFAC is attempting to develop widespread adoption of generally accepted accounting standards.

8. Credit analysts are concerned about cash flows, and not all cash accounting is considered bad. For example, state and local governments in Mexico are on a conservative system that accrues expenditures but treats revenues on a cash basis. This treatment is viewed favorably by rating agencies since it understates revenues while fully accounting for costs as they are incurred (interview with Jane Eddy, Standard & Poor's, March 25, 2002).

9. It is customary for credit analysts to restate accounting reports on a cash basis to assess the availability of cash to meet debt service payments. Revenue bond contract indentures are expressed in terms of minimums of available current revenues after meeting expenses (cash outlays) in relationship to debt service needs.

10. Asset valuation techniques differ among countries. Those that use a historical basis can greatly understate the replacement value of plant and equipment in periods of high inflation. For example, water utilities with much of their investment in underground piping and reservoirs may have major assets that have expected useful lives of 40 to 100 years. Utilities that use current market values for assets will appear to be much less leveraged (ratio of debt to total assets) than those that do not. However, their current depreciation charges are likely to be higher, which makes them appear less profitable.

11. A recent study of earnings management by local governments in Sweden and elsewhere found that use of the accrual system let governments manipulate reported earnings (deficits and surpluses) by altering depreciation rates, asset write-downs, and pension costs. The statistical analysis found that governments that were exposed to high levels of scrutiny by public groups and capital markets were less inclined to manage earnings (Stalebrink 2002).

12. The word *appropriate* is used because once beyond a simple general government balance sheet pledge (and likely even in that case), the information needed to assess risk will be specific to the local government. For example, a government that relies heavily on utility revenues will find its ability to pay debt heavily influenced by the operations of those utilities. If the raw material or labor costs are rising rapidly or users are not paying their bills, timely debt service payments may be endangered.

13. The list of items to consider can be found in various trade and professional publications. A good starting point for generic items is the Government Finance Officers Association's *Disclosure Guidelines for State and Local Government Securities* (GFOA 1991).

Part IV

Evaluating, Monitoring, and Assisting Subnational Governments

John Petersen and Marcela Huertas

Chapter 10

Credit Analysis and Credit Ratings

Credit analysis is a demand-side activity. Investors and their advisers examine information on issuers and their obligations and make judgments on the rewards and risks of investments. Credit risk, typically taken to mean the economic, legal, and political risk inherent in a particular obligation, ultimately boils down to default risk.[1] Information used in credit analysis can be garnered from a variety of sources, such as government statistical data or the local newspapers, as well as issuers and borrowers.

Credit analysis demands resources and analytical skills that many investors, especially individuals and smaller institutions, lack. Thus most investors rely on the opinions of experts (box 10.1). An independent, objective system of credit ratings of high quality is an essential component of the development of a vibrant capital market. It is especially important for security markets, with numerous investors that must rely on information provided by issuers and others. If the ratings are respected and used, the rating companies have the clout to demand full disclosure by issuers. To the degree that these companies are successful in obtaining data and that their ratings reflect legitimate risk indices, the entire market is aided by the categorization of debt and the monitoring of performance.

The role of credit ratings is not without controversy. For emerging market economies, with their chronic shortage of trained analytical staff, rating agencies offer a pool of skilled analysts who can assess credit quality on behalf of all investors, using a standard methodology (at least standard to each agency). On the negative side this concentration of opinion, using methods that are proprietary and not fully disclosed, can lead to a dangerous dependence on a handful of experts who can influence the market without an effective check.[2]

International rating agencies are sensitive about their impact on the markets. They have had considerable difficulty with "regulatory rating" (a requirement that bonds be rated before they can be listed on the exchanges or sold to the investing public), which can lead to "shopping" for the highest rating or an acceptable rating at the lowest cost. Requirements for mandatory ratings can lead to the creation of national agencies that are not technically competent and can be politically influenced. The major agencies prefer a free market for their opinions, with investors deciding which agencies' opinions are worthwhile;the agencies themselves are leery of being regulated by anyone other than the market.

The development of credit ratings in emerging markets has followed two often overlapping tracks. Along one track are various market participants who create a domestic rating agency, sometimes in alliance with an established international rating agency. The focus of these homegrown agencies has been on meeting domestic regulatory requirements. Generally, the opinions of these domestic agencies have carried little weight internationally. Along the second, more common, track are the major international rating agencies that have opened national offices or acquired local rating firms.

Subsovereign Ratings

The appeal of credit ratings is clear: they provide a third-party opinion by experts that informs investors without the skills or resources to carry out their own investigations of the relative creditworthiness of competing investment opportunities. Their appeal is especially strong to investors that have a diverse portfolio of securities, where each represents only a small part of the total holdings. Furthermore, credit ratings have positive effects on the working of subnational governments. Preparing the data for ratings and undergoing review help instill discipline in subnational government officials and staff. The rating agencies' demands for continual updating (with the threat of a down-grading if a government's performance is subpar or the required information is not provided) can strongly encourage good behavior. The rating agencies, for good reason, place considerable emphasis on governments keeping them well informed as a measure of good financial management.

The concept of creditworthiness is important. It measures the comparative risk of "payments difficulties." Rating agencies do not rate the comparative market values of securities or general market risks *per se*. Each agency

Box 10.1. Emerging Market Ratings and Bond Insurance

International credit ratings began in the 1980s with Western European countries and corporations that were active in the Euromarket. There were very few subsovereign credits to rate, since most subnational governments relied exclusively on bank lending and sovereign guarantees.

The rating agencies later entered the emerging markets by first rating sovereign borrowing in hard currencies and then the public or private corporations that seemed likely to generate hard currency to pay back international bondholders. The next instrument to be developed was the asset-backed security (ABS), which is secured by pools of underlying loans aggregated by the issuer. The ABSs started off with car loans, credit card accounts, and mortgages. These markets soon were flooded at the higher end, mainly by U.S. and Western European issuers, and margins were very thin. Attention again turned to emerging markets.

The assets that back ABSs are typically dollar-denominated securities consisting of export receivables, credit cards, and telephone receivables. The ABS approach allowed issuers to borrow at much lower rates than in the domestic markets. However, access to these markets requires having a credit rating, and getting a rating has usually required obtaining credit enhancements from third parties. The need for enhancements in turn stimulated the growth of bond insurance.

This was accomplished by structuring the debt through an offshore origination and securing the debt by receivables gathered through a trust. The future receivables are held by an offshore trust, and obligors are required to make payments to the trust. Payments never enter the country of the issuer, thereby avoiding problems of convertibility and mitigating sovereign risk. These obligations thus are not constrained by the sovereign rating of the borrower's country. The device has been used successfully by Argentine provinces that were able to pledge offshore oil revenues to repay bonds sold internationally. The funds were received offshore and so escaped the convertibility restrictions imposed by the Argentine national government in late 2001.

Source: Authors.

has its own formula for weighing various factors, but the agencies typically look at the same factors in rating subsovereign credit risk.

Except in the United States and a few other developed countries, the rating of subsovereign government risk is very much in its infancy. For emerging and transitioning countries, the number of subnational bond ratings by recognized international rating agencies, while growing, is still low. Nonetheless, the rating agencies have been staking out the subsovereign government area, and many observers believe that progress in the development of subsovereign securities markets will depend on establishing a culture of ratings to guide the market. According to the rating agencies, quite a few subnational governments also are seeking ratings to bolster their overall visibility and credibility.[3]

Each rating agency has its own rating formula. Reflecting prospects for ultimate or partial repayment, ratings range from AAA for the highest category, which is usually conferred only on sovereign credits, down to C or D categories, which are assigned to bonds that are in default. While the major agencies have different ways of weighting each factor, they agree on the major analytical underpinnings for judging the creditworthiness of subsovereign credits:[4]

- *Sovereign rating ceiling:* The rating of the national government usually sets the top limit on the rating that a subsovereign government can enjoy. National governments set monetary and fiscal policy and usually have first claim on foreign exchange. They also can change the rules of the game for subnational governments. Exceptions can arise if the debt is secured by offshore assets or hard currency revenue streams.
- *Economy:* Fiscal health is usually closely linked to the health of the subnational economy. Diversification in activity, which often comes with size, helps balance the economy's performance. Demographics are important. A high dependency population (the very young and very old) and a population growing too rapidly for a country's capacity are both negatives. Higher income and more educated populations are a plus, as are an acceptable distribution and rate of growth in income.
- *Structure and management:* An assignment of functional spending responsibilities consistent with revenue resources is a positive. Intergovernmental transfers are examined for their size and predictability. The willingness and ability of the national government to detect and stem financial emergencies is a positive. The rigor and timeliness of

budgetary and financial laws are examined and can be either a positive or negative, depending on the flexibility they provide to localities. Past performance in achieving budgetary balance is important. The timeliness and comprehensiveness of financial reporting and the application of consistent standards are all positives.

- *Fiscal performance:* Revenue composition and trends are considered. The ability to set rates at the local level is a positive. Tax burdens should be in balance with those in neighboring regions. Effective use of charges and fees is viewed favorably, but large transfers of general funds to local enterprises are not. Composition and trends in expenditure are reviewed for consistency and pace: high and rising program costs are worrisome; steady shares among programs and slow growth are reassuring. Capital spending and maintenance spending are positives; a large wage bill is a negative. The ability to budget and to meet budgets is a positive. Surpluses in current operating budgets are a strong positive, as are capital budget planning and making many expenditures from current revenues.

- *Financial position:* Liquid assets and marketable real assets are favorable factors, as are healthy reserves in relation to annual expenditures. Outstanding debt is considered. Short-term debt is a concern if not periodically retired. Long-term debt and contingent debt (guarantees) is generally a negative unless used in support of productive (self-supporting) activities. Short maturity debt with principal due at term, called *bullet maturity*, is a negative because of continuing pressure to refinance and the potential burden on current revenues. Overlapping debt of other governments that relies on the same economic base is considered.

- *Legal framework:* The lack of clear laws, legal precedent, or an effective judicial system is a major impediment, especially where there are restricted revenue or enterprise-based pledges. A history of repudiations or insolvencies is a large negative. Approval of borrowings by higher level governments and other restrictions on local borrowing may be positive factors if carried out in an efficient and nonpolitical fashion, but these can be negatives if the process is complex and political.

- *Accounting and financial reporting:* The basis and quality of financial records are examined, and prompt, consistent reports are a positive. So are timely and independent audits. Cash flow information or cash basis accounting that provides reliable information on cash available to pay debt service is a positive. Evaluation of liquid assets and accounts receivable can influence credit assessments because required investments in government bonds can be risky and accounts may be in arrears.

Opinions on credit quality are not static, and the relative importance of factors can change over time. A range of national policies not directly related to local debt can alter the mix and weighting of credit factors. For example, laws governing purchasing policies, public employee retirement benefits or wages, or the reassignment of functions and revenue sources all can shift the focus of analysts.

Credit rating analysts are especially sensitive to the changing missions and roles of subnational governments, especially as part of fiscal adjustment. For example, the responsibilities of subnational governments for infrastructure provision have increased greatly in many transitioning countries. Meeting these needs has led to changing balance sheets and operating statements, as subnational governments assume more debt to meet capital spending requirements. The increasing levels of indebtedness and debt service at the subnational government level are seen as a natural development and not necessarily as indicators of deteriorating credit quality. The important issues are the purposes for which the debt is used and how surely and quickly the revenues to pay debt service are growing.

Expanding the Market for Ratings

International rating agencies have been establishing beachheads in subnational markets, both to cover the changing circumstances of subnational borrowers and in anticipation of new markets. This process is illustrated in South Africa. CA Ratings (now affiliated with Standard and Poor's), Fitch Ratings, and Duff & Phelps (absorbed by Fitch Ratings) actively promoted their products, even though the South African municipal bond market was moribund. Despite the market's small size and cloudy prospects, the agencies continued to show substantial commitment to following municipal debt.

One role for the rating agencies in South Africa was to monitor outstanding debt for banks, insurance companies, and other institutional investors that had neither the analytical capacity nor the desire to invest in any. Before 1994 South African municipal bonds carried an implicit sovereign guarantee. When that was revoked, investors suddenly had to distinguish among municipal credits that, for all intents and purposes, had been homogeneous in the presumption of carrying no default risk. The transformation into a new government structure presented new elements of risk. The rating agencies pooled the credit research for their subscribers, who had little interest in following individual credits on their own.

During the late 1990s more insurance companies were formed to handle nontraditional business, including emerging markets. These insurers handle non-investment-grade paper (rated in the fourth tier of ratings, BBB or Baa, or higher), and no longer price under the assumption of zero loss.[5] Non-investment-grade paper requires higher reserves and may have less than the highest bond rating. Insurers make money where the perception of risk exceeds the actual risk and can alter the actual risk through close monitoring and direct involvement. Risk perceptions may be institutionalized in various prudential restrictions placed on lending institutions and investors. These perceptions and restrictions cause credit spreads, that is, the differentials in interest rates, among classes of debt. The insurer, by superior access to information, deeper analysis, and ability to diversify risk, can effectively narrow these spreads by "renting out" the use of its credit rating. It charges premiums for this service, thereby enjoying a return on the capital it commits (in addition to its interest earnings).

The difficulties of the Asian financial crisis in 1997 and the Russian default of 1998 sent the international financial markets, particularly the emerging markets, into a prolonged decline, with severe effects on subnational government borrowing. Nevertheless, interest in new debt issues remains in some corners. Fitch Ratings provides ratings for the privately financed South African bond bank, Infrastructure Corporation of Africa (INCA), on its municipal investments and holdings. With the rapid change in the South African subnational government structure, investors want to stay current under the assumption that once the government structure settles down there will be a flood of new issues. Borrowers, too, are anxious to position themselves favorably and are keeping ratings up to date. Each agency has compiled data for more municipalities than it has been called on to rate, and each makes an effort to recast data reported in standard formats.

However, not all segments of the investor community are familiar with or convinced by rating resources and opinions. Some investors express reservations about the value of credit ratings in general. Once the ratings are published, all investors must be aware of them and calculate the effects into their pricing decisions. It seldom pays to bet against the rating of a respected agency.

Rating agencies suffer from inherent difficulties that go with being both financially viable and having a powerful effect on market behavior. First, their methodologies are necessarily proprietary. If everyone could apply the rating formula, no one would pay for a rating. Second, important factors used in ratings can be largely subjective. What is the risk of political instability, including debt repudiation? (Even when the "right people" win control in a country, bondholders and creditors can lose if the terms of outstanding debt are unilaterally changed.) Third, in publishing opinions the rating organizations generally assume that certain conditions and relationships will prevail. In a rapidly changing world, the assumptions may not hold. These problems are compounded for small agencies in developing countries, where there are few users of ratings and few issues to rate. The economics do not justify retaining skilled employees, and there is too little business to sustain competition among opinions.

Credibility of Ratings

The problem of credibility arises from cases where rating agencies have failed to foresee financial disruptions or have lagged behind rapidly moving events, calling the rating process into question. Recent events in the U.S. market have shown that the rating agencies are not infallible and that investors and regulators are a goad to better performance.[6] Another example of the fallibility of ratings is the precipitous downgrading of several sovereign credits in Asia during the ongoing financial turmoil. In December 1996 all of the countries were listed as having either stable (nothing on the horizon to suggest a downgrading) or positive (indications that the rating may be upgraded) credit outlooks. Not only were the ratings reduced over the next two years, but the countries also went through a continuing period of negative outlook (indications that the rating may be reduced) on Standard & Poor's Creditwatch, which exacerbated the uncertainty about how far they would fall. The precipitous declines in the ratings of Indonesia and the Republic of Korea and the serious slides of Malaysia and Thailand caused havoc for them in the markets (table 10.1).

Several other emerging market sovereign ratings have been downgraded in recent years. The drops were especially sharp following the Russian devaluation and default in the summer of 1998, which sent all the emerging markets into a tailspin. Prior to its currency and credit crash, Russia had investment grade sovereign ratings from both Standard & Poor's and Moody's on some of its Euromarket obligations. Governments, trying to protect currencies, depleted foreign reserves. Depletions were followed by devaluations, flights of capital, and widespread concerns over domestic firms and

Table 10.1. Credit Rating Volatility in Asia: Selected Standard and Poor's Long-Term Foreign Currency Sovereign Ratings

	December 1996	September 1997	December 1997	September 1998
India	BB+	BB+	BB+	BB+
Indonesia	BBB	BBB	BB+	CCC
Korea, Rep. of	AA-	AA-	B+	BB+
Malaysia	A+	A+	A-	BBB-
Philippines	BB+	BB+	BB+	BB+
Thailand	A	A-	BBB	BBB-

Note: The dividing line between "investment grade" and "noninvestment grade" is drawn between the BBB and BB categories, using the Standard and Poor's nomenclature. The equivalent dividing line for Moody's is between Baa and Ba. Duff & Phelps and Fitch Ratings use the same symbols and demarcation points as does Standard and Poor's.

Source: Standard and Poor's.

banks making payments in foreign currencies and, ultimately, domestic currency.

Subsovereign government credit ratings were also lowered, but selectively. Typically because of the lowered sovereign rating, the effective estimate of "macro" creditworthiness and the cap on the subsovereign ratings both fell. Between October 1997 and October 1998 Standard & Poor's lowered seven of the 18 ratings on subsovereign governments (two in Korea and five in Russia). Subnational government ratings in Central Europe and South American were not affected.

Whether changes in credit ratings anticipated, coincided with, or stimulated turmoil in the financial markets is an important question, and it is being asked with increasing frequency. Once rated, issuers run the risk that the agencies may change their minds as economic and political conditions change. Relatively well-rated Malaysia was shocked to have its rating dropped from A to BBB– just days before a large international bond offering, a move that was sure to cost the country higher interest rates. The Malaysian prime minister called for controls over the market power exerted by the rating companies. The ratings for some lower-rated Asian borrowers were not changed amid the market tumult: evidently the rating agencies got it right for India and the Philippines in the first place. Both of these on-the-fringe-of-creditworthiness countries had lagged behind the formerly high-rated "tigers" in economic growth and the pace of capital market development.

Unfortunately, neither the financial markets nor the rating agencies have enjoyed any respite from the turbulent market conditions and recurring crises of the last five years. After a few years in the mid-1990s of what can best be described as euphoria in the emerging markets, growth has failed to occur.[7] The South American credits have been especially hard hit, and several subnational borrowers have defaulted. Nonetheless, there are some bright spots, with Mexico a leading recent example. Furthermore, the difficulties in the international markets have underscored the need to develop domestic markets. Without stronger domestic markets, a resumption of access to the international markets is unlikely.

Private Bond Insurance

Allied with the development of international credit ratings has been the development of commercial bond insurance. Bond insurance acts as a third-party guarantee that debt service will be paid on time. The attraction is that the insurer carries a high credit rating from the internationally recognized rating agencies. This third-party guarantee of debt with a high credit rating lowers the cost of borrowing by more than the cost of the insurance premium.

Growth of Bond Insurance

Bond insurance originated in the United States and has been tremendously successful in the municipal securities market. Insurance covers half of the dollar volume of municipal bonds. For bond insurance to catch on, investors must find value in the promise of insurers to meet the debt service payments, and investors must perceive differences in credit quality among issuers, usually expressed in different rates of interest demanded to offset the perceived differences in risk. The commercial insurer has a high rating from the recognized rating agencies that carries with it the promise of a lower interest rate for the insured borrower. While these are accepted notions in the highly developed subsovereign markets in the United States, they are still novel ideas in emerging markets. Not surprisingly, the idea of bond insurance has been most successfully applied to sales in international currency markets.

In the 1990s bond insurers underwent a transformation and began to take a much broader approach. Commercial bond insurance became an international commodity as the U.S. bond market became saturated and international markets became larger and more complicated. While all major insurers had an AAA rating and stringent reserve requirements, some of the smaller insurance firms that emerged had less than prime grade and covered credit risks of less than investment grade. The international bond insurance market appeared promising until 1997 and the Asian financial crisis.

In 1996, Standard & Poor's asked chief executives of the international insurance industry for their view of future international expansion. At the time, international business made up about 2 percent of the bond insurance companies' "book" (Smith 1998, p. 5). The executives estimated rapid growth to 9 percent of outstanding business in 2000 and 17 percent by 2005. The rapid expansion was expected to come in Asian markets. In 1996 a consortium of firms started up ASIA Ltd., which was to be a nonprime grade competitor for Asia business. Also, the relatively small insurer Capital Markets Assurance Company (CapMAC) reached heavily into the international markets in hopes of opening up new frontiers of profits. The Asia turmoil laid both ASIA Ltd. and CapMAC low, and CapMAC was subsequently absorbed by the bond insurance giant MBIA.

Problems in Emerging Markets

The international financial turmoil of 1997 sent a strong warning that the risks of the new emerging market frontier may not have been adequately understood. On the other hand, the slow entry of the major companies was well rewarded since they avoided large capital charges and the downgrading that crippled ASIA Ltd. The insurance industry had a bad experience once before, when it entered the real estate market. While the growth of private insurance can be expected to continue, it is likely to be much slower in the emerging market area than had originally been thought (Veno and Smith 1998).

The primary bond insurers were not too seriously affected by the 1997 and 1998 plunges. The primary companies had only 3 percent of their par exposures in foreign-based insurance policies. Municipal-type international business is about two and half times as profitable as domestic work and has been largely restricted to superior, investment-grade issuers. With somewhat less competition in the field, the possibility of higher premiums appeared to improve.

The crises in the Asian bond markets in 1997 was followed by the broad-scale emerging markets crisis of the summer of 1998, precipitated by the Russian government's devaluation and default. The major insurers were spared the fallout because they had been slow to add Asian credits to their risk portfolios, but ASIA Ltd. was caught in the downdraft because of its regional concentration. Although given a respectable A rating by Standard & Poor's on its creation in 1996, ASIA's rating was lowered to BA the next year as rating downgrades of the policies in its portfolio caused a major erosion of its capital position. Short of widespread defaults, a massive systemic downgrading of credits is the worst thing that can happen to an emerging market insurer.[8]

As with international financial markets generally, there was a sharp contraction in international private market insurance at the turn of the twenty-first century. The major insurance companies are not risk takers. They are really "rating upgraders" and "credit endorsers" rather than insurers in the classic sense. If they can avoid risk, they will. Underwriting policies and supplying enhancements on an international scale to government borrowers with less than investment grade issues is extremely costly since the rating agencies make much heavier exactions in terms of reserves that are required to be set aside to offset the higher risks. As a result, the use of insurance is likely to develop in emerging market economies as part of domestic schemes to encourage market access.

Notes

1. *Credit risk* is distinct from *market risk* or *interest rate risk*, which usually pertains to how the entire debt market (interest rates and exchange rates, in the case of foreign currency denominated debt) will perform.

2. The rating agencies have come under close examination and criticism regarding both their methods and influence on markets (see While 2001 and International Monetary Fund 1999). Liu and Ferri (2002) question the dominant influence of sovereign ratings (country ceiling effect) on the ratings of firms.

3. In addition to bond-specific purposes, governments may use credit ratings to promote general investor confidence achieve name recognition, improve communications, and strengthen their ability to negotiate lines of credit or bolster the credit capacity of enterprises they own (see Eddy 2000).

4. The rating agencies publish articles and reports that outline their rating criteria for various markets and instruments (see, for example, Moody's 1998).

5. By convention the value of this paper can be carried on the books at purchase price by financial institutions. With the emphasis on marking all securities "to market" (current prices), that practice has fallen out of favor.

6. The rating agencies missed badly on Enron, keeping its debt at investment grade until just days before its bankruptcy. In congressional hearings

the agencies maintained that they were duped along with others by the fraudulent financial information put out by the company. Nonetheless, the Securities and Exchange Commission is undertaking a study of the rating agencies and the need for more federal oversight of their activities.

7. Net long-term private sector resource (liability transactions of one-year or more original maturity) flows from capital markets to developing countries declined from approximately $160 billion in 1996 to zero in 2001. In other words, new long-term lending was completely offset by re-payments of outstanding debt (see World Bank 2002a).

8. The involvement of the Asian Development Bank and other owners of ASIA Ltd. was hoped to provide a certain degree of insulation because of the "management insights" and one would suppose the political clutch that the owners represented. The tumble in Asian ratings had terrible con-sequences for ASIA's insured portfolio.

Chapter 11

Monitoring and Intervening in Subnational Government Finances

A national government has a justifiable interest in subsovereign finances in general and in subsovereign indebtedness in particular.. The kinds of information required to understand the financial condition of subnational governments and subsovereign debt are much the same for governments and investors. As a result of this common interest, an active securities market is an important way to stimulate continuing interest in local financial condition. Subjecting governments to continuing scrutiny and applying pressure for greater transparency are viewed as advantages of a securities market system that relies on private capital. Furthermore, what the central government is willing and able to do to avoid and cure the financial problems of subnational governments is of fundamental concern to investors.

Financial monitoring may focus only on borrowing localities or on financial reporting by all localities, including annual budget and expenditure reviews. Much of the information needed for local debt monitoring can be generated by an active municipal securities market that demands continuing disclosure and by the availability of audited, standardized financial statements. The evolution of the credit market may be the major factor in the evolution of the relationship between the central government and its subnational partners. Once market-dictated transparency and regular reporting are achieved, there should be less need for ongoing direct supervision or regulation of subnational jurisdictions. Central government leadership in prescribing reporting practices and making reports available to the public can advance the development of private markets.

The political and financial relationships between sovereign and subsovereign governments are rich and varied. They are evolving along new lines, many of them unique to a country's tradition and position along the devolutionary scale. National government oversight and intervention in subnational government financial affairs vary fundamentally in federal systems, which leave important prerogatives to the states and their subnational governments, and in unitary governments, which have a strong sovereign center. The United States, Canada, India, and several Latin American countries, for example, have a federal system of government with specific powers and prerogatives reserved to each level. Local governments are typically subordinate to state or provincial governments, although often possessing some degree of independence. In unitary systems all powers of the state are derived from the central government, which has oversight over subnational governments. Rather than prescribe a single approach to monitoring and oversight of subsovereign conditions, therefore, this chapter first reviews international experience in developed and emerging market economies and then draws some guidelines.

Examples from the United States

Oversight and intervention by the states in the affairs of local governments vary greatly in the United States. As a general rule the older states in the Eastern part of the country (the original colonies) have tighter controls and oversight over local governments. In these so-called "Dillon Rule" states local governments are the progeny of the parent states and have only the powers expressly given to them in the state constitutions and by the legislatures.[1] Since the local governments are seen as accountable to the state, they often have strict reporting requirements to the states. If a local government gets into trouble, the state is typically in a position, if it chooses, to step in and take over government operations, including removing locally elected and appointed officials.

Direct Intervention

Because the administration and finances of local governments in the United States have been at a high level since the Great Depression of the 1930s, there are only a few examples of direct intervention. However, it can be very sweeping when used.

The state appropriates functions and monitors. In the mid-1970s the State of New York stepped in to help resolve the financial crisis in New York City, establishing a control board for the city with approval power over all financial decisions. The control board remained until the city had enjoyed two years of budgetary balance, a total of five years. The state took back the city sales tax and used it to secure the city's debts. A new financing vehicle, the Municipal Assistance Corporation, was created to sell bonds backed by the special sales tax and to refund outstanding city notes as they came due. Debt service payments on the refunding bonds had first call on the sales tax revenues; the city had access only to what remained. The federal government initially refused to provide special assistance, though it did accommodate the workout of the financial problem by providing a liquidity facility to the city. It also sponsored federal legislation that permitted the city's pension system to invest in city and Municipal Assistance Corporation securities without violating federal prudential standards. The pension systems financed most of the recovery and bought some $4 billion in Municipal Assistance Corporation bonds.

When the city of Philadelphia faced a financial emergency in the 1980s, it too came under a New York City–style state control board with oversight of all spending decisions. Washington, D.C. also had a financial control board that had to approve budgets and expenditures and that took over day to day control of key city services. Elected officials effectively lost control over spending decisions.

The state takes over. When the city of Chelsea, Massachusetts, was on the brink of insolvency in 1991 (it had little debt outstanding but was defaulting on payroll and vendor payments and there was widespread corruption), the state governor removed all elected officials and appointed a receiver. The receiver reported only to the governor and ran all aspects of the city, approving all contracts, tax levies, and the like. The state also created a special guarantee program to back the city's bonds, which were sold to fund several improvements. After three years a new city charter was written and approved by the state legislature, elections were held, and the city was turned back to elected officials. The city had to meet certain tests, including tests of financial operations, to stay out of receivership.

Similar strong approaches have been used in the small cities of Ecorse, Michigan, and East Saint Louis, Illinois. In both cities a receiver was appointed either by a state court (in Michigan) or by the governor (Illinois) to direct the financial affairs of the local government.

The state creates an oversight institution and strengthens it. When the city of Bridgeport, Connecticut, ran into financial difficulty in 1991, the state of Connecticut first tried to use a limited control board approach. The board had budget approval but no power to oversee or enforce implementation of the budget. The city overspent its budget and, at odds with the state, attempted to go into bankruptcy under Chapter 9 of the federal bankruptcy code, which has provisions for defaults by local governments.[2] The state of Connecticut opposed the city's bankruptcy petition, and the bankruptcy court ruled that the city was not technically insolvent.[3] The state subsequently stiffened the powers of the control board and provided transitional aid, and the city did not default on its debt.

The Nonintervention Tradition

Alongside this tradition of municipal intervention in the eastern United States is another tradition of much less oversight and nonintervention, in which local governments have much more autonomy. This appears to be especially prevalent in states west of the Mississippi River. When Orange County, in the state of California, had insufficient funds to pay its debt on time in December 1995, the county entered into bankruptcy (providing immediate protection from its creditors) and defaulted on $200 million in short-term debt. The state of California refused to become involved, and the county entered into extensive litigation and subsequent settlements on its own without state intervention or oversight.

In a similar case in the 1980s the Washington State Power Supply System, a large regional utility owned by several local governments (a combination of special districts and municipalities) in three states, defaulted on revenue bonds. The bonds had been sold to finance the construction of five nuclear power plants. The Supreme Court of the state of Washington ruled that the basic contract on which the borrowing had been secured was invalid and the borrowing itself was thus invalid (*ultra vires*).[4] Because of the limited obligation nature of the pledge, the bondholders were simply out of luck, having no recourse to the underlying municipal governments that were clearly not guarantors of the projects. Construction of the plants ceased, and no liability was incurred by the underlying jurisdictions.[5] None of the state governments tried to bail out the bondholders.

Examples of Monitoring and Oversight in Other Countries

Several other examples give a sense of the wide range of monitoring and intervention by higher levels of government.

Canada

In the Canadian federal system the provinces have parental powers over local governments and effectively control their finances. This is in contrast to relationships between the Canadian national government and the provinces, which are highly decentralized. Localities rely on the property tax (although legislation is at provincial level, local governments can set their own rates) and transfers from the provinces. Local government capital spending and borrowing are generally subject to provincial approval, and most borrowing is done through provincial intermediaries (bond banks) that provide additional security through provincial pledges.

South Africa

South Africa illustrates the pressure of a changing governmental structure on intergovernmental fiscal relationships in an emerging market economy. The country has moved from a highly centralized system of government to one whose constitution recognizes three spheres of government (national, provincial, and local). The rapid amalgamation of white municipalities with the less affluent black townships has led to a variety of problems, including nonpayment of property taxes and utility bills by the newly absorbed areas. Since South Africa's public sector financial structure places much of the fiscal responsibility on local governments, the nonpayment of taxes and charges has caused widespread fiscal stress. Insolvent local governments are under the control of the provinces, whose position is even more tenuous.

Responding to the fiscal problems at the local level, the national government has instituted "project viability," requiring quarterly reports from municipalities on their financial position. Distressed governments are subject to supervision. While the supervision provisions have not yet been tested, the quarterly financial monitoring is probably the most regular and frequent anywhere in the world.

Argentina

Argentina has a historically highly decentralized system of government, with significant powers given to the provincial governments. Much like the U.S. and Canadian systems, the provincial governments are the parents of the local governments. The provinces vary greatly in income and level of development. The central government raises taxes, most of which it then transfers to the provincial level to provide services. This financial structure obviously places great importance on intergovernmental transfer mechanisms. All three levels of government are permitted relatively free rein to borrow, which they have done primarily to cover operating deficits. Most of the financing has been through province-owned banks whose investment decisions were strongly influenced by the needs of state and provincial governments. The result has been large and increasing amounts of unsustainable debt, especially during the 1980s.

In the 1990s the central government stepped in to bail out the provinces and cities by replacing subnational debt with national debt. The national government essentially closed the window on provincial bank lending to provincial governments. However, the provinces have continued to borrow from private banks and to pledge future intergovernmental transfers. A recurring problem has been a lack of discipline in borrowing to cover current deficits. Since the provinces and municipalities have a high degree of independence, the central government's ability to control their behavior is limited. In a new approach, the federal government and the provinces have entered into numerous agreements intended to control provincial spending and borrowing.

Brazil

Like South Africa's, Brazil's constitution provides nominally equal status to all three levels of government. The country has had a long-standing if unsteady tradition of federalism. As in Argentina the lack of effective control by the central government led to the running up of high levels of indebtedness by the states and the two largest cities, followed by widespread defaults in the 1980s. The debts were rescheduled by the central government to convert short-term debt to long-term debt. A major problem was that the national government had no effective control over the amount of debt incurred by subnational governments. In the final analysis Brazil was unwilling to allow massive defaults. As in Argentina negotiations between the states and the central government are ongoing. Since 1998 and the passage of the Fiscal Responsibility Act, the central government has curbed imprudent fiscal behavior and set tight conditions for subnational government borrowing.

Transitioning Economies in Europe

The transitioning economies of Eastern and Central Europe emerged from highly centralized unitary systems where the subnational government subdivisions were service delivery points for the center and highly dependent on the central government for fiscal transfers. In addition, subnational governments owned various enterprises that generated revenues but that often operated at a loss. Financial reporting systems were designed for measuring levels of inputs or for tax purposes only and so provided little information on the financial condition of the government. Auditing was done by state offices and was notable for both low quality and frequency.[6]

Economies tended to operate on a cash basis with a small and highly centralized banking sector and no functioning capital markets. Major capital spending was financed by grants or soft loans and was directed by the central government or financed on a pay-as-you go basis by the locality in the case of smaller routine projects. Since subnational governments had no existence beyond the central government, monitoring and interventions consisted mainly in the removal of officials who failed to perform as instructed. Little consideration was given to coping with financial emergencies of subnational governments, although Hungary enacted legislation on municipal bankruptcies.

More recently, governments in these transitioning economies have been moving to greater local autonomy. Financial reporting systems have been put in place to provide more useful information about local conditions. These systems tend to follow the European model of full accrual accounting, and the balance sheets are often spotty and inaccurate because of unresolved questions of ownership, value of real assets, and accounts receivable. Capital financing has relied primarily on specialized loan funds or commercial banks (themselves often undergoing privatization and carrying suspect balance sheets) that have traditional relationships with the subnational governments. Recently, loans from the European Bank for Reconstruction and Development (EBRD) and grants related to accession to the European Union have become the dominant sources of long-term capital for subnational governments.

Establishing a Central Government System of Monitoring and Intervention

Establishing a framework for monitoring subnational performance—determining the appropriate institutional roles and authority to intervene and identifying under what circumstances and with what limited powers—can raise major issues of intergovernmental relationships and accountability.

As a practical matter the financial information routinely provided to the central government by subnational governments may be the primary source of centralized information about the current status of subnational debt. However, the information forms need to be carefully designed, correctly filled out, and promptly returned. Because debt issues have special information needs, careful consideration should be given to requiring subnational governments to report clearly specified information about the debt. If sufficiently detailed and frequent, periodic reporting by subnational governments can allow central government monitoring of their financial compliance with their debt obligations.

Information Needs

A system of reporting that provides complete and detailed information on outstanding subnational debt issues is basic to understanding the issuer's financial condition. Such systems can be structured in various ways. France requires that the annual municipal budget include a detailed annex on outstanding debt (see box 11.1). Romania plans to establish a public debt registry system.

For greatest effect, such a system should be integrated into a more comprehensive system that collects data on subnational finances in a form useful for analysis of financial condition. Reports on indebtedness might be required to include basic descriptions of the nature, terms, and other key characteristics of the debt; certification of compliance with the debt limitation; and information about the collateral pledged. Notification by both lender and borrower should be required in case of a payment default, and the information should be available to the public.

Having such a repository of information allows the central government to maintain a current inventory of outstanding subnational debt and makes it possible to enforce the debt service limit and monitor aggregate subnational borrowing as part of overall public debt management. The inventory, which could be updated annually through improved subnational debt reporting practices, should be open to the public and prospective lenders.

Ideally, financial oversight would come through market forces that demand the timely provision of information, which in turn determines access to the market, thereby exerting pressure for financial discipline. Where the institutions and market players are in the formative and untested stage, however, a "seed-planting" role for government is likely to be required. It is important not to discourage market initiatives or to weaken market incentives. Legal requirements that bond market participants disclose and send information to a central point help markets work more efficiently and prod subnational governments into assuming reporting responsibilities.

Formulating and Enforcing Intervention

While financial monitoring may identify problems, monitoring alone is unlikely to eliminate or cure all problems. Intervention may be needed

Box 11.1. Example of Information Provided in the Debt Annex of French Subnational Government Budgets

Every budget presented to the local, county, or regional councils in France (as well as to councils of local government associations) must include a debt annex on the status of all outstanding loans as of January 1 of the fiscal year that includes information on the following:

- Year the loan was contracted or bond was issued.
- Bank or financial institution that provided the loan.
- Amount of principal borrowed / debt issued.
- Purpose of the loan / bond.
- Maturity of loan / bond.
- Currency and rate if loan / bond is in foreign currency.
- Interest rate (fixed or floating).
- Index used to determine the rate, if floating.
- Payment schedule (annual, semi-annual, quarterly, or monthly payments).
- Grace period (number of months, years).
- Principal outstanding on January 1 of the fiscal year.
- Interest payment for the fiscal year.
- Principal payment for the fiscal year.
- Principal outstanding on December 31 of the fiscal year.

An annual total is calculated for the last four items above. These data also must be provided for loans guaranteed by the local government to a third party, with the name of the beneficiary of the guarantee.

Source: DeAngelis and Dunn 2002.

when a subnational government is in fiscal distress. What steps can higher-level governments (or others) take to protect citizens and creditors and to correct whatever is causing the financial malaise? While the remedies may be of most immediate interest to lenders and investors, their form and enforcement are questions of national policy interest since they affect issues of self-governance, the delivery of essential services, and the health of financial markets.

A viable municipal borrowing market need not have a detailed statutory intervention process. Rather, the parties can define the intervention and receivership processes contractually, and these processes can be customized for a particular deal. However, there may be constitutional restrictions on the ability of a subnational government to contract for intervention and further practical problems of having courts enforce the contract. So while subnational governments should be free to negotiate monitoring and intervention provisions with creditors, a codified national approach helps to demarcate the relationship between subsovereigns and the financial markets. To ensure greater certainty about creditors' and debtors' rights and to avoid the fallout that an individual default might have on other subnational jurisdictions, it is usually better if national policymakers develop an intervention process through law or regulation that provides a clear framework for dealing with subnational financial emergencies.

Claims after default: Who gets priority and how to collect? A legislated default cure process should include a ranking of creditors and remedies. Various options are available for establishing the priority of claims. In some countries subnational governments are able to put owners of bonded debt at the head of the line. In others, the depository bank or the higher level of government gets that position. In some countries domestic creditors come before foreign creditors, a position that is likely to discourage foreign lending. In the case of security, the first to take physical possession may have the advantage.

Options for remedies are numerous. Creditors could be given the right to intercept funds that are due to a jurisdiction from other levels of government (see chapters 5 and 7). They could have a right to trigger imposition of an additional tax within the defaulting jurisdiction or the appointment of a receiver to control expenditures or the operations of a jurisdiction. Citizens also need protection to preserve minimum essential services, such as public safety and water and sanitation. Creditors should have the right to apply to courts for execution on their security interests and for judicial intervention. Courts should be empowered to deal with insolvency and the priority of claims among creditors and to discharge debt where the local jurisdiction could not otherwise be made solvent.

Enforcing remedies in the event of default. Predictable and timely enforcement of remedies for nonpayment is essential to transform a psychology of nonpayment to a hard credit culture. That requires a legal framework that clearly lays out the negative consequences of a default. Failure needs to involve pain for the erring parties. Also important is the judicial system's effectiveness in enforcing financial and other commercial contracts and property rights. A lender will find comfort in a well-defined legal and political process that clarifies what happens in the event of a default and the conditions for which a lender can force a claim for payment or foreclose on collateral.

In emerging market economies there is often little or no experience in judicially enforcing financial obligations against defaulting subnational government debtors. Only a record of precedent will determine how the judiciary will enforce such claims. Until a system has acquired practical lending experience, including experience with defaults and remedies, it is difficult to know whether the laws on collateral foreclosure are adequate. Substantive and procedural defects in the legal framework for a remedial enforcement system may become apparent only after there has been practical experience with enforcement.

Providing for a bondholder representative. In the event of a default in the payment of a subnational bond issue, the legal framework should give bondholders the right to designate a representative to act on their behalf and to pursue remedies in concert. Otherwise, each bondholder would have to pursue remedies individually, at great cost to all parties involved. That could constrain the type of collateral pledged since it might suggest that collateral must be in a highly liquid form that would allow each bondholder to readily take possession of its share.

The way around this is to designate a representative bank or trustee to look out for the bondholders' interest and act as their surrogate. Not all trustees are alike, but as markets mature, investors will find that the role is increasingly valuable in protecting their interests. Having dependable and skilled trustees also will improve the market's perception of credit quality and lower the costs of borrowing for issuers (see box 11.2).

Recovery from insolvency. The insolvency of a subnational government raises concerns that do not apply to the typical corporate insolvency. Governments do not "go out of business," so procedures are needed for managing the affairs of an insolvent subnational government and its relationships with creditors and for helping it regain financial stability. Such procedures could be initiated by the central government, by the subnational government, or eventually by its creditors. The procedures should clearly define what constitutes subnational insolvency. Regulations need to cover setting deadlines and defining minimum service requirements, order of payments, and limitations on the competencies of elected officials.

Box 11.2. In Argentina Trustees Make a Difference

Having the right trustees can make a difference in protecting bondholders' interests. During its latest financial crisis, Argentina has gained important experience with how the selection of trustees influences the strength of a debt transaction.

In Argentina subnational governments use an intergovernmental payment, the co-participation payment, for securing loans and bonds. There are two ways to intercept this payment if used as security on a loan or bond. In the more common way, the intercept occurs at the source of disbursement—at the Banco de la Nación Argentina (BNA), the commercial bank of the federal government. In the second way the intercept occurs when the provincial bank or the financial agent of the province receives the revenues from the BNA.

Recent Argentine devaluations and widespread defaults have tested these trustee mechanisms. At the first intercept level at the BNA, every bond with a trustee has been honored. At the second intercept level hazards have arisen when province-owned banks were involved, but not when the banks had been privatized.

The Province of Chaco issued three bonds for which the provincial-owned bank (Banco del Chaco) was a trustee. When hard times arrived in 2001, the province unilaterally deferred amortization of the bonds and ordered the bank to return the funds collected in the trust escrow accounts. Bondholders brought suit against the province and Banco del Chaco. The province was sued because it had unilaterally deferred capital payments, and the bank was targeted because it broke the Argentine Trust Law by accepting and implementing the province's order.

There was a very different outcome when the Province of Rio Negro deferred amortization of all of its bonds in January 2002. The province had established a trust in its financial agent (Banco Patagonia), a former provincial bank that had been privatized. Banco Patagonia continued to honor payments to bondholders and to enforce the intercept provision. In other words, private banks have been resolute trustees, and creditors are aware of this.

During 2001 some commercial bank lenders proposed that the federal government permit interception of co-participation revenues at the Central Bank, before the funds ever got to the BNA. The private banks made the request because they believed that the Central Bank had greater independence than the BNA. The federal government rejected the proposal.

Source: Argentina case study, chapter 14.

A subnational government that defaults on its debt and other payments is likely to have poor financial management, overestimating its financial capacity and allowing expenditures to increase faster than revenues. It may require assistance in building a stronger financial base and in establishing good financial management policies and practices.

Procedures for addressing subnational government insolvency can vary considerably. Practices in Hungary and Latvia are informative and illustrate two very different approaches. Hungary relies on the court system, with almost no actions needed by the Ministry of Finance or the Ministry of the Interior (box 11.3). Latvia relies on the Ministry of Finance (box 11.4). In both cases a supervisor or trustee is appointed to assist the subnational government to prepare a financial remediation program and to supervise implementation of the program. Latvia offers the possibility of low- or no-interest financial facilities to aid in implementing the financial stabilization program. In France the Crédit Local de France often requires a financial protocol to stabilize subnational finances, including raising local taxes and reducing expenditures, as a condition for additional guaranteed loan financing for subnational governments in difficult financial positions.

Box 11.3. Debt Adjustment and Subnational Insolvency in Hungary

Under the provisions of the 1996 Municipal Debt Adjustment Act, debt adjustment may be initiated by the municipality or by its creditor through court petition. The conditions for meeting a default situation are defined from the point when an invoice or call for payments or an acknowledged debt has not been paid within 60 days, an obligation required by court decree is not met, or an obligation resulting from a previous bankruptcy decree is not paid. Once a series of notification conditions have been met by the city and the creditor and the court has determined that default conditions do exist, the court appoints a financial trustee. The trustee monitors the business operations of the local government and ensures the provision of mandated public services. The financial trustee must sign all obligations and payments, and the local government's bank cannot enforce any liens or make payments without the countersignature of the trustee.

For creditors the debt adjustment process means that all debts become due, and all claims continue to accrue interest and penalties. Debts must be reported to the financial trustee within 60 days. Deadlines are not extended, and a creditor who fails to report on time must wait until two years after completion of the adjustment process for enforcement of the debt.

The municipality's actions are severely limited once the debt adjustment procedure has been initiated. In particular, the municipality may not assume additional debt, create new enterprises, or purchase ownership interests in enterprises.

A debt adjustment committee (composed of the financial trustee, the mayor, the notary, the head of the council finance committee, and an additional council member) prepares a draft emergency budget, including a detailed listing of mandatory public functions and their financing. However, there are severe limitations. The emergency budget will not fund public health,

social, and educational facilities with a usage rate of less than
50 percent or facilities whose costs are more than 30 percent
higher than the national average.

Compromise negotiations are initiated to define the reorganization program and the debtor-creditor agreement, and the compromise agreement is submitted in writing to the court. If the
agreement meets the requirements of the law, the debt adjustment procedure is complete and the compromise is published
in the Enterprise Registry. The financial trustee may supervise
implementation of the compromise. A compromise agreement
may include liquidation of some assets of the local government.

Source: Hungary case study, chapter 29.

Box 11.4. Financial Stabilization to Address Sub-national Bankruptcy in Latvia

The Local Government Financial Stabilization Act of 1988 lists
three conditions as a basis for financial stabilization action: the
inability of the local government to meet its debt commitments,
a value of debts greater than the market value of local assets,
and a debt service ratio greater than 20 percent.

The troubled local government, on recommendation of the
chairman of the municipal council, the Minister of Finance, the
Minister of Special Assignment, or the state auditor may initiate
a financial stabilization process. The municipal council must
vote on the proposed application for a stabilization plan. If the
council rejects the plan, the Cabinet of Ministers may determine
that the local government nevertheless should enter a stabilization program.

(Box continues on the following page.)

The Stabilization Act sets out options that local governments should review while carrying out their stabilization program: improving tax collection capacity, promoting regional development, advancing amalgamation, privatizing municipal assets, and identifying cost efficiencies to reduce local expenditures.

A supervisor is appointed to assist the local government in developing and implementing the stabilization program. The supervisor makes proposals to improve the budget (which should include finding cost efficiencies to reduce local expenditures) and to monitor budget implementation for compliance with the stabilization program. At the request of the Minister of Finance, the supervisor also can control all municipal expenditures and sign the municipality's payment orders.

Source: DeAngelis and Dunn 2002.

Notes

1. Dillon was a state of Kansas judge who in the late nineteenth century laid out the theory of expressed and implied powers for local governments under the constitution of the states.

2. The federal municipal bankruptcy chapter is permissive in that a state can forbid a subdivision from filing under the chapter. The State of Connecticut, however, did not legislate such a provision until after Bridgeport had filed for protection. Since Bridgeport was found not to be technically bankrupt, the issue of whether a state could prohibit filing after the filing had been made was not decided. Most states have opted out of Chapter Nine.

3. In expert testimony, it was pointed out that the city had $400,000 in cash balances and had not demonstrated that it could not get more by simply raising taxes or cutting expenditures.

4. The court reasoned that the utility only had the ability to charge for electricity actually produced and distributed. It did not have the legal ability to levy charges and pay for electricity not produced or received. This

pledge of payment even in the event electricity is not produced or received (a "hell or high water" provision of payment) was necessary to meet debt service in case of delays in completing construction, as happened here because of massive engineering and construction problems and environmental concerns.

5. There was, however, securities fraud litigation. This was ultimately dismissed, since the standard for proving securities fraud is a difficult hurdle for plaintiffs when it involves government officials.

6. Noel (2000, p. 15) sees auditing as possibly the weakest link in the local government budgetary framework, with the central audit office as the culprit. A difficulty in many countries is the shortage of private sector talent and the high cost of outside auditors. The costs and difficulties of financial administration at the local level often are seen as a practical argument against having direct credit market access.

Chapter 12

Designing and Implementing Credit Assistance to Subnational Governments

Chapter 3 identifies three groups of subnational governments based on their readiness to access private financial markets as indicated by their financial condition, managerial skills, and (to a certain extent) size. The first group includes jurisdictions that already have access but could enjoy more and better options given a more supportive regulatory and policy environment. The second group could achieve access with help, including credit assistance that complements the operation of credit markets. The third group cannot access financial markets, even through market-oriented intermediaries, because of inadequate revenue sources. Borrowing programs should not be created for these subnational governments because borrowing will not solve this problem and could even exacerbate it.

The question then is how to assist subnational governments that do not now have the resources to be self-financing, possibly because they do not have an adequate tax base. If the central government chooses to assist these jurisdictions by establishing a predictable and stable system of intergovernmental transfers, even smaller governments can have adequate local revenues. Revenue streams from both local sources and intergovernmental transfers can be used for capital investment, with or without borrowing.

Once a subnational government has reliable revenue streams, it has the potential to support debt. Access to borrowed capital should be available to the extent that the amount of borrowing represents an acceptable level of risk. Private markets still may not serve these jurisdictions because of the small size of their financing needs, their inability to conduct analysis and planning, or their inability to deal with capital markets concepts and practices. For this group, market intermediaries and technical assistance could be made available to bridge these gaps. This middle group of potential borrowers is the major focus of this chapter.

National governments can provide an environment that promotes the marketability of local debt by implementing good macroeconomic and regulatory policies. Beyond that, several questions arise when considering assistance for subnational governments that do not have access to financial markets. Should assistance be given to help subnational governments gain access to credit? If so, what form should the assistance take in order to encourage private capital market participation and to minimize the crowding out of private capital providers? While designing national credit assistance programs that concentrate on the most needy governments seems a worthy policy objective, making cheap credit available from the central government is not without hazards. Whether as loans or grants, assistance programs have the potential to undermine private credit markets (see box 12.1).

Assistance can take several forms, ranging from technical assistance and financial assistance to direct lending and interest rate subsidies to encourage private market participants to join a transaction. At least three basic questions should be asked to determine whether to use a given technique:

- Does the assistance technique leverage private sector investment?
- How likely is it that the assistance will crowd out private sector capital?
- Does the technique increase the risk of moral hazard? How likely is it that it will be misinterpreted as a central government guarantee?

These questions are explored in the context of several forms of assistance that might be provided to promote private capital market development.

Technical Assistance

Technical assistance to help subnational governments become familiar with credit market practices and to become more creditworthy is the most likely form of assistance to attract private sector interest and the least likely to crowd out private capital. It is also the least likely to raise the risk of moral hazard. Technical assistance and training in accounting and budgeting, identifying and analyzing capital investment projects, and operating and managing facilities expand managerial skills and encourage more efficient financial practices.

Box 12.1. The Subnational Government Retreat from the Private Credit Market in the Czech Republic

Sometimes progress to more open markets for subnational governments can be reversed by national government policies, as happened in the Czech Republic. Immediately following liberalization commercial bank loans to subnational governments began to grow in the early 1990s. This growth was soon cut short by competition from state-based loan funds and capital grants.

Commercial loans to subnational governments had been encouraged through the formation of the Municipal Investment Fund, a USAID-supported project that provided a discount facility to commercial banks. Czech cities tend to have heavy urban infrastructure responsibilities, and capital spending accounts for a large share of their budgets, typically about 30 percent. However, the national government then chose to follow a less transparent capital grants policy, which together with low-cost loan programs that ignored creditworthiness undermined the emerging bank lending market. The soft loans from the state created moral hazard, and as conditions deteriorated, cities began to default. An estimated 73 percent of the State Environmental Fund loans to subnational governments were nonperforming, for example.

Finally, to meet the EU pre-accession Maastricht convergence requirements on government debt limitations and to conserve credit access for national government use, the central government ruled that it must approve all subnational government loans. This effectively stifled subnational government borrowing from private sources.

Source: Czech Republic case study, chapter 28.

Technical assistance works much better with practical applications than with abstract principles and when focused on creating local institutional and technical capacity. Technical assistance in capital planning, cash flow projections, and project management are particularly supportive of increased capital market access. These skills allow the subnational government to work within budget constraints, to match revenues and expenditures, to figure out how much to borrow and for what purposes, and to determine how quickly it can and should repay loans. Either public or private lending entities can help provide access to markets, especially if standardized documentation and processes are developed. Standardization helps to resolve questions of security and keep costs down.[1]

Financial Assistance

Financial assistance to help subnational governments gain access to private credit can take several forms. However, direct financial assistance that is insulated from market testing has significant drawbacks and risks, because the risks of adverse selection and moral hazard (see chapter 2) are always involved. To the degree that assistance from the center is institutionalized, it can foster a culture of long-term dependency and impede market development.

The lure of cheap credit provides an incentive for subnational governments to be or appear to be needy rather than self-sufficient. Direct assistance also creates hidden subsidies in the form of contingent guarantees and enhancements. It can crowd out the private sector, which typically sets higher credit standards and charges more for lending. Direct assistance usually is less efficient at leveraging private sector resources than is technical assistance.

Concessionary financing (with terms and conditions more favorable than those available in the commercial market) can also distort choices. Financial assistance reduces only capital costs to the borrower, not future facility operating costs, which will increase with the new investment. A borrower whose only source of credit is through preferential assistance, rather than capital from hard credit sources, may not have been required to fully investigate operating costs or to build them into budget planning. The governmental borrower may have little or no capacity to properly operate, maintain, and ultimately replace the facility, which then rapidly slips into decline.

However, concessional finance for subnational governments continues to have a role in most economies, either to encourage desirable activities or to surmount barriers. Furthermore, careful design can reduce the drawbacks and risks, even if it cannot eliminate them. Fundamentally, direct financial assistance should always have an exit strategy and a plan for shifting obligations to commercial credit markets. The assisting government can thereby absorb some of the risks that are unacceptable to the private credit market. This might mean finding a way to eliminate a narrow risk (such as environmental risk) by providing risk insurance. Alternatively, it might mean taking a junior lien in order to comfort potential private lenders or providing a guarantee on the "long end" of a debt structure if commercial lenders are able to provide short- and medium-term principal maturities.

Direct Lending

Direct lending can be an inefficient form of financial assistance and is likely to crowd out private lenders and invite moral hazard. Many direct lending programs aimed at subnational governments have been directed from the center. These loans are often made to unwilling and inattentive subnational governments, which end up treating them as grants. However, there can be constructive direct lending roles. The International Finance Corporation's A/B loan syndication and certification structures have demonstrated that leverage efficiencies can be achieved in the private sector with such instruments, if they are well designed.

To increase leverage and reduce crowding out and moral hazard, direct lending should be designed to induce cofinancing by commercial lenders. The smallest possible direct lending role required to achieve this objective will minimize the risk of crowding out and maximize the efficiency of the assistance rendered. Thus, for example, if a 5 percent junior lien position will induce the private sector to join in cofinancing a loan, the provider of this form of assistance should be prepared to forgo a larger loan program.

Although direct lending programs have had a poor record of loan repayment, the tide appears to be turning in some countries (see box 12.2). Credit discipline, if it is instilled into direct lending programs, can help prepare borrowers for the realities of the private market as long as sufficient economic inducements can be designed to enable borrowers to graduate to private market access.

Debt Service Subsidies and Public-Private Cofinancing

Debt service subsidies resemble direct lending in that they constitute ongoing payment streams to support subnational borrowing and so can be inefficient. They are more likely to lead to moral hazard than are more indirect or softer forms of financial assistance, such as insurance, partial guarantees, or technical assistance. Nonetheless, they can be useful tools if they are

Box 12.2. Moving from Soft to Hard Credit through Enforcement of Loan Collections: South Africa's Experience

Development banks have had a very poor loan repayment record, which has made many observers skeptical of the ability of subnational governments to make the transition into private markets with hard credit demands. However, some countries are seeking to correct the situation by holding delinquent borrowers responsible. South Africa demonstrates one way of doing this.

In January 1996 the Development Bank of Southern Africa (DBSA) inherited the Ministry of Finance's development loan portfolio for subnational governments. The portfolio consisted of some 390 loans representing about 900 million rand ($50 million) that had been made to subnational governments primarily under the pre-1994 regime. At the time of the transfer most borrowers were on time with their payments.

Amid the turmoil of the transition to the new governmental structure, many of the subnational government obligors began to go into default. The DBSA, which saw itself as a bank with commercial incentives and a capital position to protect, recoiled at the growing delinquency rate. While the original terms of the loans might have been concessionary, the DBSA's role was to keep the payments on schedule and to instill discipline into borrowers. DBSA was not expected to lose money and erode its capital base; its goal was to make reasonable returns to capital, while promoting longer term, socially useful development.

Accordingly, DBSA moved to deal with the subnational authorities to bring loan payments back on schedule. Loan officers were assigned to each region and given procedures for going after overdue loans. In three provinces, 32 of the 40 loans that had defaulted were put back on a timely basis using technical assistance and the threat of closing off future credit. In South Africa both government and private lenders have the power to seize assets of borrowers.

Source: Petersen and Crihfield 2000.

well designed to provide the smallest subsidy necessary to induce private capital market participation and if they are used solely when this is the only tool that will make the borrower creditworthy.

Linked deposits and co-lending programs are two devices used to subsidize interest costs through the private credit system. With linked deposits, a commercial bank might receive a deposit from a government intermediary that agrees to a reduced rate of interest if the bank agrees to use the deposited funds to make a loan for a particular purpose to a subnational government. The private institution still takes the credit risk, does the credit analysis, and administers the loan. With co-lending, the government intermediary makes a loan for a portion of the principal amount at a reduced rate of interest, while the private lender makes its share of the loan at the conventional rates. The borrower gets the advantage of the blended rate on its loan. The private lender, however, still has its principal at risk and administers the loan, with the intermediary as a partner in the transaction.

Major public-private infrastructure projects often have capital needs that exceed the financing capacity of a developing country's nascent credit market or banking system. A cornerstone of a credit assistance program should be a lending facility designed to attract rather then supplant private capital in financing subnational government infrastructure projects. Thus, in another creative use of cooperative devices, donors could require recipients of their credit to design loans to attract private sector participation in infrastructure projects. This participation might be by private financial institutions or by project proponents that may bring their own equity and debt financing, such as in a public-private project-financing scheme.

Such loans could be coursed through a government financial entity (GFI), which could retail the loan directly to a qualifying project (figure 12.1) or wholesale the loan proceeds to a private financial institution (PFI), which would then on-lend to a project (figure 12.2). The government finance institution, as a condition for receiving the loan from the donor, could be required to construct deals that attract private sector participation in infrastructure projects. The cofinancing approach could entail bank loans or bond issues where there are different tranches with different lien positions, maturity structures, and loan repayment mechanisms.[2] The idea is for the government finance institution to leverage private sector funds by taking various cofinancing positions in the transactions that provide comfort to the private participants or by taking positions with greater risk or less liquidity. The government finance institution is able to better absorb the added exposure because the donor credit line has been constructed for that purpose.[3]

For these "market-friendly" co-participation variants to succeed, the return on investment to private sector participants needs to be competitive with that obtainable elsewhere. Thus, the government finance institution, in taking the long view and acting as a catalyst for financial market development, would need to act as companion and facilitation lender and design issues that would stimulate private participation. For many such institutions, accustomed to market monopolies when lending to subnational governments, this would be a difficult role.

The use of an on-lending facility is customary practice for donor-based loans, but the active engagement of private sector banks and financial institutions is not. Getting the government finance institution to behave in this market-building way, perhaps compensating it for its catalyst role, would need to be wired into the donor's loan conditions.[4] A combination of inducements and requirements might be built into the loan, to encourage use of the facility while ensuring that the government finance institution does not gain all the advantages of long-term money and drive out investment through commercial banks and the bond market.

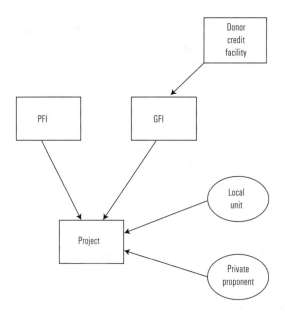

Note: In this example, a subnational government and a private participant join in a project, financed by funds from a private finance institution and from a government financing institution. The government financing institution looks to a donor credit facility for loan funds or enhancements.

Figure 12.1. Retail On-Lending by the Government Financing Institution

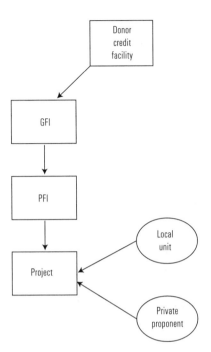

Note: In this example, a subnational government and a private participant join in a project, financed by a private finance institution from funds that have been on-lent in part from a government financing institution. The government financing institution looks to a donor credit facility for loan funds or enhancements.

Figure 12.2. Wholesale On-Lending by the Government Finance Institution

Guarantees, Insurance, and Intercepts

Guarantees are a traditional and important form of financial assistance (see chapters 5 and 10). Their contingent nature makes their cost difficult to measure at the time the guarantee is given. While guarantees can lead to lax lending practices and impede the development of effective private markets, guaranteeing specific risks or specific maturities may be worth consideration. The ability of a credit assistance provider to reduce or eliminate specific risks in a transaction (such as certain environmental hazards or the repudiation of certain contractual obligations) or to back maturities that the domestic private sector is unwilling to provide can leverage private capital investment. Properly designed and implemented such use of guarantees can reduce the risks of crowding out and moral hazard. Some of the World Bank's guarantee operations have begun to demonstrate the utility of guaranteeing specific risks or maturities as a means of inducing private capital providers to participate.

One way to reduce the risk that such credit enhancements will crowd out commercial lenders is to price them according to the degree of risk presented by each borrower. In this way local borrowers and commercial lenders see the costs involved in securing guarantees and so are more likely to treat the guarantees as having a cost. When this is done according to commercial standards, with costs and expected losses reflected in the fees charged, the guarantee is transformed into a form of insurance. While some might oppose the idea of charging needier borrowers more than those that are better off, there must be incentives to improve financial operations if subnational governments are ever to stand on their own in credit markets. Buying down part of the costs with grants but making the issuers borrow at risk-adjusted rates on the margin may be one way to force governments to pay attention to market interest rates and to scale projects accordingly. Another option is to price enhancements with "seasoning" premiums that can be partially rebated as borrowers live up to their obligations and see their circumstances improve.

As discussed in chapter 5, intercepts of national payments to subnational governments are a form of financial assistance that need not have any significant cost to the national government.[5] Intercepts can be a powerful credit enhancement—and an almost essential one, given the highly centralized system of tax collection in many emerging market economies.[6] A stream of stable, predictable intergovernmental transfers can be made pledgeable and interceptable, which can enhance creditworthiness so long as the use of the transfer is not overly restricted. Significant penalties or administrative fees when the intercept is exercised could encourage subnational governments to manage the debt payments in a businesslike fashion and not to misuse the intercept mechanism to cover lax practices. An intercept mechanism can leverage private sector funding rather than crowd it out. In the Philippines intercepts are being combined with guarantees, in the form of bond insurance, to enhance bonds sold by subnational governments (see box 12.3). To qualify for insurance, borrowers must achieve a minimum credit rating and pledge a portion of their future intercept payments to debt service. In case of default, the insurance company continues to pay the debt service to investors and assumes their rights to receive the intercept.

Box 12.3. The Philippine Local Government Unit Guarantee Corporation

Under the sponsorship of the Philippine Bankers Association, a banking consortium of 22 domestic and foreign banks has created the Local Government Unit Guarantee Corporation to provide guarantees on loans made by participating financial institutions to local governments. Some 230 million pesos were raised by subscription from the participating banks, deposited into a special account, and made available for backstopping the guarantees.

The guarantee is expected to stimulate private commercial bank interest in local government credits. For institutional and regulatory reasons, local governments have been borrowing only from government financial institutions. The government and government financial institutions are under pressure to open up the local government debt market to greater competition and to develop a municipal bond market. The government financial institutions are being privatized.

The guarantee program gives comfort to the private banks as they start lending to local governments. The program is expected to serve as an enhancement for bond issues. The guarantee depends in large part on the pre-assignment of the local government's intergovernmental transfers to the corporation, so that the transfers can be tapped in the event of default. The initial program was geared to the 120 largest local governments;once the guarantee system was in place, however, the program soon reached down to smaller government units.

As of early 2003 the corporation had insured 11 bond issues amounting to over 1.6 billion pesos (about US$35 million). Bond issue activity slowed during the political turmoil and economic slowdown of the early 2000s, but the insured bonds are paying debt service on time and in full. As a result, the use of the program in the case of a default remains to be tested.

Source: Philippines case study, chapter 26.

Intermediaries for Small Borrowers

Should a special intermediary be created for jurisdictions that cannot access credit markets through existing market mechanisms? Special intermediaries should complement rather than replace existing commercial lending and underwriting institutions. In some countries the private sector may be able to provide such intermediation, without the need to create a new government agency or function. While this may be desirable in principle, a small issue may not attract the market's attention because it would not be economical to finance in the formal securities markets.

Many intermediary models are available, including bond banks (see below), bond pools, revolving loan funds, and municipal lending institutions. Such an institution might borrow in its own name and use the proceeds to purchase debt instruments of subnational borrowers (bond banks), or it might assemble and repackage municipal debt instruments and make them available to the market (bond pools). A major attraction of such structures is that they can provide economies of scale in issuance and, because of the larger size of issuance, improve the chances of attracting interest from secondary markets.

Any intermediary function has costs, which may include administrative costs, subsidized re-lending rates, or credit enhancement costs. However, with a properly designed and efficiently run intermediary, the costs will likely be less than those involved in outright capital grants. Intermediaries have the additional virtue of helping local officials understand the trade-offs involved in debt finance (Noel 2000).

Intermediaries can be designed to provide several services to subnational governments (see box 12.4), including access to capital markets for governments that otherwise would not have access, savings on the fixed costs of debt issuance, streamlined and standardized borrowing procedures and documentation, assistance with capital planning and cash-flow projections, and pre-structuring of loan packages. The higher-level government also may decide to offer direct financial assistance, such as credit enhancement (see chapter 11) or the re-lending of intermediaries' funds at subsidized interest rates. The more passive the financial assistance and the more it is used in tandem with normal credit channels, the better, to avoid the moral hazard risks associated with direct financial assistance that is insulated from market forces. Overall, it is better to expose the novice borrower to the actual costs of capital and the discipline of the market, at least on the margin.

If the objective is to promote local self-sufficiency, it is generally advisable to avoid enhancement methods that are nontransparent, reward dysfunctional governments, or crowd out private investment. If there is a stream of stable, predictable intergovernmental transfers for jurisdictions lacking the resources to be self-sufficient, these transfers could be made pledgeable and interceptable. This would enhance creditworthiness and leverage private sector funding at little or no cost to the national government. However, the extent to which otherwise impecunious governments should be encouraged to borrow remains a judgment call. For subnational governments with slim prospects for financial self-sufficiency, it may simply be a way for the higher level providing the transfers to pass the buck of indebtedness.

Box 12.4. The Tamil Nadu Urban Development Fund, India

The Tamil Nadu Urban Development Fund evolved from a municipal trust fund to a fund financed and managed by the public and private sectors. The initial fund was financed entirely by the public sector, and while it was financially viable, it was too small to meet the demand for urban infrastructure investment.

To increase the impact of the fund, it was converted into an autonomous financial intermediary. The new fund has 30 percent participation by the private sector and is managed by Tamil Nadu Urban Infrastructure Financial Service Ltd., a private management company. Operations have been widened to include urban infrastructure projects sponsored by private investors. To further pursue the project's objective of poverty alleviation, a new grant fund was established to finance poverty alleviation projects for specific low-income populations. In addition, the participating financial institutions have committed to contribute an amount equal to 44 percent of the Tamil Nadu government's initial contribution. The ultimate objective of the fund is to provide self-sustainable financing while mobilizing private savings for urban infrastructure investment.

(Box continues on the following page.)

> The fund is administered by a board of trustees nominated by the government of Tamil Nadu and the participating financial institutions. The participating financial institutions include Industrial Credit and Investment Corporation of India, Ltd., the leading managing partner of the Tamil Nadu Urban Infrastructure Financial Service Ltd.; Infrastructure Leasing and Financial Services, a leader in the development and financing of private infrastructure projects in India on a limited recourse basis; and the Housing Development Finance Corporation, a leading finance corporation in housing and regional development. The strong reputation of these institutions in India's business and financial community should help the fund raise additional resources from other private investors.
>
> Source: India case study, chapter 24.

Securitized Loan Pool

Another mechanism for credit assistance to subnational governments is the securitized loan pool. *Securitization* means the sale of a bundle of future cash flows arising from a specified underlying pool of loans. Proceeds from the loan payments are passed through to the investor in the form of interest and principal payments. Several variations are possible: the debt service payments may or may not be secured by the underlying loans themselves (and the underlying security that they individually provide) and may or may not have recourse to the issuer.

Certain restrictions are placed on the loans admitted to the pool, either for the benefit of the investor (nonrecourse) or at the insistence of the pool sponsor or enhancer (where the pool is enhanced). The pool can be accessed either directly by individual subnational governments borrowing or indirectly by borrowing from a government finance institution (GFI) or private financial institution (PFI) that holds the pooled loan portfolios (figure 12.3).

Several configurations of securitization are possible, from pooled issues carrying an "umbrella" guarantee or access to a liquidity facility or bond insurance to strictly nonrecourse pooled securities that provide an "over-

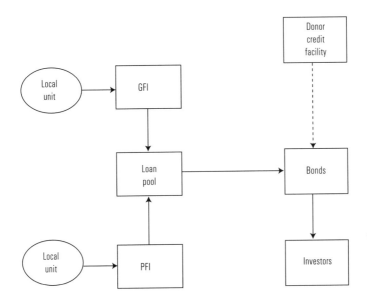

Figure 12.3. Securitization of a Loan Pool

pledge" of revenues to the underlying subnational government securities. An overpledge means that the flow of payments on the underlying loans is fractionally higher than that on the securitized debt. Thus qualifying loans would generate more debt service than the bonds sold by the pool. The excess earnings over the debt service could be used to pay the debt off faster or could be retained as income by the government financial institution that originated the pool. The pool of loan obligations can be open or closed, with an open pool permitting replacement of debt that matures or defaults with comparable loans. As depicted in figure 12.3, the pool could be backed up by a donor-based enhancement to increase the marketability of the bonds.

Securitization makes possible relatively large bond issues that create the potential for large trading volumes. Bond pools help investors become familiar with subnational government credits and provide comfort for entering into future transactions. For example, the prospect of future pool financing would permit banks to extend the maturities on the new subnational government underlying loans. The pooling and securitization technique could be especially useful in devising standard form documentation and in providing better market access to small borrowers. The pool approach would provide economical access to the credit markets for smaller localities that are creditworthy, extend maturities on loans, and ultimately work to reduce their loan costs.[7]

A bond pool has potential drawbacks, however. First, sale of the subnational government loan assets might encounter resistance from existing lenders, in some cases eroding balance sheets by reducing the stock of performing loans among their assets.[8] Thus, successful bank lending experience can work as an impediment to expanding the market options for subnational government borrowers. A second concern is the need to establish the legal status of a bond pool with respect to securities and banking regulations.[9] This proved to be an impediment in efforts to create a pool of loans to subnational governments in Poland (DeAngelis and Putnam 1999).

Bond Banks

Another mechanism for assistance to subnational government is the bond bank, which borrows in its own name and uses the proceeds to purchase debt instruments of subnational borrowers. Bond banks originated in the United States to improve access to the financial markets for small local governments. The operation and scope of bond banks have varied, depending on relative financial priorities and their legal and political environments. As the bond banks gained experience, they frequently took on specialized areas of activity, such as financing environmental activities, local schools, short-term borrowing, and equipment leasing. They also moved into limited obligations, structured transactions, and credit enhancements (see box 12.5).

A survey of state bond banks in the United States shows a variety of administrative and program structures and financing experience that can be useful to municipal credit markets in emerging market economies (Petersen 1998). Because bond banks compete with private lenders and dealers and often can finance at lower costs or on better terms, bond banks have been resisted by commercial banks and securities dealers in many states.[10] After early adoptions in several states, the bond bank movement in the United States slowed in the face of opposition from competing interests and concerns about stretching state credit enhancements too thin. More recently, interest at the national level in replacing recurring capital grants from the central government with revolving funds has reactivated interest in state-based financial intermediaries, including the traditional bond banks.

The bond bank concept has been slow to catch on in developing and emerging market economies, for a variety of reasons. First, in transitioning economies subnational government credit needs have been an orphan. The

---

Box 12.5. Assisting Small Bond Issuers: The Bond Bank Option

The United States is often thought to have a highly sophisticated financial market, with knowledgeable and skilled investors and issuers. However, that is not necessarily the case for the estimated 40,000 subnational government issuers in the U.S. bond market, many of them small and unsophisticated. Their access to markets has improved as a result of well-established legal and regulatory processes, the availability of skilled advisers, and competition among potential lenders. A combination of state-backed financial intermediaries such as bond banks, private bond insurance, and preferential federal tax policy keeps competitive pressure on dealers and banks to provide services to small issuers. As a result, the typical U.S. small local government credit has become very competitive in the markets.

To encourage this largely market-driven process, a good deal of attention has been given to upgrading local government financial management practices and reporting. States have long had an oversight function for local governments in their jurisdictions but have worked at it with increasing vigor in recent decades. Bond banks, bond insurance, and other organized lending and credit enhancing programs have required local governments to report their financial condition regularly following generally accepted accounting principles. These developments, along with the widespread use of credit ratings and recently adopted securities-related reporting requirements of the U.S. Securities and Exchange Commission, have also worked to standardize and regularize financial reports.

Source: Petersen 1998.

---

initial thrust was to create equity markets to handle the new private interests, and the need to finance the central government has taken precedence in debt markets.

Second, disruption in the political and fiscal structures in transitioning economies has made subnational governments appear to be poor credit risks. There was no clear sense from one year to the next just what responsibilities and powers subnational governments would have in the emerging regime. Such issues as ownership of property, for example, placed a cloud over lending practices that traditionally had been tied to the provision of physical collateral. In the absence of information and experience, the "name" and size of a subnational government have had disproportionate importance. Third, the economics of transactions—it is more efficient to do the due diligence and promotion of one large loan or bond deal than to round up several smaller transactions—has resulted in a strong tendency to leave the smaller subsovereign loans to the commercial banking system or municipal development funds and to use the bond markets only for larger, more profitable transactions.

Fourth, in many transitioning countries domestically derived or donor-induced development funds offering loans on concessional terms and associated grant programs have effectively undercut competition from the private sector. Long-term loans, much larger and on more favorable terms than commercial markets can offer, are frequently tied into grants.[11]

Fifth, a legacy of protection afforded by "special" municipal borrowing windows, such as development funds, have shielded local governments from the temptations and tribulations of private sector financial markets. The difficulty is that the new fiscal order calls for local governments to be more self-reliant and market-oriented. The bond bank approach offers an opportunity for smaller subnational governments to enter the market together, enjoying the benefits of a broader market appeal while minimizing the risks of a single mistake or misfortune. With experience, stronger governments may find it better to borrow on their own in the markets. These and other inducements to prudential behavior by governments can be built into the mechanics of the bond bank operations.

Liquidity Facilities

Various credit enhancements can be used to help financial markets mature and better meet the needs of subnational borrowers. Emerging markets are chronically short of long-term investible funds, as both institutional and individual investors are leery of making long-term commitments of their cash. Thus, one approach is to enlist their short-term investments into long-term capital for borrowers. A useful tool is the "put" or "tender" option, which allows investors to cash in their holdings of bonds at set dates prior to the debt's maturity date. Put options are usually found in variable-rate interest markets, where bonds are repriced on a recurring basis according to interest rate fluctuations.[12] Bonds carrying the option, no matter what their final maturity, trade like comparable obligations that are due at the next put/repricing date.[13]

Put options allow investors an "early out" and so, by definition, provide market "liquidity." The presence of the liquidity facility, which is typically a bank stand-by loan agreement or letter of credit, ensures the current bondholder, if it elects to put the bonds, that a purchaser for the bonds will always be there and the money will be returned quickly on demand. Unless the issuer pays off the bond, the bond that is put back can either be resold by a repricing agent (usually a securities firm hired for that purpose) at the prevailing rates of interest or converted into a bank loan from the liquidity facility to "warehouse" the security until a buyer is found.[14]

There are many mechanical details in designing and operating a liquidity facility, but where markets are thin, the put option can provide investors with liquidity where a secondary market has yet to take root. It provides some intriguing possibilities among the arsenal of forms of donor credit assistance. For example, a credit facility provided by a domestic bank might be backed up by a donor-assisted loan facility. Under the terms of a "put" option that would be incorporated into bond issues, the liquidity facility could be availed by "qualifying" subnational government bonds.[15]

The basic mechanics of a liquidity facility are depicted in figure 12.4. The figure shows the alternative pathways that a bond might take, depending on borrower needs and market conditions. The issuer first sells bonds with a put option to investor 1 (pathway A). Under normal circumstances (pathway B), the repricing agent reprices the bonds to maintain a market acceptance for them, and if investor 1 puts its bonds, they are resold to investor 2. However, if the repricing agent is unsuccessful in immediately reselling the bonds, the liquidity-providing bank provides a loan to pay off investor 1 (pathway C). Were the liquidity facility itself to be incapacitated for some reason, the stand-by loan agreement, in this case provided by a donor providing a stand-by commitment, would be activated (pathway D).

Put options and liquidity facilities involve fees, and the economics of such a devices are improved when there is a relatively large volume of securities involved, such as with a pool or a bond bank. The repricing of bond issues at the time of the put date means that the debt service payments will change for the underlying borrower after each put and repric-

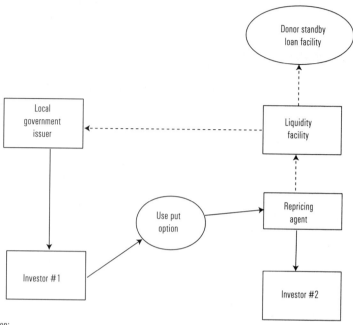

Explanation:

A. Issuer sells bonds to Investor #1 that have a put option.
B. If investor elects to exercise put, bonds are placed with repricing agent and resold to Investor #2.
C. If repricing agent is unable to place bonds with an investor, the bonds are placed with the liquidity provider, which in turn activates a loan to the issuer. The loan is repaid when the bond is resold or paid off.
D. If liquidity provider has insufficient assets to carry the bond until it can be resold, then it can borrow from donor standby loan facility.

Figure 12.4. Mechanics of a Liquidity Facility

ing. However, repricing reflects only changing interest charges, and the changes in debt service are easier to absorb if the principal component is much smaller in the first place; that can happen if the maturity of debt is stretched out.

The great advantage to the put option is its ability to extend the maturity of debt. A liquidity facility allows the bond, if it is otherwise creditworthy (current in its debt service payments) to be priced as short-term debt, while it allows for a longer maturity, that is, the date when the issuer must by contract repay the principal.[16] Having a bond's principal payable in a series of installments over 10 to 15 years, as opposed to 2 to 3 years, dramatically lowers the annual debt service.

Grant and Loan Integration

Of great importance in inculcating credit market discipline is to ensure that the availability of grants does not undercut the use of credit at market rates by subnational governments and projects that can afford it. Grants should be tailored to meet the needs of projects that are not creditworthy or that have capital costs that, once sufficiently reduced through grant assistance, can be partially financed at market rates.

Capital subsidies come in a number of forms, from paying explicit subsidies to offset interest rates, to extending credit on very favorable terms, such as below-market rates and with extended grace periods, to providing longer maturities than are available in capital markets. The form of the subsidies has operational implications.

Gains from Integrating Loans and Grants

Encouraging efficient use of resources and access to credit markets argues for integrating grants and loans.[17] A conscious regimen of exposing subnational governments to private market demand and credit expectations will benefit the development of both private lenders and government borrowers. To foster that process, grants generally should take the form of an initial capital grant that lowers capital costs to levels that can be financed by a loan. The conditions on the loan should be similar to those in private markets, with the exception that the loan will likely be of longer maturity. While the concept is generally applicable to both revenue- and non-revenue-producing projects, the initial application will likely be limited to non-revenue-producing projects. The grant also might take the form of loan "forgiveness," with a proportion of the original debt principal written down if the borrower meets its debt obligations on time. The idea is to create positive incentives for the borrower to be faithful in meeting its obligations.

While the advantages of integrating grants and loans are easy to see, actually accomplishing the integration requires technical guidance and data on project costs, benefits, and the resources of customer groups (see box 12.6).[18] Such data are likely to be sketchy, but formulating general parameters will help in decisionmaking. Perhaps one of the more straightforward applications of integration would be in such utilities as water supply and waste disposal, typically large users of capital. However, the integration concept should be applicable not only to most enterprise activities that generate some revenues but also to social or non-revenue-producing facilities that are supported by general revenues and transfers.

Box 12.6. A Brief Illustration of Grant-Loan Integration: An Example from Indonesia

It is useful to illustrate some of the concepts and terminologies of the grant-loan integration concept. The example is based on Indonesia, although the technique is generic in concept.

Determining "market-proxy" costs. Suppose that constructing and equipping a facility will cost 20 billion rupiahs (Rps) if it is built in an efficient manner to meet projected demands. Suppose also that its annual operating (*O&M*) costs (labor, materials, energy, routine maintenance) will be Rps 1 billion, again with efficient operation and adequate maintenance. These construction and operating figures are derived from a feasibility study conducted for the project. Note that the cost figures are calculated irrespective of how the facility is financed and are based solely on technical and economic efficiency grounds. In addition to the annual operation and maintenance costs, there is a potential annual debt service (*DS*) component. Thus, were the project to be totally financed at "market rates" and on a long-term basis (the economic life of the asset), then the full "market-proxy" annual debt service would be *DS'*, applying a standard level debt service schedule.

Leaving aside any equity contribution to be made by the community, the capital cost is first estimated at 100 percent debt-financing over the useful life of the improvement.

$$K = D'$$

where K is the capital cost of the facility and D' is the debt amount. An annual cost to repay the debt can now be derived, depending on the interest rate and the maturity. For comparison purposes using the market proxy approach, an annual level debt service factor can be applied that is designed to pay interest and principal at approximately constant amounts over the life of the loan (see chapter 6).

A 20-year loan at a 15 percent rate of interest would require an annual payment equal to 0.1598 of the principal each year. At level debt service the "market proxy" annual debt service cost is about Rps 320 million a year on a 20-year Rps 20 billion loan.

Thus, with the market-proxy financing calculation, the annual total combined operating cost (Rps 1 billion) and capital cost (Rps 0.32 billion) of the facility (E') would be

$$E' = O\&M + DS'$$

or total annual expenditures of Rps 1.32 billion.

This annual market proxy cost is a standardized starting point of the analysis. It is intended to replicate what the full costs would be annually were the project financed at market interest rates. Therefore, it represents a proxy for the cost of capital in the economy, making allowance for the fact that long-term financing (that is, financing for the useful economic life of the facility) is unlikely to be possible in the immediate future. The next step is to compare this full cost concept with what is affordable.

Determining affordability. The project's full annual cost needs to be compared with what the community and users can afford. This can be the most difficult part of the process. Assume that the facility will charge tariffs based on charges to residential and commercial sectors and their expected volumes of usage. The first step is to determine whether annual revenue, R, would cover the full market-proxy costs, E', which includes the market proxy debt service, DS'.

While a certain portion of users will be able to afford the costs at the stipulated rates and volumes, there may be a large number of users who will not, and cross-subsidization may not be practical or may be too burdensome. Adjustment of the revenue for the means-tested revenue constraint shows that it is feasible to raise annual revenues only to equal R^*.

The amount of debt service that is affordable under the projected performance of the project and the affordability revenue constraints is calculated as affordable annual revenue minus

(Box continues on the following page.)

Box 12.6. (*continued*)

operating costs ($R^* - O\&M = DS^*$). The constrained value can then be used to determine the amount of grant that is needed to make the overall or "blended" annual cost of the project affordable.

Amount of the capital grant. Assuming that the affordable margin of debt is borrowed on market-proxy terms, the ratio of affordable debt service to market-based debt service (DS^*/DS') also yields the ratio of affordable debt service in the project to debt services that would be required at full market rates. Accordingly, the ratio of D^*/D' (where $D' = K$, assuming that the project were to be fully debt financed) represents the ratio of affordable debt to the entire project cost, which is equal to the ratio of affordable debt service to the market-based debt service. Thus, if $D^* = 0.5$ of D', the capital grant will need to equal half of the initial project costs. The capital grant is calculated leaving the interest rate, maturity, and debt service structure unchanged. In other words, the debt borrowed *at the margin* is on market terms (with the notable exception that the maturity is longer than normally obtainable).

The affordable annual debt service (and hence overall annual revenue) is achieved by buying down the capital cost of the project through a grant. The capital grant to fill the gap equals the full capital cost minus the amount of debt that can be borrowed under the affordability criterion: $G = K - D^*$.

If the community can afford only Rps 116 million a year in total revenue, the project will need a capital grant that will reduce the debt service to half the market-proxy level, or a capital grant of Rps 10 billion. The facility's operating costs would be the same (Rps 100 million), but the required debt service would be Rps 16 million instead of the full market proxy amount of Rps 32 million.

Technical and Market Analysis

Subnational government projects need to be subjected to an affordability analysis. This "means testing" of project costs against reasonably available local resources helps ensure that the availability of grants does not discourage creditworthy governments from borrowing and does not create a culture of subsidy dependence that retards the development of capital markets. In a variant of adverse selection (see chapter 2), projects that could be financed at least partially at market rates in commercial markets elect not to borrow because they believe they can get grants. This not only reduces the overall grant funds available to needy subnational government projects, but it delays realization of projects. Grant funds should be reserved for needy projects and for projects that would become affordable to subnational government with a partial grant subsidy. Grants can also assist subnational governments to fund projects that may not be affordable in their early years but become so as they mature and as financial markets develop.

Technical and affordability analysis has two phases. First, technical parameters, based on engineering best practices, are needed to determine the most efficient operation at various scales and alternative processes and the associated reasonable costs for constructing the facilities. This analysis is the stuff of standard feasibility studies and yields a standardized annual cost function and the required capital stock investment and its cost.[19]

The second phase is the most critical in establishing the needed amount of the grant. The required capital investment is translated into a standardized annual debt service cost by applying a factor that reflects a commercial cost of capital on the assumption that the debt could be borrowed for a period of time that corresponds to the useful life of the project. Thus in addition to the facility's operating and capital cost figures, studies are needed of the likely usage and applicable rate structure in order to project operating revenues. Facilities that have a high proportion of low-income users are the most likely candidates for grants.[20] The subsidies to facilities will be "means tested," and the subsidy will come from lowering (or in some cases removing completely) future debt service through a capital grant that reduces the amount to be borrowed. This up-front grant is suggested rather than subsidized interest rates or operating subsidies, which require ongoing administration and surveillance and tend to conceal the amount of subsidy (Varley 2001).[21]

To decide how large the capital grant should be, an objective measure is needed of an "acceptable burden" of user charges that may be paid annually by the poorest users (residential and commercial). These constraints on the affordable charges then are converted into a constraint on the overall annual revenues that will be available to pay the operating and debt service costs. This constrained sum is then compared with annual operating costs (assuming efficient technical and economic operation) and the prototype "market-proxy" annual debt service, for a combined annual revenue requirement. The excess of annual revenue requirements using market proxy values over the needs-constrained revenue projections is the proportion by which the annual debt service must be reduced to qualify the project for debt financing. Where the acceptable level of annual charges is equal to or less than anticipated operating costs (excluding any debt service), it is unlikely that any part of the project should be considered for debt financing.

Planning projects on a self-sustaining basis depends heavily on the ability to develop skills in engineering and financial consultancies. Often the subnational government is unable to fund the study from the project's own resources. However, if it did, this might present a moral hazard problem, since any subnational government will prefer grant to loan funding. The long-term efficiency of an integrated grant-loan program might best be served by having the central government commission and pay for an objective third-party analysis of need and affordability. Sometimes standardized "prefeasibility" analysis provides an acceptable level of analysis. Such studies are routinely done by registered engineering firms that use cost curves to estimate facility costs under varying conditions and sizes. Costs are often adjusted for local factor costs and specific items such as land.

The analysis should be required for all capital grant programs seeking project financing. For determining the amount of the grant, project costs should be calculated at the annual amount of revenue that would be needed in the absence of the grant at some "indicative interest rate." Only after the affordability test has been applied, taking into consideration the likely amount that could be charged in tariffs or taxes, should the amount of the grant be calculated. If the independent feasibility or prefeasibility study finds that the subnational government and its enterprise can pay for a portion of the facility through a loan, then receipt of the grant should be contingent on also taking out a loan (or finding another way to pay for its share of the project).

Notes

1. The costs of developing pioneer bond issues are considerable since they represent for public and private parties alike a heavy investment in learning skills, developing documentation, and charting new procedures. In the Philippines, these costs for four relatively small bond issues ranged from 4 to 5 percent of the total issue proceeds. Bond issues are very much subject to economies of scale since the novelty and complexity of a deal may have little to do with the size of the issue (see Financial Executives Institute of the Philippines).

2. For example, the Asian Development Bank advocates the use of public-private financing vehicles. See Asian Development Bank *Commercial Cofinancing and Guarantees* (1999) and ADB, Office of Co-financing *IED Seminar on Commercial Co-financing and Guarantees* (12 May 1999). Similar structures are used by other international agencies, including the World Bank, USAID in its Development Credit Assistance program, and by various state governments in the United States.

3. It should be recognized that the credit line in this case amounts to a letter of credit or stand-by loan facility. The donor then looks primarily to fee income from the credit line, not the actual exercise of a loan. Any loan would be at commercial rates set high enough to discourage use of the facility except in emergency. By its very presence, the facility is intended to lend confidence to the market and obviate its use. Furthermore, having the imprimatur of a highly rated bank and its surveillance of the arrangements creates a halo effect in ensuring the markets of the facility's prudent operation.

4. It is useful to note that some roles can be accomplished under existing domestic market conditions, but others may be more realistic with the Bank's employing credit line assistance.

5. If the aid is to be provided anyway, making it pledgeable and interceptable does not add to the cost. Any administrative costs could be borne by the borrower.

6. Traditionally, rating agency analysis gave intercepts of intergovernmental transfers only modest credit-enhancing power in the United States. However, the power of an intercept is substantially increased if the flow goes through a trustee-administered "lock box" arrangement in which debt holders have first access to the revenue. This provision, coupled with the historical record of intergovernmental payments, led to the intercept gaining greatly in stature as an enhancement device. It is almost universally used for local school financing in the United States.

7. This has been the experience with pools and bond banks in the United States, which are usually run by state entities. Some private banks and investment firms have formed pools (mutual funds) as well.

8. In the Philippines, one of the major government finance institutions, the Land Bank of the Philippines, for example, had high nonperforming loan rates for commercial loans (17 percent) and agricultural sector loans (34 percent) as of 2000. The nonperforming loan rate for local governments, by contrast, was virtually zero.

9. The Philippine securities and exchange authority declared that local government securities are "exempt" entities for purposes of registration but that securitization of private sector loans is subject to special registration procedures that can make securitization a cumbersome and lengthy process, with tax implications as well.

10. Because they aggregate small issues into one large issue, bond banks can provide economies of scale, but that process reduces the amount of business available to regional dealers and banks. On the other hand, large money center dealers may support the creation of bond banks if they think they will get the underwriting business. The money market dealers have little political influence, however, compared with local investment firms.

11. For example, loans from the European Bank for Reconstruction and Development are frequently tied to grants that reduce the effective interest costs to very low levels. This is advantageous to the few subnational governments that get the financing but not to the governments that press ahead for loans that do not fit into the donor's particular game plan (Noel 2000).

12. The pricing can be based on a formula relating to the reference rate, such as short-term government securities. A problem with that approach is that the rate may go out of touch with the market if the government refuses to accept bids for its notes. Another approach is having a repricing agent set the rate at whatever level it takes to sell the bonds. If a buyer cannot be found, the repricing agent puts the bonds to the liquidity facility, which lends the money to pay off the investor that is cashing in the security.

13. Puts may be at any prestated value and a put at par or a slight discount is commonly used. For example, a put at a discount is one way to discourage puts from being exercised too often.

14. The loan rate from the liquidity facility is usually set at a market index plus several points. There is also a fee for making the facility available.

15. Qualifying obligation might be defined to be bonds sold for infrastructure purposes that are timely in payments and that meet certain dis-

closure and credit criteria. An important by-product of the liquidity facility is that it can help generate demand of disclosure and for credit ratings.

16. For example, there might be substantial investor interest in fixed-rate investments of a medium maturity (five years). A 15-year bond with a one-time put at year five would be attractive, and the annual debt service much lower. To work, the liquidity facility must be backed by a very high-grade credit so that there is no doubt that the facility will be there to operate. It is for this backing that a donor stand-by loan could be very effective. It is difficult to see how the systemic risk would be any greater than with a direct loan made by the donor. Also, the private sector would be stakeholders, unlike the direct loan scenario.

17. Analysts looking at Indonesia have argued that the availability of grants can be a significant disadvantage in starting a credit market culture (see Smoke 1999, pp. 1561–85). On grants undercutting loans as a problem in credit market development (see Weitz 2001, p. 5). Lewis (2002) encourages the use of market-proxy loan rates on on-lent donor funds in order to help develop private market access by local governments and discusses the need to blend loans and grants, with the size of the grants conditioned by national priorities, benefit spillovers, and the fiscal capacity of the local governments. A recent World Bank (2002a) Project Concept Document states approvingly that it appears that capital grants for the Specific Purpose Grant Fund (Dana Alokasi Khusus, or DAK) would depend on the income of governments and the nature of the project, with wealthier governments eligible for only limited grants since they qualify for commercial borrowing on most investments. The report also looks at improved integration of municipal credit with the capital market, "including closer to market determined rates" (p. 22).

18. To the extent that certain projects might be considered national public goods, they might be candidates for a national subsidy irrespective of local resources. These are points of judgment and national policy, but the initial assumption is that most projects will have large components of local benefit and that these benefits should be weighed against local resources to pay for them.

19. These technical studies often result in "cost curve" studies that provide a baseline for the costing of services and facilities under specified conditions. Deviations in individual projects are obviously to be expected, but there is a baseline from which to start.

20. Note that there may be a good deal of cross-subsidy at the local level as richer users subsidize poorer ones. The idea is that there are limits on

how much cross-subsidy can occur in a locality without driving out the richer ratepayers and that in some localities there will be too few rich users to offset the costs of serving the poor.

21. Varley (2001, p. 5) argues that subsidized rates and other soft terms lead to buildups of hidden liabilities and crowd out private sector suppliers of credit.

Part V

Policy Guidelines

John Petersen and Mila Freire

Chapter 13

Concluding Observations and Policy Guides

Subnational government borrowing is not an end in itself. Ideally, it should be used to obtain long-term capital for expenditures that provide benefits that stretch into the future. Repaying debts represents the fulfilling of an intergenerational contract obligating those who benefit from improvements to pay their share of costs over time. Subnational governments are the legitimate parties to effectuate the obligation and the agents to see that its terms are fulfilled.

Successfully incurring and paying off debt—raising funds in capital markets, employing the funds in useful improvements, and repaying the debt according to the contract—is an affirmation that the subnational government is capable of planning for the future and fulfilling its obligations. Successful debt transactions are both products of financial prudence and foresight and installments toward financial independence (DeAngelis and Dunn 2002).

That said, the gap between the ideal and the real in subnational government borrowing in private financial markets is great. Subnational governments, as junior and often freshly minted government units, must find ways to enter financial markets that are themselves young and troubled in legal and economic environments that are often in transition.

Credit market access has been approached from various angles: the needs of potential borrowers, the organization and regulation of the securities market, likely investor groups and their regulation, the need for information to analyze credit, and the rating and private insuring of securities. This book examines, in particular, the tools that senior governments and donors might choose in developing markets, looking at forms of credit assistance and methods by which higher level governments monitor and, when necessary, intervene in the affairs of subnational governments.

While it is clear that different structures of government and levels of credit market development affect the particular circumstances of each country, the following observations on policies and practices can serve as a point of departure in appraising a country's willingness and readiness to promote markets for subnational government securities. They also can stimulate debate on existing markets and on how access to them might be improved and new markets for subnational securities might best be engendered.

Security Pledges, Instruments, and Methods of Sale: From What Sources Should Subnational Debt Be Paid, What Forms Should It Take, and How Should It Be Sold?

Determining the appropriate scope and pace of subnational government borrowing and the forms it should take has presented problems for national governments, financial markets, and subnational government borrowers. Over-regulation and encrustations of out-of-date, ill-defined, and conflicting laws have caused problems. Subnational credit access has often been an afterthought, in terms of both fiscal powers and financial market development. Overall, generic laws with broad formulations of policies and simple parameters based on easily obtainable and objective criteria are better than specific procedures that must be followed with respect to borrowing.

Governing laws should make clear the *legal status and remedies* available to investors in subnational government obligations. This is frequently not the case, especially where subnational government obligations once carried explicit or implicit sovereign guarantees. The ultimate security and the enforcement process for creditors should be explicit and easy to call on. *Flexibility is important* in setting the boundaries of prudential behavior. Parties to debt transactions should be able to design security provisions to meet specific needs and circumstances, as well as general requirements. Essential services, for example, can be defined and minimum service levels protected in the case of assets and intergovernmental transfers used for pledges.

In addition to general obligation debt (supported by general revenue), local jurisdictions should be able to offer *limited obligation security* arrangements (revenue bonds) that do not involve a pledge of general revenues. Subnational governments should be able to enter into tariff setting and other covenants for limited obligation debt. If higher level governments retain ratemaking approval, provisions should be made for prior approval of rate adjustments or for some indemnification against default where the subnational government lacks the ability to adjust rates. The issues involved in rate setting and minimum service levels are thorny in low-income countries, but full costs need to be identified and any subsidies made explicit.

Subnational governments should generally be able to *assign revenue*. This includes having the ability to pledge *intercepts of intergovernmental revenue transfers*. However, certain limitations on such pledges make sense. An exception can be made for revenues that are necessary to provide minimum essential services. This could be achieved through a regulation specifying a maximum share of transfers that may be pledged to debt service payments.[1] So long as intergovernmental transfers constitute a large proportion of local revenues, as is usually the case, any prohibition against pledging funds from these sources effectively foreshortens the fiscal planning horizons of subnational governments.

Subnational governments should have the ability to create or to join with others in creating *special service districts* to address service needs related to specific areas or activities. Where government jurisdictions do not correspond with the rational service area, subnational governments should be strongly encouraged to cooperate. Applying the benefit principle, they should have revenue powers that allow them to capture a share of the value created by their activities and investments made within or on behalf of those districts. In both developing and developed countries electorates frequently are more supportive of taxes and charges that are directly related to specific physical improvements and service betterments.

The financial marketplace should be free to decide on the types of instruments and associated payment mechanisms to employ. Unless there are compelling reasons to place restrictions on all borrowers, there is no basis for treating subnational governments differently than other borrowers so long as there is *full disclosure and competitive norms* are met. However, if there is no effective competition in financial markets (including a reasonable basis of shared knowledge by borrowers and lenders), then more oversight is likely to be needed. At a minimum, strict rules are required on *public notice and disclosure of proposed transactions*.

Wherever possible, it is best to introduce competition into financial markets. As a first step, competition can be promoted by requiring subnational governments to use *formal solicitation and bidding procedures* for banking services, underwriters, advisers, investment services, and other professional specialties. Clearly, public and timely reporting on the terms and conditions of loans and bond offerings is a necessary complement to supporting a competitive regime. Even where financial markets are not fully developed and effective competition is limited, the bidding process and full disclosure of transactions should help prevent monopolistic behavior and encourage entry by private lenders.

Borrowing Power: How Much Can Be Borrowed, and Who Must Approve?

Restrictions on borrowing powers are appropriate in many emerging market economies, where the objective is to balance local self-determination with limited experience and shallow capacity in financial markets. At the same time, the object of political devolution is to link self-determination with fiscal self-sufficiency and local accountability. If financial markets are developing in the right direction, this goal may best be accomplished by using incentives that operate through the market. The issues are ones of sequence and scope: within what boundaries should the market decide on lending, and how should those boundaries change as the market matures?

While the focus of much of this book is on long-term borrowing to meet infrastructure needs, many subnational governments now rely on short-term loans to meet cash cycle needs or to finance budget shortfalls. Such *short-term borrowing*, while a useful tool when responsibly limited to a single fiscal year, has often been the Achilles heel in budgetary discipline. Short-term debt should be used only to meet cash flow shortfalls in anticipation of realistic income streams within the fiscal period. That means that under most non-emergency circumstances, short-term debt should be paid off by the close of the fiscal year.

The corollary, often built into governing law, is that *long-term debt should be limited to capital investment in property, plant, and equipment.* It should not be used to finance operating deficits except as part of a financial emergency recovery plan as defined by statute and regulation. Effective enforcement of such provisions on the appropriate use of debt requires regular reporting of borrowing and the purposes for which it is undertaken. The reporting should be based on a chart of accounts that is clear and analytically meaningful.

Limitations on outstanding debt constitute a basic form of restriction for debt that is secured by general revenues. The restriction should be related to the tax base (where the subnational government is largely self-reliant and has control over its revenue resources) or some measure of recurring revenues (which is more typically the case where localities rely on intergovernmental payments). However, limitations on total debt are only a rough gauge of permissible debt burden. Where possible, the limitation should be expressed in terms of *annual or maximum debt service.* For example, total debt service (principal and interest) on general obligation long-term debt should be limited to a maximum percentage of projected recurring annual revenues. For self-supporting debt issued to finance revenue-generating projects, however, the market should determine acceptable ratios of debt service coverage. Such projects will vary according to the technical and economic aspects of the improvement being financed and the security being pledged. Definitions matter, and the terms used in limitations need to be precisely defined.

Guarantees constitute a problem in the application of debt limitations, since the extent of guarantees is usually a missing link in debt limitation calculations. There are few quantitative restrictions on the use of guarantees. The common solution is to value against the debt limit that portion of guarantees that appears likely to be called on within a given fiscal period and to treat the remainder as contingent debt that is in effect self-supporting and not counted against the debt limit. Again, the problem is less the guarantees themselves than the reporting of the guarantees.

Approval of borrowing by a jurisdiction's legislative body is sufficient in most cases to obligate the unit, so long as the debt outstanding after the proposed borrowing falls within pre-stated legal parameters. Some countries have provisions for citizen referendum, although this is not customary in most countries and can be expensive and disruptive. Some countries require that the local budget be approved by a central government agency and that anticipated borrowings be included in the budget. Such routine budgetary review by national authorities, so long as it observes broad and general parameters, need not be overly intrusive and can help in the timely reporting of information and in the formation of macroeconomic policy. However, requiring specific prior approval of transactions by senior levels of government diminishes local flexibility and responsibility and opens the door to delay and political manipulation. Waivers of limitations in unusual cases by cognizant state or national authorities may help flexibility.

Financial Market Regulation and Disclosure: What Should the Market Look Like, and How Will It Perform?

In most developing and transitioning countries banks dominate the financial system, but with a nascent securities market beginning to broaden the financing landscape. For the most part, financial markets still do not meet the long-term credit needs of local governments. That gap is filled by national or regional government-administered on-lending programs funded by multinational donors. The observations here assume a desire to develop the securities markets as an effective alternative to a near-exclusive reliance on the banking sector or a specialized lending institution.

The *regulatory framework* for banking and securities markets should apply to subnational government borrowers just as it does to other borrowers. That framework seeks to foster the competitive norms of market efficiency and development while preserving the integrity of the payment system and protecting investors. Generally, subnational governments should enter financial markets on an equal footing with private firms, while recognizing the distinctions that flow from their taxing and governing powers. Where banking and financial regulations favor the national government, consideration could be given to according the same benefits to subnational governments, along with appropriate limitations.

A *secondary market for securities* is important to investor liquidity, but establishing such markets is inherently difficult where financial markets are small. Formal listing of subnational securities on exchanges should be required only where the potential size of secondary activity justifies the time and expense involved. Furthermore, the practical limitations on attracting long-term investments in local currency need to be considered. Alternatives might include intermediaries capable of borrowing on behalf of subnational governments on domestic and international markets and a liquidity facility to back up instruments that provide built-in liquidity, such as put-option bonds.

In some cases a secondary market for subnational debt can be developed as part of the over-the-counter markets that operate among banks and security dealers. These are likely to be more efficient for smaller issuers, whose bonds are traded infrequently. Investor protection needs to be balanced with economical access for smaller issuers, which should be a fundamental tenet of both registration and disclosure requirements.

A key concern in securities market regulation is proper disclosure. Like other securities, subsovereign securities should be subject to *disclosure standards* that require both information at the time of the initial offering and regular reporting to investors subsequently. The standards should focus on the process and generic needs. Some of the information required of governments is different from that required of private firms, and disclosure requirements should reflect that. The actual data needs for meeting such standards may best be left to self-regulatory bodies in the market and to participants in individual transactions.

Subnational government financial information needs to be reported in clear, consistent formats and promptly after the close of the fiscal period. For debt-monitoring purposes reporting on a cash or modified accrual basis is especially useful, as are cash-flow statements. Charts of accounts should reflect the needs of debt analysis, terms should be clearly defined, and users should be trained in their application. Audits should be independent, recurring, and punctual. Where governments are too small to afford independent audits, borrowing is most likely to be successful thorough a market intermediary or trustee relationships that allow for funds to be sequestered to ensure payment.

A *central repository* of financial information on government borrowers is a useful tool in promoting efficient disclosure. The repository should have current data on debt outstanding and information on security pledges and liens against real and personal property if that information is not recorded elsewhere. Markets will not thrive without information, and making information broadly available is good public policy.

Credit Analysis, Credit Ratings, and Bond Insurance: How Can Risk be Measured and Mitigated?

Credit analysis is a product of the credit market's need to assess risk. A financial market becomes viable only when there is a variety of competing investors and, similarly, investments with different risk and reward characteristics. Where there are large numbers of "passive" investors in securities that are widely held and transactions are diverse and numerous, these investors generally rely on the opinions of specialists. This need is often reinforced by various prudential requirements that are framed to ensure the investment quality of institutional portfolios.

Credit ratings, typically shorthand expressions of relative ranking among credits, are the leading form of institutionalized credit analysis. They assist in developing an active securities market by pooling skills to develop opinions. Credit ratings play an important role. They focus on credit risk (risk of payment delay or default), which then is used to help judge overall risk and reward. The use of ratings has grown steadily as markets have expanded, and they promise to play an increasing role in the regulation of banks and institutional investors.

Credit ratings have the *positive side benefit* of ranking governments on their perceived ability and willingness to pay their debts and avoid financial difficulties. The ratings are easily understood—hence their popular appeal—and contribute to the essential task of improving finances by providing an incentive to upgrade one's rating. However, credit ratings tend to centralize and dominate credit analysis, and the precise basis for the ratings is not always clear since their calculation is based on proprietary criteria. Credibility requires accuracy, a reputation for objectivity, and freedom from influence. The demand for ratings should derive from the market itself (even if part of that demand is a function of regulatory requirements on institutional investors), with competition among ratings companies. In domestic financial markets, it is not a good idea to have "official rating agencies" or to have the government set standards for ratings. Foreign markets are likely to require internationally accepted ratings.

Private sector *bond insurance* and other forms of *credit enhancement* are important in developed financial markets and may have application to subsovereign credits. The major bond insurance companies were seeking opportunities in emerging market economies during the 1980s and 1990s until the financial crises of the late 1990s dulled their appetites. With the possibility for diversification of holdings within countries limited and confidence in many currencies eroded, commercial bond insurance will be slow to take hold. Furthermore, the private bond insurance industry is highly dependent on credit ratings of their portfolios. The volatility and generally lower-rung ratings given to emerging market credits create heavy capital requirements and make it difficult for companies to price their products competitively. However, domestic credit enhancement programs that have sufficient capital, are market-oriented, and use insurance principles in determining appropriate charges may hasten development. Domestic bond insurance in the Philippines is a promising "home-grown" alternative that can assist local borrowers (see Philippines case study, chapter 26).

Financial Oversight, Monitoring, and Intervention: How Should the Central Authorities Monitor Subnational Financial Conditions and React to Financial Emergencies?

Even in countries where the credit operations of subnational governments are largely autonomous and subject to general rules, positive action by higher-level government has a place. This is especially so in requiring the collection of timely, complete, and pertinent financial information. Without comparable and consistent information on borrowers, financial markets operate in a cloud of uncertainty, with personal and political relationships dominating decisions rather than objectively measured conditions and results.

A *regular and universal reporting system for subnational governments*, founded on an accounting system relevant to the information needs of investors and prepared by properly trained officials, is a prerequisite for market development. Most important is the ability to report direct and contingent debts outstanding, current debt service requirements, and cash funds available to meet those demands as well as baseline operating expenses. While the ability to support other measures of performance and conditions is highly desirable, reliable basic data on meeting pending debt obligations and regular operating needs are indispensable to market development.

Gathered data should be made public. In countries with active financial markets for subnational obligations, disclosures may suffice since self-interested participants conduct the reviews and analysis. However, in most cases these data should also be *subject to review* by the appropriate national-level agencies to ensure that the numbers are right and to monitor the conditions of governments. Such monitoring need not be intrusive, but it can provide a warning if subnational governments are violating the rules or showing signs of financial weakness.

Intervention by higher levels of government in a subnational government financial emergency should be comprehensive and thought out in advance. Interests need to be balanced to avoid moral hazard. The responsible parties should bear the risk, sharing the pain of mistakes and bad fortune with those that would have enjoyed the fruits of investments. Intervention measures should provide for *creditor rights, remedies, and workouts*, as well as for the financial recovery or dissolution of the debtor unit. There should be added flexibility in terms of making specific pledges of security and remedies a matter of contract. However, it is best to have in place a statutory framework to define rights, essential services, and the procedure for recomposition of debt. Interventions should be rare, and not be used as a backdoor means for the higher-level government to bail out subnational governments and their creditors.

Credit Assistance and Financial Interventions: How Can Credit Assistance Encourage the Development of Private Capital Markets?

For most emerging market economies subnational government access to private financial markets is an achievable goal. However, it is not achievable overnight and may not be achievable for all subnational governments. Meanwhile, many emerging and transitioning countries will continue to depend on various forms of assistance to help satisfy the capital financing needs of subsovereign governments. For the most part, such aid will either be sanctioned or administered by central government agencies and, in all likelihood, will be funded by multilateral and bilateral assistance agencies. These sources of funds are not adequate to meet all needs, but the prospect of grants and loans on concessionary terms makes them attractive. The longer-term policy objective, of course, is to make subnational government borrowers self-reliant and the markets in which they borrow adequate suppliers of long-term capital. How best to move in that direction?

Credit assistance should be provided only to the level needed to permit a subnational government to access private credit markets. This requires *integration of grants* that might be given with the loans. Subnational governments, to the extent possible, should face the costs and demands of private credit markets at the margin in meeting their financing needs. Borrowing is not appropriate in many settings. Subnational governments that are too poor and too small to borrow in the private market should not be encouraged to borrow until their underlying financial situation makes that feasible.

Direct lending, interest subsidies, guarantees, insurance, and other financial assistance should be designed to provide subnational governments with *incentives to access the market* on their own. Such assistance should recognize *differences in creditworthiness* and reflect those differences in the interest rate and loan amount. Debt contracts, even if given on preferential terms, need to be written to commercial standards and enforced. The goal of exposing subnational government borrowers to the discipline of private markets needs to be encouraged at every step.

Financial intermediaries that pool smaller loans into larger offerings, as in *bond banks,* can provide economies of scale and give investors opportunities for greater depth and liquidity in the secondary market. *Bond banks and loan pools* can be sponsored by either the public sector or the private sector but should function as financial institutions and be subject to credit market discipline.

Other devices work through private financial markets and encourage their development. These include *government-sponsored co-lending programs, credit enhancements, and liquidity support facilities.* Their success will depend on private sector investors gaining confidence in the domestic market as a place to put long-term capital and in subnational government issues and loans as prudent and profitable investments. Donor lending programs need to promote innovations in assistance that advance the enlistment of private capital market sources. Skillful use of enhancements that leverage the amount of donor aid to encourage private market participation needs to be encouraged further.

Note

1. This is akin to a minimum coverage requirement often found in limited obligation bonds.

Part VI

Country Case Studies

Chapter 14

Latin America and the Caribbean
Argentina

A weak central government, declining economy, and uncontrolled deficits undermine the role of the credit markets in subnational finance.

Rodrigo Trelles Zabala

Lessons

Long plagued by macroeconomic instability and political upheavals, Argentina appeared to have set the right course with the Convertibility Plan in 1991, undertaking a number of reforms and pegging the Argentine peso to the U.S. dollar. However, the solutions to the country's many related structural problems either never took hold or proved to be the wrong ones. A declining economy and growing government deficits undermined the national administration, and the ensuing devaluation and default not only closed the international financial markets to Argentine borrowers but also crippled the domestic markets.

Subnational borrowers have played a major part in the nation's recurring financial crises. The reasons for this include the loose federal structure of government (in which the provinces, not the federal government, form the core of the system), the appetite for deficit spending, and the extensive government ownership of assets, including commercial banks. Argentine subnational governments have borrowed heavily from the banks, in the domestic bond market, and abroad, and by 2001 debt service was absorbing 25 percent of provincial spending. Devaluation and high domestic rates of interest (due to variable rate bank loans) pushed debt service beyond sustainable levels, precipitating widespread defaults, and in November 2002 the national government took the ultimate step of defaulting on multilateral loans.

In Argentina the weak federal government has no effective control over provincial borrowing, which it monitors but cannot regulate. Provinces historically have owned captive banks, which they have tapped for funds. While bank loans make up only part of subnational borrowing, the high interest rates and the shutting down of the domestic market were a disaster for subnational governments. The crisis has led provinces to resume the practice of issuing interest-bearing notes that serve as a substitute currency, undermining the central government's monetary policy.

Argentina provides a vivid reminder that fixes at the top or in one sector cannot cure systemic problems—and that the subnational credit market may be not only a victim of a financial crisis but also a contributor to it. An elastic revenue system; heavy reliance on negotiated transfers from the central government; and a large, expensive, and protected public workforce have reduced the ability of subnational governments to manage their finances responsibly. In addition, the bottom-up political structure has not provided the public will to make the changes needed.

Case studies look at the experience of three Argentine subnational borrowers—the province of Salta, the city of Buenos Aires, and the province of Buenos Aires—that were able to access international capital markets during the interval between crises in the mid- to late 1990s. The cases show what happened when the reforms that investors were betting on at both national and subnational levels failed to materialize. The national experience shows that extensive rebuilding is needed to solve the problems endemic to the Argentine political system if it is to cope with the challenges of a modern open economy.

Until the early 1990s Argentina experienced recurring periods of slow economic growth and high inflation, a cycle that led to the devaluation of the Argentine peso and the imposition of exchange controls. The Convertibility Plan, introduced in 1991, marked a sharp change. It appeared to finally get macroeconomic management right. Based on tighter monetary policy, tax system reforms, privatization, and liberalization of the economy, the plan reduced inflation rates from more than 1,300 percent in 1990 to 0 percent in 1996 and pushed GDP growth from 0.1 percent in 1990 to more than 7 percent a year in 1991–94. Foreign direct investment increased fivefold, reaching US$6 billion in 1993. The Convertibility Plan fixed the exchange rate to the U.S. dollar, established the independence of the Central Bank, and made the monetary base equal to the external reserves.

In the mid-1990s it also appeared that the new government could handle shocks when they arose. The Mexican crisis in 1994–95 led to a sharp recession in Argentina marked by capital outflows, declining bank deposits, rising interest rates, reduced liquidity, and increased market volatility. GDP fell by 4 percent in 1995, and the unemployment rate reached a record 18.4 percent. The government responded quickly and effectively, restoring financial equilibrium with cuts in government spending, tax increases, and proactive measures to promote fiscal discipline at the provincial level.

After a temporary recovery, conditions deteriorated sharply in the rest of the 1990s. Exports fell, the trade deficit grew, GDP growth plunged to 0.5 percent in 2000 (in part because of the Brazilian devaluation), and the fiscal deficit reached 3 percent of GDP. The central government's total outstanding debt, not including provincial debt, reached US$132 billion in June 2001, with interest payments absorbing 22 percent of the annual budget. A combination of political factors and economic mismanagement deepened the economic crisis, leading to general unrest among Argentines and to the fall of the de la Rua government at the end of 2001.

Political turmoil—involving the establishment of two interim governments—and the persisting economic crisis led to the devaluation of the peso, which soared to an exchange rate of more than 3 to 1 with the U.S. dollar from the initial parity it had held for 10 years. In late 2002 the government was holding ongoing negotiations with the international financial community, led by the International Monetary Fund (IMF), on how to correct the huge fiscal imbalances and put the economy back on track. In November 2002 the country defaulted on loans from the World Bank and the Inter-American Development Bank. In the midst of this crisis the federal government had to reduce its budget deficit, a difficult task given the constitutionally defined independence of provinces. Payments to provinces were under close scrutiny, and the government felt the need to reduce discretionary federal transfers (those that do not depend on constitutional provisions). This put further pressure on provincial budgets and make timely servicing of provincial bonds difficult.

Intergovernmental Relations

Argentina's government comprises three levels: the federal government; 24 provinces, including the city of Buenos Aires, which has the rank of province; and 1,911 local governments (municipalities) with borrowing powers. Provincial governments form the core of the country's political organization. Provinces have their own constitutions and executive and legislative branches of government. Provincial governors and legislators are elected directly to four-year terms. The municipalities are dependent on the provinces, which dictate their organization and taxing powers and, in some cases (such as the province of Chubut), have delegated taxing powers to municipalities. According to the Constitution, the federal government can intervene, with the approval of the Congress, "in the territory of a province in order to guarantee the republican form of Government." As a result, the federal government is able to assume control of a province at any time and replace an elected governor with a federal appointee.

Subnational Revenues: The Coparticipation Scheme

Argentine provinces have three major sources of direct own-source revenues: the sales tax, the property tax, and the vehicle registration tax. The sales tax is the most important, accounting for about 60 percent of total direct revenue. Indirect revenues come in the form of federal transfers: two unconditional and 10 conditional transfers. Unconditional transfers, representing 70 percent of the total, include general treasury support and the coparticipation revenue, which is the cornerstone of subnational finance in Argentina.

The gross coparticipation[1] transfer accounts for 90 percent of federal transfers to provinces and 52 percent of provincial revenues. The coparticipation law mandates that 89 percent of revenues from the federal value added tax, 64 percent of income tax revenues (after a fixed reduction), and 50 percent of a variety of other revenues go into the gross coparticipation fund. Of this, some 15 percent is retained at the federal level to finance the social security system, and another 546 million Argentine pesos (Arg$) a year is allocated to a fiscal imbalance compensation fund distributed to the provinces under a separate formula. The balance, the net coparticipation fund, is shared among the federal government (42.3 percent), the provinces (54.7 percent), and special emergency and equalization funds (3 percent) (figure 14.1).

The distribution of the coparticipation revenues among provinces was set in 1988 based on fixed percentages reflecting each province's share of total spending at the time: 43.7 percent for the more developed provinces (such as Buenos Aires, Santa Fe, Mendoza, Córdoba, and the city of Buenos Aires); 19.1 percent for the intermediate provinces; 27.3 percent for the low-density provinces; and 9.9 percent for the less developed provinces. As a result of subsequent adjustments to this formula, the current distribution of resources among provinces is based on arbitrary criteria emerging from bilateral negotiations between each province and the federal government.

Provincial governments also have coparticipation schemes, for transferring revenues to their municipalities (three provinces, Jujuy, La Rioja, and San Juan, have no coparticipation system). Unlike the national coparticipation scheme, the provincial systems allocate payments to municipalities on

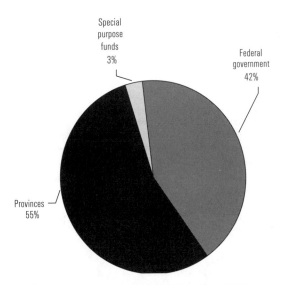

Source: World Bank staff estimates based on Argentine Ministry of Economy data.

Figure 14.1. Distribution of Shareable Taxes under the Coparticipation Scheme, Argentina

the basis of objective indicators such as area, population, other municipal revenues, and similar factors.

Expenditure Responsibilities

Under the Constitution the provinces have jurisdiction over education, municipal institutions, provincial police, provincial courts, and other matters of purely provincial or local concern (table 14.1). The federal government has jurisdiction only over the areas explicitly assigned by the Constitution: customs, national defense, foreign relations, issuance of currency, federal public debt and property, regulation of shipping and ports, regulation of banks and banking activity, and regulation of international and interprovincial trade and commerce. Responsibility for the remaining public services is shared among the three levels of government.

There has been extensive devolution of public services to the provincial level in Argentina. The share of the federal government in public sector spending fell from more than 70 percent in 1986 to less than 55 percent in the 1990s. Provinces and municipalities are responsible for the other 45 percent. Since the provinces' direct revenues account for only 18 percent of their total revenue, they depend heavily on federal transfers. Recently provinces have used proceeds from privatizations to reduce deficits and cover capital spending.

Table 14.1. Allocation of Responsibilities among Levels of Government, Argentina

Federal government	Federal and provincial governments	Provincial and municipal governments	Municipal governments
Defense	Higher education	Basic education	Markets
Foreign affairs	Preventive health	Health care	Cemeteries
Currency and banking	Economic	Water and sewerage	Solid waste collection
regulations	development	Regional and local	and disposal
Public debt	Justice and	roads	Local streets and
Interprovincial	security	Land use	drainage
transport	Housing	Fire control	Parks
Trade regulation	Passenger and		
Mail and telex	cargo terminals		
	Gas and electricity		

Source: World Bank.

Regulatory Framework for Subnational Debt

There are no national regulations on the ability of subsovereign entities in Argentina to raise debt. Under the 1991 Convertibility Plan, however, the provinces were prevented from rolling over existing borrowings from local banks and had limited access to provincial banks, their traditional source of financing.

The Constitution allows each province jurisdiction over its borrowing. Approval procedures vary among provinces, but most provinces need a favorable opinion from their controller institution (general accountant office or general prosecutor office, for example). These procedures establish that debt should not finance current expenditures and that the debt stock cannot exceed a certain share of annual revenue, a limit that usually ranges from 20 percent to 25 percent.[2] For municipal borrowing, authorization is required from the municipal council and, in some cases, from provincial financial authorities. Foreign currency debt requires the approval of the Ministry of Economy under Resolution 1075/93 of the ministry. Banks are prohibited by the Central Bank from lending to subnational governments in either foreign or local currency and from underwriting provincial bonds (Central Bank Rule A 3054) unless the Ministry of Economy authorizes the transaction or the bond issue on an exceptional basis.

Another important rule is Resolution 571/95 of the Ministry of Economy, which sets the criteria for lenders to subnational borrowers. Among these, the most notable are experience in local or international subnational debt markets, a sound financial position, and "good" loan terms (interest rate, maturity, amount, interest payments, amortization payments, and upfront fees). In cooperation with the largest Argentine bond custody company and the major stock exchanges, the Ministry of Economy has developed ways to better monitor provincial bonds. The bottom line is that the Ministry of Economy can monitor, but not control, subnational borrowers.

Subnational Indebtedness

Argentina's provincial debt reached US$29.4 billion (100 percent of consolidated provincial revenue) at the end of 2001, while the consolidated provincial fiscal deficit rose to US$6.5 billion (2.4 percent of GDP).[3] Few provinces have made an effort to cut spending, with 60 percent of expenditures in 2001 going to salaries and interest payments. All provinces ran a fiscal deficit in 2001. Figure 14.2 shows the relative position of provinces based on their operating deficit and accumulated debt as a share of their total revenue.

The provinces have pursued different debt strategies. The province of Buenos Aires accessed the bond market in 2001, issuing four bonds for a total of US$737 million. In the second half of the year the bond market was closed, and the province had to issue compulsory money bonds (Patacones) to pay salaries, contractors, and suppliers (see section below on compulsory money bonds). Córdoba tried to privatize its provincial bank and its electricity company to pay short-term commercial bank loans with bullet amortizations. Because of the high country risk, the privatizations never took place. Some provinces—such as La Pampa, San Luis, and the city of Buenos Aires, which had run fiscal surpluses in previous years— faced a sharp fall in revenues and had to fund their fiscal deficits in an adverse financial environment.

The situation is complicated, especially since the peso devaluation in January 2002. Still, the situation of provinces has improved as a result of a federal rescue through a debt swap. Formosa faces the worst situation, and

Debt as percentage of total revenues

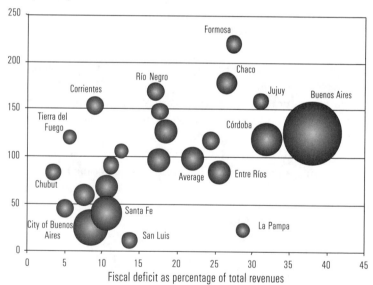

Note: The size of the bubbles represents the relative size of provincial revenue.
Source: World Bank staff estimates based on Argentine Ministry of Economy data.

Figure 14.2. Relative Fiscal and Debt Situations of Provinces, Argentina, 2001

the provinces of Chaco, Córdoba, Buenos Aires, and Jujuy also confront large problems. During the first half of 2001 many provinces tapped the bond and banking markets, but during the second half financial conditions tightened and most provinces returned to issuing money bonds.

Bonds account for the largest share of provincial indebtedness, which totaled US$29.4 billion at the end of 2001 (figure 14.3). However, the debt with banks is the most expensive because it is linked to the average rate for certificates of deposit (as published by the Argentine Central Bank) plus a rate spread or adjusted by a rate multiplier. These floating rates are recalculated every month. During the second half of 2001, when Argentine sovereign risk increased dramatically, some provinces faced real annual interest rates of 45 percent. More than 30 banks have made loans to provinces, but four banks—Banco de la Nación Argentina, Banco de Galicia, Banco Frances, and Banco Rio—clearly dominate the market, with almost 60 percent of total bank lending to provincial governments.

In 2000 the federal government implemented a voluntary refinancing program for provinces through the Provincial Development Fund. The

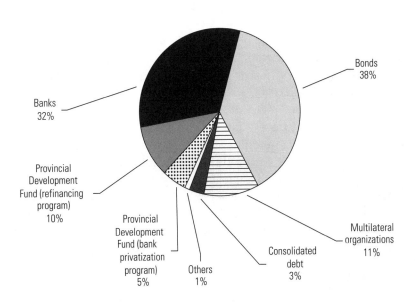

Note: The figure excludes short-term debt with suppliers and employees.
Source: World Bank staff estimates based on Argentine Ministry of Economy data.

Figure 14.3. Provincial Indebtedness by Type of Debt or Lender, Argentina, December 2001

nine participating provinces (Catamarca, Chaco, Chubut, Formosa, Jujuy, Neuquén, Río Negro, Tierra del Fuego, and Tucumán) made commitments to reduce their 1999 deficits by 20 percent, to borrow no money other than that provided by the Provincial Development Fund, to implement certain structural reforms, and to keep increases in their debt stock to no more than their 2000 fiscal deficit. In return, the fund committed to finance the provinces' 2000 fiscal deficits and the rollover of debt principal payments. The program was repeated in 2001, and two more provinces (Misiones and San Juan) joined the scheme. Both programs were unsuccessful, for two main reasons: the federal government lacked the enforcement capacity to ensure that the provinces met their targets, and politically negotiated waivers were given. Although a few provinces met their fiscal targets, most did not because there was no system to reward those that did and punish those that did not.

Multilateral lenders are also important sources of credit, accounting for 11 percent of provincial indebtedness. Until the recent devaluation of the Argentine peso, this type of debt had the lowest cost and longest maturity. However, devaluation greatly increased the cost of servicing this debt in domestic currency. Under an agreement between the federal government and the provinces signed on 27 February 2002, the federal government will provide some kind of hedging to help provinces meet the cost of this debt. Although some municipalities have borrowed indirectly from multilateral organizations, no province has indicated whether it will help its municipalities with such debt.

The debt under the Provincial Development Fund's bank privatization program[4] has a long term and low cost (7.6 percent annual fixed interest rate) because the funds were provided by multilateral organizations (the World Bank and the Inter-American Development Bank). Some 17 of the 24 provinces have been involved in programs to privatize provincial banks. The largest provincial banks (Banco de la Provincia de Buenos Aires, Banco Ciudad de Buenos Aires, and Banco de Córdoba) were not privatized, and other banks returned to provincial ownership because of the poor performance of some private managers and the nontransparent process of privatization.

Debt Service

In 2001, before the most recent debt swap, debt service payments absorbed more than 25 percent of the operating revenue of provinces. More than 45 percent of the debt service payments went to commercial banks, often for short-term loans subject to refinancing risk. There was no possibility of refinancing such loans because of the run on deposits during the second half of 2001. In addition, banks that were active players in the provincial lending market were also active players in the sovereign bond market, a situation that complicated the refinancing of provincial debt. The average life of provincial debts at the end of 2001 was six years, but some provinces had to face important due dates with no possibility of refinancing those payments. Thus at the end of 2001, as the federal government worked out a swap for sovereign debt, most of the provinces followed suit in a provincial debt swap.

Provincial Debt Swap

In establishing the criteria for the debt swap, the federal government extended eligibility only to bank loans, provincial bonds denominated in Argentine pesos and U.S. dollars, and provincial debt with the Provincial Development Fund. Bonds and bank loans would be exchanged for loans issued by the Provincial Development Fund with a federal government guarantee. In exchange for this better guarantee, creditors agreed to extend the maturities of their loans and bonds by three years, established a three-year grace period for principal payments, and lowered interest rates (70% of the original interest rate with a maximum of 7% for fixed interest rates and a maximum of London interbank offered rate, or LIBOR, plus 3 percent for floating rates).

The transaction involved 18 provinces and US$18 billion. By 14 December 2001, the last day on which creditors could enter the provincial swap, more than 450 bank loans and 70 provincial bond had entered the swap.

International credit rating agencies (Fitch Ratings, Standard & Poor's, and Moody's) considered the debt swap a "selective default" because it involved a reduction in net present value for creditors. As a result, some borrowers (such as the city of Buenos Aires) did not enter the swap. On 19 November 2001 Fitch Ratings published a press release explaining its concerns about the debt swap stemming from the change in terms and conditions of bonds and loans and the reduction in net present value of the debt exchanged.

Impact of the Devaluation

Among the first economic actions by the new government was to devalue the Argentine peso and establish a new parity for exchanging dollar-denominated debt for peso-denominated debt. Parity was set at Arg$1.4 to US$1. Some provincial debts were excluded from the exchange parity because they were incurred under foreign laws (including all multilateral loans and some provincial bonds).

After the devaluation, provincial debt instantly increased (figure 14.4). The debt stock, which had been Arg$29.4 billion at the end of December 2001, rose to Arg$62 billion by June 2002. Most provinces could no longer afford to service their debt. For international debt, ultimate responsibility rests with the federal government, which acts as guarantor. Indeed, before the present financial crisis the central government had implicitly bailed out some provinces by making their payments to multilateral lenders and then intercepting coparticipation revenues to cover the debt service costs.

Collateral for Subnational Borrowing

Two main types of collateral back provincial loans and bonds: coparticipation revenues and hydrocarbon royalties. Most subnational borrowing is backed by pledged coparticipation revenues.

Coparticipation Revenues. There are two basic mechanisms for collateralizing a borrowing with coparticipation payments (figure 14.5). The first, and the more common and safer of the two, is the intercept at the source of the

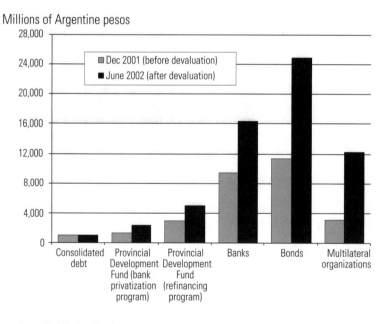

Millions of Argentine pesos

Source: World Bank staff estimates based on Argentine Ministry of Economy data.

Figure 14.4. Impact of the Devaluation on Provincial Debt, Argentina

disbursements: Banco de la Nación Argentina, the commercial bank of the federal government. The second is the intercept at the provincial bank (or the financial agent of the province) that receives the coparticipation revenues from Banco de la Nación Argentina.

These mechanisms have been tested as a result of the recent Argentine default, and some interesting differences have appeared. At the first level of interception every bond with a trustee has been honored. At the second level, however, behavior has differed depending on whether the provincial bank had been privatized, and moral hazard problems have arisen. Privatized provincial banks did not follow provincial instructions to default on bonds for which those banks served as trustee. In contrast, provincial banks that had not been privatized followed provincial instructions to default on bonds for which they were the trustee.

The province of Chaco issued three bonds for which the provincially owned bank (Banco del Chaco) acted as trustee. When hard times came in 2001, the provincial government issued two decrees (1845/01 and 1869/01) unilaterally deferring payments on the bonds and ordering its bank to return to the province the amount collected in the trust escrow accounts.[5] Contrast the experience of the province of Río Negro, which had established a trust with its financial agent, Banco Patagonia (its former provincial bank). In January 2002 the province postponed principal and in-

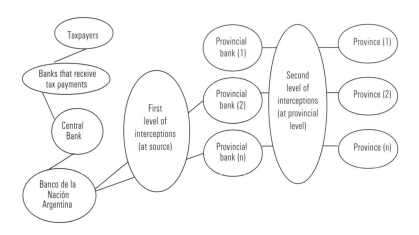

Source: World Bank staff estimates based on Argentine Ministry of Economy data.

Figure 14.5. Disbursement of Coparticipation Revenues, Argentina

terest payments on all its bonds except those for which Banco Patagonia acted as trustee, because the bank would not follow provincial instructions to default on the bonds covered by the trust.

In 2001 some commercial banks proposed that the federal government intercept coparticipation revenues at the level of the Central Bank. Clearly, they perceived the Central Bank as having greater independence than Banco de la Nación Argentina. The federal government rejected the proposal.

Municipal governments receive their share of coparticipation revenues through the financial agent of their province. Two interesting cases are the provinces of Buenos Aires and Mendoza. Because these provinces allow their municipalities to pledge their share of coparticipation revenues at the first level of disbursement (Banco de la Nación Argentina), lenders see these municipalities as more secure, enabling them to reduce their borrowing costs.

Hydrocarbon Royalties. Four provinces have issued bonds backed by hydrocarbon royalties (oil and gas) as collateral (Mendoza, Neuquén, Salta, and Tierra del Fuego). Although transactions backed by hydrocarbon royalties are much more complicated to structure than those backed by coparticipation revenues, all the bond issues were successful because investors perceive this type of collateral as the safest.[6] Hydrocarbon royalties back the most successful Argentine provincial bond issue, the Salta Hydrocarbon Royalty Trust.

One of the main advantages of hydrocarbon royalties is that concessionaires pay the royalties to the provinces through private local banks (including offshore banks), avoiding federal and provincial government interference. During the financial crisis affecting provinces in the second half of 2001 and the first half of 2002, there were no defaults on loans and bonds backed by hydrocarbon royalties.

Still, the use of hydrocarbon royalties as collateral is rare, mainly because only 10 provinces receive such royalties. Neuquén receives the largest amount, more than US$400 million in 2001.

Experience with Subnational Bonds

Argentine provincial bonds are of two types: those known as compulsory bonds, for which the investor must accept the terms and conditions offered, and those issued by conventionally accessing capital markets. At the end of 2001 more than 135 provincial bond issues were outstanding, with a total value of US$11.4 billion, and bond issues in international and domestic capital markets accounted for 40 percent of the bond debt (figure 14.6).

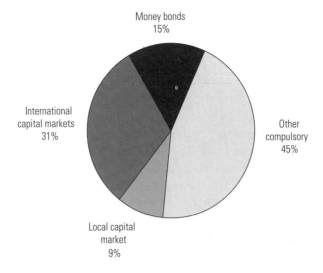

Source: World Bank staff estimates based on Argentine Ministry of Economy data.

Figure 14.6. Provincial Bond Debt Outstanding by Type, Argentina, End of 2001

Few local governments have floated bond issues in the capital market; most of the municipal bonds that have been issued have been compulsory bonds. At the end of 2001 the municipal bond debt outstanding reached US$110.5 million, and no municipality had accessed the international market.

Compulsory Money Bonds. In 2001, facing revenue shortages, many provinces began to issue bearer bonds, reviving an old scheme of using bonds to pay salaries and other expenses.[7] Money bonds are printed at the same size as Argentine pesos—indeed, they look like currency. Money bonds can be used to pay provincial taxes and are commonly accepted as money at their face value. The most well-known provincial money bond is the Patacon, issued by the Buenos Aires provincial treasury. Patacones are the only money bonds that can be used to pay federal taxes, and federal transfers to the province of Buenos Aires are made in Patacones. Most money bonds are short-term notes that pay a fixed interest rate and are backed by the full faith of provincial treasuries. This backing means little, however, because most provincial treasuries have defaulted on their bonds.

Provinces such as Tucumán never gave up using money bonds, while provinces that have done better in managing debt and accessing capital markets in the past decade, such as Buenos Aires, only recently became active issuers of money bonds. Buenos Aires has been the largest issuer: at the end of 2001 its debt outstanding in money bonds reached almost Arg$1 billion. By comparison, the debt outstanding of all provinces in this type of bonds on the same date was Arg$1.8 billion. The Provincial Development Fund has also issued money bonds (Letra de Cancelación de Obligaciones Provinciales) to pay coparticipation revenues. In all, some Arg$4.3 billion in money bonds were outstanding at the end of 2001.

Local revenues continued to decline in the first half of 2002, and at the end of June the stock of money bonds (excluding those issued by the Provincial Development Fund) reached Arg$4.1 billion and Arg$ 7.4 billion including those issued by the Provincial Development Fund. Some of these bonds, such as those issued by Buenos Aires, Córdoba, and the Provincial Development Fund, have wide acceptance and a liquid secondary market with low volatility. Nonetheless, these bonds adversely affect monetary policy, not only because they prevent open market policies but also because they can be used to buy U.S. dollars. For this reason, under an IMF financial rescue package for Argentina, provinces would stop issuing money bonds. The IMF and the Ministry of Economy have discussed options such as buy-back programs for retiring these money bonds from the market.

Other Compulsory Bonds. Other compulsory bonds typically are the result of debt consolidation related to judicial decisions, debt restructurings, and old provincial debts. Because of their compulsory nature, most of these bonds replicate the terms and conditions of consolidation bonds issued by the federal government (table 14.2).

Although the compulsory bonds were not issued in the capital market, many were listed on the Buenos Aires Stock Exchange and in the Buenos Aires over-the-counter market (Mercado Abierto Electrónico). These listings helped provinces gain knowledge about bond issuance.

Bonds Issued in the Capital Market. Capital markets have proved to be a good avenue for lowering the cost of funds and extending debt maturities for Argentine provinces: in the past several years 12 provinces have accessed the bond market, and seven of them have reached international capital markets (table 14.3). The earliest and most active issuer is the province of Buenos Aires, which launched its first issue in 1994; the province is the second largest issuer, after the city of Buenos Aires. Because of the size of its fiscal deficits, Buenos Aires cannot finance them through

Table 14.2. Terms and Conditions of the Typical Consolidation Bond, Argentina

Most common name	BOCON (bonos de consolidación)
Currency	U.S. dollar or Argentine peso
Interest rate	30-day U.S. dollar London interbank offered rate (LIBOR) or average interest rate for savings accounts in Argentine pesos
Maturity	16 years
Grace period for principal	6 years
Grace period for interest	6 years
Interest payments	Monthly, beginning in month 73; 119 payments of 0.84 percent of the principal and a final payment of 0.04 percent of principal
Period of capitalization	During the first 72 months
Collateral	None
Status	General obligation

Source: Argentine Ministry of Economy.

Table 14.3. Provincial Bond Issues in Domestic and International Capital Markets, Argentina, 1994–2001

Year	Issues	Issuers	Total amount (millions of U.S. dollars)	Average issue (millions of U.S. dollars)	Average interest rate (percent)	Average life (years)
1994	1	Buenos Aires	100	100	9.83	3.00
1995	4	Buenos Aires, Neuquén	283	71	10.15	3.17
1996	3	Buenos Aires, Mendoza	479	160	9.25	5.08
1997	8	City of Buenos Aires, Mendoza, Tierra del Fuego, Tucumán	1,156	144	10.64	7.43
1998	2	Buenos Aires	164	82	7.83	4.34
1999	10	Buenos Aires, Formosa, Misiones, San Juan, Santiago del Estero	946	95	12.88	5.09
2000	9	Buenos Aires, City of Buenos Aires, Chaco	1,306	145	12.05	5.96
2001	4	Buenos Aires, Salta	859	215	11.84	6.12

Note: The table excludes treasury bills.
Source: World Bank based on Argentine Ministry of Economy data.

the banking system. Thus it is a regular issuer in the bond market, while other provinces are opportunistic issuers.

The bond issued by the province of Buenos Aires in 1994, a U.S.-dollar fixed-rate bullet bond, was the only provincial one issued that year. Four bond issues were launched in 1995: three by Buenos Aires and one by

Neuquén. The Neuquén bond was the first (and still the only one) backed by coparticipation revenues and hydrocarbon royalties. It was also the first with a trust structure under the Argentine Trust Law (Law 24441). Neuquén was the first subnational issuer to use the largest Argentine custody house, Caja de Valores, as trustee. In 1996 Mendoza province issued its first bond, collateralized by hydrocarbon royalties. The bonds, due July 2002, were reportedly fully repaid despite the Argentine default and devaluation, demonstrating the strength of security arrangements through offshore trusts.

The province of Buenos Aires has issued bonds in the market every year except 1997, when the province achieved a fiscal surplus as a result of its privatization program. In that year, the most successful in the 1990s for bond issues, four provinces accessed the market. The market confidence prompted Mendoza to issue a bond with no collateral. (Unfortunately, the confidence proved to be misplaced.) The city of Buenos Aires launched four bonds, one denominated in Argentine pesos, two in Italian lire, and the last in U.S. dollars. All general obligation bonds, they were sold to fund an accumulated deficit. Tierra del Fuego completed a successful transaction in October 1997, offering a fixed rate bond backed by hydrocarbon royalties. Tucumán became the first province to tap international capital markets, backing its bonds with coparticipation revenues. Its program included two bonds (US$200 million each), one issued with a fixed interest rate and the other with a floating rate.

In 1998 financial conditions tightened because of the Asian, Russian, and hedge fund crises. Most of the provinces refinanced their loans in the banking market, with the province of Buenos Aires the only subnational government accessing the market. The next year, 1999, was a complicated one for Argentine provinces not only because of the Brazilian devaluation but also because of presidential and gubernatorial elections.

Also a very difficult year was 2001. The Argentine financial problem was the eye of the hurricane. Despite the turmoil, Salta launched the first Argentine subsovereign bond rated better than the sovereign. Indeed, the bond received investment-grade ratings from the three major rating agencies. The bond was denominated in U.S. dollars and backed by hydrocarbon royalties.

Among these provincial bonds, 85 percent were issued with fixed interest rates and the most common currency used was the U.S. dollar. The debt in dollar-denominated bonds increased significantly after the currency devaluation. In addition to bonds in Argentine pesos and U.S. dollars, the province of Buenos Aires and the city of Buenos Aires issued bonds in deutsche marks, yen, Swiss francs, Italian lire, and euros. Coparticipation revenues, hydrocarbon royalties, or both were usually used as collateral. The offering process often was protracted and challenging. Except for the province of Buenos Aires, subnational governments that accessed capital markets lacked experienced and permanent debt offices and reliable information. The lack of well-trained and properly prepared subnational debt offices has hampered the expansion of the subnational bond market in Argentina.

Every local bond issue used a trust scheme, which has proved to be a safe measure, especially during a financial crisis. While many provinces defaulted on their bonds after the sovereign default, there was no default on bonds with a trust scheme. There has been no common approach to dealing with the defaults. A few provinces have taken actions to reschedule their payments, others have done nothing, and still others have deferred payments.

Most bond issuing activity has been at the provincial level, with just three municipalities—Guaymallén, Bariloche, and Bahía Blanca—accessing local bond markets. Bahía Blanca is the only one with debt still outstanding as of June 2002.

Recent Developments in Subnational Finance (Up to End-2002)

Although all provinces face a deep liquidity crisis, their fiscal situation varies. The province of Buenos Aires, with the largest economy (35 percent of GDP), has accounted for two-thirds of the total provincial deficit in the past three years (1999 through 2001) on average. Even so, the relative performance of other provinces is much worse. While the central government has made efforts to rationalize spending, mainly by cutting salaries for civil servants, only a few provinces have followed this example. Many others have financed their imbalances by issuing money bonds.

The federal government's dwindling resources and its declining ability to assist subnational governments are major concerns in the protracted crisis. After the second half of 2001, because of the dramatic decline in federal revenues, the federal government failed to transfer the minimum amounts required under the federal compromise, an agreement fixing the monthly transfers owed to the provinces.[8] At the end of 2001 most of the provinces (including the city of Buenos Aires) signed a new agreement with the federal government allowing it to use notes to pay all past-due amounts to provinces and up to 40 percent of the amounts due after November 2001. The agreement also allowed the federal government to reduce transfers due after January 2002 by up to 13 percent of the total (as long as it makes corresponding reductions in the federal budget) and allowed provinces to use these reductions as a credit on debt service payments to the Provincial Development Fund.

The persisting economic crisis was causing problems in the coparticipation scheme. To address these problems, the federal government signed an agreement with provinces on 27 February 2002 aimed at sharing the costs of the crisis. The agreement includes restructuring provincial debt through the issuance of a central government bond that will be used to assume provincial debt in a new debt swap. A precondition for the debt restructuring is a reduction in the provincial fiscal deficit of about 60 percent. A deadline of the end of 2002 was set for passing a new coparticipation law. The law was not passed, and the system remains unchanged.

To guarantee their debts, the provinces pledged 15 percent of their gross coparticipation revenues. However, the amounts to be collected from provinces will be inadequate to pay the bond launched by the federal government, and the national Treasury will face imbalances beginning in the fourth year after the issue.

The agreement also calls for the central government to provide currency hedging for provincial multilateral debt. Provincial debt issued in foreign markets will receive the same treatment as central government debt.

At the end of August 2002 the federal government issued a decree (1579/02) establishing the terms and conditions for the debt-restructuring program:

- The bond issuer is the Provincial Development Fund.
- The interest rate is 2 percent annually.
- The grace period for interest payments is 7 months, and for principal payments, 36 months.
- The maturity is 16 years.
- The amortization is monthly in 13 years.
- The principal is to be adjusted by an index based on the consumer price index.
- The issue date is 4 February 2002.

An important difference between the 2001 and 2002 debt swaps is that the latter extended eligibility to debts denominated in any currency.

To reach an agreement with the IMF, the federal government was required to sign an agreement with each province establishing an ordered financial package. The aim was to avoid the issuance of provincial money bonds and to reduce fiscal deficits by up to 60 percent of the 2001 fiscal deficit. The provinces appear to be better situated than in previous years to achieve these goals: Some of them receive oil royalties that are settled in U.S. dollars. Because of inflation, tax revenues are again growing. The interest payments for the 2002 debt swap are much lower (almost 40 percent less) than those for the 2001 debt swap; salaries, which account for 50 percent of spending, have not been increased or indexed to inflation. Nonetheless, a sound monetary policy and a real commitment from the federal government to cut spending are required to avoid hyperinflation pressures and to change the situation dramatically for both the federal government and the provinces.

Key Issues for the Viability of Subnational Bonds

During the 1990s Argentina addressed several reforms that had positive effects on capital markets. Nevertheless, other major reforms are still pending.

Among the structural problems facing Argentina, building a workable fiscal relationship between the federal government and the provinces is one of the most pressing. Structural change is needed to make the revenue-sharing mechanism simpler and more equitable. Despite a constitutional requirement for change in the structure of the coparticipation scheme, there has been a political stalemate: such changes require approval by the federal government and all the provinces, something very difficult to achieve politically. Unless additional revenues are allocated to the coparticipation funds, which can happen only after economic growth resumes, the issue will remain unresolved because no province is likely to agree to reduce its share of revenues to benefit another.

The federal government's need to balance its fiscal accounts in the face of falling tax revenues and lack of external financing requires cost-cutting efforts that also involve the provinces. These efforts are complicated by the institutional inconsistency in Argentina, where provinces depend on the central government for most of their revenues but have constitutionally granted economic and financial independence and thus are not subject to central government interference.

An agreement with the provinces on the structure of the intergovernmental fiscal relationship will have to wait until institutional changes are supported by a consensus on the urgency of reform. That consensus has not yet emerged. Meanwhile, provinces need to increase local tax revenue but lack a sound structure for collecting taxes and appear unable to curb tax evasion. There is continual renegotiation of the compensation that the federal government assigns to the provinces for service responsibilities that have been decentralized. In some cases this issue is holding up further decentralization, such as for police and judicial services in the city of Buenos Aires. No agreement has been reached on how much additional funding the city should be awarded to provide these services.

The default and devaluation raised important questions relating to subnational bonds. Some provinces (such as Salta and Tierra del Fuego) are doing their best to avoid defaulting on their bonds, but will this effort be recognized by rating agencies and investors in the future? With just a few provinces having debt management offices, what would have happened if provinces had had well-trained debt managers? With independent trusts playing a key role in avoiding provincial defaults, will these structures lead to the reconstruction of the Argentine subnational debt market? Can the provinces manage the currency risks of multilateral loans, or will the federal government bail out provinces again? Regardless of the answers, it is clear that Argentina needs to rebuild its bond market. The challenge is to learn from the past and improve on it.

Province of Salta: A Bond Issue Backed by Hydrocarbon Royalties

The province of Salta had its first public debt issue in February 2001. The bond was issued by the Salta Hydrocarbon Royalty Trust with a targeted maturity of 12 years but an actual maturity of 15 (table 14.4). It is the first asset-backed structure for an Argentine subnational issuer rated higher than the federal government. The structure includes a strong security package enabling the bond to just reach international investment grade (figure 14.7). The transaction was considered very successful not only for its long maturity but also for its relatively low cost for an Argentine province at the time. However, the marketing period was long because of the financial problems Argentina experienced at the end of 2000.

The Province

Salta is one of Argentina's major provinces, with an area of 155,488 square kilometers and 3 percent of the country's population. At the time of the issue the province was managed by a strong administration, elected in 1999 for a second four-year term and with a positive record in financial management and administrative reform.

Table 14.4. Features of the Bond Issue by the Salta Hydrocarbon Royalty Trust

Feature	Details
Issuer	Salta Hydrocarbon Royalty Trust, a trust established in the U.S. state of Delaware
Amount	US$234 million
Market	Qualified investors in Europe and the United States
Issue date	28 December 2000; offered and closed in February 2001
Issue price	100 percent
Interest rate	Fixed at 11.55 percent a year
Interest payment period	Quarterly on 28 December, March, June, and September
Maturity date	28 December 2015
Expected maturity date	28 December 2012
Amortization	Bullet
Targeted amortization	Starting 2.25 years after the issue date, with the first targeted amortization on 28 March 2003
Ranking	Direct and unsubordinated
Credit ratings	• Moody's: Baa3 (global)
	• Standard and Poor's: BBB– (global)
	• Fitch Ratings: BBB– (global)

Sources: Salta Hydrocarbon Royalty Trust offering circular, Moody's, Standard & Poor's, and Fitch IBCA.

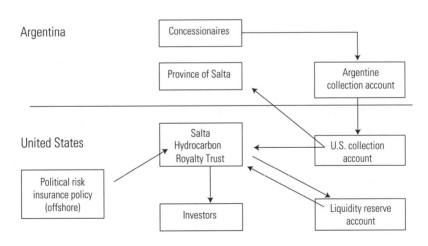

Source: Salta Hydrocarbon Royalty Trust offering circular.

Figure 14.7. Flow of Funds for the Salta Hydrocarbon Royalty Trust Bonds

Economic Performance. Following several years of robust economic growth, Salta suffered an economic downturn in 1995, paralleling the national recession triggered by the Mexican crisis. Like all Argentine provinces, Salta was deeply affected by the capital flight from the banking system and the reduced availability of international liquidity. Salta has a diversified economy by Argentine standards, but its per capita income and education levels are below the national average. Manufacturing is its main activity, accounting for almost a fourth of its production. Its chief exports are agricultural products, industrial products, and fuel and energy. Brazil has historically been Salta's most important export market, accounting for 30 percent of total exports, followed by the United States at 10.6 percent and Bolivia at 9.2 percent. Hydrocarbon production and exploration activities in the province increased sharply with the deregulation of the 1990s. As a result, hydrocarbon royalties rose from US$16 million in 1991 to US$20.7 million in 1995 and US$37.5 million in 1999.

Financial Performance. At the time of the bond issue the province derived current revenues from three main sources: gross coparticipation transfers (71 percent, with net coparticipation transfers accounting for 44 percent), provincial taxes (15 percent), and provincial nontax revenues (5 percent). Current spending goes primarily to personnel costs (54 percent in 2000) and transfers to municipalities (11 percent).

Salta had strong revenue growth in the early 1990s, reflecting national economic trends following the implementation of the Convertibility Plan in 1991. The province has maintained a relatively small fiscal deficit compared with other provinces, and it achieved a fiscal surplus in 1996 as a result of its privatization program and the transfer of its pension fund to the federal government. The privatization program, considered very successful, included two banks, a water supply company, and an electricity utility.

Debt Profile. Salta's debt stock increased by 85 percent in 1995–2000 as a result of fiscal deficits in those years (table 14.5). The province has been reducing its debt with the national government, its bond debt, and its consolidated debt while increasing its bank and multilateral debt. The growth in its commercial bank debt implies a higher cost of funding and shorter maturities.

Salta's ratio of debt to economic production is worse than the average for Argentine provinces (figure 14.8). However, thanks to the tight administration by its government, its ratio of debt service to operating revenue matches the national average. Moreover, the province has a slightly lower cost of funding than the average.

Table 14.5. Debt by Source, Salta, 1995–2001
(millions of Argentine pesos[9])

Source	1995	1996	1997	1998	1999	2000	2001
Banks	34.5	146.1	247.5	268.9	361.6	435.7	350.6
Multilateral lenders	8.8	31.6	21.4	74.1	105.3	105.4	147.4
Provincial Development Fund (bank privatization program)	16.7	50.0	50.9	50.9	50.9	50.9	49.3
Bonds	99.3	100.3	123.5	93.7	76.2	82.0	324.0
Other debt	375.6	234.2	104.6	83.7	92.8	90.0	74.9
Total	534.8	562.0	547.9	571.3	686.8	764.0	946.2

Note: Data are as of the end of December of each year.
Source: World Bank staff estimates based on Argentine Ministry of Economy data.

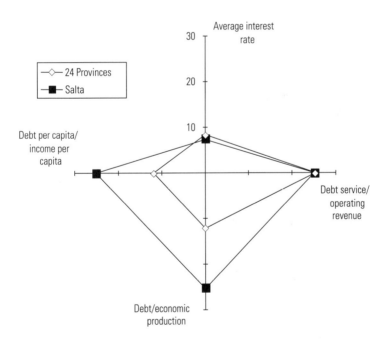

Source: World Bank staff estimates based on Argentine Ministry of Economy data.

Figure 14.8. Selected Debt Indicators, Salta and All Provinces, End-2001
(percent)

Issue Development

The Salta bond issue represented the first time that a subnational Argentine government was involved in a true sale of its future royalties. This made legal due diligence particularly important. The transaction was analyzed by Argentine and U.S. counsel, with both focusing on key aspects of the hydrocarbon concessions (terms and conditions, validity of permits, hydrocarbon royalties), the relevant hydrocarbon laws, the province's rights to the hydrocarbon royalties and other revenues, and the validity of the collateral documents and arrangements. Also important was the regulatory and constitutional framework governing the province's revenue-raising powers and expenditure responsibilities.

The structure of the notes was the key to their receiving the first global investment grade for an Argentine subnational bond. The notes were structured as a U.S. dollar issue to tap a deep and mature market, important for a first international issue. The structure included four innovative features that had never been used before in Argentina:

- The province sold its hydrocarbon royalties to a trust in a true sale under Argentine law.
- The trust, established in the U.S. state of Delaware, issued the notes.
- Target amortizations were scheduled to be due in 2015, but failure to make a targeted principal payment does not constitute an event of default.
- Salta used a political risk insurance policy for its bond, the first Argentine subnational issuer to do so.

Reasons for the Issue. Like other subnational governments, the province was facing an increasingly short-term and high-cost debt structure because of the large share of its debt contracted from commercial banks. This made an international bond issue with a longer maturity and a fixed cost of funding an attractive alternative. The province also viewed the issue as a good opportunity to gain credibility in international markets. The issue was structured as a single transaction, and all the funds raised were used to prepay commercial bank loans.

Credit Rating. The Salta bond issue was the first Argentine transaction simultaneously rated by the three major rating agencies—Fitch Ratings, Moody's, and Standard & Poor's. All ratings just reached international investment grade. The main factors supporting the ratings were these:

- The true sale of the royalties, which mitigated the risk of provincial interference with the transaction.
- The convertibility and transferability insurance policy covering 31 months of interest payments.
- The reserve liquidity fund covering six months of interest payments.
- The irrevocable and unconditional payment instructions delivered by the province to all the concessionaires with concessions dedicated to bond repayment.
- A flexible amortization schedule, which means that failure to pay targeted amortizations is not an event of default.
- Levels of collateralization that can sustain significant drops in oil and gas prices and lack of growth in oil and gas demand.
- Proven reserves representing 29 years of gas production and 33 years of oil production at 1999 levels.

Underwriting and Marketing. The syndicate acting as lead manager charged a gross fee of 2.75 percent, considered high by industry standards. The issuance took almost a year. The issue was marketed to qualified institutional investors in the United States under Rule 144A and outside the United States under Regulation S. In line with common practice, road shows were the main presales marketing technique used. Interestingly, investors formally requested a meeting about the issue with the Ministry of Economy, and it was the first time such a request had been made for an Argentine provincial bond issue. Seven large institutional investors subscribed to the offer, and all attended the meeting held in Buenos Aires at the Ministry of Economy. The lead manager made presentations to the investors and took them to the province to build knowledge and confidence.

Key Factors Affecting the Issue

Salta had little tax authority or revenue flexibility, and its expenditures were rigid. These fiscal constraints, together with the province's lack of visibility in the international markets, prompted the decision to use hydrocarbon royalties as collateral and issue the bond through a trust.

The regulatory framework also played a key role in the bond issue for several reasons. Two sets of regulations—those for oil and gas—had to be taken into account. The transaction was the first involving a true sale of royalties by a subnational government, and possible changes in hydrocarbon royalties and currency exchange transfers were being contemplated.

The perception in international capital markets of Argentina's financial condition had a large influence on the offer price and coupon rate of the issue. In addition, after the 1997 Asian crisis and the ensuing crises in other emerging markets (Russia in 1998, Brazil in 1999), investors had become cautious about emerging market bonds and demanded larger spreads over U.S. treasury bonds. However, while the issue was adversely affected by the weak sovereign position at the time of the launch, the province was considered highly competent and gained broad credibility during the road shows. There were several reasons for this. The province, which was well managed by a strong team, had implemented a series of reforms aimed at improving tax collection and controlling spending. The province had privatized its bank and other provincial companies and transferred its pension fund to the national government.

Despite competent management, the province still had a lot of work to do in financial reporting and disclosure. Financial statements were not prepared or audited in accordance with international standards, and the budgeting process was still elementary. The insufficient and inconsistent statistical and financial information on the province complicated financial and economic due diligence. Given these inadequacies, the security structure of the issue was the key to its success.

Recent Developments

In 1999 and 2000 the effects of the Brazilian devaluation and the slowdown of the Argentine economy led to a worsening of Salta's fiscal position and increased its fiscal imbalances. Debt (excluding short-term arrears to suppliers and employees) was equal to 76 percent of provincial revenue, and debt service absorbed 20 percent of revenue. In December 2001 the province's total debt stock reached Arg$946 million.

To improve its debt profile, the province decided to participate in the debt swap program promoted by the Argentine government in December 2001. However, it could include only commercial bank debt and consolidation bonds in this swap. On 27 February 2002 Moody's downgraded the Salta Hydrocarbon Royalty Trust from Baa3 to Caa1 because of the redenomination of dollar-denominated contracts between private parties at the exchange rate of 1 to 1.

While most private companies found it impossible to obtain authorization from the Central Bank to transfer money overseas to pay their debts, most provinces received authorization from the Ministry of Economy to pay their international bonds. This shows that at times of deep crisis such as that experienced in Argentina, the strength of the credit arrangements backing a bond and its overall security structure is as important as the political will to make good on payments.

City of Buenos Aires: A Debut in the International Bond Markets

The city of Buenos Aires made its debut in the international bond market with a euro medium-term note program in March 1997 equivalent to US$500 million (table 14.6). The city launched four issues from April to June 1997 and a fifth and final one in July 2000. The notes could be issued in a variety of currencies, including the Argentine peso, U.S. dollar, Italian lira, and euro. The first series was issued in U.S. dollars and targeted primarily to the U.S. market (table 14.7). The purpose of the program was to refinance the city's debt stock and restructure its bank, Banco Ciudad de Buenos Aires. It was also aimed at gaining credibility and a sound reputation for the city among global investors.

Table 14.6. Key Features of the Bond Program of the City of Buenos Aires

Feature	Details
Issuer	City of Buenos Aires
Arranger	Chase Manhattan International/Chase Bank AG
Dealer	Chase Manhattan International
Currency	Various hard currencies, including the U.S. dollar, Argentine peso, Italian lira, pound sterling, Swiss franc, yen, and euro
Amount	Up to US$500 million equivalent in series
Maturity	Variable by series (up to 30 years)
Issue price	At par, discount, or premium over par by series
Method of issue	Continuous basis with syndication if needed and minimum offerings of US$10 million equivalent
Interest rate	Fixed, variable, or zero coupon, depending on the series
Fixed rate notes	Payable in arrears on agreed dates
Variable rate notes	Interest borne separately in each series by reference to such benchmarks as the LIBOR and London interbank bid rate (LIBID)
Interest periods	As agreed between issuer and dealers
Zero coupon notes	Bear no interest and normally issued at a discount
Status	Direct, unconditional, unsecured, unsubordinated ranking pari passu with all obligations of issuer

Source: City of Buenos Aires offering circular.

Table 14.7. Main Characteristics of the Bond Issues by the City of Buenos Aires

	First issue	Second issue	Third issue	Fourth issue	Fifth issue
Currency	U.S. dollar	Italian lira	Argentine peso	Italian lira	Euro
Hedging		Swap		Swap	Swap
Amount in					
original currency	250 million	100 billion	150 million	69 billion	100 million
Issue date	11 April 1997	23 May 1997	28 May 1997	10 June 1997	7 July 2000
Maturity date	11 April 2007	23 May 2004	28 May 2004	10 June 2005	7 July 2003
Interest	Semiannual	Annual	Annual	Annual	Annual
	11.25 percent	10 percent	10.5 percent	9.5 percent	9.5 percent
Amortization			Bullet		
Listing			Luxembourg Stock Exchange/PORTAL		
Arranger			Chase Manhattan International		
Rating			Moody's: B1; Standard & Poor's: BB–		

Source: City of Buenos Aires offering circulars.

Each of the issues sold well, thanks to the city's good international reputation and low indebtedness. Despite the city's growing fiscal deficit, its debt at the time of the issue was equal to only 1.4 percent of its annual economic production. This, coupled with a targeted reform program, helped achieve reasonable ratings, which strengthened market perceptions. The notes were placed at a fairly large spread over the benchmark U.S. treasury bonds, but the city was more interested in achieving a placement well diversified by region and investor than in minimizing costs.

The Issuer

The city of Buenos Aires, located at the mouth of Rio de la Plata, was founded in 1580 and has been the capital district of Argentina since 1880. Its population of 3 million represents 8.6 percent of the country's total. The city is administratively independent from the province of Buenos Aires and has no fiscal or political relationship with it.

The city was granted its autonomous status (similar to that of a province) following constitutional reforms in 1994. Before these administrative changes the president of Argentina appointed its mayor, and the federal government made most key decisions. The city's constitution, approved in October 1996, provides for executive, legislative, and judicial branches. The city has a decentralized administration consisting of "communities" managed by an elected seven-member administrative board. These communities are responsible for secondary services, such as maintaining streets and parks, but have no independent revenue-raising powers.

Economic Performance. Besides being the federal capital and key financial center of the country, the city is a major driver of the economy, contributing more than a quarter of GDP. Thanks to a strong concentration of services and industry, the city's per capita income grew by 90 percent over the past decade to reach Arg$22,400 in 2001, about three times the national average. The city was affected by the Mexican crisis of 1995 but less so than other parts of the country; its production fell by 1 percent, while national GDP declined by 4.4 percent. Production growth in the city averaged a strong 5.7 percent in 1992–98. Argentina's most recent economic crisis, which led to a contraction in GDP of 3.4 percent in 1999 and 0.5 percent in 2000, started to affect the city's finances only in 2001.

Financial Performance. At the time the bond program was launched in 1997, the city of Buenos Aires derived more than 90 percent of its revenue from local taxes, mainly turnover taxes (57 percent), property taxes (16 percent), and motor vehicle licensing fees (9 percent). Federal transfers contributed only 6 percent of revenue, far less than the 50 percent typical for most other provinces. The city is a net contributor to Argentina's subnational system: while the federal government collects about a third of its total tax revenue in the city, it gives back to the city only 1 percent of its total transfers to provinces.

The city maintained a solid financial position from 1996 when it received autonomy to 2001 when it was affected by the Argentine crisis, with operational surpluses each year. The situation was sharply different before 1996. The city had large structural deficits amounting to US$1 billion over the period 1991–96. It generally funded the deficits through late payments to suppliers and short-term loans. Growing spending coupled with shrinking revenues led to a surge in the fiscal deficit—from US$9 million in 1995 to US$349 million (13 percent of revenue) in 1996.

Debt Profile. When the bond program was launched, the city had a moderate level of direct debt by national and international standards, with a debt stock of US$1.16 billion, about 1.4 percent of annual economic production (table 14.8). The moderate level of debt was possible because of the substantial transfer of outstanding debts to the federal government that occurred when the city's new constitution was adopted. This debt was later refinanced as part of the Brady bond program, in exchange for offsetting claims against the federal authorities.

At the end of 2001, before the debt swap and devaluation, the city of Buenos Aires had a strong debt position relative to the average for Argentine provinces (figure 14.9). The only debt indicator on which the

Table 14.8. Debt by Source, City of Buenos Aires, 1995–2001 (millions of Argentine pesos)

Source	1995	1996	1997	1998	1999	2000	2001
Banks	448.9	591.1	226.1	119.0	35.5	13.8	12.8
Multilateral lenders	31.8	23.2	19.2	17.6	22.9	45.2	55.0
Bonds	0.0	0.0	450.7	450.7	450.7	545.8	545.8
Other debts	264.5	481.3	420.6	340.3	498.9	451.6	780.7
Total	745.2	1,095.6	1,116.6	927.6	1,008.0	1,056.4	1,394.3

Note: Data are as of the end of December of each year.
Source: World Bank staff estimates based on Argentine Ministry of Economy data.

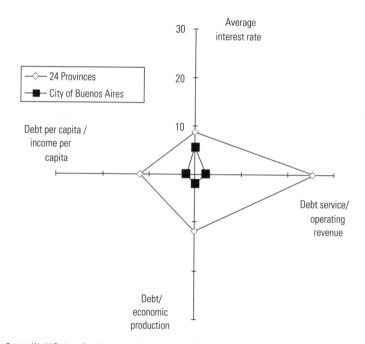

Source: World Bank staff estimates based on Argentine Ministry of Economy data.

Figure 14.9. Selected Debt Indicators, City of Buenos Aires and All Provinces, End-2001 (percent)

city's performance was close to the provincial average was the cost of funding.

At the time of the bond sale the city's financial management and reporting systems were reasonably effective by Argentine standards. However, there were problems stemming from the different accounting treatment of revenues and expenditures, the incompleteness and inconsistency of some of the information, and the lack of audited financial statements.

Issue Development

The bond issues, used to capitalize Banco Ciudad de Buenos Aires (US$100 million) and restructure short-term obligations, reduced the city's exposure to short-term volatility in interest rates and market appetite, but they increased the city's exposure to currency risk.[10] Moreover, the longer-term obligations require that the city accelerate reform in order to meet its liabilities. The city's de facto assumption of the obligations of its bank was a concern, because it could create a precedent for future bailouts. The bank had a large share of nonperforming loans, a small capital base, and narrow profitability.

Moody's and Standard & Poor's, generally optimistic about the prospects of Argentina and the city, rated the bonds B1 and BB–. These ratings were a major factor in the eventual placement of the issues. Nonetheless, both rating agencies expressed concerns about the city's ability to tackle fundamental structural problems in revenues and expenditures and about the inefficiencies of Banco Ciudad de Buenos Aires.

The first issue under the program (US$250 million) sold extremely well in the market despite a rapid weakening of the benchmark U.S. treasuries that increased the spread from 330 basis points to 370. Even at the larger spread and in a tightening market, however, the issue was a resounding success. The issue was twice oversubscribed, and more than two-thirds was sold to U.S. investors. An important feature was that it attracted new money rather than investors selling out of existing portfolios.

The second issue, a peso issue equivalent to US$150 million, was struck in record time, with marketing starting on a Friday and price-fixing taking place on the following Monday. The second issue had a narrower spread over the benchmark 2006 Argentine treasury bonds (95 basis points, compared with 140 basis points for the first issue). In line with the strategy of market diversification, the peso transaction was followed by lira issues, which also performed well.

The transaction as a whole was considered highly successful. Book demand was high in all cases, with issues oversubscribed about twice, and all series of notes were sold out. Interest in the bonds came mainly from institutional investors, which purchased about 90 percent of the issues on average.

Key Factors Affecting the Issues

Macroeconomic conditions in the country and the city played a major part in the success of the bond issues. Especially significant were the economy's resilience to the Mexican crisis and the importance of the city to national GDP, employment, and income. Another key factor was the city's strong revenue raising powers, a sign that repayment did not depend on central government transfers.

Conditions in the bond market affected placement dates and price-fixing arrangements and determined the underwriting and marketing process. Because the bond sale was relatively small and a debut for the issuer, a full underwriting commitment could not be obtained from the arrangers. Instead, the bonds were sold on a best-efforts basis.

The city's reputation and its plans for reform also contributed to the success of the issues, despite the city's less-than-optimal financial performance. Among the greatest concerns for the rating agencies was the fiscal deficit, considered a sign of structural problems and a constraint on reform. The city's financial reporting system, while needing improvement, did not adversely affect the issues, though it slowed the due diligence and rating process.

Recent Developments

In 1999 and 2000 the city of Buenos Aires was able to maintain a strong fiscal position despite the economic crisis in Argentina. By cutting capital spending and reducing the budget for noncore activities, it achieved surpluses of 2.3 percent of total revenue. In 2001, however, a decline in own-source revenue led to a deficit of almost Arg$250 million, equivalent to 8.4 percent of total revenue. While revenues remained relatively stable in the first half of 2001, they started to decline in August 2001, when they averaged 9 percent less than in August 2000, and fell sharply for the rest of the year. In December 2001 revenues were 46 percent less than in the same month in 2000. With the city of Buenos Aires deriving 90 percent of its revenues from own sources, this dramatic decline in own-source revenues had a big impact on the city's solvency.

City authorities decided not to participate in the provincial debt swap promoted by the federal government in November 2001, which the rating agencies considered a partial default. The city's debt stock was sustainable. Annual debt service reached US$196 million at the end of 2000, equivalent to 6.1 percent of current revenue. Almost all debt had been issued at a fixed rate, and about 46 percent was denominated in Argentine pesos.

At the end of December 2001 the city council approved the Economic and Social Emergency Law, which allows the executive body to issue bonds to pay employees and suppliers and to contract additional debt of up to US$218 million. In February 2002, in response to the deterioration in economic activity in Argentina, Standard & Poor's reduced its rating of the Buenos Aires foreign currency bonds to CCC+ on the global scale, and in June 2002 Moody's rated the city Ca. In late 2002 the city was conducting negotiations with investors to restructure its bonds.

Province of Buenos Aires: An Extensive International Bond Program

The province of Buenos Aires launched a euro medium-term note program in 1994 totaling US$3.2 billion. The intention was to finance provincial needs but also to gain credibility and a sound reputation in global markets. The notes could be structured with maturities ranging from 30 days to 30 years and issued in currencies including the Argentine peso, U.S. dollar, euro, yen, deutsche mark, Swiss franc, and Italian lira. All issues under the note program (except for the 30th) were sold at fixed rates, and all bonds had bullet maturities. In addition, the province engaged in a wide variety of debt swaps, all against the U.S. dollar.

Under this note program Buenos Aires had frequent recourse to the international bond market in recent years (table 14.9). Its record as an issuer in those years shows that it was a relatively regular issuer, it had strong debt management capacity, and its exposure to currency risk was very high, which led it to declare a default after the Argentine devaluation.

The Issuer

Buenos Aires is the largest province in Argentina, with a population of 13.8 million. The province is a net contributor to Argentina's subnational system, receiving only 23 percent of federal transfers, well below its share of the national population (38 percent) and GDP (35 percent).

Economic Performance. Buenos Aires is the main driver of the Argentine economy, contributing more than a third of GDP. Per capita income in the province reached Arg$6,980 in 2001, a little less than the national average. The service sector accounted for almost 50 percent of production in the province in 2001, with finance, real estate, and insurance alone contributing almost 20 percent. Manufacturing is the main economic activity, representing more than 31 percent of economic production.

Table 14.9. Access to the Bond Market by the Province of Buenos Aires, 1994–2001

Issue number[a]		Currency	Amount in original currency (millions)	Amount in U.S. dollars (millions)	Issue date	Due date	Interest rate (percent)
1		U.S. dollar	100	100.0	14/07/94	14/07/97	9.50
2		U.S. dollar	15	15.0	16/08/95	16/08/98	11.50
3		U.S. dollar	100	100.0	19/10/95	20/10/98	11.50
4	(swap)	Deutsche mark	150	104.5	07/12/95	07/12/98	10.00
5	(swap)	Deutsche mark	250	170.2	05/03/96	05/03/01	10.00
6		Swiss franc	200	159.0	23/10/96	23/10/03	7.75
7		Euro	100	108.8	13/07/98	12/07/02	7.88
8 –	Reopening 6	Swiss franc	75	55.7	23/12/98	23/10/03	7.75
9		U.S. dollar	150	150.0	19/03/99	15/03/02	12.50
10	(swap)	Euro	175	185.0	06/05/99	06/05/04	9.75
11	(swap)	Euro	150	151.9	12/07/99	12/07/06	10.63
13	(swap)	Euro	300	289.7	03/03/00	03/03/05	10.75
14		U.S. dollar	350	350.0	29/03/00	29/03/10	13.25
15 –	Reopening 13 (swap)	Euro	50	48.3	14/04/00	03/03/05	10.75
16		Yen	3,000	27.9	24/05/00	27/05/03	4.25
18	(swap)	Euro	100	96.5	05/07/00	05/07/04	10.00
21		U.S. dollar	100	100.0	27/09/00	01/08/03	12.75
22		U.S. dollar	160	160.0	31/08/00	05/09/07	13.75
23		Euro	100	89.4	06/09/00	06/09/02	9.00
27	(swap)	Euro	300	276.3	30/01/01	30/01/03	10.25
28	(swap)	Euro	300	274.4	23/02/01	23/02/04	10.38
30		U.S. dollar	74	74.0	28/09/01	28/09/06	24.17

a. Numbers missing from the sequence in the column correspond to the number of a treasury bill issued by the province.
Source: Province of Buenos Aires Public Credit Office.

Financial Performance. The province derives more than 55 percent of its revenue from provincial taxes, mainly turnover taxes (23 percent), property taxes (7 percent), and motor vehicle licensing fees (5 percent). Federal transfers provide the other 45 percent, a share similar to that for most other provinces. Buenos Aires was strongly affected by the fall in its own revenues since 1999. From 1998 to 2001 operating revenues fell by more than 15 percent, while operating expenditures rose by 11.7 percent. Even so, total expenditures increased by only 2.3 percent, reflecting cuts in capital spending and investments. During this period the accumulated fiscal deficit totaled almost Arg$8 billion.

The province privatized its electricity utility (for more than US$1.2 billion) and its water company (US$440 million). However, the province still owns several companies (railroads, a bank, a hotel, and a shipyard). Moreover, it retains ownership of Banco de la Provincia de Buenos Aires, the second largest Argentine bank. From time to time the bank generates significant costs to the province because of nonperforming loans resulting from unsound credit management practices. In the second half of 2002 the province bought the bank's nonperforming loan portfolio by issuing a provincial bond for US$1.3 billion.

Because Buenos Aires predates the Argentine republic and joined the Argentine confederation only after the national Constitution was adopted, it has certain prerogatives. One of them is that its provincial bank is not governed by the Argentine Central Bank. Because of the provincial bank's importance, however, the two banks maintain close coordination.

Debt Profile. Buenos Aires has a stable and well-trained debt management team that has gained much experience in debt markets since 1994 as the province has pursued a debt strategy focusing on bonds. The province's financial management and reporting system are reasonably effective by Argentine standards, though it has problems resulting from the different accounting treatment of revenues and expenditures, the incompleteness and lack of consistency of some information, and the absence of audited financial statements.

Huge provincial deficits have led to substantial growth in the debt stock of Buenos Aires. In 2001 the province's indebtedness increased sharply because of its enormous deficit and the capitalization of the provincial bank (table 14.10). Almost US$3.7 billion of the province's debt at the end of 2001 was issued under foreign laws; accordingly, this part of the debt increases as the Argentine peso is devalued. Even so, at the end of 2001, before the debt swap and the Argentine devaluation, Buenos Aires had debt indicators similar to the average for provinces. The exception was debt service as a share of operating revenue, where Buenos Aires exceeded the average (figure 14.10).

Buenos Aires was the first province to sign the agreement with the federal government required as a condition of the negotiations with the IMF on a financial assistance program. Like most of the provinces that later signed such agreements, Buenos Aires committed to reduce its fiscal deficit by up to 60 percent of the 2001 deficit. It achieved a substantial part of the deficit reduction by defaulting on bond and loan payments. Without structural reform the reduction is unsustainable, because the main problems that led to those deficits remain unsolved.

Key Factors Affecting the Issues

Moody's and Standard & Poor's are the credit rating agencies that rate Buenos Aires. Since the province's first launch under the program, provin-

Table 14.10. Debt by Source, Province of Buenos Aires, 1995–2001 (millions of Argentine pesos)

Source	1995	1996	1997	1998	1999	2000	2001
Banks	2,108.8	2,053.5	2,024.4	2,046.7	2,030.1	2,341.9	2,631.2
Multilateral lenders	169.2	173.8	330.3	450.2	727.2	907.2	968.7
Provincial Development Fund (refinancing program)	0.0	0.0	0.0	0.0	0.0	0.0	421.3
Bonds	319.4	694.4	735.3	725.7	1,385.1	3,340.6	6,412.8
Other debts	587.3	688.7	692.5	770.9	844.1	886.9	1,087.2
Total	3,184.7	3,610.4	3,782.4	3,993.5	4,986.5	7,476.5	11,521.3

Note: Data are as of the end of December of each year.

Source: World Bank staff estimates based on Argentine Ministry of Economy and Province of Buenos Aires Public Credit Office data.

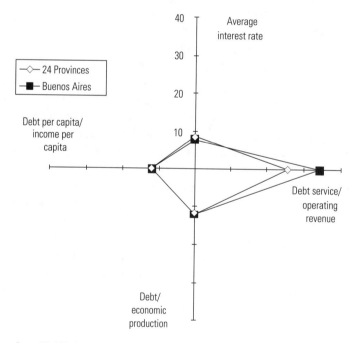

Source: World Bank staff estimates based on Argentine Ministry of Economy and Province of Buenos Aires data.

Figure 14.10. Selected Debt Indicators, Buenos Aires and All Provinces, End-2001 (percent)

cial ratings have generally changed with the sovereign Argentine rating. The rating agencies have expressed concerns about the province's ability to tackle fundamental structural problems in revenues and expenditures and about the inefficiencies of Banco de la Provincia de Buenos Aires. During the first issues the ratings were an important factor in accessing the market.

The key factors have been the significant revenue raising powers of the province, its large tax base, and its strong negotiating position with the federal government. Buenos Aires usually leads every negotiation between the provinces and the federal government. Moreover, Buenos Aires is by far the best-known Argentine subnational debt issuer.

The provincial administration's commitment to reform has proved to be weak. While the province privatized some of the companies it owned, it continues to own Banco de la Provincia de Buenos Aires, its largest source of quasi-fiscal deficits, as well as other corporations that are not a core part of provincial activity. Provincial authorities have been unable to cut fiscal deficits or implement serious reform since 1999. They have tried to reduce fiscal deficits by cutting capital spending, but year after year the decline in revenues has exceeded the spending cuts.

Like the other provinces, Buenos Aires has much work to do in improving financial reporting and disclosure. Its financial statements still are not prepared or audited in accordance with international standards.

Recent Developments

In recent years the province has maintained stable expenditures by cutting capital spending, but the fall in revenues forced it to finance substantial fiscal deficits. Provincial authorities decided to participate in the provincial debt swap promoted by the federal government in November 2001. As usual Buenos Aires was the largest player, entering the debt swap with a targeted amount of more than US$6.4 billion.

On 29 January 2002 the province declared a default on some bond payments, initiating the largest Argentine provincial default in history. During the first half of 2002 the province continued issuing money bonds (Patacones) to finance its fiscal deficit. At the end of June 2002 the outstanding debt in Patacones reached Arg$2.4 billion (2.5 percent of annual economic production in the province). On 25 July 2002 the first tranche of Patacones was due, for an estimated amount of Arg$500 million, but because of its financial situation the province had to exchange these bonds for a second tranche (Patacones B).

The province has been greatly affected by the Argentine devaluation. According to the province, its outstanding debt reached Arg$21.3 billion at the end of March 2002. Unlike other bond issuers that were already involved in debt restructuring, such as Santiago del Estero and the city of Buenos Aires, the province of Buenos Aires declared that it would wait for the sovereign debt restructuring before renegotiating its debt. In February 2002 Standard & Poor's reduced its rating of the Buenos Aires long-term foreign currency bonds to CCC+ on the global scale, reflecting the deterioration of economic activity in Argentina. In June 2002 Moody's downgraded the province's foreign currency debt rating to Ca.

Notes

1. Gross coparticipation includes different programs such as the National Fund for Housing (FONAVI) that were historically earmarked revenues, but since 2000 these revenues have been converted to nonearmarked revenues.

2. Most provinces have their own interpretations of the terms *revenues* and *debt service.*

3. The exchange rate at the end of 2001 was US$1 to Arg$1.

4. The privatization program was created in the mid-1990s to encourage provinces to privatize their financial institutions. Originally funded by the World Bank, the Provincial Development Fund later was capitalized by the national treasury. Thus in the late 1990s, the fund supported provincial bank privatization using its own assets.

5. Some bondholders brought suit against the province and its bank—against the province for unilaterally deferring payments and against the bank for breaking the Argentine Trust Law (Law 24.441) by carrying out the province's order.

6. Bond issuance in Argentine provinces typically takes an average of four to six months if the bonds are backed by coparticipation revenues, and six to nine months if backed by oil revenues.

7. The money bond is not unique to Argentina. They have been used in unusual circumstances in the United States. The states of Michigan (in the 1980s) and California (in the early 1990s) issued "warrants" to pay employees and suppliers during cash crises. The warrants were very short term and were issued at a discount. Banks accepted the warrants from the payees and then cashed them in at maturity.

8. In December 1999 the provinces and the federal government signed a federal compromise fixing the total monthly transfers owed to the provinces until the end of 2000. By the end of the period fiscal difficulties in Argentina and the pending negotiations with the IMF on a financial rescue package brought provincial transfers under tough scrutiny. In November 2000 a second federal compromise was signed that fixed total transfers to provinces for 2001, obligated provinces to pursue fiscal discipline, and required the federal government to increase funds for unemployment and social programs and to allow provinces to administer part of these funds.

9. From April 1991 to January 2002 the Argentine peso and the U.S. dollar were at parity.

10. The city was able to hedge euro and Italian lira debt against the U.S. dollar, but it could not hedge its U.S. dollar debts. Thus after the devaluation its indebtedness increased dramatically.

Chapter 15

Latin America and the Caribbean
Brazil

A past of excessive borrowing by a few large states makes the future difficult for all subnational entities.

Rodrigo Trelles Zabala and Giovanni Giovanelli

Lessons

Brazil's experience with subnational borrowing serves as a cautionary tale of the deep and lasting effects that weak central control, macroeconomic instability, fiscal indiscipline, and insufficient regulation can have on a country's public finances. This story in large part reflects the legacy left by imprudent lending by state banks and failure to subject the states to the discipline of the capital market. It also reflects the gyrations of Brazil's political system as it alternated between decentralization and recentralization.

The latest phase of democratization has led to advanced devolution of political and fiscal authority to the states, giving them substantial power to generate revenue and a large degree of autonomy. Subnational borrowing powers have traditionally been extensive and flexible. There was abundant borrowing in the 1960s and 1970s, with both domestic and foreign bond issues permitted as well as financing from state-owned banks, which often amounted to "lending to oneself." Financing by state-owned banks proved to be a key source of fiscal indiscipline, exacerbating already weak central controls and the ambiguous intergovernmental framework, where the assignment of expenditure responsibilities is particularly opaque. In addition, pressures on state budgets, such as generous pension plans for retired public servants, made balancing the budgets difficult.

Brazil has suffered multiple bouts of macroeconomic instability, starting with debt defaults by the central government in the 1980s and hyperinflation in the mid-1990s. This instability has pushed local finances over the edge, leading to a need for three rounds of bailouts in recent years. The moral hazard that central guarantees and recurring bailouts have introduced in local fiscal behavior has been difficult to erase. Credit enhancements—such as the Central Bank's appropriation of intergovernmental transfers to guarantee repayment—have removed incentives for creditors to factor local fiscal health into their financing decisions. As a result of the most recent default, however, the central government prohibited any additional borrowing (with the exception of refinancing existing debt) until 2010. It also instituted stricter controls for managing outstanding local debt and placed a cap on state spending.

Several characteristics of the crises serve as useful lessons. Although 30 percent of local debt took the form of bonds, the bond debt problem was concentrated in a handful of states accounting for 90 percent of this debt. A large share of debt was incurred with state banks that lacked incentives to perform competent analyses of local financial conditions and, in many cases, resulted in the obvious conflict of having a governing body lend to itself. Additionally, the absence of the private sector from subnational lending eliminated a potential source of evaluation and control. This last characteristic is a curious one, since Brazil's financial markets are relatively developed by Latin American standards.

The central government's current stranglehold on local debt and financial operations has not addressed the underlying problems of Brazilian states, particularly the inability to cure persistent fiscal deficits and the continued rollover of highly subsidized debt. Legislation has focused on administrative controls and restrictions, and little has been done to correct the deficiencies in market mechanisms. Regulatory reforms have been proposed—including laws relating to bankruptcy, contracts, and disclosure—to foster a prudent, market-based institutional framework. Some headway has been made in these areas, and there is hope that further reform, together with improvements in local fiscal health and retirement of the existing debt burden, will open the door to a sustainable capital market for local obligations in the medium term.

Sovereign Context

Brazil is politically structured as a federation. While the revenue sources of the different tiers of government are reasonably well laid out by the Constitution, there is much overlap in the provision of services. The country has a large municipal sector with around 5,500 units—ranging from small rural enclaves to the massive urban centers of São Paulo and Rio de Janeiro. These two megacities have tended to overshadow much of the rest of the country economically and politically and, not coincidentally, account for more than two-thirds of the municipal debt. Much of the political history of the country has been marked by a tug-of-war over resources and influence between the wealthier regions in the Southeast and the poor regions in the Northeast.

Brazil has been plagued by a history of fiscal and financial instability. The large debts accumulated in the past by some of the provinces and the two largest cities have imposed a big burden on the country's finances, and their refinancing through a series of federal bailouts has led to major macroeconomic problems. The highly decentralized public sector and heavy personnel expenditures have contributed to persistent public sector deficits. Transfers from the central government dominate local revenues, accounting for about two-thirds on average, and the many very small municipalities depend heavily on them.

As a result of recent financial reform efforts, direct borrowing from the financial markets is now tightly regulated and municipal borrowing is curtailed. Borrowing is limited to subsidized loans from two state-controlled banks—in effect, the government lending to itself. Private lending to municipalities is thereby effectively precluded. Efforts to introduce private lending require changes in the concessionary loan practices as well as other reforms to improve creditworthiness. The moral hazard resulting from a tradition of interference and bailouts of troubled loans presents a major obstacle to creating an efficient market for subsovereign credits.

Macroeconomic Conditions

The Brazilian economy is the largest in Latin America and the tenth largest in the world by GDP, with a strong export-oriented private sector. Before the introduction of the Real Plan in 1994 Brazil's economic performance had been characterized by macroeconomic instability. The events of the 1970s and 1980s—the oil shock, the debt crisis, the rise in real interest rates, and the decline in foreign direct investment and credit—caused a drastic contraction of the economy. State intervention, poor fiscal management, exchange rate management, and general indexation of wages contributed to hyperinflation and state and federal fiscal deficits. In 1980–88 annual inflation averaged 200 percent, and in 1989–94 it soared to an average 1,260.3 percent. After the Real Plan was introduced in 1994, however, inflation decelerated, falling to a manageable 9 percent in 1996, the year that Rio de Janeiro floated a municipal bond issue in the international bond markets.

Aimed at curbing inflation and building a foundation for sustained economic growth, the Real Plan was designed to address persistent deficits in the federal government's accounts, expansive credit policies, and widespread backward-looking indexation. The plan was implemented in three phases. The first, addressing the fiscal deficits, had as its centerpiece the creation of the Emergency Social Fund by constitutional amendment in February 1994. The second phase, initiated in March 1994, began a process of monetary reform by introducing a new index, the real unit of value, aimed at eliminating the distortions in relative prices in the economy. In July 1994 the federal government initiated the third phase of the Real Plan by adopting a new currency, the *real*, with an initial ceiling of parity with the U.S. dollar, and removed the real unit of value. By promoting deindexation of most prices and adopting a floating exchange rate subject to a parity cap, the federal government was able to orchestrate an abrupt deceleration of inflation, a convergence in the growth rates of tradable and nontradable goods, and greater competition in all sectors.

Large imbalances remained in public finance. Brazil's current account, which ran an average deficit of 0.02 percent of GDP between 1990 and 1994, deteriorated to a deficit of 2.5 percent in 1995 and 3.2 percent in 1996. In addition, Brazil's external debt ratios remained relatively high. At the end of 1996 total external debt stood at $178.1 billion, equivalent to 322.7 percent of exports, up from 296 percent the year before. Annual debt service obligations were also heavy, reaching 49.3 percent of exports in 1996 and 57.3 percent in 1997.

In the fall of 1997 the Brazilian currency came under attack as a result of the general anxiety about emerging markets that grew out of the East Asian crisis. Unlike Argentina, Brazil had not tied its currency to the dollar but allowed its targeted exchange value to crawl downward, allowing some room for inflation. It raised interest rates to defend the currency and appeared to be faring well until the Russian crisis in the summer of 1998 brought on another crisis in confidence, intensified by the threat of Minas Gerais to default on its debt to the federal government.

In January 1999 Brazil devalued its currency. Assisted by a loan from the International Monetary Fund, it immediately implemented a targeted inflation monetary policy that contained inflation: in 1999 the consumer price index rose by 4.9 percent, in 2000 by 6.2 percent, and in 2001 by 9.4 percent. Brazil's debt management strategy focused on extending the maturities of federal debt by indexing government securities to the U.S. dollar and the inflation rate. That debt structure, combined with the Argentine default at the end of 2001, led to a new Brazilian debt crisis. In August 2002 the federal government received a package of financial assistance from the International Monetary Fund: a $30 billion loan that was to be disbursed in two installments, the first ($6 billion) before the presidential election and the second ($24 billion) when the newly elected president took office. Meanwhile, anticipating political change, the international financial markets reacted nervously to the election campaign and the *real* faced continued downward pressure in world markets.

Structural Reforms

In the 1990s Brazil undertook myriad reforms as it attempted to liberalize its economy and contain the size of its government sector. The Cardoso administration, entering office in October 1994 with a clear agenda of reform, made great progress in privatizing state-owned enterprises and improving the climate for foreign investment. However, other initiatives critical for consolidating the public sector were not implemented, including cutting public sector payrolls, reforming the tax structure, overhauling the social security system, and reforming the civil service.

Brazil's privatization program is among the largest and most comprehensive in the developing world. The government has eliminated several distortions in the program, most notably the distinction between resident and nonresident ownership of companies, which had prevented foreign participation in such sectors as mining, transport, petroleum, electricity, and telecommunications. It also improved the regulatory regime and introduced tax exemptions and incentives for investments in less developed regions and export-oriented zones.

Between 1991 and 1995 Brazil privatized 41 companies, for total revenues of $9.2 billion; privatizations in 1996 raised another $6 billion. The privatizations also transferred $8.1 billion in debt to the private sector. Foreign direct investment, which rose from $2.2 billion in 1994 to $17 billion in 1997, accounted for a third of the privatization proceeds. However, difficulties in the public sector persisted, proving to be largely impervious to reform.

Intergovernmental Relations

The Brazilian federal structure, established by the 1988 Constitution, consists of the federal government, 26 states, one federal district, and an undefined number of municipalities (roughly 5,500 today). The 1988 Constitution set the powers of the federal government, which include national defense, social security, monetary policy, control of public debt, interstate and foreign trade, and the establishment of general norms for civil servants. It granted states all powers not otherwise reserved for the federal government. The Constitution also delineated some concurrent responsibilities of the federal government and states, including education, tax legislation, and social assistance, and it specified that federal law, while limited to general norms, prevails in case of conflict with state legislation.

Unlike other federal constitutions, which typically subject municipalities to the control of their state, the 1988 Constitution recognized municipalities as a third tier of government with the same constitutional status as states. Accordingly, states cannot impose on or prohibit the actions of the municipalities within their jurisdiction. The Constitution left the division of functions and responsibilities between states and municipalities ambiguous, merely reserving for municipalities the power to legislate on subjects of local interest and provide for local services. The loose controls on the local sector led to the emergence of a large number of small municipalities, an outcome fostered by the intergovernmental transfer system.[1]

Revenue Raising Capabilities

The 1988 Constitution explicitly defined the division of tax responsibilities between the levels of government. In addition to assigning a specific tax base to each level of government, the Constitution created a system of revenue sharing that redistributes resources among levels of government and geographic regions.

Direct Revenues. The Constitution assigned states receipts from the value added tax and authorized them to tax automobiles and real estate. Since the value-added tax is the highest yielding tax in Brazil, this assignment gave states much independence, particularly in the wealthy Southeast. States retained some flexibility to set the rates on interstate sales, subject to the minimum and maximum limits established by the Senate.

Municipalities were assigned a tax on services, an urban property tax, and a real estate transaction tax. These are all locally assessed and collected, although the tax on services is subject to a maximum established by federal law.

Revenue Sharing System. The 1988 Constitution substantially increased the amount of taxes shared by the federal government. Brazil's revenue-sharing system has two main parts: the participation funds and the state value added tax.

The participation funds consist of fixed shares of the federal government's two principal taxes: the income tax and the industrial product tax. Under the 1988 Constitution the federal government is required to transfer 21.5 percent of the participation funds to the states. Within each group of states, 95 percent of the funds are distributed among states on the basis of population and per capita income, with poorer states receiving a larger share. The other 5 percent is distributed in proportion to the area of states, to cover the relatively higher expenditures associated with a dispersed population. The federal government distributes another 22.5 percent of the participation funds to municipalities, transferring 10 percent of this amount to state capitals and distributing the other 90 percent among all other municipalities on the basis of population and the state's per capita income.

The participation funds represent a substantial redistribution of revenues among regions. On average, the less wealthy states of the North, Northeast, and West-Central regions receive twice as much as the states of the South and Southeast. The participation funds doubled in size between 1967 and 1992 and have been a predictable and reliable source of income over the past 10 years.

The state value-added tax is the second major tax-sharing arrangement. Under the Constitution states are required to transfer 25 percent of their proceeds from the value-added tax to the municipalities within their territory. Of this amount, 75 percent must be distributed on the basis of the origin of tax collections. The other 25 percent is distributed according to formulas established by each state legislature. The Constitution expanded the base of the state value-added tax by abolishing federal taxes on fuel, mining, transport, and electricity and incorporating these into the state value-added tax.

Expenditure Responsibilities

In contrast to the explicit provisions on revenue sharing, the Constitution leaves unclear how expenditure responsibilities are to be divided between federal and subnational governments and between states and municipalities. This ambiguity has led to friction over their roles. To match the increase in revenue sharing mandated by the 1988 Constitution, the federal government proposed a program of decentralizing expenditures. When this proposal was rejected by the Congress, the federal government transferred some expenditure responsibilities to states and municipalities on an ad-hoc basis. These included suburban railways and highways in São Paulo and Rio de Janeiro, transferred to their state governments, and federal hospitals in Rio de Janeiro, transferred to the state and municipality. The federal government also unloaded some health care costs onto subnational governments by reducing federal compensation payments.

Despite the federal government's decentralization efforts, the 1988 Constitution extended central control over two main areas: personnel and state debt. Under the Constitution state and local governments cannot dismiss redundant civil servants or reduce nominal salaries. Public employees have the right to retire after 35 years of employment (30 years for women and teachers) and to receive a pension equal to their final salary plus any subsequent constitutionally mandated increases. This mandate has proved to be onerous, substantially reducing the fiscal flexibility of states and municipalities. Pension benefits are particularly troublesome: constitutionally protected, very liberal, and unfunded, they represent an ongoing drain on current revenues.[2] Reforms have been undertaken, but they are forward looking, and civil servants employed at the time the 1988 Constitution was adopted continue to be protected by its provisions (World Bank 2001). To restrict growth in the protected classes of civil servants, local governments reportedly are attempting to privatize services and hire workers on a temporary basis.

In response to the profligate borrowing of the past, the 1988 Constitution also provided that any state or municipal government wishing to borrow, domestically or internationally, must obtain approval from the Senate. Subsequent tightening of statutes and regulations has sought to rein in subnational borrowing and reduce the need for further bailouts by the national government.

Regulatory Framework for Subnational Borrowing

Brazilian states and municipalities traditionally have had access to a wide variety of debt funding sources:

- Domestic bond issues.
- Domestic private commercial banks.
- Federal intermediaries, such as the Federal Housing and Savings Bank and the Federal Development Bank.
- State-owned commercial banks.
- Foreign institutions, including multilateral development banks and private commercial banks.
- Informal sources, such as arrears on salaries and on payments to suppliers.

Under the 1988 Constitution the Senate retained the authority to regulate state borrowing. It adopted a resolution regulating such borrowing on the basis of a state's existing debt stock, its revenues, and its capacity to service debt. However, the Senate reserved the right to grant exceptions, and it often did so.

In 1998 the Senate adopted several new measures to control subnational debt. One of these, Senate Resolution 78, prohibits the issuance of new subnational bonds until the end of 2010 except to finance the rollover of previously issued bonds. In addition, Resolution 78 contains the following:

- Prohibits borrowing from own enterprises or suppliers.
- Limits new debt to no more than 18 percent of real net revenues.[3]
- Limits annual debt service to no more than 13 percent of real net revenues.

- Limits debt outstanding to no more than 2 times real net revenues.[4]
- Prohibits governments in default from accessing new borrowing.
- Requires governments to have a primary surplus before obtaining new loans.[5]
- Prohibits governments from contracting new debt during the last six months of their term.

The Law of Fiscal Responsibility, adopted in 2000 by the Senate, takes a more comprehensive approach, extending beyond subnational governments to the federal government as well. The law contains the following:

- Limits all personnel costs—including pensions and permanent and temporary personnel—to 60 percent of current revenues.
- Limits the net stock of debt to no more than 2 times net current revenues for states and 1.2 times for municipalities.
- Allows states and municipalities that exceed the debt stock limit 15 years to adjust to the requirements.
- Authorizes new debt only when debt service does not exceed 11.5 percent of current revenues.
- Forbids borrowing between levels of government, except for federal institutions.

External borrowing by states is largely exempt from federal regulation unless it requires a federal guarantee, in which case the Ministry of Finance has the authority to grant or deny federal backing. Still, the National Monetary Council of Brazil, in its Resolution 2280, established conditions for the external credit operations of states and municipalities. The two most important provisions of this resolution are the following:

- The proceeds of the external credit must be used to refinance the issuer's outstanding domestic financial obligations, with preference given to the obligations with a higher cost of funding or shorter maturity than the external debt.
- In cases where the issuer has no credit rating, the issuer must establish a sinking fund escrow account with a balance equivalent to the monthly debt service obligation (principal and interest).

The federal government and the Central Bank have attempted to tighten regulations on the supply side. Central Bank Resolution 2461, adopted in 1998, prohibits private banks from increasing their holdings of state debt other than bonds. However, it does allow them to adjust the composition of their state debt portfolios as existing debt matures. Central Bank regulations also prohibit states from borrowing from their own commercial banks, although this rule has not been strictly enforced.

In addition, the Central Bank prohibits public sector banks and financial institutions from having more than 45 percent of their equity in the form of loans to or investments in public sector entities. The Federal Housing and Savings Bank and the Federal Development Bank are both subject to this limitation. Municipal development funds are not subject, though they are limited by the Fiscal Responsibility Law. The Central Bank also controls borrowing in its capacity as adviser to the Senate: every borrowing request must be directed to the Central Bank, which analyzes each case and makes a recommendation to the Senate.

Interestingly, all limitations on subnational borrowing are based on administrative controls, with no market-oriented mechanisms in place. Introducing a market-based system of credit allocation remains a dream as the country continues to try to dig itself out of a legacy of fiscal profligacy.

Recurring Subnational Debt Crises

The regulatory framework to control subnational debt emerged as a consequence of three bailouts by the federal government during the 1980s and 1990s. The first followed the debt crisis in 1989, caused by the heavy domestic and international borrowing in the 1970s and the shocks to the economy in the early 1980s. When the federal government defaulted on its external debt in the 1980s, subnational governments did the same; when the federal government reached an agreement with foreign creditors, it had to assume the subnational foreign debt of $19 billion. The outstanding debt plus arrears were rescheduled for up to 30 years. This initial bailout included only the foreign debt of states and municipalities.[6]

After this first bailout subnational governments started to pressure the federal government to reschedule their debt held by federal institutions. In 1991 a second round of negotiations began, concluding in 1993 with another bailout, this time covering only debt with federal institutions ($28 billion). As in the previous bailout, the debt was rescheduled for up to 30 years and interest rates were subsidized.

As part of this second bailout the federal government took steps aimed at reducing the need for future bailouts: it prohibited itself from lending to states and municipalities in default, and it adopted a constitutional provision allowing itself to intercept intergovernmental transfers to pay debt service. The limits that the Senate established relating to debt service permitted the capitalization of debt service obligations that could not be met.

During the negotiations that began in 1991 the states made several attempts to include their bonds. These attempts failed, and, not surprisingly, these bonds led to another subnational debt crisis. By the mid-1990s the high interest rates that states faced and the capitalization clause had led to a dramatic increase in their stock of debt. Bonds accounted for 30 percent of the debt not yet refinanced, and the domestic bonded debt of states rose from 2.3 percent of GDP in 1991 to 5.4 percent by mid-1996. However, the debt in bonds was not a widespread problem: four states accounted for more than 90 percent of the almost $30 billion in debt stock in bonds (figure 15.1).

This time the solution was a conditional bailout that included a fiscal and financial restructuring program, privatization of public companies, and the sale of state-owned banks, and the negotiations were held on a state-by-state basis. Another important difference was the requirement

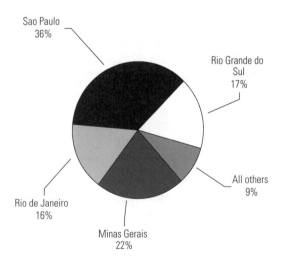

Source: Central Bank of Brazil.

Figure 15.1. Distribution of the Debt Stock in Bonds by State, Brazil, End of 1996

that states entering the program make a down payment equal to 20 percent of the debt to be rescheduled. This requirement led to the privatization of state-owned companies and banks. Again the debt was rescheduled for up to 30 years, with a fixed real interest rate equal to 6 percent. This interest rate was heavily subsidized, since the debt of the federal government carried much higher rates. Some 25 states and 180 municipalities participated in the refinancing program.

All states and municipalities offered their own revenues and revenue transfers as guarantees, but only up to a maximum of 15 percent of their revenues. At the end of 2001 the debt restructured under this program had amounted to more than $100 billion, and a series of new rules had been imposed to control subnational debt (see section on regulatory framework).

The Fiscal Responsibility Law represents a landmark in the control of subnational debt. Even so, rules cannot be seen as a solution to the underlying fiscal problem of persistent operating deficits. At best, rules can restore confidence and encourage better fiscal and financial management practices. Subnational governments' inability to achieve surpluses and their continued rolling over of debt, coupled with the large federal subsidy on outstanding debt, are fundamental problems that Brazil has not yet addressed.

Subnational Credit Market

While a few states and municipalities have tapped international credit and bond markets, subnational governments have financed their needs mostly through public financial institutions or loans provided by the federal government. The debt of states has steadily increased as a share of GDP since 1998, while that of municipalities has remained a fairly constant share (figure 15.2).

During the past decade states have issued bonds underwritten by their own banks and then sold to investors and other market participants. Municipalities have relied mainly on funds provided by the Federal Housing and Savings Bank and Federal Development Bank and by municipal development funds established with grants from the World Bank and the Inter-American Development Bank. Private banks have played almost no role—surprising, given the Brazilian financial sector's size and level of development.

Why have commercial private banks stayed away from the subnational credit market? There are several plausible explanations:

Percent

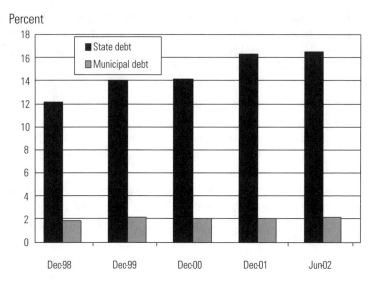

Note: Figure excludes the debt of state-owned companies.
Sources: World Bank and Central Bank of Brazil.

Figure 15.2 Subnational Debt as a Share of GDP, Brazil, 1998–2002 (percent)

- States and municipalities borrow funds at subsidized, below-market interest rates, making it impossible for private banks to compete for their business.
- Private banks have been "burned" in the past by several subnational defaults.
- The private sector offers loan maturities that tend to be much shorter than those offered by public financial institutions.
- Private financial institutions generally do not offer grace periods for repaying loan principal.

Meanwhile, public banks are under close scrutiny by the federal government, which is trying to prevent the public sector from lending to itself. The government's strategy for doing so is to have public banks lend to privatized infrastructure companies at subsidized interest rates. However, these below-market interest rates imply that some projects and capital investments being financed are not economically efficient. A credit policy requiring market interest rates ensures that projects are economically efficient and that capital investments are carefully selected and analyzed. The high real interest rates seen in Brazil in 2002, however, make most capital investment projects unviable.

Brazil, then, presents a paradox. It has large financial markets, but those markets are not tapped by municipal governments and access to them is very restricted for states. Subnational borrowing is dominated by state-owned and federal banks and an assortment of specialized funds that lend at subsidized rates (table 15.1). Still, the subnational credit market is clearly a big market in Brazil and the biggest in Latin America. To further expand that market, the federal government should promote a market-oriented funding policy to help break away from the old tradition of borrowing from public institutions. Ending that tradition will be difficult without numerous public sector reforms, but surely could be part of a package of such reforms.

Table 15.1. Municipal Sources of Funds, Brazil, 1999

Program	Source of funds	Lending rate	How the rate was determined
Caixa Economica Federal (Federal Housing and Savings Bank)	Mandatory workers' contributions to FGTS; credit from Inter-American Development Bank (IADB)	8–12 percent	Margin over the cost of funds
BNDES (Federal Development Bank)	PIS-PASEP and FAR employer social insurance contributions	5–8 percent for subsidized regions and activities; up to 16 percent for standard loans	2.5 percent margin. FAT funds carry rate of TJLP plus 2.5 percent, although only part has to be paid in cash. Remainder is capitalized indefinitely.
Federal Treasury bailout	Federal budget	6–9 percent	Political negotiation
Paraná municipal development fund	IADB (formerly World Bank)	10.14 percent	3.5 percent over IADB reference loan rate
Minas Gerais municipal development fund	World Bank	9.04 percent	3 percent over World Bank reference loan rate
Ceará Development Bank and municipal development fund	World Bank and Federal Development Bank	9 percent	Spread over base rate
Private sector commercial loans	Market	34.5 percent for two-year commercial loans to prime borrowers	Market

Source: World Bank 2000.

In addition, subnational governments need to develop better fiscal and financial management practices to generate confidence among private lenders, which are both skeptical of government credits and conditioned to expecting bailouts. As a result of this lack of confidence, municipalities did not have access to medium- and long-term private funds to finance their capital investments. Moreover, in contrast with many other countries, where large cities have been encouraged to borrow from private banks, in Brazil large cities borrow proportionally more from public banks than smaller municipalities do.

Interestingly, the Central Bank's ability to intercept intergovernmental transfers to service subnational debt provides investors with a much better safeguard than those available in other Latin American countries with subnational credit markets at similar levels of development (such as Argentina). This type of credit enhancement, however, also has costs. It eliminates the incentives for lenders to analyze potential subnational creditors, because they think that their loans will be repaid no matter how the loan proceeds are invested. Further, it eliminates the incentives for state and local governments to analyze their projects, because they know they can gain access to the credit market by pledging their revenues to the Central Bank.

All this makes clear that Brazil's subnational credit market has a low level of financial intermediation and efficiency—and that measures are needed to reduce the cost of funds and increase efficiency. A recent World Bank study (2001) proposed the following initiatives:

- Strengthening contract enforcement.
- Reforming the bankruptcy law.
- Extending the maturities of commercial bank loans.
- Increasing the efficiency of the judicial sector.
- Strengthening the rights of secured and unsecured creditors.
- Improving the quality of information provided to the market.
- Introducing better accounting standards and practices.
- Developing a stronger framework for sharing creditor information among financial institutions.
- Adopting a new, more comprehensive securities law.

These recommendations point to the importance of the legal and regulatory framework in developing local credit markets. A clear priority is reform of creditors' rights to rank secured creditors first. Another is reform of the bankruptcy law, to move away from the tradition in Brazilian legislation of favoring debtors, and there is a clear need for a comprehensive securities law. Today legislation relating to securities is dispersed among the civil code, commercial laws, financial sector rules, and special laws applying to particular financial instruments.

The quality and availability of information need to be improved not only to reduce uncertainty but also to add greater transparency to the credit system. Some initiatives already have been taken in this area. For example, the Central Bank has created the Credit Risk Data Center, a system that provides monthly information on credit operations of 20,000 *real* (equivalent to roughly $6,500 today) and above. Finally, extending the maturities of debt will help achieve a more stable macroeconomic framework.

Clearly, much work needs to be done to develop a private credit market for subnational borrowers. In an important step, the authorities appear to recognize the need to move away from captive sources of funding in the medium term. A market-oriented funding policy will lead to a better allocation of funds and a better assessment of investment projects by subnational governments as well as lenders. Limits need to be imposed on debt not to reduce or discourage municipal borrowing but to ensure that loans are used to fund capital investments and that the investments financed are economically efficient.

Notes

1. The mechanism for distributing federal aid is an unintended but effective inducement to form small municipalities. This mechanism favors small municipalities, which derive up to 90 percent of their revenues from transfers. Lenient requirements for incorporation allow the federal transfers to become a revenue source and thus a means of employment for would-be government officials and workers.

2. In the municipality of Rio de Janeiro retiree payments, fixed at the level of the retirees' final salary and indexed to salary increases for their last position, grew from 26 percent of payroll in 1993 to 35 percent in 1997. Since the city bureaucracy is growing slowly, the number of retirees will one day surpass the number of employed workers. See World Bank (2001, p. 23).

3. Real net revenues are total revenues less receipts from credit operations less property sales less transfers for specific purposes less specific grants for specific projects.

4. The limit declines by 0.1 annually until 2008, when it reaches 1.0.

5. The primary deficit or surplus is equal to total revenues less total expenditures less interest payments.

6. The rules of the bailout were set by Law 7978 (27 December 1989). Those of the second and third bailouts were set by Law 8727 (5 November 1993) and Law 9496 (11 November 1997).

Chapter 16

Latin America and the Caribbean
Colombia

Despite fiscal difficulties, the country has succeeded in using the private market mechanism to raise funds while limiting local borrowing.

Rodrigo Trelles Zabala

Lessons

Colombia has made a significant shift—though with restrictions—toward decentralization, but the consequent shift to substantial transfers has caused fiscal imbalances for the central government. Strong central control curbed an earlier acceleration in subnational borrowing. Continuing deficiencies in the regulatory framework surprisingly have not led to widespread fiscal difficulties, though decentralization and mandated spending have continued to strain fiscal balances.

Use of credit by subnational governments grew sharply in the 1990s because of inflexibility in local expenditures. Borrowing restrictions were lax because of legislated mandates to increase central transfers to finance required expenditures, and private banks, provided with an intercept mechanism, were content to lend. As a result, subnational borrowing doubled relative to GDP. The substantial increase in debt led to enactment of a law requiring approval from the Ministry of Finance for additional debt and tying borrowing controls to the fiscal health of local governments. In addition, new rules required banks to increase capital reserves for riskier subnational loans, increasing the cost of borrowing from commercial banks.

The new law slowed the growth of subnational debt substantially, and the central government has been able to avoid large bailouts of subnational governments. In contrast to Argentina and Brazil, Colombia essentially used a market-based mechanism to impose limits on local borrowing, allowing borrowing to continue in a controlled environment.

Findeter, an innovative government financial intermediary, has played an important role in facilitating local borrowing by providing loans to subnational governments that cannot access the private market and by discounting loans made by private banks. However, it has experienced some difficulties in recent years. For the central government, chronic fiscal imbalances have been a continued concern. In 2001 it implemented new laws to streamline the intergovernmental transfer regime and free up extra revenues to address its imbalances.

Bogotá is the star of Colombian subnational borrowing. It has successfully issued domestic debt and in 2001 became the first and only Colombian city to issue an international bond. The city is in the rare position of having its credit rating constrained by the sovereign rating (which is dampened by political instability). More recently, macroeconomic instability has put a strain on Bogotá's financial position, but this does not detract from its history of fiscal prudence and several years of operating surpluses. Its record of competent management has secured its position as one of the strongest municipal borrowers in Latin America. Indeed, even in the face of refinancing pressures stemming from the short-term maturity of its obligations, the city has successfully managed the currency and interest rate risks on its outstanding debt.

Colombia is a unitary country with 43 million inhabitants, 75 percent of whom live in urban areas. Although beset by domestic turmoil, and despite the flagging world economy, the country has generally turned in a good economic performance in the past few years. Inflation has been declining, dropping from nearly 17 percent in 1999 to 8 percent in 2001, but economic growth also has been slowing, from 3.4 percent in 1999 to 1.6 percent in 2001.

In 2002, thanks to the tight monetary policy of the Central Bank, inflation remained relatively low (7 percent). However, the country had another year of slow economic growth (an estimated 1.6 percent), with adverse effects on public revenues and expenditures. Recent forecasts put the fiscal deficit for 2002 at 4 percent of GDP, well above the target of 2.6 percent. Two of the main sources of pressure on the national budget are growing military spending and a rise in pensions. President Alvaro Uribe Velez, elected in May 2002, focused his presidential campaign on fighting drugs, guerrillas, and paramilitaries, which explains the increase in military spending. The government plans to solve the pension problem with a national referendum to reform the pension system in 2003.

In Colombia all levels of government, including subnational units, rely heavily on domestic debt markets to fund their deficits. In addition, the federal government has been working toward a domestic government bond market since 1995—with much success compared with other governments in the region. However, Colombia's economic and political situation undermines investor confidence, a situation exacerbated by the crises in other Latin American countries, such as Argentina, Brazil, and República Bolivariana de Venezuela. As a result, the voluntary government bond market has remained closed since August 2002. The national government needs to restore public confidence, particularly investor confidence, because it is almost impossible for the government to forgo borrowing from the domestic debt market.

Intergovernmental Relations

Colombia's 1991 Constitution defines three types of subnational territories: departments (states), districts (municipalities with the status of departments), and municipalities.[1] The country has four districts: Bogotá (capital district), Barranquilla, Cartagena, and Santa Marta. The Constitution commits the central government to providing compensating resources when it imposes spending or service requirements on subnational governments. The central government has honored this commitment so far, but continued fiscal imbalances could lead to exceptions or limits. Colombia's recently launched and still incomplete process of decentralization has led to problems in maintaining fiscal balances at the national level because of resource transfers to subnational governments as well as problems in avoiding unsustainable deficits at the subnational level (Dillinger and Webb 1999).

The decentralization was begun in 1983 several years after the military lost control of the government. An early landmark in the process was Law 78 of 1986, which required that mayors be elected by the people rather than appointed by the governors of departments. Similarly, the 1991 Constitution mandated that governors of departments be elected rather than appointed by the president. In addition, the Constitution committed the central government to expanding the revenue sharing system (*situado fiscal,* or "situado") to ensure adequate provision of the services it is intended to support.

Revenues

Since 1983 departments have collected taxes on liquor, cigarettes, vehicles, and lottery sales; these taxes form the core of departments' own revenues. In addition, departments receive transfers from the central government through the revenue sharing system, established in 1971 by Law 46 to transfer 13 percent of the central government's ordinary revenues. The 1991 Constitution and Law 60 of 1993 expanded the revenue sharing system by adding the income, customs, and value-added taxes, increasing the system's share of the central government's revenues to 22.1 percent in 1993 and to 24.5 percent in 1996. Law 60 required that 15 percent of the shared revenues be distributed equally among the departments and the other 85 percent according to specific social indicators.[2] The Congress is required to review this sharing formula every five years.

In addition, under Colombian law all hydrocarbon royalties must be distributed to subnational governments according to a formula directing 47.5 percent of royalties to producer departments, 12.5 percent to producer municipalities, and 8 percent to municipalities that are ports, with the other 32 percent redistributed across the country. The discovery of oil has increased the importance of this revenue source.

For municipalities, locally raised taxes cover about a third of expenditures in the aggregate. Wealthier municipalities raise more, poorer ones less. The primary sources of local tax revenue are the property tax and the business tax (on gross turnover). The many other local taxes tend to be unproductive. An interesting exception is the *contribucion de valorization,* a local betterment fee based on the user-pays or benefit principle. Some observers believe this tax could be used more extensively (Ahmed and Baer 1997).

In the mid-1990s municipal spending was equal to about 6 percent of GDP, but municipal tax revenues were only about 2 percent of GDP. For most municipalities, then, transfers from the central government are critical. Under Law 60, 60 percent of the shared revenues *(participaciones municipales)* transferred by the central government to municipalities are to be distributed according to the number of inhabitants with unsatisfied basic needs, and the other 40 percent according to such indicators as population size, administrative efficiency, and improvements in the quality of life. Transfers to municipalities were expected to grow until 2002.

Thus as a result of the new arrangements introduced by the 1991 Constitution and Law 60, the central government has been transferring almost 47 percent of its total revenues to subnational governments. In addition, the rules mandate that any increase in its tax base must be shared with subnational units. These heavy demands have caused continuing fiscal problems for the central government.

Expenditures

Subnational governments have little autonomy in managing their expenditures. Consider this example in education: subnational governments are responsible for paying teachers' salaries, but the size of the salaries is determined through negotiations between the central government and the national teachers' union. As part of the ongoing decentralization process, the central government transferred responsibility for education, health care, and investments in water and sewerage to subnational governments in the 1990s. However, a lack of capacity to handle these services led to reconsideration of the transfers to some municipalities. After a review, the services were transferred only to departments and to some larger municipalities with proven management capacities.

The revenue-sharing system stipulates how resources transferred by the central government are to be spent. Departments are required to spend 60 percent of the revenues for education, 20 percent for health care, and the remaining 20 percent for other purposes. Municipalities must apply the transfers to basic education (30 percent); health (25 percent); water supply (20 percent); physical education (5 percent); and housing, welfare, debt service, and other uses (20 percent). The earmarking and tight rules have made it difficult for departments to balance their budgets. Part of the difficulty stems from the fact that the central government continues to set workers' wages and the terms of employment.

For subnational governments, the budgetary inflexibility resulting from the earmarking of most of their revenues and the mandated spending linked to transfers can lead to unsustainable fiscal deficits, reflected in rising levels of debt. Only 12 departments achieved a fiscal surplus in 2000. Among the 20 that had fiscal imbalances, 9 had deficits exceeding 15 percent of their total revenue, and for Vichada the fiscal deficit was almost 150 percent of revenue (figure 16.1). Subnational governments also suffered serious effects from the country's slow economic growth in 1999 and 2000.

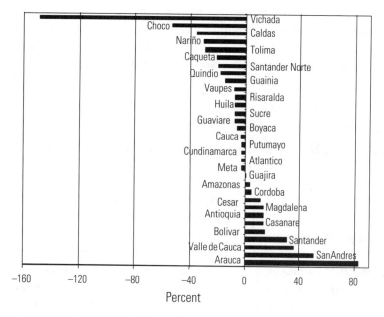

Source: World Bank based on Colombian Ministry of Finance.

Figure 16.1. Fiscal Balance as a Share of Total Revenue by Department, Colombia, 2000

Regulatory Framework for Subnational Debt

The earmarking of revenues and the centrally determined use of transfers encouraged growing use of credit in the early 1990s. Banks expanded their lending on the strength of the constitutional mandates to increase transfers to local governments. The weak reporting by and control over local governments and the ability to use intergovernmental revenue transfers to secure debt also loosened constraints on borrowing (Ahmad and Baer 1997).

Subnational borrowing had been rare in the past, but during the 1990s subnational bank debt rose as a share of GDP—from 2.6 percent in 1991 to 4.6 percent in 1997, including indirect debt and the debt of subnational government-owned companies; direct debt in 1997 was 3 percent of GDP (Dillinger, Perry, and Webb 2001). Until 1997 the central government required prior approval from the Ministry of Finance for any subnational borrowing.

In 1997 a new law, Law 358, was enacted to curb the excessive use of credit by subnational governments. Under this law, called the "traffic light" law, the Ministry of Finance analyzes two indicators of indebtedness before approving subnational borrowing:

- Capacity to pay, measured by the ratio of interest payments to operating surplus (the operating surplus is defined as current revenues less fixed current expenses).
- Sustainability of debt, measured by the ratio of debt outstanding to current revenues.

Based on these indicators, a subnational government might be free to borrow or might face restrictions (table 16.1).

On the supply side the Central Bank implemented various policies relating to subnational borrowing in the past decade. Since 1999, however, it has tightened regulations, requiring that banks maintain capital reserves for the full amount of any loans to subnational governments with a "red light." This regulation has made the loans costly to lenders and thus to borrowers, supporting the effectiveness of the traffic-light system. In Colombia, unlike in Argentina and Brazil, the Central Bank has always been prohibited from lending to subnational governments.

Table 16.1. The "Traffic Light" System for Regulating Subnational Borrowing, Colombia

Rating	Indicator	Result
Green	Interest as % of operational savings less than 40% and debt stock/current revenues equal or less than 80%	No restrictions on lending
Yellow	Interest as % of operational savings equal or greater than 40% but less than 60% and debt stock/current revenues equal or less than 80%	Lending only with Ministry of Finance's authorization
Red	Interest as % of operational savings greater than 60% or debt stock as % of current revenues greater than 80%	No lending, unless the subnational agrees to adjustment plan

Source: Law 358 of 1997.

Subnational Debt

The growth in subnational debt was a direct consequence of the decentralization. The inflexibility in local expenditures made it difficult to adjust spending, resulting in fiscal imbalances. Also contributing to the growth in debt was the regulatory framework. The framework had been poorly defined until 1997 and the passage of Law 358, which introduced a stricter approach to regulating subnational borrowing. On the positive side, in Colombia, unlike in Argentina and Brazil, subnational governments did not own banks, so nontransparent lending practices were avoided.

According to the Ministry of Finance, commercial banks account for more than 50 percent of total lending to subnational governments, and financial corporations account for more than 15 percent. Public and private banks lend to subnational governments at variable interest rates and require that they pledge specific revenue sources to repay loans. Some governments have pledged shared revenues even though they had only limited ability to use these earmarked resources for debt service.

Subnational indebtedness grew during the second half of the 1990s, but the "traffic-light" controls under Law 358 appear to have put on the brakes (figure 16.2). The increase in indebtedness between 1996 and 1997 was the largest of the period in both relative terms (74 percent) and absolute terms (1.6 billion Colombian pesos [Co$]).[3] Subnational borrowing then tightened, and despite the recession of 1999, subnational indebtedness as a share of Colombia's GDP remained stable from 1999 to 2001. Because of

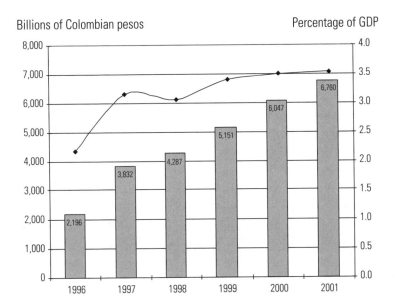

Source: World Bank based on Colombian Ministry of Finance.

Figure 16.2. Direct Subnational Debt, Colombia, 1996–2001

the limits established by the traffic light law, debt service requirements for most departments are less than 10 percent of their total revenue. In 2000 only two departments devoted more than 10 percent of their total spending to interest payments (for Valle de Cauca the share was 42.10 percent, and for Arauca, 54.87 percent).

Despite the pressures facing subnational governments, the central government has not had to conduct comprehensive bailouts. During 1998 the departments of Valle de Cauca and Santander Norte were not servicing their debt. Valle de Cauca renegotiated the terms of its debt with the banks and at the end of that year reached a restructuring agreement with them. This market solution to a subnational debt problem differed from the approaches adopted in such Latin American countries as Argentina and Brazil.

Findeter: A Financial Intermediary for Subnational Credit

In 1989, under Law 57, the Colombian government created Findeter (Financiera de Desarrollo Territorial) as a second-tier financial institution to finance or rediscount commercial bank loans made for municipal capital projects. The central government owns 92.53 percent of the company, and the departments own the remaining shares.

Findeter has evolved from a municipal development fund that disbursed credit at subsidized rates to a bank that provides credit at market rates as well as technical advisory services. It also has improved its efficiency. In the past gaining access to funds took an average of 18 months, but in recent years Findeter has reduced the wait to approximately 6 to 8 months. While the institution's original purpose was to lend to local governments, today it can serve a broader range of borrowers, including the private sector (table 16.2).

Since its inception Findeter has provided credit, directly or indirectly, amounting to almost Co$3.7 trillion, allocated across a variety of uses (figure 16.3). Subnational governments that cannot access the private credit market finance most of their projects through Findeter. The terms and conditions of the loans it provides differ substantially from those provided by commercial banks, because most bank loans are short to medium term while Findeter's are medium to long term (table 16.3).

As a second-tier lender, Findeter rediscounts commercial bank loans for subnational governments for up to 100 percent of the loan. However, the commercial banks perform the financial and risk analysis and bear the full credit risk (a key factor in reducing moral hazard). Findeter thereby provides a ready market for the loan but does not assume the credit risk of the counterpart commercial bank.

Subnational governments have seen the relative interest rates on their loans decline. Two factors have contributed to this. Because most subna-

Table 16.2. Potential Borrowers from Findeter

Private sector	Public sector	Others
Companies and individuals involved in education	Departments Districts	NGOs dedicated to such activities as local cultural activities
Private companies that provide public services	Municipalities Municipal associations	
Nongovernmental organizations (NGOs) involved in public services	Metropolitan areas Decentralized organisms (not included in the federal budget, such as housing agencies)	

Source: World Bank based on Findeter.

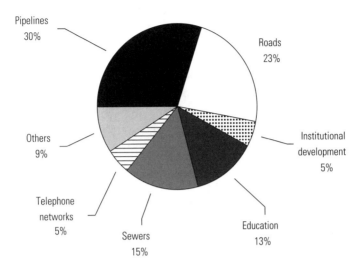

Note: Underlying values are in 1999 Colombian pesos.
Source: World Bank, based on Findeter data.

Figure 16.3 Allocation of Credit from Findeter 1989–99

Table 16.3. Terms and Conditions of Findeter Loans

Credit amount	Up to 100 percent of the project cost
Amortization	Up to 12 years, including 3 years' grace for principal payments Up to 6 years, including 1 year's grace for principal payments for preinvestment projects
Amortization system	Quarterly
Interest payments	Quarterly
Rediscounts	Up to 100 percent of the credit
Annual interest rate (rediscounts)	Average fixed interest rate for bank certificates of deposit plus 2.5 percent
Fees	Surveillance: flat fee of 1 percent of the credit amount Commitment: annual fee of 0.75 percent of the undisbursed amount

Source: Findeter.

tional governments have pledged shared revenues for loan repayment and banks can intercept these revenues, subnational governments are seen as strong credits. Findeter has an outstanding track record in refinancing municipal loans, with only 2 percent of its loans nonperforming in 1996. Because of its low rate of nonperforming loans during the past decade and its medium- and long-term investment perspective, Findeter was able to encourage commercial banks to extend maturities and lend directly to local governments.

Although the scheme in which commercial banks performed the financial and risk analysis and retained the credit risk worked initially, recently Findeter has found it difficult to have commercial banks as intermediaries. Because of excess liquidity, the commercial banks' portfolio in Colombia declined by 8 percent between November 2000 and December 2001. Findeter's credit line now has to compete with commercial banks in the market. In the current economic cycle, with local governments already carrying excessive debt and having no additional revenue streams to pledge, commercial banks are not finding adequate guarantees to act as intermediaries.[4]

Recent Developments

In 2000 the Colombian Congress passed Law 617 to establish a regulatory framework for making fiscal adjustments at the subnational level. The main goal is to provide a long-term solution for subnational fiscal imbalances. The law was designed to free current revenues to fund operating expenditures fully and capital investments partially. The law sets specific limits, such as restricting personnel expenditures to no more than 50 percent of nonearmarked current revenues by 2004. In addition, it establishes a prohibition on funding current expenditures with debt and restricts short-term treasury borrowings. To encourage fiscal discipline, the central government restructured more than Co$849 billion of subnational debt through the fiscal adjustment program. According to the law, the central government can provide guarantees for subnational governments if they agree to the following requirements:

- Implement a fiscal adjustment program.
- Reduce operating expenditures.
- Adjust legislative expenditures to enable a reduction in the expenditures of legislators.
- Reschedule debt to improve payment capacity.
- Obtain new credits from banks to finance the fiscal adjustment program.

In June 2001 a legislative act was approved requiring that the three types of intergovernmental transfers be combined in a new general participation system. The system became effective in January 2002. The funds will grow annually by the average annual percentage change in national current revenues in the previous four years. During a transition period (2002–08) transfers will grow by the rate of inflation plus 2 percent in 2002–05 and by the rate of inflation plus 2.5 percent in 2006–08.

Since the new general participation system is still being tested, its results are uncertain. Nonetheless, the new scheme clearly allows the central government to reduce its fiscal imbalances, since the system does not include the additional revenues that have resulted from the national tax reform introduced by Law 633. Thus subnational governments will benefit less than the central government.

Capital District of Santa Fe de Bogotá: First Subnational Issuer in the International Bond Market

Unlike many other municipalities, Bogotá sought to take full advantage of the greater opportunities offered by the decentralization process that began in Colombia in 1983.[5] Decentralization gave residents the chance to choose local representatives through elections every three years, and it granted municipalities more independence to address the needs of their residents along with full responsibility for financial management. (A new law aimed at extending the term of elected municipal representatives and allowing greater flexibility in seeking reelection is to be implemented in 2004.) The Law of Urban Reform of 1989 was designed to help municipalities improve their operations through such mechanisms as expropriation, land banks, land readjustment, land improvement taxes, designation of priority areas for urban expansion, and transfer of construction and development rights.

For both political and technical reasons, however, many Colombian municipalities never made full use of their ability to improve financial self-sufficiency through their own tax base, cost recovery policies, and other initiatives. Instead, they preferred to continue their dependence on mandatory revenue sharing by the central government. For many of them the consequence was a precarious financial situation—a result of fluctuating transfers and large municipal debts, most of which are guaranteed by future national transfers.

Bogotá is one of the few municipalities that undertook tax reform, sought out new revenue sources, reorganized and streamlined sectoral institutions, and found ways to improve its operations to the point where it was able to successfully float local and international bond issues to cover some of its funding needs. Despite these positive actions, Bogotá's financial health deteriorated recently as a result of macroeconomic problems in the country that affected direct transfers as well as property values and business activity, two key factors in determining own revenue for Bogotá. Moreover, the city's revenue structure is incompatible with its growing financial needs. Recent reluctance by the city council to approve several new tax and cost-cutting initiatives has added to the problem. In addition, the capital investments completed in the past few years will demand greater current spending for operation and maintenance.

Despite these dampening factors, the city's experience with bond issues illustrates its relative strength in municipal financing. In 2001 Bogotá sold US$100 million in bonds in the international market, becoming the first and so far only Colombian city to access that market. Despite the 2001 devaluation of the Colombian peso, the city saw a good opportunity in the international market. It undertook the bond issue not only because of the sound financial condition it had achieved, but also as a marketing strategy to show itself to the world. While this was Bogotá's first time borrowing abroad, the city has a strong record in bond issues, having earlier launched 11 bond issues in the local bond market.

Features of the Bond Issue

The launch was very successful and obtained a low interest rate of 9.5 percent (table 16.4). The issue did not carry a sovereign guarantee. Given the uncertain situation in Colombia and the difficult straits of the emerging economies of Latin America, the market reception was gratifying. The city was able to issue the bond at a fixed interest rate, a very important feature because almost all of its debt has variable interest rates. Nonetheless, this bond clearly implies more currency risk exposure for the city. Bogotá's authorities are working to reduce the risk exposure.

The Issuer

Bogotá, the capital district of Colombia, had an estimated population of 6.6 million in 2001, 16 percent of the country's total, and occupies an area of 1,732 square kilometers. Administratively, the city is not part of the department of Cundinamarca but has direct fiscal and political relationships with the central government. The city was granted its autonomous status, similar to that of a department or municipality, following constitutional reforms in 1991. The city is a net contributor to Colombia's subnational sys-

Table 16.4. Features of the Bond Issue by the Capital District of Santa Fe de Bogotá

Feature	Details
Date of issue	2001
Issuer	Capital District of Santa Fe de Bogotá
Currency	U.S. dollar
Amount	US$100 million
Maturity	2006
Amortization	Bullet
Interest rate	9.5 percent annually
Interest periods	Semiannual
Market	International bond market. The notes were issued under the U.S. Securities and Exchange Commission Rule 144A and Regulation S.
Purpose	Funding infrastructure projects.
Status	Direct, unconditional, unsecured, unsubordinated ranking pari passu with all obligations of the issuer. No sovereign guarantee.
Covenants	The district will not allow liens on its assets or revenues to secure any of its external indebtedness in the form of securities unless the notes are secured equally. Other covenants exist.
Cross-default	Failure to pay any public external indebtedness or external debt constituting guarantees of the district for amounts greater than US$20 million.
Governing law	State of New York
Rating	Fitch Ratings: BB+ (global) Standard & Poor's: BB (global)

Source: World Bank based on Moody's and Standard & Poor's.

tem: it accounts for more than 20 percent of GDP but for only a small percentage of central government transfers.

Bogotá owns eight independent companies that provide a wide range of services, including water, housing, energy, telephone, television, and mass transit. All are controlled by an independent board of directors but subject to budgetary oversight by the district.

The mayor is elected for a three-year term and cannot be reelected to consecutive terms. Council members are also elected for a three-year period.

Economic Performance. As the country's capital and main financial center, the city is a major economic engine, contributing more than 20 percent of the country's GDP with less than 17 percent of its population. During the first half of the 1990s Bogotá's economy grew faster than that of the nation. During the second half of the decade, however, the gap between the national and city growth rates narrowed, and Bogotá could not avoid the economic recession that began in 1997. The city's per capita income is 50 percent higher than the national average.

Manufacturing accounts for 16 percent of the city's economic activity, and finance and real estate account for almost 30 percent. Other services represent 27 percent (transport and communications 10 percent, construction 7 percent, and trade 10 percent). Although exports do not play a key role in Bogotá's economic base, the city administration is committed to increasing exports by promoting agreements with the Cundinamarca department to improve transport, communications, and infrastructure.

Bogotá is by far the largest urban center in the country. Since 1990 its population has grown by almost a third. Immigration into the city is a concern for authorities because of the demands it imposes on infrastructure. Immigration also has an impact on labor indicators. In June 2001 the unemployment rate in Bogotá reached 18 percent, compared with a national rate of 15 percent.

Financial Performance. The city has a positive track record of sound financial and fiscal management, reflected in the string of operating surpluses it has achieved since the early 1990s. In addition, Bogotá has an aggressive investment plan to meet the needs of its growing population. However, the fall in revenues since 1997 has hampered implementation of the investment plan and caused rescheduling and deferral of some projects.

Current revenues reached their peak in 1998 at US$1.3 billion, while total revenues reached their highest level in 1999 at US$1.9 billion (table 16.5). The economic recession that began in 1997 affected revenues, but the administration was able to cut some expenditures to offset the decline. National transfers to the city reached their peak in 2000, accounting for 35 percent of current revenues that year. In 2001, in response to the economic

Table 16.5. Revenues and Expenditures, Capital District of Santa Fe de Bogotá, 1995–2001 (millions of U.S. dollars)

Item	1995	1996	1997	1998	1999	2000	2001
Current revenues	770	1,058	1,271	1,274	1,108	995	1,033
Current expenditures	586	773	859	882	925	782	715
Operating balance	94	186	330	297	112	155	231
Capital revenues	85	254	223	234	820	554	613
Capital expenditures	336	584	702	743	961	769	570
Total revenues	854	1,312	1,493	1,509	1,928	1,548	1,646
Total expenditures	922	1,357	1,562	1,625	1,885	1,550	1,285
Fiscal balance	−158					−144	−150

downturn, the central government took initiatives to reduce its transfers. Bogotá's capital revenues stem from dividends from its enterprises, income from financial assets, asset sales, and reductions in the capital maintained in certain companies.

Bogotá has cut not only current spending but also capital spending to maintain a sound fiscal and financial position. In 1999 the city was planning to sell its telecommunications company (Empresa de Teléfonos de Bogotá, or ETB), but the financial crisis triggered by the Brazilian devaluation and the ripple effects on Latin American economies adversely affected the deal. During the past decade the city financed most of its investments through a pay-as-you-go scheme, making it possible to maintain stable debt service levels.

Projections for 2001 showed that the city would achieve an operating surplus for the eighth consecutive year and also enjoy a fiscal surplus that would allow it to make its debt payments (US$80 million) while saving money for further investments.

Debt Profile. Because the city has not financed its capital investments through borrowing, its debt has remained sustainable. The composition of its debt stock changed during 1995–2001. The share of external debt increased, reaching a peak in 1999 (figure 16.4), but external debt declined in both relative and absolute terms in 2000 and remained stable in 2001. The external debt consists of a syndicated loan arranged in 1997, the bond issue, and multilateral loans.

Bogotá's debt service payments have remained smooth in recent years as a result of its conservative debt policy (figure 16.5). The city estimates that its ratio of interest payments to operating surplus will peak in 2002, at 30 percent, and then decline to 24 percent by 2004, well below the 40 percent ceiling established by Law 358 of 1997 (the "traffic-light" law). City authorities generally are more concerned about hedging interest rate risks than hedging currency risks because only 3.6 percent of the debt stock bears interest at fixed rates while almost 55 percent of the debt is denominated in Colombian pesos. The authorities are also taking refinancing risk into account. More than 35 percent of the debt outstanding is due during 2002–04, and almost 90 percent is due during 2002–06. Accordingly, city officials are planning to refinance the debt by contracting loans with multilateral agencies and issuing bonds in the domestic market.

Recent Developments

As noted, the central government took several initiatives in 2001 and 2002 to limit its transfers to subnational governments. How great an impact the

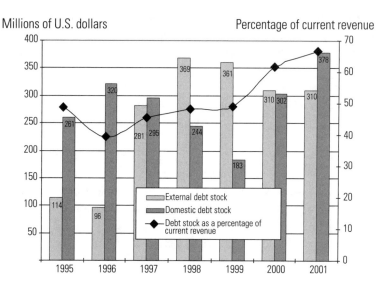

Source: World Bank based on Fitch Ratings.

Figure 16.4. Debt Stock, Capital District of Santa Fe de Bogotá, 1995–2001

Millions of U.S. dollars

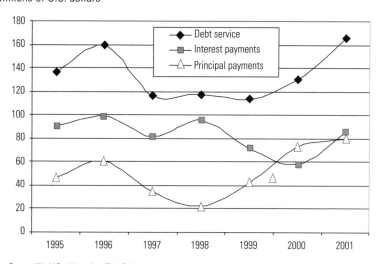

Source: World Bank based on Fitch Ratings.

Figure 16.5. Debt Service, Capital District of Santa Fe de Bogotá, 1995–2001

cut in transfers will have on Bogotá's finances remains unclear. Conservative estimates forecast losses of Co$644 billion for Bogotá during the transition period (2002–08) for the new regime established by the national government. This figure represents a 14 percent decline in transfers during the full transition period.

Beyond the changes under the new transfer scheme, Bogotá has seen a downward trend since 1997 in the national transfers it has received, in both relative and absolute terms (for example, shared revenues covered half of the city's education expenditures in 1990 but only 38 percent in 2001). Because the city must rely increasingly on its own revenues, authorities are committed to improving tax collections, cutting certain costs (in 2001, for example, the city eliminated 4,058 permanent positions), and expanding the tax base.

Credit Ratings

The U.S. dollar bond issue was globally rated by Standard & Poor's (BB) and Fitch Ratings (BB+). Their analyses reflected concerns about the economic recession and violence affecting the country at the time of the issue, but both agencies concurred that the city has shown a great commitment to maintaining prudent financial management.

According to the rating analyses, the ratings took into account the following positive factors:[6]

- Satisfactory fiscal operations.
- Proven ability to manage severe economic downturns.
- Manageable and affordable debt position.
- Valuable assets.
- The city's status as Colombia's main economic center.

The ratings also reflected some negative factors:

- A weak local economy that suffered the effects of the national economic recession.
- Significant pension liabilities.
- The potential adverse effects of the reform of the government transfer system.
- Country risk.
- The increasing service needs of a growing population.

According to one of the rating agencies, Bogotá deserves an investment-grade rating. However, because the sovereign's rating imposes the ceiling, the country's weak financial situation and its macroeconomic conditions undermined the credit status of the city. The devaluation of the Colombian peso, the economic recession, and the violence in the country all had adverse effects on the issue.

In recent years the international bond market for emerging market economies has been very volatile, and several Latin American economies have experienced financial crises and problems that have affected the entire region. Nonetheless, Bogotá was able to launch a successful bond issue. The transaction suggests that even in the face of trying national and regional conditions, strong subnational borrowers can gain access to the market.

The city administration's reputation was a major factor in the success of the issue. Even after several years of economic recession the city's management was able to cut spending and boost revenues to offset the decline not only in its own revenues but also in those received from the central government. The city's experience in the domestic bond market helped it prepare the bond offering. In addition, its financing policy for capital expenditure helped maintain relatively low levels of debt, considered a positive factor at the time of the issue. Its comprehensive investment plan and maintenance of valuable assets also were viewed positively by investors.

Notes

This chapter relies on information provided by the World Bank, Fitch Ratings Colombia, Standard & Poor's, the Colombian Securities and Exchange Commission, and the Colombian Ministry of Economy and Public Credit.

1. Departments are the main territorial divisions of Colombia. They were created in 1831, when the country was divided into five departments: Cundinamarca, Boyacá, Magdalena, Cauca, and Itsmo.

2. The number of students enrolled, the number of school-age children not attending school, the number of patients seen by health units, and the number of potential patients based on population.

3. In 1997 inflation (based on the consumer price index) was 18.5 percent.

4. World Bank consultant reports as reported in www.findeter.gov.co.

5. Much of this introductory section draws from World Bank sources.

6. Based on credit reports by Fitch Ratings and Standard & Poor's.

Chapter 17

Latin American and the Caribbean
Mexico

*Using credit ratings can be an effective means of instilling a
culture of creditworthiness.*

Steven Hochman and Miguel Valadez

Lessons

Mexico has traditionally been a highly centralized state, with the
states and local governments having centrally assigned duties
and limited fiscal autonomy. Except for the local property tax,
local revenue options are limited, and the states especially are
heavily dependent on federal transfers. However, reforms in recent years are improving financial flexibility at the municipal
level and increasing capacity to borrow in private markets.

In the 1990s Mexico's federal government inadvertently involved itself in the decisionmaking for subnational borrowing
through pledged transfers and the implicit guarantee of local
government bailouts that came with them. Accordingly, creditors took little time to conduct thorough evaluations of subnational finances, and some local governments borrowed beyond
their means. The 1994–95 financial crisis exposed these deficiencies and necessitated a costly federal bailout program that
forced a rethinking of subnational lending parameters.

To avoid a recurrence of the fiscal indiscipline and to remove itself from the local lending equation, the Mexican government instituted reforms that induced subnational governments to acquire internationally recognized credit ratings. The mandate placed the onus on banks, and thus subnational borrowers, by requiring that loans be supported by risk-weighted reserves that raised the cost of borrowing. Loans without credit ratings were assigned the highest reserve ratio. In addition, further reform to the intergovernmental transfer regime added clarity to local finances.

These positive steps, particularly the institution of credit rating requirements, have sparked the beginnings of a credit rating culture and spurred a nascent domestic capital market for subnational debt. Indeed, subnational governments have discovered that they can finance large projects more cheaply through bond issues than through bank loans. To encourage prudent local borrowing, the government has created a conservative trust fund structure for local government debt issues, a structure that is viewed favorably by international credit rating agencies and has boosted the ratings for several issues.

As the case study shows, the strong mechanisms inherent in the trust fund raise the certainty of repayment and lower risks. Thus despite the remaining institutional deficiencies in intergovernmental relations and judicial processes, a borrowing framework that demonstrates a political will to repay has allowed a viable market for subnational debt to begin to operate.

Mexico is the world's thirteenth largest economy, eighth largest exporter of goods and services, and fourth largest producer of oil. Far-reaching stabilization and structural reform efforts since the late 1980s have been rapidly transforming the Mexican economy and putting it on a faster growth track. Despite the massive setback from the 1994–95 financial crisis, the economy grew by an average of nearly 3 percent a year in the 1990s after virtually stagnating in the 1980s. The initially export-led recovery after the 1994–95 financial crisis has brought the economic growth trend close to 5 percent.

Mexico has benefited from its increasing integration with the North American economy, especially that of the United States. Trade liberalization, particularly through the North American Free Trade Agreement, has clearly contributed to Mexico's rapid economic transformation.[1]

Decentralization

In the past two decades the relationship between the federal and subnational governments in Mexico has changed significantly. The enactment of the Fiscal Coordination Law in 1980, the decentralization of public services initiated in 1992, the financial bailouts of states and municipalities in 1995 and 1997, and, most recently, the introduction of credit ratings as a factor in obtaining loans all have reshaped the institutional framework.

For decades Mexico has been constitutionally a federation. However, until the 1980s there had been a trend of increasing centralization (see Giugale and others 2001). This trend has been reversed most noticeably since the mid-1990s, when the country began devolving significant spending responsibilities to the local level. Nonetheless, the federal government still dominates the fiscal landscape, raising about 94 percent of all revenues and accounting for about 70 percent of all direct spending in the country (table 17.1). As a result, the states and municipalities rely greatly on transfer payments from the central government.

Table 17.1. Spending and Own-Source Revenues as a Share of GDP by Level of Government, Mexico, Selected Years, 1991–97
(percent)

	1991	1994	1997
Own spending			
Federal	8.4	11.5	11.5
State	3.0	3.2	4.9[a]
Municipal	—	1.2	—
Own revenues			
Federal	—	16.9	15.8
State	—	0.2	1.0[a]
Municipal	—	0.3	—

— Not available.
a. Data are for state and municipal governments combined.
Sources: Giugale and others 2001; Amieva-Huerta 1997.

Even as Mexico progresses toward greater local autonomy, fiscal responsibility, and accountability, there continues to be a noticeable lack of institutional elements to strengthen the state and local sector. Mexico has 31 states in addition to the federal district and more than 2,400 municipalities. These range widely in skills and resources. Many lack training programs, reliable information systems, agencies for coordination, and a legal and statutory framework (Giugale and others 2001). Without these, devolution remains immature and fragile. Decentralization policies have applied almost exclusively to the state level. Most municipalities received few new responsibilities even after the reforms of 1998, when a large share of the new resources allocated to municipalities were directed to federally mandated expenditures. Meanwhile, large municipalities take on many critical tasks without additional funding from the center.

Moreover, despite the increased devolution of spending, effective decentralization for Mexican states decreased throughout the 1990s. On average, states receive 85–95 percent of their revenues from federal transfers. Most transfers from the central government to the states are earmarked for specific purposes, typically to finance federally mandated employees in municipalities or for matching grants programs. The center still mandates how states are to fulfill their fiscal obligations, which is inconsistent with states' increasing political and economic power. In addition, the fiscal transfer regime is seen as too complex and opaque, based on historical inputs rather than performance or caseloads, and subject to political manipulation.[2] Until the late 1990s states rarely had a clear picture of how much funding they would receive, and the discretionary nature of transfers discouraged efficiency.

Revenues and Responsibilities: The Fiscal Coordination Law of 1980

Mexico's Fiscal Coordination Law provides for a revenue-sharing system in which all states and municipalities participate. This system enables states and municipalities to receive a share of the federal revenue collected from various sources, the most important being the value added tax and oil revenues. About 20 percent of the federal revenue collected goes into the General Fund for Shared Revenues *(Fondo General de Participaciones),* which is distributed to the states under a formula that takes into account population, the collection effort for certain taxes *(impuestos asignables),* and a compensatory mechanism that effectively subsidizes poorer states. While states may spend these shared federal revenues, called *participaciones,* as they please, they must pass on to their municipalities at least a fifth of the shared revenues they receive.

Decentralization initiatives have led to a notable increase since 1995 in spending responsibilities shared by the states and the federal government, particularly in health and education. Expenses in these areas are covered primarily by specifically appropriated funds, or *aportaciones*. State responsibilities also include administration, state infrastructure, and security, while water supply and treatment are often municipal responsibilities. In addition, the federal government provides discretionary financing for investment in basic infrastructure programs.

There are important distinctions among these three categories of funding. Shared revenues are a recurrent revenue source but subject to fluctuation with the level of tax collections. From the perspective of state governments, they represent a flexible resource that may be used for any purpose. Appropriated funds are also recurrent but are subject to yearly appropriations. Because the use of appropriated funds is federally determined, they are a less flexible revenue source for states than are shared revenues. Discretionary financing is nonrecurring, and the amount available for a state depends on the effectiveness of its lobbying efforts. These resources are the least flexible for states, since the funds are directed to specific projects and often must be matched by state funds.

The most important tax levied by states is the payroll tax, while the most important one for municipalities is the property tax. States and municipalities also collect fees and user charges and earn interest income from financial investments. In addition, state governments use federal taxes collected at the state level that are transferred fully (such as taxes on new vehicle registrations) or partially (such as those on alcoholic beverages); there are also significant state taxes in northern border states (on cross-border activity, such as trade and tourism) and oil-producing states (on oil).

Despite the gains in financial autonomy, states and municipalities continue to have only weak revenue-raising powers, with few revenue sources, low rates, poor financial record keeping, and inefficient revenue collection procedures. Municipalities have traditionally relied on the property tax, which is levied at low rates and often (along with user charges) subject to relief.[3] Nonetheless, in the larger municipalities property taxes can account for 20 to 40 percent of revenue.[4] The potential exists for better collections, particularly for property taxes and some excises and user charges, if the political will for reform can be mustered.

Overview of Subnational Borrowing

Until recently subnational borrowing was a product of Mexico's top-down intergovernmental relations, with the central government largely setting the rules and making the decisions—on an ad hoc basis and through negotiations between players belonging to the same political party (Giugale and others 2001). However, the increased political competition in Mexico and the devolution and greater subnational autonomy led to a need for stricter and more transparent rules for governing subnational borrowing. In 2000 the Mexican Treasury promulgated a new subnational borrowing framework. The new regulations eliminated discretionary federal transfers, required lending institutions to adopt prudential limits and get risk assessments (ratings) on state debt, and provided incentives for regular financial reporting by states and municipalities.

As Mexico moved toward greater decentralization, its total subnational debt doubled between 1994 and 1998, but the debt is concentrated in a few subnational entities. Three states—the Federal District, Mexico, and Nuevo León—together account for 65 percent of the outstanding debt (figure 17.1).

The Problem of Indiscipline: Credit Markets and Debt before and after the 1994–95 Financial Crisis

Federal transfers—general revenue-sharing funds and specifically appropriated funds—typically represent roughly 90 percent of total revenue for state governments and perhaps 70 percent or more for all but the most

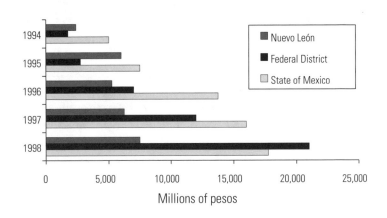

Source: World Bank.

Figure 17.1. Borrowing by Three State Governments, Mexico, 1994-98

property-rich municipal governments. Subnational governments typically finance their major capital spending requirements through bank loans, both from commercial banks and from the government development bank, Banobras. The Mexican Constitution prohibits state and municipal governments from borrowing from foreign sources or in foreign currency. Denied access to international credit markets—markets that customarily insist on credit ratings as a lending requirement—Mexican governments that borrowed had little incentive until recently to seek independent evaluations of their credit standing.

Federal Revenue-Sharing Funds as Collateral

Bank loans to Mexican states and municipalities have generally included a collateral pledge of the borrower's federal revenue-sharing funds as a debt guarantee. Lenders and borrowers alike viewed the involvement of the federal government in the process as an implicit guarantee, a perception that led some states and municipalities to borrow beyond their means and banks to lend without proper credit assessments. These factors exacerbated the financial turmoil experienced by most state governments in the fiscal crisis of 1995.

The importance of federal revenue sharing for state revenues and its relative reliability as a revenue source contributed to its use as collateral for state borrowing. The institutional arrangement supporting this practice was based on article 9 of the Fiscal Coordination Law, which authorized lenders, in the event of nonpayment by a state or municipality, to direct the federal government to deduct pledged shared revenues from state revenues and use them to pay the overdue debt service. When a government failed to pay its debt, the lender invoked the collateral pledge and intercepted that government's flow of federal funds. That left some governments with insufficient funds to pay for essential services. As a result, they sought additional financial support from the federal government, which was forced to come to their rescue. In the most recent rescues of note, mounted in 1995–97 in response to the fiscal crisis following the Mexican peso devaluation of late 1994, all states were bailed out. Many states have since refrained from borrowing, but a few have borrowed heavily.

Subnational Debt Profile in the Mid-1990s

At the end of 1994 subnational (state and municipal) debt in Mexico totaled 25 billion pesos, an amount equivalent to 72.7 percent of the shared revenues received by the states that year. More than half the debt was attributable to borrowers in four major states that had high ratios of debt to shared revenues: Sonora (254 percent), Nuevo León (125 percent), Jalisco (116 percent), and Mexico State (115 percent). While municipalities and smaller states tended to have lower ratios of debt to shared revenues, some had similarly high ones: Querétaro (215 percent), Quintana Roo (136 percent), Baja California Sur (121 percent), and Campeche (101 percent).

Even among states with low ratios of debt to shared revenues, some were vulnerable because they had very short debt maturities: San Luis Potosí (2.7 years), Durango (3.8), Chihuahua (4.4), and Colima (4.7 years). The average debt maturity at the end of 1994 was only 6.6 years. Assuming a constant payment schedule, subnational governments would have had to devote more than 11 percent of their annual shared revenues on average just to cover their principal payments. Further complicating the debt profile, nearly all the debt carried floating interest rates, leaving states and municipalities with sizable interest rate exposure.

Subnational Debt Relief Programs, 1995–98

This debt profile points to a high degree of vulnerability. Adverse developments in late 1994 that persisted through 1997 created a situation that made debt payments unsustainable. On 20 December 1994 the Mexican peso was devalued as the exchange rate against the U.S. dollar went into freefall, sending the nation into a fiscal crisis. Short-term interest rates rose sharply in 1995, peaking at nearly 75 percent in April. An economic crisis caused federal tax revenues—and thereby the pool of shareable revenues— to contract sharply; inflation—and thereby the cost of providing government services—rose rapidly.

During 1995 most states and many municipalities, including some with relatively little debt, missed principal or interest payments or both. In some cases the default period lasted only a few weeks; in others it extended over a year. The defaults resulted from the combination of heavy debt, shrinking revenues, and soaring interest payments. Some also may have occurred in part because of a belief that the federal government would step in and provide financial assistance.

In late 1995 the federal government put together the first of two debt relief programs for states and municipalities. It offered the program to all subnational governments regardless of their level of debt. Most states and many municipalities joined the program, which involved converting old debt into a new, inflation-adjusted unit of account (*Unidad de Inversión*, or UDI) that carried fixed interest rates and extending debt maturities. This arrangement spread debt service payments over a longer period, though at the expense of increasing the peso cost of the debt (because UDIs were adjusted for inflation). In return, state and municipal governments agreed to restore fiscal discipline, increase transparency, and improve their financial reporting.

In addition, the federal government provided direct financial assistance to many states. The amount of this aid, often earmarked for debt payment, varied with states' financial need. In 1998 the federal government sponsored a second debt relief program that lowered the interest rates charged on UDIs and further extended debt maturities, up to 18 years.

As a result of the debt relief programs and the better revenue performance after the crisis, the debt profile of Mexico's subnational governments improved substantially. The average ratio of debt to shared revenues declined from 72.7 percent in 1994 to just 38.7 percent by the end of 2001. The average debt maturity almost doubled, from 6.6 years before the financial crisis to 12.5 years in 2001.

Reform of Financial Legislation: Reasons, Objectives, and Preliminary Outcomes

To avoid a need for rescues of subnational borrowers in the future, the federal government searched for a way to accomplish the following:

- Encourage banks to give greater weight to the evaluation of intrinsic credit factors in their decisions on lending to state and local governments.
- Give state and local governments added incentives to keep their finances in order and avoid excessive borrowing.
- Reduce the likelihood of financial problems arising at the state and local levels that would require federal intervention.

Collateral Procedures

Since the end of the debt relief program in 1998 the federal government has put in place several reforms aimed at preventing a need for new bailouts. As a first step it modified article 9 of the Fiscal Coordination Law, ending a bank's ability to request a direct transfer from the federal Treasury of a state or municipal government's shared revenues. The aim was to reduce the federal government's involvement in the credit relationship between lenders and government borrowers.

Instead, state governments and the banks were to determine beforehand what collateral procedures would apply if arrears emerged. However, the new arrangement did not work as expected. Commercial banks, reluctant to participate, curtailed their lending to state governments and municipalities. As a transitional mechanism, the federal government accepted a temporary "mandate" from the states to transfer pledged shared revenues, a modified version of the original scheme that did not remove the federal government from the process.

In late 1999 the federal government notified states and municipalities that it would terminate the mandate arrangement in March 2000 and announced its intention to develop a new mechanism that would minimize the federal government's role. The mechanism, a master trust agreement (*Fideicomiso Maestro*), would enable subnational governments to use their shared revenues as debt collateral by channeling a share of these funds directly to the trust.

Subnational Credit Ratings

In December 1999 Mexico's Treasury introduced new bank regulations, the latest in a series of steps to enhance transparency in credit and capital markets and encourage state and local governments to assume greater responsibility for their own affairs. The regulations, which took effect in April 2000, require that a bank lending to a state or local government set aside capital reserves according to the risk-weighted credit exposure represented by the loan. Independently issued credit ratings serve as the measure of risk. The new regulations relate each state or local government's credit rating to that of the federal government and require banks to set aside reserves determined by the rating gap that results. The larger the gap, the higher the capitalization requirement.

The regulations do not require state or local governments to obtain credit ratings. However, borrowers without a rating are penalized, since banks must apply the highest capital reserves—and in all likelihood will charge the highest interest rates—for these loans. The use of ratings was intended to encourage banks to give greater weight to credit factors in their lending decisions and to give state and local governments added incentives to keep their finances in order and reduce the likelihood of a new federal bailout.

Since the new regulations took effect, most states and many municipalities have obtained credit ratings. By late May 2002 all but three of Mexico's 32 federal entities (31 states and the Federal District) had been assigned credit ratings by at least one and, in most cases, two internationally recognized rating agencies (one state has three ratings). Some cities also have been assigned ratings, and these reveal important differences in creditworthiness between state and municipal governments. The three agencies assigning the ratings are Moody's Investors Service, Standard & Poor's, and Fitch Ratings.

A handful of negotiable debt offerings—certificates whose payment relies on state or municipal financial backing—also have been rated. As governments have grown increasingly aware that, for a large project, a certificate issue can offer lower interest costs than a bank loan, more certificate offerings are being prepared. A capital market for state and municipal governments is developing in Mexico.

Since the initial assignment of ratings, some have been raised and others lowered. When a rating is assigned or changed, the rating agencies publish press releases or reports explaining what factors support the rating and what trends may affect the rating in the future. Using these explanations and other data, some market observers have published predictions of future rating assignments for issuers not yet rated.

Growing numbers of subnational governments are submitting their financial statements to independent audits. State and municipal finance officials—and lenders—are developing the habit of asking, "What can be done to improve this rating?" or "If we borrow this much more, or if we take these steps involving government finances or debt, how would that affect the rating?" These are signs that a new credit culture is developing among state and municipal governments in Mexico.

While it is still early, it appears that the Mexican government's goals in requiring credit ratings—promoting a new credit culture and removing the federal government from the credit relationship between state and local governments and their lenders—are being realized to an extent beyond some of the most optimistic expectations.

Recent Subnational Borrowing Experience, 2000–02

The chief federal restrictions on subnational borrowing in Mexico are the ban on foreign currency loans and the requirement that the proceeds of borrowing be used solely for capital investment.[5] State-enacted debt laws also regulate state and municipal borrowing, requiring approval by the state congress for state borrowing in most cases and establishing parameters for short-term borrowing. Municipal borrowing typically requires only local legislative approval if the loan is payable within the term of the borrowing administration, but longer-term debt issuance requires both municipal and state approval.

The recent legislation to improve financial and, by extension, subnational borrowing mechanisms has led to the first local government bond issues. Three subnational entities have issued debt under the master trust fund structure that the federal government proposed in 2000 (table 17.2). The Aguascalientes and San Pedro bond issues received ratings on a par with the national rating and are direct, fully binding obligations of the jurisdictions. The issues were assigned a comparatively high rating for two main reasons. Both municipalities have relatively large own-source revenues (San Pedro's are among the largest in Mexico, and Aguascalientes has robust property tax revenue). Even more crucial, however, is the secure structure provided by the trust fund arrangement.

For both municipal bond issues, the trustee of the fund is given rights to 100 percent of the municipality's shared revenues from the federal government, and all these revenues are pledged so that they can be used as a guarantee for issue repayment. Legal provisions add further security. The state government, which distributes shared revenues to municipalities, is contractually obligated to redirect the funds from the municipal treasury to the trust fund. The Fiscal Coordination Law reinforces the obligation for

Table 17.2. Subnational Bond Issues, Mexico, 2002

Entity	Date of issue	Type of instrument	Rating	Amount (millions of pesos)	Term (years)
Municipality of Aguascalientes (Aguascalientes)	11 December 2002	Certificado Bursatil (Capital Market Certificate)	Moody's: Aaamx; S&P: AAA	90	5
State of Morelos	11 December 2002	Certificates of Participation	Fitch: AA+(mex); Moody's: Aa2mx	216	7
Municipality of San Pedro (Nuevo León)	24 July 2002	Certificado Bursatil (Capital Market Certificate)	Fitch: AAA (mex); Moody's; Aaamx	110	7
Total				416	

Source: Serrano Castro 2002.

timely revenue transfers. In addition, both the Nuevo León and Aguascalientes state governments have a history of good fiscal health and timely payment of shared revenues. Moreover, any modification to the trust's rights to shared revenues must be approved by all creditors under the trust. Both issues state that additional debt can be acquired only if debt and debt service limits have not been reached (these vary with the jurisdiction) and that the new debt must follow the same trust fund structure.

Added security for all three issues in any events that threaten the repayment schedule is provided by a trigger for advance trapping of cash for the trust (for San Pedro and Aguascalientes, at 1.5 times the monthly amount required in the repayment accounts). Bondholders can respond to serious threats to their security (such as attempts to invalidate the trust contract or provide false information) by appropriating the full share of shared revenues allowed by the bond contract to accelerate full repayment.

For all three bond issues, cross-collateralized reserve funds limit the risk of nonpayment due to revenue shortfalls. One of the more interesting differences among the issues is the payment structure. Aguascalientes uses a bullet structure that pays periodic interest until the maturity, when the full principal is paid. Both Morelos and San Pedro use amortized structures with a three-year grace period on principal. A more significant difference relates to the Morelos issue. This issue stands out not only because it does not specify debt limits but because it has a lower rating—in part because the trust for this issue does not have access to 100 percent of shared revenues even in the event of nonpayment. The maximum that the trust can request is 30 percent of the revenues pledged to and received by the state's master trust fund. That amounts to 16.4 percent of the state's shared revenues.

Accordingly, the repayment contingencies for the Morelos issue are somewhat weaker and, with a two-tier trust fund structure, subject to competing financing needs. Nonetheless, nonpayment risk is quite low because the legal structure commits 30 percent of the revenue of the master trust fund to the issue offering. Moreover, the contract cannot be changed without the approval of senior lien creditors and the state congress. This contrasts with the other two issues, for which proposed changes require unanimous creditor approval. Significantly, the purpose of the San Pedro and Morelos issues is to refinance or retire outstanding loan obligations rather than provide direct project financing.

These examples of local borrowing in Mexico show that even with deficiencies in enforcement and institutional development, subnational borrowing in the bond markets is possible. What is needed is a credible payment mechanism that demonstrates the political will to ensure timely and complete repayment of debt obligations.

Notes

1. As a reflection of the opening of the economy, Mexico's trade (imports plus exports) as a share of GDP tripled between 1980 and 2000, reaching 40 percent.

2. At least until 1999 politically favored states were able to receive ad hoc transfers that thwarted the incentives to manage well and enhance local revenue (Giugale and others 2001).

3. The effective property tax rate in the mid-1990s was estimated to range between 0.03 and 0.05 percent. Rural areas are taxed at half the effective rate. The rates are grossly inadequate, but authorities do not want to deal with the political problems of raising them. See Amieva-Huerta (1997, p. 575).

4. Cities have been given greater ability to control land use and to determine property tax values and rates under recent constitutional amendments (article 115, approved in 1999), powers traditionally exercised by the states. But property tax rates are still subject to state approval. The reforms are seen as providing the larger cities more revenue raising power and flexibility and more discretion over revenues. See Aldrete-Sanchez (2000).

5. This section is based in large part on Moody's Investors Service rating reports for the relevant municipal bond issues.

Chapter 18

Sub-Saharan Africa
South Africa

Despite sophisticated financial markets, the country is slow to reinvigorate its municipal bond market amid rapid changes in its political and fiscal structure.

Matthew Glaser and Roland White

Lessons

In marked contrast to other countries of Sub-Saharan Africa, South Africa has a sophisticated private financial market. Municipal borrowing—through bonds and from intermediaries—has been a feature of local government funding for years, though before the early 1990s such borrowing was implicitly or explicitly guaranteed by the state. Aggregate lending volumes have stagnated and declined in recent years, however, primarily as a result of the interplay between a deficient policy and regulatory framework and poor budget discipline and financial management practices in local governments.

South Africa has taken measures to address these deficiencies. However, these measures, combined with ongoing reforms in the organization of the local government system (such as changes in boundaries), have led to a lack of stability, creating an uninviting investment environment for private lenders.

Today, prospects for growth in municipal borrowing are uncertain even though the potential demand for loan finance far exceeds existing volumes. South Africa has many of the basic conditions for expanded local borrowing, including a sophisticated and liquid financial sector, local authorities with substantial fiscal capacity, and a sound policy and legal framework that is soon to be introduced. Other factors, however, such as weaknesses in budgetary and financial management and the nature of certain structural and regulatory reforms, militate against growth in local borrowing. The next five years will be critical in determining the long-term outlook for municipal borrowing in South Africa.

South Africa is unique in many ways. It has the institutions and policies that many countries seek. It has efficient and vital capital markets for national government, public enterprise, and corporate bonds. It has substantial experience with municipal securities, a large and liquid financial sector eager to lend to municipalities, and clearly stated, market-oriented policies on the verge of being enacted into law.

Despite these strengths, some key indicators are headed the wrong way. The number of lenders to municipalities is shrinking. Private lending to municipalities is stagnant, and the government-owned lender is actively competing for the business of large and creditworthy municipalities while the market's structure is becoming steadily desecuritized.

All this points to a need for clear, stable, and effective legal and financial arrangements within which municipalities can plan. The disruptions of the post-apartheid transition period since 1994 have been unavoidable, and South Africa has managed this transition fairly well. Long-term borrowing and lending, however, depend on long-term predictability. Successive changes in municipal borders, powers, and functions have made it difficult for municipalities or investors to anticipate the future. These changes have made municipal borrowing expensive and have caused many private lenders to withdraw from the market, at least until conditions stabilize. Clear remedies for defaults have not yet filled the vacuum created by the disappearance of implicit government guarantees. With the finalization of legislation expected during 2003, the new municipalities and their legal framework will be settled. The municipalities then must be allowed time to find their footing. Any further uncertainty could prevent municipalities from obtaining long-term credit for infrastructure.

Efforts are also needed at the municipal level. If the supply of "bankable" projects and municipal debt securities is to grow significantly, municipalities must develop the basic skills and experience in accounting, planning, reporting, and marketing that support wise borrowing choices. Demand for credit should be the natural consequence of careful and informed municipal capital planning. Borrowing may be the most powerful tool in a municipality's financial toolbox, for it can lay the foundation for economic development and a virtuous cycle of growth. If used unwisely, however, it can leave crippling debt for the next generation (box 18.1).

Once the legal framework is finalized and stabilized and the basic skills and experience are developed, investors will have no reason not to come to the table. Assuming that borrowing does expand, financial crises will eventually occur in some municipalities, as they do in any country. How well South Africa deals with these crises will indicate the likelihood of long-term success. If sound financial emergency mechanisms are in place and if they prove effective, some diminution in loan volumes still may occur, but that would probably be followed by a resumption of steady growth in South Africa's municipal credit market.

Local Government. Before the advent of democracy in 1994 South Africa had a variety of local government systems, with about 1,300 municipalities throughout the country. In urban areas separate white and black local authorities were subsidiary to the four provinces that then existed. White local authorities included the core cities and virtually all the economic activity. These local authorities had their own councils, staff, and revenue sources, including property taxes and revenue from utility services. Black local authorities, often located nearby and providing cheap labor for the core cities, had limited services and widespread poverty. Other areas where black people lived were included in "independent homelands" and "self-governing territories," where a variety of administrative and traditional authorities provided local governance and limited services.

Since 1994 the legal and financial underpinnings of municipalities have undergone a series of changes aimed at democratizing and deracializing municipalities. In 1994 the "homelands" were reincorporated into the republic, and negotiations were initiated to determine local government boundaries. This process resulted in the creation of 843 municipalities after local govern-

Box 18.1. A South African Parable

Not long ago a district councilor asked his municipality's accounting firm for help. Collections of budgeted revenues had been falling steadily, while expenditures and responsibilities for providing services had increased with the addition of new territory. Every month the municipality was spending more money than was coming in. Unpaid suppliers threatened to withhold services, and local banks refused to extend more credit. Fortunately, he told the accountant, the municipality had been offered a lifeline—a euro-denominated loan at only 3 percent interest from an overseas development agency. The councilor wanted help building a case for South Africa's National Treasury to guarantee the loan, as required by the development agency. With the loan proceeds, the municipality could launch tourism projects necessary for its economic development.

The hard truth is that this municipality can ill afford a 3 percent euro interest rate (which could amount to 50 percent a year in South African rand if the exchange rate were to fall at the rate it did in 2001). In fact, municipalities are legally barred from borrowing in a foreign currency. Nor was the municipality able to convince the National Treasury to guarantee the loan: government policy. It is clear that municipalities' access to credit must depend on their own creditworthiness. Before the municipality borrows, it must increase its revenues, cut its expenditures, or both, even if that means delaying important projects.

The loan the overseas agency had offered to the district council is part of a "low-cost" lending program intended to help South African municipalities build infrastructure and pursue economic development projects. The agency's project officer in South Africa is under heavy pressure from his agency and his government to place the project funds and demonstrate concrete successes.

Well-intentioned development programs that make credit available to the noncreditworthy do South African municipalities no service. Some development programs do more to support employment and careers in development agencies than to help build sustainable systems and structures. This loan would be a negative-sum transaction: The donor has spent large amounts to create and staff the lending program, and lending the money at the 3 percent euro interest rate would create additional cost. The municipality would be asked to assume additional debt when it cannot even meet its existing obligations, a step that would probably accelerate its developing financial crisis. Unfortunately, neither the council nor the management staff has the training and experience to recognize that the "low-cost" loan could turn out to be quite expensive. The municipality, reluctant to believe that the infusion of cash would not relieve its budget crisis, continues to search for a sympathetic ear in the national government.

ment elections in 1995. Neighboring white and black urban areas were amalgamated, with the intention that revenues generated in the core cities could be used to extend services to underserved areas. In 1996 a new constitution established a decentralized system of government featuring autonomous local, provincial, and national spheres of government. In 2000 a second step in the consolidation of municipalities reduced the number from 843 to 284 and, in many cases, integrated rural and urban areas.

These 284 new municipalities consist of three groups:

- Local municipalities (232).
- District municipalities (46), which typically include several local municipalities within their borders.
- Metropolitan municipalities (6), which include South Africa's largest cities.

This series of changes has brought clarity and certainty to the institutional framework for the six metropolitan municipalities. For the 278 local and district municipalities, however, which cover the same territory, an important step remains—sorting out their respective powers and functions. Although recent amendments to the Municipal Structures Act have created a legal framework within which district municipalities will eventually provide most services, in many cases services are still provided by local municipalities. By ministerial regulation, legal authority remains mainly with local municipalities for the present time.

How the eventual transfer of responsibility from local to district municipalities will occur, and what it will mean for fiscal powers, are being debated. The uncertainty associated with this ongoing transition makes it difficult for local and district municipalities to plan capital spending strategically and to borrow to finance their capital investment plans.

Local Government Revenues and Expenditures

Municipalities spend a little less than a quarter of the total budgets of all three spheres of the South African government. In the 2000/01 financial year aggregate municipal spending was budgeted at some 61.8 billion rand (R), while national government spending was budgeted at R 84.3 billion, and provincial spending at R 110.5 billion

Municipal revenues in South Africa come from own-source revenues (local government taxes and tariffs) and from intergovernmental transfers, mostly from the national sphere.

Own-Source Revenues

While municipalities generate about 92 percent of their own revenues in the aggregate, the experience of large urban centers differs from that of other municipalities. The six metropolitan municipalities, with strong revenue bases, generate some 97 percent of their own revenues, while municipalities with annual budgets of less than R 300 million generate only 65 percent of their own revenues in the aggregate. Many poor and rural municipalities generate less than 10 percent of their own revenues.

Most of the own-source revenues of municipalities come from tariffs for utility services such as water, sewerage, and solid waste disposal. National policy, reflected in legislation, calls for these services to be self-financing.[1] In some cases they generate a surplus, and in others, losses. Much depends on the ability of the served population to pay and the seriousness with which the municipality pursues collections. Many municipalities provide electricity service to their residents, though this function is to be transferred to new regional service entities. This prospect causes concern among municipalities that make a profit on electricity service or that rely on the threat of cutting it off to collect other taxes and tariffs.

The second biggest source of municipal revenues is the property tax, but this tax is available only to local and metropolitan municipalities. With the December 2000 advent of "wall-to-wall" municipalities, property taxes now may be imposed on essentially all property in the country. This represents a significant expansion of the tax base compared with that of apartheid-era local authorities, which generally included only urban areas. Historically, some municipalities imposed taxes on land value only, though most imposed taxes on both land and improvements, often using different rates. National legislation is expected to soon provide uniform regulations to replace the patchwork of apartheid-era provincial ordinances, but such legislation will leave tax policy decisions largely to local councils.[2]

For district municipalities own-source revenues come mainly from the regional services council levy, a business tax also used by metropolitan municipalities. It is generally recognized that this tax is in need of reform.

Intergovernmental Transfers

The national government transferred some R 6.5 billion to municipalities in the 2000/01 financial year. These transfers, and their share in the national budget, have been increasing and are expected to continue to grow for at least the next three years. The transfers come from many small programs that South Africa's National Treasury has been working to consolidate. There are three basic types of transfers, and ultimately there may be as few as three transfer programs:

- Unconditional transfers, generally determined by a poverty-based formula and often described as subsidies for providing basic municipal services to people who cannot afford to pay the full cost. These transfers account for 57 percent of the national transfers to local government. The largest is the "equitable share" transfer, guaranteed by the Constitution.
- Conditional transfers intended to help municipalities build infrastructure. The largest conditional transfer is the Consolidated Municipal Infrastructure Programme grant. Infrastructure-related transfers make up 35 percent of the national transfers to local governments.
- Conditional transfers intended to help municipalities improve their capacity or restructure their operations. These account for 8 percent of the national transfers to municipalities.

In addition to consolidating the transfer programs, the National Treasury is committed to making the transfers as predictable as possible to facilitate local planning and capital investment decisions. This predictability is particularly important for poor municipalities that rely heavily on national transfers for general operating revenues and, potentially, to secure borrowing.[3]

Provincial transfers to local government, made at the discretion of each province, are less well documented. The total in the 2000/01 financial year was estimated at R 1.2 billion. These transfers are usually tied to arrangements under which a municipality delivers a service on behalf of the province, though they also have been used to provide assistance to financially troubled municipalities.

Role of Municipal Borrowing in Financing Capital Investment

All municipalities in South Africa—metropolitan, district, and local—have infrastructure responsibilities. Municipalities are responsible for local services such as potable water supplies, wastewater and solid waste disposal, city streets and street lighting, and, in many cases, electricity. All these responsibilities require physical facilities, which in turn require capital investment.[4]

Extending services to unserved and underserved areas has received the most attention recently and, given South Africa's history, is the most pressing need. However, at least three other types of investment needs also must be considered. First, services above the basic level must be available to those who can afford to pay for them. Second, if South Africa is to create the conditions for increasing employment and thereby lifting more people out of poverty, well-chosen investments must be made in economic infrastructure that will help generate private direct investment. Third, and often overlooked in current debates, ongoing investment is needed to upgrade infrastructure that has reached the end of its useful life. While some attempt has been made to quantify the "backlog" investment needed to extend services to underserved areas,[5] little has been done to quantify the need for strategic or replacement investment. Even the "backlog" analysis may be of little use; demand for infrastructure probably has no practical limits, and the experience of industrial countries suggests that backlog investment grows in proportion to a country's wealth rather than reaching some theoretical ultimate state.

How are South African municipalities to finance such capital investment if they lack the current resources to do so? Like municipalities elsewhere, they can look for private equity investors, apply for intergovernmental grants, or turn to the municipal debt market.

Private Equity Investment through Public-Private Partnerships

Public-private partnerships are one important channel through which private equity investment can contribute to the provision of local infrastructure. In the three years that South Africa's Municipal Infrastructure Investment Unit has been tracking the local infrastructure sector, projects using public-private partnerships have attracted some R 1.69 billion in private investment (including the projected capital investment over the lifetime of the contracts). The public-private partnerships that South African municipalities recently have entered into can be broadly divided into three groups:

- Short-term partnerships that do not involve capital investment and usually require the municipality to make payments to the contractor for services rendered.
- Long-term partnerships requiring fee payments to the municipality or investment in municipal infrastructure.
- Divestiture arrangements under which the municipality transfers a facility to a private firm, though it may retain some regulatory role.

Notable examples of public-private partnerships have been formed in the municipalities of Nelspruit, Richards Bay, and Johannesburg.

In 1995, as a result of the redrawing of municipal boundaries, Nelspruit's land area increased eightfold and its official population increased tenfold to 240,000, but its income grew by only 38 percent. Many newly incorporated areas had never received water and sanitation services. To extend service to all residents, Nelspruit needed to make large-scale investments in infrastructure. However, many residents of the new areas are very poor and can contribute little toward the cost of new infrastructure. To deal with these problems, in 1999 Nelspruit granted a concession for water and sanitation services, the largest long-term municipal public-private partnership in South Africa. The contract calls for a private firm, the Greater Nelspruit Concession Company, to take over, manage, maintain, build, rehabilitate, and, after 30 years, transfer back to the municipality all of Nelspruit's water and sanitation assets. Every resident is to receive basic service within five years. By early 2002, R 35 million had been invested, but the project has not attracted private finance; most of the funding has been put up by the government-owned Development Bank of Southern Africa. The main barrier to private investment appears to be the possibility that the national government will impose tariff caps. Although the government has never done so, South African legislation provides for this possibility.

In 2000 the municipality of Richards Bay signed a 20-year concession contract for the operation, maintenance, and development of its airport. The contract involves R 13 million in payments to the municipality, which will be used to repay debts associated with the facility. Another R 7 million will probably be invested in upgrading runways, depending on the results of an independent assessment later in the contract period. In addition, 20 percent of the concession firm's equity and 20 percent of its dividends will go to a trust fund for the development and support of local communities, particularly traditional communities near the airport.

In 2000 Johannesburg sold Metro Gas, a gas distribution business serving approximately 15,000 business and residential customers, to U.S.-based Cinergy Global Power for R 110 million. The new owner is expected to invest another R 276 million in the facility over 10 years, making the deal arguably the biggest municipal privatization in South Africa.

Experience has shown that the ability of municipalities to make wise and effective use of public-private partnerships depends on their ability to identify and articulate their needs, negotiate with potential partners, live up to the commitments they make in their agreements,[6] and manage the contracts they establish with private service providers. Local politics in South Africa, as elsewhere, can be turbulent, and public-private contracts have sometimes become political touchstones. Implementing any public-private partnership necessarily involves some tension between the municipal council's short-term interests in keeping tariffs low and service levels high, and the concessionaire's interest in earning a return for investors, so it is essential that contracts be clear and thorough. It is also critical that key decisions related to the partnership—such as tariff and collection policy—have broad support from the community. Finally, it is important that the community be able to give the private investor reasonable assurances, based on the community's legal standing and the commercial viability of the services involved, that the revenue streams for repaying the investment will be adequate.

The prognosis for private equity projects in South Africa is unclear. For investors, it may depend on South Africa's willingness to clarify tariff issues.[7] It also will depend on whether a significant number of municipal projects can be identified that will generate reliable cash flows. For municipalities, policy considerations may come into play, with some municipal councils preferring to retain ownership and control over essential municipal assets. For others, political interests may be at stake. South Africa's powerful labor unions, for example, often see public-private partnerships as a threat. All these limitations suggest that public-private partnerships will provide only a fraction of the investments needed—and that most infrastructure investment must be funded from other resources.

Intergovernmental Transfers for Infrastructure

In the 2000/01 financial year the national government provided only about R 2.4 billion in infrastructure transfers to local government. Infrastructure grants are made through a number of separate (generally sectoral) programs and are tied to specific projects. South Africa's National Treasury is committed to consolidating these grant programs and allowing municipalities more discretion in deciding how to allocate funds and what infrastructure they most need to build, and efforts to ensure this are under way. The aim is to avoid the bottlenecks and unintended results that sometimes have occurred under the current system, which may make grants available for extending one service to an area but not other services.

With the consolidation of these grant programs into one or two, it might be possible to reshape the infrastructure transfers into predictable revenue streams that the municipalities could then leverage through borrowing. In contrast to lump sum grants, this approach would allow more municipalities to receive simultaneous streams of revenue, helping the local government sphere build infrastructure more quickly.

Municipal Borrowing

Public-private partnerships will clearly finance only a fraction of South Africa's infrastructure investment needs in the foreseeable future. Infrastructure transfers are also small relative to investment needs. In most cases, therefore, municipalities will have to finance infrastructure from taxes and tariffs. Borrowing against these revenue streams, and possibly against infrastructure transfer streams as well, would allow municipalities to build infrastructure more quickly and distribute the financial burden more equitably across the generations that will use it.

South African municipalities generally understand that borrowing is not a new or separate source of revenue and that borrowed capital and interest must be repaid with revenues from taxes, tariffs, and intergovernmental transfers. The good news is that municipalities in South Africa, unlike those in many other African countries, have significant recurring revenue streams available for leveraging. Borrowing, provided it is done wisely, can help these municipalities deliver tangibly on the promise of democracy.

The South African policy on municipal borrowing, as laid out in the government's 1998 *White Paper on Local Government* and its 2000 *Policy*

Framework for Municipal Borrowing and Financial Emergencies, clearly calls for such borrowing to be based on a market system, with lenders pricing credit to reflect the perceived risks.

Potential Size of the Municipal Debt Market. Outstanding long-term municipal debt (to the public and private sector) in South Africa was estimated to be around R 19 billion by mid-1997. Though relatively stable for years, this figure declined slightly after June 2000, in the run-up to the December 2000 municipal elections. In the aggregate, municipalities clearly have the financial capacity to responsibly service a great deal more long-term debt.

Quantifying the potential size of the South African municipal debt market is inevitably a speculative exercise, but some indication of that size can be gleaned from municipal capital budgets. For the 2000/01 financial year these totaled some R 13.7 billion. Budgeted amounts may be higher than actual spending, but the previous year's actual capital expenditures are estimated at R 10.3 billion. If half of all capital spending were debt financed and the other half "pay as you go," this would suggest a potential debt service capacity of R 5.1–6.8 billion a year.

Based on these debt service capacity figures and a 10 to 12 percent annual interest rate on 20-year financing (a reasonable rate for low-risk debt in the South African capital market), total municipal debt capacity could be expected to be between R 38 billion and R 85 billion—two to four times the current outstanding debt of South African municipalities in 2000. If municipal budgets continue to grow, debt service capacity also will grow. Naturally, much depends on assumptions about interest rates, the term of the debt, and the degree of leverage. Still, it is not unreasonable to conclude that the financial capacity of South African municipalities could support a municipal debt market around three times the current size.

Trends in Municipal Borrowing. Actual lending in the municipal sector, however, has fallen far short of the performance that these figures imply. Long-term private lending to South Africa's municipalities has been essentially flat for at least four years. National Treasury data, collected since 1997, show that municipal debt owed to the private sector generally remained between R 11 billion and R 12 billion during 1997–2000. At the same time debt owed to public sector institutions, including the Development Bank of Southern Africa, grew significantly, from R 5.6 billion to R 8.1 billion (figure 18.1).

This increasing reliance on public sector lending to municipalities is worrisome given South Africa's goal of expanding private investment. The

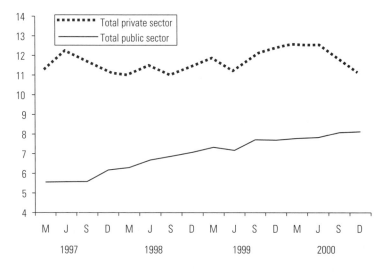

Source: South African National Treasury.

Figure 18.1 Outstanding Municipal Debt, South Africa, 1997-2000 (billions of rand)

Development Bank of Southern Africa accounted for more than 30 percent of outstanding municipal debt by the end of 2000, a share that had nearly doubled since 1997. Most of its portfolio is with large, relatively robust metropolitan municipalities. Several of these municipalities have reported recent price competition by the Development Bank for their borrowing needs in cases where private lenders have been ready and willing to lend. In the short term, having a discount lender willing to "beat any price in town" because of historical or current advantages conferred on it by the state (such as a lower cost of capital) is advantageous for municipal borrowers. In the long term, however, this will undermine the development of private lending. Private lenders will have no incentive to spend time considering a potential loan if they are consistently undercut by a government-owned lender.

Most new private lending since 1997/98 originated through a single specialized entity, the Infrastructure Corporation of Africa. The company's appetite for debt, through originating new loans and acquiring existing debt, has helped offset the exit from the market by other actors, and its market share has grown even faster than that of the Development Bank of Southern Africa. Like the bank, the Infrastructure Corporation of Africa extends most of its municipal loans to large metropolitan municipalities. Together, the two institutions now account for about half of all outstanding municipal debt. Insurance companies have sold most of their municipal debt holdings, and pension funds have cut theirs significantly. This increasing concentration of municipal debt stock in the hands of a few lenders does not bode well for the South African government's goal of "a vibrant and innovative primary and secondary market for short- and long-term municipal debt" (South Africa 1998).

Another undesirable trend is the changing nature of the debt stock. Municipal securities, which are (at least potentially) freely tradable on South Africa's capital markets, have steadily declined, while loans, which are less mobile and generally remain in the originator's portfolio, have increased markedly (figure 18.2). Because securities can be traded, term risk is lessened where there is a market for the bondholder to sell the bond if neces-

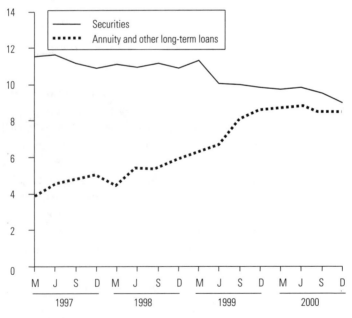

Source: South African National Treasury.

Figure 18.2 Outstanding Municipal Debt by Form, South Africa, 1997–2000 (billions of rand)

sary. This liquidity brings more potential investors into the picture, which is highly desirable in South Africa.

The shift to loans can be attributed to two main factors. First, the reliable and public accounting, budgeting, and financial information that investors and rating agencies need is not readily available for most municipalities. Thus investors' due diligence requires analysis and often proprietary recasting of municipal financial statements. That leads to high transaction costs in originating loans and transferring them among investors. This situation favors large, specialized investors with experience lending to municipalities over casual investors that otherwise might be willing to buy a relatively small amount of rated municipal debt as part of their portfolios.[8]

Second, there is a lack of clear remedies in a municipal default, and some institutional investors have dealt with this legal gap by structuring highly secured loans that are specific to the originating institution.[9] Some of these specialized structures could be securitized, but the excess of capital supply over municipal demand means that there is little incentive to go to the effort.

Assessment

This discussion raises an obvious question: Why has such a large discrepancy arisen between the potential size of the municipal debt market and actual lending activity? If there is so much scope for additional borrowing, why has it not happened? Four main factors appear to be responsible.

Local Government Reform

Local government in South Africa has been subjected to continuous reform since 1994, a process that has involved all key parts of the sector—institutional, fiscal, and organizational. Two aspects of this reform have affected municipal lending activity. First, the process of change has created a great deal of uncertainty for investors, discouraging exposure to municipal risk. Second, some of the reforms themselves, such as those related to boundary demarcation, have adversely affected the structural basis of many municipalities' financial positions (depressing ratios of revenue to population, for example), reducing their credit capacity. While the effects have been relatively minor for large metropolitan areas, they have been significant for many secondary cities and towns, which previously had been viable credit risks and which, after the metropolitan municipalities, represented the largest sector of the market for municipal credit.

Thus both the fact of continuous reform and the nature of that reform have curbed lending. That is not to argue against such reforms. However, it does suggest that the impact of the reform and the length of the process can have long-lasting adverse effects on the ability of local governments to finance and deliver much-needed infrastructure and that such reform should be carefully assessed and guided in light of these effects.

Budgetary Performance and Financial Management

A combination of poor budgetary performance and weak financial management has undermined the creditworthiness of a significant number of local authorities in South Africa. Some local governments are well managed and pursue disciplined fiscal policies. However, these tend to be the exceptions, and poor fiscal management and discipline are common throughout the municipal sector, even in the larger urban centers. Johannesburg, for example, ran into major financial difficulties in the second half of the 1990s, though its performance has since improved considerably. Many municipalities run budget deficits—while disguising them with formal budgets that unrealistically inflate revenues to achieve budget "balance" as required by law. Most municipalities have limited human resources and systems capacity and a flawed municipal accounting system that undermines their ability to provide financial data that investors can regard with confidence.

Legal and Regulatory Framework for Municipal Borrowing

South Africa still has not enacted a sound, comprehensive legal and regulatory framework for municipal borrowing. Uncertainties relating to processes and the rights and recourses of borrowers and lenders in the municipal sector remain, discouraging lending. For example, because rich, white local authorities rarely defaulted on debts under the apartheid regime, and because municipal debts were viewed as guaranteed by the national and provincial governments, South Africa's law on remedies in the event of municipal defaults is underdeveloped. This has led to prolonged uncertainty and ineffective remedies in some recent municipal financial crises. Work initiated in 1998 to develop a comprehensive municipal borrowing framework resulted in a "best-practice" policy framework and draft legislation promulgated by the Cabinet in mid-2000. Constitutional and political difficulties, however, halted the progress of this legislation, and by early 2003 it still had not been enacted.

Activities of Public Sector Lenders

The Development Bank of Southern Africa has advantages over private lenders as a result of its connection to the government and its ability to compete directly with these institutions for municipal clients. These advantages have led to complaints that the bank is "squeezing out" such players from the market and thereby suppressing the development of private activity in the sector.

Challenges

Beyond the four factors discussed in the previous section, others also may have played some part in stifling the development of the municipal debt market in South Africa, such as high real interest rates and poor capital planning by local authorities. In early 2003 there were several reasons to hope that South African municipalities' access to private credit could improve in the short to medium term:

- The December 2000 demarcations resolved long-pending amalgamation and boundary questions. The division of functions between local and district municipalities still needs to be clarified if they are to access capital markets autonomously. However, for metropolitan municipalities (and for local and district municipalities willing to cooperate on debt issues), the chronic uncertainty relating to boundaries is over.
- The December 2000 municipal elections put municipal councils in place for five-year terms. This placed councils in an excellent strategic position to assess their infrastructure needs and debt capacity and plan for the responsible use of debt as part of their strategies for service delivery and economic development.
- South Africa's National Treasury has begun providing three-year indicative allocations for most intergovernmental transfer programs. For municipalities that cannot rely on own-source revenues from taxes and tariffs, predictability in intergovernmental transfers is key. Clear indications of future transfers could enable these municipalities to access credit at whatever scale fits their capital needs.
- A November 2001 constitutional amendment empowers municipal councils to make legally binding commitments relating to future budgets and revenues that will secure debt. Before this amendment,

the weight of legal opinion was that a municipal council could not make such binding commitments, a restriction that would clearly limit investors' willingness to invest in long-term municipal debt.

- Legislation to give effect to the government's policy framework on municipal borrowing, including in the event of municipal default, is included in the Municipal Finance Management Bill, which was approved by South Africa's Cabinet in 2001 and was due to be enacted in 2003.

All these factors point to a potential for significant expansion of South Africa's municipal debt market. Three main challenges must be addressed if this is to occur.

Finalizing the Legal Framework

South Africa's government set out a clear vision for a legal framework for municipal borrowing in its 1998 *White Paper on Local Government* and its 2000 *Policy Framework for Municipal Borrowing and Financial Emergencies*, but not all the policies described in these documents have been enacted into law. The most important legislation is the Municipal Finance Management Bill. This bill has three key parts:

- *Finance management.* The bill regulates the budgeting, accounting, and financial reporting of local governments, requiring clear and consistently formatted information about municipalities' financial condition. This information should facilitate municipal borrowing by enabling lenders, rating agencies, and other players to make investment decisions more quickly and efficiently.
- *Borrowing.* The bill regulates short- and long-term municipal borrowing, implementing the elements of the government's policy framework that relate to borrowing. Key provisions of the bill limit short-term borrowing to cash flow management within the financial year; limit long-term borrowing to financing property, plant, and equipment; and allow municipal councils, under certain conditions, to pledge assets and future revenue streams to secure debt. A constitutional amendment paving the way for these security provisions was adopted by Parliament in November 2001.
- *Financial emergencies.* The bill creates a process, including an agency within the National Treasury, to deal with municipalities in financial crisis, implementing the financial emergency provisions of the policy

framework. The goal is to restore a municipality to financial health as soon as possible while balancing the interests of citizens, the municipal council, creditors, and other stakeholders. It remains to be seen whether the provisions of the bill, once enacted, will provide a framework that is sufficiently robust and efficient to build investor confidence in municipal debt.

In addition to enacting the Municipal Finance Management Bill, a few other loose ends need to be taken care of if South Africa is to create a legislative framework that enables municipalities to freely access private credit. These include the following:

- Drafting disclosure regulations and providing mechanisms for disseminating information. If active trading in municipal securities is to occur, potential buyers of municipal bonds must have ready access to reliable information that is material to investment decisions.
- Clarifying the ability of municipalities to commit to future tariffs or to tariff setting mechanisms. The recent constitutional amendment may help, but uncertainties remain. The tariff capping provisions of the Water Services Act and Municipal Systems Act that are troublesome to private equity investors are of concern to debt investors.
- Clarifying the powers and functions of local and district municipalities in a way that limits the potential for future uncertainty and change.
- Reviewing old legislation for inconsistency with policy and revising it where necessary.[10]

Strengthening Local Government Capacity and the Budget Culture

Some South African municipalities prepare and use capital and operating budgets and financial reports. Only a few, however, have developed comprehensive capital investment programs that address their needs since the December 2000 amalgamations. These basic planning and accounting processes should be in place before a municipality goes to the capital markets, because any municipality considering infrastructure borrowing should be in a position to understand how debt service and operational expenses for infrastructure will affect its budget. The municipality must be able to realistically project the revenue from the new investment. To achieve efficiencies and plan strategically, the municipality should be able to analyze different infrastructure options and financing scenarios. Municipalities that lack these skills are not equipped to make the best decisions for their community. Both municipal councilors and managers need these skills, though at different levels of detail. A council that can ask the right questions is more likely to get the information it needs to make good decisions.

The December 2000 amalgamations exacerbated the effects of the lack of financial experience and capacity in some municipalities. This round of urban-rural consolidation blended an average of three municipalities and significant unincorporated territory into one new local municipality. This change meant that the new municipalities would have to consolidate financial information of varying quality from several sources, a process that could take a year or more. Even then it would be several years before municipalities or potential investors could discern trends in revenues or expenses. Ultimately, municipalities that want to borrow at reasonable rates, and have a choice of investors, must be able to produce a reliable record of financial performance.

The amalgamations also pose a challenge in identifying capital needs. Most municipalities include newly incorporated areas whose infrastructure needs must be considered systematically as well as previously incorporated areas whose needs must be reprioritized in the context of the new municipality. South Africa's Municipal Systems Act requires municipalities to develop integrated development plans that include capital plans. However, many municipalities have not yet completed integrated development plans; among the plans that have been developed, not all are of high quality or represent a true community consensus on needs and priorities.

Another concern is the "culture of nonpayment" in some parts of South Africa, a legacy of resistance from the apartheid era. In a few municipalities council members have encouraged citizens not to pay their tariffs and taxes. In many more, council members have failed to take the lead in helping citizens understand the need to pay for services. The practice of budgeting realistically and spending within the limits of available resources must become embedded in both the political and the management cultures of local government in South Africa.

Many of South Africa's municipalities need sustained technical assistance, training, and experience to identify their capital needs and financing options and to effectively articulate their need for credit. To borrow wisely and efficiently and to be able to pay their debts when due, municipalities in South Africa, like those everywhere, must have strong skills in the following areas:

- Budgeting and accounting.
- Identifying, analyzing, and prioritizing community needs.
- Planning an appropriate mix and sequence of projects and funding options.
- Developing specifications suitable for competitive procurement of construction and financing.
- Managing procurement issues.
- Managing projects during and after construction.
- Marketing the municipality, its projects, and its debt instruments to investors.
- Legal drafting and negotiation.

Developing these skills will take time and effort, but the payoff will be good government, well-chosen projects, and appropriate financing. Shortcuts could result in poor projects, expensive financing, and little support in local communities or the country as a whole for further municipal borrowing.

Foreign and domestic development agencies seeking to make a sustainable contribution to South Africa's municipalities would do well to consider mentoring and support to develop these basic skills. South Africa's National Treasury has launched a pilot program that is bringing experienced municipal finance managers from other countries to work with their South African colleagues. These managers will stay for one to two years, helping to get newly amalgamated municipalities' budgets and accounts in order and into compliance with the reporting requirements of the Municipal Finance Management Bill. This kind of ground-level support and capacity building is essential for financially healthy municipalities, for sound, information-based local policy decisions, and for wise borrowing.

Facing South Africa's Ambivalence about Markets

These challenges—dealing with imperfections in the legal framework and building municipal capacity—will be familiar to anyone who has worked on municipal debt policy anywhere. A more difficult issue needing to be addressed in South Africa is the society's ambivalence about the market-oriented policies being pursued. This ambivalence mirrors, and is reinforced by, global debates about economic integration and deregulation.

South Africans have mixed feelings about their private financial institutions. Many are proud of their "first-world" capabilities. The South African economy boasts well-functioning stock and bond markets, commercial and investment banks, insurance companies, rating agencies, and regulatory bodies. Many others, however, see these institutions, which developed under an oppressive regime, as instruments and beneficiaries of that repression. A deep-seated mistrust of capitalism and resentment of the role that some capitalists played in the apartheid era persist in some quarters. This history has made it difficult for many South Africans to embrace market-oriented financial institutions.[11]

Although government policy endorses the need to attract private finance, there is little confidence that the private sector will come to the table.[12] There are concerns that private lending to subnational governments will develop slowly or not at all, even if the correct policies are put into place and the necessary capacity built. Moreover, there are concerns that even if markets provide finance for large and financially secure municipalities, small and poor municipalities will be left out.

These concerns have had several consequences. First, they have made it difficult for the government to push the necessary legislation and constitutional amendments through Parliament as quickly as had been hoped. Second, concerns about the reliability of financial markets have led some in government to consider various forms of artificial stimulus for subnational borrowing, including national government guarantees and debt insurance sponsored by the Development Bank of Southern Africa. Third, there is some support within the South African government for nonmarket approaches to subnational debt—such as government on-lending—especially for provincial governments (there is presently no provincial borrowing in South Africa, which is effectively prohibited).

These nonmarket approaches would probably prove problematic in execution. With both direct government lending and guarantees, there will inevitably be defaults, imposing future costs on the national government. These contingent costs are difficult to predict and quantify. Governments throughout the world have a poor record of managing loans to subnational borrowers—the rate of default on government or government-guaranteed loans usually exceeds that on commercial loans to the same entities. Another concern is that shifting private investors' focus from the creditworthiness of the borrower or the project to the creditworthiness of the national government will result in loans being made to subnational governments that cannot afford them, increasing their financial stress. These cures for market imperfections could easily be worse than the disease.

South Africa's ambivalence about markets, while understandable given the country's history, must be overcome if its municipalities are to attract private investment. Choosing the route of relying on capital markets would mean that the focus would have to be on improving the framework, skills, and information that those markets need to function effectively. Maintaining this focus will be more difficult than taking shortcuts such as guarantees, but it will be a more sustainable and strategic choice.

Notes

1. Municipal Systems Act, No. 32 of 2000. See especially subsection 74(2).

2. A draft Property Rates Bill was published for comment in August 2000 and is likely to be adopted in 2003.

3. These transfers must be both well targeted and predictable. But there can be a tension between these two goals. As new information becomes available that would help improve targeting, the equity of adjusting targeting must be weighed against the need to ensure that commitments can be met for infrastructure that has been begun or financed in good faith.

4. With some minor exceptions, municipalities in South Africa are not responsible for social services (such as health and education), which are provided by provinces, or for policing, which is a national function.

5. The 1996 Municipal Infrastructure Investment Framework estimated the basic need at R 38.5 billion and the full service need at R 75 billion.

6. In some cases politicians and activists have actively discouraged residents from paying utility bills, and councils have been reluctant to cut off service to enforce payment. In Fort Beaufort the municipality sued to void the concession agreement and was successful in setting aside the contract.

7. The Water Services Act provides that the minister for water affairs and forestry can regulate municipal tariffs for water services. The Municipal Systems Act provides similar authority to the minister for provincial and local government with respect to all municipal services. The potential for such regulations to interfere with negotiated arrangements between a municipality and a concessionaire limits investor interest in revenue-based public-private partnerships in South Africa.

8. The apartheid-era local authorities that issued the now-disappearing securities did not necessarily have good-quality financial information either. However, with their financial strength and implicit national and provincial support, their bonds were seen as safe investments for individuals and institutions.

9. Examples include tax-structured transactions in which a financial institution benefits from depreciation on municipal assets; pledges by munic-

ipalities to banks of property tax revenues derived from the banks' own property; and deposits by municipalities with financial institutions that, with interest, equal the principal amount of the loan at maturity, protecting investors' principal.

10. Buried legislation creates an entry barrier, at least to the uninitiated. Recently a financial institution that had not previously lent to South African municipalities negotiated a loan with one of the country's biggest cities. The lender commissioned a South African law firm to review the applicable legislation. The firm found a Transvaal ordinance from 1903 and an unused exchange control regulation that required National Treasury approval of the proposed loan. Existing lenders to the municipality, either unaware of or unconcerned by these laws, had never asked for Treasury approval, and Treasury did not want to be in a position of approving—and perhaps implicitly endorsing—local borrowing decisions.

11. Investors from such countries as the United Kingdom and the United States are not necessarily viewed more favorably. While it is accepted that foreign investors found the stigma of white racism unappealing, they are nevertheless seen as benefiting from the perceived stability and low labor costs of that era, and their investments in South Africa as propping up the apartheid regime.

12. In an interesting contrast, in Eastern Europe and the former Soviet Union a broad perception that communism had failed left the typical person willing to accept more market-oriented solutions. In South Africa capitalism was seen as part of the problem, and the expected coming of democracy was often linked to diminution of the power of capitalists.

Chapter 19

Sub-Saharan Africa
Zimbabwe

*A centrally prescribed and unsustainable credit market
succumbs to political and economic turmoil.*

Roland White and Matthew Glaser

Lessons

Although Zimbabwe neighbors South Africa, its recent experience in local government borrowing is very different from that
country's. In Zimbabwe local government borrowing has been
premised on a policy and regulatory regime—most evident in
central government guarantees and prescribed assets for institutional investors—that is inimical to the development of sustainable municipal credit markets. The country's two largest
cities have been able to successfully issue a limited volume of
securities for many years, but this has come at the cost of accumulating liabilities for the central government and significant financial losses for investors. When a default by Harare in 1998
prompted the government to withdraw its implicit guarantee of
local bond issues, interest rates immediately jumped, making
local government borrowing prohibitively expensive. Not until
2001 did the central government again begin to underwrite mu-

---

nicipal debt issues, this time explicitly. Moral hazard has thus become embedded in the subnational lending system.

The economic and political crisis that Zimbabwe now confronts makes it difficult to talk about prospects for sustainable subnational borrowing in the country. The most recent bond issues suggest that borrowing has ceased to be an affordable source of funding for long-term investment programs. The policy and regulatory environment for subnational borrowing in Zimbabwe has fostered a "false" municipal bond market in which investors rely on the financial position of the central government rather than the creditworthiness of the municipal issuer. The sustainability problems that this has created have been greatly exacerbated by the deterioration in the country's economic and political climate.

Starting in early 2001 economic and political conditions in Zimbabwe began to deteriorate dramatically. In February 2002 the official annualized inflation rate stood at around 110 percent, GDP had shrunk by 5 percent over the previous year, and one in four jobs in the formal economy had disappeared. Under conditions such as these, the prospects for sustainable, cost-effective subnational borrowing are remote. Whether the municipal finance market will regain any of the momentum it began to show in the 1990s—though in a problematic policy environment—remains unclear.

Institutional Framework for the Financial Sector

Until recently Zimbabwe had a relatively stable financial system based on a long tradition of high savings and a well-diversified financial sector. Complementing the substantial and relatively sophisticated banking system are near-banks (nonbank financial institutions), insurance and pension funds, a well-established stock market, and a range of other market participants. The system has become increasingly competitive, though with a growing amount of risk. The government's National Economic Structural Adjustment Program, implemented in the early 1990s, introduced some economic deregulation, enhancing competition, allowing market conditions to influence financial prices, and increasing the diversity of market participants and financial services (World Bank 1998). During the 1990s assets held by deposit-taking institutions grew significantly in real terms (table 19.1).

Financial Institutions and Instruments

The financial sector remains segmented, with legal restrictions on the kinds of transactions that different types of institutions can undertake.

- *Commercial banks.* The seven commercial banks in operation in 1999 were the largest institutions in the banking system. At that time they held 32 percent of the assets in the financial system and 60 percent of loans and advances, and 49 percent of deposits, in the banking system. Permitted to undertake most types of financial intermediation (except financial leasing and hire purchase), commercial banks are important lenders to subnational governments for short-term facilities, such as overdrafts and bridge financing.
- *Merchant banks.* With six existing in 1999, merchant banks perform the second largest volume of financial intermediation but cannot offer checking accounts. They tend to cater to larger enterprises by providing tailored services and trade financing.
- *Discount houses.* There were six discount houses in 1999. Their primary role is to act as a market maker for commercial and merchant bank liquidity and as the main receiver and dealer of treasury bills from the central bank, the Reserve Bank of Zimbabwe. (Until 1999 dis-

Table 19.1. Assets of Deposit-Taking Institutions, Zimbabwe, 1992–97 (millions of Zimbabwe dollars)

Type of institution	1992	1993	1994	1995	1996	1997 (Sept.)
Commercial banks	8,062	14,900	20,275	24,669	32,648	40,533
Merchant banks	1,961	6,126	7,756	10,361	17,051	18,349
Discount houses	716	1,347	1,674	3,781	3,161	2,958
Finance houses	1,491	1,498	1,908	2,866	4,270	5,420
Building societies	2,916	3,892	5,808	10,088	13,843	15,666
Post Office Savings Bank	2,315	2,977	3,662	4,466	6,227	6,927
Total	17,460	30,740	41,082	56,230	77,200	89,852

Source: Reserve Bank of Zimbabwe 1997.

count houses had exclusive access to the Reserve Bank and would purchase treasury bills and rediscount them into the rest of the financial market. Now, however, all financial institutions have access to the Reserve Bank.) The discount houses play an important market-making role in the municipal finance market, assisting subnational governments in issuing long-term bonds for capital development. In 2001 one of the discount houses was licensed to assist local authorities in seeking funding for infrastructure and to create a market for local government securities (such as municipal bonds and municipal treasury bills). Discount houses held around 3.3 percent of the assets of deposit-taking institutions in 1997.

- *Finance houses.* The four finance houses existing in 1999 function largely as fixed asset financing arms of commercial banks, financing equipment and vehicle loans and collateralized lending. The finance houses hold about 3.1 percent of the assets in the financial system (excluding the Reserve Bank of Zimbabwe).
- *Building societies.* There were five building societies in 1999. These institutions accept share, savings, and fixed deposits and negotiable certificates of deposit. They lend for residential and commercial mortgages, purchase treasury bills, provide other loans to the government, place funds in the money market, and finance low-income housing projects. In 1997 they held approximately 17 percent of the assets in deposit-taking institutions.
- *Post Office Savings Bank.* A government-owned institution, the Post Office Savings Bank mobilizes funds from small savers throughout the country and offers both savings and fixed deposit facilities. In 1997 it held 7.7 percent of the assets in deposit-taking institutions.
- *Development finance corporations.* The development finance corporations specialize in term financing, often with support from the government or donors. These include the Agricultural Finance Corporation, Zimbabwe Development Bank, and Small Enterprises Development Corporation.

Instruments traded in the market include treasury bills and government bonds, bank acceptances, certificates of deposit, and a limited amount of commercial paper. Treasury bills dominate the market and have had a crowding-out effect on competing investments. Maturities range from 30 to 91 days for treasury bills and from 1 to 16 years for fixed-income debt stock.

Prescribed Assets Regime

The government of Zimbabwe, to regulate interest rates in its favor, has maintained a "prescribed assets" regime. Institutional investors (pension funds and insurance companies) in Zimbabwe are required to keep 45 percent of their holdings in prescribed assets, which have generally included long-term bonds (with maturities of more than six years) of the central government, parastatals, and local governments (this share has been reduced from 55 percent in 1997 and 65 percent before that).[1] This requirement originally had some validity, as a way to ensure safe investments by financial institutions. However, its continued use guarantees the public sector preferential access to domestic financial markets.

Throughout the 1990s there were insufficient prescribed assets in the market to satisfy the statutory requirements. This, coupled with the government guarantee implicit in the prescribed asset requirements, has made pricing these assets difficult. A recent World Bank (1998) review of the financial sector concluded that

> . . . [T]he contradiction between investors holding fewer prescribed assets than required and the inability of [the] Government to place long-term stock suggests that market participants are reticent to hold long-term instruments except at very high yields and [that the] Government is reticent to pay such a premium for long-term funds.

The availability of prescribed assets has tended to fluctuate. During shortages municipal bonds, for example, have often been oversubscribed when first issued, depressing interest rates (Phelps 1997). There is no secondary bond market in Zimbabwe because most institutional investors find it difficult to meet the required 45 percent share for prescribed assets and therefore adopt a "buy-and-hold" strategy.

Intergovernmental Structure

Zimbabwe has a two-tier system of elected government: the central government (with line functions devolved to both the provincial and the district level) and local governments. The local governments consist of 57 rural district councils and 23 urban councils—city and town councils, town boards, and local boards.

The councils are elected on the basis of ward constituencies, with all adults having the right to vote. Their functions and responsibilities are set out in the Rural District Councils Act and the Urban Councils Act. Local governments are responsible for administering the areas under their jurisdiction. However, the central government maintains strategic control of boundaries and the hiring and firing of local government senior staff.

The urban councils have a broad range of responsibilities—street lighting, street cleaning, physical planning, emergency services, municipal police, low-cost housing, primary education, primary health care, solid waste management, road maintenance and expansion, and water and sewerage services. They also operate enterprises, including farms and beer gardens.

Subnational Funding Sources

Local authorities have three main sources of funds for financing current and capital expenditure: internal revenues, external revenues, and borrowing.

Internal Revenues

Local governments derive internal revenues primarily from taxes and service charges. They do not have complete autonomy over these revenue sources: to increase taxes, property assessments, and service charges for low-income areas, local governments must obtain the approval of the minister of local government, whose ministry oversees their operations on behalf of the central government.

- *Assessment rates and supplementary charges.* Assessment rates, applied to the ratable value of property within the municipal boundaries, are levied on commercial properties and on residential properties in high-income areas. Flat unit charges on properties (known as "supplementary charges") are levied on residential properties in low-income areas. Any increases of more than 20 percent in either of the charges must receive prior approval by the minister of local government, often leading to delays that result in revenue shortfalls. Assessment rates and supplementary charges account for around 20 percent of subnational income.
- *General service revenue.* Local authorities generate increasing revenues from charges for "economically viable" services, such as sewerage and refuse collection. Sewerage contributes around 7 percent of subnational income, refuse removal and housing income around 6 percent each, and income from health and welfare and other general services around 24 percent.

- *Trading income.* Profits from water distribution are by far the largest source of trading income. Some councils also run such trading operations as farms and beer gardens, although these typically contribute only a minor share of budgets.
- *Other internal revenue sources.* From time to time local authorities also derive income from the sale of fixed property, primarily land.

External Revenues

External revenues come through intergovernmental transfers, which have recently declined precipitously to insignificant levels (table 19.2). In transferring responsibility for health care services to local authorities, for example, the central government initially agreed to fund a share of the salary costs through grants. Within a year, however, these grants had ceased to flow, and the health funds of local authorities now operate at significant deficits.

In general, intergovernmental transfers are a much less important source of revenue for larger, urban councils than for rural councils. Harare, for example, received no intergovernmental transfers in 1995–97, and for Kwekwe such transfers accounted for less than 1 percent of revenue during that time.

Borrowing

Local authorities can turn to three main sources for borrowing:

- *Government loans.* Government loans have accounted for around 90 percent of local authorities' total borrowing for capital development over the past two decades. The funds for these loans have been obtained mostly from aid agencies, then on-lent to local authorities at

**Table 19.2. Local Government Revenues by Source, Zimbabwe, 1995–98
(percentage of total)**

Revenue source	1995	1996	1997	1998
Assessment rates and supplementary charges	24	25	22	31
General services	35	44	36	56
Trading income	22	7	6	8
Intergovernmental transfers	18	24	35	6

Source: Zimbabwe Central Statistical Office accounts.

concessional rates through the General Loan Development Fund and National Housing Fund.

- *Bank overdrafts and short-term loan finance.* Overdrafts and short-term borrowings are capped at the local authority's income from rates in the previous year (unless otherwise authorized by the minister of local government) and are intended to be temporary. These funds may be used for capital expenditure only if borrowing power for that expenditure has been obtained from both the Ministry of Finance and the Ministry of Local Government. Between 1994 and 1997 subnational revenue grew by 26 percent while outstanding debt grew by 78 percent. Much of this deficit is being financed by overdraft facilities.
- *Long-term finance.* Local authorities can raise long-term finance from private investors by issuing bonds or by borrowing directly from financial intermediaries, including the Local Authorities Pension Fund.

Local Government Borrowing

The Urban Councils Act and Rural District Councils Act provide broad borrowing powers to local governments. Local governments are permitted to borrow for capital works or improvements, acquisition of fixed property, certain kinds of advances, payment of compensation (excluding that for permanent employees), liquidation of previous loans, relief of general distress (caused by a natural disaster, for example), and acquisition of plant, equipment, and vehicles.

Regulation and Oversight

Before a local government can borrow, however, the local council must pass a formal resolution of its intention to borrow, give public notice of its intention, including the purpose for which the borrowed funds will be used, and invite comments from its constituents. Before borrowing from the central government, the Local Authorities Pension Fund, a municipal provident fund, a medical aid society, or another local authority, the council must obtain permission from the Ministries of Local Government, Public Construction, and National Housing. If the council intends to issue bonds, stock, or debentures, it must obtain authority from the Ministries of Finance and Local Government. Four of Zimbabwe's five major cities—Harare, Bulawayo, Gweru, and Kwekwe—have issued bonds in local capital markets. Indeed, Harare and Bulawayo have been raising bond finance since the late 1960s or early 1970s. By contrast, short-term overdraft facilities require central government approval if they exceed the previous year's income from rates.

The requirement for central government approval, along with the prescribed assets regime, has provided a foundation for the primary market for municipal debt in Zimbabwe because it has led to a market assumption of an implicit central government guarantee of such debt. The phrasing of issues has often reinforced this impression. For example, the prospectus prepared by Kwekwe for its 1998 issue stated that "[w]hile the Government does not explicitly guarantee this stock issue, it has the moral responsibility to ensure that the local authority meets its external obligations." Prud'homme (1999, p. 14) has argued that the local government bond market in Zimbabwe is really a "false" market in which "[f]or all practical purposes, municipal bonds . . . are basically a variety of central government bonds, and are seen as such by the financial community."

Borrowing Trends

Faced with deteriorating revenue bases and increasingly unfunded mandates in the social sectors, local governments have been forced to increase their debt over time (table 19.3). Of the total debt, an average of 47 percent is held in bond issues in the domestic markets (registered stock) and 53 percent is from other sources (including the central government and private sources, such as the Local Government Pension Fund). Long-term borrowing from private financial institutions is therefore an important source of finance, particularly for the five largest councils (table 19.4).

Table 19.3. Gross Public Debt of Local Authorities, Zimbabwe, 1994–97 (millions of Zimbabwe dollars)

	1994	1995	1996	1997
Long-term borrowing	1,376.7	1,559.4	1,767.5	2,293.4
Registered bonds	553.5	543.5	629.5	815.6
Central government	713.4	871.1	945.6	1,287.4
Private	109.7	144.8	192.4	190.4
Short-term borrowing	4.8	50.7	43.8	169.5
Total	1,381.5	1,610.1	1,811.3	2,462.9

Source: Zimbabwe Central Statistical Office 1999.

Table 19.4. Bond Issues by Local Governments, Zimbabwe, 1990–2001

Year	City	Issues	Total amount (millions of Zimbabwe dollars)	Total amount (millions of U.S. dollars)	Coupon rate (percent)	Inflation rate (percent)	Term (years)
1990	Harare	1	46	17	15.3		19
1991	Bulawayo	1	10	1.98	17		10
1993	Harare	1	90	12.98	32	27.6	5
1994	Harare	1	120	14.30	17	22.3	7
1994	Bulawayo	1	100	1.92	18	22.3	10
1996	Harare	1	100	9.93	18	21.4	17
1996	Bulawayo	1	100	9.93	20	21.4	10
1997	Bulawayo	1	100	8.04	14	18.9	15
1998	Kwekwe	1	28	1.15	28	30	10
1998	Gweru	1	50	2.05	23	30	10
2001	Harare[a]	10	249	1.84	13.4–18	60.8–112.4	1–13
2001	Bulawayo	2	250	1.388	28–32	60.8–112.4	

a. All these bonds carried an explicit government guarantee. The official Zimbabwe dollar–U.S. dollar exchange rate was pegged in January 2001. The U.S. dollar figures here reflect the parallel market rate.
Source: Reserve Bank of Zimbabwe.

According to data collected from the local authorities and one of the discount houses, local government bonds in issue in September 2001 stood as follows:

City	Millions of Zimbabwe dollars
Harare	539
Bulawayo	630
Gweru	50
Kwekwe	36
	1,255

However, municipal bonds constitute a very small share of the instrument base of the lending institutions (about 5 percent of their portfolios), and the instruments are rarely traded. The secondary trades that have occurred have been transacted at significant discounts, probably reflecting the market risk perception of municipal bonds. Nearly all the bonds are held by pension funds, with banks preferring a short-term investment horizon. As a result, it has become extremely difficult to price existing stocks and to compute the cost of funds for new issues.

The implicit government guarantee has always ensured a lower cost of borrowing for local governments compared with the yield curve. This has been changing, particularly since a much-publicized default by Harare on the redemption of locally registered bonds in August 1998.

Most financial market participants have access to very little information on municipal bonds or securities in issue and consequently have very little information on the operations and performance of urban councils. This lack of information limits the market's capacity to price municipal securities and, more important, limits the financial sector's ability to design and offer services to the municipal sector. There is interest in developing loans for urban councils, but municipal bonds account for only about 3 percent of institutional investors' portfolios on average (PADCO and Techfin Research 1999).

Design of Municipal Debt

The Urban Councils Act and Rural District Councils Act specify that "all loans made by authorities are secured and charged upon the assets of the Council and all securities granted by the Council in respect of such loans shall rank equally without priority." This pledge is similar to the security for general obligation bonds in the United States. However, this statutory language appears to prevent the issue of revenue bonds in Zimbabwe—bonds for which the issuer pledges a particular revenue source. Nor do the acts anticipate the use of innovative security structures that would dedicate a separate revenue stream to an escrow account for future debt offerings (Johnson and Kimberley 1999). Even so, this type of security enhancement is under review by Harare, where potential investors in a proposed bond offering are suggesting that the water fees of the 20 largest users be paid directly to an escrow agent as security for payment of the debt service on the new bonds.

The general pledge or parity bond provision is modified by other provisions of the Urban Councils Act relating to the creation of separate estate and parking accounts into which a council's income from specified sources flows. Money in these accounts can be directed only to specified costs and expenditures. Although these accounts may be considered dedicated income streams for purposes of a revenue bond financing, there is no case law to support this conclusion or the conclusion that these accounts are assets of the council and therefore subject to the general pledge provision (Johnson and Kimberley 1999).

In some cases, however, a dedicated revenue stream other than property taxes (for example, revenue from water fees) might be more attractive to investors than a general obligation pledge of the local government. Moreover, given the decline in the general balance sheets of local governments, a project investment financed from a dedicated revenue stream might be more acceptable to investors than the general obligation bonds now authorized. Revenue bonds have therefore attracted growing interest from local governments, though no such bonds have been issued yet. All bonds have been for general development purposes, issued on a pari passu basis (with a ranking equal to that of all others).

The legislation allows subnational governments to establish and operate a consolidated loan fund, used to separately account for all money borrowed and principal and interest payments made. Only Harare has established such a fund; other local governments use sinking funds to repay loans. They pay annual installments into the sinking fund, sufficient to pay off the debt over the period for which the money was borrowed, and then use the fund for final (bullet) redemption.

The amount of issues is usually lower than the amount authorized by the Ministries of Local Government and Finance. The authorizations usually remain valid for several years (in principle, for an unspecified number of years). A local government then can opt to use up only part of its right to issue bonds, either because it does not want to run the risk of failing to sell all its bonds or because it does not want to commit itself to excessively high interest payments in the coming years. For example, Kwekwe, which obtained authorization to float bonds for 55 million Zimbabwe dollars (Z$) in 1998, chose to go to the market for only Z$28 million that year and planned to go to the market for the rest at a later date.

Bond Issuance and Trading

Local governments that have issued bonds prepare the issue in-house or have discount houses assist them by drawing up the prospectus, undertaking the initial canvassing, and processing the initial public offering. Trading takes place mainly over the telephone, and settlement is conducted on the same trading day. There is no central depository, nor is there a well-defined settlement system. Because of liquidity problems, some financial institutions have encountered situations in which transactions have been confirmed only after funds have been cleared.

In principle, bonds are allocated to prospective investors through bidding. Interested investors fill in a stock auction application form indicating the price they are prepared to pay for the bonds of a nominal value of US$100 and the number of bonds they want, enclosing a check for the appropriate amount. The bonds are then allocated to those offering the highest price. In practice, the prices offered appear to be very close to the nominal value of the issue. The Kwekwe issue of Z$28 million, for example, sold for Z$28.92 million. Most bond issues have reportedly closed at somewhat below par, at about 95 to 97 percent.

The prospectus for a bond issue states the purpose of the issue, the amount to be raised, the interest rate, the issue price, the opening and closing dates for applications, and the maturity date. It explains where, when, and how to file applications. Payment is often 10 percent on application, and the balance three months later. The prospectus also gives details about the allocation of bonds and any refunds of payments made on application. Interest is normally calculated on a daily basis at the stated rate and paid semiannually. The prospectus states the redemption date, on which payment is made against surrender of the bond certificate. The prospectus expressly states that the debt will rank pari passu (equal) with all existing debt and form a charge on the rents, rates, and general revenue of the local authority and that it will be further secured on all its assets.

The level of disclosure in a typical prospectus (generally four to five pages long) for a local authority bond offering in Zimbabwe falls far short of international norms and often fails to meet listing requirements of the Zimbabwe Stock Exchange. The quality of prospectuses reflects an underlying assumption by investors that the creditworthiness of the issuer is immaterial because of the sovereign guarantee implicit in the prescribed assets regime and approval requirements for borrowing. Moreover, in Zimbabwe there is no authority that verifies the facts provided in prospectuses.

No bonds issued in Zimbabwe have been supported by an independent credit rating. Indeed, with the central government guarantee, there has been no need to verify the financial information. In 1999–2002, 17 of the urban councils were independently rated. Contrary to expectations, the rating agency Duff & Phelps (1999) found that some of the smaller local governments "reflect lower costs structures, more efficient collection procedures, and more pragmatic financial planning than their large counterparts." The rated councils have used the associated management reports as guides for improving their internal operating efficiency.

Even though all local municipal long-term bonds are listed on the Zimbabwe Stock Exchange, there is virtually no trading. The Stock Exchange and its members tend to ignore municipal bonds. If secondary trading in local debt securities develops, there will be a need for continuing disclosure to allow the market to reassess the value of securities on the basis of developments since the initial prospectus. Even an initial prospectus that properly and fully disclosed relevant information would not contain information relevant to investors years after the bonds were first sold. Just as for initial disclosure, standards for continuing disclosure do not need to be established by statute.

Assessment and Prospects

Toward the end of the 1990s and through 2001 central government funding of local authorities in Zimbabwe began to decline precipitously. Grants fell both because of policy decisions by the government and because of its increasingly strained fiscal position. Public sector loans declined mainly as a result of the closure of donor-funded projects that had been the source of the intergovernmental loans and because of the diminished donor interest in the country. Moreover, while no accurate data are available on the repayment performance of local authorities, there have been reports of an increasing number of effective defaults on public sector loan obligations—a common phenomenon in Africa and indeed globally.

Under these circumstances—and given the advantages of the policy environment for local borrowers due to the prescribed assets regime and central guarantees—it might have been expected that local governments would make greater recourse to the bond market. However, this has not occurred. Real borrowing in 1998–2001 was substantially lower than in the 1980s and early 1990s. This decline probably reflects the deterioration of the financial sector's position resulting from the deterioration in the wider economy as well as the central government's difficulties in fully enforcing its prescribed assets policy. It probably also reflects factors specific to the municipal bond sector, such as the fallout from the Harare default in 1998. It is impossible to disentangle these effects and weigh their relative importance. Moreover, attempting to establish what would have happened in the municipal debt market if Zimbabwe's macroeconomic situation had not deteriorated would be a largely speculative exercise.

Only a small number of local governments have floated bonds in Zimbabwe, and until 1997 only Harare and Bulawayo had done so. The value of bonds in issue constitutes a relatively small share of capital investment financing by local governments. For example, Prud'homme (1999) has calculated that in 1990–96 bonds accounted for only around 20 percent of capital investment by local governments. During this period subnational governments made capital investments amounting to US$298 million while issuing US$60 million in bonds.

This amount seems relatively small when compared with the reported investment needs of local governments—around US$55 million a year (PADCO and Techfin Research 1999). A World Bank–funded program financing infrastructure investments in all 23 urban centers in Zimbabwe disbursed a similar amount (also around US$60 million) in 1994–98, so the nascent municipal finance market in Zimbabwe was able to match this large public sector program in dollars invested.

The domestic financial market has the potential to make significant financing available for the investment needs of local governments, but current stocks of municipal bonds have been acquired largely on the back of government guarantees and the prescribed assets regime. Private investors have shown a reluctance to take municipal paper on its own merits. Further development of the municipal finance market in Zimbabwe (feasible only when macroeconomic stability is recovered) would depend on a number of measures, including introducing a more transparent and predictable intergovernmental fiscal transfer system, amending the legislation to allow for the ring-fencing of infrastructure projects through the issuance of dedicated revenue bonds, introducing credit enhancement measures such as municipal bond insurance, and strengthening financial management and disclosure by local governments.

A False Municipal Bond Market

As Prud'homme (1999) has argued, the central authorization, central guarantee, and prescribed assets policies that have provided the foundation for private lending to local governments have created a "false" municipal bond market in Zimbabwe: investors have lent on the basis of these policies rather than on the basis of the risk presented by a local authority. The importance and impact of this policy environment became clear in the Harare default of 1998. The central government did not make good on its implicit guarantee, with the consequence that all Harare bond issues since then have had to carry its explicit guarantee. The only other city that has been able to raise bond finance since that time (Bulawayo) had to pay a large premium for the privilege and commit to special arrangements that may or may not be replicable.

Broader economic circumstances aside, the policy regime governing subsovereign borrowing in Zimbabwe has created an unsustainable situation. Prescribed assets have created general problems for the financial sector. Actions by the central government aimed at strengthening the municipal finance sector (authorizations and implicit and explicit guarantees) have increased rather than diminished the government's liabilities while making it almost impossible to price municipal risk. Even if the macroeconomic situation in Zimbabwe improves dramatically, this policy environment needs to be fundamentally reformed if a sustainable municipal debt market is to emerge.

Market Discipline

The policy regime also appears to have contributed to a decline in the quality of local financial management and budgetary discipline. The period 1996–98 was characterized both by fairly high levels of borrowing from the public and private sectors and by deteriorating financial positions of many larger urban councils and growing local fiscal deficits, funded by short- and long-term debt.[2] In 1995–97, for example, Kwekwe's annual budget deficit grew from Z\$1.7 million to Z\$13.8 million, and its aggregate debt burden from Z\$2.3 million to Z\$17.8 million (Steffenson and Trollegaard 2000). Harare has consistently been both the most active local borrower and the one with the worst financial record (Prud'homme 1999).[3]

Thus in a regulatory environment where the ability of a local authority to borrow on the markets has been determined by the actions and financial position of the central government rather than the soundness of the authority's own financial position, access to debt finance has failed to exert a disciplinary effect on local government borrowers. As Prud'homme (1999) has noted, "Recourse to the bond market does not seem to have been [driven by] financial wisdom and discipline. [Nor has] the ability of a city to go to the market [been] constrained by the soundness of its financial position and the existence of healthy accounts."

Bond Issues and Inflation

Until 1998, as a result of the prescribed assets regime, local governments were generally able to access the market at interest rates close to or below the inflation rate, borrowing at zero or negative interest rates and thereby benefiting from a hidden tax on financial institutions. Interest rates rose sharply on new issues after the 1998 Harare default. Once again in 2001, when the central government reduced and strictly regulated interest rates in an effort to contain its own soaring domestic debt, local governments benefited substantially from the spread between the real cost of money and the rates on their bond issues.[4] Prud'homme (1999) has calculated that in real terms, with an annual inflation rate of 20 percent, a 15-year bond of US$100 is reimbursed for about US$6.

This is clearly not a sustainable situation for financial institutions in the long term. Of course, the policy of prescribing financial assets is a concern that extends beyond the municipal sector. However, like many other monetary and fiscal policy questions, it requires serious attention if a sustainable municipal debt market is to emerge in Zimbabwe. Only after fundamental reforms in the overall policy environment will it be possible to address the issues that relate specifically to municipal borrowing: the intergovernmental fiscal structure, the powers of local governments to budget and issue debt, the regulation of market participants, and procedures in the event of default. Serious and detailed reform in all these areas is essential before a sustainable debt market can emerge in Zimbabwe, but under today's circumstances this is unlikely to happen in the short or even the medium term.

Notes

1. These long-term bonds are known as "registered stocks" in Zimbabwe.

2. An analysis of the financial statements of 13 of the largest urban councils for fiscal 1998 confirmed the weak financial position of most of the councils. Of the 13 assessed, only 2 reported (modest) surpluses in fiscal 1998. Of the 11 councils in deficit, 4 were carrying deficits of more than Z$20 million.

3. In June 1999 the entire Harare council was dismissed by the central government on the basis of an extremely adverse report on the city's financial position by Deloitte and Touche.

4. For example, in January 2002 interest on 90-day negotiable certificates of deposit was 23 percent, while the annualized inflation rate was 112.4 percent.

Chapter 20

Middle East and North Africa
Morocco

In a developing financial market with good potential, private investors are reluctant to lend to local governments that have little fiscal autonomy.

Samir El Daher

Lessons

In Morocco, a unitary state with highly centralized governance, a national lending agency has dominated local government borrowing. The country is working to decentralize its governance and is still developing its domestic financial markets, which have had little experience in lending to subnational governments. Municipalities depend heavily on centrally collected and administered revenues and have little flexibility in setting local rates. Even so, local governments are important service providers, with large capital spending needs.

Morocco relies on a municipal development fund, the Communal Infrastructure Fund, as a vehicle for ensuring access to credit for municipalities that are too small or too heavily dependent on the central government to tap credit markets directly. The country's experience with its lending program has been fairly positive, but resource constraints threaten to crimp future growth. The Communal Infrastructure Fund, almost the only source for long-term credit to subnational governments, has relied for resources largely on government funding and on lines of credit from official bilateral sources and multilateral institutions. Now diversifying its funding sources, it has been tapping domestic financial markets for long-term credit. The fund has issued medium- and long-term securities on domestic markets without government guarantee and has been steadily improving its management of financial risks and conforming with prudential regulations.

Deficiencies in financial management and reporting by subnational governments hamper their access to private credit, and centrally provided credit has limitations. Prescriptions of ways to address these shortcomings and limitations provide insight into the choices policymakers need to confront to make subnational access to credit more feasible.

In the more than 20 years since Morocco introduced the basic laws for municipalities—the Law on Municipal Organization and the Law on Organization of the Finances of Local Governments—it has experimented with and gradually extended the fiscal and administrative framework of decentralization. During this period the country has strengthened decentralization by reforming local revenues, adopting formula-based intergovernmental transfers, and establishing a stable system of credit financing. Decentralization both poses great challenges and offers great potential—because of tight budgets, disparities in access to basic services, and the increased demand for basic services that has arisen with Morocco's rapid urbanization. The challenges of development require a good framework for budgetary processes, intergovernmental fiscal relations, the assignment of expenditures and revenues, and the development of subnational credit markets.

In Morocco urban municipalities depend for 40 percent of their revenues on three centrally administered taxes: two shared taxes—an urban tax and a business tax—and a local property-based tax. They derive another third of their revenues from intergovernmental transfers, and the rest from local fees and taxes. The share of revenues from own sources for local governments in Morocco appears to be comparable to that in many OECD countries. Local governments in Morocco depend less on central transfers than do municipalities in Latin America, for example, where transfers account for more than half of revenues on average. However, these governments have limited fiscal autonomy, with little discretion in determining the base or rate for shared and local taxes or even for user charges and fees for municipal services. An estimated 70 percent of local government revenues are subject to centrally set rates.

If local governments are to meet their financing needs, they will have to rely more on local revenues. Most own-source revenues are fees and charges for services or for periodic activities (such as annual fairs), and motor vehicle taxes generally accrue to the central level. Thus the most immediate prospect for increasing local revenues appears to be raising existing property taxes. Local governments also need greater freedom to determine local fees and charges for services.

Morocco has recently reformed its intergovernmental transfer system to remove the perverse incentives for deficit spending and unwise borrowing. By eliminating the budget deficit subsidy, the reforms have imposed a hard budget constraint on local governments and ensured that they would bear the full cost of borrowing. The reforms have also introduced a formula for distributing value added tax revenue that has improved the equity of fiscal transfers to local governments as well as the predictability and transparency of local revenues.

Subnational Government Borrowing

While Morocco has been liberalizing its financial sector and reforming its local government sector, the ability of subnational governments to access private credit remains largely untested. That ability depends on the quality of the fiscal and financial management, the budgetary and control systems, and the planning and implementation of their investment programs. One of the main determinants of subnational governments' creditworthiness and access to private funding under market conditions, however, is the legal and regulatory framework in which they generate revenues, manage assets, and finance and provide services.

Morocco's relatively developed financial markets provide a potentially good base of long-term funding for subnational governments. Total bank credit in the country averaged around $15 billion, or about 50 percent of

GDP, over the past five years. However, with the exception of a small number of direct bond issues by Casablanca,[1] local government borrowing has taken place predominantly through loans from the publicly owned, specialized financial intermediary, the Communal Infrastructure Fund. Although no legal restrictions prevent subnational governments from borrowing from other financial institutions, borrowings from commercial banks have been limited, mainly because of regulatory and institutional impediments affecting the risk associated with subnational borrowers. Foremost among these impediments are the limited autonomy and authority of subnational governments in mobilizing revenues and managing expenditures.

To foster a more efficient subnational finance system, the central government has embarked on reforms to help expand the bankable demand for private credit and increase the participation of private financial institutions in subnational investment funding. Success in these reforms will be critical given the pressing need to reach beyond budgetary resources to meet the large investment funding requirements. The hope is that, in an appropriate enabling environment, commercial banks would be interested in the potentially growing subnational finance market—previously too fragmented and unknown to justify large commitments and investments in systems development and know-how.

Main Issues in Subnational Borrowing

In Morocco credit financing accounted for about 8 percent of the total resources of subnational governments, and debt service for 19 percent of their current expenditures, over the five-year period from 1996–2000. While there is both potential and scope for further expansion of subnational credit markets, this expansion would need to be supported by regulations and instruments adapted to the investment financing needs of subnational governments. It also would require easing the demand-side constraints that impede their access to credit. These constraints relate mainly to the following:

- Subnational governments' lack of autonomy in fiscal decisionmaking coupled with poor planning and operating capabilities.
- Inadequate, ad hoc, or inconsistent economic selection criteria and benchmarks used by the central government in its review of subnational investment programs.
- The inefficiency of asset management by subnational governments.

- The absence of performance standards for locally provided monopoly services, which has resulted in poor quality of service delivery.
- The inadequacy of cost recovery practices and their lack of differentiation between revenue-generating services and public goods.
- Inadequate collection levels for user fees.

In addition, mobilizing private resources for subnational infrastructure in Morocco is likely to require a greater role for private providers of services—through greater use of concession arrangements, for example. The provision of services remains too centralized and uncompetitive.

Reforms aimed at improving local revenue mobilization and financial management focus on accounting, payment, financial control, and audit systems and on the incentives needed for timely collection of resources and reduced payment delays. Particularly important is greater capacity to generate own-source revenues through rational bases and rates for local taxes and adequate collection levels. The recently approved formula-based distribution of value added tax revenue has improved the predictability of part of the revenues of local governments, though more needs to be done for other sources of shared revenues. In addition, the central government has been working to improve the efficiency and transparency of its extensive administrative, financial, and budgetary controls, with a view particularly to reducing perceptions among potential private lenders that the government implicitly guarantees subnational borrowings.

Regulatory Environment for Subnational Borrowing

On the supply side an increase in subnational borrowing in the domestic financial markets will depend on adjustments to laws and regulations related to borrowing authority and the issuance, registration, and servicing of debt. The governance and transparency of financial markets need to be improved through rules that avoid creating distortions by remaining neutral between market participants and between instruments (such as between loans and bonds). Moreover, the regulatory and supervisory framework for subnational borrowing needs to be strengthened through sound bankruptcy laws and prudential regulations.

Bankruptcy of subnational governments needs to be governed by regulations on debt adjustments, bankruptcy initiation, debt workout plans, and allowed expenditures during bankruptcy proceedings. The protection of creditors' rights needs to be clarified by addressing such things as the authority to pledge assets as security for borrowing, to set up independent trusts to handle the recurrent revenues of projects, and to establish sinking funds to amortize repayments of principal. In particular, the authority to pledge assets needs to be defined by regulations that differentiate between categories of subnational assets, such as core assets that may not be sold or used as debt collateral and noncore assets that may be used as collateral. In addition, measures are needed to improve the reliability of asset registration and valuation.

In the area of prudential regulations the central government has imposed limits and controls on subnational government borrowing, primarily through regulations relating to the receipt of loans from the Communal Infrastructure Fund. Debt service payments associated with subnational government borrowing must be treated as obligatory expenditures recorded in local budgets. Funds are not sequestered, but the local government must approve the budget, and debt service is a priority expenditure. Although this budgetary commitment does not guarantee against default—since expenditures related to debt service still need to be authorized by the local government—it does make default less likely. Moreover, regardless of the implied comfort, private creditors can set their own exposure limits. The prudential rules of the Communal Infrastructure Fund, for example, limit eligibility for borrowing to subnational governments whose debt service does not exceed 40 percent of their combined own-source and value added tax revenues. Debt service is estimated to be in the range of 20 to 25 percent of total local budgets.

Several reforms are needed to encourage private participation in subnational borrowing. An important focus of the regulatory reforms should be information to prospective creditors about the financial situation of subnational borrowers, particularly their indebtedness—whether direct liabilities or contingent liabilities such as guarantees. Disclosure rules should distinguish between publicly and privately placed offerings, with private placements subject to less stringent disclosure. Disclosure also would provide a useful basis for credit rating, which in time might become a statutory requirement to allow creditors to assess their exposure to local governments. Audits are required, but they should be conducted by a government agency rather than an independent party.

Types of Subnational Borrowing

Most subnational borrowings in Morocco have been earmarked for specific infrastructure investments. Even so, the financial industry has not sought to develop specific infrastructure finance instruments that would entail a distinction between tax-supported (general obligation) and revenue-based (limited obligation) borrowing schemes. Tax-supported borrowings allow subnational governments to service debt out of general revenues. They are often used to finance "public-good" projects that indirectly produce tax revenue (such as by increasing real estate values or stimulating economic growth and business investments) that can help meet debt service. In Morocco the prospects for effective tax-based funding schemes are not promising. Because subnational governments lack the authority to determine the bases and rates for locally collected taxes and to ensure adequate collection levels, they are unlikely to capture the benefits of many public-good projects.

Revenue-based borrowing, not yet used in Morocco, allows the borrower to meet debt service obligations from the revenues of the project financed by the debt. As a means of credit enhancement, these revenues are pledged to creditors as senior debt collateral. This requires segregating the revenues in an account out of which debt holders would be paid on a priority basis. Under existing laws, however, it is unclear whether subnational governments in Morocco can pledge future revenues as security for borrowing.

Revenue-based borrowings can be structured on a nonrecourse basis, in which creditors' claims are limited to the project's revenues or, at most, the project entity's assets. Because these revenues and assets can be segregated from other subnational government assets, nonrecourse finance can shield the central government from implicit contingent liabilities associated with subnational debt.

Communal Infrastructure Fund: Intermediary for Subnational Borrowing

Using a financial intermediary that can tap credit markets on behalf of subnational borrowers is one way to foster market access for small and medium-size municipalities that still cannot directly access Morocco's long-term credit markets. The Communal Infrastructure Fund, which has been almost the only source of long-term credit for subnational governments, has relied for resources largely on government funding and on lines of credit from official bilateral sources and multilateral institutions. Recently it has sought to diversify its funding sources, and as part of its strategy it has been tapping the domestic financial markets for long-term credit.

The Communal Infrastructure Fund has issued medium- and long-term securities (variable rate notes and certificates of deposit), without government guarantee, at small spreads over government debt issues. It has been steadily improving its management of financial risks, conforming with the prudential regulations of the banking authorities. Its issues, amounting to a dozen so far, have been relatively evenly spaced. In the 1990s the fund's lending accounted for some 20 to 25 percent of total investment outlays by subnational (principally municipal) governments. In the past few years subnational credit has declined somewhat in real terms (as has subnational investment), despite expectations that the volume of credit would grow as a result of the reforms in the intergovernmental transfer and local revenue schemes.

The subnational credit market in Morocco remains relatively small, with the Communal Infrastructure Fund's portfolio of $500 million representing about 3 percent of outstanding bank credit. Its annual loan commitments range between $100 million and $200 million. Most of the fund's lending has gone to urban municipalities, which account for about 70 percent of outstanding credit. Rural communes, with small projects and limited debt service capacity, account for about 25 percent of outstanding credit. (The balance of the fund's lending goes to municipal corporations.) However, rural communes hold more than half the outstanding loans by number.

The loans extended by the Communal Infrastructure Fund in the 1990s were largely for non-revenue-generating projects—roads (32 percent of total loans), electricity (16 percent, mainly to rural communes participating in national electrification programs), solid waste management (10 percent), sewerage (9 percent), sports facilities (6 percent), urban transport (3 percent), and water supply (2 percent). This sectoral distribution shows that the fund has been a relatively important source of financing for sewerage and solid waste projects. The small share of financing for water supply reflects the fact that water investments are the responsibility of the national water authority, which does not borrow from the fund. Loans for commercial infrastructure (such as local markets) have accounted for some 15 percent of the total.

The Communal Infrastructure Fund has the potential to take on an increasingly important role in subnational finance. It has a valuable franchise with subnational governments, specialized knowledge, a strong equity base, and a broad and diversified project portfolio. It has been the preferred lending vehicle for subnational governments and can continue to mobilize funds on behalf of local governments, mainly from official bilateral and multilateral sources. Financial measures have been taken to strengthen its autonomy, financial viability, and capital base. Government guarantees are no longer provided for its domestic bond issues, and its provisions on loan arrears are now in line with the prudential requirements for the banking sector. Its repayment experience is good, with few loans in arrears.

With further reforms, the Communal Infrastructure Fund might be able to play more of a developmental role in subnational finance in the context of an open, competitive financial sector. The fund is expected to make its operations increasingly sustainable and to leverage its capital by issuing debt in private credit markets and lending the proceeds to subnational governments. It could expand its menu of services to include nonlending products, such as fee-based financial advisory services and technical assistance to larger municipalities. In time it could expand its range of borrowers beyond subnational governments to other providers of local services, whether public entities or private concessionaires.

As a provider of long-term credit to subnational governments, the Communal Infrastructure Fund could participate in and sometimes lead banking syndicates for larger loans to subnational governments and concessions for local infrastructure and possibly help in underwriting subnational bond issues. In pooling the credit demand of subnational borrowers, the fund could act as a bridge between subnational governments and institutional investors. This would be especially useful where subnational governments have little potential for directly accessing private credit markets and where institutional investors are in no position to assess the risk of individual subnational governments but might be willing to assume, through the Communal Infrastructure Fund, a diversified exposure to the subnational government sector.

Private Financial Institutions in Subnational Borrowing

Commercial banks have shown little interest in lending to local governments in Morocco. Among the main factors inhibiting such lending are the limited autonomy of subnational governments, the weak institutional and management capacity, the lack of transparency and weak auditing standards, and the lack of access to timely and reliable information on subnational governments' financial and operational performance. Added to these are the generic difficulties of perfecting collateral interests through cumbersome and uncertain recourse to the judicial system. Accordingly, despite the banks' large liquidity and their financial advantages over the Communal Infrastructure Fund (which lacks access to lower-cost deposits and cannot finance private concessions), the few attempts by banks to enter the subnational finance market have been inconclusive. Most commercial bank term lending for infrastructure has been restricted to private concessions and, occasionally, municipal corporations. As a result, banks still lack familiarity with the legal, institutional, and regulatory framework in which subnational governments operate.

Yet commercial banks' interest and involvement in the subnational finance market could grow in line with demand if the demand is at a scale sufficient to sustain the business development costs involved for banks entering and competing in the infrastructure sector (particularly in water, sewerage, and solid waste, where future investments by subnational governments are expected to be substantial). Depending on the depth and effectiveness of reforms in the subnational government sector, banks also could be attracted by prospects for increased profitability resulting from the expectation of greater credit demand, lower operational costs, and more manageable credit risks.

Potential Role for the Bond Markets in Subnational Borrowing

The institutional savings in Morocco could potentially provide a substantial funding pool for investments in subnational government projects. Indeed, given the shortage of attractive fixed income securities for pension funds, insurance companies, and mutual funds, debt securities issued by subnational governments could be appealing, particularly those issued by large urban municipalities with sufficient and stable resources. First, however, obstacles to issuing public debt must be removed and regulations governing financial transactions by subnational governments introduced (in such areas as financial disclosure, registration, underwriting, distribution, instruments). The capital market regulations now in effect do not respond to the needs of subnational issuers, particularly with respect to procedures and disclosure requirements.

Because of limited technical capabilities and high transaction costs, only a few subnational governments in Morocco—the largest urban municipalities—would be likely to access the bond markets directly. Nonetheless, the development of a subnational securities market could foster the broader reforms—in disclosure, financial transparency, management quality, auditing, asset collateralization, and credit rating capabilities—that are needed for independent assessment of the creditworthiness of local governments.

Note

1. These bonds are not listed on an exchange and were distributed solely domestically.

Chapter 21

Middle East and North Africa
Tunisia

Meeting most local government capital needs,
the municipal development fund starts to borrow in
the domestic capital markets.

Samir El Daher

Lessons

A unitary and highly centralized state, Tunisia is making efforts
to decentralize its governance and to develop its domestic financial markets. Private financial institutions have had little experience in lending to subnational governments, which have relied for credit finance almost exclusively on a municipal
development fund. Local governments rely heavily on centrally
collected and administered revenues and have little freedom to
set local rates.

The municipal development fund in Tunisia is the cornerstone
of the system for financing subnational investment, carried out
as part of national planning. Combining loans and grants, the
fund executes the central government's policy on financing
subnational capital investment. Although the fund has little experience in raising capital, it recently has issued bonds on the
domestic market.

The fund's sustainability would be enhanced by diversifying capital sources, broadening the range of services to local borrowers, and expanding its client base. Transforming the fund into an autonomous, commercially viable specialized financial institution may offer the best prospects for sustainability. Properly done, the development of the fund into a market-based institution—able to mobilize long-term resources on behalf of subnational borrowers—could catalyze the emergence and growth of a local government bond market in Tunisia.

In Tunisia subnational governments have relatively limited responsibilities for financing and providing services and so have relatively limited needs for long-term borrowing. The main urban services—such as water, transport, sanitation, and electricity—are provided by national agencies. Investments in health and education are also a national responsibility. Subnational governments are responsible mainly for roads, drainage, public order, pollution control, solid waste collection, and street cleaning and lighting. Their capital expenditures represent about 50 percent of their current revenues on average, though the share varies depending on the jurisdiction, with large urban centers devoting a bigger part of their budgets to investment spending than small rural entities.

The central government plays a major role in allocating resources and credit to subnational governments. Borrowing by subnational governments has occurred almost exclusively through a specialized financial intermediary wholly owned by the government, the Fund for Loans and Support to Local Communities (Caisse de Prêts et Soutien aux Collectivités Locales, or CPSCL). The CPSCL is also the main channel through which the central government transfers resources to subnational governments to finance their capital expenditures. Tunisia has no local government bond market in which subnational governments can issue debt, although it does have long-term credit markets for central government and corporate debt. The CPSCL's resources consist of a relatively large equity base provided by the government and external local government lines of credit provided by bilateral and multilateral financial institutions.

Tunisia has 256 local governments, representing about 60 percent of the country's population; the other 40 percent live in unincorporated areas. Local governments are managed by governing councils that elect a president. The governments have inadequate financial management capacity, with accounting systems that need to be improved. For example, while tax registers have been computerized in local governments, tax receipts are still processed manually.

Local governments depend on direct taxes for 32 percent of their resources. These include the hotel tax; the real estate tax; the undeveloped real estate tax; and the industrial, commercial, and professional establishments taxes. The taxes on real estate and undeveloped real estate were recently reformed, improving collections. Legislative and administrative changes in assessment values and improvements in accounting and computerization would also boost collections. Indirect taxes, mainly license fees for several types of small businesses, account for 8 percent of local government revenue. Many of these local levies are of little value and could be eliminated to allow local governments to focus on those with the greatest revenue potential. As in Morocco, local governments need greater freedom to fix rates in accordance with local ability to pay. Fees for public services, such as a surtax on electricity and a tax for removal of industrial waste, account for 24 percent of local government revenue.

In addition, subnational governments receive two types of financial transfers from the state. Transfers for operating expenditures are made through a dedicated fund, the Common Fund for Local Communities, which provided 27 percent of local government revenue in 2000. The formula for distributing these transfers includes an incentive for improved tax collections and an element of cross-subsidy to aid the poorer local governments. Transfers for investment financing come through one of two channels: the sectoral ministries, which deposit funds directly with local governments for financing certain types of equipment, or the CPSCL, which provides both grant financing and loans.

The fiscal situation of subnational governments remains precarious, reflecting their weak savings and borrowing capacity. Their current expenditures rose faster than their current revenues in 1992–2002. Their investments, though relatively small in volume, also increased more rapidly than their current revenues, with estimates suggesting that they doubled in current value in the same period. Moreover, a decline in the savings capacity of subnational governments has undermined their finances. Even so, the outlook for growth in subnational investment—and thus in subnational borrowing—remains good. Progress, however, will depend on further institutional reforms addressing such aspects as decentralizing authority and involving the private sector in the provision of services through concessions, management contracts with capital expenditures, and other arrangements.

Framework for Subnational Finance

The capital investment projects of subnational governments and unincorporated rural areas are listed in the Communal Investment Plan as part of a national five-year economic development plan. Once the projects of subnational governments are included in the Communal Investment Plan, they are entitled to receive financing from the program. The financing plan for capital investment projects is based on a formula that outlines the following:

- The share to come from self-financing or a subnational government's own resources (about 30 percent).
- The share to come from grants or the central government's contribution (30 to 40 percent).
- The loan component granted by the CPSCL (30 to 40 percent).

Local projects outside the framework of the Communal Investment Plan are revenue-generating (commercial) schemes, such as slaughterhouses or public markets.

The Role of Credit in Financing Subnational Investment

At 30 to 40 percent, borrowing represents a significant share of the financing of subnational investment projects. Debt service accounts for some 15 to 20 percent of current revenues for subnational governments. Given limited savings capacity, repayments of principal need to be spread out over six years on average, so as not to undermine budgets.

Credit is allocated to subnational governments according to their size, a distribution policy intended to provide small subnational governments with the basic equipment needed even at the risk of increasing their debt relative to their own resources. Large cities have more room for maneuver but nevertheless are hampered by the rigidity of their resources from local taxes and intergovernmental transfers. The capacity of subnational governments to finance their capital projects in line with the investment plans set out in the Communal Investment Plan, and to repay their debt, will depend on a real increase in their revenue receipts. In turn, that will require increasing central government transfers and subsidies, widening tax bases, and improving tax collection.

Constraints on Subnational Governments' Access to Investment Finance

The great diversity among Tunisia's subnational governments—in population size, economic resources, and the range of public services provided to residents—is mirrored in disparities in the capital bases and solvency. As a result, some subnational governments are better able than others to access credit, and a small number might be deemed creditworthy by potential creditors. However, the needs of these potentially creditworthy entities are large relative to the total demand for credit by subnational governments.

For subnational governments with a substantial capital base, the central government could conceivably decide not to finance investments in projects that have a strong potential of attracting private financing, such as solid waste treatment projects. In this case such projects might be financed by the CPSCL through arrangements involving private concessionaires and delegated service providers, although reforms would be needed to lay the groundwork for such private participation.

Indeed, the government is considering possible changes in the way subnational investments are financed. One option might be to progressively reduce, for a given period, the volume of CPSCL lending in a way congruent with the currently weak borrowing capacity of some subnational governments. An assessment should be made of the extent to which large subnational governments might be able to take advantage of more flexible financing plans than those provided for under the Communal Investment Plan—and greater freedom in the choice of investments.

For the subnational sector as a whole, the main constraint on investment financing relates to the financial situation of governments. Substantial financial adjustments will be crucial to enable subnational governments to carry out their investment programs.

The Role of the Municipal Development Fund

As Tunisia's municipal development fund, the CPSCL is the cornerstone of the system for financing subnational investment. Combining credit and grants, the CPSCL carries out the government policy on financing subnational capital investment under a set of procedures aimed at ensuring efficient distribution of investment credits. Since the CPSCL was created in 1975, the institutional framework governing its operations (legal status, procedures manual, investment guide) has been amended twice, in 1992 and 1997. These amendments increased the resources available to the CP-SCL but failed to endow it with sufficient autonomy in decisionmaking. Its mandate is still part of the relatively rigid framework under which the Communal Investment Plan is implemented. As the partner of subnational governments in financing their capital investments, the CPSCL ought to have greater autonomy.

The CPSCL's activities remain relatively modest in scope because large infrastructure investments are outside the purview of subnational governments and do not receive CPSCL financing. The policy on subnational capital investment under the Communal Investment Plans has been giving priority to bringing infrastructure and basic equipment up to a common level across subnational governments. The CPSCL distributes its financing among the 256 subnational governments in accordance with the government policy on financing subnational capital investment. Tunis alone accounts for 12 percent of debt outstanding, and the country's 10 next largest towns for another 35 percent. With the investment effort by subnational governments exceeding 40 percent of their current revenues, it can be realized only by combining loans and grants to achieve a high average rate of subsidy.

The CPSCL's financial prospects are linked to the resources and solvency of the subnational governments that are its customers. A recent strategic study commissioned by the CPSCL from expert consultants in local government finance looked at the CPSCL's prospects for change and sustainability. The study led to proposals for redistributing tax revenue and charges between the central and subnational levels of government (with an increase in financial transfers from the central government) and between subnational governments and other institutions or authorities providing public services at the local level. Strengthening the borrowing capacity of subnational governments—and the growth potential of the CPSCL—also would require increasing their tax revenue and tax collection levels. Without such measures, the CPSCL's activities could expand only very slowly or even decline, with serious repercussions for its profit margins and financial equilibrium.

An Expanded Framework for the Operations of the Municipal Development Fund

A review of the financial situation of subnational governments, particularly their debt ratios and their capacity to self-finance investments, suggests that the CPSCL needs to move beyond the uniform method of financing that it has been using. Introducing several different financing "windows" would allow the CPSCL to adapt its assistance to the varied financial situations of subnational governments. It would also enable the CPSCL to identify new opportunities and to broaden the range of its activities, products, and clients. The CPSCL, for example, might have two windows:

- One window, providing financing under the Communal Investment Plan, involving all transfers or subsidies provided on an off–balance sheet basis and for which the CPSCL would be acting as an agent for the government against a management fee.
- A second window for more commercial financial operations, for financing investments outside the Communal Investment Plan, on terms reflecting the cost of resources mobilized by the CPSCL on private credit markets.

In addition, the CPSCL might consider introducing instruments and products enabling it to offer its clientele a broader range of financial engineering and technical assistance services. As the CPSCL evolves, there might be a possibility of a third line of activities for financing operations by other categories of borrowers or clients, such as private entities to which subnational services are subcontracted. Such financing could occur only after reforms allowing private concessionaires and subcontracted service providers to participate in subnational investment programs.

By ensuring a reliable channel for credit for priority projects, the CPSCL has brought about significant improvements in the financing of subnational investments, often in difficult circumstances arising from the weak technical capabilities and financial and institutional constraints of subnational governments. For the CPSCL to be sustainable, however, it will need to boost its capacity to mobilize long-term financing and broaden its capital base by diversifying the resources on which it draws. If the CPSCL is to take on an enhanced role as a specialized financial institution and gain access to other types of resources, subnational finances must undergo adjustments. The capacity of subnational governments to finance their capital investments and repay their debts depends on a significant increase in subnational receipts.

Diversification of Activities, Products, and Clients

Under the proposed strategy for making the CPSCL financially sustainable, efforts should be made to strengthen the CPSCL's authority in committing resources. Requests by subnational governments for financing investments outside the Communal Investment Plan should be eligible for loans from the CPSCL to the extent that they meet its eligibility criteria, particularly the criteria relating to economic and financial returns (some of the projects now under the Communal Investment Plan might not fully comply with the CPSCL's standards). Moreover, these loans should be granted on terms reflecting the true cost of borrowing by the CPSCL on private credit markets.

The prospects for diversifying the CPSCL's clientele are limited in the short term. Consideration should be given to making CPSCL loans available to private concessionaires providing local public services, subject to limits on the share of such loans in the CPSCL's activities. This financing of concessionaires would be unlikely to crowd out other options for subnational governments if it were limited to resources that the CPSCL could borrow on private credit markets.

Financing requests from the most solvent subnational governments are expected to attract the interest of commercial banks and other sources of capital market financing over the next few years. Even so, the development of lending activity directed at the subnational sector remains a commitment that few domestic financial institutions are inclined to undertake. For this reason the CPSCL is still the agency best placed to respond to the financing needs of subnational governments, even if its skills in subnational financing may still need improvement.

The CPSCL has yet to acquire all the characteristics and assets of an effective specialized financial institution. Its lending activities and debt outstanding with subnational governments remain modest, reflecting the small share of subnational capital spending in the national investment effort. Moreover, its portfolio is subject to credit risks arising from the precarious financial situation of many of its borrowers. While its activities are now governed by centralized administrative procedures and financing policies under the Communal Investment Plan, under a new market-oriented regime the CPSCL would need to enhance its skills in the analysis of subnational finances, the evaluation of credit risk, and financial engineering, particularly in project structuring.

The continued importance of the policy of state subsidy of subnational investments means that the CPSCL would have to continue to finance subnational investments through a combination of loans and grants. However, this role should not preclude the diversification of its financial products. The CPSCL should aim at steady growth in its turnover, by offering a wider range of options to subnational governments and by expanding its clientele to include private concessionaires and larger projects.

Diversification of Resources

The CPSCL needs to diversify its financing sources in domestic markets not only to finance its loans to subnational governments and respond to growing demand from clients but also to ensure its sustainability in Tunisia's evolving financial sector. Because the CPSCL cannot rely indefinitely or exclusively on lines of credit from external donors, developing the ability in the medium term to tap the bond market appears to be essential for continuing and sustaining its activity. The way in which the CPSCL finances its operations has not yet required specific skills for capital mobilization; if the institution is to grow and change, however, it will need to acquire these skills.

The CPSCL, as part of its efforts to diversify its resources, is seeking to mobilize credit through bond issues on the domestic financial market. It recently floated its first public bond issue in the local currency, with a maturity of seven years. For this purpose it obtained a credit rating from the Maghreb Rating Agency. The favorable rating of AA will permit the CPSCL to launch future bond issues under attractive terms. Nonetheless, the quality of its credit, as perceived by potential investors, will depend largely on the quality of its clients and their solvency.

Transformation into a Market-Based Specialized Financial Institution

The strategic study commissioned by the CPSCL concluded that the best path was to transform the institution into a market-based specialized financial intermediary for subnational governments. In this scenario a possible strategic alliance could be considered between the CPSCL and another financial institution interested in financing subnational governments' programs and projects, especially if the CPSCL were to broaden its activities to include other categories of borrowers and clients. As a specialized market-based institution, the CPSCL could envisage forming such an alliance on the basis of its comparative and competitive advantages in financing subnational investments—potentially attractive factors for banking institutions. This approach would avoid the prohibitive costs involved in setting up a bank while still affording the CPSCL access to an attractive source of funds, the deposits of the allied banking institution. The alliance would also allow the CPSCL to participate with its partner in loan syndications, for example, expanding the range of its activities to include operations of a scope and risk profile that would preclude the CPSCL from being the sole creditor.

The transformation of the CPSCL into an autonomous, commercially viable specialized financial institution should be accompanied by institutional and regulatory strengthening. Changes are needed in the CPSCL's statutes, for example, to progressively transform the CPSCL into a limited liability company, allowing it to strengthen its capital base by attracting new partners that would shore up its position in the financial sector. The CPSCL's capital market skills need to be enhanced in anticipation of the diversification of its resources and access to private credit markets. Also needed is the development of policies, guidelines, and procedures reflecting the CPSCL's current method of financing and expected changes (for example, addressing issues relating to project financing and financial engineering, including financial restructuring plans for subnational governments in difficulty). Done properly, the development of the CPSCL into a market-based institution—able to mobilize long-term resources on behalf of subnational borrowers—could serve as a catalyst for the emergence and growth of a local government bond market in Tunisia.

Chapter 22

Asia
People's Republic of China

This nation is characterized by huge needs, vast potentials, and a changing governmental system that is sorting out how to go about financing infrastructure.

John Petersen

Lessons Learned

China's intergovernmental system, like its economic system, has been evolving over the past 20 years. As the economy has moved from central planning and direction to a more open, market-based regime, so has there been greater decentralization of governmental decisionmaking and more local fiscal autonomy. However, the matching of public sector resources to spending assignments has been imperfect at best, leaving heavy spending loads on some localities that have few resources of their own, while helping others achieve relatively strong financial positions.

The combination of constrained formal budgets and the ability to decentralize functions and assets to government-owned companies led to the evolution in much of China's subnational sector of a parallel sphere of "off-budget" self-supporting, quasi-government activities. This "off-budget" sphere, relying on extra budgetary funds, has been especially important in the operation and financing of asset-heavy infrastructure investment. Legally precluded from borrowing using their own credits, subnational governments have resorted to a combination of bank lending and bond issues by the companies they own as a means of financing infrastructure.

Resorting to off-budget finance has been a mixed blessing. On the one hand, the techniques are legally penumbraed and operationally opaque, as the borrowing entities are not subject to regular oversight and reporting. On the other, subnational borrowers have gained early experience in the financial markets (albeit, in controlled ones) and at running commercial, fee-based operations. In the area of highway transportation, funds have been raised from a remarkable array of public and private sources, including the stock markets and foreign investors. The joint venture and asset-based financings are seen as models for self-liquidating projects.

Despite impressive growth, the Chinese financial markets continue to be both bank-dominated and restricted in scope, with few instruments and a limited large institutional investors. The credit markets are administered, with interest rates being set by the authorities, issuances allowed on a case-by-case basis, and credit decisions taken on other than economic grounds.

Establishing a local government bond market is being given special impetus because of the concerns about the Chinese banking system and how it will perform under the stress of impending international competition. Bank loans, a large proportion of which are to non-performing state-owned companies and are extended at concessionary rates, are seen as an increasingly undependable source of funds for infrastructure financing. Meanwhile, the small but growing Chinese bond market appears to offer a viable alternative to the rolling over of bank loans. Rationalizing and regularizing local government access to the long-term domestic bond markets is an important priority for both financing capital needs and broadening the nation's bond markets.

Over the past two decades, China has taken a deliberate path toward developing both a market economy and fiscal decentralization of its government. Its model of "market socialism" and the retention of centralized controls in the economy have given it a special status among developing nations. Despite (or, some argue, because of) its cautious approach and measured structural changes, it has enjoyed a sustained and rapid rate of economic growth that places it in a league enjoyed by few nations, namely post-war Japan and Korea. It was able to avoid the worst bumps of the Asian crisis and has maintained relative high levels of foreign investment into the early twenty-first century.[1]

Nonetheless, as the economy modernizes, urbanization continues, and the country opens to the rest of the world, China finds itself grappling with continuing issues of how to balance state control with responsiveness in meeting the needs of fast growing urban areas and a more prosperous citizenry. How subnational governments, which are charged with providing the bulk of services to the population and businesses, will respond to these challenges and meet the swiftly mounting demands for infrastructure is a critical part of the picture.

Government Structure and Decentralization

China is unusual in many ways, not the least of which is its multi-tiered governmental structure. A unitary state, its vast size and variety have led to a necessary looseness in its structure below the top. Beneath the national government, the subnational government administration is divided into four tiers: (i) provinces, regions, and municipalities that are directly under the central government; (ii) prefectures and cities under the provinces and regions; (iii) counties, county-level cities, and districts under prefectures and cities; (iv) towns and townships under (autonomous) counties. There are 31 provinces,[2] autonomous regions and municipalities directly under the central government; 333 prefectures and 695 cities (259 cities at prefecture level, 400 cities at county level); 2,074 counties; and over 40,000 towns and townships. Under and amid the layers are tucked hundreds of thousands of communes and settlements, products of the collective past that still bind people to their housing, jobs, and basic social services.

Fiscal Framework

As befits a sprawling nation of 1.3 billion people, China's fiscal system is highly decentralized. That was not always the case with taxation, and, until recently, little spending discretion was given the local level.[3] However, the reforms of the last two decades have gradually loosened the structure. The Budget Law of 1992 gave substantial autonomy to the subnational units, but it is an autonomy that is constrained in a latticework of "nested" oversight. Each level of government has an independent budget that must be approved by the People's congress at that level but is subject to oversight by the next higher level. Accordingly, the National People's Congress approves only the central budget.[4] The central government determines the broad outline of the revenue sharing system, but it deals directly only with the provincial administrations that are immediately below it. Thus, although China has a unitary system of government, the dispersal of intergovernmental fiscal arrangements gives it a strong federal character.

Another dimension in Chinese subnational government that is critical to understanding its structure is the "horizontal characteristic" of local governments; these governments have corporate branches (companies) that operate off the budget. In addition, with a heritage of state ownership and control of business, there are other, less formal relationships that are important in understanding the complex economic and fiscal relationships at the subnational level.[5]

In 1994, China adopted tax reform, the centerpiece of which was the Tax Sharing System, where the central government and subnational governments have separate tax-collection powers over certain categories of taxes. This reform, which was followed by buoyant economic conditions, led to the rapid increase in tax revenues at both the central and subnational levels. However, due to the asymmetry between fiscal power and expenditure assignment, the ratio of subnational revenues to the total revenues has averaged around 50 percent, while the ratio of local fiscal expenditure to the total remained high at about 70 percent (table 22.1) Of the 70 percent of total public expenditure that takes place at the subnational level (provincial, prefecture, county and township), more than 55 percent is at subprovincial levels.

The fiscal gap between revenues and spending is mostly filled in the aggregate by transfers from the central government to the localities. However, the system is far from comprehensive in achieving balance; some local units run surpluses, while many others are in deficit. County and township governments, in particular, have faced huge fiscal deficits, partly financed by borrowings from state-owned commercial banks and government financial institutions (trust and investment companies). These deficits in the formal fiscal budget can be supplemented by deficits in local government

Table 22.1. Subnational Revenues and Expenditures, 1993 to 2001 (Yuan billion)

	1993	1994	1995	1996	1997	1998	1999	2000	2001
Subnational fiscal revenues	339.1	231.1	298.6	374.6	442.4	498.4	559.5	639.4	779.3
Total government revenues	78%	44%	48%	51%	51%	51%	49%	48%	48%
Subnational fiscal exps.	333.0	403.8	482.8	578.6	670.1	767.3	903.5	1036.5	1309.0
Total government expenditures	72%	70%	71%	73%	73%	71%	69%	65%	69%
Fiscal gap (revenues − expenditures)	6.1	−172.7	−184.3	−203.9	−227.7	−268.9	−344.0	−397.1	−529.7

Source: Kang 2002.

companies, further complicating the analysis and adding a dimension of contingent obligation to the equation.

Subnational Revenue Sources

Subnational tax revenues are a composite of both own-sources taxes over which the localities have power and those taxes that are administered by and shared with the central government (Kang 2002, Appendix 7). The composition of major local tax sources to subnational governments in 1999 was as follows:

- Business tax,[6] which is 100 percent local, accounted for 34 percent of the total local tax revenues.
- Value added tax, which is split between central (75 percent) and local (25 percent), accounted for 23 percent of the total.
- Enterprise income tax (EIT) on enterprises subordinated to the local governments (which was formerly only local but became shared in 2002), accounted for 13 percent of the total.
- Various taxes levied on properties, income, and activities that account for the remaining local tax revenues.[7]

As noted, the fiscal gap at the subnational level government level is filled by the transfer payment or internal revenue allotment from the central government,[8] which amounted to Y 518 billion in 2001.[9] The two major components of transfers are the rebate of shared taxes and earmarked grants for specific purposes. The tax rebates are origin-based and thus favor the richer cities and regions; these rebates represent about 50 percent of the payments received from the center. The earmarked grants, which are specific-purpose transfers paid out of central funds, have grown even more rapidly in importance. They amounted to approximately Y 256 billion or about 50 percent of all transfers in the 2001 budget (World Bank 2003b).

Three further caveats are appropriate in examining the revenue and expenditure balance. First, while the assignment of tax sources in the 1994 reform straightened out the revenue side of the equation, a similar redesign and sorting out of service responsibilities did not occur. China retains a system where social services such as education, health, and pensions that constitute the "social safety net" are both supplied and financed at the local level. So, too, are the major infrastructure activities of water, sewers, local roads, and electric power. Second, the revenues assigned to the local level only go down to the provincial level. Below that level, it is up to the provinces to design the sharing and/or assignment systems for the subordinate city and county units; similarly, the cities and counties do as they wish with the districts and townships. Not surprisingly, this latitude at the lower levels leads to vast differences in fiscal capacity and the nature and menu of the services provided.

Third, governments in China have concentrated on industry as a source of raising revenue, which harkens back to the country's collectivist history, where direct taxes were rare and the state supported itself by industry profits. A danger is that taxes can be subject to future cycles in manufacturing. However, in 1994 there was a move toward a much broader spectrum of taxes. Furthermore, when both budgetary and off-budget activities are considered the existing system has a broader, if not always transparent, revenue-raising capacity.

Extra Budget Revenues

The formal budgets of governments in China tell only half the local financing story. Local governments are highly dependent on extra-budgetary funds (EBFs), which nationally amount to 20 percent of GDP (about two-thirds of which accrue to local governments). These off-budget revenues finance local services, help bridge the gap between the revenue and expenditure, and are critical to financing infrastructure investments. Local governments (including municipal districts and villages) enjoy near-autonomy in the imposition of EBFs. Despite the prevalence of fees and levies found in government budgets, conventional user charges (such as for water, sewage, garbage removal) are relatively underutilized.[10]

Given the historical dynamics of revenue sharing, local governments have had a powerful incentive to keep these funds off-budget. Central agencies, which have their own set of EBFs, have begun to implement measures to integrate EBFs into the budget.[11] Self-raised funds consist mainly of special fees, charges, taxes on enterprises that are owned by that government, leases of land, and profit distributions from local government owned businesses.[12] Also included are surtaxes and charges on enterprises within the government's jurisdiction. While the legal authority can be murky, these charges essentially are outside of the formal budget and rely on extra-legal means of collection and enforcement or, more simply, the operation of a market, where the company can have locational and political advantages.

There are differences of opinion regarding the probity and efficiency of EBFs. One view is that the off-budget activity is a marker along the road of the long march toward the market economy, since many industries and businesses are, in fact, products of the governmental system. Collecting charges for specific services and spending them locally is an application of the benefit principle and makes for a closer link between locally perceived needs and resources. It also keeps decisionmaking at the local level and makes it quicker and less subject to outside interference.

Offsetting these advantages are several disadvantages. There is little up-to-date information on EBFs, and their relationship to their local government owners is often opaque, sometimes apparently tied to personal and political relationships. Moreover, the charges, fees, and impact on profits represent a growing burden. It has been estimated that extra budgetary exactions eat up perhaps 50 percent of corporate profits in the country (Irwin 2002).

National leaders are concerned about EBFs and the cloudy fringe of local government-owned business. There is a desire to integrate EBFs back into the comprehensive state budget. However, if this rubric is applied to local owned enterprises, it could mark a step backward, a recentralization of the country's public finances and the center-based mandates. A compromise solution might be to formalize the EBF process and make assignment of duties to companies clearer, financial reporting and accounting consistent, and relationships more uniform throughout the country.[13]

Infrastructure Financing

China faces many issues in reforming its economy to be more market-based, strengthening and liberalizing its financial system, and ensuring adequate basic services. Improved infrastructure is a fundamental need and vital to China's continued economic development and social welfare. Although the country is still largely rural, there is increasing pressure to urbanize; the urban population grew from 17 to 33 percent of the total from 1980 to 2000. In addition to the problems of increasing density and resulting congestion, the growing household income demands more and improved urban services. The increased trade and communication connections both internally and globally depend on improved transportation services. Internally, it is still difficult to get goods to and from markets, which restricts growth in more remote areas.

Paradoxically, local governments are responsible for providing infrastructure, but the existing fiscal and financial systems allow few ways to assume that responsibility directly. Local governments are generally responsible for meeting the capital-intensive, lumpy-expenditure needs of environmental structures, roads, drainage, and power. With limited budgetary means, how they go about doing so varies dramatically. While local governments are not permitted to borrow on their own behalf, large amounts of local borrowing have been occurring through government-owned enterprises, project entities, and other channels that are able to operate "off budget." Project financing using foreign funds has also been a distinguishing feature and is especially important in the transportation area.

Infrastructure finance at the local level is arranged through the following avenues:

- Medium-term "policy" lending executed through the China Development Bank (CDB), which loans are funded through Policy Financial Bonds that it issues periodically. The "F" bonds have a 5- to 10-year maturity and carry an implicit central government guarantee.
- Commercial bank loans to government-owned entities that are medium-term (mostly 3- to 5-year) commercial loans.
- Use of on-budget and off-budget current revenues. Formal budgetary resources have played a declining role in infrastructure finance in recent years, as the activities of government-owned enterprises have blossomed.

- Various public-private arrangements (usually with local government-owned businesses) that range from concessions given private investors to joint ventures and build-own-operate schemes. In yet other cases, companies may borrow funds for purposes of *de facto* relending to the parent government.
- Donor-based on-lending activities that are channeled through government companies.

The above list reflects that Chinese infrastructure finance is an inherently complex area, one where the distinctions between the private and public sectors are blurred.

Local Borrowing Powers and Arrangements

Local governments are not allowed to borrow against their general revenues.[14] However, they may borrow for special projects indirectly either through asset-holding companies that they own or through a Special Purpose Vehicle (SPV). These are often named Urban Development and Investment Corporations at the municipal level and act on behalf of the local government in funding for infrastructure and other investments. Thus, while general-credit borrowing is prohibited, "special fund" borrowing—in the guise of locally owned enterprises—is practiced.

Some local governments evade the borrowing prohibition clause by setting up a special entity to effectively borrow for them by issuing corporate bonds. Such bonds are dubbed *transmuted bonds*. The issuing corporations have ties with the local authority, and bond proceeds are used, in turn, to lend to the local government or its affiliated government-owned company. Repayment of the bonds comes from the repayment of the underlying loans and, eventually, from the parent owner's fiscal funds. The marketplace and the Chinese Ministry of Finance view the debt as contingent liabilities of the parent local government unit (Kang 2002).

Getting a quantitative handle on the extent of this activity is a challenge, since these SPV units and companies neither exist as part of the formal governmental structure nor do they systematically and publicly report their financial results or conditions. Also, they can occupy a spectrum of business success, from enterprises that contribute to local revenues through taxes and the distribution of profits to fiscal sinkholes that require subsidies and soft loans to remain in existence.

There are concerns that the efforts to restructure the banking system in China will cut off bank lending to the off-budget enterprises and effectively to the many local governments that depend on them. Understanding the full extent of these government-company activities and figuring out a way to rationalize them is a leading challenge in Chinese subnational finance. Whether by rationalizing the use of the SUV and off-budget funds or permitting direct borrowing powers by on-budget local governments, there is a need to allow responsible and well-regulated borrowing at the subnational level.

Highway Finance

Highway finance in China illustrates both a major national effort in infrastructure spending and an ingenious blend of traditional and new funding sources, including access to foreign private capital and the domestic stock market. During the interval from 1996 to 2000, China invested Y 805 billion in highway construction, more than five times the total for the previous 15 years combined. The methods of project financing used for highways may hold promise for wider applications to other forms of infrastructure.

Highway construction in China historically has been supported by using combinations of government grants and loans and user charges. Major reliance has been on three user charges, the road maintenance fee (levied on commercial transports), the vehicle annual use fee, and the new vehicle purchase fee.[15] These three user fees represented, as of 1998, some $25 billion in revenues, or about 75 percent of the funds used for highway construction and meeting debt service costs. The use of tolls has grown rapidly in importance. Almost all high-grade highways, including new expressways, are toll facilities. In 1998, tolls generated $2 billion revenue annually and were expected to reach $20 billion by 2010. Tolling new high-use highways to generate revenues for amortizing the debt portion of finance is well established in China and perhaps a precedent to other self-supporting activities (World Bank 2003a).

The tolling mechanism and the established system of user charges have helped to attract private capital flows into highways, especially in the rapidly growing coastal areas, where private developers were awarded early concessions.[16] These capital flows into highway construction often come in the form of joint ventures, where the governments or their asset companies link up with foreign investors in projects to build and finance the improvements. The public-private projects are also generating securities in both the domestic and international securities markets.

Since 1990, over 80 joint venture projects (with provincial and municipal agencies, including Hong Kong developers) have been organized in 14 provinces. The total capital cost of these projects is estimated at Y 95 billion, of which Y 75 billion is from private sources. The public sector provides, under terms of a concession, land and highway facilities in need of rehabilitation and construction; external sources, such as the private sector and mainland agencies, provide the capital for reconstruction and expansion. The private investor almost always participates in operational activities with provincial partners and in toll collection facilities. The private partner takes a lead in the contribution of equity and in some cases makes shareholder loans to the project; the provincial and municipal agencies contribute their own funds, generally in the form of repayable equity or debt to the project. Figure 22.1 illustrates the typical relationship of public and private sector parties in a cooperative toll road joint venture.

Cooperative joint ventures are "cooperative" and "joint" and have featured a number of incentives to give foreign partners security in their investment over the period of the concession, which is most often 20 to 25

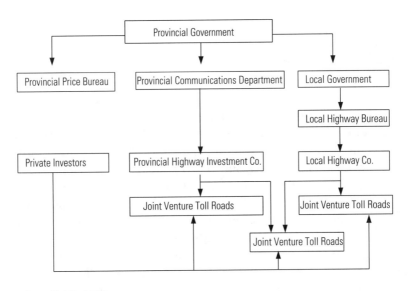

Source: World Bank 2003a.

Figure 22.1. Typical Cooperative Joint Venture Arrangement for Expressway Development

years. These incentives include minimum profit guarantees, guaranteed repayment of capital, tax incentives, exchange loss protection, and preferential loan repayment.

Provincial governments have turned increasingly to asset-backed financing for new high-grade toll highway projects, using toll revenues of the existing highways as security to raise new debt and equity.[17] The preferred method of financing highways is through expressway companies, which is a form of joint venture, with the provincial governments providing equity and private participants providing a mixture of equity (with stock offered on the Hong Kong or Shenzhen stock exchange) and debt.[18]

Share prices of the expressway companies listed in Hong Kong appreciated initially. In the years subsequent to the Asian financial crisis, and as a result of the large number of new entries to the Hong Kong market by provinces with interest in highway asset securitization, share prices fell sharply and investors became cautious. In response, Chinese authorities have directed more shareholding companies to the A and B share markets located in Shenzhen in order to attract local investors. International investors have access to the B share market in Shenzhen. To expand the investor base, one company (Zhejiang Expressway Company) applied to Britain's listing authority to have its H shares traded on the London Stock Exchange (World Bank 2003b).

The Financial Sector

Before 1979, China's financial system functioned as a mono-banking regime. Characteristically of a centrally managed system, China's financial sector was "repressed," that is, markets were not allowed to function (they in fact were banned), interest rates were kept below market rates, and exchange was cleared at official rates that did not reflect the market. In the 1980s, the country began sweeping economic reforms geared toward more decentralized economic management and a market-driven, albeit socialist, economy. As part of the package, Chinese authorities wished to replicate the western financial system, complete with diversified financial intermediaries, a competitive financial market structure, and an effective regulatory and supervisory framework (Xu 2002). China has approached reform by using an "empirical gradualism" based on "laboratory experiments," in which reform policies were paced, tested first in selected sectors and widely adopted only if experiments confirmed that the policies were viable (Wei 2000 p. 31).

Restructuring the financial sector involved reorganizing the existing banking institutions and creating new financial intermediaries. The job was huge. It required the following:

- Transforming the interest-free and non-repayable grants into interest-bearing bank credits, promoting self-finance, and attracting foreign capital.
- Restructuring the mono-bank system into a two-tier banking system to separate central banking and commercial banking.
- Developing financial instruments and markets, including money, bonds, and the stock market.
- Creating a legal and institutional framework for the financial sector and financial supervision (Wei 2000).

Banking System

Before the reform of 1979, the People's Bank of China (PBC) was the sole financial institution in the Chinese planned economy and market-based financial activities were banned. With a plan to transform the PBC into a central bank, the State Council dispersed the commercial banking activities, once operated by the PBC, to four "specialized banks" (Xu 1998, pp. 19–20). China's banks and financial institutions now are sorted into the following groups:

- Four state-owned banks, formally known as four "specialized banks": the Agricultural Bank of China (ABC), the Industrial and Commercial Bank of China (ICBC), the Bank of China (BOC), and the People's Construction Bank of China (PCBC).
- Two "policy" banks.
- Share ownership commercial banks.
- Urban co-operative banks.
- International trust and investment corporations.

Comparing deposits to GDP, China's banking system is one of the world's largest; the unusually high ratio of bank assets to GDP (130 percent) is a reflection of both China's high savings rate and the lack of alternative uses of those savings. However, China's capacity to handle forthcoming foreign competition, which will be rapidly arriving with its entry into the WTO, is providing the country's banking system with major immediate problems.[19]

China's banking system, which dominates the financial landscape, presents a large number of structural and operational problems. The central bank, the PBC, is not independent. The State Council still sets monetary and exchange rate policy, although both policies are supposed to be the province of the PBC. Decisions are made on political grounds by government authorities at various levels, and the freedom to choose among loan opportunities is limited. Although price controls have largely been removed, government authorities instead of market mechanisms still command the interest rates on bank deposits and loans. Generally, the banks are unprofitable operations; the rate of return on assets of China's four largest state-owned banks has been low and falling. There have been lapses in the supervision of financial sector operations, which became problematic during the 1990s.[20]

Perhaps the most intractable problem in China's banking system is a huge amount of bad loans. The non-performing loans (NPL) continue to grow, with NPLs estimated at about 24 percent of bank footings. These are largely a result of bank lending to unproductive State Owned Enterprises (SOE) and the banks' generally unprofitable operations. Government control of credit allocation and influence in bank lending decisions have meant that the SOEs received about 70 percent of total bank loans at subsidized interest rates (Li-Gang 2002). This would not be a problem had the SOEs not incurred large losses and been so highly indebted. Much of the lending was heedless: debt-to-equity ratios rose quickly from 19 percent in 1980 to 79 percent in 1994 (Huang 1998, p. 6). At the same time, most of these troubled SOEs kept their businesses running by means of state bank loans or government subsidies.

According to some observers, SOE managers and employees had no motivation to reform; they felt no pressure to repay the bank loans because both banks and enterprises are owned by the state (Huang 1998). Reforming the Chinese state-owned enterprise system has proceeded slowly and the banks have acted as buffers in the process. Since China lacks "social safety nets," a rapid push on SOE reform could raise unemployment rates and trigger unrest. Ultimately, the SOEs must be restructured, either through imposing hard-budget constraints, downsizing, or outright closure.

Capital Markets

Besides the formation of the two-tiered banking system, creating financial markets was a key objective in reform. However, this reform proved slow in arriving, as China seemed less than committed to having financial markets as alternative means of financial intermediation. In the early 1990s, the securities markets emerged with the institution of the Shanghai and Shenzhen securities exchanges. China's stock market is now the second largest in Asia, second only to that of Japan. The Shanghai stock market and its smaller counterpart in Shenzhen have 1,200 listings and a market capitalization of approximately $500 billion. As was noted, the domestic stock market is of special interest to local government finance in China because of the recourse made to it by government-owned companies. This has been particularly the case with highway transportation and expressway companies.

On the other hand, the size of the Chinese domestic bond market is small compared to the bank loans and equity markets (table 22.3). Outstanding bond debt in 2000 was equal to 25 percent of GDP (corporate and government), while bank credit equaled 133 percent of GDP. Equity market capitalization has soared to 53 percent of GDP.

Bond Market

The potential domestic bond investor base is already large, although options are restricted largely to either bank savings accounts or government bonds. The average national savings rate has been around 35 percent and reached Y 8 trillion in 2002. Major institutional investors in bonds are security investment funds, insurance funds, social security funds, and commercial banks (which, however, are prohibited from buying corporate bonds). Individuals hold Y 0.8 trillion worth of bonds.

Despite the market's growth, channels for investment continue to be limited. Corporate bonds are viewed as risky, as are common stocks (80 percent of which are shares in state-owned companies). Governments may want to privatize their company equity holdings but they must sell their

Table 22.3. Market Capitalization, Bonds, and Domestic Bank Credit as Percentages of GDP: 1995–2000

Item/Year :	1995	2000
Stock Market Capitalization	5.9%	53.8%
Corporate Bonds*/	4.0	9.2
Government Bonds	5.6	5.3
Domestic Credit	91.1	132.7

*/ Includes government-owned institutions and enterprises.
Source: Shiria 2002.

ownership, which would depress stock market prices. Thus, slow liquidation of ownership, to the extent that it takes place, seems to be in order (Shiria 2002).

There are three major types of bonds (table 22.4):

- *Treasury bonds or T-Bonds:* Two thirds of outstanding debt in China is the state Treasury bonds of various types with maturity of 6 months to 30 years, with largest amount being in the 3- to 5-year range.[21]
- *Financial bonds or F-bonds:* These account for one third of outstanding debt and are from China's policy banks, the China Development Bank (CBD) and Export-Import bank of China. These support infrastructure projects or are used to develop strategic industries. CBD accounts for 95 percent of the F-bond issuance with maturity of 6 months to 30 years.[22] The F-bonds are considered to be quasi-government bonds and carry an implicit guarantee.
- *Corporate bonds:* These account for only 4 percent of the outstanding bonds and consist of central corporate bonds issued by enterprises owned by the central government (such as CITIC, State Power, and Three Gorges), local corporate bonds issued by enterprises owned at the local level, and corporate short-term bonds. The usual maturity of central corporate and local corporate bonds is 3 to 5 years, although there have been 8-year issues.

The issuance of corporate bonds is governed by strict procedures, which in part explains the small market share. For issuance of larger than Y 100 million (about US$12 million), corporate bond issues can seek CSRC approval for stock exchange listings.

Table 22.4. Outstanding Domestic Bonds and Issuance in 2001 (Yuan billion)

	Outstanding	Percentage	New Issues	Percentage
T-Bond	1,561.8	62.1	488.4	64.2
Policy F-Bond	853.4	33.9	259.0	33.9
Corporate Bond	100.9	4.0	14.7	1.9
Total	2,561.1	100.0	762.1	100.0

Source: Shirai 2002.

Credit Quality and Ratings

The stock exchanges require that all listed debt securities be at least A-rated by the domestic credit rating agencies. Given the competition to meet minimum rating mandates and a lack of industry standardization, however, most corporate issues can get a minimum of single-A rating. The practice of credit rating in China started in 1987, but most rating agencies remain poorly managed and underfunded. A rating may be given at the time of a new offering, but maintenance research is not supported by secondary market activities, nor does the market in pricing seem to acknowledge the value of credit rating. Two services in China providing more credible opinions service in the nascent market include China Chengxin (which is owned 30 percent by Fitch Ratings and 10 percent by the IFC) and Dagong International (which is a joint venture with Moody's).

Interest rates are administered and coupons are capped at 1.4 times the rate of savings deposits of the same term, but they are lower than the rates on bank loans. All bonds are issued at interest rates dictated by the PBC, which takes into account macroeconomic conditions but does not distinguish by credit risk or allow the market to price to reflect the risk. All bond issues must be approved on a case-by-case basis by the State Development Planning Commission (SDPC) and, depending on the sector that is borrowing, by other national level institutions.

Municipal Bonds: Today and Tomorrow

China has limited experience with municipal bonds, including a brief surge of municipal bond issuance in the early 1990s that led to a number of defaults or near-defaults by the issuers. This led to imposition of the tight regulatory controls on municipal bonds that amounted to their being outlawed. Under the twenty-eighth provision of the 1995 Budgetary Law: "Budgets of all local government units should be {balanced} and, without the exceptional permission from the law or the State Council, no local government should issue bonds."[23]

Existing "municipal" bonds are seen as a subset of the corporate market and are now those bonds that are issued by SPVs and local government-owned companies. They are bought on the reputation of the issuer and an implied guarantee that the municipality will not let the issuer fail. There appears to be little market scrutiny of underlying financial conditions and little information upon which to base such judgment. The risk is seen as ultimately transferred back to the owner government. The Shanghai Urban Development Investment Corporation (UDIC), a company owned by the City of Shanghai, has issued bonds to help finance infrastructure investments primarily in the transport area. Many other localities have issued bonds through SPVs and their companies, using the corporate bond model.

Given the existing regulatory framework, the regulations on bond issuance that appear most pertinent to issuances by local governments are as follows (World Bank 2003b):

- Local government bonds may only be issued by asset-owning companies and the local governments have divorced asset ownership from service delivery (by use of SPV) to meet this requirement.
- Bonds must be issued with the guarantee of a third-party asset-owning company or financial enterprise, which local governments have configured themselves to do.
- A borrower must have three years of profitable operation, which is an impediment to new start-ups.
- Cumulative outstanding bonds may not exceed 40 percent of the issuing institution's assets.
- Bonds may not exceed 30 percent of project cost.

The above restrictions favor older state-owned companies that have assets to which some value can be affixed. To meet the requirements, local governments create companies and economic vehicles that can take ownership of assets. After seasoning, projects then are headed to the stock or bond markets, if permission is received.

Whatever the limitations and impediments, using the domestic bond markets is critical for large-scale infrastructure projects. As a practical matter, governmental units or companies entering into three-year bank loans have little revenue to pay off loans and are forced to roll over their bank debt, which exposes them to short-term rate fluctuations. Moreover, the impending WTO agreements on financial systems, entailing international competition and standards for the domestic financial sector, will force state-owned banks to be stricter in the terms of loans and will expose their weakness as large amounts of short-term loans being renewed will not be able to be paid since consumers cannot pay tariffs required to repay three-year loans. All these considerations point to the importance of recourse to the bond markets and less dependence on the state-owned banks.

A representative of the Chinese Ministry of Finance has observed the need for a municipal bond market and made recommendations on how that might come about and what it would look like in China. Responsible subnational borrowers could be fit into a framework of controlled issuances, which essentially involves selectively relaxing the prohibition for qualifying borrowers. These issuances would be self-liquidating (revenue bonds), and the credit quality would fit between that of the riskless sovereign debt and riskier corporate debt. Characteristic of the Chinese approach, the municipal bond market would open slowly and selectively (Kang 2002).

An issue in formulating a municipal bond market is the quality of financial management and transparency. The Chinese central government has committed to budgetary reforms, and some significant progress has been made strengthening the public expenditure management system. A detailed Government Financial System has been designed to provide a system for the preparation and execution of the government budget at both central and provincial levels. The financial system was effectively adopted and became effective in fiscal 2002. Modernized procedures for payment processing and accounting have been adopted. The design of a government financial management information system is being piloted in ministries and some provinces. Local levels have adopted "zero-based" budgeting approaches to better prioritize the use of available resources, decrease the importance of EBFs by converting fees and charges into regular taxes, and bring the funds into fiscal accounts. Obviously, some subnational borrowers will achieve improved management and transparency earlier, and it is likely to be these (or their companies and projects) that achieve early bond market entry. In fact, the promise of such entry can hasten the reforms.

Shanghai: Bond Financing Environmental Improvements

Movement toward a more formal, regularized, and transparent municipal bond market in China requires pioneer issuers of size and stature. The City of Shanghai may fill that role. The World Bank has been working with the City on a large-scale environmental financing program. Shanghai municipality is one of four cities in China that have provincial-level status. It has a registered population of 14 million urban dwellers with another 3 million in temporary residents. An important industrial and trade center, it accounts for about 1 percent of the nation's population and 5 percent of its GDP. However, there are pressing needs to improve urban service delivery, notably on water and sanitation. Only about 11 percent of the sewerage flow receives secondary treatment; the quality of the surface-drawn drinking water is rapidly deteriorating, and the municipality has severe solid waste disposal problems (World Bank 2003a).

The need for environmental improvements and their large geographic scope have led the city to consider a region-wide approach to water pollution problems and, in particular, the use of an on-lending facility by the central city unit to assist the suburban units in meeting their share of the improvements. Use of the Shanghai UDIC to bring together several of its suburban areas into a joint financing program is now a priority. Over the next 5 years, UDIC will need to finance some $4.85 billion in improvements. Capital budgets indicate that the municipality can provide perhaps $3.5 billion, which leaves a gap of over $1 billion to be financed. The desire is to tap the domestic bond markets to do this.

Shanghai city's investment activities have previously used bonds for transportation, hotel investments, and manufacturing, the debt having been issued by UDIC. The current proposal is for UDIC to have an environmental subsidiary, the Shanghai Water Assets Operation and Development Company (SWOAD), to issue bonds. The added need is seen for a district-wide financing vehicle that will permit the city and suburbs, the region, to enter into a financing plan. Arranging for adequate security for on-lent funds in view of the constraints on formal budgets is a challenge.

The World Bank's endeavors to assist the Shanghai area are also aimed at supporting continuing financial sector reform and expanding the capacity of the markets to finance long-term improvements. The effort is in pushing ahead the creation of a municipal bond market to free the project needs from dependency on short-term bank loans, to tap into long-term savings, and to enliven the non-governmental long-term bond market, making it a more viable long-term lender.

Notes

1. See Rodrick (2003) on the distinctive Chinese economic approach. Due to efficiency gains, high rates of savings and investment, buoyant export growth and foreign direct investment, and a vast supply of semi-skilled labor, the People's Republic of China's growth has been outstanding. Between 1978 and 2000 it averaged more than an 8 percent growth rate in GDP, one of the highest sustained growth rates in the twentieth century, matched only by Japan and Korea (Li-Gang 2002, p. 10).

2. Includes 22 provinces, 5 Autonomous Regions, and 4 Municipalities: Beijing, Shanghai, Tianjin, and Chongquing. Some provinces are larger than most nations: Guangdong Province has 70 million people and Henan has 93 million.

3. Under the centrally planned economy (1957 to 1979), taxes were industry-centered, and the value-added was simply tapped by the state at the industry level and surpluses used to cover government costs. Tax administration was simple. Taxes were paid by the state-owned enterprises (SOE) and with planned output, mandated sales, and fixed prices, surpluses were easy to determine. See World Bank 2002, p. 7.

4. The intergovernmental fiscal system has gone through many changes. The fiscal-decentralization reforms beginning in the 1980s led to declines in both the ratio of total fiscal revenues to the GDP and that of central government fiscal revenues to the country's total fiscal revenues. To correct the decline, measures were taken to direct a large lump of tax revenues to the central level and more fiscal spending responsibilities were devolved to the local level.

5. There is the added parallel relationship of the Communist party that is present at each level of government. There are also what are known as the "off-off-budget" companies that are run by officials in an unofficial capacity but that rely on governmental contacts and informal channels. See Irwin 2000.

6. A gross receipts tax falling mainly on service sectors not covered by the value added tax; rates range from 3 percent to 20 percent.

7. The "property" tax on urban land use and rural land occupancy generates only 2 percent of local own-source revenues (Kang 2002, p. 9).

8. The central government collects 50 to 55 percent of total revenues and accounts for about 30 percent of direct expenditures; the rest is transferred to local governments.

9. The Chinese currency, Renmindi, is denominate in Yuan (Y). In 2002, US$1 equaled Y 8.3.

10. This is due to regulatory constraints that have kept fees that appear in budgets well below cost-recovery levels.

11. In 1999, the Ministry of Finance began to formulate organizational budgets that show all budgetary, extra-budgetary, and other resources and spending for each ministry, starting with four national Ministries (Education, Science and Technology, Labor and Social Security, and Agriculture). In 2000, the list was extended to 26 agencies.

12. See Wong (1999) for an analysis of EBFs and their role in transitioning economies.

13. The recognized EBFs are but part of the problem. According to Irwin 2000 (p. 169), "off-off-budget" represents another layer, which often amounts to arm-twisting to get businesses to pay up and may require extra-legal mandatory loans that may or may not be repaid. These "second generation" or "off–off-budget" activities may equal up to 25 percent of a government's formal budget in some cases.

14. Budgetary Law in 1995 (28th provision) prohibits local government from issuing bonds. Furthermore, debt that is owned or guaranteed by the local government is illegal and invalid.

15. The National People's Congress approved a fuel tax in October 1999 to replace the fees, but the fuel tax has not been implemented (sharing between the central government and provincial governments has not been decided).

16. It appears that much of the cream has been taken of the toll road market in China. With the most "profitable" opportunities already built or committed, remaining roads will require mixed private/public financing if private sector finance is to be attracted (World Bank 2003a).

17. Once the tolled expressways mature and traffic levels are reached, provinces usually attempt to refinance these segments through the formulation of listed expressway companies and a stock offering.

18. Eight provincial expressway companies have raised the equivalent of $1.6 billion in equity capital through 2002 for the rehabilitation and expansion of the highways (World Bank 2003b).

19. Under the WTO agreements, by 2005 China is to meet a series of requirements to open its banking system and financial markets to international competition.

20. In 1993 and 1996, China's financial sector was disrupted as the country's banks and non-bank financial institutions were subject to illegal speculation in both stock and real estate markets. This disruption was caused by the Chinese banking supervisors failing to inspect banks' lending policies; consequently, it triggered two large Chinese financial institutions going into bankruptcy (Wei 2000, p. 7).

21. The Ministry of Finance issued its first 10-year issue in 1999, followed by fixed-rate 15- and 20-year issues in 2001, and fixed rate 30-year issue in 2002. In January–October 2002, 12 T-bonds were issued in the aggregate amount of Y 282 billion, in 3–5 years and for bonds with 10- to 30-year maturity. Coupon rates were set at 1.9 percent (2-year issued in May) to 2.9 percent (30-year issued in May) (see World Bank 2003b).

22. In January through October 2002, 15 "F-bonds" were issued by CDB in the aggregate amount of Y 195 billion. Coupon rates were set at 2.15 percent (10-year issued in June) to 4.5 percent (30-year issued in March).

23. Kang 2002, p. 13.

Chapter 23

Asia
Republic of Korea

A centralized fiscal system, tight controls on borrowing, and preferential loans from the center have curbed the interest in subnational borrowing in the credit markets.

John Petersen

Lessons Learned

The Republic of Korea is a unitary state that started on the path to devolution relatively recently. One of the rapid-growth "Asian Tigers," it has developed impressive economic power and a good-sized domestic capital market and banking system. Having this financial system in place, however, does not mean that subnational governments will access it. Local borrowing decisions, and subnational finances generally, are closely supervised and regulated by central government authorities. Most local borrowing occurs through specialized government-owned institutions that are tied into national line ministries. These typically offer better rates and longer loan terms than are available in the markets. Thus local borrowing decisions are largely choreographed by a network of centrally controlled regulations and inducements. Given Korean concerns about the national economy and the strong tradition of centralization, fiscal decentralization does not appear to be imminent.

Even so, as devolution continues, the twin forces of greater local autonomy and a need to raise capital more efficiently are likely to increase interest in developing more competitive markets for local debt. The country's robust economic growth and urbanization require heavy capital outlays, and capital investment projects account for a large share of local spending. While these outlays are heavily supported by central government transfers, the need for credit will grow. Moreover, large Korean cities have experience in raising capital funds locally through compulsory bonds, a borrowing instrument unique to Korea.

Seoul illustrates some of the features of subnational financing. Responding to the crises of the late 1990s, it rapidly restructured its operations, reduced its workforce, pushed capital spending out to corporations (public and private), and paid down debt. With the swift recovery in the Korean economy, it has seen its revenues rebound and its bond rating upgraded. Although its bonds are not guaranteed by the central government, its creditworthiness, at least as perceived by the credit rating agencies, benefits from the strict state oversight of its operations.

A democratic and highly centralized Asian country that has enjoyed record-setting economic growth, the Republic of Korea has elected to fiscally decentralize its governmental structure slowly and carefully. While spending activities have been increasingly devolved to local government units, these units act in many ways as agents of the center. The central government has retained a tight grip on their spending decisions, fiscal systems, and borrowing authority.

Nonetheless, there are pressures for further devolution, with the hope of achieving the greater political accountability and spending efficiency expected with greater local autonomy. The nation's relatively well-developed capital markets provide a potential mechanism for helping to accomplish this, although access to capital markets by local authorities has been both limited and closely supervised by the central government. State-owned specialized lending institutions, offering attractive terms to local government units whose capital plans are blessed by the central government, still dominate the local government credit scene.

Subnational Finances

Korea has come to decentralization and devolution relatively late. Aside from a brief experiment in the 1960s, Korea has long remained a highly centralized unitary government, with relatively little autonomy at the local level.[1] Starting with local elections in 1994, Korea moved toward a system of political decentralization. But that decentralization has been largely administrative, involving little in the way of local fiscal autonomy. Local finances are still controlled from the center, with minimal local control over revenue and spending decisions.

Local government in Korea is organized at two levels. The first level, the regional governments, consists of Seoul and five other large cities and nine provinces. In the second level are 250 smaller district, city, and county units, known as the local governments. (Both types of government are generally referred to as local governments here.) As in most decentralized unitary states, each tier has its responsibilities and some own resources. However, as is true in many unitary states, the lines of demarcation between local responsibilities and those of the central state are vague (Kim 2002). The system depends heavily on transfer payments from higher levels of government. In Korea the entire network is thoroughly regulated and overseen by the central authorities.

In Korea, as in many countries, local economies and fiscal resources vary widely. The capital region of Seoul, with a population of 10 million, accounts for about 22 percent of the nation's population, 25 percent of its GDP, and 22 percent of local government spending. The focal point of much of the country's development, Seoul weighs disproportionately heavy in its economic development plans.

Revenue Sources

The system's high degree of centralization is reflected in the disparity between local government spending and own-source revenues: although local governments account for about 50 percent of total general government spending, they raise only 20 percent of revenues from their own sources, with the rest derived from central government transfer payments. The intergovernmental transfers are largely specific and conditional, and the central government exercises considerable administrative control over local activity. A large share of local unit spending is for capital projects, which are tied into national planning processes and requirements. This emphasis on capital projects limits the revenues available for operating purposes (Chu and Norregard 1997).

Local taxes are heavily skewed toward real, personal, and commercial property. These taxes are applied both *ad rem* and *ad valorem* on tax bases, with varying rates of assessment, and especially on property transactions. Local tax revenues have been growing in significance in Korea but are still relatively small as a share of GDP (4 percent) compared with those in other OECD countries. Although local units may set rates within wide ranges, all were using the same standard rates at least until the mid-1990s. Because expenditures are largely controlled by central decisionmaking, there is little local initiative to alter local tax rates (Kim 2002).

The Korean intergovernmental transfer system is complex. It takes into account expenditure needs and resource capacities and excludes several better-off jurisdictions (including Pusan and Seoul) from the distributive calculations. It also has provisions for funding special projects, over which members of the legislature have influence. The national transfer system is largely duplicated by a mandated regional transfer scheme under which regions make transfers to their local governments. Thus, all transfers are strictly regulated by the national government (Chu and Norregard 1997).

The current system of governance, with little devolution of fiscal authority to the local level, has been criticized for not reaping the efficiency advantages that should come with greater local autonomy. Subnational borrowing is subject to a complex regulatory framework and process in which consistency with national development plans takes precedence. The Ministry of Government Administration and Home Affairs takes the lead regulatory role, and local governments must obtain both its approval and that of local councils before undertaking borrowing (for international borrowing, the Ministry of Finance and Economy is the key player). Line agencies of the national government (such as the Ministry of Transportation and Environment) also get involved in particular projects and in the extension of subsidized credit.

Because of the historically close integration of the central and local governments and the center's approval process and close oversight, the financial risks in subnational lending are viewed as shared between the local and national governments, even in the absence of a formal central government guarantee. However, given the close national supervision and the little latitude afforded local governments, the risk of moral hazard appears to be minimal. The center is firmly in control of what is being done and the risks being taken.

One result of the firm central controls has been that the growth in subnational government debt has been subdued and its relationship to the economy has remained fairly constant. Local government debt as of 2001 represented only 3.3 percent of GDP compared to the central government debt of 20.7 percent. Local debt over the past few years has grown at roughly the same pace as the economy, while central government debt doubled in relationship to GDP between 1995 and 2001 (Kim 2002).

A market-oriented system of local borrowing would help increase the accountability and efficiency of local governments. Although the existing system of highly regulated and largely subsidized local borrowing has kept close control over local activities, Korea lacks a good credit allocation system in which local units would benefit from market terms and conditions. In the mid-1990s local units were borrowing at 6 percent with long grace periods, while market interest rates were at 9 percent. Moreover, the method of offering local bonds—usually through negotiation with banks with which the bond issuers have customary relationships—suffers from a lack of competitiveness (Chu and Norregard 1997).

Central Domination through Carrots and Sticks

Korea's developed economy could provide the financial basis—sufficient savings, large capital flows, and a developed market infrastructure—for developing a local credit market. Countering these advantages is the strong central political control of local government affairs. This domination is exercised both by controlling access to preferred financing from government-owned banks and through close monitoring and approval of local government debt issuance and detailed project review.

Government-owned banks and institutions provide about three-quarters of local government credit, and bonds issued by the local governments provide most of the remaining quarter.[2] The terms of the loans from government banks and institutions are more favorable than those available on bonds. The loans carry interest rates in the range of 3 to 7 percent, with tenors of up to 30 years. In contrast, bonds have interest rates of up to 10 percent and tenors of 10 years.

Government control is manifested through bureaucratic guidelines and edicts of the Ministry of Government Administration and Home Affairs on the eligible source of funding for specific projects. These essentially induce—if not direct—local government units to borrow on favorable terms from government sources, inhibiting the development of the private market for loans and bonds. Nonetheless, Korea has the largest domestic subnational government bond market by volume in Asia, even though this market is a small fraction (about 0.5 percent in 1999) of the overall Korean bond market.

Contrast the Korean approach with that in the United States, for example, where the federal government controls project development primarily through programmatic control of grants (as in the allocation of funds for transport) rather than through direct control of local government project funding or of the local debt market. If the federal bureaucracy ever gets involved, it does so only to require local governments to show how they can fund a project before it provides a grant. It does not monitor, control, or interfere in the local municipal credit market.

Legal and Regulatory Framework for Subnational Borrowing

Many broad legal and regulatory issues condition the development of a local government credit market. These include banking and municipal regulations that determine where subnational governments can deposit their funds and from whom and how much, if any, they can borrow; requirements for approvals by government (central, regional, and local); eligible uses of loan proceeds; types of borrowing instruments; repayment mechanics; and regulations relating to private loans and underwriting.

Korea has several laws relating to local government borrowing, codified in the Local Autonomy Act, the Local Financial Act, and the Enforcement Decree of the Local Financial Act. These acts define the procedures for borrowing by local governments and the approvals they must obtain from higher levels of government. The acts also define the general terms and conditions of the loans, eligible projects, and other details. Generally, the laws are very restrictive and local borrowing is tightly controlled by the central government.[3]

The borrowing procedures used in Korea are bureaucratic and complex, involving multiple approvals by both local and central government agencies. Although the local city council has the final say on whether a municipality will borrow funds for a specific project, the Ministry of Government Administration and Home Affairs reviews project plans and budget estimates and approves central government loans, which often involves other central government ministries and agencies. Since these loans are on favorable terms, the Ministry encourages their use. However, the Ministry of

Government Administration and Home Affairs also decides what projects are "appropriate" for any incurrence of local debt, so they have effective veto power over all local borrowing (Kim 2002).

One purpose of reviewing projects at the planning stage is to compile nationwide data on required borrowing from government financial institutions for input into the central government's annual budget cycle. This gives the Ministry of Finance a sense of the maximum demand for funds and the impact that local borrowing may have on credit supply. The Ministry of Government Administration and Home Affairs approves specific projects, but the Ministry of Finance clearly has overall control.

The elaborate project review and approval process illustrates the high level of central government involvement in local government capital budgeting. Although local governments make the final decision on projects, the central government and its institutions, primarily the financial institutions, still have much influence over what types of projects local governments may pursue and how they will be financed.[4]

The national government uses a set of regulations to determine whether local governments can borrow. Under these regulations a local government may borrow if it meets the following conditions (Darche 2002):

- It is not delinquent on principal and interest payments.
- The ratio of its average annual debt service (principal and interest payments) in the past four years to its average annual local revenue (local taxes, general shared taxes, current revenue, and grants) in the past four years does not exceed 20 percent.
- The ratio of its general fund balance (revenue minus expenditure) in the past fiscal year, minus its local fund balance carried forward to the next fiscal year, to its local revenue in the past fiscal year is greater than –10 percent.
- Its local tax revenue in the past fiscal year is more than 90 percent of that in the previous fiscal year.
- It has not violated laws and regulations relating to subsovereign borrowing.

While it is unclear what documents the Ministry of Government Administration and Home Affairs uses to ensure that local governments meet these conditions, project applications probably require financial statements or other financial information to measure compliance with these debt indicators.

Different types of subnational borrowing instruments are authorized by different laws. For example, compulsory bonds are authorized by article 19 of the Local Finance Act, and regional bonds are authorized by article 12 of the Urban Railway Act. These laws demonstrate the diversity of legal and procedural requirements faced by local government units in Korea, consistent with the advanced development of the country's financial system. The laws define such things as the eligible use of the proceeds and the security for repayment (whether collateral or a pledge of specific revenues). Borrowing in both the domestic and the international bond market requires adequate disclosure. Bank loans are less transparent, but borrowing is subject to local legislative approval.

Local Government Debt Instruments

Subnational units in Korea may use a large number of debt instruments, although two basic types—bonds and loans—may be used in two types of markets—domestic and foreign. The diversity of debt instruments reflects the relatively high development level of the Korean capital markets. The forms of security can vary as well, with the debt being secured on the general account, special accounts, or enterprise revenues.

Korea has a well-developed private domestic bank lending system, though it was radically restructured after the 1997 East Asian crisis. However, the private banking system rarely provides loans to regional and local units. Local units may borrow from private banks, but these loans are a small share of their total borrowing. Government-owned financial institutions dominate subnational borrowing, accounting for more than 80 percent of borrowed funds. Other financial institutions (private mutual and other funds, housing societies, pension funds, domestic contractual savings institutions) also lend to local governments through direct placement or bond purchases.

The government financial institutions and local government units negotiate the terms of loans. Private banks prepare bids based on the prime rate, often higher than the interest rates local governments can obtain from the government financial institutions, and local governments must compete with regular commercial customers. Almost all bank loans are secured by a "full faith and credit" pledge, which, given the high level of central government oversight, has political as well as financial implications.

The full faith and credit pledge assumes that the political relationship between the lending bank and the local unit is sufficiently strong to ensure

loan repayment. Although no data are available on the performance of local government loans during the Korean financial crisis beginning in 1997,
the government financial institutions do not appear to have had any significant loan delinquency problems. One reason may be the political (and
perhaps financial) support of local units by higher-level governments. Another may be that, by delaying projects, local governments could use the
large capital-spending component of their budgets as a buffer. Moreover,
while the 1998–99 downturn in the Korean economy was sharp, it was also
brief and followed by a vigorous recovery.

Local governments can also borrow from foreign banks, but these loans
are rare and available only to the larger metropolitan areas. Korean cities
have also ventured into the international bond markets. Any foreign borrowing, whether bank loans or bond issues, requires approval by the Ministry of Finance and the Ministry of Government Administration and
Home Affairs.

Korea has three types of domestic bonds—public, compulsory, and government compensation—and two primary types of foreign bonds. For public bonds, also known as flotation bonds, the issuer hires a securities firm
that solicits purchase offers from investors. These are general obligation
bonds secured by the full faith and credit of the issuer. Compulsory bonds
are unique to Korean finance. Their name comes from the fact that purchase of the bonds is compulsory for individuals and firms receiving certain services or privileges from the borrower, such as when purchasing a
car, receiving a license, or registering a local company. The proceeds from
these bonds are used to fund water services, subways, and other regional
projects in the 15 largest metropolitan areas and major cities. These bonds
are supposedly secured with the revenues generated by the improvements
they finance and may be seen as an early application of the benefit principle. The issuing government sets the terms, typically a sub-market interest
rate and extended grace periods.

Compensation bonds are used in construction financing. A form of vendor financing, they are given in lieu of direct cash payments to construction companies that build urban infrastructure. The city using these bonds
negotiates their terms and conditions with the construction company.
Compensation bonds have interest rates of 0 to 10 percent and tenors of
one to five years.

Foreign bonds, issues payable in foreign currency, are sold in both domestic and international markets. The metropolitan governments of Seoul
and Taegu have issued foreign currency general obligation bonds in inter-

national markets. These bonds received the sovereign ceiling rating because of the cities' status in Korea and the strong central government oversight.[5] Foreign borrowing, in both bank loans and bonds, represents only about 4 percent of all subnational debt; since the financial crisis of the late 1990s, interest in this source has declined (Kim 2002).

Debt proceeds fund a variety of activities. Seoul uses loans and bonds to fund construction of its subway, water, and sewerage systems, and other projects. The major metropolitan areas use debt proceeds mostly for housing and for agricultural and industrial estates, while the provinces use them primarily for housing and water and sewerage systems.

Debt Marketing and Sales

Korea's advanced bank and bond markets have led to the establishment of a large debt financing "skills infrastructure" to service these markets. There are numerous underwriting firms, financial advisers, and trust banks on the sell side, and institutional and retail investors on the buy side. However, to date, most local unit borrowing is done through special central government funds or through the use of the compulsory and compensation bonds.

The marketing process for local government bonds can be quite complex. Private bond placements are negotiated with the lending party (a public or private pension fund or some other contractual savings entity), with the bond terms and conditions usually based on current market rates. For public offerings a number of marketing devices may be used. In some cases the local unit hires an underwriter (or a private bank), one with which it may have a long-term relationship, to negotiate the sale of the bonds to its institutional and retail clients. In other cases the local borrower offers a competitive tender for underwriting services, which means that the financial agent takes on the marketing risk of reselling the bonds in the capital markets.

For compulsory bonds, the terms are set by the issuing government, and the retail buyers (purchasers of cars and houses, for example) must purchase the bonds at the given rates. In other words, local governments use their regulatory powers to compel a "tied-in" bond sale on preferential terms. For compensation bonds the issuing government negotiates the terms and conditions with the contractor. It is unclear whether these terms and conditions are negotiated with the price of the contract or only after the contract is awarded to the company. For foreign bonds underwriters are selected on a negotiated basis and then provide the borrower with either a firm price for the sale of the securities on the international markets or a "best efforts" underwriting basis, depending on the terms of the underwriting agreement between the issuing government and the senior underwriter.

Seoul's Management of Debt and Capital Spending

As the national capital, Seoul represents the largest local government in Korea. The city is the economic and political heart of the country and its largest local government borrower. Like other local governments in Korea, Seoul directs much of its spending to capital projects. Capital spending has accounted for about 40 percent of the total, though that share has declined in recent years.

The international currency crises of 1998 caused a sharp but short retrenchment for Seoul, which then recovered rapidly along with the rest of the country.[6] The city took quick and dramatic steps to restructure during the crisis. Besides delaying capital projects, it reduced its workforce by 22 percent. Although the crisis slowed borrowing and investment, the strong recovery greatly increased current revenues, and Seoul recently has been able to pay down debt and restore its investment program. Between 1998 and 2001 the unemployment rate fell from the crisis level of 7.6 percent to 4.5 percent, and in 1999–2001 the city generated substantial surpluses.

After earlier rapid growth, net debt outstanding has peaked and is being reduced (table 23.1). Debt outstanding as a share of total revenues, which was as high as 110 percent at the time of the crisis, fell to pre-crisis levels (about 87 percent) in 2001 and was projected to continue dropping. In the fall of 2002 Moody's rewarded Seoul with an upgrade of its foreign currency debt rating to A-3, recognizing its rapid recovery and generally sound prospects (Moody's Investors Service 2002).

Seoul has achieved greater autonomy in recent years, but this has not resulted in a larger city government. It is shifting more infrastructure spending to public corporations responsible for rapid transit services and, following the reduction in its workforce, has been outsourcing activity to the private sector. Moreover, the central government maintains close oversight, a factor that figures prominently and positively in its credit rating:

> Although Seoul's debt is not guaranteed by Korea, the national government's role in requiring budgetary balance, monitoring the city's budget condition, and approving borrowings is an important contributor to the [city's] rating (Moody's 2002, p.3).

Table 23.1. Debt and Capital Spending of the Seoul Metropolitan Government, Republic of Korea, Fiscal Years 1996–2001
(billions of won, except where otherwise specified)

Indicator	1996	1997	1998	1999	2000	2001
Net debt outstanding	4,865	5,635	5,609	5,969	6,197	6,075
Total revenues	5,665	5,595	5,178	6,107	6,994	7,015
Debt as a share of total revenues (percent)	86.4	100.7	110.6	96.7	88.6	86.6
Capital expenditures	—	2,869	2,116	1,982	1,982	2,105
Capital expenditures as a share of total expenditures (percent)	48.2	40.9	36.2	32.1	23.7	20.2

— Not available.
Source: Moody's Investors Service credit reports for Seoul Metropolitan Government.

Seoul has tapped offshore financing, through the sale of Yankee bonds (dollar-denominated bonds sold in the New York market) in the amount of $500 million in 1994. In August 1999 investors opted to exercise a five-year put option for $158 million, which Seoul met by drawing on reserves and floating a local currency bond issue. In mid-2000 more than 90 percent of the city's debt was denominated in Korean won.

Seoul relies on compulsory bonds as well as domestic bond sales and bank loans, an array of credit sources that gives it much flexibility in debt management. The large share of capital spending in its annual budget, much of it financed from current sources, provides a cushion of postponable expenditures if times get rough. In response to the events of the late 1990s, the city sharply reduced its capital investments as it redirected funds to repaying debt, shifted projects to corporations, and privatized some functions. Given the large menu of capital needs for which it is responsible, this flexibility is critical.

Prospects for a Stronger Subnational Government Credit Market

With a well-developed infrastructure of financial markets and intermediaries, Korea has good prospects for developing an extensive subnational government credit market if that were a national priority. The important elements of such a market are all in place: high per capita GDP and savings, well-developed and competitive financial intermediaries, a well-developed legal and regulatory system to support this competitiveness, and competitive public and private contractual savings institutions.

However, having the framework for a subnational debt market in place does not mean that the market will function. There are other pieces to the puzzle. For a market to develop also depends on effective demand for funds. This, in turn, depends on such things as the degree of effective decentralization of the municipal finance system, the regulation of municipal financial activities, and the political relationship between central and local government officials. Furthermore, the young Korean decentralization must contend with the perception that local borrowing is in fact a means of receiving central government grants over time and, correspondingly, that there is little need for, or interest in, raising local taxes or fees when central subsidies are on the horizon (Kim 2002). These factors hold back the development of subnational finance in Korea. Perhaps the biggest constraint on the development of a local credit market is the limited capacity of (and incentives for) local government officials to manage revenues and expenditures to achieve financial viability and creditworthiness. Lack of local fiscal autonomy and managerial capacity impedes the development of credit markets in which local governments would rely on private capital and be accountable to the market.

Korea illustrates the tradeoffs between securing macroeconomic stability and control and undertaking a more liberal process of political and fiscal devolution. It illustrates the development of a local government credit market that is closely controlled by the central government and relies primarily on the relationships among government-owned banks, special funds, and local government units. The top-down political relationship between the central and local governments has constrained the development of a more efficient local credit market. Subsidized interest rates and extended loan tenors that are unavailable in the private markets have made continued dependence attractive.

Notes

1. The Korean Constitution spends little time on the question of local autonomy. The relevant section (article 117) essentially states that subnational governments should exist at regional and local levels, should have

powers to serve local needs, and should have their own legislative bodies. Until 1994 the chief local officials were appointed by the central government. The framework and powers of subnational governments are defined by national legislation (the Law on Local Government Autonomy).

2. The government-owned banks and institutions include the Housing and Commercial Bank, Industrial Bank, Small and Medium Industry Promotion Corporation, Energy Management Corporation, and Environment Management Corporation. The specialized agencies tend to be organized by financing purpose and have close ties with the government line agencies.

3. Article 115 of the Local Autonomy Act states that governments can incur debt, with central government permission either when a permanent improvement in citizens' welfare is guaranteed or in the event of natural disaster. Article 7 of the Local Government Act declares a "no debt principle" that local budgets must be balanced (except in cases allowed under Article 115).

4. In interpreting what is an appropriate use of local debt, the Ministry can be flexible. All the soccer stadiums for the 2002 World Cup were financed by local government borrowing and a 30 percent national subsidy (see Kim 2002, p. 28).

5. Moody's Investors, "Service Web site, Seoul Metropolitan Government: Global Credit Report" (November 2002) .

6. Korean real GDP grew by 5 percent in 1998, shrank by 7 percent in 1999, and then snapped back, growing by 11 percent in 2000 and 9 percent in 2001.

Chapter 24

Asia
India

Experiments in local governments accessing the private capital markets provide promising results.

Pryianka Sood

Lessons

Experience in India with municipal credit is limited primarily because of a lack of decentralization beyond the state level. Most states, though financially weak, have significant autonomy—but this autonomy is not passed down to municipalities. Some states have taken steps to augment the power of lower levels of government, however, and these few exceptions have added positive chapters to the evolving story of local credit in India. The formation of municipal corporations with borrowing powers and the creation of successful municipal development funds are promising beginnings.

Although municipal governments continue to depend on revenue transfers from state governments, they have been assigned significant expenditure responsibilities, compounded in many cases by increasingly pressing infrastructure needs. Meanwhile, the country's debt market remains dominated by

---

the central government and public enterprises. To establish an effective municipal bond market, the government needs to create tax incentives for investing in bonds and regulations that support debt issuance, such as by providing for guarantees and establishing a market regulator. In the absence of these conditions, some states and municipalities have turned to financial intermediaries for funding for urban infrastructure.

While only the central government can tap international credit markets, local governments may borrow domestically. Ahmedabad was a pioneer in issuing bonds. The city undertook reforms that strengthened municipal tax revenue and sought a credit rating to enable it to issue bonds. The improvement in the city's fiscal position won it a strong credit rating, and its successful issuance of debt provided a model for other cities in India.

Two entities have facilitated municipal borrowing. The Municipal Urban Development Fund, created to provide infrastructure financing to local governments under the World Bank–financed Tamil Nadu Urban Development Project, functioned as a state-owned revolving fund. Providing a combination of loans and grants, with no state guarantee for lending, the fund achieved high repayment rates. However, while the fund proved financially viable, its scope and depth were limited by its reliance on state grants for funding. In addition, the fund's state ownership and management meant that its operations lacked autonomy, were weighed down by bureaucracy, and proved subject to political interference.

To address these shortcomings, the fund was converted into an autonomous, privately managed financial intermediary, the Tamil Nadu Urban Development Fund. Larger in scope, boasting solid performance indicators, and with a long list of potential borrowers, the new fund has attracted substantial private funding and has successfully linked private capital with local public infrastructure needs. The fund's structure, however, does not accommodate non-revenue-generating projects and limits its accessibility to smaller municipalities that cannot issue bonds. A key challenge is to create mechanisms allowing these small local governments to access private sources of capital.

Even so, the Tamil Nadu Urban Development Fund has done much to improve municipalities' access to private capital for financing infrastructure investments. Its success points to the importance of a comprehensive approach that divides tasks between government and the private sector.

India has a three-tier structure of government comprising the center, the states, and the local governments—the *panchayati raj* institutions (rural local bodies) and municipalities (urban local bodies). Until the passage of constitutional amendments in 1992, however, the government system functioned essentially as a two-tier federal structure with powers, functions, and responsibilities divided between the central government and the states. This division largely satisfied the principles of both federal finance and fiscal federalism.

The central government is responsible for all functions with national importance and large economies of scale, while states bear the main responsibility for delivering basic public services, such as public order, public health and sanitation, and water supply and irrigation. However, the division is not absolute. States have concurrent jurisdiction with the center in such areas as education, electricity, economic and social planning, and population control and family planning. Where conflicts arise, however, the central government's power overrides that of the state governments, and any powers not delegated explicitly to state governments reside with the center.

Revenue raising powers are based on the principle of separation of revenue systems, with tax bases assigned exclusively to the center or to the states. Most revenue sources with a mobile tax base are assigned to the center, while those with an immobile or local tax base (liquor excise, motor vehicle tax, agricultural land and income taxes) are assigned to the states. The use of mobility as a criterion for dividing the tax base has resulted in powers to levy most broad-based taxes (income tax, corporation tax, customs and excise) coming to rest with the center, with the retail sales tax the only major exception. The assignment of revenue powers has been asymmetric: states are charged with functional responsibilities that entail larger expenditures than they can meet from their own resources.

Even though states can levy taxes and duties that have substantial revenue potential, the revenue from these sources meets only about 50 to 60 percent of their current spending needs on average. Moreover, the principle of separation is applicable only in a legal sense, not an economic one. For example, while the center can levy taxes on production (excise duties), only the states can levy taxes on the sale or purchase of goods. Similarly, only the states can levy taxes on agricultural income and wealth, and only the central government can levy taxes on nonagricultural income and wealth.

The assignments of tax and expenditure authority have led to a vertical fiscal imbalance. In the financial year 1997/98 the states raised about 31 percent of total government revenue in India, but incurred about 57 percent of total expenditure. Transfers from the center made up the balance. The ability of the states to finance their current spending from own sources of revenue has declined over time, with own-source revenue falling from 69 percent of state spending in 1955/56 to around 55 percent in the 1990s (Rao 2000).

Recognizing that the revenue raising powers assigned to states are inadequate to meet their expenditure responsibilities, the Constitution provides for transfers from the center to state governments through tax devolution and grants in aid. To ensure that the transfers are allocated fairly, the Constitution requires that the president appoint a finance commission at least every five years to review central and state government finances and make recommendations on transfers to states for the next five years. In addition to these transfers, states receive assistance from the Planning Commission based on a formula determined by the National Development Council and transfers for specific purposes under programs implemented by national ministries.

Decentralization and Subnational Government

The Constitution of India that came into force in 1950 made detailed provisions for the democratic functioning of the central and state legislatures, but it did not make urban government a clear constitutional obligation. Even though the municipal acts of various states provided for regular elections to urban local bodies, or municipalities, these acts were often superseded for indefinite periods. Therefore, while the third tier of government existed in India, it took the form primarily of rural local bodies, or panchayats. Indeed, article 40 of the Constitution requires states to "organize village Panchayats (rural local bodies) and endow them with such power and authority as may be necessary to enable them to function as units of self-government." In keeping with these constitutional requirements, many states enacted legislation for the creation of panchayati raj institutions and the devolution of functions and responsibilities to them, and state governments devolved some revenue and expenditure powers to these subnational units.

However, these initial decentralization efforts remained limited to a few states. The system remained far from representative, and there was no mechanism to prevent state governments from superseding elected local governments. Moreover, the fiscal powers devolved to these lower levels of government remained inadequate, so that they continued to depend on grants from the state government to meet their development spending needs.

Decentralization under the Constitutional Amendments of 1992

The constitutional amendments of 1992 (the 73rd and 74th), perhaps the boldest democracy initiative in the world, gave concrete shape to the Indian government's commitment to vest power in the hands of the people. The amendments made the creation of elected urban local bodies a constitutional obligation and recognized both rural local bodies (panchayats) and urban local bodies (municipalities) as institutions of self-government. [The amendments defined three types of urban local bodies, depending on such criteria as population density, revenue generated for local administration, and the share of population engaged in nonagricultural activities: *nagar* (town) panchayats for areas in transition from rural to urban, municipal councils for smaller urban areas, and municipal corporations for large urban areas.] In the two-tier federal structure local governments below the level of the state had functioned merely as agencies of the state government. States now are required to hold regular elections for these local governments, with mandatory representation of women and disadvantaged groups (the scheduled castes, scheduled tribes, and backward classes). In 2000 India had more than 250,000 rural and urban local bodies (table 24.1).

The amendments set out an illustrative list of functions for urban and rural local governments. State finance commissions, regularly appointed by the state governments, ensure the devolution of financial resources to these local governments. The commissions review the finances of the local au-

Table 24.1. Third Tier of Government, India, 2000

Type of local authority	Number
Rural local bodies	247,033
Panchayats	238,682
Village level	232,278
Intermediate level	5,905
District level	499
Autonomous councils[a]	8,351
Village councils	8,310
Block advisory committees	25
Autonomous development councils	16
Urban local bodies	3,682
Municipal corporations	96
Municipal councils	1,494
Nagar panchayats	2,092

a. In autonomous district council areas, for weaker sections and tribal areas.
Source: India, Ministry of Finance 2000.

thorities and make recommendations on the distribution of the state revenues between the state and local governments and among local governments, the assignment of tax and other powers to rural and urban local bodies, and the grants in aid to local governments.

The empowerment of the panchayats and municipalities to function as institutions of self-government has been slow (India, Ministry of Finance 2000). While there has been a downward push of power, it falls well short of a federal devolution.

Functional and Fiscal Decentralization

The Indian Constitution has allowed considerable fiscal decentralization to the state level. Despite the constitutional amendments, fiscal decentralization has not gone further. While states raised nearly 31 percent of total government revenue in 1997/98 and had command over 55 percent of the revenue for spending purposes, local governments raised only 3 percent of the total and had about 10.4 percent at their disposal (table 24.2).

Thus local governments have very little revenue power. Decentralization notwithstanding, rural and urban local bodies in India face significant financing gaps (table 24.3).

In recognition of both the increased responsibilities and the financing gaps faced by local governments, the constitutional amendments were aimed at setting in motion a series of steps to improve the financial status

Table 24.2. Fiscal Decentralization, India, 1997/98

Level of government	Revenue collected (percentage of GDP)	Revenue accrued (percentage of GDP)	Revenue collected (percentage of total)	Revenue accrued (percentage of total)
Central	11.4	6.8	62.5	34.5
State	6.3	10.9	34.5	55.1
Local	0.6	2.1	3.0	10.4
Urban	0.5	0.8	2.7	4.0
Rural	0.04	1.3	0.3	6.4
Total	18.3	19.8	100.0	100.0

Sources: India, Ministry of Finance 2000; Rao 2000.

Table 24.3. Finances of Local Bodies, India, 1990/91 and 1997/98

	1990/91		1997/98	
	Total (crore rupees)	Share of GDP (percent)	Total (crore rupees)	Share of GDP (percent)
Rural local bodies				
Total expenditure	7,147	1.33	20,931	1.38
Expenditure on core services[a]	417	0.08	1,555	0.10
Other expenditure	6,730	1.26	19,377	1.28
Total revenue	6,614	1.24	19,356	1.28
Own revenue	370	0.07	677	0.05
Tax	238	0.04	377	0.02
Nontax	132	0.02	300	0.02
Other revenue	6,244	1.17	18,679	1.23
Urban local bodies				
Total expenditure	24,395	4.56	151,308	10.00
Expenditure on core services[a]	9,988	1.87	101,224	6.68
Other expenditure	14,407	2.69	50,085	3.30
Total revenue	3,931	0.73	12,179	0.80
Own revenue	2,736	0.51	7,599	0.50
Tax	1,935	0.36	5,892	0.39
Nontax	801	0.15	2,127	0.14
Other revenue	1,195	0.22	3,608	0.30

Note: One crore = 10 million rupees.
a. Roads, sanitation, water supply, and street lighting.
Source: India, Ministry of Finance 2000.

of local governments and their performance. The Eleventh Finance Commission (India, Ministry of Finance 2000) recommended the statutory provision of 1,600 crore rupees (Rs) to rural local bodies and Rs 400 crore to urban local bodies each year in 2000–05, to be distributed among states using the following criteria and weights:[1]

Criterion	Weight (percent)
Population	40
Index of decentralization	20
Distance from highest per capita income	20
Revenue effort	10
Geographic area	10

In addition, the amendments mandate that tax assignments, revenue sharing, and grants in aid to local governments are to be based on the recommendations of the state finance commissions and that central grants are to be linked to duly elected and empowered local bodies. However, because of the lack of clarity in the functional jurisdictions of local bodies, implementation of the constitutional amendments remains far from effective.

Moreover, the devolution of powers and functions to local governments has varied widely across states, reflecting the variation in the willingness of state governments to devolve. In many states the "conformity acts" enacted to give effect to the constitutional amendments have sought to restrict the autonomy of local governments, particularly panchayats, through provisions at odds with the amendments (Rao 2000). Several state acts effectively treat the panchayats as agents of the government rather than as self-governing institutions. India's experience with decentralization spans a broad spectrum: at one extreme is Kerala, where decentralization has been very successful; at the other are Uttar Pradesh, where local bodies have failed, and Bihar, where even the mandatory decentralization has not been completed.

Despite this dismal record, the 73rd and 74th constitutional amendments have been important in framing the decentralization process and strengthening local governments. The aim is to make subnational governments focal institutions in the provision of public services by endowing them with authority commensurate with their responsibilities and involving people at the local level. The amendments seek to transform local governments from constrained and indifferent institutions of governance into freer and more responsive ones.

Decentralization and Government Borrowing

The Constitution of India assigns borrowing powers to both the central and the state governments. However, while the central government may borrow from any source within the country as well as from abroad, state governments are restricted to borrowing within the country. Subject to conditions imposed by law, the central government can make loans to any state. It also can give guarantees on loans raised by any state as long as these do not exceed limits fixed under the Constitution (article 292). Central government loans to states are charged against the consolidated fund of India, a fund consisting of all revenues received by the central government, including loans.

While state governments have constitutional powers to borrow, the central government exercises overall control over their borrowing. A state cannot raise a loan without the consent of the central government if the state has an outstanding loan made by, or guaranteed by, the central government.

Local governments, with the exception of municipal corporations, are not vested with borrowing powers by the Constitution. Instead, they are wholly dependent on state governments for capital loans. The borrowing powers of municipal corporations are governed by the Local Authorities Loans Act of 1914, which permits them to borrow on security of their funds for public works that they are legally authorized to carry out, for relief works in times of famine or scarcity, for the prevention of outbreak of any dangerous epidemic diseases, and for the repayment of lawfully incurred debt.

Despite the borrowing powers under the Local Authorities Loans Act, municipal corporations must obtain the prior approval of their state government to borrow. The act requires municipal corporations to submit to their state government such details as the purpose for which the loan is sought, the amount of the loan, information about the loan security, the schedule for loan disbursement, loan terms, revenue receipts, and expenditure profile. The limits on borrowing are determined by annual ratable value (a measure of the value of a property, based on expected gross annual rent, on which the property tax is based), the value of municipal properties and assets, own revenues, and the general financial position of the municipal corporation. The act does not permit municipal corporations to use debt instruments to raise finance for services and infrastructure.

Municipal corporations and municipal councils also have raised loans from banks and other financial institutions and from government agencies such as the Housing and Urban Development Corporation, with the approval of state governments and with state guarantees for the debt. Local governments thus continue to depend heavily on higher levels of government. While the dependence on intergovernmental transfers ranges from 60 to 65 percent of recurrent expenditures for municipalities, rural local bodies (panchayats) depend almost entirely on transfers to meet recurrent expenditures. Since decentralization was initiated, some states, such as Gujarat and Maharashtra, have adopted legislative provisions explicitly authorizing local authorities to undertake open market borrowing. However, there have been no serious attempts to encourage or empower local bodies to use debt instruments even within the limits of the Local Authorities Loans Act of 1914 (Mathur 1999).

Domestic Debt Markets

While India's equities market attracts the participation and interest of a large number of retail investors, its debt market has traditionally remained a wholesale market, with the government and public enterprises the predominant borrowers. Despite being the third largest market in Asia by outstanding debt issued, the Indian debt market until recently was largely a captive one (Analyst 2002). The statutory liquidity ratio requirements of the Reserve Bank of India, under which banks must invest part of their deposits in central and state government bonds and other approved securities, resulted in a captive investor base of a few hundred banks and institutional investors.

A retail debt market existed in the country in the late 1950s and 1960s, when individual investors accounted for more than half the holdings of government securities. However, the administered interest rate regime, which lowered yields on government securities, and the availability of other financial instruments led to the disappearance of this market.

Although it is not difficult to see why the debt market in India remains immature, interest and participation in the market have increased markedly in recent years. Annual trading volumes more than doubled from Rs 450,000 crore in 2000/01 to Rs 700,000 crore in the first seven to eight months of 2001/02. This growing interest reflects in part the downtrend in stock markets, which has led investors to look for safer investments. The deregulation of interest rates has also quickened the development of the market. Lending and borrowing rates now are determined by the market with the Reserve Bank of India's bank rate (or refinance rate) serving as the benchmark.

A healthy, vibrant, and efficient domestic debt market is essential for a strong economic future for India. The devolution of functions and powers to lower levels of government has come with a corresponding decline in central government grants, subsidies, loans, and other transfers. In response to the need to generate domestic finance for development, particularly the enormous amounts of long-term finance needed for infrastructure, efforts are under way to stimulate the development of domestic debt markets. Efforts are also aimed at designing and financing pilot projects that are commercially viable and ensuring that participating municipal governments are creditworthy borrowers (Analyst 2002).

As the debt market expands to include insurance companies, pension funds, mutual funds, banks, primary dealers, provident funds, and corporations, its focus can be expected to widen beyond the current focus on government securities to incorporate a repurchase market, commercial paper, debentures, bonds, and securitized debt (India, Ministry of Finance 1997, 2001).

In a significant step in developing domestic bond markets, municipal bonds are beginning to emerge as important instruments for mobilizing resources for local governments' development spending needs. As noted, some states (including Gujarat and Maharashtra) have explicit legislation governing borrowing by local authorities in the open market. It is amendment of the Local Authorities Loans Act of 1914, however, that is most likely to foster the growth of the municipal bond market. Such an amendment should promote the development of a fully fledged municipal bond market through tax incentives encouraging individual and institutional investors to invest in bonds. Regulatory measures providing for bond guarantees and insurance and a specific regulatory role for the Securities and Exchange Board of India or the establishment of a similar regulatory authority would also be necessary (India, Ministry of Finance 1997).[2]

The First Local Bond Issue: The Experience of Ahmedabad

Bangalore was the first city in India to obtain a credit rating and issue municipal bonds. The Municipal Corporation of Ahmedabad, the largest city in Gujarat, followed suit. However, unlike the Bangalore municipality, which issued bonds subscribed to by private investors alone, the Ahmedabad Municipal Corporation issued bonds subscribed to by both public and private investors. By doing so, it became the first urban local body in South Asia to raise funds through a public issue (its issue is therefore generally referred to as the first bond issue).

The Ahmedabad Municipal Corporation turned to borrowing in the open market as part of its efforts to recover from a deteriorating financial condition. Despite having sound finances until the early 1980s, its current revenue deficit had reached Rs 60 million by the end of 1993/94. Revenue yields from its two main taxes—the property tax and the *octroi* tax (a tax on the entry of goods into a local area for consumption or sale)—were proving inadequate, in part because of lax administration and enforcement of municipal taxes and the corporation's poorly trained management staff. Moreover, the city's expenditure needs were growing. In the second half of the 1980s the city's slum population doubled, and living conditions for poor people became dangerously unhealthy. To compound matters, the city government had neither plans nor funds to undertake the investment needed to address the situation.

Given the enormity of the problems, the state changed the administrative leadership and management of the Ahmedabad Municipal Corporation in 1994, and a general reform program was instituted. The municipal corporation initiated a $145 million capital improvement plan covering water supply, sewerage, bridges, overpasses, and a slum development project. It also acted to strengthen the property tax base and improve the administration, enforcement, and collection of both property and octroi taxes (Mathur 1999). Most important, the municipal corporation decided to take advantage of statutory provisions allowing it to raise finance.

In 1996 the Ahmedabad Municipal Corporation asked the Credit Rating Information Service of India to rate the institution's inherent creditworthiness and its financial position, becoming the first Asian urban local body to receive a credit rating for a proposed domestic bond issue.[3] Initially the municipal corporation obtained a credit rating of A+, signifying "adequate safety with regard to timely payment of interest and principal amount." Based on its financial performance in 1996/97, however, the rating agency upgraded its rating to AA (SO), indicating a "high degree of certainty regarding timely payment of financial obligations on the investment."

The proceeds of the Rs 100 crore ($29 million) bond issue were to fund part of the capital improvement plan, with the rest of the costs to be met from internal accruals and assistance from multilateral financial institutions (USAID 1997). In addition, a U.S. government $22.5 million loan guarantee allowed matching support from private U.S. lenders.

The Ahmedabad bond issue was designed as a structured obligation with octroi revenues from 10 collection points earmarked for servicing the issue and kept in an escrow account. Placement was both private and public, with 75 percent (Rs 750 million) privately placed and 25 percent (Rs 250 million) sold in the retail market (table 24.4). The bond issuance process was supported by the U.S. Agency for International Development (USAID),

Table 24.4. Terms of the Bond Issue by the Ahmedabad Municipal Corporation

Issue size	Rs 1,000 million (Rs 750 million on a firm allotment basis)
Commitment	Net public offer of Rs 250 million fully underwritten
Face value	Rs 1,000 at par
Maturity	Seven years, with repayment in thirds in the fifth, sixth, and seventh years
Redemption	In three installments: Rs 333 at the end of the fifth year, Rs 333 at the end of the sixth year, and Rs 334 at the end of the seventh year
Interest or coupon rate	14 percent a year, payable semiannually on the outstanding principal (At 14 percent, the coupon rate was substantially higher than the 10.7 percent being offered on government bonds of comparable maturity.)
Tax exemption	None
Credit rating	AA (SO) by Credit Rating Information Service of India
Security	Charge or mortgage on physical assets of the Ahmedabad Municipal Corporation
Structured	Escrow on octroi revenues of the Ahmedabad Municipal Corporation
Listing	Ahmedabad Stock Exchange and National Stock Exchange
Regulation	Securities and Exchange Board of India

Note: SO indicates structured obligation.
Source: Ahmedabad Municipal Corporation 1999.

which helped adapt U.S. municipal bond financing techniques to the Indian capital markets.

A Model for Municipal Bond Issues

Ahmedabad's municipal bond financing has developed into a model for India. More than 30 Indian cities have sought credit ratings as the basis for issuing municipal bonds or as a guide to improving their financial condition. The growing interest in municipal bonds among India's institutional investors is gradually opening a substantial new source of financing for the development of Indian cities. In addition to Ahmedabad and Bangalore, several other cities—Ludhiana, Nagpur, Nasik, Madurai, and Surat—have raised funds from the Indian capital market through municipal bonds.

Municipal bonds are not the only avenue through which local governments in India are seeking to gain greater access to credit markets. They are also looking at innovative mechanisms that bundle underlying loans and involve greater private sector participation. One such mechanism is the Municipal Urban Development Fund, conceived in the late 1980s as part of the Tamil Nadu Urban Development Project. The fund and its successor have been used to finance infrastructure projects in municipalities throughout the state of Tamil Nadu.

Tamil Nadu's Experience with Urban Development Funds

Tamil Nadu is the third most urbanized state in India (after Maharashtra and Gujarat), with 40 percent of its population in urban areas. Sixty percent of the state's urban population lives in towns of more than 100,000, and about 15 percent lives in Chennai (formerly Madras), the capital of Tamil Nadu. The urban poor constitute 30 percent of the population of Tamil Nadu.

Challenges in Urban Infrastructure

The urban population in Tamil Nadu has been growing steadily for a century, increasing sixtyfold between 1901 and 1991. Many small towns have emerged, with a small economic base and little ability to generate employment or invest in infrastructure. The infrastructure needs are great. Per capita water supplies fall significantly below the norms. Only 16 percent of the population has access to adequate sanitation in town panchayat areas, 32 percent in municipal council areas, and 57 percent in municipal corporation areas. While 70 percent of the solid waste generated is collected, most local bodies do not have organized disposal facilities, and less than 50 percent of the roads are provided with storm drains (Malathi 2000).

Several factors account for the huge backlog in infrastructure investment. Urban infrastructure has been neglected in the state because urban areas have lacked political lobbying power proportionate to the size of the urban population and because the central and state governments have tended to give priority to investments in rural infrastructure. The underinvestment also results from constraints on the generation of resources for financing urban infrastructure, including unpredictable and discretionary government resource transfer systems, weak financial accountability, inappropriate methods of property tax assessment, inadequate user charges, and poor billing and collection systems. Also contributing are the weak managerial and administrative capacity of urban local bodies, the lack of long-term finance, and the limited options for municipal finance.

Moreover, there are unrealistic expectations about the ability of improvements to pay for themselves. Municipal corporations and councils seek to finance capital investments in urban infrastructure entirely through debt, relying on user charges or general tax revenues to cover the debt and operation and management costs. This strategy ignores the divergence between private and social benefits (or costs) and the lack of buoyancy in local tax revenues.[4] As a result of these factors, coupled with the outdatedness of laws governing local administration, urban local bodies have remained almost entirely dependent on the state government for their survival.

Decentralization and Its Financial Implications

The Tamil Nadu state government's decentralization strategy has been to empower urban local bodies by recognizing their constitutional governance and by increasing the amount and predictability of financial transfers while holding the local bodies accountable for meeting minimum requirements in delivering services. The Second State Finance Commission recommended a level of transfers to enable the local bodies to meet their revenue expenditure needs and part of their investment needs. Most of the transfers (87 percent) would take the form of untied funds but with suitable monitoring mechanisms and greater accountability. The balance (13 percent) would be disbursed through various funds to meet the wide-ranging needs of local bodies (Tamil Nadu, Finance Department 2000).

Some of the major recommendations of the State Finance Commission implemented since 1997/98 include the transfer of 3.6 percent of the state's tax revenue to urban local bodies; the allocation of transfers on the basis of population, per capita expenditure, and per capita revenue; the setting aside of 15 percent as an equalization and incentive fund to reward performance and build the capacity of weak and unviable urban local bodies; and the transfer of 90 percent of the entertainment tax to local bodies (Malathi 2000; Tamil Nadu, Finance Department 2000).

Despite the additional resources channeled to urban areas, the available financing falls far short of investment needs (table 24.5). The state finance commission estimated that in 1996–2001, Rs 4,810 crore ($1.3 billion) would be required for investments in core urban infrastructure facilities. Table 24.6 gives an indication of the size and type of investments needed for some of these core infrastructure requirements.

Power of Local Authorities to Borrow

In Tamil Nadu local bodies are empowered to raise money from financial institutions under the Tamil Nadu Urban Local Bodies Act of 1998 (Act 9 of 1999). This act was enacted by repealing the Tamil Nadu District Municipalities Act of 1920 (which had earlier empowered local bodies to raise money) and the municipal corporation acts of Chennai, Madurai, Coimbatore, Tiruchirapalli, Tirunelveli, and Selam. The new act brings all the state's urban local bodies—town panchayats, municipal councils, and municipal corporations—under one common, comprehensive act.

Table 24.5. Estimated Gap in Urban Infrastructure Financing, Tamil Nadu, 2002 (crore rupees)

Type of local body	Investment needs	Borrowing capacity	Financing gap
Municipal corporations	2,653	1,698	955
Municipal councils	1,351	419	932
Total	4,004	2,117	1,887

Source: Rajivan 1999.

Table 24.6. Infrastructure Investment Requirements by Type of Urban Local Body and Sector, Tamil Nadu, 1996–2001 (crore rupees, except where otherwise indicated)

	Municipal corporations	Municipal councils	Town panchayats	Total	Share of total (percent)
Water supply and sewerage	522	212	167	901	24
Sanitation	875	520	127	1,522	40
Solid waste management	40	32	24	96	2
Storm drains	287	81	192	560	15
Roads	337	197	62	596	16
Lighting	26	21	63	110	3
Total	2,087	1,063	635	3,785	100

Note: Annual inflation during the period covered was 12 percent.
Source: Tamil Nadu, Finance Department 1996.

Under the Tamil Nadu Urban Local Bodies Act of 1998 a municipal corporation may, by resolution, borrow through debentures or other means secured on various revenues (taxes, duties, fees, and dues authorized by the act) funds required for construction works, acquisition of land, payment of government dues, or repayment of existing loans. Borrowings must be approved by the state government, along with their terms and conditions, date of flotation, and time and method of repayment. The act limits the repayment period of a loan to no more than 60 years and the maximum amount that can be borrowed to 12.5 percent of the ratable value of property in the municipality.

The Local Authority Loans Rules specify that for loans from nongovernment sources that are not repayable by annuities, the local government is to create a sinking fund to ensure adequate funds for debt service. The local government is expected to make semiannual or annual payments into this fund sufficient to repay the loan within the term fixed for repayment. (Under present regulations, however, it is not obligatory for all municipalities to create sinking funds for resources raised after 1981/82.) The accountant general, who audits the accounts of municipalities, may instruct the local authority to transfer money from its income into the sinking fund in the event of a shortfall. However, objections raised during audits usually are not taken seriously because the accountant general lacks the power to summon and question the responsible officials (India, National Commission to Review the Working of the Constitution 2001).

Municipalities face borrowing limits based on the ratable value of property within their boundaries. However, evidence suggests that this debt limit has not been effectively enforced. For example, in Chennai the ratable value of property was estimated at Rs 3,842 million in 1995/96. This implies a borrowing ceiling of Rs 480 million—but the Chennai Municipal Corporation's outstanding debt in 1995/96 was Rs 856.2 million. An alternative standard, used by the Municipal Urban Development Fund, is a ceiling on the debt service ratio (the ratio of debt service requirements to own-source revenues). For the Chennai Municipal Corporation the projected debt service ratio has been between 17 percent (in 1995) and 36 percent (in 2000).

A debt ceiling linked to the performance of the municipal corporation, as determined by the debt service ratio or debt service coverage ratio (the ratio of cash flow available for debt payments to the total debt payments due), appears to be a better measure for limiting local borrowing than one linked to the annual ratable value. The reason is that a debt ceiling linked to the debt service or debt service coverage ratio, by definition, acts as a check on the amount that a municipality would borrow. In contrast, the annual ratable value measure generally will not. As noted, the annual ratable value method for valuing property in a municipality (and thus estimating its ability to repay debt) is inappropriate in India.

Municipal Urban Development Fund

The main challenges in the urban sector in Tamil Nadu, as elsewhere in India, are to reduce the massive backlog of infrastructure investment and improve the delivery of basic urban services. To improve urban infrastructure throughout the state, the government of Tamil Nadu in 1988 launched the Tamil Nadu Urban Development Project, financed by the International Development Association, the concessional lending arm of the World Bank. As part of this project, the Municipal Urban Development Fund was conceived as an innovative mechanism for financing revenue-generating infrastructure projects proposed by municipalities throughout the state.

The Municipal Urban Development Fund was set up on a pilot basis as a wholly state-owned revolving fund to provide long-term capital for municipal infrastructure projects. The fund was embedded in the machinery of the government, managed by the project management group and administered by the director of municipal administration. The fund provided subsidized loans combined with grants, with no state or other guarantees. It proved to be popular with municipalities because it gave them access to new capital and on terms and conditions they found acceptable. Debt repayment rates were high (about 90 percent). In the first five years the fund disbursed about $63 million for more than 500 subprojects.

Conceived as an experiment, the Municipal Urban Development Fund proved to be a financially viable municipal credit scheme. Before it could become a sustainable independent financial intermediary, however, it needed to overcome several obstacles (World Bank 2002):

- The fund's lending capacity was far too small compared with the potential demand for investment financing.
- The fund's mobilization and deployment of funds were not optimal. It relied heavily on grants from the government of Tamil Nadu, and its outflows comprised a mix of grants and subsidized loans.
- The fund depended entirely on public financing, including financing on-lent from an International Development Association credit line.
- Located within the administrative machinery of the government, the fund lacked autonomy and faced a risk of political interference.
- The fund's staff were subject to the constraints of the civil service system.

Tamil Nadu Urban Development Fund

In 1996, with the aim of achieving managerial efficiency and attracting private capital to urban infrastructure, the Municipal Urban Development Fund was converted into an autonomous financial intermediary—the Tamil Nadu Urban Development Fund. The new entity was established as a trust fund with private equity participation—the first public-private partnership in India providing long-term municipal financing for infrastructure without state guarantees. In addition, the scope of operations was widened to include urban infrastructure projects sponsored by public undertakings (entities in which the government has at least 51 percent ownership) and private investors. The restructured fund has three main purposes:

- To finance urban infrastructure projects that improve living standards.
- To facilitate private participation in infrastructure through public-private partnerships and joint ventures.
- To operate a complementary window, a grant fund, to finance poverty alleviation projects for specific low-income population groups.

Eligible borrowers include urban local bodies, statutory boards, public undertakings, and private corporations. Eligible sectors include transport, sanitation, water supply, solid waste management, integrated area development projects, roads and bridges, and sites and services.

In contrast with the Municipal Urban Development Fund, the Tamil Nadu Urban Development Fund is located outside the government. The fund is managed by Tamil Nadu Urban Infrastructure Financial Services, an asset management company set up under the Companies Act of 1956. The company is a joint venture between the government of Tamil Nadu (with an equity stake of 49 percent) and three financial institutions—the Industrial Credit and Investment Corporation of India (21 percent), the Housing Development Finance Corporation (15 percent), and Infrastructure Leasing and Financial Services (15 percent). The government's equity stake is restricted to 49 percent to facilitate a private sector orientation in investment decisions.

The arrangement has enabled the Tamil Nadu government to retain experienced financial institutions whose strong reputation in India's business and financial community is expected to help the fund raise additional resources from other private investors (World Bank 2002). The Industrial Credit and Investment Corporation of India is the lead managing partner of the asset management company. The Housing Development Finance Corporation is a leading finance corporation in housing and regional development. Infrastructure Leasing and Financial Services is a rapidly growing financial institution that specializes in developing and financing private infrastructure projects in India on a limited recourse basis.

The Tamil Nadu Urban Development Fund, which is similar to state revolving funds in the United States and municipal banks in Europe that finance infrastructure projects, is expected to develop into a self-standing financial intermediary capable of financing viable urban infrastructure projects. The basic infrastructure investments undertaken by the fund are based on city development strategies or corporate plans. These plans identify the key issues facing a city and help establish priorities through a consultative process involving elected officials, municipal officers, government agencies, community and professional groups, and business and industry representatives.

Lending Policies and Terms. The Tamil Nadu Urban Development Fund lends only for capital expenditure purposes. It does not finance land acquisition costs, operation and maintenance expenditures, and other expenditures such as salaries. The fund's management company ensures that a project to be funded meets several eligibility requirements: The project must be a high-priority capital expenditure program of an urban local body or statutory body. It must be an urban infrastructure project (excluding power and telecommunications) that will contribute to an improvement in the living standards of the urban population. It must have obtained appropriate statutory and environmental clearances, documented in the project evaluation report, and must comply with the environmental, resettlement, and social standards specified by the Tamil Nadu Urban Development Fund. Moreover, it must adopt technology and technical norms that are appropriate, proven, and the most cost effective. In addition, projects with quantifiable benefits are required to have an economic rate of return of at least 12 percent (rate of return calculations are not required for projects of less than $500,000; World Bank 2002).

Borrowers also must meet eligibility requirements: they must maintain a ratio of total expenditures to total revenues of less than 1, and a ratio of debt service (interest and principal payments) to total revenues of less than 30 percent. Security mechanisms include escrow accounts of revenues from such sources as property taxes and water charges. Pledges of movable assets provide another source of security. The lending terms of the Tamil Nadu Urban Development Fund vary depending on the type of borrower and project (table 24.7).

The loans can be given in conjunction with grants from the grant fund, operated by the Tamil Nadu Urban Development Fund and owned by the government of Tamil Nadu. The grant fund seeks to do the following:

- Strengthen and upgrade the financial, technical, managerial, and service delivery capabilities of localities through training and through computerization of municipal accounts and basic records such as births and deaths.
- Finance projects that directly benefit low-income urban population groups, such as sanitation, water supply, storm drainage, street lighting, and sewerage systems.

Table 24.7. Lending Terms of the Tamil Nadu Urban Development Fund since 1998/99

Interest rate	Overdue interest	Annuity (principal and interest)
Urban local bodies 16 percent a year for water supply and sewerage	18.5 percent a year on the overdue amount charged from the date of the scheduled payment until the date of actual payment	*Service projects* [a] One-year moratorium and 15-year repayment
16.5 percent a year for other projects		Water supply and sewerage projects Five-year moratorium and 16-year repayment
Private sector Market-determined rates		

a. Service projects are those that do not require initial (lumpy) investments like those needed for water supply and sewerage projects and the like.
Source: Rajivan 1999.

The grant fund covers the cost of preparing projects financed by the Tamil Nadu Urban Development Fund and those that seek private participation, while the Tamil Nadu Urban Development Fund finances the costs of resettlement and rehabilitation.

The Tamil Nadu Urban Development Fund structures its investments on the basis of the debt service capacity of urban local bodies, carrying out elementary budgeting exercises based on demand analyses. When urban local bodies have established clear, direct benefits to the urban poor from proposed projects, the fund has supplemented loans with a grant, reducing the effective interest rate. In the belief that investments in basic infrastructure can be sustained only through better project management performance, the fund has supported capacity building efforts for local bodies, such as the computerization of accounts and training programs to manage environmental and social issues.

Performance of the Fund. By the end of 2001/02 the Tamil Nadu Urban Development Fund had approved 179 projects at a total project cost of Rs 675.02 crore and had disbursed Rs 447.28 crore for 172 projects. These projects encompassed more than 500 subprojects in 90 of the 110 municipalities in Tamil Nadu—such projects as storm drains, sewerage and solid waste management schemes, commercial ventures (such as wholesale markets), and transport infrastructure including roads and bridges (figure 24.1; box 24.1). In 2002/03 the fund proposed approvals of about Rs 50 crore for approximately 20 projects. Figure 24.2 shows the value of capital works executed by municipalities with financing from the fund.

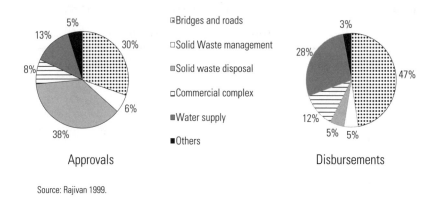

Approvals   Disbursements

Source: Rajivan 1999.

Figure 24.1. Funding Approvals and Disbursements by the Tamil Nadu Urban Development Fund by Sector as of 31 March 1999

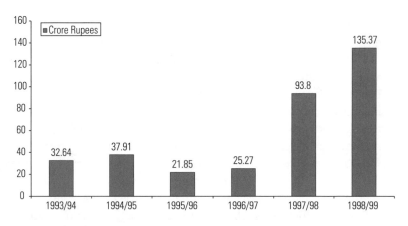

Note: Data for 1998/99 are provisional.
Source: World Bank 2000.

Figure 24.2. Value of Capital Works Executed by Municipalities with Funding from the Tamil Nadu Urban Development Fund, 1993/94 to 1998/99 (crore rupees)

Financial projections for the Tamil Nadu Urban Development Fund indicate that the fund's total annual income will increase from Rs 30.7 crore in 1997/98 to Rs 124.5 crore in 2002/03, that its profits will rise from Rs 23.6 crore to Rs 84.8 crore in the same period, and that its loans outstand-

Box 24.1. Recent Projects Financed by the Tamil Nadu Urban Development Fund

Among the projects being financed by the Tamil Nadu Urban Development Fund are three prototypes—the Karur Municipality Bridge, the Madurai Bypass (Inner Ring) Road (a toll road), and the Alandur Sewerage Project—all involving private participation.

Karur Municipality Bridge. The Karur Municipality Bridge, the first toll bridge to be constructed on a build-operate-transfer (BOT) basis by an urban local body in India, is expected to generate predictable cash flows for the operator, since it will be used by freight drivers with the capacity to pay and will substantially reduce vehicle operating costs and time. The Tamil Nadu State Toll Act has been amended to allow municipalities to enter into BOT contracts, providing a stable regulatory framework for investors. The concession was awarded through competitive bidding for a 14-year term, including the construction period. The Tamil Nadu Urban Development Fund approved a loan of Rs 100 lacs (Rs 1 crore = 100 lacs) to meet part of the project costs. The project financing has helped free municipal resources for pressing investments in core infrastructure services (Tamil Nadu Urban Development Fund 1999).

Madurai Bypass (Inner Ring) Road. The Tamil Nadu Urban Development Fund has also funded the first toll road in Tamil Nadu—the 27-kilometer Madurai Bypass (Inner Ring) Road—at an estimated project cost of Rs 47 crore. The fund provided financing through a 15-year construction loan to the Madurai Municipal Corporation. However, after construction was completed and toll revenues began to come in, the municipal corporation issued 15-year bonds to replace the construction loan. The bonds carry 12.25 percent annual interest, payable semiannually, while the loan carried an interest of 15.5 percent a year. This innovative financing mechanism not only helped reduce loan costs but also freed up fund resources for other projects.

(Box continues on the following page.)

Box 24.1. (*continued*)

The project financing is structured on a nonrecourse basis so that lenders have recourse only to the project revenues, not to the general revenue flows of the Madurai Municipal Corporation. The second and third phases of the project are being developed on a BOT basis, with a pledge of the revenues from the first phase as security to encourage private participation.

Alandur Sewerage Project. The financing scheme for the Alandur Sewerage Project, now under construction, involves user charges, private equity for the BOT segment of the project, and up-front payments by customers. The proposed tariff rates are designed to cover operation and maintenance expenses, debt service, and payments into a sinking fund. The tariff structure includes cross-subsidies, with tariffs for commercial users three times—and tariffs for industrial users five times—those for households. Deposits of Rs 5,000 have been raised from households and Rs 10,000 from commercial and industrial customers.

Contracts were awarded through competitive bidding consistent with World Bank guidelines. The sewage treatment plant is being constructed under a BOT contract backed by a user-pay mechanism and fixed annual fees to cover operation and maintenance over a five-year period. The works are being supervised by an independent, private project management consultant.

---

ing on 31 March 2003 will be Rs 908 crore. In addition, its debt-equity ratio will be satisfactory (at 2.86) on that date, and the government of Tamil Nadu will hold 56.5 percent of the paid-up contribution, with the financial institutions holding 43.4 percent.

These financial projections assume the availability of a World Bank credit line of $80 million as the primary source of long-term finance and that the entire amount drawn in a year from this credit line is disbursed to sub-borrowers in the same year. They further assume that the profits of the government of Tamil Nadu are transferred to the grant fund while the profits of the financial institutions are plowed back into the trust fund (Rajivan 1999).

Assessment of the Tamil Nadu Urban Development Fund

The Tamil Nadu Urban Development Fund has increased private capital flows into the state's urban sector and leveraged the World Bank's resources by issuing bonds and other debt instruments (World Bank 2002). The bond issue of the Madurai Municipal Corporation in November 2000 is a case in point. Facilitated by the fund, the bond issue—the first by an urban local body in Tamil Nadu—raised $23 million for the Madurai Municipal Corporation's Bypass (Inner Ring) Road Project (table 24.8). The three financial institutions participating in the fund provided guarantees or other credit enhancement or risk participation mechanisms. This support, along with the role of the Tamil Nadu Urban Development Fund, helped garner a rating of AA+ for the bond issue (box 24.2).

The bond issue was oversubscribed, in large part because of its AA+ rating. Investors in the issue included commercial banks (70.5 percent), contributors to the Tamil Nadu Urban Development Fund (11 percent), regional rural banks (9.5 percent), insurance companies (8 percent), cooperative banks (0.95 percent), a private company (0.05 percent), and others (4 percent).

Raising financing through domestic bond issues is in line with one of the fund's main objectives: securing sustainable funding for urban infrastructure investments beyond the World Bank's line of credit. Indeed, a loan covenant with the World Bank for the second phase of the Tamil Nadu Urban Development Project requires that the fund raise $50 million from private sources.

Table 24.8. Terms of the Bond Issue by the Madurai Municipal Corporation

Issue size	Rs 100 crore ($23 million), private placement
Instrument	Nonconvertible
Face value	Rs 1,000 at par
Maturity	15 years
Redemption	In five equal annual installments
Interest or coupon rate	11.85 percent a year, payable semiannually
Tax exemption	None
Credit rating	LAA+ (SO) by Investment Information and Credit Rating Agency (Rating is equivalent to AA+, indicating high safety and modest risk.)
Put or call option	After 8 years
Regulation	Securities and Exchange Board of India

Note: SO indicates structured obligation.
Source: Pradhan 2002.

Box 24.2. Basis for the AA+ Rating of the Madurai Municipal Corporation Bond Issue

- The issue is backed by a credit enhancement and structured payment mechanism requiring the Tamil Nadu Urban Development Fund to maintain a bond service fund equivalent to one year's principal and interest payments as collateral throughout the life of the bonds.
- The fund has achieved a high collection efficiency (ratio of collections to total debt service due), thanks to such mechanisms as a no-lien escrow account for the property tax revenues of urban local bodies, and has few nonperforming assets.
- The fund's low gearing ratio (total debt to total net worth), efficient collection mechanisms, and surplus funds provide a comfortable liquidity position.
- The fund's accounting practices, including its asset classification norms, are conservative.
- The fund has no major funding constraints or asset-liability mismatches, and it has access to long-term financing through the World Bank loan.
- The government of Tamil Nadu firmly supports and is committed to the success of the Tamil Nadu Urban Development Project and to urban sector reforms in general.
- The system of financial devolution, based on the recommendations of the state finance commissions, is being implemented successfully and has enhanced the finances of urban local bodies.
- The fund manager has a qualified team of professionals carrying out credit assessments and project appraisals. It also has a well-defined organizational structure and well-defined roles for its officials.

Source: World Bank 2001.

Lessons and Conclusions

The Tamil Nadu Urban Development Fund has positioned itself as a strategic intermediary linking capital markets with local urban infrastructure needs. Its performance in achieving lending targets, high repayment rates, and high quality in the infrastructure constructed has enabled it to access the market for resources. Its loan recovery rate of nearly 100 percent is a clear indicator of its success as a financial intermediary (table 24.9). It is hoped that its success as a self-standing financial intermediary will encourage other private financial institutions to enter the new municipal financing market.

One factor instrumental to the success of the fund is that, as an autonomous financial intermediary managed by a private asset management company (unlike the Municipal Urban Development Fund), it is insulated from government interference. Management by a private company has proved to be advantageous. The company has the freedom to recruit the best staff members and to pay market rates to retain them, and private management eliminates the bureaucratic element that plagues most government-run entities.

Table 24.9. Financial Indicators for the Tamil Nadu Urban Development Fund as of March 2002

	Indicator	1998/99	1999/2000	2000/01	2001/02
Disbursements (crore rupees)	Benchmark	19.0	92.0	89.0	83.0
	Actual	20.0	56.0	219.0	20.0
Cumulative disbursements	Benchmark	19.0	111.0	200.0	283.0
(crore rupees)	Actual	20.0	76.0	295.0	315.0[a]
Ratio of net profit to	Benchmark	12.9	13.4	14.8	13.0
net worth	Actual	16.0	15.3	13.4	16.8
Ratio of net profit to	Benchmark	5.4	5.9	5.6	4.7
average assets	Actual	6.1	5.7	4.0	6.0
Loan recovery rate (percent)	Benchmark	78.0	84.0	90.0	90.0
	Actual	99.0	100.0	100.0	99.8
Ratio of debt to equity	Benchmark	1.3	1.5	1.7	1.8
	Actual	1.4	1.3	1.7	2.2
Debt service coverage ratio	Benchmark	3.3	2.4	2.0	1.5
	Actual	1.3	2.9	2.4	1.4

Note: Benchmark values are used to determine the financial viability and efficacy of the fund.
a. Excludes disbursements before 1998/99 because projections were not made until that year.
Source: Rajivan 1999.

Equity participation by leading Indian financial institutions has also contributed to the fund's successful performance and indicates the private sector's commitment to the fund. Private equity participation is scarce in India, but the three financial institutions participating in the fund have contributed 30 percent of its equity. Private financial institutions' ownership share in the fund was expected to rise to 44 percent by 2003.

Nonetheless, despite several innovative financing mechanisms to mobilize private resources, the fund's debt financing depends mainly on the security provided by the limited operating surplus of municipal borrowers. Small projects can be financed in this way, but large, lumpy, and non-revenue-generating investments cannot be. For example, the fund can provide long-term loans, but its interest rate is unattractive for most sewerage projects sponsored by municipalities. This corporate-bank-style approach can be used to finance only limited types of municipal infrastructure projects. Moreover, while large municipalities can finance their investment needs through direct bond issues backed by project revenues and general revenues—with the fund taking the construction risk, if necessary, by providing an initial loan later replaced by capital market debt, as for the Madurai Bypass (Inner Ring) Road Project—more innovative mechanisms are needed for small municipalities. To provide such a mechanism, in 2001/02 the fund's management company created a pooled financing facility with credit enhancement. This financing scheme pools the infrastructure investment projects of small and medium-size towns to give them access to debt raised in the market. The aim is to reduce the transaction and borrowing costs for essential infrastructure, particularly sewerage projects, which require substantial funds over a long period, often more than 20 years (figure 24.3).

Under this scheme, guarantee funds are put up by the government or an intercept of state transfers to municipalities is used to provide security. The financial institutions participating in the Tamil Nadu Urban Development Fund not only help municipalities raise finance for their projects but also provide advisory services (project structuring and technical assistance) for these projects.

A trust called the Water and Sanitation Pooled Fund has already been registered under this pooled financing scheme, to link municipal financing needs with the capital market (table 24.10). Subscribers to the fund include banks (Rs 30.25 crore) and the Provident Fund Trust (Rs 0.16 crore).

In addition, the Tamil Nadu Urban Development Fund seeks to expand its activities beyond the state of Tamil Nadu. It intends to create a new fi-

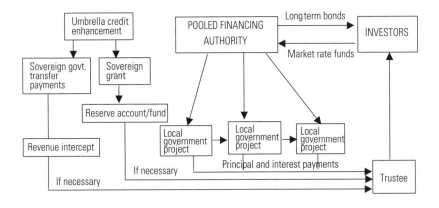

Source: Rajivan 2003.

Figure 24.3. Simplified Flow of Funds in the Pooled Financing Scheme

Table 24.10. Terms of Issue of the Water and Sanitation Pooled Fund

Maturity	15 years
Put or call option	After 10 years
Redemption	In 15 equal annual installments
Interest payment	Annually on diminishing balance
Face value of bond	Rs 100,000
Credit rating	AA (SO) by Investment Information and Credit Rating Agency; AA (SO) by Fitch Ratings
Guarantee	50 percent of the principal guaranteed by USAID; the government of Tamil Nadu to top up shortfalls through interception of transfers
Debt service reserve fund	Rs 6.90 crore to be invested in highly secured and liquid investments

Note: SO indicates structured obligation.
Source: Rajivan 2003.

nancing window—similar to a mutual fund—to finance municipal infrastructure projects in other states.

The experience of the Tamil Nadu Urban Development Fund has shown that financing infrastructure investments requires a comprehensive approach—one that includes sector reforms involving decentralization and a symbiotic "division of labor" between the government and the private sector. While the appropriate division of labor varies from one country to another, generally the government (central and state) needs to work on the policy and regulatory fronts in raising finance and building the capacity of local bodies, especially in project management and accounting, while the private sector needs to be involved as a market developer and innovator to attract greater private investment in local infrastructure. Depending on the circumstances and the project, private participation can take the form of direct investment, such as in BOT projects, or financial investment, such as loans and bond purchases.

The Tamil Nadu Urban Development Fund has had good success in its role as a specialized financial intermediary, not only in performing fund supervision and management functions but also in providing advisory and technical assistance to infrastructure projects. The challenge for the fund is to retain its ability to function as an autonomous financial intermediary with adequate freedom and an equity stake. The key to its long-term sustainability lies in its ability to integrate with the financial sector by aligning its interest rates and loan terms with those of the market. The separation of grant finance and debt finance is a step in this direction. The fund's long-term sustainability also will require the government and the private sector to work together on several fronts, including strengthening the financial position of municipalities, building the capacity to develop and implement sound projects, and ensuring high loan recovery rates—all essential for a strong financial performance by the fund.

Notes

1. One crore = 10 million rupees.

2. Established under the SEBI Act in 1988, the Securities and Exchange Board of India is charged with protecting the interests of the investors in the securities markets and regulating and promoting the development of the capital market in the country. It is mandated to check unfair and fraudulent trade practices and impose monetary penalties on erring market players.

3. The oldest and most well-known domestic rating agency in India, the Credit Rating Information Service of India is associated with Standard & Poor's, which holds equity in the rating agency.

4. Most infrastructure projects produce benefits over and above those that accrue to private individuals. These benefits, known as social benefits, often are not measurable. If social benefits are included in cost-benefit analyses done to determine user charges, the charges are bound to be lower than needed to recover the costs of investment and operation.

Chapter 25

Asia
Indonesia

*After crises, decentralization and renewed efforts seek to bring
local governments to the capital market.*

Robert Kehew and John Petersen

Lessons

In Indonesia, which has a tradition of strong unitary government
and central control, meaningful political and fiscal decentralization is just beginning. The great challenge is not only to establish a new system of subnational fiscal autonomy and fiscal
transfers, but to do so in a disrupted political system struggling
to emerge from the financial crises of the late 1990s. For subnational credit, the legacy of national on-lending programs that
have gone awry makes reformulating the debt market difficult.

In the mid-1990s the national government attempted to move
local utilities into the emerging domestic bond market. However, the 1997 economic and political crises dealt the prospects
for this market a severe blow. The financial markets and banking system were decimated, and the corporate market experienced heavy defaults. The rate of default by local governments
on their borrowings from the central government's develop-

---

ment funds (which had effectively been the only long-term lenders available to them) steadily increased. The heavy arrears on these loans, coupled with the failure to deal with this situation, have eroded the perceived creditworthiness of local governments and introduced considerable moral hazard. With little appetite or capacity to finance local government debt, private credit markets are unlikely to be a source of funds in the near future. Improving that prospect requires redesigning grant and loan programs to stimulate rather than crowd out the participation of private credit markets.

As Indonesia redesigns its intergovernmental system, consulting economists are urging that officials consider integrating grants and loans in ways that promote access to private credit markets. Getting this integration process right, however, requires data and analyses that typically have not been produced in the past and that would require funding in the future. Poor financial management and reporting practices and a lack of competent human resources also impair prospects for local governments gaining access to credit markets any time soon.

On a more positive note, Indonesia is committed to political and fiscal decentralization. When local governments' spending responsibilities and revenue sources are settled and their financial management is improved, their creditworthiness, real and perceived, should improve as well. However, care will need to be taken to avoid repeating the mistakes of the past in parceling out assisted credit and insulating local governments from the costs and demands of private capital markets.

Indonesia is the world's fourth most populous country, with a population of approximately 210 million according to the 2000 census.[1] An apparent economic pacesetter during much of the 1980s and 1990s, Indonesia saw its economy swiftly and devastatingly derailed in the East Asian crisis of the late 1990s. The crisis led to the toppling of the Suharto regime and rapid political change.

A unitary state, Indonesia is divided into about 30 provinces and more than 360 local government units, including cities (*kota*) and more rural regencies or districts (*kabupaten*). Together, provinces, cities, and districts are referred to as regional authorities. In addition, some local services are provided by locally owned enterprises (*badan usaha milik daerah*).

Until very recently Indonesia was highly centralized, with regional authorities generally lacking meaningful political or fiscal autonomy. The administration of local government was tightly controlled from the top down, with the national government having substantial presence at the local level. Regional authorities relied on central government transfers for 70 percent or more of their revenues. Almost all subnational investment projects were funded by grants or loans from the central government, a policy that has left a legacy of moral hazard following the recent regime change.

The economic and political turmoil in the years since 1997 has led to considerable loosening of restrictions on local spending and revenue raising powers. In addition, intergovernmental transfers have been increased to promote more local decisionmaking. These changes have been made in part to try to counter the separatist mentality that has spread throughout parts of the country and in reaction to the former top-down controls. Thanks to the greater intergovernmental transfers and expanded local taxing powers, some local governments now have more resources to finance their needs. Others remain impoverished. Meanwhile, the difficult economic circumstances (and the conditions imposed by the International Monetary Fund in its rescue activities) have caused the central government to reduce its own spending and subsidies.

The political restructuring and devolution in Indonesia have arrested the earlier efforts at development of the subnational credit markets. However, they also provide the potential for erecting these markets on a sounder foundation in the future.

Characteristics of Subnational Government Borrowing

Despite some early efforts by local governments to enter private credit markets, almost all the funds they have borrowed in the past 20 years or so have passed through one of two central government mechanisms:[2]

- Regional Development Account (RDA), the government's channel for lending state budget funds (some derived initially from donor funding) to regional governments and their enterprises.[3]

- Subsidiary loan agreements (SLAs), the mechanism for on-lending funds from major donors and lenders (mainly sovereign loan funds from the World Bank and the Asian Development Bank) for qualified regional infrastructure projects.

These two loan windows are operated out of the Ministry of Finance. There is no separate financial institution that focuses on lending to local governments. While regional governments have borrowed a small amount from other sources, such as regional development, state, or commercial banks, most of this borrowing has occurred in response to short-term needs, such as the management of cash flow, rather than long-term capital investment needs. Bank loans, which are relatively expensive and short term, more often go to locally owned enterprises.

Following the first SLA loan in 1978 and the initial RDA transaction in 1980, the first decade of SLA and RDA operations saw only modest borrowing. Since 1987 the volume of lending from these windows has increased: the 315,011 million rupiah (Rp) lent in 1999 was fairly typical (table 25.1). In 1978–99 the central government made some 814 loans worth around Rp 4.6 billion.[4] Most of the loans that have been made have gone to locally owned enterprises in the water sector. By 1999 about two-thirds (63.4 percent) of the country's 292 cities and rural districts had borrowed from these windows, while the rest had no experience in RDA and SLA borrowing.

To place matters in context: the volume of RDA and SLA loans that have been made does not reflect a large market, even in relative terms. Lewis

Table 25.1. Central Government Lending to Local Governments, Indonesia, Selected Years, 1980–99

Year	Loans per year SLA	Loans per year RDA	Annual disbursements (millions of rupiah)	Cumulative arrears Millions of rupiah	Cumulative arrears Rate (percent)[a]
1980	0	1	18,930	16,181	47.5
1985	3	6	23,903	82,049	24.7
1990	12	27	546,003	428,499	32.6
1995	16	6	266,117	812,482	41.5
1999	15	12	315,011	843,269	41.9
Total (for 1978–99)	387	427	4,599,864	843,269	41.9

a. Arrears as a percentage of payments due (principal, interest, penalties, and the like).
Source: Lewis 2001, p. 5.

(2001) points out that total lending to regional governments as of 1999 represented only about 0.5 percent of Indonesia's GDP for that year. In South Africa for that year, by contrast, regional debt represented about 4.0 percent of GDP.

The RDA and SLA loans do not reflect market terms and conditions. Since 1989 the central government has set interest rates at 11.5 percent for both types of loans (SLA loans often carry an additional 0.25 percent interest charge, remitted to a local bank that administers repayment collections). Maturities typically range from 18 to 20 years. Grace periods on interest and principal payments are normally 3 to 5 years, with interest usually capitalized during grace periods. The government levies commitment fees on undisbursed balances. Contrast these conditions with those in the commercial market, where rates in 2002 stood at around 18 percent a year and loan maturities were much less than half those for the RDA and SLA loans.

A key problem with RDA and SLA lending is the unacceptably high level of arrears. Cumulative arrears on loan repayments (including principal, interest, and penalties), already high in the early years of RDA and SLA lending, grew steadily to more than 40 percent in 1999. At the end of 2000 subnational borrowers were at least 6 months late in making payments on some 640 loans—80 percent of the 802 loans being monitored by the central government. This high arrearage rate occurs despite substantial penalties on arrears. For RDA loans the penalty on overdue principal is 6.5 percent a year, and that on overdue interest 18.0 percent. For SLA loans the penalty is 2.0 percent over the annual interest charges. The high level of arrears taints the creditworthiness of the entire local government sector, discouraging the formation of a subnational government credit market.

Factors Shaping the Subnational Government Credit Market

Efforts to build a local government credit market are not new. The legacy of earlier efforts and recent political and economic events have led to a number of conditions that are shaping the nature and pace of the development of the subnational government credit market.

Early Efforts to Create a Market

Indonesia had a booming economy throughout the 1980s and early 1990s and was held up as one of the more successful development stories in Asia. In the late 1980s, as part of its national central planning initiative, the country undertook limited devolution aimed at increasing local technical and administrative capacity and transferring greater authority to local governments, including the ability to market debt in the financial markets. Part of the motivation was to take some of the excess demand load off the SLA and RDA loan funds and to move self-supporting activities into the expanding commercial credit markets (Ardiwinata 1997).[5] The central government took the lead in establishing a regulatory framework for local bond issues, fostered market interest, and promoted the first generation of borrowers. The initial borrowers were to be local water utilities, which were to sell self-supporting revenue bonds.[6]

After a review of some 300 local water utilities, 25 were selected as financially healthy and therefore prime candidates for issuing bonds. Hopes were high: it was estimated that the potential demand for funds over the first three years would be about Rp 1 trillion ($300 million at the prevailing exchange rate). Three local water utilities were initially selected for the first batch of issues, but the number was reduced to two when one candidate was instead put up for privatization. The two remaining bond issues were to have been completed in 1997. However, the bond deals went awry during the financial crisis and the ensuing political turmoil of that year and the next.

At the time economists acknowledged that the true costs of issuing municipal bonds compared with those of other financing alternatives were largely obscured by distortions in the lending programs and the credit markets. The subsidized RDA and SLA loans led to an uneven playing field and fostered both long waits for assistance and political manipulation to get to the head of the line. In addition, private investors were actively promoting concession and build-operate-transfer (BOT) contracts that were not based on strictly economic merits and could have political advantages. Moreover, the high domestic interest rates favored a heavy reliance on offshore financing, which entailed substantial exchange risk—as was clearly demonstrated in the aftermath of the 1997 crisis and the devaluation.

Macroeconomic Conditions: Weak Economy and Financial Markets

Indonesia's economy was hurt severely by the 1997 economic crisis. Data from the Asian Development Bank indicate that Indonesia's real per capita GDP plummeted from $1,110 in 1997 to $600 in 1999 (Asian Development Bank 2002). In two years the country lost what had been a decade's gain in living standards.

The economic crisis affected all aspects of the economy, including Indonesia's financial and capital markets. It crippled the banking system, which, as a result of a huge bailout program, is now dominated by the central government. At the end of March 2001 government-controlled banks held about two-thirds of the system's assets (table 25.2). This reflects a sharp increase from five years earlier, when government-controlled banks held only about 45 percent of assets. This situation, a result of actions taken by the government in response to the 1997 economic crisis, reflects the underlying weakness of the banking sector.

Of the government banks, the four state banks are controlled by the Ministry of State-Owned Enterprises. The others, formerly private banks taken over in the aftermath of the 1997 crisis, are now controlled by the Indonesian Bank Restructuring Agency. The agency has a policy of divesting itself of the banks it holds, and it has begun to do so. Successful bank divestitures are a sign of the returning health of the banking sector, since divested banks had to be sufficiently healthy to attract buyers. Restructuring should pave the way for injections of private capital into the market.

The banking system remains highly vulnerable and faces liquidity problems. Bank assets are dominated by recapitalization bonds issued by the government in response to the 1997 crisis. The shares of nonperforming loans are high, with the weighted average for the government banks about 17 percent (World Bank 2001). Private banks also face problems of liquidity and nonperforming loans.

Few debt instruments of any kind are traded in the capital market, in part because the market is dominated by the recapitalization bonds. Trading in these central government debt instruments has been minimal, largely because of the combined effect of high interest rates (which mean that the recapitalization bonds with fixed rates of interest would trade at a

Table 25.2. Banking Sector Assets by Type of Bank, Indonesia, End of March 2001

Type of bank	Assets (trillions of rupiah)	Share of total (percent)
Government banks	730.5	66
State banks (4)	470.8	43
Banks controlled by the Indonesian Bank Restructuring Agency (7)	259.7	23
Other banks[a]	370.0[b]	34
Total	1,100[b]	100

a. Includes private domestic and foreign banks and public regional development banks.
b. Estimated.
Source: World Bank 2001.

heavy discount) and banks' small effective capital ratios. There has been no primary market (much less a secondary one) for bonds issued by local governments or locally owned enterprises.

The central government is restructuring its massive public debt, which has affected the prospects for developing a long-term debt market. Under this restructuring the government expects to repay a portion of the recapitalization bonds upon maturity. It plans to roll over another portion of its maturing debt into variable interest rate bonds with longer maturities. This action should increase liquidity. While it will also increase investors' familiarity with longer-term debt instruments (a strength in the long term), in the immediate future it could absorb what little demand now exists for longer-term debt (a weakness in the short term). The government also plans to issue treasury bills, which will promote the development of the capital and financial markets by setting benchmark interest rates and increasing liquidity. Treasury bills will be issued only after approval of a sovereign debt securities law, now being developed.

The framework and infrastructure for a capital market—dating from before the 1997 crisis—is still in place. The government has developed a regulation and procedure for corporate bonds that would also apply to bonds issued by locally owned enterprises, though not those issued by local governments. Before the 1997 crisis corporate bonds were floated on the market; Darche (2002) reports corporate bond issues of Rp 15,887 billion in 1997. Indonesia has both equity and fixed income securities markets. It also has experienced underwriters that could serve as financial advisers to local governments and two local credit rating agencies operating in its securities markets, one of which (Perfindo) is trying to develop rating criteria for local governments.

The Indonesian institutional investment sector is relatively small and conservative, with combined assets of only about 6.9 percent of GDP in December 1999. In a sign of the sector's conservative practices, in 2001 the two largest public pension programs kept some 97 percent of their assets in bank deposits (which are insured by the central government). While perhaps prudent given the present uncertainties, this posture is not conducive to the formation of a long-term debt market.

The weakness of the banking sector and capital markets helps explain why banks and investors have lent only small amounts to local governments and locally owned enterprises, particularly after the 1997 crisis. Financiers also mention other reasons for the limited lending to subnational entities:

- A perception that local entities are generally not creditworthy.
- Inadequate financial reporting and disclosure.
- The disparity between public and private sector accounting and auditing practices and the resulting lack of familiarity with local governments as potential borrowers.[7]

Decentralization Policy

In contrast to the largely cosmetic efforts of the early 1990s, the government of Indonesia initiated a "big bang" approach to decentralization in 2001, aimed at transferring spending responsibilities, resources, assets, and some 2 million of its employees to the local level. While this process has not yet translated into a subnational government debt market, it may do so eventually. Undergirding the decentralization process are Laws 22 and 25 of 1999, which deal with administrative and fiscal decentralization.

Law 22 of 1999 begins to define local responsibilities—crucial for enabling local governments to define their capital investment needs and thus to borrow effectively. The law defines several broad "sectors" (such as education and public works) that local governments must implement. Regulations and decrees have begun to define functional responsibilities within these broad sectors, though more work is required.

Law 25 of 1999 is designed to strengthen local government revenues in support of decentralization. The law articulates a key goal of decentralization: "to make even the fiscal capacities of regional governments to finance their expenditure needs." While the fact that local responsibilities have not yet been fully defined makes it difficult to assess the sufficiency of the resources provided, the sources so far assigned to local governments have provided substantial resources. In addition, some local governments are reportedly taking matters into their own hands and have substantially raised local taxes and charges, arguing that they are free to do so under the new decentralization regime. Aside from creating greater horizontal imbalances, this is seen as harmful to local economies and internal commerce (Firdausy 2002).

A major tool for meeting the goals of vertical and horizontal fiscal balance is the general allocation grant. Law 25 of 1999 requires the central government to direct at least 25 percent of its revenues to the general allocation grant—a substantial amount. The law allows local governments to decide how best to use these resources. In principle, operating surpluses could be used to secure debt or for pay-as-you-go financing of capital investment. In practice, however, the prohibition on dismissing employees transferred from the central government to the local level has meant that, on average, local governments use more than half the resources from the general allocation grant to pay for employee salaries and benefits.

New revenue sources under decentralization include some that the central government is to share with subnational governments, such as property-related taxes, natural resource revenues, and a tax on personal income. The revenue sharing is aimed in part at responding to regional aspirations for greater access to and control over revenues derived locally (such as through petroleum extraction). Because the bases of these shared revenues (property value, natural resources, personal income) are unevenly distributed in Indonesia, the chosen approach to revenue sharing will tend to exacerbate differences in per capita income among governments. As a result, when a subnational credit market eventually develops, that market may be segmented, with richer local governments better able to access private sources of capital than poorer ones. A strategy for rationally allocating credit and grant resources among local governments will need to take into account these differences in their access to resources.

The government of Indonesia has thus taken big strides toward providing local governments with additional resources. However, it has not yet devolved the portion of the development budget corresponding to local areas of responsibility. Lewis (2001, p. 40) estimates that some Rp 15–25 trillion of the Rp 52.3 trillion budgeted by the central government in 2001 for development expenditures corresponds to areas of responsibility that are now being decentralized. Closely related to this circumstance, a specific-purpose grant, contemplated by Law 25 and earmarked for financing specific types of capital investment, has not yet been made fully operational. Thus, responsibility for capital investment in areas of local responsibility (along with the corresponding resources) has not yet been fully defined and consolidated at the local level.

Transfers and shared revenues dominate local revenues in Indonesia, with own-source revenues contributing only around 5 percent of the total on average. Analysts generally expect local taxes and user charges to produce more flexible and reliable income streams than transfers or shared revenues from the central government. Thus, until the shared taxes and transfers become fully institutionalized, this situation hurts the creditworthiness of local governments. The Ministry of Finance is evaluating alternatives for new or devolved taxes that could serve as a cornerstone for a system of local government finance.

Legal and Regulatory Framework Governing Debt Transactions

Law 25 of 1999 generally confers on local governments the right to borrow without excessive central government interference; Regulation 107 of 2000 further clarifies this right. This right, however, has been temporarily countermanded by a partial moratorium on borrowing by local governments. Responding in large part to post-1997 concerns about excessive public debt, a Ministry of Finance decree prohibits new borrowing by local governments from domestic or foreign sources until the end of 2002. Exempted from this prohibition are borrowing through an on-lending vehicle (such as the SLA) and short-term borrowing for cash flow management. Borrowing by locally owned enterprises is also exempted.

With this moratorium scheduled to be lifted, a review of the legal and regulatory framework is warranted to see whether it provides for well-constructed, enforceable, and transparent credit transactions with local governments—a precondition for the emergence of a local government debt market. This review points to several areas in which laws and regulations should be revised or clarified to allow better credit transactions and the development of a market for local government credit.

Regulation 107 in effect requires that the terms and conditions of a foreign loan that is to be on-lent to local governments be passed on to the local borrowers, including foreign exchange risk. This is a heavy burden to impose, and it has complicated recent efforts to reactivate RDA and SLA lending, which have been constrained by the moratorium. Moreover, it runs contrary to typical practices for on-lending international public resources to local governments.

A lender to a local government will seek as much security for the loan as possible. If loans cannot be sufficiently secured, a local government debt market probably will not take root. Local governments face excessive restrictions on the assets they can pledge to secure debt. Existing regulations do not clearly establish their right to pledge expected future revenues.

Nor does the law provide sufficiently for the use of a trust mechanism in local government debt transactions. Such a mechanism can help to ensure that borrowers use funds for the purposes intended and comply with loan terms and conditions, including debt service payment schedules. Trust mechanisms are particularly important in countries where rule of law is poorly developed, such as Indonesia. While the Capital Markets Law includes trust provisions, their applicability to local government debt transactions is not clearly established.[8]

Another potential route to help secure debt is a revenue intercept provision, allowing creditors to intercept revenue transfers to local governments to pay debt service. Law 25 of 1999 and Regulation 107 provide for intercept of general allocation grant funds. While encouraging, this provision appears to give the central government (as a lender through, for example, its RDA window) a senior position relative to other creditors of a local government. This situation does not encourage private entry into the local government credit market. Moreover, the intercept provision has not yet been made fully operational or tested.

Also needing further clarification is the applicability of financial reporting and disclosure provisions in the Capital Markets Law to local governments. Adequate disclosure is essential for the economic decisionmaking that allows a sustainable debt market to flourish. Weak coordination among central government oversight units adds to the difficulties. At present, oversight responsibilities for local financial reporting are shared by the Ministry of Home Affairs and the Ministry if Finance, and the two have not agreed on what accounting and reporting standards to follow. Adding to the difficulties is the low level of managerial and financial competency in many local governments, a problem that needs to be resolved by training and instilling a greater sense of professionalism.[9]

Reforming Public Lending Programs

The heavy arrears on the RDA and SLA loans have been attributed to a number of factors. One of the most important is organizational: the fact that the RDA and SLA loan windows operate out of a multipurpose government agency, the Ministry of Finance, may impede effective loan administration. Unlike a specialized entity, the Ministry of Finance must try to satisfy multiple—and sometimes conflicting—objectives. For example, the ministry is responsible for allocating the general allocation grant, a mandate that could complicate the exercise of authority to intercept funds from this source to enforce loan repayment. Other factors also play a part:

- Local officials argue that they should not be held responsible for the outstanding loans that predate decentralization, because the loans were made with little meaningful local participation or agreement.

- Most loan agreements have been uncollateralized and therefore virtually unenforceable. (Recent loan agreements provide for an intercept of general allocation grant transfers, though this mechanism has not yet been used.)
- The system and criteria used to evaluate the creditworthiness of potential borrowers and project proposals were inadequate. In the past many SLA and RDA loans were awarded to local governments and locally owned enterprises that had significant arrears on existing loans or whose creditworthiness was otherwise not adequately assessed. More recently the government established a policy of making no additional loans to borrowers in arrears on previous loans. However, some local entities have received new loans despite being in arrears.
- Inability to pay does not help explain nonpayment by local governments. Lewis (2001) finds that the average amount borrowed by local governments in the 1990s was only Rp 1,580 million, while the average operating surplus was Rp 3,444 million, suggesting that local governments borrowed well within their capacity to repay. He concludes that "poor repayment of debts is more a function of unwillingness to repay than it is fiscal inability to make good on repayments . . ." (Lewis 2001, p. 21). Local governments in Indonesia have learned over time that they do not need to repay.
- While the government has approved a small number of debt restructuring plans for local water utilities, it has not yet put in place a comprehensive policy and program to deal with the loan arrears. This policy of indecision in effect penalizes local governments that continue to pay off their loans.

Integration of Loans and Grants

Among the many unfinished pieces of the Indonesian subnational loan agenda is how to better integrate loans with grants, to avoid having the availability of grants impede rather than support the development of capital markets. One proposed approach is to transform interest rate subsidies into a "buy-down" of the capital that a local government must borrow for a project. (The amount of that buy-down and thus the size of the subsidy could be based on various indicators of the project's affordability to the local population.) The local government would then borrow the remaining amount at prevailing commercial rates from private entities. This technique has the virtue of providing the subsidy in one lump at the outset and exposing local governments to market conditions on the margin of their financing needs.[10]

The integration of grants and loans is not an original idea. Others looking at Indonesia have argued that a significant disadvantage in developing a credit market culture is the real or potential availability of grants that scuttle the demand for loans at prevailing market rates.[11] The indiscriminate use of grants, it is argued, builds a culture of dependence on subsidies and hinders the development of notions of cost recovery. It also can stymie efforts to induce local governments to enter the capital markets. By the same token, a conscious regimen of exposing local governments to private market demands and credit expectations will benefit the development of both private lenders and government borrowers.

Integrating grants and loans for projects would require a combination of technical and affordability analyses. First, technical parameters, based on best practices in engineering, are needed to determine what operation is most efficient at different scales and with different processes and what costs are reasonable for constructing the project facilities. The analysis, the stuff of standard feasibility and engineering studies, would determine standardized annual cost functions, the capital investment needed, and its cost.

Second, in the more critical step for determining the size of the grant needed, the capital investment required would be translated into a standardized annual debt service cost. This is done by applying a factor that reflects a commercial cost of capital on the assumption that the debt could be borrowed for a period corresponding to the useful life of the project. Thus in addition to the operating and capital cost figures, a study is needed of the likely use of the facility and the applicable rate structure to determine the likely operating revenues.

The underlying idea is that for certain classes of users (say, residential users in the lowest income brackets) the potential for revenue generation may be severely limited. Facilities with a large share of low-income users would be the most likely candidates for grants (that is, some form of capital subsidies).[12] Thus the subsidies to facilities would be "means tested" and the subsidy would come from lowering (or in some cases eliminating) future debt service payments by providing a one-time capital grant that reduces the amount to be borrowed. This up-front grant is suggested rather than subsidized interest rates or operating subsidies because both of these must be extended into the future, require ongoing administration and monitoring, and tend to conceal the amount of subsidy.[13]

The critical question is, how large should the capital grant be? To decide this, an objective measure needs to be developed for an acceptable burden of water charges paid annually by the poorest users (residential and commercial). These affordable charges then can be "backed through" the revenue system to form a constraint on the annual revenues available to pay the operating and debt service costs. This constrained sum would be compared with the sum of annual operating costs (assuming efficient technical and economic operation) and the prototype "market proxy" annual debt service—or the required annual revenue. The extent by which the required annual revenue exceeds the needs-constrained revenue represents the proportion by which annual debt service must be reduced to make the facility feasible for debt financing (at least in part). Where the acceptable level of annual charges is equal to or less than the expected operating costs of the facility (without including debt service), it is unlikely that any of the project should be considered for debt financing.[14]

In the present era of reform in Indonesia, it is hoped that new approaches to integrating grants and loans will be used and that the mistakes of the past will not be perpetuated in the future. Twin reforms in intergovernmental finance and the financial system have the potential to be mutually reinforcing and beneficial.

Prospects for a Local Government Debt Market

The prospects for developing a local government debt market in Indonesia are undoubtedly mixed. These prospects were dealt a severe blow by the 1997 economic crisis, the after-effects of which will linger for some time. In addition, the heavy arrears on RDA and SLA loans, coupled with the lack of a comprehensive program to deal with this issue, have eroded the perceived creditworthiness of local governments. The legacy of unpaid concessional loans, rampant moral hazard, unsettled intergovernmental relations, and a weakened financial sector conspires to make achieving a market-based credit system for local governments a difficult feat, at least in the near to intermediate term.

Still, there are reasons for hope. Indonesia has embarked on true decentralization. When the implications of this process are fully realized—that is, when local governments have a clearer list of local responsibilities, a stronger set of own-source revenues, and a more effective approach to financial management—these governments will have a chance to improve their creditworthiness. When these strengthened local governments encounter a revived private sector and a rationalized public sector, Indonesia should see the emergence of a market for local government credit.

Notes

1. This section draws heavily on Lewis (2001).

2. This section draws from Kehew and others (2002).

3. The predecessor of the Regional Development Account was the Investment Funds Account. In this chapter loans made through the earlier account are grouped with RDA loans.

4. RDA and SLA loans also mobilized additional resources, typically requiring a 10 to 25 percent match from the central government, the local borrower, or both.

5. Indonesia had a small but growing corporate debt market and some institutional buyers at the time and was trying to develop its securities markets.

6. Local general governments (that is, regional authorities other than certain self-supporting utilities such as the local water utilities) were seen as having revenue systems too weak and inflexible to support bond issues. Moreover, it was thought that investors would better understand the accounting systems of the local water utilities.

7. Other factors, such as the lack of a well-established intercept mechanism for intergovernmental revenue transfers, are discussed below.

8. The early plans for using revenue bonds did include contracts that acted like trusts. Because there was no established trust law in Indonesia, each contract was unique. The mechanism and the enforcement of the trusts were never tested.

9. See Firdusay (2002, p. 82). Financial management at the local level is portrayed as often not only incompetent, but also corrupt. The head of the capital markets supervisory agency (BAPEPAM) cites the inability of local finance offices to do proper accounting and financial reporting as an impediment to their entering the financial markets.

10. See Johnson and Petersen (2002). The following section draws heavily from that report.

11. On the case of Indonesia, see Smoke (1999). On grants undercutting loans as a problem in credit market development, see Weitz (2001, p. 5). A recent World Bank document (2002, annex 2-3, pp. 40–41) states approvingly that it appears that the specific-purpose capital grants would depend on the income of governments and the nature of the project and that

wealthier governments would qualify for only limited grants because they qualify for commercial borrowing on most investments.

12. There may be a good deal of cross-subsidy at the local level, with richer users subsidizing poorer ones. But there are limits on how much cross-subsidy can occur in a locality without driving out the richer ratepayers, and in some localities there may be too few rich users to offset the costs of serving the poor.

13. See Varley (2001, p. 5), who argues that subsidized rates and other soft terms lead to the buildup of hidden liabilities and crowd out private suppliers of credit.

14. It is conceivable that a project could generate insufficient revenue to pay the everyday operation and maintenance costs, let alone debt service costs. In that case operating costs as well as capital costs may need to be subsidized. It is best to identify these two components separately and to try to make the project self-supporting at least to the level of operation. In Indonesia general allocation grants could be used to subsidize operations, while specific-purpose grants should be project specific, means tested, and used only for one-time capital grants.

Chapter 26

Asia
The Philippines

An innovative insurance program is critical in starting a local government bond market.

John Petersen

Lessons

In the Philippines the Local Government Code of 1991 ushered in a new framework for intergovernmental relations, extending more responsibilities and decisionmaking power to local governments. It established a system of transfers that has been stable and predictable and that contributes a large share of local budgets. The law also opened prospects for local government financing from private sources, with relatively few restrictions. Despite growing capital spending needs, however, substantial barriers remain. Perhaps most important is the restriction of depository banking to government-owned banks, which has effectively limited local governments to two such banks for their credit needs.

Nevertheless, efforts have been made to expand access to private financing. The desire of the private banking system to enter the local government credit market, coupled with earlier

---

efforts by the Department of Finance, contributed to the formation of a small but energetic municipal bond market toward the end of the 1990s. This development was largely made possible by the creation of a specialized bond insurer, the Local Government Unit Guarantee Corporation, with joint public and private ownership. The corporation, which insures investors for a fee, has instituted proprietary credit ratings used to determine eligible credits and set insurance fees.

Despite early successes, continued growth in the Philippine municipal bond market will remain difficult as long as the government banks retain their dominant depository and lending relationships with local governments. The vision formed by the Philippine government in the mid-1990s foresaw the government financial institutions limiting their lending to short-term financing and small projects that did not qualify for municipal bonds. However, these banks have found local government loans, backed by the assignment of transfer payments, very profitable and are not anxious to have the local government market made competitive.

Another impediment is the availability of concessionary loans through the Municipal Development Fund or through concessionary loan programs routed through government-owned banks. These loans create a risk for private lenders, which might develop local government projects only to see them picked off by government financial institutions able to lend on concessionary terms.

The municipal securities market in the Philippines, fueled by the innovative insurance provided by the Local Government Unit Guarantee Corporation, will remain an "infant industry" for some time, needing active steps to make private underwriting of bonds competitive. The Local Government Unit Guarantee Corporation has provided a focal point for increasing the competition for such lending and for building the foundations of a market. At the very least the competitive advantages bestowed on government lenders should be reduced, as should the tax advantages given to investments routed through banks.

During the 1980s the Philippines underwent turbulent political change that led to a powerful movement toward greater democracy, a more open economy, and political devolution. Beset with economic difficulties and heir to a large government sector, persistent trade deficits, and heavy international debt from the despotic Marcos years, the reform-minded nation steered a course toward political decentralization, trade liberalization, and debt repayment.

The keystone of the political reform was the passage of the Local Government Code of 1991, which shifted resources and responsibilities to local governments. Implementing the new code has been a challenge, as the legacy of central government primacy and involvement in local affairs has continued and the national government's deficits have persisted.

A largely peaceful popular revolt occurred in 2000, in response to the corruption of the Estrada regime and poor economic performance, bringing a change in national leadership. Overall, the country has made steady if slow progress, and it suffered less from the East Asian crisis than did its neighbors. However, it continues to be dogged by a sluggish economy and difficult political situation.

Structure and Finances of Local Governments

The Philippines is a unitary state with a hierarchical system in which local governments are directly under the control of the national government, though with certain constitutional protections. The local sector consists of three levels: the provinces and major cities, the municipalities, and the *barangays* (essentially neighborhood organizations). The country has more than 1,600 local governments (in addition to the 42,000 barangays), including 78 provinces, 82 cities, and 1,525 municipalities.

The Local Government Code of 1991 assigned greater responsibilities for service provision to local governments and also entitled them, under the internal revenue allotment (IRA) scheme, to receive 40 percent of the state's income and value added tax revenues, which are distributed on the basis of a formula. The code also gave local governments expanded powers for setting local tax rates and collecting own-source revenues. The mainstays of local revenues are the property tax, the business tax, and taxes on vehicles.

The program of formula-based revenue sharing led to local governments largely substituting the new revenues from the central government for own-source revenues, especially the local property tax. In 1990–96 local own-source revenues declined from 50 percent of total local revenue to 30 percent, while local governments' share of total government spending grew from 6 percent to 16 percent. (With spending at 3 percent of GDP, the size of the local sector remains modest.) The aggregate revenue numbers mask big differences among the local jurisdictions. Cities derive about 50 percent of their revenues from own sources, compared with only about 30 percent for provinces.

One motivation for the new intergovernmental structure was to get local governments to assume a greater share of the burden of financing infrastructure. It was thought that this might be accomplished by permitting local governments broad powers to borrow without the approval of the national government. To that end the Philippine Department of Finance, with considerable donor support, led the way on initiatives to expand local governments' access to credit, following a policy articulated in 1996 (Llanto and others 1998).

The Power to Borrow

Although the Local Government Code provides substantial borrowing powers to local governments, there are some restrictions. Section 324 imposes a limit on local governments' borrowing capacity, stipulating that their appropriations for debt service should not exceed 20 percent of their regular income. In addition, a local government must budget for all contracted-for debt service; otherwise its budget is considered void, and it cannot lawfully spend funds.

Regulation of bond issuance is indirectly implied by section 296 of the Local Government Code, which subjects such debt to regulation by the Securities and Exchange Commission and the Central Bank. Until recently these regulatory provisions were not energetically exercised, however. The Securities and Exchange Commission has held that local government bond issues were exempt from its registration procedures, but in late 2000 the Department of Finance requested the commission to "delegate" its approval powers to the department for purposes of developing a registration procedure.

In addition, the Central Bank Act (Act 7653) requires that, as a condition of borrowing, the monetary board render an opinion on the impact of the borrowing on monetary aggregates, the price level, and the balance of payments. For a sovereign guarantee there is a more rigorous test and approval is required from the secretary of finance. No local government has borrowed with such a guarantee, nor has any borrowed in foreign currency.

Lending to Local Governments

The Local Government Code of 1991 appeared to open several avenues for local governments to access credit finance from bank credits and "other similar forms of credits" and also from bonds and "other securities." Local governments can use credit financing for two purposes—liquidity and capital projects. Meeting liquidity needs involves credit financing of a local government's current spending in advance of expected releases of intergovernmental (primarily IRA) payments or the receipt of taxes. Borrowing by local governments has been modest, accounting for only 3 to 5 percent of their receipts.

A review of access to credit by local governments should start with lending activity by the government financial institutions, by far the most important source of loan funds. Local governments naturally made initial credit requests to government financial institutions, since these hold their cash accounts. As these financial institutions regained confidence in local governments, they began to finance their capital projects. Today the main sources of non-donor-based credit financing are two government financial institutions, the Landbank of the Philippines and the Development Bank of the Philippines, and two specialized on-lending institutions, the Local Water Utilities Administration and the Municipal Development Fund. The Local Water Utilities Administration channels development assistance to local water supply projects and has offered long loan terms that match those of the underlying development assistance loans.

In the early years after the Local Government Code was implemented, the Philippine National Bank and the Landbank were the largest providers of credit to local governments. In 1995 the Philippine National Bank held about 5.9 billion pesos (P) in loans to local governments, the Landbank about P 4.7 billion, and the Development Bank about P 0.2 billion (Llanto 1996). The Municipal Development Fund had P 1.8 billion in loans, and the Local Water Utilities Administration about P 8 billion in water sector loans.

The government financial institutions, reopening their lending windows to local governments after the defaults of the 1980s, focused on those with higher incomes, as shown by the large average loan size in their local government loan portfolios. Interest rates on these loans were about the same as those on their prime commercial loans, suggesting that they assign a low risk premium to local governments. The average tenors were longer than those for commercial loans, at about two to four years.

After 1995 the growth of lending accelerated for the Landbank and the Development Bank, in part because of the rapid withdrawal of the Philippine National Bank from the local government credit market following the bank's privatization. By the end of 2000 these three financial institutions had total outstanding loans to local governments of around P 16.5 billion (table 26.1).[1] The Landbank has been the most aggressive in lending to local governments and securing deposits from them. It had more than P 22 billion in approved loans to local governments at the end of April 2000, of which about P 10 billion had not been availed. The Development Bank and the Philippine National Bank are also actively soliciting local government business, although their loans to local governments are smaller and growing less rapidly.

The Landbank has the largest share of local government loans in its loan portfolio, at 9.6 percent in mid-2000. This share is smaller for the Development Bank and the Philippine National Bank. However, since default rates on local government loans are extremely low, and since large shares of the commercial loans held by the government financial institutions are nonperforming, local governments account for a much larger share of performing loans.[2]

The loans by the government financial institutions to local governments are equal to about 40 percent of their deposits with these banks, although the share varies. Thus at first glance it appears that the banks value local governments more for their depository relationship than for the ability to earn returns on lending to them.

The government financial institutions use the depository relationship and government reporting to create credit and investment instruments. They base credits for capital projects on the IRA and revenue flows of the local government rather than on the revenue flows of the project. They make available short-term credit facilities tied to future budget releases that allow local governments to draw funds in advance of revenues. And, moreover, they enable local governments to arbitrage on interest rates and on financial reporting by, for example, granting loans secured on their deposits, allowing the local governments to earn spreads on their investments and still report high deposit balances. These practices help the government financial institutions manage the risk of lending to local governments, while enabling the local governments to venture into commercial borrowing and financing of capital projects.

For the Local Water Utilities Administration, ongoing structural problems prevented it from expanding its participation in financing local water supply projects. Lending by the Municipal Development Fund also grew slowly, reaching P 2.7 billion in 1999. Among other possible sources, the

Table 26.1. Local Government Loans and Deposits with Selected Financial Institutions, Philippines, 2000

Financial institution	Local government loans outstanding, December 2000 (billions of pesos)	Local government loans as a share of total loans, June 2000 (percent)	Local government deposits, late 2000 (billions of pesos)
Landbank of the Philippines	11.9	9.6	28
Philippine National Bank	3.0	2.8	8
Development Bank of the Philippines	1.6	4.3	7
Total	16.5	—	43

— Not available.
Source: ARD, Government Finance Group 2001, pp. 56–57.

government pension funds, which had shown early interest, were content to invest in high-yield government obligations and made heavy commitments to the commercial property sector and equity investments. These factors impeded their participation in the growing local government credit market.

Private commercial banks carry out almost no direct lending to local governments. A regulation restricting local governments' depository accounts to government financial institutions as well as other impediments have precluded their access to private banks. (However, private banks are the main purchasers of the municipal securities that have been issued.) Thus policy and institutional factors have led to a de facto duopoly by the Landbank and the Development Bank in local government deposits and credits.

Like many emerging markets, the Philippine bond market is dominated by the central government and its need to finance its deficit. There are also a few corporate bonds. There is an active treasury bill market in which short-term bills are sold competitively at maturities ranging from 31 days to one year. Small-denomination bonds to attract individual savers were introduced in 1999. The treasury bill rates serve as the benchmarks for loans, which are typically sold in a variable rate format with 182-day adjustments.

The growing institutional investor base is led by government-owned contractual savings institutions. The Social Security System and the Government Service Insurance System had combined assets of about P 290 billion at the end of 1999. Prudential requirements and the high rates on treasury bills have precluded much diversification away from government securities, although the funds have recently invested in equities and real estate.

The Philippine banking system at first appeared to come through the East Asian financial crisis of the late 1990s relatively unscathed. However, the slow growth of the economy, recurring fiscal problems, and political instability have taken their toll on the condition of banks. Several factors contributed to Philippine banks' early resistance to the Asian downturn: the banks' generally prudent lending policies (especially with respect to real estate), high reserve requirements, good accounting and transparency practices, high profitability, and a penchant for holding large amounts of government debt rather than direct loans.[3] Nonetheless, commercial loan payment difficulties emerged as the economy continued to lag in the early 2000s. While the overall ratio of non-performing loans has not exceeded 20 percent, many loans had to be restructured by mid-2000. Meanwhile, banks have been kept busy financing the large and continuing deficit of the national government.

One result of the economic slowdown at the end of the 1990s was that it made the local government loans held by the government financial institutions look better and better. With their nearly flawless repayment record during the 1990s, as is discussed below, these loans have come to be recognized as a lucrative form of lending for the government financial institutions and have taken precedence over much riskier private sector loans. Banks can lend to local governments at 2 to 6 points above the treasury bill rate (the same as commercial loan rates) and typically pay savers rates that are 3 points or more below that rate. Thus banks enjoy a huge interest spread, one that an effective capital market should be able to shave through disintermediation.

Early Development of a Municipal Bond Market

Municipal bonds have a history in the Philippines. Sections of the Local Government Code of 1991 replaced the Marcos Executive Order 725 of 1975 that had permitted local governments to issue tax-exempt municipal bonds. These sections of the code authorize local governments to issue taxable, revenue-based municipal bonds subject to any applicable rules issued by the Securities and Exchange Commission and the Central Bank. Such bonds are specifically the obligation of the local government, not of the national government. Local governments must use bonds for self-liquidating, revenue-generating purposes (section 299). However, they may create debt and use other credit facilities for any "infrastructure and other socioeconomic development purpose" as long as it accords with the local development plan (section 296). Local governments were also granted considerable latitude to enter into public-private arrangements.

Municipal bonds were expected to become a major source of infrastructure capital, substituting economically responsive local decisionmaking and rate setting for central government provision of capital funds. Adoption of the new law on revenue-based municipal bonds was followed by an extensive orientation effort to inform officials of local governments, private commercial banks, the investment houses, the Securities and Exchange Commission, the Central Bank, the Department of Finance, the Central Office of Audit, and other national entities about the opportunities and requirements associated with developing and issuing municipal bonds. The Securities and Exchange Commission and Central Bank formulated rules to facilitate rapid review and clearance of proposed revenue-based municipal bonds.

Despite heavy promotion, in the ensuing years of the mid-1990s only five small municipal bond issues took place. These were very small (P 8 to 26 million) and of short maturity (two to three years) (Petersen 1998). Four of the issues, as government-guaranteed bonds sold for housing projects, were partially tax-exempt, and only one issue was unenhanced and fully taxable.[4] Early interest shown by the investment houses in municipal bonds after the passage of the Local Government Code of 1991 faded away.

A variety of institutional and economic factors led to the lethargy in starting up the municipal bond market. Four "environmental" impediments had a particularly important effect in abating private market interest in municipal bonds:

- *The greater appeal of private sector financings for finance professionals in the Philippines.* The equity markets and private banking, both domestically and abroad, attracted the top Filipino talents.
- *Ignorance and caution.* Both sides of the credit market were faced with the new phenomenon of local governments raising money in securities markets that were inexperienced in lending to them. Potential lenders and investors continue to have grave doubts about local political units' fiscal discipline and willingness to pay.[5] Local governments were used to obtaining grants or concessionary loans from Manila and generally are unskilled in planning for and raising capital funds on their own.
- *The small number (and small scale) of viable projects and the rigors and costs of bond issues.* Marketing bond issues involved large costs that neither the public nor the private sector could profitably absorb.

Good revenue-producing projects were few in number and, once they surfaced, subject to being "poached" by government lending institutions on concessionary terms.

- *Oligopolistic behavior by the government financial institutions.* With origins in a centralized and nationalized banking system that met all the banking needs of local governments, the government financial institutions dominate the provision of credit and other banking services to local governments, which are familiar and valuable clients.

Creditworthiness of Local Governments

Despite these impediments, the local government credit market has continued to tantalize many private bankers because, as a group, local governments appear to be a very good credit risk. Creditors' experience with local governments over the past decade has been excellent. Local government debt has been secure and profitable, and creditors have had relatively few problems in achieving high rates of timely payment on loans. Of course, this experience is almost exclusively that of government-owned institutions, which alone have the ability to hold local governments' deposits. The Landbank reported that only 0.18 percent of its outstanding local government loans were past due at the end of 2000. The Development Bank reported no past-due local government loans at the end of November 2000. The Philippine National Bank indicated that its portfolio had a couple of "defaults" but virtually "no losses," although some earlier loans had been restructured. The Municipal Development Fund claimed a similarly good repayment record, reporting defaults of less than 1 percent in the late 1990s (see World Bank 1999b).[6]

This strong debt repayment performance by local governments is the result of a mix of factors. Many local governments are prudent about going into debt and do not overextend themselves. Others have limited capital needs and prefer to use IRA payments or grants to fund these needs, usually restricted to small projects. The relative prosperity and political stability of the 1990s also helped. The most important factor may have been the conditions enforced by the government financial institutions: rapid payback periods on loans, a conservative lending stance (for a period in the 1980s the government financial institutions did not lend to local governments), and the strong security provided by the ability of government financial institutions to intercept the IRA payments.

These repayment records, though established exclusively with government financial institutions, provide evidence that at current levels of borrowing and pledges of security, there is little reason to characterize local governments as weak or undependable credits. However, current levels of local government debt are low by international standards and the security pledged has always been general obligation, with a heavy reliance on IRA payments. Thus it is unlikely that the strong repayment records reflect financial management acumen on the part of the borrowers.

Role of Private Banks

Private commercial banks in the Philippines, though they would very much like to make loans, have been cautious (if not skeptical) about the possibilities of revenue-based municipal bond financing. They view local government lending as an unknown commodity, and without an explicit ability to hold local government deposits or intercept central government payments, they consider local governments to be high risk. Moreover, local governments offer poor income prospects compared with the nonrisk returns of 10 to 15 percent on treasury bills.

Private banks are similarly cautious about underwriting bond issues for local governments. The costs of preparing revenue-producing bond issues are relatively high, and private underwriters face a risk that government financial institutions will pick off local government bond issues by coming in late and offering attractive loan terms. For a time the roles were reversed, and the private sector was underwriting a growing number of local government bond issues. The slowdown in economic activity and political turmoil in the early part of the present decade appeared to abate the bond market's growth.

Still, circumstances are moving in the direction of greater private market access. One recent change has made municipal bonds more attractive to private banks. The Agri-Agra law (Presidential Decree 717) requires private banks to maintain 25 percent of their portfolio in loans to the agricultural and agribusiness sector. It has been difficult, however, for banks to develop loans of this type, and in the late 1990s there was reportedly a P 20 billion deficit in their holdings of Agri-Agra loans. A Central Bank ruling in 2000 now permits banks to use municipal bonds toward the Agri-Agra requirements, stimulating demand for such bonds.

Local Government Unit Guarantee Corporation

The Bankers Association of the Philippines had long been interested in developing mechanisms to insure against the risks to its member institutions in dealing with local governments. In 1997 the Department of Finance, intent on developing a municipal bond market, began an initiative that culminated in the formation of the Local Government Unit Guarantee Corporation, a company that underwrites investor insurance of local government bonds. The company was capitalized at P 250 million (about $7 million) in March 1998 and began an extensive marketing campaign targeting both banks and local governments.

The Local Government Unit Guarantee Corporation added several interesting ingredients to the development of the Philippine bond market. To write guarantee policies and set its premiums, it had to develop credit criteria and a credit rating system (see section on credit ratings). The premium for the guarantee depends on the rating and the scale of the transaction, with around 1.0 to 1.5 percent of the outstanding principal being the target level for premiums. By March 2001, the corporation had closed on eight bond issues involving its guarantees.[7] As of mid-year 2003, Local Government Unit Guarantee Corporation–insured bonds amounted to about P 1.7 billion (about $33 million) in insured principal outstanding.[8] At its current level of capitalization the corporation could guarantee around P 2.5 billion in loans or bond issues and believes that it needs more capital.[9]

In 1999 the Local Government Unit Guarantee Corporation engaged in negotiations with the U.S. Agency for International Development (USAID) on the use of USAID's new credit enhancement program, which would allow U.S. government backup on its guarantees. USAID requested that the two government financial institutions holding equity in the corporation (the Landbank and the Development Bank) divest their interests in it. Concerned about possible government interference, it asked that the corporation divest itself of the bond rating function, if possible. (That decision will depend on the financial viability of the rating function.) In late 1999 the corporation entered into an agreement with USAID and has paid the fees to receive its 30 percent backup on qualifying bond issues.

The Local Government Unit Guarantee Corporation represents an innovation of international significance in local government finance. It has provided a way to involve private commercial banks in local government capital financing despite the barriers to establishing banking relationships. Its enhancements bring early homogeneity to a potentially disparate market and the promise of some liquidity to an otherwise comatose secondary market. If its selection of credits to insure proves dependable, it will go a long way toward building investor confidence. The corporation also operates an internal rating system that is unique in the scope and detail of its credit assessments. The rating system could become commercially viable if the volume of bond financing is sustained.

Multilateral and Bilateral Initiatives: The Municipal Development Fund and Technical Assistance

The Philippine Municipal Development Fund is an initiative of the World Bank and other donor institutions dating to 1984 (Gavino 1998). While the donor institutions set up the fund because of the underdeveloped capital market in the country, in the end it wants local governments to access the capital market. The fund uses different modes of assistance, combining loans and grants to correspond with the revenue-generating and non-revenue-generating (social and environmental) components of projects. For projects with large social and environmental components (relating to schools, dump sites, and public markets, for example), grants can cover up to 70 percent of the project cost. The loans are tied to the grants. There also has been a concerted effort to inject more private capital and managerial expertise into the financing and operations of infrastructure facilities.[10]

Working with the Development Bank of the Philippines, the World Bank has been experimenting in using the Municipal Development Fund to aid local government infrastructure projects. One example is the Local Government Unit Urban Water and Sanitation Project, which finances facilities that are not part of the water districts financed by the Local Water Utilities Administration. The project requires privatized operation under a design, build, and operate scheme in which lease payments from the operators are used to repay the local government's loan. Another example is the Water Districts Development Project, an initiative dating from 1993 that the World Bank has undertaken with the Landbank of the Philippines. This project has added sewage treatment to existing water districts. The project has had problems because of collection difficulties and changes in local government leadership. Yet another example is the flood control project in San Fernando, Pampanga. Because all these are inherently non-revenue-generating projects, they encounter difficulties when political problems arise, because the funds need to be allocated to the projects from the local governments' current operations.

While the ultimate aim in setting up the Municipal Development Fund was to have local governments access private capital, there appears to be no clear mechanism for inducing them to do so. Implementing a credit program that features submarket lending terms while attempting to develop a private capital market for the more creditworthy borrowers poses major difficulties. Two types of moral hazard are present. For program administrators, there is a desire to lend to good projects and to show responsible use of funds by achieving good repayment records. Proponents of such projects are typically the more creditworthy local governments. For local government borrowers, there is a desire to qualify for the program so as to avail themselves of the preferential (submarket) terms. They understandably resist having to borrow at higher interest rates and for shorter periods.

The World Bank and others are also providing technical assistance aimed at improving access to credit, however. Part of the World Bank's Local Government Finance Development Fund (LOGOFIND) project is directed toward technical assistance and training programs to bolster local government financial administration. One objective is to develop more professional planning and analytical capacity at both the national and the local government level, which would enhance credit-related policies and implementation.

The GOLD (Governance and Local Democracy) Investment Promotion and Prioritization Program, sponsored by USAID, has worked for several years in five provinces (Bohol, Capiz, Lanao del Norte, Nueva Vizcaya, and Palawan). Although the program has provided no credit assistance, it has promoted better practices in capital budgeting and in accessing alternative credit sources. The project developed participatory methods for identifying and developing possible local government investment projects that could be financed through loans, joint ventures, build-operate-transfer (BOT) arrangements, and municipal bonds. Of 50 investment projects analyzed, only one emerged as a possible candidate for revenue-based municipal bond funding. However, several smaller projects might be candidates for bank loans or for loan pooling devices.

In a related effort in 2000, a project funded by USAID and undertaken by the Financial Executives Association of the Philippines prepared a comprehensive manual of practice in the municipal bond market (Financial Executives Institute of the Philippines 2000). The manual explains step by step how issues are developed and marketed and what roles different participants play. It includes copies of the typical documents needed in bond offerings and explains legal authorities and constraints. It also shows the range of costs that have been incurred in bond sales.

Appraisal of Local Governments' Access to the Credit Market

Loan funds from the government financial institutions appear to have been generally available to local governments, at least through late 2001. The constraints appeared to be in the development of bankable projects and the reluctance of local governments to borrow to finance projects at the rates and on the terms offered by the government financial institutions. Moreover, despite continuing perceptions to the contrary in the private sector, credit quality does not appear to be an issue, although this proposition has not been tested by widespread borrowing in large amounts. The bonds and bank loans have done well with respect to repayment, but borrowing is at very modest levels and well secured by the IRA payments.

The supply of projects that are good candidates for debt financing is constrained by the limited ability of local governments to formulate projects and put them into satisfactory technical shape for financing. This problem has many sources, including lack of skills among local government officials and the cost and difficulty of procuring professional services. Not surprisingly, smaller local governments normally give preference to small, simple capital projects and the purchase of equipment (such as earth-moving machinery). Moreover, the assignment of government responsibilities places the provision of major infrastructure facilities outside the purview of local governments, putting these facilities in special districts (such as water and sewerage) or leaving them with national agencies (ports and terminals). Thus, to be technically feasible, projects often require the cooperation of local governments in regional schemes and perhaps the cooperation of national agencies as well.

The capacity of local governments to pledge credible security is limited because of the reliance on IRA (which itself has proved to be a strong security) and the resulting weakness in own-source revenue raising systems. Creditors may nominally prefer self-supporting projects and physical collateral (and revenue-generating projects are supposedly required for bond issues).[11] As a practical matter, however, both government financial institutions and bond investors look to the IRA pledge for security. Thus there have been no local government loans that are pure revenue bonds—that is, bonds based solely on project earnings and assets. There are also some legal issues. The legal ability of local governments to have separate, restricted funds for debt service is unclear, and the existing accounting system used in local governments does not recognize the separate fund doctrine nor do financial reporting formats facilitate separate reporting.

Political risk ("willingness to pay") continues to be the paramount concern among potential private sector lenders. Perhaps because of the institutional and regulatory barriers in dealing with local governments, private creditors are generally leery of extending credit to them. Private market investors see local politics as volatile and undependable and still subject to the national government's intrusion or to changes in the rules of the game. Without the private sector as a direct stakeholder (creditor) relying on the viability of local governments, the chances for such changes may be increased.

Private commercial banks, aside from their participation in the Local Government Unit Guarantee Corporation and their role as underwriters of municipal bond deals, have been effectively blocked from lending directly to local governments. The main constraint is the regulation restricting local governments' depository accounts to the two government banks, the Landbank and the Development Bank, and one private bank, the Philippine National Bank. Inability to hold these accounts means that private commercial banks cannot establish customer relationships, enjoy the economic benefits of holding deposits, or have the benefits of IRA intercepts and offsets against deposits as collateral against loans (though banks can enjoy the benefits of the IRA intercept if they hold bonds insured by the Local Government Unit Guarantee Corporation). Commercial banks have attempted to circumvent this restriction by underwriting and investing in bonds. Neither activity establishes broader relationships with local governments or provides the benefits of holding deposits. As long as the depository restriction remains in place, issuing securities will be the only way for local governments to tap private capital.

The local government bond market appears capable of sustained growth, although potential obstacles have arisen. Recent events have caused uncertainty about what procedures are to be followed in the municipal bond market operation, and the central government may be having second thoughts about allowing the market to develop without active oversight. The Department of Finance indicated that it would issue an executive order regulating the municipal bond market. The Central Bank, by resolution, referred requests for its waiver on a proposed municipal bond sale (Caloocan) to the Department of Finance, seeking prior "endorsements" from the department before granting the waiver.[12] Still, the Department of Finance showed a willingness to discuss and negotiate the bond regulation and approval process with the private underwriters and financial advisers.

In the long term the national government needs to follow through on implementing its capital access plan for local governments. That plan argued that credits for commercially viable local governments should be financed by private capital sources (private commercial banks and the bond market). Progress was made in improving access to the capital markets for local governments, primarily through the Local Government Unit Guarantee Corporation. The Municipal Development Fund intends to tighten its focus on smaller, less creditworthy local governments, but private commercial banks continue to be excluded from the local government loan market by their inability to hold local government deposits except under exceptional circumstances.

The market should include participation by commercial banks (as both direct lenders and investors in securities) and other private and public investors that local governments can best access through a domestic bond market. The direct lending and on-lending systems, funded by development assistance and operated exclusively by the government financial institutions and the Municipal Development Fund, inhibit growth in the domestic markets and the tapping of domestic private capital.

Credit Ratings

There has been interest in the Philippines in creating a system of credit ratings and an independent rating agency to rate local government securities, to help create investor confidence, and to provide criteria for setting price differentials. Two independent rating agencies operate in the Philippines, but neither of these rates local government credits. Specializing in rating corporate obligations, these private rating agencies have no particular competence in rating local government credits and are too expensive. Philippine financial institutions, including the two government financial institutions, use internal rating systems to classify the creditworthiness of local governments, but no entity publishes credit scores or bond ratings for local governments (see ARD, Government Finance Group 2001, section 3). However, the Local Government Unit Guarantee Corporation has indicated that it would like to spin off its rating activity if the service can be made financially viable, to make it independent of the company's insurance business (Tirona 2001).

The rating system used by the Local Government Unit Guarantee Corporation is the most developed one. The system is based on a two-step approach. First, an indicators screen based on secondary data is used to screen potential candidates for guarantees (the screen has data for about 160 of the largest local governments). This produces scores. Second, a full-blown credit analysis is performed on applicants for insurance coverage. This provides a rating for the local governments. The company also judges the creditworthiness of projects to be financed by bond proceeds, although it does not assign ratings to such projects.

By early 2001 the Local Government Unit Guarantee Corporation had rated eight local governments for purposes of insured bond sales. These ratings are not made public, but the requirement is that the local governments be "investment grade" to secure insurance.[13] The costs of preparing ratings (approximately P 40,000–50,000) have been incorporated into the insurance premium.

To be effective and credible, a credit rating system must meet four criteria:

- *Sound methodology.* The system must be logically sound in what it measures, and the analysis used must be relevant to judging ability and willingness to pay.
- *Competent and professional administration.* The system must be applied rigorously by individuals who have the necessary skill and judgment and the required data.
- *Objectivity and independence.* The system must be free of political and economic pressure. It will earn no respect if it is manipulated for political or financial ends.
- *Financial sustainability.* The system must be financially viable to meet the first three criteria. That means that it must be self-supporting or subsidized in a way that protects its independence and at a level enabling it to pay for the professional skills required.

Meeting these four criteria is difficult for the Philippines when it comes to rating local government securities because there is insufficient demand to support an independent, professionally run rating agency. There are few bond issues, they tend to be small, and the ratings now given are a tie-in of the bond insurance, which all recent bond issues have used. Moreover, the government financial institutions, which make all bank loans to local governments, have their own internal systems (and yet still rely mostly on the IRA assignment). There is no requirement for investors or issuers to be rated. The rating system of the Local Government Unit Guarantee Corporation is in place only because of an internal prudential requirement, reinforced by a reinsurance requirement by USAID. Thus a rating agency would need to be founded on direct or indirect regulatory requirements.

The most successful route, however, may be the credit ratings "cart" following the credit market "horse." Published credit ratings are most important to current and potential holders of securities—passive investors that do not have direct lending relationships with the borrower like those that a bank has. Until the securities market, consisting of many passive investors with substantial holdings, becomes more important as a source of capital to local governments, there will be little effective demand for published external ratings.

Rating systems, whether internal or proprietary, will be greatly helped by improvements in the data on local governments made available by the national data gathering agencies, the Bureau of Local Government Finance and the Central Office of Audit. Without better data, particularly on debt service payments and self-balancing funds for local government enterprises, quantitative analysis will continue to have severe limitations.

Other Impediments to Local Governments' Access to the Credit Market—and Possible Remedies

The main obstacles to expanding local governments' access to private capital markets have been discussed—difficulties surrounding the banking depository relationships, perceptions of credit quality, and lack of credit ratings. There are other institutional and regulatory impediments as well, some of which are intertwined.

Exclusive Rights of Assignment of Central Government Payments

Only the government financial institutions and the Municipal Development Fund are permitted to use IRA deeds of assignment as security on loans extended to local governments. This privilege allows the government financial institutions to dominate the local government credit market and restricts competition on loans, deposit rates, trustee relationships, and other measures that help local governments better manage their fiscal resources and strengthen their creditworthiness.

The government financial institutions are reluctant to give up this competitive advantage. However, the same rights of assignment and interception of funds should be extended to private banks and investment houses, though perhaps constrained by prudential limits allowing such rights only to qualifying private banks.

Inadequate Financial Accounting and Reporting

The system of financial record-keeping and reporting prescribed by the Central Office of Audit for local governments does not lend itself to the financial statement reporting required by banks, investment houses, and investors in municipal bonds. The Central Office of Audit, in consultation with private banks and investment houses, should develop guidelines for financial record-keeping to support the analysis of debt obligations. The existing local government accounting system, an adaptation of that used by the central government, reports only highly aggregated results. Revamping the system to allow for self-balancing and freestanding enterprise funds and to shift the focus from ensuring legal compliance to reporting financial condition would do much to aid bond financing techniques.

High Front-End Costs of Bond Issuance

To prepare revenue-based municipal bond packages for marketing, local governments must invest in preliminary project identification, prefeasibility and feasibility studies, and financial preparations. Some of this work can be done in-house, but in every case there comes a time when the local government must engage external specialists (financial analysts, bond underwriters, and the like). However, the procurement process presents a problem. Many local governments lack the capacity to put out competitive solicitations for underwriting services—and as a result are not allowed to hire experts to help them. Moreover, the costs of preparing and floating bond issues are high relative to the amounts borrowed, especially for small issues.

Private banks and investment houses generally will not put up these front-end costs unless the project has very large potential (P 250 million and above). Even in these cases local governments will have to finance some of the costs, a process complicated by the procurement laws. Because of the high front-end costs, local governments are reluctant to explore major development projects.

Taxation of Securities Transfers

The documentary stamp tax (levied on legal documents and associated financial transactions, such as stock or bond certificate transfers) hampers the development of an investor market in stocks and bonds by creating a disincentive for investors to take risks. Continuing the tax will further dampen the chances for developing a vigorous capital market, including municipal bonds. The present tax system favors continued intermediation through banks, since investments made through banks (such as certificates of deposit or savings accounts of more than five years' maturity) are exempt from the documentary stamp tax.

Lack of a Secondary Bond Market

Establishing a secondary market for municipal bonds would encourage more individual and institutional investors to invest in such bonds, particularly those wanting options on how long they remain invested in a single bond. A secondary market cannot emerge until there is a primary market supplying a volume of tradable securities. Even so, the first steps toward developing a secondary market for municipal bonds need to be taken. The Philippine Securities and Exchange Commission, in collaboration with the Philippines Stock Exchange, is exploring the start-up of trading operations in bonds, including revenue-based municipal bonds. This might be aided by establishing a "bond pool" that would combine small local government loans into packages of sufficient size to attract investor interest and an active secondary market. The existing tax law is not conducive to secondary trading, however.

Lack of Procedures for Financial Emergencies of Local Governments

There is little guidance on what procedures to follow in the event of a financial emergency at the local level. Section 531 of the Local Government Code of 1991, which deals with debt relief for local government units, might have been adequate for debt management problems encountered in the Marcos era. However, the expanded use of credit finance by local governments today calls for a comprehensive procedure for dealing with local governments that run into serious financial difficulty.

The procedure should be designed so that it does not intrude on the fiscal autonomy granted to local governments under the Local Government Code but does hold them accountable for willful actions of default. It should be structured to lend comfort to investors on economic and natural calamities *(force majeure)* beyond the control of local governments but not on political succession problems at the local level (where trust accounts and legally enforceable contracts can provide protection).

Tax Treatment of Local Government Interest Payments

The government treasury bill market and investor practices have favored short-term maturities and high interest returns, and there are no incentives designed to foster investment in longer-term maturities at somewhat lower interest rates. This situation inhibits the wide adoption of revenue-based municipal bond financing by local governments. Revenue-producing projects often need several years of gestation for design, construction, operation, and cash flow generation. They need the bond-created funds at interest rates lower than those prevailing in the regular bank loan market and with maturities much longer than the usual two- to five-year loan period.

There are several ways to attack this impediment. One way is to set up tax exemption incentives for long-term bonds with maturities of, say, four to five years. Individual investors, given current credit finance practices in the market and the absence of a secondary market, probably would not wish to tie up their funds in such long-term maturities. Major institutional investors, such as the Social Security System and the Government Service Insurance System, however, have expressed interest in reserving small slices of their portfolios for investment in sound revenue-based municipal bonds, given appropriate incentives.

Two possible options are giving a blanket tax exemption to all revenue-based municipal bonds or setting up a graduated system of exemptions for bonds with maturities of 7 to 15 years. Although always controversial, tax exemption is used extensively by sovereigns to enhance the market for their bond issues. Applied surgically, it might be good "bait" for drawing investor funds out to longer maturities.

Weak Incentive for Investor Due Diligence

The ability to intercept IRA payments is a mixed blessing. It enhances the credit of local governments, but it can lead investors to rely on the intercept mechanism as the only source of security and remove the incentive to conduct due diligence to ensure that projects are self-supporting. One possible cure is to exempt projects that are self-supporting from the ceiling on debt service, discussed next. The idea would be to ensure that projects are self-supporting and kept apart from any pledged support from general revenues. Without such a tax pledge, there would be no need to restrict project borrowing by the availability of general tax revenues, as is now done.

Ceiling on Local Government Debt Service

Section 324(b) of the Local Government Code imposes a limit on the debt incurred by a local government by restricting annual appropriations for debt service to no more than 20 percent of its regular income. For some provinces and large cities, this cap is reportedly beginning to constrain development initiatives.

Municipal bonds are restricted to "revenue-producing" activities. Precisely how that phrase is to be interpreted is unclear, since the revenues produced may well be insufficient to pay operating expenses and debt service. For activities that generate sufficient revenue to cover operating expenses and debt service, the debt service might be exempted from the ceiling. This is customary practice in the United States. Similarly, in the European Union the debt of self-supporting government-owned utilities is not counted against the national debt ceiling.

Prospects for Developing the Private Credit Market

The Local Government Code, at least on paper, opened prospects for a market for local government obligations. It created a potential for local government financing from private sources both for expenditures in advance of revenues and for capital projects, but serious structural barriers remain. Particularly important is the restriction of depository banking to government financial institutions, which has effectively limited local governments to two such institutions for their credit needs. Nonetheless, local governments gained experience as borrowers in the 1990s and saw the development of a range of credit and security structures. This experience contributed to the emergence of municipal bonds toward the end of the decade.

Starting up the municipal bond market in the Philippines will remain difficult as long as the government financial institutions retain their dominant depository and lending relationships with local governments. The vision formed by the Philippine Department of Finance in the mid-1990s foresaw the government financial institutions limiting their lending to short-term financing and small projects that did not qualify for municipal bonds (Philippines, Department of Finance 1996). The problem is that the government financial institutions have found local government loans, backed by the assignment of government transfers, to be very profitable and are not anxious to have the local government loan market made competitive.

Another impediment to the development of the private capital market is the continued availability of concessionary loans from the Municipal Development Fund or through concessionary loan programs routed through the government financial institutions. These loans create a risk for private lenders, which might develop local government projects only to see them picked off by government financial institutions able to lend on concessionary terms. For a time the reverse was the case, with government financial institutions being undercut by aggressive bond issues. However, the most recent evidence is that the government financial institutions, with funds to spare, have been refinancing outstanding local government bond issues at lower interest rates.[14]

The municipal securities market in the Philippines, fueled by the innovative insurance provided by the Local Government Unit Guarantee Corporation, will remain an "infant industry" for some time, needing active steps to make underwriting and trading of bonds competitive. The Local Government Unit Guarantee Corporation has provided a focal point for increasing the competition for local government lending and for building the foundations of a municipal bond market. At the very least the competitive advantages bestowed on government financial institutions should be reduced, as should the tax advantages given to investments routed through banks.

Notes

1. Although there are other government financial institutions, such as the Veterans Bank and Amanah Bank, they are small and do not offer the full range of services provided by universal banks such as the Landbank of the Philippines and the Development Bank of the Philippines.

2. On 30 June 2000 nonperforming loans for the Philippine National Bank were 35 percent of total loans; for the Landbank of the Philippines, 19 percent; and for the Development Bank of the Philippines, 9 percent (*Business World, Special Report for Q2 2000*, 16 August 2000).

3. For a discussion of the Philippine banking system and its good performance during the recent crisis, see Delhaise (1998).

4. Victorias Pabahay (P 8 million), Santo Domingo (P 10 million), Calavaria (P 20 million), Puerto Princesa (P 20 million), and Lagaspi Suerta (P 26 million). Santo Domingo's issue did not carry a guarantee or the partial tax exemption. The guaranteed bonds were guaranteed for principal and up to 8.5 percentage points of the interest rate, and 8.5 percentage points of the interest was exempt from the 20 percent withholding tax. The bonds ranged in final maturity from two to three years and carried interest rates of 14 to 16 percent. See Gavino (1998, pp. 27–28).

5. There has been a persistent negative perception in the Philippine municipal bond market of the 1991 Cebu bond deal, which briefly threatened default at the time of the changeover in governor of that province. There was no default, though there was a reduction in the land collateral pledged by the province. The political rhetoric of the time and selective memories overshadowed the actual outcome. While much is made about the terrors

of political succession and repudiation of debt, the repayment record for the few local government bonds issued has been spotless—and that for loans, nearly perfect—in the past decade.

6. The 15-year period of strong performance that began in 1985 followed an inglorious one in which there were widespread defaults on local government loans in the early 1980s. Burdened by loans from the Marcos era, local governments refused to pay debt service to the government financial institutions. They were largely relieved of that burden in the mid-1980s, when the central government forgave many of the debts.

7. The policies cover debt service insurance, which amounts to a guarantee of debt service payments. In any given year these are much less than the outstanding principal, but they will sum up to much more over the life of the bonds.

8. See Tirona (2003, p. 2). Thus far, the default rate has been zero. As of mid-2003, the Local Government Unit Guarantee Corporation anticipated P 2.5 billion in guaranteed local government debt by the end of the year.

9. The business plan of the Local Government Unit Guarantee Corporation includes a commitment by the 22 member banks to subscribe more capital when it is called for. With its roughly $7 million capitalization, the corporation is very small by industry standards. However, given the IRA-secured loans, its potential portfolio appears to be of high quality, though dependent on the stability of the country's intergovernmental payments system.

10. See Gavino 1998 for a discussion of various infrastructure financing initiatives, including build-operate-transfer and other privatization schemes. While much has been done at the national level, privatization projects have been slow to materialize at the local level.

11. Although projects to be financed are to be "self-liquidating, income-producing or livelihood projects," there is plenty of room to maneuver in interpreting these terms, none of which is defined. See Local Government Code of 1991, section 397.

12. Monetary Board Resolution 1442 (25 August 2000).

13. A condition of the USAID reinsurance is that the local government bond issues be for allowable purposes and occupy one of the top three rating categories (AAA, AA, A). The Local Government Unit Guarantee Corporation has insured bonds at a slightly lower rating grade (B), forgoing the USAID reinsurance in at least one case.

14. Jesus Tirona, president of the Local Government Unit Guarantee Corporation, correspondence, Manila, October 2002.

Chapter 27

Eastern and Central Europe
Bulgaria

*With the exception of Sophia, weak local finances,
uncertain transfers, and a fragile banking system
stall local government borrowing.*

Peter D. Ellis and Kremena Ionkova

Lessons

Decentralization in Bulgaria during the 1990s was slow and
painful, occurring amid political instability and stressful economic conditions. A unitary state with a tradition of highly centralized control, Bulgaria has been reluctant to adopt new policies and implement reforms. The ad hoc design of
intergovernmental relations has greatly limited the autonomy of
local governments, which face many fiscal guidelines imposed
by the central government. Local governments rely heavily on
transfers from the center (shared taxes and grants), which have
been subject to uncertainty and lack of transparency. As macroeconomic conditions have improved, the intergovernmental fiscal system has recently stabilized, but tight central government
control continues to constrain local authorities in developing
and implementing their budgets.

The economic upheavals and fiscal pressures of the early 1990s led to widespread deferral and cancellation of capital projects, and infrastructure in all cities in Bulgaria—including its capital, Sofia—has deteriorated. The limited fiscal flexibility of local governments will make it difficult for them to meet investment needs in infrastructure.

Despite large capital investment needs and growing contributions to the nation's revenue equalization system, Sofia has managed its budget prudently since the late 1990s. Relatively debt free, it has successfully entered the international bond markets. As the capital city it has unique advantages. Elsewhere in the country municipal borrowing has been virtually absent—hampered by weak local finances, a fragile banking system, and an unsettled and untested legal and regulatory framework.

What Bulgaria and especially Sofia need is an intergovernmental system providing local governments with greater fiscal autonomy and predictability. Central government rules and regulations, once reduced in scope and detail, should be made less arbitrary and enforced more strictly. The emergence of significant borrowing activity will probably depend on the development of own sources of revenue and healthier financial markets. However, as Sofia's experience shows, good management and improving economic conditions are also key.

Among the formerly communist countries of Central Europe, Bulgaria came late to political decentralization and the shift to a market-based economy, earning the label of an "uncertain decentralizer" (World Bank 2001c, p. 55).[1] With a heavily centralized economy tied into an industrial trade system based on the old communist trading bloc, this relatively small country of 8 million found privatization and market liberalization difficult hurdles to surmount while it struggled to protect old industries and employment. After a rocky start down the path of reform and a period of high inflation and negative real economic growth in the early to mid-1990s, the country began to make significant progress by the end of that decade.

Like the rest of Bulgaria, Sofia has undergone major structural transformations in its economy along with rapid changes in its administrative and fiscal responsibilities. These changes were linked early on with the transition to a market economy and more recently with preparation for accession to the European Union (EU). Despite the uncertainties associated with reform, especially with respect to local government regulations and finance, Sofia has managed to capitalize on the opportunities offered by reform, producing economic growth and maintaining sound fiscal balances. Its success in tapping the international bond markets has been both a part and a product of this positive management.

Like all municipalities in Bulgaria, Sofia faces strict central government guidelines on its budget process, though it also receives many exemptions from central government regulations. Tight budgetary controls combined with changing regulatory constraints have led to uncertainty in planning and executing annual budgets. Even so, Sofia successfully floated and repaid a eurobond of 50 million euros (EUR). During the lifetime of the bond, however, the city benefited from a highly stable macroeconomic environment free of adverse shocks.

Transition from a Planned to a Market Economy

During the first half of the 1990s structural reforms in Bulgaria proceeded slowly in the face of economic stress and political turbulence. Economic contraction had led to large deficits and rampant inflation.[2] The socialist party, which remained in power except for a brief interlude, was generally reluctant to follow through on ambitious reforms, espoused by forces that tended to be centered in the larger cities. After the severe banking and foreign exchange crisis that erupted in 1996–97, the government began to pursue sound economic policies and a comprehensive structural reform program.

Along with the stresses and shocks of the transition to a market economy, Bulgaria also faces the challenge of preparing for EU accession. As part of both these efforts, the country needs to undertake substantial public investment to upgrade its capital and infrastructure stock while also strengthening central administration, local governments, and the judicial system. Bulgaria's large national public debt poses a challenge for sound debt management and implies that the country must accept either a slow pace of investment in fixed assets or a slow pace of national debt reduction.

As Bulgaria began the transition from a planned to a market economy, it redefined the role of its national government to facilitate economic liberalization, a goal that it hoped to achieve while maintaining economic and social stability and ensuring distributional equity. Increasing local autonomy and citizen participation was seen as an integral part of the transformation. Fiscal and administrative decentralization has led to fundamental changes in the way the economy and local governments function. Perhaps the most significant change, especially for Sofia and other large cities, has been the increasing responsibility assumed by local authorities for providing public services.

Recent national and subnational reforms have raised Bulgaria's ranking among the transitioning economies in democracy, financial development, economic liberalization, and private sector share of GDP. However, much remains to be done in achieving meaningful fiscal devolution.

Local Governments

Bulgaria initiated local government reforms in 1991, at the beginning of the transition period. These reforms led to direct elections of mayors and the emergence of municipal councils as the locally elected legislative bodies. Administrative and territorial reform followed in 1995 with the adoption of the Administrative and Territorial Structure Act, which redefined the new regional units in the country. In 1999 a new administrative division increased the number of regions from 9 to 28. The 28 regions were then aggregated into 6 planning regions (oblasts) to facilitate the use of EU structural funds within the context of the country's negotiations for EU accession.[3] Municipal self-determination led to further divisions at the local government level, including the establishment of districts (rayons) in larger municipalities such as Sofia, Varna, and Plovdiv.

The Regional Development Act of 1999 defines the new planning regions as spatial units created for the purpose of regional development of infrastructure, the creation of enabling environments for investment at subnational levels, and the utilization of local, national, and foreign resources. Local authorities and nongovernmental organizations are expected to participate in defining regional priorities. In practice, however, municipalities feel excluded from this process, and most regional plans that have been developed have been driven by a top-down approach.

The 28 regions carry out the regional policy of the national government. As branches of the central administration, they do not have revenue raising powers. Each region is administered by a governor (appointed by the prime minister), whose main functions are to ensure that all decisions made by the municipal council are legal and do not exceed its authority and to bear responsibility for all state property in the municipality.

Local governments are the main institutions responsible for urban planning and management and have statutory responsibility for providing and maintaining infrastructure and some urban social services. Most municipalities have acquired ownership of the fixed assets of public housing, public transport, and water and sewerage companies.

Local Government Finances

The preparation of both the state (central government) budget and municipal budgets in Bulgaria involves significant limitations. The state budget is planned and implemented annually, discouraging long-term investment programs. Fiscal discipline has been lax. Local governments are allowed to plan a deficit of 10 percent of expenditures in their budget, regardless of whether the deficit results from operating or investment outlays. Local governments use cash accounting, leaving open the possibility of unfunded and unaccounted-for liabilities. Revenue sources and expenditure assignments at the local level are often mismatched, in part because of the budgeting process but also because of weak management capacity, poor accountability, and inadequate financial control. In 2000 the central government provided additional revenue (beyond the budgeted amounts) to municipalities equal to roughly 1 percent of GDP. These end-of-year payments to localities are opaque and have been criticized as leading to soft budget constraints and political manipulation (Bogetic 1997).

Local budgets are drawn up on the assumption that the municipality will receive the full amount of the state subsidy stated in the annual budget law. However, in practice the municipality may receive less than expected, since only 90 percent of state subsidies are allocated according to the budget law. The other 10 percent are distributed at the end of the year on an ad hoc basis, and the procedure used in these allocations is unclear. Moreover, with year-to-year budgeting there is no guarantee that targeted investment subsidies for a two-year project will be included in the second year's budget law. Local government expenditures account for about 8 percent of GDP, in line with the share in other transitioning economies, and for 20 percent of the nation's consolidated public expenditures (figure 27.1).

Central control over local budgets is pervasive. As a result, local governments lack the flexibility to respond efficiently to local demands and priorities. Their expenditure assignments are limited to payment for services

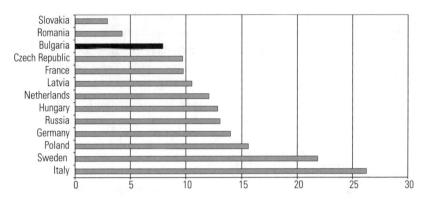

Source: Authors' calculations based on data from IMF 2002a and 2002b.

Figure 27.1 Local Government Expenditure as a Share of GDP, Selected Countries, Various Years, 1998–2002
(percent)

identified at the national level, and their spending resources are also centrally determined. Central authorities cite two reasons for limiting local autonomy: the need to limit accumulated arrears incurred by municipal governments and the insufficient local management and technical capacity.

As in many countries in Central and Eastern Europe, the intergovernmental finance system in Bulgaria continues to evolve, leading to continual change in revenue sources and funding responsibilities for municipalities. The intergovernmental finance system is based on an equalization mechanism, an explicit attempt by the central government to redistribute wealth to poorer municipalities through a formula incorporating need-based factors. This formula, however, which is subject to ad hoc changes from year to year, does not provide predictability in transfers.

Municipalities all generally have the same set of responsibilities: education (not beyond secondary), social welfare, cultural institutions (such as museums and libraries), public utilities, transport, and sports and leisure. Transfers from the central government to subnational authorities take the form of grants, with targeted capital and social assistance transfers exceeding general grants. Shared service mandates create additional problems. Important consequences are the difficulties in matching expenditure assignments and revenue responsibilities.

In principle, the decentralization of expenditure responsibilities should involve either greater local authority to raise revenues or sufficient and stable intergovernmental transfers. However, municipalities in Bulgaria have very limited authority to raise local revenues, and the central transfers leave substantial unfunded mandates. As a result, the intergovernmental system results in a mismatch between assigned functions and their financing.

The state budget law provides the amount of central government transfers annually, including shared taxes—the personal income tax and the corporate income tax. As the nation's capital, Sofia has a large share of national employment and thus a large share of the personal income tax revenue. Bulgarian municipalities depend excessively on central government transfers, absorbing about a fifth of consolidated public revenues in the form of shared taxes and grants. National transfers and shared taxes account for about 90 percent of total local government revenues, while own-source revenues make up only about 10 percent (World Bank 2001c). Local revenues consist of shared taxes (personal and corporate income taxes), local taxes, local fees, other revenues (property sales, fines, and the like), and state transfers. All local taxes are controlled by national limits on rates and bases.

Since the municipalities have limited revenue and expenditure authority, it is difficult for them to accumulate net savings. Nonetheless, Sofia's capital expenditures account for almost a fifth of its total spending, which is 10 percentage points higher than the average for all municipalities in Bulgaria and in line with the level of local investment in other transitioning economies.

The state budget limits the amount that local governments can devote to capital investments. In 1999 the limit was 10 percent of own revenues, which, according to the Ministry of Finance, includes shared taxes. This limit was reduced to 5 percent in 2000. (Sofia was the only municipality exempted from this rule in 2000, so that it could spend the remaining 60 million Bulgarian leva [BGN] from its eurobond issue.) The restriction on capital investments is aimed at preventing irresponsible local governance and maintaining macroeconomic stability. However, it limits the ability of all local governments, including those in good financial health, to effectively invest in and develop local infrastructure and services, an effect compounded by the unpredictability of the capital investment ceiling.

While local governments have the power to borrow, they may do so only for capital purposes and when there are "insufficiencies" in the local budget (World Bank 2001c, p. 41). Until recently local governments carried out little or no borrowing from banks, borrowing only from the central government. High interest rates, a weak banking sector, unstable transfer systems, and problems in defining assets that can be pledged as security on debt have all conspired against the creation of a domestic credit market for subnational borrowers (Bogetic 1997).

Sofia and the Transition

As the capital of Bulgaria, Sofia serves as its economic, financial, and cultural center. Favorably located at the intersection of three main road transport corridors, Sofia is Bulgaria's largest metropolis, with a population of roughly 1.2 million. According to the 2001 census, the city's population had contracted by 0.2 percent since 1991, less than the national decline of 0.8 percent.

Structure of the City Government

According to the Local Self-Government and Local Government Act, the Sofia municipality (the city) is an administrative and territorial unit with the status of a region (oblast), comprising 4 towns and 34 human settlements. Sofia's local government consists of elected representatives (the municipal council) and the mayor, who performs executive functions with the support of appointed officials and the municipal administration. A lower tier of local government includes districts, a municipal administration, and mayoralties. The Sofia municipality is a legal entity with its own property and is responsible for managing its own budget.

The *municipal council* approves strategic and development plans, the annual budget, the fees charged on services, the acquisition and disposal of municipal property, service contracts and concessions, indebtedness, and the management of municipal companies. It also passes subacts—such as ordinances, decisions, and instructions—and elects standing and ad hoc committees.

The *mayor*, elected directly by the citizens of Sofia, performs the executive functions. The mayor's primary responsibilities relate to maintaining public order, implementing the municipal budget, managing long-term programs, and the like. The municipal council has elected six deputy mayors, nominated by the mayor, who are responsible for finance and business affairs; transportation and infrastructure; education and culture; investment and construction; ecology, environment, and land reform; and public health care and social assistance.

Sofia is divided into 24 *districts* (rayons), each of which has a district mayor nominated by the mayor of Sofia and approved by the municipal council. The districts implement municipal policies and administer the budget. In addition, district mayors assist Sofia's mayor in the provision of services to the district population. Some of the larger districts have a significant administrative apparatus.

The *mayoralties* (kmetstvos) extend direct self-government to the level of human settlements, especially those too small to be a distinct municipality. The scope and type of responsibilities of the 34 mayoralties in the Sofia oblast vary considerably. Their mayors, directly elected by a majority of registered voters, may attend municipal council meetings but have no vote. Their activities are coordinated by the mayor of Sofia.

The *municipal administration* drafts and implements policies on health, education, social assistance, municipal development, environmental protection, management of municipal property, enterprises and finances, and public works and utilities. The municipal administration and the 24 district administrations together constitute one of the largest employers in Sofia, with roughly 1,700 employees.

All this conveys a sense of fragmentation in Sofia's governance structure. The 34 mayoralties are only marginally represented in the decisionmaking process. Most district governments are too small to operate basic services independently or to implement local policies. Instead, they can be seen as a mechanism to foster coordination with the region and economies of scale in management. Some of the districts (such as Lozenetz, Sredetz, and Krasna Poljana) have the population, economic activities, and diversity of land uses to justify a relatively independent tier of local government. Others (such as Kremikovtzi and Studentska) tend to have uniform land uses—being predominantly industrial or residential, for example—and do not function as self-sufficient entities. Moreover, the administrative boundaries of the districts do not conform to the urban development patterns or natural landscape of Sofia and are perceived as superimposed divisions that preclude efficient urban planning and management.

Economic Development

Sofia serves as the main engine of economic growth for the national economy, contributing an estimated one-fifth of Bulgaria's GDP. The city's economy benefited from the national economic recovery toward the end of the 1990s and from the country's increasing macroeconomic stability. Although no official time-series data exist on Sofia's gross regional product, experts estimate the city's real growth rate to be about double the national growth rate. Estimates by Sofia's regional statistical office put the city's gross regional product per capita in 1999 at BGN 4,917, compared with the national GDP per capita of BGN 2,841. Thanks to the city's more rapid growth, its unemployment rate in 2001 (4.5 percent) was much lower than that in the rest of the country (17.8 percent). Similarly, the city's poverty rate in 2001 (5.0 percent) was less than half the national rate (12.8 percent).

In earlier decades Sofia pursued an intensive strategy of industrial development, and its rapid industrialization in the 1960s and 1970s led to brisk in-migration from rural areas. This strategy resulted in an economy dependent on manufacturing and heavy industries but also created an administrative and intellectual hub. The city's strong ties to export markets in the former Soviet Union made the transformation from a highly centralized command economy to an open, market-driven one difficult. Once these captive markets were lost, Sofia and the rest of the country had to struggle to find new customers in a competitive market. While painful, the shift in Bulgaria's foreign trade was nonetheless relatively rapid, and by 1997 more than 60 percent of its exports were going to markets of the Organisation for Economic Co-operation and Development (OECD).

With Bulgaria slow to embrace privatization, less than half the manufacturing in Sofia has been privatized. Still, about half of Sofia's employment was in the private sector by 1998. Sofia generally receives a large share of the foreign investment flowing into Bulgaria. In 1992–2000 the city attracted about half of the country's foreign direct investment, though it accounts for only 15 percent of the nation's population (Standard & Poor's 2002). Of the total investment of $1.1 billion in Bulgaria in 2000, Sofia attracted $693 million. About a third of the foreign direct investment in the city has gone to the financial sector as foreign banks enter the market, followed by trade, tourism, and light industry—all potential growth sectors for the city's economy.

Sofia's shift to a service-based economy has been slow, and its economy still has a large share of manufacturing employment, concentrated in a few large state-owned enterprises. Trade and transport are the most developed sectors, accounting for almost a third of employment. Construction is growing and employs about 7 percent of the city's workforce, compared with about 5.4 percent for Bulgaria as a whole. Industry, with 19 percent of employment, is largely concentrated in a single, loss-making steel company, Kremikovtzi. The city needs to further improve the competitiveness of its economy by developing a more sophisticated service sector and industries with greater value added.

Financial Situation

Like all local governments in Bulgaria, Sofia has seen its financial responsibilities increase significantly since the beginning of the reforms, encompassing a wide range of social and infrastructure tasks.[4] Moreover, the functions assigned to the municipality are not always well defined, and laws and regulations guiding the division of functional mandates are sometimes conflicting. The unfunded mandates are undesired and should be eliminated in full. A related problem is the lack of clarity about which level of local government is responsible for delivering a service, a situation that tends to reduce accountability. Assigning clear responsibility to a unit of government for a specific service is important to enable constituencies to hold that unit accountable.

In 1998 grants from the central government accounted for 23 percent of Sofia's revenue. By 2000, however, such grants accounted for only 3 percent of the city's revenue as the newly created equalization mechanism began to redistribute resources from cities like Sofia to poorer regions. In 2001 Sofia received no grants, becoming a net contributor to the central budget. Of the 262 local governments in Bulgaria, only 19 do not receive grants. Sofia is expected to remain a contributor to the central budget, since the equalization mechanism is likely to stay in place for the foreseeable future.

Taxes (including shared taxes) contributed more than four-fifths of the city's revenue of BGN 398 million in 2001. The city's tax revenues have been increasing faster than the inflation rate, growing by more than 15 percent a year, and their share in total revenue increased from 70 percent in 1995 to more than 80 percent in 2001. Driving the growth in tax revenues are higher collection rates, an expanding economy, and the corresponding rise in income. The city's income tax base supports revenue stability. In 1999–2001 personal income tax revenues rose by 27 percent, from BGN 150 million to BGN 190 million, or about 15 percent in real terms. Total tax revenues grew by 13 percent in real terms during the same period.

Although the city has a good tax base, it has limited revenue and expenditure flexibility. All local and shared taxes are determined by national legislation that specifies their base and a range for the rate. The central government exerts tight control over the allocation of local revenues and expenditures. In addition, Sofia faces liquidity constraints resulting from seasonal fluctuations in its tax revenues, low cash balances, and a limited ability to borrow from local financial institutions to cover short-term financing gaps.

Capital revenues, like current revenues, have been unpredictable and not necessarily linked to the level of economic activity in the city. Local capital receipts, which come mainly from property sales and are accounted for in the extrabudgetary privatization fund, dropped from BGN 12 million to BGN 5 million between 1999 and 2001. These receipts are likely to continue to decline until 2012, when privatization sales are expected to be completed. Another source of capital revenue is the state capital expenditure grant, a transfer from the central government. This revenue has varied from BGN 29 million in 1999 to BGN 16 million in 2000. With no set rules for allocating this grant among local authorities, the distribution appears to be the outcome of annual negotiations between the municipalities and the Ministry of Finance.

Despite the constricting expenditure requirements by the state, Sofia has been capable of prudent fiscal management. In 2000 the city had an operating surplus of 4.3 percent and a deficit after capital expenditure of 13.5 percent (table 27.1). The deficit after capital expenditure in 2000 was attributable to the city's investment program, largely financed by its eurobond sale. In 2001 and the first part of 2002 the city curtailed its investment program to accumulate funds for repayment of its eurobond. Sofia should therefore show surpluses after capital expenditures for 2001 and 2002.

Debt Management

Sofia is among the few municipalities in Bulgaria that have successfully borrowed funds independent of the central government. The municipality has received three loans—two loans from local banks in 1994 and a syndicated loan from local banks in 1998—and issued one bond—the only municipal eurobond issued in Bulgaria so far. The 1998 syndicated loan, from Lead Bank and Bulbank, was for cash management purposes (road rehabilitation and repair) and used two forms of collateral. Two public facilities (a hospital and a kindergarten) were pledged as half the collateral, and shares in municipal companies were pledged as the other half. The eurobond of

Table 27.1. Financial Performance Indicators for Sofia, 1996–2001
(percent)

Indicator	1996	1997	1998	1999	2000	2001[a]
Ratio of operating surplus to operating revenue	3.6	3.7	8.6	7.2	4.3	31.0
Ratio of surplus after capital expenditure to total revenue	2.2	4.3	0.7	10.5	−13.5	24.6
Ratio of overall balance to total revenue	0.1	2.6	−5.6	−11.9	−13.7	24.6

a. Data refer to the first three quarters only.
Sources: Regional Statistical Office of Sofia; Standard & Poor's Ratings Direct.

BGN 100 million was an important source of capital funds for the city between 1999 and 2001.

Neither the 1998 loan nor the later eurobond sale was guaranteed by the national government. However, since Bulgaria has no legislation definitively prohibiting central government bailouts, national and international lenders may be more willing to lend to municipalities than they would be if the country had such legislation. In any case there has been no need for central government bailouts of Sofia.

In contrast to the national government, which has a high level of public debt, Sofia has a small debt burden by international standards. Sofia's conservative debt position is reflected in its credit rating relative to those of other cities (table 27.2). The only debt the city had outstanding at the end of 2001was the EUR 50 million note at 9.75 percent interest, which was issued in May 1999 and matured in June 2002. The eurobond, issued to help fund the city's capital investment program, financed mostly small transport-related infrastructure projects. With the eurobond outstanding, the city's debt burden, as measured by the ratio of debt to operating revenue, stood at 26 percent in 2001. In that year the city repaid BGN 10 million from the budget, and in 2002 it repaid BGN 40 million from the budget and other revenue sources, such as its extrabudgetary privatization fund. The lifetime of the eurobond coincided with a period of macroeconomic stability during which the city enjoyed steady growth. These conditions made it easier for the city to save and accumulate funds to repay the bond.

In early 2002 Sofia signed two new loans. The first is a EUR 35 million loan from the European Bank for Reconstruction and Development to finance an extension of the subway and the purchase of new buses. This

Table 27.2. Credit Ratings of Selected Local Governments, 2001

	Date	Local currency rating	Foreign currency rating
Sofia	7 November	BB/Stable/—	BB–/Stable/—
Moscow	19 December	—	B+/Stable/—
St. Petersburg	19 December	B+/Stable/—	B+/Stable/—
Samara Oblast			
(Russian Federation)	13 November	—	B/Positive/—
Istanbul	14 December	B–/Stable/—	B–/Stable/—
Rio de Janeiro	9 August	BB+/Negative/—	BB–/Negative/—

Note: Table shows local governments with non-investment-grade ratings only.
Source: Standard & Poor's Ratings Direct.

loan, to be disbursed over the period 2002–04, has an estimated 7 percent interest rate, a 10-year payback period, and a 3-year grace period for the principal. The second is a loan for 12.9 billion yen (roughly BGN 210 million) from the Japan Bank for International Cooperation, to be disbursed in 2002–06. It is estimated to carry a 1.5 percent interest rate over 30 years, with 10 years' grace. Even with zero real growth over the next 30 years, the debt service for these two new loans, which have highly favorable terms, will be less than 6 percent of total revenue. These loans probably will serve as a catalyst for new lending from multilateral institutions in the immediate future—just as has happened in many other transitioning economies—although Sofia may increasingly tap private credit as its financial conditions warrant.

What Local Governments Need

Political decentralization in Bulgaria has proceeded with no comprehensive policy framework and in the midst of political instability and tough economic conditions. The impromptu design of intergovernmental relations that has emerged is defective, causing administrative and fiscal bottlenecks that limit the effectiveness of local governments and thereby constrain the economic development of cities. The central government imposes many fiscal guidelines on municipalities, including Sofia, but also grants exemptions from its rules, making it difficult for local authorities to develop an appropriate set of internal rules to alleviate these bottlenecks. In Sofia an additional problem is the hierarchical structure of decisionmaking, with almost no devolution of authority within the municipality.

Sofia, like the rest of Bulgaria, has a deteriorated stock of infrastructure. The economic upheavals and fiscal pressures of the early 1990s led to widespread deferrals and cancellations of capital investment projects (Bogetic 1997). To upgrade its infrastructure stock, Sofia needs to undertake major investments, but the limited fiscal flexibility allowed by the central government will make it difficult for the city to make the expenditures needed. Dealing with the backlog of investment needs also will limit the city's ability to meet other expenditure needs. Despite its large capital investment needs and its increasing contribution to the revenue equalization system, Sofia has managed its budget prudently over the past five years. The city's financial performance has benefited greatly from the improving macroeconomic environment and from the greater stability and flexibility of the intergovernmental system since 1998.

While the intergovernmental finance system has become fairly stable recently, with little change since 1998, Bulgaria's municipalities had to cope with significant change earlier in the 1990s. Tight control by the central government continues to constrain local authorities in developing their budgets. At the same time the lack of enforcement of central government regulations and the selective exemptions from rules have created uncertainty in revenue and expenditure flows for local governments. What Bulgaria and especially Sofia need is a system where local governments enjoy greater fiscal autonomy but where the remaining central government rules and regulations are more strictly enforced, with fewer arbitrary exemptions.

Notes

The analysis refers to the situation in Sofia as it existed until the end of 2001. The chapter draws on World Bank reports; the recently produced city strategy for Sofia, which was prepared with the assistance of the Cities Alliance (as well as the World Bank and the United Nations Human Settlements Programme); Urban Institute studies commissioned by the U.S. Agency for International Development; statistical reports of the city of Sofia; and reports of the credit rating agency Standard & Poor's.

1. "Uncertain decentralizers" are defined as countries that need substantial changes in intergovernmental finances and face major macroeconomic challenges that may take precedence over granting more local autonomy (World Bank 2001c).

2. In part because of the loss of trade with the Russian Federation, which also was in decline, Bulgaria saw its GDP shrink by 40 percent in 1990–93. Government revenues fell by even more, and the government's deficit ballooned to 14 percent of GDP in 1991.

3. The structural funds work toward the goal of achieving economic and social cohesion in the EU. Resources are targeted to actions that help bridge the gaps between the more developed regions and the less developed ones and promote equal employment opportunities for different social groups.

4. Much of the earlier decentralization policy essentially consisted of pushing the central government's deficit down to the local level as service responsibilities and norms were assigned (or, in the case of such norms as wages, dictated) without corresponding increases in transfers.

Chapter 28

Eastern and Central Europe
Czech Republic

Unfettered local borrowing powers prove illusory without
credible investor security and effective market regulation.

João Carmo Oliveira and Jorge Martinez-Vazquez

Lessons

The case of the Czech Republic illustrates the difficulties of balancing liberal subnational borrowing provisions with the practical realities of developing sufficient regulation and oversight of local finances—regulation and oversight needed to maintain macroeconomic stability and a functioning subnational credit market.

The Czech government has not carried decentralization far. One problem has to do with size and wealth. While a few large cities have substantial own-source revenues, most local governments are small and heavily dependent on the central government. Changes under way should lead to greater decentralization.

The Czech Constitution declares municipal borrowing a legally protected right, but having a right to access credit and having an effective framework for doing so are two different things. An inability to pledge future revenues, which the law does not recognize as a source of collateral, has constrained local credit. Despite such problems with debt security, local borrowing grew rapidly in the 1990s. Some small municipalities ran up unsupportable debt and may be insolvent. Others borrowed heavily for tourism infrastructure and in expectation of the revenue it would bring. A few large municipalities issued bonds to fund substantial capital spending.

The early rapid increase in bond debt ran counter to the central government's fiscal adjustment goals, and the government imposed a temporary ban on new bond issues in the late 1990s. The ban was rescinded by 2000 as local debt leveled off. However, continuing shortcomings in public finances and the regulatory framework leave a potentially risky fiscal situation, which has dimmed creditors' enthusiasm. One reason creditors are reluctant to lend to local governments is that the existing bankruptcy law does not apply to subnational units.

Policy and regulatory shortcomings have softened budget constraints and introduced moral hazard. These shortcomings include a lack of transparency in local finances because of accounting practices, the absence of an entity to monitor local finances, an unstable and idiosyncratic intergovernmental transfer system, and the limited restrictions on local borrowing. Lack of transparency makes it difficult to analyze the financial situation of local governments and may explain the rapid increase in local debt. There is little legal basis for central control, which is exerted indirectly.

A combination of pro-market mechanisms and regulatory controls would foster a sustainable subnational credit market, and several reforms are suggested. These include restricting loans to capital expenditures, clarifying security provisions, imposing limits on local government debt, introducing prudential requirements on lending to local governments, and instituting bankruptcy provisions and disclosure provisions. Also recommended is establishing a monitoring agency and the use of credit ratings to encourage fiscal prudence.

The Czech Republic began its transition to democracy and a market economy in 1989 from what many considered the most favorable position among the prominent transitioning economies now vying for membership in the European Union (EU) . While not without difficulties and disappointments, the transition has been largely successful, revealing a country with a wealthy and diverse economy, a strong industrial base, and a skilled labor force.

In 2001 unemployment fell for the first time since the transition began, to 8.1 percent. Inflation remained fairly low at less than 4 percent. A high level of foreign direct investment (among the highest in the region) has increased productivity and competitiveness, facilitating the restructuring of industry. These positive forces notwithstanding, the Czech Republic underwent a recession in 1997–99 that eased only in 2001, with strong domestic demand and investment-driven real growth of 3.6 percent. However, the current account balance worsened in 2001 for the third consecutive year, showing a deficit of 4.7 percent of GDP.

The Czech Republic has had its share of difficulties in entering the global economy. Immediately after its transition to democracy and free markets, the country latched onto fixed exchange rates, believed to be needed to encourage foreign investment. A surge of investment and an immature financial system led to a sharp rise in inflation. This was soon countered by high interest rates to defend the currency. Rather than simply slowing inflation, however, the tight monetary policy led to severe deflationary pressures and, coupled with imprudent lending practices, resulted in many business failures.[1]

The transition to a market economy is not complete in the Czech Republic. Important structural deficiencies remain, including a need to carry out judicial reforms that already have been enacted and to curb corruption and citizens' resulting distrust in government and in the process of privatization. Crucially, events relating to the three-year recession have called into question the effectiveness of bankruptcy laws and the quality of corporate governance and transparency. In the early 1990s, when privatizations surged, the structure of the privatizations allowed the state-controlled banking sector to take indirect control of many state enterprises. This situation encouraged poor lending decisions by banks. As the recession set in, the banks' fragile loan portfolios were exposed, revealing questionable corporate practices that fueled citizens' distrust. The government responded with tighter regulation and supervision of banks. A large state bailout of banks followed, contributing to a deterioration in public finances. This deterioration could adversely affect government debt and already is reflected in an unspectacular (though stable) national credit rating.

Subnational Government and Fiscal Management

The overall level of subnational debt needs to be seen as the product of local government decisions, which in turn reflect the structure of inter-governmental fiscal relations in the country and the effectiveness of the overall fiscal management and budgeting.

Intergovernmental Relations

The autonomy of local governments in the Czech Republic is still evolving. Immediately after the communist regime, and the breakup with the Slovak Federal Republic in 1993, the country administration was structured into two levels of government: the central government and 6,191 municipalities. The government structure was highly centralized, and municipalities had no capacity to raise revenue other than collecting local fees and charges. In 1994–2000 local expenditures made up a little more than 20 percent of the national consolidated budget, comparing unfavorably with some other transitioning economies such as Poland and Hungary. However, tax amendments in recent years have reduced municipal reliance on central transfers, and additional planned tax changes will increase local fiscal autonomy. Prague alone accounted for almost 17 percent of municipal expenditure in 2000, highlighting its importance in the national economy.

The structure of local government is undergoing reform. The 73 state district offices, which had little revenue raising capacity and only limited responsibilities under centralization, are being replaced with 14 newly created regional governments. With this change comes the prospect of significant devolution of revenues and responsibilities. Own-source revenues have been fairly small, with the central government determining major tax rates and bases and collecting most revenues. Under new legislation, however, a portion of state tax revenues is to be shared among the 14 regions as control of regional transport and other infrastructure is passed to them starting in 2001–2002. Beginning in 2002–2003 the plan has been to give regional governments their own tax revenues and perhaps introduce new municipal taxes.

Local governments already have some service responsibilities, including primary and secondary education, urban development (housing with water and sewerage infrastructure), some social services, and control of small state institutions (for example, agricultural education institutions). The gradual decentralization has not been burdensome to local governments because revenues have been increased to match the expanded responsibilities, sustaining sound local budgets.

Public Sector Debt

During the 1990s public debt outstanding in the Czech Republic averaged around 13.5 percent of GDP, with local government debt—a relatively new phenomenon in the country—increasing from 0.3 percent of GDP in 1993 to 2.2 percent in 1999 (table 28.1). Thus the Czech Republic appears to do well with respect to the Maastricht general criterion for fiscal discipline.[2] Nonetheless, a more conclusive assessment of both local financial sustainability and macroeconomic stability would require also taking into account all forms of contingent liabilities in the Czech Republic, at each level of government.[3]

Table 28.1. Public Debt Outstanding, Czech Republic, 1993–99

Debt item	1993	1994	1995	1996	1997	1998	1999
(billions of koruny)							
Municipal	**3.4**	**14.3**	**20.3**	**28.3**	**34.4**	**39.0**	**40.0**
Loans	2.5	4.9	8.7	11.6	13.5	18.0	17.6
Bonds	0	7.6	8.5	11.9	13.2	11.9	10.9
Others	0.9	1.8	3.1	4.8	7.7	9.1	11 5
State	**158.9**	**157.3.**	**154.4**	**155.2**	**173.1**	**194.7**	**228.4**
(percentage of GDP)							
Municipal	**0.3**	**1.2**	**1.5**	**1.8**	**2.1**	**2.2**	**2.2**
Loans	0.2	0.4	0.6	0.7	0.8	1.0	1.0
Bonds	0	0.6	0.6	0.8	0.8	0.7	0.6
Others	0.1	0.2	0.2	0.3	0.5	0.5	0.6
State	**15.9**	**13.3**	**11.2**	**9.9**	**10.4**	**10.8**	**12.4**
Total	**16.2**	**14.5**	**12.6**	**11.7**	**12.4**	**13.0**	**14.6**
(percentage of state debt)							
Municipal	**2.1**	**9.1**	**13.1**	**18.2**	**19.9**	**20**	**17.5**
Loans	1.6	3.1	5.6	7.5	7.8	9.2	7.7
Bonds	0	4.8	5.5	7.7	7.6	6.1	4.8
Others	0.6	1.1	2.0	3.1	4.4	4.7	5.0
(percentage of municipal revenue)							
Municipal	**4.5**	**15.4**	**19.1**	**24.8**	**27.8**	**28.3**	**23.6**
Loans	3.3	5.3	8.2	10.2	10.9	13	10.4
Bonds	0	8.2	.8.0	10.4	10.7	8.6	6.4
Others	1.2	1.9 .	2.9	4.2	6.2	6.6	6.8
(percentage of municipal tax revenue)							
Municipal	**11.4**	**31.6**	**34.8**	**45.1**	**52.3**	**54.1**	**52.9**
Loans	8.4	10.8	14.9	18.5	20.5	25.0	23.3
Bonds	0	16.8	14.6	19.0	20.1	16.5	14.4
Others	3.0	4.0	5.3	7.6	11 .7	12:06	15.2

Sources: Czech Republic Ministry of Finance; World Bank staff estimates.

As in many other unitary countries, in the Czech Republic local governments have had only limited discretion in financing their expenditure. Since local governments cannot print money and have very limited tax autonomy, their most important option for financing local fiscal imbalances has been to borrow. Commercial sources of borrowing include loans and credit from banks and other sources, including bond issues. Noncommercial sources include interest-free or subsidized loans from the state, mainly under programs operated by the Ministry of Finance and the State Environmental Fund. In addition, municipalities have often provided guarantees and assumed contingent liabilities that may expand their effective financial exposure. Although this exposure does not appear yet to have been excessive, it represents a potential fiscal risk to macroeconomic stability that the central government should monitor. Whether local government debt becomes a macroeconomic threat depends on how the economic system perceives the debt and whether indebted local governments are explicitly or implicitly backed by the central government.

Local Fiscal Imbalances and Debt Accumulation

In the Czech Republic municipalities, as self-governing entities, are the only local governments that can borrow. District offices do not have the power to assume contractual financial obligations of their own because they are merely administrative bodies of state territorial administration. In the future, as the new regions substitute for the old districts, it is likely that these intermediate levels of government also will acquire the right to borrow.

Growth of Municipal Debt

The outstanding debt of Czech municipalities grew steadily in 1993–99, rising from 11 percent of municipal tax revenue to 53 percent. In 1999 this debt was equal to 2.2 percent of GDP and almost 20 percent of the state debt (figures 28.1 and 28.2).[4]

Although municipal debt still may be considered too small to be an immediate threat to macroeconomic stability, its rapid growth in 1993–99 (by tenfold) is worrisome. The stabilization of municipal debt outstanding relative to GDP in 1999 (and even the slight drop relative to municipal tax revenue) appears to have been a result of significant sales of financial assets during that year (including stockholder rights in shares of energy distribution companies). These sales enabled municipalities to meet their entire financial needs for the year, including some debt amortization. More worri-

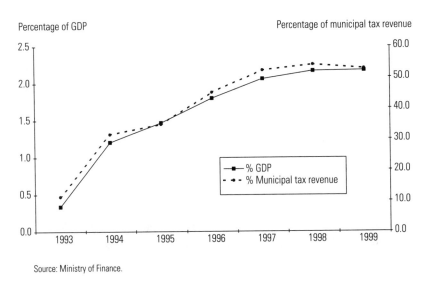

Source: Ministry of Finance.

Figure 28.1. Municipal Debt Outstanding, Czech Republic 1993–99

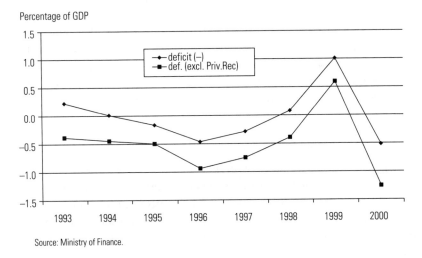

Source: Ministry of Finance.

Figure 28.2. Local Fiscal Deficits, Czech Republic 1993–2000

some, however, is that the reasons that municipal debt outstanding grew so rapidly during the decade are not entirely transparent. There is no evident correspondence between the imbalances in municipalities' fiscal accounting flows (reflected in figure 28.2) and their accumulation of debt (see figure 28.1). While fiscal flow statistics show that municipalities' fiscal position was reasonably stable during the 1990s (that is, with small deficits alternating with small surpluses), aggregate municipal debt outstanding accumulated quite rapidly. This apparent statistical discrepancy may reflect lack of uniformity in accounting and lack of transparency, which could be due to several causes:

- Differing interpretations by municipalities of accounting procedures and terminology.
- Off-budget financial operations, including reimbursable components of grants from the state budget and extrabudgetary funds inadequately recorded as revenue by some municipalities.
- Credit guarantees to budgetary and nonbudgetary organizations (and other off-budget contingent liabilities) effectively assumed by municipalities only when these guarantees were called.

The lack of uniformity in accounting and the absence of full transparency in fiscal operations (including those affecting assets and liabilities of public entities) could, at some point, represent a major macroeconomic risk. In such situations statistics tend to become unreliable, and nontransparent contingent liabilities tend to show up as direct municipal liabilities only when the obligations are called. Since nontransparent contingent liabilities have not been properly reflected in the fiscal accounting flows, there is no early warning system to indicate the level of risk to which municipalities are exposed.[5]

Composition of Municipal Debt

During the 1990s all forms of municipal debt expanded substantially: loans, bond issues, and other forms, including noncommercial loans and, especially, refundable transfers (concessional loans from the Ministry of Finance). Bond debt grew sharply in the mid-1990s (see table 28.1). Toward the end of the 1990s the Exchange Commission prohibited new bond issues as part of the general fiscal adjustment policy.[6] Except for the city of Prague, no municipal bond issues occurred between 1998 and early 2000, and the municipal bond debt has fallen slightly in nominal terms (figure 28.3). Only Prague issued, in 1999, bonds in the foreign financial market, a 200 million euro (EUR) sale (table 28.2). In the late 1990s municipalities' outstanding debt consisted of 45 percent loans, 29 percent issued bonds, and 26 percent other forms (figure 28.4).[7]

Percentage of municipal tax revenue

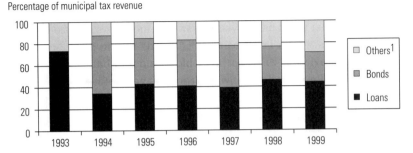

1. Includes noncommercial loans and, especially, refundable transfers from the center.
Source: Ministry of Finance.

Figure 28.3. Composition of Municipal Debt Outstanding, Czech Republic, 1993–99

While most local governments have had access to bank loans and credit, only the larger cities (Prague, Ostrava, Plzen, Bruno, Liberec, Ustinad Labem, and a few others) have issued bonds. Municipal bond issues (mainly in foreign capital markets) and municipal commercial loans (mainly domestic) have been used primarily to finance public works and transport systems.

In addition, municipalities have received two types of concessional loans from the state: programmed loans (for example, to supplement the required counterpart funding for the EU preaccession structural funds[8] for investment projects) and discretionary, ad hoc loans (such as from the State Environmental Fund and the state budget). Municipal borrowing from the State Environmental Fund has financed mainly gas and water supply systems, sewerage, and wastewater treatment plants. Municipal borrowing from the state budget has been primarily for housing.

Accounts payable, another component of local government debt (for wages and salaries as well as to suppliers), does not appear to be significant in the Czech Republic.

Access to Borrowing by Municipalities

Large Czech municipalities have had access to all financial markets and to the most sophisticated debt instruments for financing their investment projects. In contrast, small municipalities have had access (if any) only to

Table 28.2. Municipal Bonds Issued, Czech Republic, 1992–99

Year of issue	Municipality	Face value (millions of koruny, except where otherwise indicated)	Maturity (years)	Interest rate (percent)	Underwriter
1992	Ostrava	8.5	6	D + 1.5	City Hall
1993	Sumperk	20	5	18.00	CSOB
1994	Smrzovka	115	7	14.25	CS
	Liberec	100	5	14.25	CS
	Prague				
		7,300*	5	7.25	Nomura International
	Pardubice				
	Usti nad Labem	50	5	12.70	KB
		150	5	12.70	KB
					[Burzovni spolecnost pro]
	Caslav				
	Rikytnice nad Jizerou				
	Veseli nad Moravou	90	8	15.50	Kapitaloy trh
	Rychnov nad Kneznou	120	7	12.00	CS
		10	7	14.10	Velkomoravska banka
1995		100	7	13.10	KB
	Plzen				Bayerische
	Marianske Lazne				Vereinsbank
	Brno				Praha, ING CR,
	Frydek-Mistek				Capital Markets, SCFB Praha,
	Decin	500	5	11.50	KB
	Kladno	200	5	11.50	KB
	Ostrava				
1996		1,200	7	11.10	IPB
	Zidlochovice	150	5	11.80	CS
	Prague	250	7	12.50	CSOB
		250	7	12.50	CSOB
		1,318.2**	5	LIBOR + 0.2 [25.00]	ING Barings
1997		40	10	12.90	
1999		EUR 200 million	5	4.63	CMZRB ING Barings

Note: LIBOR is the London interbank offered rate.
Note: D interest rate base index.
*Valued at US$250 million. Czech Equivalent cited.
**Valued at DM 75 million. Czech Equivalent cited.
Source: Czech Republic Ministry of Finance.

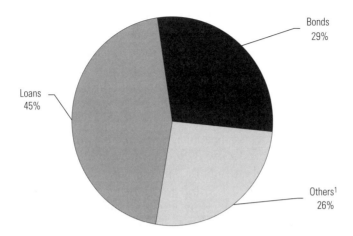

1. Includes noncommercial loans and, especially, refundable transfers from the center.
Source: Ministry of Finance.

Figure 28.4. Average Composition of Municipal Debt Outstanding, Czech Republic, 1998–99

local banking and noncommercial credit sources. This difference is reflected at least in part in the vast disparity in creditworthiness between these two groups of municipalities. Large municipalities have inherited substantial assets and have buoyant tax bases, with good revenue performance from shared taxes (mainly the personal and corporate income taxes). Small municipalities have insufficient assets and meager revenue and tax capacity, inadequate to support credit operations.

Moreover, there has been a perception that the Czech commercial code restricts collateral for credit operations to assets existing at the time the debt agreement is signed—that is, that it does not recognize future revenue as collateral (Kamenickova 1999a). This perception (though not confirmed by current regulations), together with the limited tax autonomy of local governments, may be a factor in preventing small and medium-size municipalities from improving their access to financial markets. For banking sector representatives, these issues are a major concern when dealing with municipalities' credit. They have argued for allowing municipalities to have greater control over their own tax bases, in the place of continued reliance on state transfers.[9]

Nonetheless, most small and medium-size municipalities appear to be indebted—beyond their ability to service the debt. Indeed, some of the weaker municipalities appear to be insolvent. The perception in the banking sector is that only a few small municipalities have shown good creditworthiness in the recent past, thanks to their development potential as tourist centers. Some of these municipalities (such as Jizerou, Rokytnice, and Smrzovka) are already borrowing heavily from the banking system, especially from Ceska Sporitelna (the Czech Savings Bank), and investing in tourism infrastructure.

In decentralized systems subnational governments, which are generally responsible for financing local public infrastructure, commonly rely on debt financing for capital expenditure. This has not always been the case in the Czech Republic, where the central government still plays a big part in financing local infrastructure, mainly through matching grants. Transferring this capital spending responsibility to subnational governments is an important step in developing a sense of ownership at the local level, which tends to result in better maintenance of the capital stock and greater efficiency in the use of facilities.

However, financing local capital needs entirely from local current revenues (without borrowing) would not be feasible—even if the local authorities had the desired autonomy in determining local tax bases and rates. Nor would it be economically efficient or equitable: since the benefits of these investments generally persist for several years or decades, future generations should contribute to their financing.

There is also a cash management argument: local government borrowing may be justified by the need to match nonsynchronized expenditure and tax flows within the same year. Moreover, borrowing may provide an important independent mechanism for fostering political accountability. The reason is that financial markets may signal the quality of the performance of local governments through credit ratings and interest rates charged or, in the extreme, by blocking the governments' access to credit.

Local government borrowing may be desirable as an instrument for allocating resources optimally across time and promoting economic growth and fiscal equity. Without clear rules and accountability, however, financial market failures and soft budget constraints can lead to irresponsible borrowing by local governments, which can easily turn into other problems. Local officials may be tempted to overspend on popular programs by borrowing excessively, leaving the bill for future taxpayers. Moreover, local governments that have engaged in uncontrolled borrowing might default on their debts, perhaps forcing the central government to assume these unpaid liabilities. This would pose big risks to macroeconomic stability, justifying the adoption of regulations and monitoring mechanisms to ensure fiscally responsible borrowing by local governments.

Management of Local Government Debt

International experience offers several approaches to the management of local government debt from which the Czech Republic might profit when designing its own model.[10] The most common approaches include allowing financial market discipline to operate freely; using strict administrative, case-by-case control; and establishing explicit, preemptive, and legally binding general rules to prevent crises and encourage good market behavior. A combination of these options might prove most advantageous for the Czech Republic.

Market Discipline

In principle, relying on market discipline would be the most preferable approach. However, at times market discipline alone can be less effective than desired, because of market failures such as these:

- *Restricted financial markets.* Market discipline will be ineffective where financial markets are not free and open, as is the case in the Czech Republic. Common market failures are restrictions on access to foreign capital markets, which limit options, and compulsory allocation of resources (including those of official financial agencies and public enterprises) to aid the placement of government bonds.
- *Lack of transparency.* Market discipline also may fail where the availability and dissemination of information are inadequate, especially information on the amount of debt outstanding and borrowers' capacity to pay. Obtaining reliable financial information in the Czech Republic—especially for local governments—is difficult. Municipalities may not use the same interpretation of the chart of accounting, may not maintain clear and uniform registers of their assets and liabilities, and may not systematically publish and disseminate reliable information on debt and capacity to pay. Moreover, much greater transparency is needed on extrabudgetary or contingent liabilities of local governments, in the form of direct or indirect guarantees.
- *Soft budget constraints and moral hazard.* Where moral hazard permeates the public sector's relationship with the financial system, market disci-

pline can be a poor instrument for checking excessive indebtedness of local governments. Ad hoc, extraordinary, and off-budget financing and central government loans, grants, and guarantees create moral hazard. Loans and guarantees made by municipalities to municipal organizations (budgetary and nonbudgetary) may do the same.

- *Insensitivity to market signals.* For market discipline to be effective, borrowers need to show sensitivity to market signals by seeking financial policies consistent with full solvency. Rising interest rates should stop a borrower or at least cause the borrower to review a borrowing decision. As elected politicians, however, municipal mayors and heads of regional executive boards are unlikely to be concerned with market signals when deciding on current expenditure programs.

Even in mature financial markets, such as that of Canada, sole reliance on market discipline has failed to check excessive indebtedness of subnational governments. In Canada in the mid-1990s subnational government debt reached 23 percent of GDP. Subnational governments were forced to adopt fiscal adjustment programs—but only after they were excluded from the market, which entailed high social costs. In Argentina and Brazil, where the necessary market conditions were lacking, the experience with subnational borrowing in the 1980s proved disastrous. The central government had to intervene with large bailouts to rescue the creditors and avoid systemic crisis.

In the Czech Republic under present market conditions, market discipline alone is unlikely to ensure responsible borrowing from the capital market by local governments. A more effective option would be to have regulation in place that can prevent excessive indebtedness (as discussed below). To the extent possible, regulation should imitate desirable market discipline, to minimize distortions and encourage market practices in the future. In addition, the government should explicitly encourage market discipline, participation by the private sector, and development of independent financial intermediaries and credit rating institutions. The government also should encourage periodic monitoring reports by independent organizations. Reports on the indebtedness and current and prospective financial situation of local governments not only can help discipline local government borrowing but also can tend to promote the development of market institutions.[11]

Administrative Controls

Some countries exercise direct control over capital market borrowing by local governments. They may require that each proposed credit operation be approved by a central agency or prohibit local governments from accessing private capital markets directly. Central agency approval, requiring evaluation of each loan contract, tends to lead to micromanagement, bureaucracy, and inefficiency. India has used this approach to oversee state borrowing because the central government is a major creditor of the states and because the Constitution provides for such approval. In the 1980s Australia prohibited direct access to capital markets, centralizing all loans and on-lending the funds to subnational governments. However, because direct control proved ineffective, Australian subnational governments have again been allowed free access to capital markets, though their borrowing is subject to aggregate controls and the borrowing of individual governments is monitored more closely.

Central governments have generally realized that exercising direct control over local governments' credit operations is impractical. It increases the centralization of financial decisions, running counter to the fiscal decentralization goals of greater accountability by local authorities and greater allocation efficiency. It involves the central government in every credit operation of local governments, increasing central bureaucracy and administrative inefficiency, and it tends to foster inefficiencies in the financial system.

Direct control of every credit operation is not recommended for the Czech Republic, whose 6,254 municipalities and 14 new regions (2001 data) would make such an approach both costly and difficult. Moreover, an indiscriminate ban on capital market borrowing appears to be incompatible with the Czech Constitution (article 101 allows local self-governments to freely operate their own properties and budget) and with parliamentary acts establishing and regulating the regions and municipalities (Acts 129/2000 and 128/2000 empower local assemblies to decide on credit and loan operations).

Rules-Based Approach

Rules governing access to capital markets can be effective only if they are transparent, legally binding, simple to follow, and applied across the board. Such rules should include clear quantitative limits and procedural norms that respect and, to the extent possible, imitate financial market discipline and creditworthiness indicators. Many countries have adopted the rules-based approach as a preventive measure or in response to a particular situation.

To preempt systemic crises, some countries limit the credit operations of local governments by prohibiting central bank financing, financing of noninvestment expenditure, short-term liquidity assistance, and external (foreign) financing. These rules are often justified. To preserve monetary stability, independent central banks should not provide direct finance to government, including local governments. Bank financing of noninvestment expenditure should be banned so as to force local governments to make necessary adjustments in their current revenues and expenditures.[12]

The Czech Republic should pursue restrictions on central bank financing and financing of noninvestment expenditure, but it may be unwise for it to prohibit short-term liquidity assistance and external financing. Short-term loans for liquidity assistance can allow local governments to smooth out cash flows during the year and can synchronize financial inflows with outflows. Such loans are quite common and appropriate in many countries, including Brazil and the United States. For liquidity assistance to perform its function well, however, there must be a contractually binding obligation on local governments to repay their short-term debt in the same fiscal year it is incurred.

The most compelling reasons for prohibiting local government access to foreign capital markets have been macroeconomic:

* Such operations can adversely effect monetary stability.
* A concerted approach to negotiating foreign financing could be beneficial for the country.
* The default of one entity might affect the creditworthiness of other entities and the sovereign risk rating.
* Multilateral financial institutions usually require a sovereign guarantee.

Still, prohibiting foreign borrowing would be counterproductive for promoting European market integration. Moreover, with the rapid development of market conditions in the Czech Republic, the imminent integration with the EU market, and the ongoing fiscal decentralization, an inability to access international capital markets would lead to the loss of opportunities. Thus rather than either prohibiting foreign borrowing or liberalizing it completely, it might be prudent for the time being to continue to require local governments to obtain permission from the Czech Exchange Commission for foreign loans.

The Czech Approach to Managing Local Government Debt

In the Czech Republic the central authorities have controlled municipalities' access to capital markets through a mix of market discipline and implicit government control, exercised through moral suasion of both financial institutions and municipal governments. In 1997 the Ministry of

Finance suspended authorization by the Exchange Commission of new foreign bond issues by local governments, and it has recommended that financial institutions stop lending to municipalities with a ratio of debt service ratio of 15 percent or more.[13] In addition, the Ministry of Finance has threatened to discontinue state grants and loans to municipalities that do not obey these "rules." Although banks apparently have followed the recommendations, the rules are not legally binding.

The Exchange Commission is the only formal instrument for monitoring and controlling local indebtedness. However, this institution only determines whether a domestic borrower may issue bonds in foreign capital markets; it does not monitor other types of municipal debt, including domestic debt. Municipalities face no formal limit on borrowing. Indeed, they can borrow from any source, for any purpose (even to finance current spending), and on any terms (Kamenickova 1999). Some of the financial operations of municipalities are guaranteed by official institutions (including Ceska Sporitelna), but most of these are not explicitly guaranteed, and it is unclear how creditors would recover their money in case of default. The Bankruptcy and Composition Act does not cover municipalities, and this omission may be one reason that banks have become increasingly reluctant to continue financing most municipalities.

Meanwhile, municipalities have been granting loans and guarantees to local businesses to support local development. Although such financial activities are subject to the approval of municipal assemblies, the procedures for such approvals are unclear. The lack of mechanisms for monitoring and supervising such lending has left room for soft budget constraints and also has introduced moral hazard—both features of a high-risk fiscal situation.

Options for Reform

The Czech Republic faces a clear need to develop a financial system that includes basic operational and supervisory rules designed for local government debt. This system should be aimed at promoting responsible access to capital markets while also keeping hard budget constraints in place. Also needed are institutional arrangements to improve the availability and reliability of information on local debt—to increase transparency and accountability in the system.

Reform should not require doing away with the basic legal structure allowing normal access to borrowing subject to approval by the local assembly. However, it is recommended that such borrowing be subject to stronger supervision by the Exchange Commission, the Central Bank , and the Ministry of Finance.

The Czech government might consider the following reforms for local government borrowing:

- *Restrict loans to high-return investment expenditures* by banning medium- and long-term loans for current expenditures by local governments and by requiring full repayment of any short-term liquidity assistance in the same fiscal year.
- *Limit the debt service ratio* (the ratio of annual debt service to own current revenue) of local governments to, say, 10 percent.[14] Beyond this limit, more debt should not be allowed, because debt service commitments probably would jeopardize the normal delivery of basic public services (such as health, education, and social assistance).
- *Limit the total debt ratio* (the ratio of debt outstanding, including contingent liabilities, to total annual revenue excluding conditional grants) of local governments to, say, 80 percent.[15] Such a limit might need to be phased in. For now, the central authorities could adopt a prudent approach by allowing only gradual increases in the total debt ratio of a subnational government.[16]
- *Limit banks' portfolio exposure* to the obligations of any local government to a certain percentage of total assets. The Central Bank should apply strict norms of supervision, especially to the official credit institutions (such as Ceska Sporitelna).
- *Enact a financial emergency or bankruptcy law* clearly defining debt workout procedures for local governments in case of default, a critical need given current conditions in the Czech capital market. (A good practical example might be the bankruptcy law adopted by Hungary.)[17] Once approved, the procedures for settling local government debts should be implemented diligently. Rules will not provide a cure if they are not enforced. Putting in place a sound bankruptcy mechanism does not reduce the need for a proper system of controls and incentives to harden the budget constraints of lower-tier governments in the Czech Republic. International experience has shown that central government oversight (including, in some cases, the temporary takeover of responsibility from local authorities) remains a key source of financial discipline.
- *Adopt a law on fiscal responsibility* aimed at limiting recurrent, excessive deficits and the imprudent buildup of local public debt. Such

laws, which make fiscal authorities and managers personally, legally accountable for their decisions, create the conditions for greater efficiency, fiscal transparency, and accountability of public administration. The law should prohibit financial guarantees by subnational governments (for their enterprises or for local businesses) and central government guarantees and bailouts of local government debt. The recent fiscal responsibility act adopted by New Zealand, and especially that adopted by Brazil, could provide guidance.

* *Review the financing rules in the commercial code,* clarifying the ability of local governments to pledge future revenues as collateral for loans. Clarification of the financing rules could strengthen the financing of public budgets by forcing local governments to be more transparent and accountable and by encouraging lenders to evaluate risks more seriously. However, this reform would be effective only if it gives local authorities sufficient fiscal autonomy to determine local tax bases and rates.

* *Encourage the dissemination of risk and credit analyses* of local governments to improve transparency, foster market discipline, and promote the practice of creditworthiness analysis. In Australia, Canada, and the United States creditworthiness analysis has been a common practice, with private risk rating companies playing a central role. Credit ratings help local governments obtain necessary financing from domestic and foreign capital markets while also monitoring the risks of excessive indebtedness. Rating the creditworthiness of municipalities has just begun in the Czech Republic and should be strongly encouraged. The government can help by regularly making available reliable information on the fiscal and financial situation of municipalities.

* *Establish an official monitoring agency* to keep records and monitor the level of local government debt, including contingent liabilities. This agency, possibly under the Ministry of Finance, could carry out statistical, coordinating, and supervisory roles and play an essential part in the systematic dissemination of reliable information on the fiscal and financial situation of municipalities. It could also help enforce the fiscal responsibility law, initiate financial emergency measures, foster market discipline, and support the development of market institutions. Through these functions, such an agency would increase transparency and create an early warning system for local government debt.

Notes

This chapter draws on Fitch Ratings reports.

1. Vaclav Havel (2002) argues that in a small, open economy like that of the Czech Republic, the fixed rate regime was inconsistent with financial liberalization, and ultimately led to excessive growth in money supply. The Central Bank, which in the initial transition years lacked experience, pursued an extremely low inflation target that sent the country into recession.

2. The Maastricht criterion for fiscal discipline (article 109j(1) of the European Community Treaty) requires the ratio of the public sector deficit to GDP to be less than 3 percent and the ratio of public sector gross debt to GDP to be less than 60 percent. These are the government finance criteria, part of the European Monetary Union's (EMU) convergence criteria to which member countries submit. The other criteria relate to price stability, exchange rates, and long-term interest rates. Although compliance with the convergence criteria is not a precondition for accession to the European Union, accession does entail accepting the objectives of the EMU, and all member states must in due course comply with them permanently.

3. For example, including the "hidden" fiscal risks of the special institutions (Konsolidacni Banka, Ceska Inkasni, National Property Fund, and Ceska Financni) as well as state guarantees, the 1997–98 estimated average "true" fiscal deficit was 5 percent of GDP (rather than the conventionally estimated average of 1.25 percent), and the "true" public sector liability, excluding local governments, was 22 percent. See Polackova Brixi, Schick, and Zlaoui (2000).

4. Even if an upper-bound level of 4 or 5 percent of GDP—including contingent liabilities—is assumed, the indebtedness of subnational governments would not appear high by international standards. For example, in Germany subnational government debt was 21 percent of GDP in 1996, and in Australia it was 11 percent.

5. On the design of a warning system, see Ma (2000).

6. The Exchange Commission is a central government agency created in 1998 to regulate access to foreign capital markets and control the country's exposure to foreign debt.

7. Accounts payable of local government debt (i.e., arrears on wages and salaries as well as suppliers) do not appear to be significant in the Czech Republic.

8. The European Union Pre-Accession Funds are grants made available to EU members to promote investment in priority areas prior to their accession to the Union. In the case of the Czech Republic, these grants are oriented for environmental and transport projects, for agricultural and rural

development, and for institution building to prepare for the larger Structural Funds once the Czech Republic enters the EU.

9. During a World Bank mission in 2000 this preference was revealed in all interviews with financial sector representatives.

10. For a survey and discussion of relevant international experience, see Ter-Minassian and Craig (1997); Lane (1993); and Giugale, Trillo, and Oliveira (2000).

11. An initiative that has contributed to disciplining municipal access to borrowing and to disseminating good market practices is the *Credit Finance Analysis Handbook for Municipalities in the Czech Republic,* developed by the Union of Towns and Communities with assistance from the U.S. Agency for International Development. The handbook provides municipalities with guidance on debt management. Another initiative contributing to the development of a healthy capital market for local governments is the dissemination of analytical work on the financial situation of different municipalities, now being developed by the Czech Rating Agency. These initiatives should be strongly supported by the Ministry of Finance, through facilitating the development of reliable data by all local governments.

12. Enforcing this rule may be difficult (because money is fungible), but the amount of loans should not exceed investment.

13. Understood as the ratio of interest on debt and repayment of principal to the municipal own current revenues.

14. Here, revenue means total local government revenue excluding conditional grants.

15. The total debt ratio reflects the burden of financial obligations, which the debt service ratio alone cannot capture because of grace periods. Together, these two indicators are important for signaling the balance between present consumption and future liabilities, and limits on these ratios can protect the solvency of local governments in the long term.

16. This prudent approach is recommended in the short run, especially for the new regions that have been borne free of debt. Otherwise, the mere announcement of limits that may be sustainable in the long run may trigger adverse fiscal and macroeconomic effects in the short run, since regional politicians may want to compete for financing in the new decentralized environment.

17. Hungary's Procedure for Settlement of Local Government Debts was initially promulgated in April 1996 (Act XXV/96), with a revision approved by the Hungarian parliament on 29 February 2000. The revised act has been effective since January 2000.

Chapter 29

Eastern and Central Europe
Hungary

Rapid decentralization, early over-extensions, and a slow econo-my lead to tighter controls and reduced borrowing.

Pryianka Sood

Lessons

Hungary's experience illustrates how myriad institutional and macroeconomic issues can converge to confound early efforts to make local governments more accountable and self-supporting. After a decade of adjustment, prospects for subnational borrow-ing in private capital markets are improving, but for most local governments the capacity to raise capital remains uncertain.

In the euphoria of the early transition from a command to a market economy, Hungary created a highly decentralized and fragmented government structure. Decentralization appeared to give local governments significant potential to raise own-source revenues. However, a high-tax central government and a slow-growth environment left them with little will to raise lo-cal taxes and dependent on central transfers. After an early burst of activity, municipal infrastructure spending declined through the 1990s.

The effects of delayed infrastructure spending became increasingly evident in the mid-1990s—as a result of urban population pressures and the emergence of the criteria for accession to the European Union (EU)—even as tight fiscal policy constrained transfers. Matters were complicated by the burdensome (and often conflicting) national mandates and extensive rules and regulations for local services, which absorb about two-thirds of local spending. Under economic stress, harnessed by restrictions, and lacking incentives to raise own revenues, local governments saw their revenues fall by 20 percent in real terms between 1993 and 1998.

Although sales of the substantial capital assets inherited by Hungary's local governments have helped to meet capital spending needs, the supply of saleable assets has dwindled. Moreover, after the unfettered ability of local governments to borrow led some to overextend, possibly threatening future stability, the government began tightening borrowing laws in 1995 and put a municipal bankruptcy law into effect. These laws are generally viewed as consonant with the development of private capital markets. But the shaky financial condition of local governments and the ease of entering bankruptcy have dampened private lending. The rapid growth in local government debt in the early 1990s was reversed in the late 1990s as local authorities began to pay it off.

Only one Hungarian city, Budapest, has entered the international capital market. Development of local credit markets is seen as essential to meet the growing capital needs related to EU accession. While EU grants and loans are forthcoming, matching funds will be required at the local level. To raise these funds will require improvements in local financial management and reporting as well as operational and lending vehicles that can serve the needs of the many fragmented localities.

Hungary was the first socialist country in Central and Eastern Europe to embark on the path of economic and political liberalization. As several features of the economy had been reformed earlier, many considered it better placed than its nearby peers, such as Poland and the former Czechoslovakia, to respond to the shocks of the transition from socialism to a market economy in 1989. Hungary had higher foreign direct investment than its neighbors, better export performance, and a vibrant domestic private sector.

However, Hungary also had problems. Unsustainable foreign debt combined with a propensity to favor present consumption over investment led to a foreign exchange crisis and forced the government to implement a stabilization program in late 1989. By 1997, after a long and costly period of adjustment, the macroeconomic and structural policies put in place by Hungary had created better conditions for sustainable growth. While the process of fiscal consolidation and convergence toward the European Union—particularly in controlling inflation—is far from over, the basic macroeconomic conditions for stability and growth are clearly in place (World Bank 2000).

Transition in the formerly socialist states in Central and Eastern Europe has been marked both by the move from a command economy to liberalized markets and by decentralization of government. For a highly centralized, state-dominated economy, adjusting to a market-based system is complicated. So is decentralization. Once political decentralization was introduced, however, it proceeded very quickly in many transitioning economies.

For every country in the region, legislation on local self-government represented a significant departure from the past. Subnational governments had existed in most of the formerly socialist economies, but they acted primarily as administrative arms of the central government, with no independent fiscal or legislative responsibilities. New legislation affirmed decentralization and local financial autonomy, freeing subnational governments from central control and allowing local democracy to flourish. However, while the trappings of democracy were quickly accepted, true fiscal decentralization—uniting local accountability for service delivery with local revenue raising power—has been slower to materialize. Fiscal decentralization has occurred in fits and starts, with more than a few accidents along the way.

Decentralization and the Local Government System

Hungary was the first of the Central European countries to start developing and implementing municipal decentralization. Launching a series of legal reforms in 1990 with the Law on Local Self-Government, the country decentralized the state administration, reestablished the autonomy of local governments, devolved greater responsibilities for public service provision to these governments, and ultimately tightened local budget constraints, in part by regulating municipal bankruptcy (Kopányi and others 2000).

Until 1990 the government in Hungary had been organized in a multitier system in which the central government controlled more than 1,523 local councils through 19 county councils. Hungary was a unitary socialist state, and the local councils had no separate legal identity. Under the old regime local units performed a wide range of expenditure functions but only in the capacity of agents of the central government. Local governments had little independent revenue, and even though they were charged with some spending responsibilities, few of these were independent spending functions. Some fees and duties were collected locally, but the rates were fixed by the central government. In the event of revenue shortfalls the funding needed to cover expenditures was negotiated with the central government and channeled from the central budget, mostly through the counties.

The passage of the Law on Local Self-Government in 1990 eliminated the middle tier of government—the 1,523 local councils that had served as the agents of the central government, carrying out its fiscal orders through the 19 county councils (the regional bodies).[1] The law not only abolished the local councils; it also scaled back the responsibilities of the regional bodies. Hungary was left with effectively two levels—the national state and a host of local units. At the same time the number of local governments increased dramatically—to 3,148 in 1993—as many of the former local councils broke up into discrete units along historical lines of community. For agglomerations with populations of 50,000 or more, 22 cities of county rank were established, with Budapest given the status of an autonomous municipality. The existence of so many small units has been identified as a major problem in rationalizing municipal services (see Davey 1990 and Peteri and Wright 1994).

The Law on Local Self-Government also redefined the rights and responsibilities of the two remaining levels of local government. Local governments (localities) now are directly responsible for most traditional local government functions. Some taxing authority has been devolved to these local governments, but most expenditure responsibilities are still met through grants from the central government. The grants, though largely unconditional, are related in part to spending norms linked to expenditure responsibilities. Localities can own, borrow, and dispose of property and establish, manage, and sell public enterprises.

The Law on Local Self-Government was the first of several laws that now frame the Hungarian intergovernmental system and lay out the terms of autonomy for local governments.[2] Broadly speaking, these laws accomplished the following:

- Established that local governments are no longer agents of the center and its ministries.
- Adopted the principle that local governments should be public service entities with assigned tasks and local taxing powers.
- Accepted the principle of subsidiarity as embodied in the European Charter.[3]
- Established sets of mandatory and voluntary service activities to be carried out by municipalities.
- Accepted the principle that municipalities can be legally obligated to perform certain tasks, but that mandates should be accompanied by fiscal or other assistance.
- Defined performance standards for voluntary tasks that are the responsibility of local citizens.
- Allowed local taxing authority.
- Established that local governments have ownership rights.
- Allowed and encouraged local governments to enter into associations with one another.
- Detailed a process for municipal bankruptcy proceedings, including the authority for workouts to avoid potential bankruptcy.

Under the Law on Local Self-Government towns, cities, the capital region and its districts, and counties have equal local government rights. In principle, this has created a system of equality among local governments, but it is one in which resources and responsibilities vary considerably.

Decentralization and Subnational Finance

Hungary has a large public sector compared with those in other European countries. General government expenditure (including social security) was about 51 percent of GDP in 1995. It declined to 43 percent in 2000, and the plan was to reduce it further to 40 percent by 2003. Correspondingly, local government expenditure fell from 16.5 percent of GDP in 1993 to 12.8 percent in 2000 (real expenditure fell by 20 percent).

The 1990 Law on Local Self-Government devolved many expenditure responsibilities to subnational governments, but it defined the tasks of local governments vaguely. The tasks are basically shared responsibilities. The central government heavily influences the legal requirements for service provision. Despite the devolution of some taxing authority to local governments, most expenditure responsibilities are still financed through grants from the central government. These grants, though unconditional, are linked to expenditure responsibilities.

The Law on Local Self-Government provided for a range of revenue sources to finance local government functions. These include five major local taxes (taxes on business, land, buildings, communal services, and tourism), user charges, revenues from entrepreneurial activities, and receipts from the disposition of rental and commercial properties. Local revenue accounted for 26 to 35 percent of total local government revenue in the late 1990s. Central government fiscal transfers accounted for most of the rest, with receipts from loans contributing 3 to 5 percent (figure 29.1).

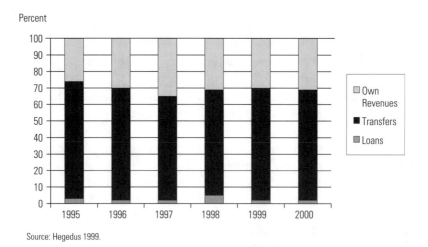

Source: Hegedus 1999.

Figure 29.1. Sources of Local Government Revenue, Hungary, 1995–2000

Between 1990 and 1998, as general government expenditure declined by 31 percent, local revenues and receipts fell by 33 percent. Locally generated revenues and borrowing proceeds could not offset the reduction in general government transfers.

As increasing responsibilities for financing and providing services and growing investment needs for local infrastructure coincided with tight fiscal policies and smaller budgetary transfers, local governments had to respond to the mounting fiscal pressure on both the expenditure and the revenue side. On the expenditure side, they improved the cost efficiency of local services. However, they also cut costs by reducing capital investments below replacement levels, adversely affecting both the quantity and the quality of many public services. By the end of the 1990s municipal investment in infrastructure fell significantly short of the rate that would be required to meet EU standards for investment.

On the revenue side, local governments made little effort to generate more own-source revenues. Local governments also faced structural problems. Most municipalities are too small to undertake investments in projects on an economically viable scale. Moreover, the specialized financial instruments and financial intermediaries needed to meet the investment demand of municipalities are lacking.

As investment rates increase as part of the EU integration strategy and as asset sales decline as a source of investment finance, local governments will have to turn increasingly to private capital to meet the growing demand for public infrastructure and upgrade the quality of service to the levels required for accession to the EU (World Bank 2000).

Evolution of Domestic Capital Markets

Capital markets in transitioning economies generally are still in the early stages of development. This is reflected in the number and variety of institutional investors (insurance companies, pension funds, mutual funds) and the resulting depth of markets. It is also reflected in the still-immature market infrastructure (primary and secondary markets, rating agencies, analysts) and market regulation (disclosure requirements) and in the markets' small capitalization, turnover, and range of products (table 29.1).

Hungary's capital markets, though put in place before the postsocialist reforms of the early 1990s, got off to a slow start. Capitalization was low as a result of several factors—the gradual approach to privatization (until late 1995), the lack of development of the institutional investment sector, and

Table 29.1. Equity and Debt Markets, Selected Countries in Central and Eastern Europe, End-1995
(millions of U.S. dollars, except where otherwise specified)

	Czech Republic	Hungary[a]	Poland[b]	Slovak Republic	Slovenia
Equities market					
Market capitalization	17,992	2,850	4,564	5,329	306
Market capitalization as a percentage of GDP	40.3	7.1	3.9	30.6	1.7
Annual trading volume	4,713	764	4,861	840	341
Number of listed shares	86	42	65	21	18
Average daily turnover	20	3	20	3	1
Bond market					
Market capitalization	3,302	1,135	5,235	6,091[c]	338
Market capitalization as a percentage of GDP	7.4	15.1	4.4	6.5	1.9
Annual turnover	2,617	1,276	1,654	521	176
Number of listed bonds	23	38	13	32	16
Average daily turnover	11	5	7	2	1

Note: Figures refer to trading at the stock exchanges and exclude the Czech and Slovak securities exchanges and the Bratislava Options Exchange.

a. Equities turnover and capitalization include shares, investment fund certificates, and compensation vouchers. Bond turnover and capitalization include government and corporate bonds and treasury bills.

b. The Poland Stock Exchange replaced the listing system with a three-market division in 1995. The shares shown as listed here trade in the main and secondary market.

c. In September 1995.

Source: Bokros and Dethier 1998.

a burdensome tax structure due to the large government sector. Capital market development also was constrained by a preference for corporate placements without the issuance of new equity shares, large foreign direct investment flows that favored joint ventures, and the bond market's focus on meeting the national government's large fiscal needs, crowding out private investment.

Nonetheless, Hungary had started out ahead of its neighbors. The government began money market and capital market reforms as early as 1983, when it allowed the reintroduction of corporate bonds. Indeed, Hungary was more effective at developing its bond (debt) markets than its equities markets. While the equities market capitalization was only $2.9 billion, or 6 percent of GDP, at the end of 1995, the bond and treasury bill market had a capitalization of about $6.5 billion in March 1996. The total debt turnover on the Budapest Stock Exchange was $1.2 billion in 1995. Over-the-counter trading accounted for another $12 billion in 1995, with turnover values in government bonds and bills 6 to 12 times those on the stock exchange.

The government dominated the debt markets. In 1995 corporate bonds accounted for less than 1 percent of bond capitalization and turnover in the Budapest Stock Exchange and 5 percent of bond turnover in over-the-counter trading. Driving the government's dominance were its large fiscal deficits and debt payments.[4] Deterioration in Hungary's macroeconomic fundamentals prompted a decline in Hungary's international credit ratings in early 1995.[5]

Local Government and the Capital Market: The Early Phase

The evolution of the municipal credit framework in Hungary can be divided into two general phases. In the first, from 1990 to 1995, controls on subnational borrowing were essentially based on market discipline. Local governments had little experience with this concept of market access, nor had they needed to worry about it. Before decentralization, the large number and amount of grants available from the central government led most municipalities to behave in ways aimed at maximizing grants. Moreover, the large receipts from the privatization of municipal assets meant that local governments had no need to access capital markets to finance their development spending. Accordingly, constraints on the demand side were the main factors in the limited use of capital markets to finance capital spending.

In 1990, however, local governments in Hungary acquired new financing needs as they became responsible for capital expenditures in the service areas assigned to them. These new expenditure responsibilities, compounded by the requirements for meeting the standards relating to EU accession conditions, brought with them huge financial needs.

The main sources of financing for local government investments in Hungary are receipts from property (sale of assets), grants from the central government, loans, and operating surpluses. In 1995–97 receipts from local government asset sales accounted for about 70 percent of total investment funds. Since 1997 this share has declined, however. The second most important source of funds is capital grants, which account for 20 percent of investment funds.

The Law on Local Self-Government granted municipalities the authority to borrow freely for capital investment projects, without approval from or registration with a higher level of government. Thus from 1990 until March 1995 municipal governments faced no absolute or formula-based limit on borrowing and could borrow for whatever purpose and on whatever terms the city council approved. (Short-term borrowing for liquidity management can be initiated by the local mayor, while long-term borrowing to finance infrastructure investments and property improvements requires the approval of the local assembly.) There were, however, restrictions against using shared revenue, transfer payments, normative grants (such as equalization grants), and infrastructure grants from the central government for repaying loans (implicitly, the central government would not finance a local government's debt). In addition, the Law on Local Self-Government stipulated that the central government would not assume responsibility for local debt.

From the outset, bank loans have been the largest source of credit. The national government provides some subsidized loans, but most funds are borrowed from banks, carry market interest rates, and have medium-term (five- to eight-year) maturities. While private banks are free to lend, state-owned banks dominate lending (as well as other intermediation services). The National Savings Bank (OTP) early on had a near monopoly of loans to local governments, accounting for 99 percent of lending to municipalities in 2001. The bank's portfolio of loans to municipalities, which has been increasing continuously since the end of 2001, grew by 35.6 percent in 2002, reaching 63.3 billion forint (Ft). However, while the total volume increased, the bank's share of the municipal loan market fell to 55 percent (OTP Bank 2003).

In obtaining loans, localities may pledge as collateral properties they own, except for vital core properties such as streets, public parks, and common areas. County guarantees for local borrowing, common in the past, remain legally possible but are not a promising security, mainly because the counties no longer have secure revenue sources. The counties' role as guarantor has diminished accordingly.

In the early 1990s some localities had strikingly high levels of debt, stemming from local councils' borrowings for projects under earlier regimes and carried over into the new framework. Under the earlier system repayments due on any borrowings approved under the national credit plan were guaranteed by the national government. After the reforms this debt became the responsibility of the new local governments, and for some it was a major burden. Moreover, given the loose regulation, it was seen as a potential threat to the national treasury.

After enactment of the Law on Local Self-Government, municipal borrowing grew quickly. In 1991 local governments took Ft 4.5 billion in credit, and in 1992, Ft 7.5 billion. Still, the amount in 1992 constituted only

1.5 percent of total local budget receipts. In 1993 the share of borrowing rose to 4 percent.

Most localities used their borrowing authority cautiously. However, the changes in—and uncertainty about—the revenue system and the abolition of credit planning and central guarantees for local investment put municipalities in a new position. By the mid-1990s some municipalities had begun to borrow long term to finance short-term operating deficits, a practice that at the time was not prohibited. Other borrowing was largely to finance investments in nonmandatory infrastructure (activities not mandated by the state).

As a result of the unfettered freedom of local governments to manage their assets and budgets, the central government faced the possibility of dealing with hundreds of cases of contingent liabilities and directly carrying out mandatory local tasks if local governments failed. Indeed, localities began to default, and both creditors and debtors began to lobby for large-scale state bailouts. Representatives of several commercial banks explicitly stated that loans to these localities were for the public benefit and therefore ought to be bailed out by the state.

In late 1994 and 1995 the Hungarian government had several policy options for controlling municipal borrowing and protecting the solvency of the state budget. One was to declare "no responsibility" for borrowings by local governments. A second was to impose restrictions under existing legislation and create a monitoring and enforcement mechanism. A third option was to rely on an informal agreement with the major financial institutions involved with local governments, asking them to enforce debt limits and restrain excessive borrowing. A fourth option was to rely on market discipline and transparency to screen out risky clients and penalize bad decisions by borrowers and lenders.

Municipal Debt Financing: The Post-1995 Phase

In the second phase of municipal borrowing, following 1995, the central government instituted regulation of local government borrowing and dealt with the consequences of impending municipal defaults. New laws, along with the tight fiscal conditions in the country, placed curbs on the growth in subnational borrowing and began to rein in its use. The government enacted three key measures: a limit on debt service for local governments in 1995, the Municipal Debt Adjustment Act in 1996, and the Securities Act in 1997 (which included rules on issuing municipal bonds).

With the Law on Local Self-Government of 1990, Hungary's local governments had become independent entities subject only to the supervision of the Parliament, with no intermediate layer of government or administration to approve, monitor, or intervene in their financial activities. Nonetheless, some national oversight continued. The State Audit Office monitors the technical, accounting, and reporting aspects of the use of state funds by local governments. However, while it issues opinions on the use of funds, it cannot punish violations. The Public Administration Offices issue opinions about the formal compliance of local government decisions with the Constitution and other laws but do not comment on the effectiveness, content, or reasonableness of local government actions (Jókay, Szepesi, and Szmetana 2000).

Without the political will or the ability to tightly control local government borrowing and business practices by constitutional and legislative fiat, the Hungarian government decided to propose a municipal debt adjustment (bankruptcy) law that would be invoked if prudence and other preemptive measures failed. Hungary's corporate bankruptcy law, in force since the late 1980s, did not entirely apply to municipal borrowers, since they could not be liquidated unless the state took over their duties. Because every citizen has a constitutional right to representation at the local level, local government cannot be liquidated like a commercial enterprise. Accordingly, a coherent policy geared to governments was needed to define debt adjustment procedures.

The state's aim was to avoid having to take on the contingent liabilities of local governments and to ensure the continuance of vital public services without additional strain on the national budget. Thus its approach was to regulate the process wherever possible and to allow market actors to assume risk. The debt adjustment law would protect debtors, creditors, and the state budget while making it entirely clear what would happen in the case of municipal default. Rather than the tight allocation regulations known in Europe, the Hungarian government decided that both lenders and borrowers should be held responsible for their decisions, while it put in place mechanisms for ultimately protecting mandatory services.

The Municipal Debt Adjustment Act of 1996, in effect since mid-1996, is the centerpiece of the new municipal borrowing framework. The law defines a debt adjustment process aimed at allowing local governments to regain their financial health while also protecting the rights of creditors. Its provisions, which impose definite costs on local governments that default on debt or other payments, also lend protections to debtors and limit the powers of creditors. There is strong evidence that the law has prevented bankruptcy filings by encouraging both creditors and debtors to seek redress outside the court system and take steps to ensure solvency and operational efficiency.

Under the new legal framework, municipalities stopped borrowing beyond their capacity to service debt (Kópanyi and others 2000). Debt service as a share of own-source revenue has been well below the limit of 70 percent authorized in the 1996 amendment.[6] In 1998 local government debt service as a whole was well under 30 percent of own-source revenue.[7] By early 2000 there had been only 9 court filings for bankruptcy and about 60 bankruptcy threats that resulted in out-of-court agreements between the local government and its creditors.

Nonetheless, the municipal bankruptcy law is not without its drawbacks. It has been criticized, for example, for essentially eliminating municipal capital borrowing. Since 1995 municipal medium- and long-term borrowing has been limited largely to a few big cities. Recent experience with municipal finance shows that the bankruptcy act has prompted even the smallest communities to put in place effective preventive measures to avoid the risk of asset liquidation. Moreover, financial institutions have been more prudent in lending to municipalities (particularly for gas and wastewater projects). The municipal bankruptcy framework has performed effectively in Hungary's market-oriented legislative and institutional environment.

Bond Issue by the Municipality of Budapest

Budapest, the capital of Hungary, is home to 2 million inhabitants and a consumer market of around 5 million. With more than 90 percent of the nation's service industry and 60 percent of its research and development capacity, Budapest produces more than a third of Hungary's GDP. In Budapest services account for a large share of income and employment—a share nearly 20 percent larger than the national average—and the unemployment rate is much lower (Pallai 2000).

The challenge for Budapest, as for other municipalities, was to use the framework created by the Law on Local Self-Government of 1990 to transform the financial and administrative system it had inherited from the socialist era. Since only fiscal stability and independence could provide the basis for political independence and greater fiscal autonomy, it was clear that own-source revenues would have to be increased. Greater own-source revenues were needed to ensure not only financial independence but also the long-term security of services for which municipalities were now responsible.

While Hungary faced serious macroeconomic and fiscal problems in the mid-1990s, Budapest also confronted a structural deficit. Part of the strategy to remedy the situation was to focus on increasing its own revenues through taxes and charges rather than fighting to restore earlier levels of central transfers. The new financial strategy was aimed at shifting to an active borrowing policy, entering the capital markets as a fully autonomous entity, and building a loan portfolio that spread financing risk. To adopt an active borrowing policy, Budapest had to increase its financial reserves to the equivalent of at least one year's debt service obligations.

Until 1996 the municipality borrowed primarily from domestic banks (domestic currency loans) and from two international financial institutions, the European Bank for Reconstruction and Development (in 1993) and the World Bank (in 1995).[8] The loans were raised on the principle of negative pledge; only the assets created through the project financing were pledged, not tax revenue or assets of the municipality.

In 1996–97, with a relatively small debt burden, a large investment portfolio, a well-regarded privatization process, and growing confidence in the country, Budapest appeared ready to enter the international bond market to raise finance. In 1996 the city decided to issue its first bonds in the eurobond market, targeting public investors. Budapest also decided to issue bonds without a rating because the city could not get a higher credit rating than the country. A two-round tender was conducted to select the lead manager. Ultimately, however, the issue had to be postponed because of a change in the national tax law.

In 1998, after amendment of the tax law, Budapest decided to launch its eurobond issue (table 29.2). In the meantime Hungary's sovereign rating had improved from speculative to investment grade (Moody's Baa2), and the city's financial status had strengthened. The municipality did not seek a rating of its own, but it compiled an information memorandum for the sale. The five-year bonds were issued at a 57–basis point "surcharge" over the Bundesbank bond of the same term and obtained a 35–basis point premium over the London interbank offered rate (LIBOR). The Hungarian National Bank issue in February 1998 had a 31– to 33–basis point premium over LIBOR. Thus the market assessed the risk of the municipality's bond as similar to the country risk. Institutional investors subscribed to 20 percent of the bond issue, and private investors, mainly on the German and Austrian money markets, to the remaining 80 percent (Pallai 2000).

Bond Issue by the Municipality of Pecs

With a population of about 160,000, Pecs is the fifth largest city in Hungary. It is situated in the south of the country, close to the Croatian border.

Table 29.2. Terms of the Bond Issue by the Municipality of Budapest

Amount	DM 150 million	**Paying agent**	Deutsche Genossenschaft
Type of bond	Fixed rate		Bank
Form or		**Debt service**	0.37 percent of 1999 budget
denomination	Global bearer bond	**Authorization**	General assembly, mayor's
Issue date	23 July 1998		office
Maturity	Five years	**Supervision**	Capital Market Supervisory
Amortization	None; bullet		Board
Interest rate	4.75 percent	**Purpose**	General funding purposes
Interest payment	Annual	**Use of proceeds**	Infrastructure and financial
Rating	None		reserves
Security	Unsecured	**Performance**	Punctual
Cross-default	Capital market obligation	**Other debt (as of**	
Law	German	**1 January 2000)**	Ft 4,093 million
Listing	Frankfurt Stock Exchange	*Long term (more than*	
Lead manager	Deutsche Genossenschaft	*one year)*	1.63 percent of total budget
	Bank	**Other debt service**	0.13 percent of total budget

Source: Pallai 2000.

Since coal and uranium mining were discontinued in the early 1990s, light industry and the service sector have grown, complementing the traditional food, tobacco, and leather industries.

Pecs floated its first bond issue of Ft 150 million in 1997, using the proceeds for general purposes (table 29.3). The bond issue amounted to only 1 percent of its 1997 budget and therefore had no material impact on its financial situation. Of the municipality's total revenue in 1997, 40 percent came from central government subsidies, 16 percent from local taxes and fees, 16 percent from privatization receipts and other capital revenues, 14 percent from municipal services and other operating income, and 13 percent from personal income taxes. Of its total expenditure, 34 percent went to salaries and wages, 26 percent to maintenance, 16 percent to social security, 12 percent to investments and associated costs, and 10 percent to operating expenses. At the time of the bond issue the municipality had more than Ft 1.5 billion in outstanding debt.

No credit rating was contemplated for the issue because of its small size, its private placement, and the fact that it was guaranteed. Moreover, as a private placement, the issue required only the standard minimal documentation and limited due diligence and was fully underwritten by the manager.[9] Because there were only a few potential investors for this unlisted issue

Table 29.3. Terms of the Bond Issue by the Municipality of Pecs

Issue date	6 February 1997
Issue	Ft 150 million in bonds at 16.4 percent annual interest, fixed rate, at par
Purpose	General funding purposes
Status and security	General obligation and guarantee
Form and denomination	Registered notes; Ft 10 million
Guarantor	Raiffeisen Unicbank Rt.
Market	Hungarian domestic market, direct placement
Maturity	Five years (6 February 2002)
Amortization	Bullet due at term
Rating	None
Law	Hungarian
Listing	None
Lead manager	RSI Hungary Securities Ltd.
Paying agent	Raiffeisen Unicbank Rt.
Performance	Punctual
Public participation	None
Other debt at 1 January 1999	Short term (less than one year)
Total amount	Ft 908 million
Total amount as a percentage of the 1999 budget	6.3 percent

Source: Municipality of Pecs [http://www.fornax.hu/].

(primarily insurance companies), no public marketing took place. Indeed, the issue was a "bought deal"—that is, it was placed with one insurance company as the sole investor. The offered price was considered competitive and therefore was accepted by the city. Since the investor planned to hold the issue until maturity, no trading and no secondary market could develop. The size of the transaction (less than $1 million) made an international placement infeasible.

When Pecs had considered its funding alternatives in mid-1997, market conditions favored bonds over loans. Short-term rates were slightly above 20 percent, and the benchmark five-year forint government bond was trading at about 16 percent. The bond offer, including the guarantee fee, was considered to be at least 75 basis points cheaper than a bank loan with a similar maturity.[10] The lead manager offered a five-year fixed rate bond issue—the standard for the municipal private placement market. The municipality had received bond offers at even more advantageous terms relative to loans. Since the fixed rate bond seemed substantially cheaper than floating rate notes, it accepted the offer.

The Pecs issue was guaranteed by a commercial bank, and both the guarantor and the lead manager are subsidiaries of a foreign bank. Like all domestic, privately placed municipal debt issues until then, the Pecs issue carried a bank guarantee. The bond issue for Budapest that followed in 1998 was placed without such a guarantee.

Prospects for a Larger Municipal Credit Market

Local government finance in Hungary remains in transition, and much still needs to be done to ensure that the decentralization of government activities is economically efficient and politically sustainable. Under the Law on Local Self-Government localities assumed far greater spending responsibilities. With local own-source revenues inadequate and the sale of assets coming to an end, new sources are needed to pay for these responsibilities. While local governments, needing to catch up on deferred investments and anxious to meet EU accession requirements, have looked to domestic capital markets to meet their investment needs, private investors' interest in supporting these needs remains unclear.

Several trends have had powerful effects on municipalities in Hungary. These include the declining contributions to municipal budgets from the central government, the drop in income from the one-time sale of public assets, and the growing needs for project and infrastructure development. Strapped for funds to meet operating needs and unable or unwilling to raise local taxes, localities have seen investment in infrastructure shrink as a share of GDP, from 3 percent in 1991 to about 2 percent in 1997. Hungary's municipal debt market remains embryonic. There have been few bond sales, and bank loans have remained the dominant source of borrowing for local governments.

However, a growing number of factors, on both the supply and the demand side, may encourage a larger municipal credit market in the near future. Hungary has taken steps toward regulation that leaves capital markets relatively untrammeled and has sought to clarify the allocation of risk. Such regulation is part of the legal, regulatory, and institutional framework critical to the development of an efficient subnational capital market—a framework that provides the foundations for a market in which private investors and financial intermediaries compete to mobilize financial resources from savers. The goal is to correctly price the extension of credit and efficiently allocate capital among subnational government investments.

Several pieces remain to be fitted into this mosaic, however. At the national level the burden of excessive regulation and a costly central government needs to be eased to give local governments greater fiscal flexibility. The excessive fragmentation of local government, which inhibits economies of scale and the efficient delivery of services, needs to be cured. At the subnational level the capacities of local governments to finance projects, program investments, manage financial policy, and manage revenue and debt must be strengthened.

Notes

1. Budapest enjoyed special status as a county and municipality and was directly represented in the central government planning process.

2. The others include the laws on Local Taxes (1990), Elections of Self-Governments (1990), Property Transfer (1991), Tasks and Authorities Competencies (1991), the Capital City and Its Districts (1991), Municipal Bankruptcy (1996), and Debt Management (1996). See Ebel, Varfalvi, and Varga 1998.

3. The principle of subsidiarity calls for examining two criteria when considering which governing body should have jurisdiction over a problem. First is the size of the problem: if an issue encompasses many local communities or extends over a large geographic area, the involvement of a higher level of government may be necessary. Second is the resources or political will of a local community: if they are inadequate for addressing the problem, a higher level of government may intervene.

4. To provide incentives to investors to purchase government securities, the government provided two tax breaks: up to 30 percent of income on government bonds held for more than three years and a 10 percent tax on government paper (as compared with the 10 to 20 percent tax applied to equities).

5. Hungary has a positive reputation for debt service in international capital markets. Standard and Poor's has given it a BB+ rating with a stable outlook. Moody's has rated Hungary's sovereign unsecure rating A1 rating for both local and exchange currency issues.

6. Debt is defined as including loans, bonds, guarantees issued on behalf of third parties, and lease agreements. Own current revenues are defined as including local taxes, duties, interest revenues, environmental fines, and other own revenues. This definition excludes the revenues of institutions (rent, user fees), although these are also included in local government bud-

get tables as part of own local revenues. Own local revenues are "corrected" by subtracting short-term liabilities (not including cash flow credits, which are used to ensure funding of local government operations).

7. These data do not include guarantees and leases, so the available borrowing capacity is lower than can be directly estimated (Pigey 1999).

8. These initial loans from the European Bank for Reconstruction and Development and the World Bank were for investments in public transport.

9. The manager's commission and the annual guarantee fee are part of the overall pricing but were not disclosed.

10. This figure is an estimate, since the precise size of the guarantee fee was not disclosed.

Chapter 30

Eastern and Central Europe
Poland

*National policies and a difficult economy slow but do not halt
the growing use of credit markets by local governments.*

Miguel Valadez and John Petersen

Lessons

By most measures Poland has made a successful transition from
a centrally planned economy to a decentralized, market-based
system. This success is the product of several factors. Fiscal
management problems inherited from the centrally planned system were reversed by a combination of technical assistance from
Europe and the United States, the incentives for reform created
by the desire for accession to the European Union (EU), and laws
enacted to satisfy EU criteria for public finance and organization.
Just as for Mexico and the North American Free Trade Area, the
proximity to the EU and the increasing integration with the EU
economy have provided incentives for well-framed regulatory reform and for competent and conservative fiscal management.
These factors, together with Poland's robust economic performance over the past decade, provide a stable foundation for developing local government capital markets.

Although political decentralization in Poland has been methodical and reasonably well supported by the central government, it is not complete. The process has emphasized devolution of spending responsibilities and limits on local own-source revenues. For the typical urban powiat (major city), the local government with the most fiscal autonomy, own-source revenues amount to only a third of the total. Stability in local fiscal management has been enforced by legislation that limits local debt and encourages fiscal prudence. This preference for prudence over fiscal flexibility has restricted local governments' ability to use debt to meet capital spending needs.

Short case studies of several Polish cities provide an overview of the fiscal situation of local governments and their experience with subnational borrowing. Key fiscal characteristics include low revenue flexibility, high operating expenditures relative to total expenditure, increased spending responsibilities not fully supported by central transfers, and significant infrastructure needs. Local governments face strict statutory limits on borrowing, which make no distinction between operating deficits and capital expenditure financing. Nonetheless, several Polish cities have borrowed in the markets and carry international credit ratings, though foreign currency issues were prohibited by law as of 2002.

Most local financing comes from bank loans initiated through technical assistance and government financial institutions. Municipal bond issues have grown substantially since 2001 as a cheaper alternative for financing extensive capital spending in the current climate of tight budgets. These early steps in a well-regulated and closely monitored environment suggest that the prospects are good for further development of Poland's municipal capital market and its ultimate integration with the EU financial markets.

In the transition from a centralized economy to a decentralized, market-based economy, Poland had a jump start over many of its Eastern European neighbors. In the mid- to late 1990s Poland had among the highest economic growth rates in the region (GDP grew 5 percent a year in 1990–2000), demonstrating the rewards of a successful transition. Structural reforms, macroeconomic stabilization policies, and a dynamic private sector all combined to make the transition one of the most successful in Eastern Europe.

In the early part of the present decade the economy underwent a marked downward shift. High growth rates, strong domestic demand, and high inflation gave way to low (though still positive) real growth, weak demand, high unemployment, rapidly falling inflation, high real interest rates, and a significant appreciation of the zloty. The zloty's appreciation reduced external competitiveness and slowed economic growth, necessitating cost cutting by firms and thus worsening unemployment. Meanwhile, high interest rates increased the cost of servicing domestic debt, which accounts for 55 percent of all public debt. In 2002 debt service costs for domestic borrowing were four times those for foreign debt.

The poor economic environment led to a need for more public sector spending, resulting in deteriorating finances and budgetary problems. The general government deficit for all governments increased sharply, to 6 percent of GDP in 2001, reversing what had been a steady decline in general government debt. Meanwhile, fiscal tightening exposed fiscal management problems at the national level. The 2001 budget proved unrealistic. It was based on poorly informed assumptions about future revenues and on uncontrolled spending increases. To address this lack of fiscal discipline, the minister of finance had proposed limiting nominal spending increases by pegging them to inflation, starting with the 2003 budget. However, in 2002 the Parliament circumvented this proposal by increasing spending beyond the proposed limits. The struggle to rein in deficits extended into 2003, and the future of a framework for limiting spending remains uncertain. Poland needs to restore fiscal balance on its way to accession to the European Union (EU), planned for 2007. In the process it needs to free up 31 billon zloty (PLN), or about $8 billion, to contribute to the EU budget and billions more to meet matching requirements on EU grants (Reed 2003).

Placing further pressure on fiscal resources, political influence has hampered the ability to cut back certain expenditures (particularly sensitive are insurance for farmers and pension payments). Around 80 percent of state spending is in the form of entitlements and is not discretionary, undercutting prudent fiscal behavior.[1] Nonetheless, the Polish fiscal system includes a measure of discipline—statutory restrictions on deficit levels that are triggered when government debt reaches specified limits. These restrictions, coupled with the need to adhere to the membership requirements of the European Union for future accession, may impose a tangible spending ceiling and provide a measure of fiscal stability. The legislative framework, crafted in an atmosphere of dominant fiscal demands and stress at the national level, has supported conservative fiscal and debt management practices at the local level. While the framework is effective in maintaining fiscal prudence, it has also slowed the use of debt by local governments and constrained their efforts to address the nation's infrastructure needs.

Local Government System and Decentralization

The political upheaval that greeted the early 1980s in Poland (and led to the imposition of martial law) forced a rethinking of the country's economic and political system.[2] A combination of communism and market-based democracy emerged that, by the late 1980s, had planted the seeds of decentralization.

Earlier Poland had a unitary government structure. The government was segmented into several different spheres: the central level, 17 voivodships (regions), 330 powiats (intermediate-level administrations), and nearly 3,700 gminas (municipalities and towns), all acting as an arm of the central government within their geographic reach. By the late 1970s powiats had been abolished and their functions assumed by the voivodships. The unrest of the 1980s led to further reorganization of government and the introduction of some power sharing among different levels—and fostered the goal of improving fiscal mechanisms.

The devolution of fiscal authority that followed allowed voivodships to hold own-source revenues for the first time, substantially increasing their financial autonomy in handling such responsibilities as health, welfare, and regional transport. By the late 1980s there had been a significant shift of power to the voivodships, in large part because of the political limitations of central intervention. State-owned enterprises also were given a measure of autonomy, but because they were not exposed to competition and hard budget constraints, the gains in operational efficiency were limited. Gminas received greater responsibilities for sanitation and public housing maintenance, but this proved to be little more than deconcentration; control remained with the central government. In the end the reforms stalled, in part because the centrally planned system precluded the establishment of property rights. Without these, the incentives for fiscal discipline could not be fostered.

Indeed, intergovernmental relations remained murky and devoid of incentives. Revenue allocations were based on bargaining between the local and national levels, and the reforms of the 1980s served only to weaken central control. Unsurprisingly, local governments (and higher levels) lacked a good understanding of sound financial management. These factors made the need for new, strongly enforced fiscal rules clearly apparent. However, the existing intergovernmental system hampered further reform and would plague the transition to come. The incomplete reform and the exposure to market forces combined to create economic upheaval in the late 1980s. The result was hyperinflation.

Transition

In 1990, after the communist collapse, Poland held its first democratic elections. At this time public service provision was inefficient and still highly centralized. Local governments faced difficult challenges—such as the obscure legal status of state enterprises, a distorted budgetary revenue structure, and the question of what to do with massive stocks of public housing. The newly elected government began to address these issues through new laws.

The Law on Local Self-Government of 1990 embedded decentralization into the country's governance structure, establishing legally protected local autonomy for gminas and clear responsibilities for local public functions. A new legal framework separated local budgets from the center and eliminated extrabudgetary arrangements. The framework, put fully in place a year after the first law was enacted, included the Act on Local Revenues and Rules of Financing of 1990, the Budget Law Act of 1991, and the Act on Taxes and Local Fees of 1991. Responsibilities assigned to local governments included health, housing, energy, education, sanitation, water supply, local transport, and social assistance. These responsibilities were typically financed by a combination of own-source revenues, shared taxes, and transfers from the center.

In areas such as public transport, gminas were likely to have autonomy in pricing and provision, while in such areas as education their autonomy tended to be fairly limited. Moreover, the extent of local control depended on the gmina. Some were granted substantial fiscal autonomy, while others had little more than tasks delegated by the center. Indeed, decentralization proved to be necessarily conditioned by a gmina's political, financial, and technical realities. To facilitate the process of decentralization, the Office of Public Administration Reform was established to coordinate the sharing of information between levels of government during the early years of the transition.

Despite these efforts, the new rules of the game were vague. Echoing the historical murkiness in local-central relations, ambiguities in the assignment of responsibilities reduced accountability and limited the benefits of decentralization (Barbone and Hicks 1995). Even so, there were notable successes, particularly in public transport, where local governments achieved high cost recovery, and in centrally legislated welfare programs, where local administration increased efficiency.

Present Framework

Decentralization in Poland continues to move forward. Recent legislation has reduced the local administrative presence of the central government. The re-creation of urban and rural powiats, through the Law on Local Government Revenues of 1999, has led to further devolution of revenues and expenditures. Urban powiats, which include the larger cities, have both gmina and powiat responsibilities (table 30.1). The gminas, the lowest level of government, have achieved the greatest fiscal autonomy as a result of their expanded authority to set tax rates. However, fiscal autonomy at all levels remains low; for example, the central government places caps on tax rates set by gminas.

While public expenditures have been highly decentralized, revenues have not been decentralized at an equal pace. Still, this has not imposed an undue burden on most local governments, because the central government has tended to provide the means for meeting their growing expenditure responsibilities. However, there are some notable exceptions. Some local governments have not received matching funds and have had to use tariffs to make up the shortfall, such as for water supply in the early 1990s. More recently, education responsibilities given to urban powiats have not led to matching transfers from the central government, which has necessitated moving resources earmarked for other uses to make up the shortfall. In an apparent paradox, as expenditure responsibilities and own-source revenues have increased, they have fallen as a share of total revenue, as the case of Szczecin illustrates (figure 30.1).

The current intergovernmental arrangement for revenue sharing and expenditure responsibilities was supposed to last two years (1999–2000), but in 2002 it was simply extended. Decentralization is likely to deepen in the

Table 30.1. Current Structure of Subnational Government, Poland

Level of government	Main responsibilities	Revenue sources	Financial authority
Voivodships (16 regions)	Regional economy, international economic relations, social welfare	• Subsidies tied to regional tax revenues (source of the largest share of revenue) • 1.5 percent share of local personal income tax • 0.5 percent share of local corporate tax	Borrowing capacity and extensive infrastructure responsibilities
Powiats (373 intermediate administrations)	Secondary education, social welfare, public order and security, public health, county roads, flood and fire response	• 1 percent share of local personal income tax • Subsidies tied to: – Powiat tax revenues (source of the largest share of revenue) – Social welfare expenses – Equalization component	No tax collection or rate setting authority but large expenditure responsibilities
Gminas (around 2,500 towns and municipalities)	Land development, municipal roads, water provision, sewerage, heating and electricity, waste disposal, local public transport, primary health care and social welfare, municipal housing, primary education	• 27.6 percent share of local personal income tax • 5 percent share of corporate tax • Subsidies tied to local conditions with progressive component for gminas with low own-source revenues	Can set local taxes and fees (property tax is most important) for 35 percent of total revenue, but maximums are set by central government

Source: Standard & Poor's 1999.

coming years, with more revenue independence for voivodships and powiats expected.[3] For cities (urban powiats), however, changes in the revenue structure are not expected to be significant.

Banking and the Financial Markets

Poland's banks have been the most important source of credit since municipal borrowing took off in the mid-1990s. Their stability and maturity are crucial for developing Poland's local credit market. As Poland's financial system deepens, it will more readily and efficiently provide funding for market-oriented credit instruments such as bond issues.

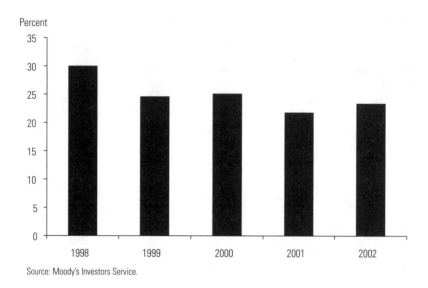

Source: Moody's Investors Service.

Figure 30.1. Own-Source Revenue as a Share of Total Revenue, Szczecin, 1998–2002

Banking

Poland's banking sector, made up of many small banks and a handful of larger ones, is relatively small compared with those of other countries.[4] Bank assets were equal to only 60 percent of GDP in 2000 (by comparison, in Spain the ratio is well over 100 percent), and a third of Poles do not use banks (Fitch Ratings 2000). Thus there is an obvious need for greater expansion and deepening of the banking sector, although this may also mean consolidation of the many small banks. Despite a large foreign bank presence, some banks continue to be at least partially state owned, and political interference in their operations in the past has undermined a long-term corporate strategy. Corporate governance has been weak, and the legal framework for banks has not fully clarified issues relating to ownership, rights, and duties. These problems have been exacerbated by lack of transparency in some banking group structures.

To strengthen the Polish banking system, partial foreign ownership of banks has been permitted. Because of political sensitivity, however, foreign participation has been limited, and thus so too have been the restructuring and modernization of Poland's banks. Despite public reluctance, foreign participation in banking will increase in the coming years and, through greater competition, probably will induce significant consolidation in the sector. The supervision of banking in Poland (by the General Inspectorate of Banking Supervision) earns favorable reports. However, ensuring continued success will require a legal framework for supervision of consolidated entities. Tellingly, a recent bank failure (Bank Staropolski) points to the need for greater transparency and for further measures to allow effective supervision. Neverthetheless, most current prudential regulations are in line with EU directives, and the rest are moving toward convergence. The Banking Act of 1997 outlines the regulatory framework for bank operations, including audits and disclosure requirements. Its roots lie in the Act on Accounting of 1994, which established a basic accounting framework for companies in accordance with EU directives. Poland's central bank is charged (by the National Bank of Poland Act) with establishing detailed regulations for banks.

Financial Markets

Poland's equities market is the largest in Central Europe. In 2000 there were 200 large and 26 small entities listed on the national exchange, the Warsaw Stock Exchange. The capitalization of the equities market in 2000, at 25 percent of GDP, was smaller than banking sector assets, reflecting its relative immaturity. The market is regulated by the Law on Public Trading and Securities of 1997.

The asset-backed securities debt market remains at an early stage of development, in part because of uncertainties in the legal framework. By early 2003, however, the growth of mortgage lending and mutual funds appeared to herald a much stronger and more diversified financial market.[5] A corporate bond market exists, but provisions in the corporate bond law mandating bank representation for debt issues have limited the use of debt because of banks' unwillingness to take on the risk. Until recently the law permitted the issuance of only specific-purpose debt. However, a new bond act in effect since August 2000 has liberalized bond issues, and the use of bonds is growing.

As in many transitioning and emerging market economies, in Poland the concept of a bond market for municipal obligations developed on the margins, following the earlier efforts to establish markets for corporate securities and national government obligations. With no history of local government bond issues since the 1930s, Poland had little practical experience on which to build. Nonetheless, technical assistance provided a major boost,[6] and by the mid-1990s commercial interest had emerged among both domestic and foreign banking and investment firms (Fitch Ratings 2000). With the aid of technical assistance, the Polish Securities Commission designed registration requirements and disclosure guidelines for local government securities that were adopted by the Parliament in 1998. However, the requirements for listing securities on the exchange proved to be too rigorous and expensive for municipal issuers, and few have opted to pursue such a listing.

Subnational Borrowing Experience

Transition and decentralization have opened new financing options. Western-style public finance instruments began to emerge in the early 1990s, including a more decentralized tax regime and government financial institutions oriented toward assisting localities. Among the most important of these institutions was ECOBANK, which provided funds for local governments through the Environment Fund.

The relative stability in fiscal relations between the central and local governments in the early 1990s prompted the introduction of legislation in 1994 allowing local governments to access domestic capital markets. Initially the national government appeared to be willing to provide guarantees for borrowing by local governments as long as their debt service did not exceed 15 percent of their revenue and they pledged appropriate fiscal transfers as collateral. However, this provision was never activated, and only a handful of gminas ever applied (World Bank 2001c). Nevertheless, several large cities tried to enter the bond markets, both domestic and international, in the mid-1990s. Meanwhile, bank loans (often in the form of privately placed bond issues) were a major source of funding.

Trends in Subnational Borrowing

In 1990–95 the local government sector in Poland grew rapidly as devolution took hold. The Law on Municipal Finance of 1993 gave localities a general right to issue securities, though it restricted issuance by limiting debt service to 15 percent of regular revenues on issues and loans not secured by real property. In 1995 municipal issuance was further regulated by the Law on Bonds. A subnational credit market began to emerge with the privatization of commercial bank lending to larger cities, and a few pioneering bond issues began to appear (see Bitner 1998). These early bond issues had short maturities (two to three years) and high interest rates (more than 20 percent), reflecting the inflation rates of the period. Despite the active interest in selling bonds, the provision of credit was dominated by direct bank lending and by concessionary financing from state and voivodship environmental lending programs.

More recently, maturities have been extended to up to 15 years. Krakow, Lodz, and 25 other large and medium-size cities have sold bond issues, and five Polish cities carry international bond ratings. The slowdown in the economy and in the international credit markets has curbed the growth in the bond market, but total municipal credit, estimated at only 0.6 percent of GDP in 1996, has expanded to around 2 percent of GDP.[7] Credit appears to have grown quite rapidly since 1998, in part because of the new responsibilities putting pressure on local budgets.

Municipal interest in bonds has also been steadily increasing. Although commercial bank credits and loans accounted for 75 percent of municipal debt in 2001, that year saw a marked jump in municipal bond issues. The value of the subnational bond market increased from around PLN 860 million in 2000 to PLN 1,463 million in 2001, and the number of issuers from 89 to 140, with PKO Bank Polski the largest lead manager of municipal bond issues.[8] According to the Central European Rating Agency, gminas have become increasingly interested in issuing debt. At the end of 2001 some 35 gminas (including Czestochowa, Lublin, Poznan, Rzeszow, Szczecin, Walbrzych, and Wroclaw), 5 powiats, and 2 voivodships planned to issue bonds. The growing interest reflected the cost advantage of selling bonds over taking direct loans.[9] Nonetheless, bond issues still make up a relatively small share of total municipal debt (figure 30.2).

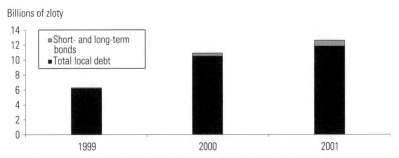

Note: The credit values reported by the International Monetary Fund are lower than those reported by Fitch Polska and cited in the text. But the data from both sources illustrate the positive trend in bond financing.
Source: International Monetary Fund, Government Finance Statistics database.

Figure 30.2. Local Government Debt by Source, Poland, 1999–2001

Regulatory Limits

The early efforts in Poland to develop a legal and regulatory framework for bond issuance, with the Polish Securities Commission attempting to devise securities regulations and disclosure guidelines suited to the issuance of subnational debt, helped lay the foundations for market development. Many of the requirements, however, proved to be burdensome for localities (Bitner 1998, p. 80). A 1999 law prohibited issuance of debt denominated in foreign currencies, even though Krakow had successfully issued a bond denominated in deutsche marks in 1998 (Standard & Poor's 1999).

The Public Finance Law of 1998, reflecting a desire to meet EU standards, clearly limits general government debt to an absolute maximum of 60 percent of GDP. It limits local government debt to 60 percent of total revenue and local debt service to 15 percent of total revenue. The law includes triggers to avoid exceeding the 60 percent target at the national level. If combined government debt reaches 50 percent of GDP, local governments are prohibited from approving budgets with a higher deficit-to-revenue ratio the following year. If debt reaches 55 percent of GDP, the state budget cannot result in an increase in state debt, local governments must reduce their deficits, and the limit on local governments' annual debt service drops from 15 percent of revenue to 12 percent. If debt rises to 60 percent of GDP, there can be no deficits and borrowing stops. In addition, the government must create a strategy for reducing the debt and present that strategy to the Parliament.[10] As the city case studies in this chapter illustrate, this fiscal prudence has been passed on to local governments. In some cases a city will impose even stricter controls on its borrowing than those set forth by the central government.

Outlook for Subnational Borrowing

As Poland's cities have seen their expenditure responsibilities increase, their own-source revenues have not kept up. Cities face increasingly pressing infrastructure needs, but they have little revenue flexibility. Indeed, many Polish cities have already reached the centrally imposed limit on local rates and thus have no further revenue flexibility in local taxes and fees. Future debt financing needs are evident. The major credit rating agencies now rate at least half a dozen Polish cities (despite the present ban on foreign borrowing), clearly viewing the upcoming EU accession as a promising development for Polish city finances. EU assistance will ease the financial burden on local governments by providing targeted funds that should reduce dependence on the center. This increase in own-source revenues also should also expand future borrowing capacity.

With the economy sputtering in the past couple of years, tax receipts have fallen and economic woes have added to the fiscal burden of Polish cities. For urban powiats this increased burden has been exacerbated by new education responsibilities that have not been met with matching support from the central government. Cities' flexibility in operational expenditures has been particularly weakened because salaries now make up a large part of total spending (as much as 60 percent in some cases). The large wage component of the budget makes it more difficult to vary expenditures because employees (who also vote) object to being laid off or given lower wages. In contrast, a road, bridge, or sewer that goes years without repair is less noisy about the neglect. Nonetheless, for the most part Polish cities have been able to manage the new responsibilities. Indeed, the well-designed and well-functioning regulatory framework for subnational borrowing and the conservative fiscal practices of local officials minimize the dangers of subnational overborrowing and fiscal collapse. Credit ratings, as monitors of financial health, provide added incentives for fiscal discipline.

Polish cities tend to have fairly narrow operating surpluses because of their relatively large current spending needs, such as in education and social services. In the Czech Republic and Hungary, where capital outlays are more prominent in local budgets, cities tend to have larger operating margins. For Polish cities the less capital-intensive nature of their operations means that debt service will make up a smaller share of their annual budgets. The large demands of current expenditures on their budgets probably mean that, in time, Polish localities may find it more attractive to borrow as a means of financing capital improvements.

Key Definitions

The limits imposed on local deficits mean that Poland's regulatory scheme for local governments has had to contend with the question of what an appropriate measure of a deficit is at the local level. This definition is important in formulating regulations.

Public budgeting usually makes a distinction between recurring (current) and nonrecurring revenues and expenditures. Current revenues and expenditures are perceived as growing smoothly and changing fairly slowly. In contrast, capital expenses are more volatile and cyclical because of elections, changes in mandates, and episodic needs for replacement (because of deterioration, emergencies, or the demands of growth). Capital spending can also vary from year to year because of changes in the economic environment, such as in inflation, economic growth, and interest rates. Capital outlays can be postponed, one reason that capital spending is often insufficient during periods of sustained fiscal pressure.

Capital spending can change dramatically from one year to the next. For example, a small town that replaces its investments only at intervals of several years may decide to build a new town hall. This decision will lead to a big jump in its total spending and in its debt and debt service. How should the financial health of the town—its margin of safety in financing the new expenditure—be judged?

The surplus from current operations is often seen as the best way to assess the financial capacity of a local authority to absorb extra expenditures without putting great stress on its revenues or existing spending. The operating surplus (current operating revenue minus operating expenditure) represents the margin of safety for the following outlays:

- Repayment of existing debt (and the future debt to be incurred).
- Emergency increases in spending (rebuilding after a natural disaster, for example).
- Financing of current capital needs (since it provides resources for financing facilities that need not be financed by debt).
- A carryover of funds to the next fiscal period (if sufficient, a source of funding that may permit revenues to be reduced).

Capital spending is usually financed by a mix of current-period revenue financing, grants, and borrowing from various sources. Financing investments from current-period revenues relies on there being funds left over after operations that are not used for paying debt service on outstanding debt. This is called the *net* surplus from operations and *after* the payment of debt service. The *gross* surplus—the amount left over after operations and *before* the subtraction of any payment for debt service (both principal and interest)—is called *funds available* for debt service.[11]

Figure 30.3 shows how the surplus (both gross and net) from a government's current operations is derived from the flow of revenues and expenditures. The gross surplus after current operation expenditures are met can be used to pay capital account costs (that is, loan redemption and investment outlays) or it can be saved by placing it in reserves.[12] The net surplus from operations, calculated after payment of debt service, is available to meet investment outlays (along with borrowing proceeds and targeted funds) or can be placed in reserves (which may be used to fund investment outlays or to cover any future operating deficits). Nomenclatures can vary.

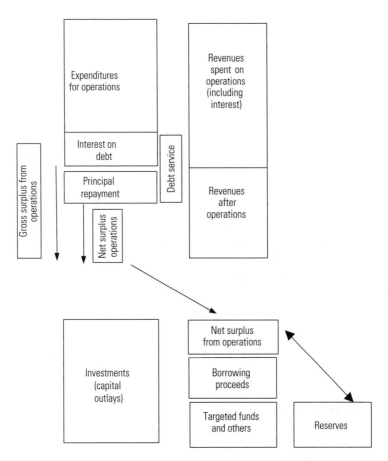

Figure 30.3. Concepts of Surplus from Operating Revenues as a Source of Funds for Capital Spending

For example, the term *gross fiscal balance* refers to all revenues (both recurring and nonrecurring) after the subtraction of all expenditures (both current and investment). Thus a city that is borrowing or selling off assets may run a significant negative fiscal balance but enjoy a substantial net operating surplus. Over time, however, current revenues need to grow to pay the debt service on the funds that are borrowed as well as to preserve the margins of safety described above.

Polish cities have traditionally financed investment outlays through central government grants or from current surpluses. Until recently there was little borrowing for infrastructure investments except by a few of the larger local governments or from specialized central government agencies and regional banks, in part because of the inherent conservatism of local authorities. The surge of interest in borrowing in domestic and foreign bond markets in the mid-1990s has been moderated by the recent recessionary conditions and by the restrictions on local government borrowing arising from the Maastricht protocols and the EU accession requirements. The European treaty (article 104, revised) requires a limit on the public deficit and the outstanding public sector debt.[13] A 1993 protocol defines the two quantitative limits as a maximum of 3 percent for the ratio of the deficit to GDP and a maximum of 60 percent for the ratio of debt outstanding to GDP. The protocol was written with the aim of achieving convergence in the fiscal policies of the countries entering the European Monetary Union.

These restrictions on debt do not distinguish between borrowing for capital needs and borrowing to fund operating deficits. Thus, any capital outlays by a local government that exceed its net operating surplus and capital grants (that is, any capital spending supported by net borrowing) count as increasing overall government debt and press against the accession limits. This has had a dampening effect on local governments' planning for the use of debt. Also contributing to the reduced use of debt is the prospect of the EU supplying capital funds, which will mean lower costs if local authorities can defer needs until these funds are available.

Local Financial Reporting

The Ministry of Finance and the Polish statistical agency both have requirements for local financial reporting and regularly collect data from gminas. The data collected by the Ministry of Finance are used primarily for tallying local government debt. They are timely, of good quality, and capable of supporting much more analysis of financial performance and condition. However, no entity in the central government is charged with performing that analysis, and the information, still treated as confidential under archaic rules, is not disseminated in a disaggregated form. So, as sometimes happens in developing markets, the information needed may be gathered, but lack of funds and good policy may preclude its being fully used (Petersen and Chomentowski 1999).

Five Cities, Five Experiences with Municipal Debt

Most of the five Polish cities with international bond ratings are struggling to keep operating costs in line with operating revenues. Overall, however, the experience in these five case studies is positive. Each case study high-lights a different aspect of debt financing as practiced by Polish cities. They are based largely on 2002 reports by credit rating agencies, which perform ongoing review and analysis of outstanding debt for the local governments that are rated.[14]

Wroclaw: The Challenge of Managing a Fiscal Deficit

Wroclaw has a well-diversified economy and is one of Poland's wealthiest cities (in terms of average worker salary). As an urban powiat, it has access to own-source revenues. In 2001 these accounted for 55 percent of operat-ing revenue. Wroclaw still relies on central government funding, which provided 41 percent of operating revenue in 2001 (figure 30.4). Wroclaw's revenue structure is fairly similar to that of many urban powiats. Moreover, like many other Polish cities, it has reached the upper limit on its local tax rate. Remaining sources of revenue flexibility include asset sales and self-supporting tariff entities such as housing rental and public transport.

Investment in infrastructure is a key part of Wroclaw's development strategy. With little revenue raising flexibility and an important capital spending program (equal to 15 percent of total revenue in 2001 and set to

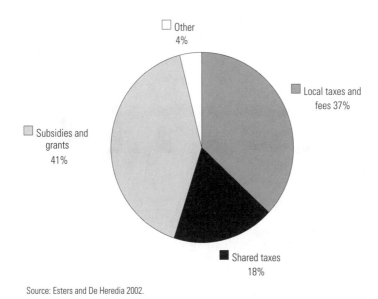

Source: Esters and De Heredia 2002.

Figure 30.4. Structure of Operating Revenue, Wroclaw, 2001

expand with investments in road building and waste management), the city has little choice but to use debt financing. The city has been running a growing gross budget deficit (that is, the fiscal balance, which includes all spending, including capital outlays financed by borrowing and asset sales) and assuming progressively more debt (figure 30.5).

Despite its growth, the debt burden is considered relatively moderate. At 38 percent of operating revenue in 2001, debt outstanding was well below the 60 percent statutory limit. After a projected increase in debt outstanding to 56 percent of operating revenue in 2002, the city expects much slower growth in the following years (with debt projected to reach 58 percent at the start of 2006). Even with the 60 percent limit on the ratio of debt to operating revenue, the city may allow the ratio to rise to 70 percent of operating revenue as long as capital revenue remains in line with projected averages. Consistent with the increase in debt, a negative gross fiscal balance is expected to persist, but projections show a progressive decline based on an ambitious goal to cut operating spending.

Interest payments on the debt were expected to amount to 3 percent of operating revenue in 2002, and total debt service to 9.3 percent. As the

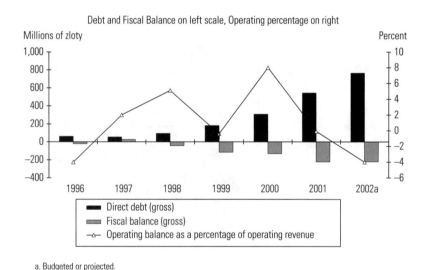

a. Budgeted or projected.
Source: Esters and De Heredia 2002.

Figure 30.5. Budget and Debt, Wroclaw, 1996–2002

debt burden has increased, so too has the share of expenditures devoted to debt service. However, because the city is expected to maintain prudent fiscal management and to control spending, the growth in debt has not raised red flags. Even so, creditors and credit rating agencies will closely monitor the city's future fiscal behavior.

Lodz: Budget Pressures and the Use of Loan Financing

Wroclaw's basic story of cyclical budgetary performance and a growing debt burden is equally applicable to Lodz and, indeed, to most Polish cities (figure 30.6). Lodz is plagued by a higher than average unemployment rate that strains social spending and by a concentration of labor in manufacturing. Because of these factors, its revenues and expenditures are more sensitive to poor economic conditions than are those of a diverse economy such as Wroclaw's.

Lodz faces an expenditure structure similar to that of many urban powiats, with education and social welfare typically around 40 to 60 percent of expenditure (figure 30.7). As noted, the expansion of municipal responsibilities in 1999 widened the gap that municipalities claim already existed between revenues and expenditures. Education responsibilities proved especially burdensome in 2000, when new legislation raised teachers' salaries. Lodz financed the resulting cash shortfall with debt. The flexibility of education and social welfare spending is clearly very limited, and Lodz and many other Polish cities also contend with this low flexibility in meeting pressing infrastructure needs.

Lodz has a debt burden far smaller than that of many of its peers, with projections putting it at 27 percent of operating revenue at the end of 2002 (figure 30.8). However, the debt burden is likely to increase with the city's ambitious infrastructure improvement program. The debt service burden is also modest (6 percent of operating revenue in 2002), in part because a large share of the city's loans come from national or voivodship environmental funds that have fixed interest rates below the rate of inflation. Some of the other loans are with foreign banks and have floating interest rates, and a significant 29 percent of loans are denominated in euros and are not hedged.

Despite these risk factors (and those endemic to local governments in Poland), the expectation is that the city will exercise prudent budget management and not expose itself to unsupportable debt. In the short term it has the capacity to make up shortfalls with increased debt. More important, the city has the budgetary means to freeze spending if needed, al-

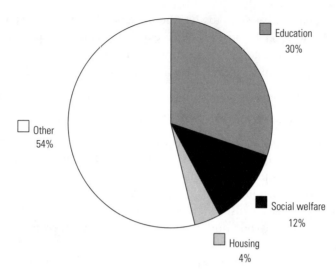

Source: De Heredia and Esters 2002a.

Figure 30.6. Structure of Operating Expenditure, Lodz, 2001

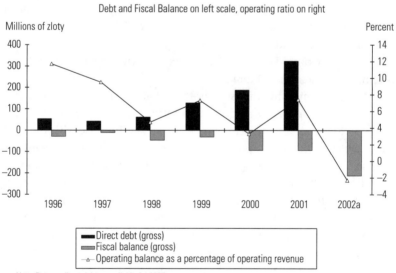

Note: Data on direct debt unavailable for 2002.
a. Budgeted or projected.
Source: De Heredia and Esters 2002a.

Figure 30.7. Budget and Debt, Lodz, 1996–2002

Percentage of operating revenue

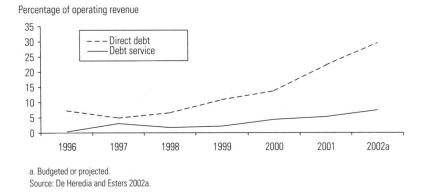

a. Budgeted or projected.
Source: De Heredia and Esters 2002a.

Figure 30.8. Debt Burden as a Share of Operating Revenue, Lodz, 1996–2002

though it will have to make structural changes to its budget to avoid unsustainable debt in the long term. The recent deterioration in its fiscal balance, together with its undiversified economy and higher than average unemployment rate, has earned the city a lower rating (BBB– from Standard & Poor's) than that of many of its peers in Poland.

Szczecin: A Move Away from Commercial Bank Credit

Szczecin is one of Poland's most developed cities. Located close to the border with Germany, it has good transport links with Western Europe that have encouraged substantial foreign investment. However, the Zachodniopomorskie voivodship of which it is a part is relatively rural and underdeveloped and has not attracted comparable attention from foreign investors.

The Szczecin city budget has been well managed, with annual operating balances at a comfortable margin until the projected deficit in 2002 (figure 30.9). Even the projected deficit in 2002 was expected to be alleviated by the sale of an asset. Though the city can similarly cover future deficits and thereby mitigate future debt pressures, it will need to control spending, particularly investment spending, to sustain the budget balance.

Szczecin's debt has been growing relatively rapidly in the past few years (figure 30.10). The rise after 1999 reflects the increasing demands imposed on the city budget by the creation of urban powiats and the new intergovernmental arrangements. Even so, Szczecin's debt has grown more slowly than that of other Polish cities; debt outstanding, projected to be 26 per-

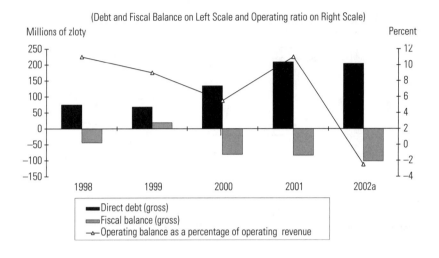

(Debt and Fiscal Balance on Left Scale and Operating ratio on Right Scale)

■ Direct debt (gross)
■ Fiscal balance (gross)
–△– Operating balance as a percentage of operating revenue

Note: Data for the operating balance as a percentage of operating revenue are approximate.
a. Budgeted or projected.
Source: De Heredia and Esters 2002b.

Figure 30.9. Budget Balance and Debt, Szczecin, 1998–2002

cent of operating revenue in 2002, is still small. Debt service costs are similarly modest, at 4.4 percent of operating revenue in 2001. Because of the city's continuing need for improvements in infrastructure, debt is expected to continue to rise in the medium term.

In 2001 Szczecin launched three bond issues representing 29 percent of the city's outstanding debt. In discussing the bond issues, the city president reported that the debt strategy was to move away from commercial credit and toward bonds. Some PLN 60 million worth of financing was issued. For the first issue—PLN 30 million, 10-year, fixed rate bonds—four offers from banks were considered. A consortium consisting of Bank Przemyslowo-Handlowy and Bankgesellschaft Berlin was chosen as issue administrator. For the second and third issues (8- and 9-year bonds with variable interest, amounting to PLN 15 million each), which attracted interest from seven banks and six banks, respectively, PKO Bank Polski was chosen as issue administrator.[15]

Despite the city's recent use of bonds for debt financing, bank loans still accounted for 70 percent of its outstanding debt in 2001. The rest of the financing takes the form of preferential loans. Some 15 percent of Szczecin's

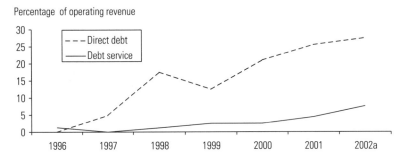

Percentage of operating revenue

Note: Data are estimates.
a. Budgeted or projected.
Source: De Heredia and Esters 2002b.

Figure 30.10. Debt and Debt Service as a Share of Operating Revenue, Szczecin, 1996–2002

debt is fixed rate, and its floating rate debt is linked to Polish treasury bills. More than a quarter of the debt is denominated in foreign currency (euros).

Even with the amount of debt expected to increase, Szczecin's stable financial situation is expected to endure, earning the city a BBB/stable rating from Standard & Poor's. According to the rating agency, an important reason for this credit rating, besides the small debt burden and the operating surpluses, is that Szczecin's fiscal managers have acted prudently and are expected to continue to do so.

Krakow: Foreign Bond Issuance and Municipal Companies

Krakow's position as one of the most important cities in Poland is reflected in its sovereign-level credit rating. With a diverse and wealthy economy and a high level of international investment, the city has been riding out the recent budget squeeze surprisingly well (figure 30.11). In 2002, however, it faced large budget deficits and increasingly limited financial flexibility. Nonetheless, a history of prudent fiscal management suggested that the city would be able to cut its costs, meet its budget targets, and contain the growth of debt.

The city was an early innovator in municipal credit. In 1997 it floated a bond issue of PLN 15 million, sold to local banks after competitive bidding.[16] In 1998 the city issued Poland's first municipal bond in the foreign market, with a value of 66 million deutsche marks. A two-year floating rate note, the issue was used to finance the city's rapid tramway system. Despite the success of this foreign bond issue, in 1999 the central government

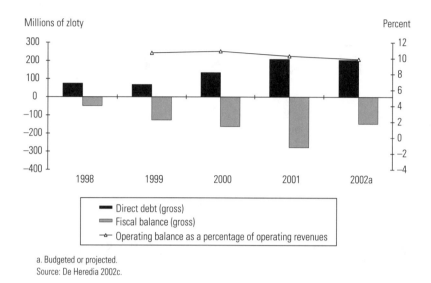

a. Budgeted or projected.
Source: De Heredia 2002c.

Figure 30.11. Budget and Debt, Krakow, 1998–2002

banned such issues. The tramway project was expected to be completed by 2002 but was delayed by a related project; the expected completion date is now 2004. By improving transport in the city, the project is expected to attract more foreign investment.

Krakow owns several companies that provide public services—a transport company, an electricity utility, and a water and sewerage utility. Only the transport company is unprofitable, largely because the city government keeps transport tariffs low, transferring budgetary funds to the company to make up the shortfall. Improvements to Krakow's sewerage infrastructure will be financed in large part with European pre-accession funds, which will cover 70 percent of the investment needs. The rest of the financing will come primarily from soft loans through domestic environmental protection funds. While the public service companies will incur more debt, most will be self-supporting. The loss-making transport company has no debt.

Poznan: Strict Borrowing Controls

Poznan is the second most important banking center in Poland. The basic story told for the other cities—good fiscal management, rising debt, and a falling operating surplus—is equally applicable to its case.

Poznan's credit experience has an interesting regulatory side. The city has enacted tougher limits on borrowing than those required by national law. Outstanding debt cannot exceed 30 percent of year-end revenue, and debt service cannot exceed 10 percent of revenue. The city intends to conform to these debt limits until 2005. The other interesting feature of Poznan's debt experience is that its debt consists entirely of domestic bank loans with floating interest rates. This means that it has no currency risk but is exposed to domestic interest rate risk. Among the city's existing capital sources, all of its self-supporting municipal companies have incurred debt. As sole owner, the city effectively acts as the guarantor of the debt, adding to its risk burden.

Notes

1. For example, the farmers' social security plan is noncontributory for farm owners and accounts for $4 billion a year in subsidies. With a ratio of workers to nonworkers of 51 percent, Poland has the lowest employment ratio of any OECD country (Reed 2003).

2. This section draws on Barbone and Hicks (1995) and Standard & Poor's (1999).

3. According to Moody's ratings reports from 2002, the Ministry of Finance was considering replacing the gmina property tax with a value-added tax, which would significantly increase local revenues.

4. This section draws on Fitch Ratings (2000).

5. Polish mutual fund assets doubled between 2001 and 2002 as consumers, responding to the low interest rate environment and changes in taxation, shifted from savings deposits to the higher-yielding funds (Spiro 2003).

6. Poland has received substantial technical assistance on municipal bonds, with early efforts centered on the Municipal Development Account, sited in the Ministry of Finance. Technical and financial assistance from the U.S. Agency for International Development and the U.K. Phare fund aided the effort, which involved both local governments and the domestic banking and finance sectors (Bitner 1998, pp. 79–80).

7. Based on the International Monetary Fund's Government Finance Statistics database and the World Bank's Global Development Finance and World Development Indicators databases.

8. Data are drawn from Fitch Polska reports.

9. Data are drawn from Fitch Polska reports.

10. A major difficulty is that these limits are defined using a cash basis and a global concept of deficit, making no distinction between borrowing for operating deficits and that for capital outlays. See Petersen and Chomentowski (1999, p. 16).

11. There are different conventions in calculating the net surplus from operations. Normally in a cash-based system the interest component of debt service is not included in the operating costs (as in the formal full accrual model), and the net operating surplus (minus interest costs) is treated as "funds available" for debt service. Debt service coverage is often calculated as the ratio of these "funds available" to annual debt service. In addition, convention subtracts nonrecurring revenues from operating revenues, such as receipts from asset sales or restricted or one-time grants.

12. The term *investment* is typically used to identify public capital expenditures in Europe. In the United States the expression is usually *capital outlay*. They mean the same thing.

13. Council of the European Community Regulation 3605/93 of 22 November 1993.

14. All 2002 figures cited are budgeted or projected estimates. These studies are based in part on rating analyses by Standard & Poor's.

15. From an interview with Edmund Runowicz, the president of Szczecin [http://www.regional-business.com.pl/nr4_47/czas_gb.html].

16. The bond award was very competitive. Local banks, intent on keeping the city's business, bid aggressively for the small bond issue, which ended up carrying a variable interest rate based in and with no markup over the rate on the government's 52-week treasury bills.

Chapter 31

Eastern and Central Europe
Russian Federation

Survivors face the consequences of early excesses and crises,
and display newfound discipline.

Asad Alam, Stepan Titov, John Petersen

Lessons

In the early 1990s regional and local governments in the Russian Federation borrowed heavily and short term to finance their substantial operating deficits. This rush to market occurred in a volatile macroeconomic environment, with heavy spending on subsidies and on the promise of large transfers from the central government. The essentially unregulated financial markets grew rapidly and haphazardly until the crisis of 1998. There also was some foreign borrowing as the cities of Moscow and St. Petersburg, for example, shifted to eurobond borrowings in an attempt to reduce debt service needs. However, this borrowing activity was based on a false premise that the exchange risks could be borne.

The events of 1998 showed the risks of the headlong rush into markets. Foreign borrowing was attractive with the fixed exchange rate, but the devaluation of the ruble in the wake of the

1998 financial crisis dramatically increased debt burdens. Meanwhile, massive defaults on domestic debt occurred among the more remote and dependent Russian regions and cities when they failed to receive anticipated transfers and shared tax receipts from the central government. Moscow and St. Petersburg, however, maintained their debt repayments. The federal government moved to curb local and regional borrowing, but only after recognizing that subnational borrowers were incurring unsustainable risks.

The subnational borrowing experience in Russia points to several lessons. First, foreign borrowing without adequate hedging arrangements in an uncertain macroeconomic environment is very risky and can be extremely costly. Second, centrally enforced prudential rules are needed to discipline borrowing, especially in a newly minted, exceedingly speculative, and unregulated securities market. Third, unfettered market access by subnational borrowers can outpace the development of sound revenue systems and adequate security.

Left largely to their own devices, some subnational borrowers have pulled through the crisis. One of these is St. Petersburg, whose experience shows that an integrated management strategy for domestic and external debt can minimize borrowing costs for the government and keep debt burdens low. It also shows that a debt management strategy must be anchored in a strategy for sharpening the development focus and efficiency of public spending.

For the rest of the Russian subnational sector, which lacks the wealth and sophistication of the major cities and has yet to establish a stable federal-local fiscal framework, the recovery remains slow and arduous.

Borrowing by Russian subnational governments, particularly the city of St. Petersburg, provides a case study of the risks of largely unfettered subnational borrowing in a volatile macroeconomic and political environment. In the early 1990s, facing fiscal imbalances stemming from low and uncertain revenues, a large share of spending on subsidies, and the use of noncash instruments in budget execution, many regional and local governments began to rely heavily on short-term borrowing to finance their spending. As a result, subnational governments, including St. Petersburg, acquired a large share of short-term debt between 1993 and 1996. Regulation of local and regional government debt was erratic and politically influenced, and the regional securities markets springing up were characterized as belonging to the "Wild West." Even in the face of high interest rates, virtually every Russian region and major city was selling bonds in the new and untested markets in a headlong rush to secure cash.

In 1997, as part of a comprehensive plan to improve its financial management, St. Petersburg sought to reduce its debt burden by opting for lower-cost external borrowings from the eurobond market and the European Bank for Reconstruction and Development (EBRD), essentially as a swap for its high-cost domestic borrowings. The city undertook this strategy in an environment of fixed exchange rates. With the 1998 devaluation, however, the city was left with a burden of high-cost external debt. Meanwhile, scores of regional and municipal borrowers, dependent on federal payments that stopped coming, simply defaulted on their domestic debt. Since 1998 St. Petersburg has reduced its debt stock and lowered its borrowing costs through prudent management of its budget and a growing economy that has helped generate greater revenues and budget surpluses. The experience in the Russian Federation has shown the challenges of subnational borrowing in the face of changing rules, market uncertainty, and a volatile macroeconomic environment.

Macroeconomic Context

The Russian Federation, with a population of about 146 million, covers a vast land area almost twice the size of Canada, the next largest country. The federation has 89 subjects—oblasts, republics, krays, autonomous okrugs, and the major cities of Moscow and St. Petersburg. These units vary in description, reflecting differences in the degree of autonomy and the ethnic mix of populations. They form the second tier of government and are referred to generally as regions. (A third tier, the local level of government, is made up of the subdivisions of the regions, municipalities, and districts in urban areas and of the rayons in rural areas.) The regions differ widely in climate, ethnic makeup, population density, natural endowments, and economic base.

Although the administrative system inherited from the former Soviet Union is formally a federation, formal relations between levels of government have been effectively based on a highly centralized, one-party, unitary government. Fiscal federalism has developed since independence, however, with important effects on fiscal management. Early efforts at devolution during the transition proved to be much more form than substance, with fiscal autonomy heavily constrained by central government controls over spending norms and the setting of levels of service, rents, prices, and salaries. Tax collection remained decentralized, but tax-sharing arrangements were established by the central government, subject to negotiation, and nontransparent. A study of the Russian Federation's fiscal system in the mid-1990s indicated that its "features render the system of local governance nontransparent and question the degree of accountability of regional and local governments" (Craig, Norregaard, and Tsibouris 1997, p. 698).

The macroeconomic environment in Russia was also marked by volatility and uncertainty. The Russian government started implementing a series of economic reforms in 1992 to stabilize the economy and spur growth. By 1997 some elements of stabilization were becoming noticeable as annual inflation fell to around 11 percent, the current account balance showed a surplus equivalent to about 0.5 percent of GDP, and GDP growth turned positive for the first time since the beginning of the transition.

Fiscal adjustment, however, lagged during this period. Even with tight monetary policies and a stable exchange rate (used as a nominal anchor during stabilization), the federal budget deficits remained at 7 to 10 percent of GDP in the second half of the 1990s. The governments started to rely heavily on domestic and external borrowing to fill the budget gap and turned increasingly to accumulation of arrears and massive use of barter and noncash offsets. Estimates suggest that these implicit subsidies reached a size of up to 10 percent of GDP (Pinto, Drebenstov, and Morozov 2000). Moreover, as the global slowdown that started in 1997 gathered steam, petroleum prices, a key factor in government revenues, began to drop with the decline in international demand for oil.

The combination of a tight monetary policy, a loose fiscal policy, a fixed exchange rate regime, and excessive public borrowing—all in a climate of intense currency speculation—led to the macroeconomic and financial crisis of August 1998. The national government defaulted on most of its domestic obligations and was forced to abandon the pegged exchange rate regime. The crisis led to a sharp real depreciation of the ruble, a major banking crisis, a subsequent drop in GDP of 4.9 percent, and a rise in inflation to 84 percent.

Since the disastrous events of 1998 the Russian economy has strengthened. Indeed, as petroleum prices have recovered and the devalued ruble has improved the economy's competitive position in world markets, Russia has emerged as one of the world's fastest growing economies. Real GDP, after falling by more than 50 percent in 1991–98, grew by 5.4 percent in 1999, 8.3 percent in 2000, and 5.0 percent in 2001. Four major factors have helped support the renewed growth: the significant real depreciation following the 1998 crisis, the oil and gas price boom that began in the second quarter of 1999, the reduced crowding out of the private sector resulting from the elimination of the government's market borrowings, and the low real prices for domestic energy.

Average inflation declined from a postcrisis peak of 86 percent in 1999 to about 20 percent in 2001. At the same time external liquidity has improved with substantial growth in the current account surplus—which increased from $1 billion (0.3 percent of GDP) in 1998 to $34 billion (11 percent of GDP) in 2001—driven largely by the export windfall resulting from higher international energy prices. This has allowed the accumulation of gross foreign exchange reserves, up from $12 billion in 1998 to about $37 billion by the end of 2001. However, the growth of the surplus has put upward pressure on the real exchange rate. Real appreciation of about 20 percent in 1999–2001 partly offset the gains from the 1998 devaluation.

The fiscal position also has been strengthened by higher tax revenues and expenditure restraint. Federal revenues increased from 13.5 percent of GDP in 1999 to about 18 percent in 2001. During the same period the primary surplus improved from 2.2 percent of GDP to 4.9 percent. An overall budget surplus was achieved for the first time in 2000 at 1.2 percent of GDP and was estimated at 2.4 percent of GDP in 2001. Moreover, all federal budget revenues raised since early 1999 have been in cash. The ratio of public debt to GDP fell sharply—from 138 percent in 1998 to 52 percent in 2001—as a result of strong growth, appreciation of the ruble, the repayment of debt, the erosion of domestic debt by inflation, and a write-off of $10.6 billion in debt under a London Club restructuring agreement.

Greater liquidity and better fiscal management have led to a significant reduction in noncash offsets on payments to budgets and in noncash transactions between enterprises. The share of barter transactions declined from 30 percent of all transactions in 1999 to 22 percent in 2001. There also are signs that noncash execution of subnational budgets declined drastically, from about 50 percent of budget revenue in 1998 to about 6 percent in 2000. However, while extrabudgetary funds and overdue payables to suppliers and the budget have been reduced in real terms, they continue to represent a significant source of vulnerability for the economy. These liabilities amounted to 22.2 percent of GDP in 2000.

The macroeconomic improvements have taken place in the context of an improving system of intergovernmental finance and stronger incentives for regional fiscal management. Legislative and administrative initiatives have sought to move fiscal federalism away from a system based on bargaining and special arrangements to one based on rules. These initiatives include tax code reforms, a new local budget code, uniform rates of tax sharing between the center and regions for all major taxes, clarification of expenditure obligations with some reduction in unfunded mandates, the introduction of competitive intergovernmental transfers, and a general tightening of budgetary discipline at the federal level.

Early Adventures in Subnational Borrowing

One casualty of the 1998 crisis and devaluation was the subnational bond market that had sprung up as part of the "shock" movement toward political devolution and a market-based economy. In the wake of the crisis and the defaults of the federal government, nearly all domestically held municipal bonds plunged into default, ending what had been a wild ride to the credit markets by many subnational borrowers.

The early market had been dominated by regional governments (oblasts), which not only were the larger subnational units but also enjoyed federal tax exemption. Regional governments started issuing bonds in 1992 (despite high inflation), and by 1997 most were using borrowed resources.[1] Several types of bonds quickly emerged, including bonds much like the federal government's treasury bills, or GKOs (short-term zero-coupon notes used primarily to cover operating deficits), housing bonds (essentially used to sell off publicly owned housing), and arbitrage bonds (which allowed governments to borrow and invest proceeds in the high-yielding federal bonds). Much of the borrowing of the era, all of which was short term, was undertaken to cover operating deficits or invest in higher-yielding assets. Little of the borrowing was done to finance capital projects.

The municipal bond market in Russia started up virtually free of any meaningful central regulation, and governments began issuing bonds under a number of laws. The tax-exempt status and what some saw as an implied federal guarantee soon became an issue for the federal authorities. The Ministry of Finance in 1995 attempted to deny tax-exempt status to all subnational bonds but relented for the regions. Requests for tax exemption subsequently were handled on a case-by-case basis.

From the outset it was clear that the fiscal capabilities of subnational borrowers varied enormously. Moscow, a relatively well-off government that ran surpluses, did not borrow until relatively late, and then only sparingly. In contrast, St. Petersburg was an avid issuer that used the proceeds of its borrowing to cover operating deficits.[2] Both cities also borrowed in the international markets in 1996.[3] Meanwhile, smaller regions and cities sold a rapidly swelling volume of bonds on the many regional stock exchanges that had sprung up overnight. In 1992–95 the Russian Ministry of Finance registered some 43 subnational bond issues. In 1997 alone some 309 issues were registered for local exchanges and another 3 were destined for the euro markets, totaling more than $5 billion in value (Tchepournykh and Simonsen 1999). These bonds, usually with maturities of a year or less and yielding as much as 95 percent in interest by mid-1998, were seen as entailing significant credit risks. It was a prediction they did not fail to fulfill when the August 1998 crisis and devaluation struck.[4]

The ensuing collapse of the subnational bond market was by no means unexpected. The World Bank, noting the lack of effective central oversight, had cautioned in a 1996 report:

> The legal framework for subnational borrowing in Russia is more permissive than in many countries. Although significant problems have not yet arisen, there is a real possibility of uncontrolled borrowing for the wrong purposes, including financing operating deficits, propping up local enterprises, and investing in activities best left to the private sector (World Bank 1996, p. 42).

There was a precipitous slide in bond ratings, reflecting the crash in the credit of subnational borrowers (table 31.1). Only a few subnational borrowers had received international credit ratings before the crisis of 1998. In late 1997 all Standard & Poor's ratings of subnational governments were speculative (in the BB category) but not overwhelmingly so. How the cities and regions responded to the financial crisis had an effect on their ratings.

Moscow and St. Petersburg were put on the "pending default" list (CCC category) at the outset of the crisis, but they managed to pull out of the nose-

Table 31.1. Standard & Poor's Credit Ratings of Subnational Borrowers, Russian Federation, 1997–2002

Borrower	December 1997	June 1998	August 1998	December 1999	January 2002
Moscow	NR	BB–	B–	CCC–	B+
St. Petersburg	BB–	B+	B–	CCC–	B+
Novograd	BB–	B+	CCC	SD	NR
Samara	BB–	B+	CCC	SD	B
Sverdlovsk	BB–	B+	CCC–	CCC	CCC+
Tartarstan	BB–	B+	CCC–	SD	CCC+
Yamal-Nenets	NR	BB–	B–	CCC–	CCC+
Irkutsk	NR	B+	CCC	CCC–	CCC+

Note: The table shows the foreign currency ratings for approximately the dates shown. NR indicates that the issuer is not rated. BB is a speculative grade just below the lowest investment grade (BBB). B is highly speculative, and CCC indicates pending default. Plus and minus signs indicate where the credit falls within each rating band. SD is selective default. Source: Standard & Poor's, various issues.

dive by continuing to honor their contracted debts. Other Russian cities and provinces went into selective default (SD), but one of these (Samara) later managed to restore its rating. Overall, however, the early batch of credit ratings had clearly overvalued the creditworthiness of Russian subnational borrowers. Only a few could muster internationally acceptable credits, and in early 2002 none was considered investment grade, though Moscow and St. Petersburg managed to keep their ratings above pending or selective default.

After the municipal and regional defaults of 1998, Russia disallowed subnational borrowing from abroad except in limited circumstances for refinancing outstanding debt. Debt service is generally limited to 15 percent of operating expenditures, and subnational borrowing is restricted to capital investment. In addition, municipally owned banks are prohibited, and the federal government does not guarantee local bonds (World Bank 2001). Russian localities continue to rely heavily on shared taxes (for about 50 percent of revenue) and transfer payments (30 percent), with own-source revenues accounting for around 20 percent of revenue. The subnational governments in the more rural and remote regions of the federation depend even more on central transfers and shared taxes.

A Survivor: The City of St. Petersburg

St. Petersburg was one of the few survivors of the carnage in the subnational bond market. It is the second largest metropolis in Russia (after Moscow), with a population of about 4.6 million. St. Petersburg and Moscow are the only two Russian cities that are also subjects of the federation, giving them the status of regions. As a result of this status, St. Petersburg has some political and fiscal characteristics that differ from those of other municipalities. The city has more powers to enact legislation on economic issues and budgets than do third-tier municipalities. It also enjoys greater fiscal autonomy, since it is only dependent on changes in federal tax legislation (unlike the municipalities that are subject to regional laws) and is allowed to levy higher tax rates than other municipalities.

The center of gravity for all of northwest Russia, St. Petersburg is considered the unofficial second capital of the country. It is one of the most advanced regions of Russia, accounting for about 3.2 percent of the country's GDP and 2.7 percent of its industrial production. In 2000 St. Petersburg's gross regional product amounted to 232.8 billion rubles (Rb), about $8 billion. The economy's strengths lie in its food processing industry; high-technology machine building and shipbuilding; and transport, financial, and telecommunications services. St. Petersburg is a global tourist attraction and an important center of education, health care, and fundamental research. It is also the second largest financial center in Russia (after Moscow), and its stock exchange is the leading subnational bond market.

During the past decade of transition to a market economy, the city experienced a dramatic decline in industrial output. The collapse in output was more pronounced than that for the Russian economy as a whole, because the city does not have developed oil, gas, and metallurgy sectors, which helped offset the fall in output in other parts of the country.[5] However, the city's growth pattern mirrored that of Russia—with growth declining until 1996, slightly positive in 1997, dropping in 1998, and then recovering in 1999–2001. The city's recovery has been stronger than the national average, with the gross regional product growing by 6.8 percent in 1999 and 10 percent in 2000, thanks to the import substitution effect following the 1998 devaluation. Major engines of economic recovery have been the chemical and petrochemical industry, food processing, and machine building and metal processing. The city's share of the foreign investment in Russia grew from 5.3 percent in 1995 to 11 percent in 2000, when it amounted to $1.14 billion.

The city ran budget deficits until 2000, when a surplus of 4.1 percent of budget revenue allowed it to repurchase part of its eurobonds. Another surplus of about 2.4 percent of budget revenue was expected in 2001. The city made substantial efforts to phase out noncash budget execution, and the noncash share of its own budget revenue fell from 17.4 percent in 1997 to 4.7 percent in 2000. Unlike many other regions, St. Petersburg has no wage arrears in its budget.

Trends in City Borrowing

St. Petersburg started borrowing domestically in 1994 to cover its budget deficit. Its leading creditors during this period were commercial banks, which provided financing through loans and purchases of city government bonds. The city's domestic borrowings increased rapidly, from Rb 212.5 million in 1994 to Rb 3,298.5 million in 1996 (table 31.2). A growing share of the portfolio was in short-term commercial bank loans and short-term municipal bonds (with average maturities of less than five months). These rose to 90 percent of total debt in 1996 (loans were about 30 percent of total debt, and short-term bonds about 60 percent). During this time external borrowing became attractive as a result of the longer maturities provided by foreign loans, the high domestic and low international interest rates, and the low perceived exchange rate risk (due to a fixed exchange rate with the U.S. dollar).

In 1997 the city decided to lengthen the maturity of its debt, diversify its financial risks, and refinance its high-cost short-term domestic commercial bank loans and short-term municipal bonds through a five-year eurobond placement of $300 million. In 1998 the city took out a $100 million credit line from the European Bank for Reconstruction and Development (of which $40 million was drawn in 1998), whose ruble proceeds would also be used to reduce domestic debt. As a result, the share of foreign currency borrowings jumped from 1 percent at the beginning of 1997 to 45 percent at the beginning of 1998 (table 31.3).

Circumstances changed dramatically in 1998 with the unfolding of the Russian financial crisis and the sharp devaluation of the ruble. St. Petersburg had no cover for foreign currency risks (such as through hedging operations or own sources of foreign exchange earnings), and the devaluation caused a sharp increase in the ruble amount of its foreign currency debt and in its debt service expenditures (table 31.4). The city continued to pay its creditors on time and in full, even as many other Russian regions defaulted on their obligations, but the debt service imposed a heavy burden on the city's finances.

Since then, improved public finances have allowed the city to reduce its debt burden and refrain from new borrowing. Both the level and the composition of its debt stock have changed substantially. Foreign debt fell from a peak

Table 31.2. Debt by Type, St. Petersburg, 1994–2001 (millions of rubles)

Type of debt	1994	1995	1996	1997	1998	1999	2000	2001
Domestic debt	212.5	1,275	3,298.5	2,352	1,692.1	1,579.2	3,089.7	5,091.4
Bank loans	109.4	414.0	993.8	71.0	262.2	71.1	0	—
Other loans	78.4	0.4	0.4	0	0	0	0	—
Bank veksels	0	77.0	19.9	0	0	0	0	—
CoF veksels	0	95.0	307.6	79.1	0.2	0.2	0.2	—
Municipal bonds	0	647.4	1,976.4	2,165	1,417.8	1,391.5	2,636.8	—
Other	24.7	41.3	0.4	37.8	11.9	0	0	—
Ruble guarantees	0	0	0	0	0	116.4	452.7	—
Foreign debt	0	0	24.0	1,951.5	7,683.3	13,227.8	9,488.4	6,794.3
Eurobonds	0	0	0	1,776.2	5,521.5	8,016.0	6,117.2	—
Loans from international financial institutions	0	0	0	130.4	2,063.7	2,167	2,398.2	—
Loans	0	0	24.0	44.9	98.1	0	0	—
Currency guarantees	0	0	0	0	3,044.8	973	—	—
Total debt	212.5	1,275.1	3,322.5	4,303.9	9,375.4	14,807.0	12,578.1	11,885.7

— Not available.

Note: Data for 2001 are not broken down by type of debt instrument.

Sources: St. Petersburg Committee of Finance; World Bank staff estimates.

Table 31.3. Structure of Debt, St. Petersburg, 1994–2001 (percentage of total debt)

Type of debt	1994	1995	1996	1997	1998	1999	2000	2001
Domestic debt	100.0	100.0	99.3	54.7	18.0	10.7	24.6	42.3
Bank loans	51.5	32.5	29.9	1.6	2.8	0.5	0	—
Other loans	36.9	0	0	0	0	0	0	—
Bank veksels	0	6.0	0.6	0	0	0	0	—
CoF veksels	0	7.5	9.3	1.8	0	0	0	—
Municipal bonds	0	50.8	59.5	50.3	15.1	9.4	21.0	—
Other	11.6	3.2		0.9	0.1	0	0	—
Ruble guarantees	0	0	0	0	0	0.8	3.6	—
Foreign debt	0	0	0.7	45.3	82.0	89.3	75.4	57.2
Eurobonds	0	0	0	41.3	58.9	54.1	48.6	—
Loans from international financial institutions	0	0	0	3.0	22.0	14.6	19.1	—
Loans	0	0	0.7	1.0	1.0	0	0	—
Currency guarantees	0	0	0	0	0	20.6	7.7	—
Total debt	100.0	100.0	100.0	100.0	100.0	100.0	100.0	100.0

— Not available.
Note: Data for 2001 are not broken down by type of debt instrument.
Source: Table 31.2.

Table 31.4. Debt Indicators, St. Petersburg, 1997–2001
(percent, except where otherwise indicated)

Indicator	Limits set by federal law	1997	1998	1999	2000	2001
Total debt (millions of rubles)		4,303.9	9,375.4	14,807.0	12,578.1	11,885.7
Debt/budget revenue	100	29.15	54.93	56.80	33.46	24.00
Debt service/budget expenditure	15	—	7.8	7.9	8.5	4.1
New borrowings/budget revenue	30	18.02	12.49	12.68	16.72	8.80
Debt/gross regional product		5.68	10.44	9.57	5.40	—
Foreign debt/total debt		45.3	82.0	89.3	75.4	57.2
Short-term debt/total debt		33.35	24.37	13.45	15.50	51.12
Average yield of open market bonds, year-end		33.27	77.12	50.7	30.98	19.65
Average duration of open market bonds (days)		325	168	305	620	796

— Not available.
Sources: St. Petersburg Committee of Finance; AVK Securities and Finance; World Bank staff estimates.

of 89 percent of the total at the beginning of 2000 to only 75.4 percent at the end of that year, with eurobonds accounting for 48.6 percent of the total.

Instruments for Domestic Borrowing. The city has used several instruments for domestic borrowing, including the following:

- *Open market bonds.* Among Russian regions, St. Petersburg is the largest issuer of open market bonds, city bonds of variable maturity that are placed on the open market and traded. Secondary trading is also permitted. The St. Petersburg bond market is among the most liquid in the Russian financial market. Different market and design options are available for trading in open market bonds, including forward contracts, repurchase operations, fixed coupon bonds, and floating coupon bonds. At the end of 2001 the city's outstanding open market bonds totaled Rb 5 billion.
- *Savings bonds.* One- to five-year bonds issued since 1999, savings bonds are targeted to both individual and institutional investors. Effective demand for such bonds has been low. At the end of 2000 the city's outstanding savings bonds amounted to Rb 70 million.
- *Special-purpose bonds.* Introduced in 1999, special-purpose bonds were provided to city enterprises as a means of offsetting their tax arrears

to the city. Holders of such bonds used them to settle two-month arrears due to the city budget for certain taxes.[6] These bonds have not been used since 2001, since all city budget revenue is now raised in cash. At the end of 2000 the city's outstanding special-purpose bonds totaled Rb 102 million.

- *Commercial bank loans.* A significant instrument in the early years, bank loans are now used by the city administration only to support short-term cash management needs.

Instruments for Foreign Borrowing. The city uses three types of instruments for foreign borrowing—commercial bank loans, eurobond issues, and borrowings from international financial institutions.

- *Commercial banks.* Commercial banks were the first source of external borrowing for the city. It borrowed $10 million under a 1995 loan agreement with the German Dresdner Bank, repaying the loan in December 1999. In 2001 the city negotiated a $35.9 million syndicated loan from a consortium of Italian banks, guaranteed by the federal budget, for repairing damage to the subway.
- *Eurobonds.* The eurobonds issued in 1997 make up the largest part of St. Petersburg's foreign currency debt. On 18 June 1997 the city placed its first issue of $300 million, with a maturity of five years and a coupon rate of 9.5 percent—a spread of 312 points over the benchmark U.S. treasury bond. The lead manager for the issue was Salomon Brothers International. With the 1998 financial crisis, the spreads rose to 800 basis points. Recent spreads have been much smaller, at about 300 basis points over the benchmark U.S. bond, but are still close to precrisis levels. In 2000 the city started a buyout of these bonds from its own budget proceeds. At the end of 2001 the outstanding amount was estimated to be about $108 million, due in June 2002.
- *International financial institutions.* The city has received several loans from the European Bank for Reconstruction and Development and the World Bank. The $100 million EBRD loan in 1997, to support the city's creditworthiness enhancement program, financed the redemption of short-term municipal bonds. The loan is only partially disbursed—the city received the first installment ($30 million) in August 1998 and the second ($10 million) in November 1998. This five-year loan carries a floating interest rate.[7] In November 2001 the city

signed an agreement with the bank converting $16 million of the loan into rubles. Borrowings from the World Bank have been for two projects—the Russian Federation's 1995 Housing Project, under which a subloan of $33.5 million was made to the city, and the 1997 City Center Reconstruction Project, involving a loan of $30 million. Disbursements under these loans totaled about $50 million by the end of 2001.

Structure of the St. Petersburg Bond Market. The St. Petersburg bond market involves the following participants:

- *Issuer:* the Committee of Finance of the St. Petersburg administration.
- *General agent:* an authorized financial institution—AVK Securities and Finance—acting as the market on account of, and on behalf of, the issuer.
- *Exchanges:* authorized institutions acting as the trading, registration, and clearing system for the primary and secondary markets and for repayment. There are two exchanges in St. Petersburg—the currency exchange and the stock exchange.
- *Settlement depository:* an authorized institution—the St. Petersburg Settlement Depository Center—carrying out a centralized accounting of operations with bonds and performing depository services.
- *Settlement center:* an authorized credit organization—the St. Petersburg Settlement Center—providing settlement services for bond transactions.
- *Depository deponents:* professional securities firms providing depository services for market participants.
- *Bond dealers:* professional securities market dealers providing services to investors. At the end of 2001 the city had 34 bond dealers, representing most of the biggest banks and financial companies operating in Russia.
- *Investors:* corporate and private clients investing in bonds.

Credit Ratings. The three major international credit rating agencies—Fitch Ratings, Moody's, and Standard & Poor's—rate the city's foreign currency debt. Credit ratings have improved in recent years, reflecting in part the improvement in sovereign ratings (table 31.5). In 1999 St. Petersburg became the first Russian region to receive a local currency rating from Standard & Poor's and Fitch Ratings.

Table 31.5. Credit Ratings, St. Petersburg, 1998–2002

Date	Fitch Ratings		Moody's Investors Service		Standard & Poor's	
	Foreign currency	Local currency	Foreign currency	Local currency	Foreign currency	Local currency
1 January 1998[a]	BB+	NR	B1	NR	BB–	NR
1 January 1999	CCC	NR	Caa1	NR	CCC–	NR
1 January 2000	CCC	CCC	Caa1	NR	CCC	CCC
1 January 2001	CCC+	CCC+	B3	NR	B–	B–
1 January 2002	NR	NR	NR	NR	B+	NR

Note: For an explanation of the ratings and other abbreviations, see table 31.1.
a. First-time rating.
Source: Credit rating agency reports.

Experience with Guarantees. St. Petersburg uses guarantees mostly for loans for commercial investment projects. Before 1997 it used guarantees for funding deferred investment. But since then it has issued them for concrete investment projects with business plans. The city has declared principles for the selection of borrowers: the borrower must have sustainable finance and no tax arrears and must provide 100 percent liquid collateral. In practice, however, the city also provides guarantees to commercially nonviable but socially important projects, such as a hospital and a research institute.

Executed guarantees amounted to Rb 258.6 million (1.5 percent of total expenditure) in 1998, Rb 2,023 million (7.7 percent) in 1999, and Rb 2,027 million (5.7 percent) in 2000. According to the city Committee of Finance, the guarantees issued in these years were concentrated in utilities, transport, construction, and the food industry. Few city-provided guarantees have been called, and the amount of outstanding guarantees has fallen, declining from Rb 3.2 billion (21.3 percent of total city debt) on 1 January 2000 to Rb 1.4 billion (11.3 percent) on 1 January 2001.

Legal Framework for Subnational Borrowing

In the Russian Federation, as in most other transitioning economies with a federal structure, federal legislation sets out the basic principles for debt management by St. Petersburg, limits the volume of new issues, and outlines some qualitative parameters for debt, such as the possible types and purposes of borrowings. The main federal laws that define these rules are the Budget Code of the Russian Federation, the Law on Budget Accounting and Standards, and the Law on Terms of Issue and Turnover of State and Municipal Securities. Uniform standards for debt accounting form a core element of the federal legislation.

The Budget Code of the Russian Federation defines debt obligations as including loan agreements and contracts, government securities, and government guarantee agreements. Before the adoption of the Budget Code in 1999, the government guarantee agreements were not included in the city's debt. The federal legislation requires that the accounting of foreign debt in local currency be carried out at the current exchange rate (the exchange rate at the date of valuation). It also requires that the regional budget law list domestic and foreign borrowings (and guarantees) for the corresponding financial year. All borrowing proceeds and debt repayments are reflected in the budget.

The federal legislation is complemented by the annual St. Petersburg budget law, which establishes the borrowing program for the year and provides information on debt operations for policymakers. The city's budget—along with the federal legislation—establishes constraints on budgetary expenditures:

- The ratio of debt outstanding to revenues (excluding transfers) is limited to 100 percent.
- Debt service expenditures may not exceed 15 percent of total budgetary expenditures.
- The budget deficit may not exceed 15 percent of budget revenues, excluding transfers from the federal budget.
- Borrowing may be used only to finance investment expenditures; current expenditures may not exceed revenues.
- Foreign borrowing is permissible only to refinance maturing external loans.
- The annual budget must specify limits on the amount of budget guarantees outstanding for the year.

These prudential limits are an attempt by the federal government to prevent regional governments from developing large deficits or building up unmanageable debt burdens. Some of these limits, such as those on external borrowing, may limit access to new investment finance and may need to be relaxed as the national debt burden declines. The legal framework for debt management appears to be broadly satisfactory for monitoring purposes and provides for integrated debt management. In time, however, it will need to be strengthened to allow more sophisticated risk management, such as for contingent liabilities arising from financial transactions of city-owned enterprises.

Institutional Framework for Subnational Borrowing

Management of St. Petersburg's debt is centralized in the Committee of Finance, which formulates the debt strategy, provides systemic portfolio analysis and decision support, and handles investor relations and public disclosure. A special unit is responsible for debt management. This debt unit is led by the deputy head of the Committee of Finance, who reports directly to the head of the committee (figure 31.1).

Debt Management Strategy. The city has a medium-term debt management strategy covering all domestic and external debts that it contracts as well as guarantees, also treated as debt. The debt management strategy has evolved with economic circumstances and now includes policy for the long-term development of domestic capital markets and a notion of risk exposure. The current strategy emphasizes:

- Minimizing the cost of financial resources to the city budget through integrated debt management and improvement of the city's credit rating.
- Reducing exposure to foreign currency risk by extending the maturity structure of foreign debt, lowering the cost of foreign borrowing, and reducing the share of foreign currency debt.
- Lessening the burden of domestic borrowings by extending the maturity of domestic bonds and reducing yields.
- Ensuring the effective use of guarantees to promote capital investment.

The debt unit of the Committee of Finance supports the implementation of this strategy through debt analysis and risk assessment. It issues periodic reports and makes them publicly available; it also makes information available on the Committee of Finance Web site. The unit actively manages risk, although its ability to do so is now limited as the repurchase of eurobonds and domestic municipal bonds reduces the share of marketable instruments in St. Petersburg's public and publicly guaranteed debt portfolio. The debt unit uses quantitative benchmarks to measure and limit specific risks and, importantly, consolidates data on external and domestic debt to create a comprehensive view of the public debt portfolio.

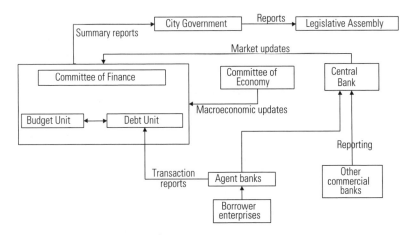

Source: St. Petersburg Committee of Finance.

Figure 31.1. Administrative Structure for Executing the Debt Strategy, St. Petersburg

The city has been successful in recent years in implementing its debt strategy. The amount of debt outstanding has declined (see table 31.2), average borrowing costs have fallen, the maturity structure of loans has been extended, and the portfolio is more diversified. In addition, the debt service burden has lessened. Diversification has been achieved primarily through domestic issues of open market bonds of variable maturity (including long-term coupons of 5 to 30 years) and the issue of new instruments such as savings bonds and special-purpose bonds. The city also repaid one of its foreign currency loans from Dresdner Bank early, in 1999, and repurchased about $190 million in eurobonds. The extension of the maturity structure has been facilitated by the long-term borrowings from the World Bank. The city undertakes medium-term debt sustainability and economic forecasts that are adequate for its current needs.

While the debt strategy has been effectively implemented, it does not capture hidden debt, such as that of unitary enterprises, and this may cause problems with the expected restructuring of these enterprises. Addressing this issue would be a welcome move toward developing an asset and liability management approach to debt.

Information and Disclosure. Disclosure of information on the public debt portfolio of St. Petersburg is complete and timely. The Committee of Finance publishes information on total debt monthly on its Web site and in the local press. It also publishes detailed annual debt management reviews. Market prices of open market bonds are published daily in information bulletins issued by the general agent, on the agent's Web site, on electronic trading sites, in local newspapers, on business Web sites, and by information agencies such as Bloomberg and Reuters. The transparency in disclosure has been a critical element in the city's progress toward creditworthiness.

From Crisis toward Recovery

The unfettered market access of subnational governments contributed to the speculative bubble in Russian financial markets that burst in 1998. Only a few survivors emerged from the wreckage of widespread defaults—most important, the great cities of Moscow and St. Petersburg. The past five years have been a period of disciplined recovery for the survivors of the great crash.

St. Petersburg has followed a strenuous fiscal path. In the early years of the transition the city borrowed short term to finance structural budget deficits in a volatile macroeconomic environment and with heavy subsidy spending. As this strategy became clearly unsustainable, the city shifted to using eurobonds and EBRD borrowings to reduce its debt service needs. As it phased out subsidies and strengthened budget and cash management, the city hoped to improve its liquidity and its creditworthiness. However, while foreign borrowing was attractive with the fixed exchange rate, the devaluation of the ruble in the wake of the 1998 financial crisis strained the city's fiscal accounts. The city maintained its debt repayments in the face of the shock and worked to develop an integrated debt management strategy. At the same time it sought to restructure its expenditures by expanding its investments in human and physical capital.

The experience of St. Petersburg teaches several lessons:

- Foreign borrowing without adequate hedging arrangements in an uncertain macroeconomic environment is very risky.
- Prudential rules for borrowing can help discipline borrowing.
- A diversified borrowing strategy helps mitigate risk.
- An integrated management strategy for domestic and external debt provides the best means to minimize borrowing costs for the government and keep debt burdens low.

- A debt management strategy must be anchored in a strategy for sharpening the development focus and efficiency of public spending.

St. Petersburg and Moscow, borrowers with ample resources and sophistication, have been able to retain access to the markets. However, the fate of other Russian subnational borrowers remains precarious. Future subnational borrowing will depend on a reliable intergovernmental revenue system and stronger own-revenue systems.

Notes

1. It was estimated that these "municipal bonds" represented about 3 to 4 percent of all market debt outstanding in the Russian Federation in 1997.

2. Together, Moscow and St. Petersburg represented 68 percent of the bonds outstanding in 1997.

3. Moscow borrowed $500 million in the euro market and was rated Ba2 by Moody's and BB– by Standard & Poor's. St. Petersburg borrowed $300 million and was rated Ba3 and BB–. The ratings were capped by the Russian Federation's rating of Ba2.

4. Expected transfers backed most of the borrowings from the central government. When these payments failed to materialize, borrowers quickly defaulted on the bonds.

5. In 2000 industrial production in St. Petersburg was about 42 percent of the level in 1991, while that in Russia was about 62 percent of the 1991 level.

6. These taxes were the land tax, profit tax, transport tax, property tax, educational institutions tax, housing and social infrastructure tax, and tax for law enforcement activity.

7. Originally the interest rate varied with changes in the London interbank offered rate (LIBOR) and the spread of Russian Federation bonds. With the 1998 crisis, the debt service on the EBRD loan became onerous, and the terms of interest calculation were renegotiated in 1999. Under the new terms the rate is LIBOR plus a fixed margin, and the margin can be reduced by meeting certain targets for financial management performance and improvements in credit ratings. The new terms have reduced debt service expenditures and the risk of interest rate fluctuations. The loan is being repaid in semiannual installments.

Bibliography

Abrahams, Mark, Francis Conway, Peter Tatian, Zdena Matouskova, and Jiri Mejstrik. 1999. "Union of Towns and Communities. 1996." *Credit Finance Analysis: Handbook for Municipalities in the Czech Republic.* Urban Institute, Washington, D.C., and Urban Research, Prague. http://www.usaid.gov/locations/europe_eurasia/dem_gov/local_gov/pdf_docs/ckcdtmnl.pdf.

Ahmad, Ehtisham, and Katherine Baer. 1997. "Colombia." In Teresa Ter-Minassian, ed., *Fiscal Federalism in Theory and Practice.* Washington, D.C.: International Monetary Fund.

Ahmedabad Municipal Corporation. 1999. "Institutionalization of Bond." [http://www.ahmedabadcity.org/institutionalisation.html].

Aldrete-Sanchez, Horacio. 2000. "Strengthening Mexican Public Finance from the Ground Up." *CreditWeek Municipal* (Standard & Poor's), 17 July, pp. 13–15.

Amieva-Huerta, Juan. 1997. "Mexico." In Teresa Ter-Minassian, ed., *Fiscal Federalism in Theory and Practice.* Washington, D.C.: International Monetary Fund.

Analyst. 2002. "Indian Debt Markets: Bonding with the Times." Institute of Chartered Financial Analysts of India, Hyderabad.

ARD, Government Finance Group. 2001. "Capacity Building in Local Government Unit Finance." TA 3349-PHI. Final Report to the Asian Development Bank, Manila.

Ardiwinata, Rusman. 1997. "Indonesia: Implementing the Municipal Revenue Bond Program." In Priscilla Phelps, ed., "Municipal Bond Market Development in Developing Countries," U. S. Agency for International Development, Washington, D.C.: Finance Working Paper.

Asian Development Bank. 2002. "Key Indicators of Developing Asian and Pacific Countries – Indonesia." [www/adb.org/research/statistics_idc].

Bahl, Roy, and Johannes Linn. 1992. *Urban Public Finance in Developing Countries.* New York: Oxford University Press.

Barbone, Luca, and James F. Hicks. 1995. "Local and Intergovernmental Finances in Poland: An Evolving Agenda." In Richard M. Bird, Robert

D. Ebel, and Christine I. Wallich, eds., *Decentralization of the Socialist State: Intergovernmental Finance in Transition Economies*. Washington, D.C.: World Bank.

Barrientos, Laura, and Yves Lemay. 2001a. "Ratings Action: Aguascalientes, Municipality of." Moody's Investors Service, New York.

———. 2001b. "Ratings Action: Morelos, State of." Moody's Investors Service, New York.

———. 2002a. "Ratings Action: Moody's Assigns Preliminary Aaa.mx National Scale Rating to Municipality of San Pedro Garza Ps. 110 Million Bond Enhanced Transaction." Moody's Investors Service, New York.

———. 2002b. "Summary Opinion: Aguascalientes, Municipality of." Moody's Investors Service, New York.

Berghof, Erik, and Patrick Bolton. 2002. "The Great Divide and Beyond: Financial Architecture in Transition." *Journal of Economic Perspectives* 16 (1).

Bird, Richard M., Robert D. Ebel, Christine I. Walich, and Richard Miller, eds. 1995. *Decentralization of the Socialist State: Intergovernmental Finance and Transition Economies*. Washington, D.C.: World Bank.

Bitner, Michael. 1998. "Poland." In Priscilla Phelps, ed., "Municipal Bond Market Development in Developing Countries." Finance Working Paper. U.S. Agency for International Development, Washington, D.C.

Bogetic, Zeljko. 1997. "Bulgaria." In Teresa Ter-Minassian, ed., *Fiscal Federalism in Theory and Practice*. Washington, D.C.: International Monetary Fund.

Bokros, Lajos, and Jean-Jacques Dethier, eds. 1998. *Public Finance Reform during the Transition, the Experience of Hungary*. Washington, D.C.: World Bank.

Borish, Michael S., Wei Ding, and Michel Noel. 1996. *On the Road to EU Accession: Financial Sector Development in Central Europe*. World Bank Discussion Paper 345. Washington, D.C.

Burke, Shahid, and Guillermo Perry. 1998. *Beyond the Washington Consensus: Institutions Matter*. Washington, D.C.: World Bank.

Chu, Ke-young, and John Norregard. 1997. "Korea." In Teresa Ter-Minassian and J. Craig, eds., *Fiscal Federalism in Theory and Practice*. Washington, D.C.: International Monetary Fund.

Craig, Jon, John Norregaard, and George Tsibouris. 1997. "Russian Federation." In Teresa Ter-Minassian, ed., *Fiscal Federalism in Theory and Practice*. Washington, D.C.: International Monetary Fund.

Darche, Benjamin. 2002 ."Southeast Asia: Lessons Learned from South Korea, Vietnam, Philippines and Indonesia." Subnational Credit Market Project. World Bank, Washington, D.C.

Davey, Kenneth. 1990. *Local Government Reform in Hungary*. Birmingham, U.K.: University of Birmingham, Institute of Local Government Studies.

Davey, Kenneth, and Peteri Gabor. 1998. *Local Government Finances: Options for Reform*. Nagykovacsi, Hungary: Local Government Know-How Fund.

De Heredia Myriam Fernandez. 1999. "Commentary: Poland's Local Government Becomes More Democratic." Standard & Poor's. RatingsDirect. New York.

———. 2002a. "Research: Lodz, City of." Standard & Poor's. RatingsDirect. New York.

———. 2002b. "Research: Szczecin, City of." Standard & Poor's. RatingsDirect. New York.

DeAngelis, Michael, and Robert Dunn. 2002. "Legal and Regulatory Framework for Subnational Government Borrowing." Subnational Credit Market Project. World Bank, Washington, D.C.

DeAngelis, Michael, and R. Fenn Putnam. 2000. "Securitization of Polish Municipal Debt." United States Agency for International Development, Warsaw.

Delhaise, Philippe. 1998. *Asia in Crisis: The Implosion of the Banking and Finance Systems*. Singapore: John Wiley & Sons (Asia).

De Heredia, Myriam Fernandez. 1999. "Commentary: Poland's Local Government Becomes More Democratic." Standard & Poor's, RatingsDirect, New York.

De Heredia, Myriam Fernandez, and Christian Esters. 2002a. "Research: Lodz, City of." Standard & Poor's, RatingsDirect, New York.

———. 2002b. "Research: Szczecin, City of." Standard & Poor's, RatingsDirect, New York.

De Mello, Luis. 2000. "Fiscal Decentralization and Intergovernmental Fiscal Relations: A Cross Country Analysis." *World Development* 28 (2): 365–80.

Dillinger, William. 1994. *Decentralization and Its Implication for Urban Service Delivery*. Washington, D.C.: World Bank.

Dillinger, William, and Steve Webb. 1999. "Decentralization and Fiscal Management in Colombia." World Bank, Latin America and the Caribbean Region, Washington, D.C.

Dillinger, William, Guillermo Perry, and Steve Webb. 2001. "Fiscal Decentralization in Latin America." Mimeo, World Bank, Latin America and the Caribbean Region, Washington, D.C.

Ding, Chengri and Garret Knapp. 2003. "Urban Land Policy Reform in China." *Land Lines* 15 (2). Lincoln Institute of Land Policy, Boston.

Duff & Phelps Credit Rating. 1999. "Credit Rating and Diagnostic Reports." Harare.

———. 2000. "Credit Ratings and Diagnostics of Local Authorities: Round II." Harare.

Ebel, Robert, and Serdar Yilmaz. 2001. "Fiscal Decentralization: Is It Happening? How Do We Know?" Conference in Honor of Richard Bird, Conference at Georgia State University, Atlanta, April 4–6. [http://isp-aysps.gsu.edu/papers/ebel2001.pdf].

Ebel, Robert, Istvan Varfalvi, and Sandor Varga. 1998. "Sorting Out Intergovernmental Roles and Responsibilities in the Hungarian Transition." In Lajos Bokros and Jean Jacques Dethier, eds., *Public Finance Reform during the Transition: The Experience of Hungary.* Washington, D.C.: World Bank.

Eddy, Jane. 2002. "Local Government Ratings in Emerging Markets." *Local and Regional Government: 2002.* Standard & Poor's Corporation, New York, NY. March, p. 13.

Esters, Christian, and Myriam Fernandez De Heredia. 2002. "Research: Wroclaw, City of." Standard & Poor's. RatingsDirect, New York.

Estirn, Saul. 2002. "Competition and Corporate Governance in Transition." *Journal of Economic Perspectives* (Winter): 77–100.

Financial Executives Institute of the Philippines. 2000. *Municipal Bonds: A Manual.* Manila.

Firdausy, Carunia Mulya. 2002. "Study of Local Government Finance and Bond Market Financing in Indonesia." Center for Economic Research – Indonesian Institute of Science, Jakarta, Indonesia.

Fitch Ratings. 2000. *The Polish Banking System.* London. [http://www.fitchratings.com]. September 2002.

Fitch Polska. 2001. News Archives, Poland. [http://www.fitchpolska.com.pl/news.htm]. November 2002.

Freire, Mila, M. Huertas, and B. Darche. 1998. *"Subnational Access to the Capital Markets: The Latin American Experience."* Paper presented at the First World Bank Conference on Capital Market Development at the Subnational Level, Santander, Spain, October.

Gavino, Carlos. 1998. "LGU Financing: Present Sources, Availability, and Terms." Coordinating Council of the Philippines Assistance Program and U.S. Agency for International Development, Manila.

GFOA (Government Finance Officers Association). 1991. *Disclosure Guidelines for State and Local Government Securities*. Chicago.

Giugale, Marcelo, F. H. Trillo, and J. C. Oliveira. 2000. *Achievements and Challenges of Fiscal Decentralization: Lessons from Mexico*. Washington, D.C.: World Bank.

Giugale, Marcelo, Olivier Lafourcade, and Nghuyen Vinh H., eds. 2001. *Mexico: A Comprehensive Development Agenda for the New Era*. Washington, D.C.: World Bank.

Giugale, Marcelo, F. H. Trillo, and J. C. Oliveira. 2000. "Subnational Borrowing and Debt Management." In Marceo Giugale and Steve Webb, eds. *Achievements and Challenges of Fiscal Decentralization: Lessons from Mexico*. Chapter 6. Washington, D.C.: World Bank.

Glasser, Matthew, ed. 1998. *Formulation of a Regulatory Framework for Municipal Borrowing in South Africa*. Research Triangle Park, N.C.: Research Triangle Institute.

Halligan, Olaim. 1996. *Municipal Bonds in Russia*. Moscow: Russian European Center for Economic Policy.

Havel, Vaclav. 2002. "The Value of Transparency in Conducting Monetary Policy: The Czech Experience." *Federal Reserve Bank of St. Louis Review* 84 (4):160–61.

Hegedus, Jozsef, and Gabor Peteri. 1997a. "Local Finance and Municipal Financial Management in Hungary." In Jozsef Hegedus and Gabor Peteri, eds., *The Modernization of Local Government Finances and Financial Management in Hungary*. Proceedings of a conference organized by the Metropolitan Research Institute, Budapest, April 1996.

Hegedus, Jozsef, and Gabor Peteri, eds. 1997b. *The Modernization of Local Government Finances and Financial Management in Hungary*. Budapest: Metropolitan Research Institute.

Hegedus, Jozsef. 1999. "Hungarian Local Governments." In Emil J. Kirchner, ed., *Decentralization and Transition: The Visegrad*. New York: Macmillan Publishers.

Heslam, David, and Sharon Raj. 2002. "Credit Analysis: Czech Republic." Fitch Ratings. New York.

Hertelendy, Zsofia, and Mihály Kópanyi. 2000. "Municipal Enterprises." World Bank, Washington, D.C.

Huang, Yiping. 1998. "Challenges for China's Financial Reform." Asia Pacific School Economics and Management: The Australian National University. Asia Pacific Press.

IMF (International Monetary Fund). 2002. *Global Financial Stability Report: Market Developments and Issues.* Washington, D.C.

———. 2002a. *Government Finance Statistics Yearbook 2002.* Washington, D.C.

———. 2002b. International Financial Statistics Yearbook 2002. Washington, D.C.

India, Ministry of Finance. 1997. *Economic Survey 1997.* New Delhi.

———. 2000. *Public Finance Statistics 1999–2000.* New Delhi.

———. 2001. *Economic Survey 2000–2001.* New Delhi.

India, National Commission to Review the Working of the Constitution. 2001. "Effectiveness of the Public Audit System in India: Reforming the Institution of the Comptroller and Auditor General (CAG)." Consultation paper. New Delhi.

India Infrastructure Report. 2003. "Governance Issues for Commercialization." 3iNetwork, Ahmedabad, India.

Irwin, Christopher. 2000. "China: Redesigning The Local Government Fiscal System." *Local and Regional Government: 2000.* Standard & Poors' Company New York.

Johnson, B., and M. Kimberley. 1999. "Analysis of Legislation and Policies Relating to Municipal Finance in Zimbabwe." Prepared for Rural Unity for Development Organization and U.S. Agency for International Development, Harare.

Johnson, Brad, and John Petersen. 2002. "On-lending Programs for Local Government Capital Investments: Creation of a Special Financial Intermediary." U.S. Agency for International Development/Indonesia, Jakarta.

Jokay, Károly. 1997. "Assessing Municipality Borrowers in Transition Economies." *Transition* 8 (5).

Jókay, Károly, Judit Kálmán, and Mihály Kopány. 1998. "Municipal Infrastructure Financing In Hungary: Four Cases." World Bank, Washington, D.C.

Jókay, Károly, Gabor Szepesi, and Gyorgy Szmetana. 2000. "Municipal Debt Management and Bankruptcy Intervention in Hungary: Case Studies and Lessons Learned (1996–2000)." World Bank, Subnational Development Program, Washington, D.C.

Kang, Jia. 2002 "Study on Local Government Debt Financing in the Peoples Republic of China." Asian Development Bank, Manila.

Kamenickova, Vera. 1999a. "Fiscal Decentralization in the Czech Republic." Project 180-0034. The Urban Institute and U.S. Agency for International Development, Washington, D.C.

————. 1999b. "Reforms of Public Administration and Establishment of Regional Self-Governments in the Czech Republic within the Framework of the E.U. Accession." In Eric Von Breska and Martin Brusis, eds., *Central and Eastern Europe on the Way into the European Union*. Munich: Centrum fur Angewandte Politikforschung, Ludwig Maximilians-Universitat.

Kehew, Robert. 2002. "Use of Betterment Fees in San Pedro Sula." Lincoln Land Institute, Case Study for the Value Capture Study. Cambridge, Mass.

Kehew, Robert, Jack Bates, Brad Johnson, John Petersen, Prima Setiawan, and Jesus Tirona. 2002. "Local Government Finance Policy Framework Study: Assessment of Current Conditions and Future Requirements." U.S. Agency for International Development/Indonesia, Jakarta.

Ke-young Chu and John Norregard. 1997. "Korea." In Teresa Ter-Minassian, ed., *Fiscal Federalism in Theory and Practice*. Washington, D.C.: International Monetary Fund.

Kim, Junghun. 2002. "Local Government Finance and Bond Market Financing in Korea. Asian Development Bank. (November).

Kopányi, Mihály, Samir El-Daher, Deborah Wetzel, Michel Noel, and Anita Papp. 2000. *Modernizing the Subnational Government System*. Washington, D.C.: World Bank.

Lane, Timothy D. 1993. "Market Discipline." *IMF Staff Papers* Vol. 40 (March 1993), 53–88.

Lardy, Nicholas R. 2002. *Integrating China into the Global Economy*. Washington D.C.: The Brookings Institution.

Leigland, James. 1998. "Municipal Bond Tax Exemption in Emerging Economies." Finance Working Paper. Report 92/42. United States Agency for International Development, Washington, D.C.

Lewis, Blane. 2001. "Local Government Borrowing and Repayment in Indonesia: Does Fiscal Capacity Matter?" U.S. Agency for International Development/RTI, Perform Project. U.S. Agency for International Development/Indonesia, Jakarta.

————. 2002. "Fiscal Decentralization: White Paper." U.S. Agency for International Development/RTI, Perform Project. U.S. Agency for International Development/Jakarta.

Li-Gang, Liu. 2003. "Avoiding Chaos: Sequencing Financial Reform in China." Asian Development Bank Institute (unpublished paper).

Li-Gang, Liu, and Giovanni Ferri. 2002. "How Do Global Credit Rating Agencies Rate Firms from Developing Countries?" (forthcoming, *Asian Economic Papers*).

Llanto, Gilbert, Rosario Manasan, Mario Lamberte, and Jaime Laya. (1998) *Local Government Units' Access to the Private Capital Markets.* Manila: Philippine Institute for Development Studies.

Ma, Jun. 2000. "Design and Implementation of a Fiscal Early Warning System for Subnational Governments." World Bank, Washington, D.C.

Malathi, S. 2000. "Urban Reforms in Tamil Nadu." World Bank Institute, Urban and City Management Program, Washington, D.C.

Mathur, O. P. 1999. "Decentralization in India: A Report Card." In D. K. Srivastava, ed., *Contemporary Fiscal Issues: Papers for the Eleventh Finance Commission.* New Delhi: Har-Anand Publications.

McCormack, James, and Sharon Raj. 2002. "Comment: The Polish Fiscal Glass—Half Empty or Half Full?" Fitch Ratings, New York.

Mihajek, Dubravko. 1997. "Japan." In Teresa Ter-Minassian and J. Craig, eds., *Fiscal Federalism in Theory and Practice.* Washington, D.C.: International Monetary Fund.

Moody's Investors Service. 1998. *Subnational Governments: A Rating Agency Perspective.* New York: Global Credit Research.

Moody's Investors Service. 2002. "Metropolitan Government of Seoul: Global Credit Report," New York (November).

Montmaur, Valerie, Lana Pukovic, and Yves Lemay. 2001. "Global Credit Research Analysis: Poznan, City of." Moody's Investors Service. New York.

Noel, Michel. 2000. "Building Subnational Debt Markets in Developing and Transition Countries: A Framework for Analysis, Policy Reform and Assistance Strategy." Policy Research Working Paper 2339. World Bank, Private and Financial Sectors Development Unit, Europe and Central Asia Region, Washington, D.C.

Okorotchenko, Elena. 2001. "Commentary: Czech Government Reform Could Lead to Significant Changes for Local Governments." Standard & Poor's RatingsDirect, New York.

Orial, Lydia. 2000. "Business Options: Mixed Signals." *Manila Bulletin,* 19 October, p. 2.

OTP Bank. 2003. Documentation for the company's annual general meeting, 25 April (translation). [http://www.fornax.hu/cgi-bin/bet_file_en.cgi?file=iksz_3399_0].

PADCO and Techfin Research. 1999. "Zimbabwe Local Government Capital Development Project: Capital Markets Study." Vol. 2. Harare.

Pallai, Katalin. 2000. "The Framework of Decentralization." World Bank, Washington, D.C.

———— 2000. Financial Management Reform in the Municipality of Budapest. Fiscal Policy Training Program 2001, Fiscal Decentralization Course July 23–August 3, 2001, Atlanta, Georgia. World Bank Institute, Washington, D.C.

Peteri, Gabor. 1993. "From the Enterprising Local Government Towards Local Economic Development." *Private Sector Development and Local Government in Hungary*. Budapest: Public Policy Institute.

Peteri, Gabor, and Glen Wright. 1994. "Local Government Issues in Hungary." Report to Hungarian Parliament Committee on Local Government, Public Administration, Internal Security and Policy, Budapest.

Petersen, John. 1998. "A Primer on State Bond Banks in the United States." Paper presented at the First Conference on Capital Market Development for Subsovereign Governments, World Bank, Santander Spain, October.

————. 1998. "Building a Municipal Bond Market in the Philippines." ARD and U.S. Agency for International Development, GOLD (Governance and Local Democracy) project, Manila.

————. 2002. "Romanian Cities Go to Market." Romania Decentralization Project. United States Agency for International Development, Washington, D.C.

Petersen, John, and Victor Chomentowski. 1999. "Local Government Debt and Financial Monitoring in Poland." Report prepared for the U.S. Agency for International Development, Poland Project. Urban Institute, Washington, D.C.

Petersen, John E., and John Crihfield. 1998. "Linkages between Subnational Governments and the Credit Markets." World Bank, Washington, D.C.

Petersen, John, and John Crihfield. 2000. *Developing Subsoverign Credit Markets*. Washington, D.C.: World Bank.

Peterson, George. 1999. "Building Local Credit Systems." World Bank, Urban Mangement Program, Washington, D.C.

Phelps, P. 1997. "Expanding Municipal Finance in Zimbabwe: Recommendations for Addressing Current Constraints." Prepared for Rural Unity for Development Organization and U.S. Agency for International Development, Harare.

Philippines, Department of Finance. 1996. "LGU Financing of Basic Services and Infrastructure Projects: A New Vision and Policy Framework." Manila.

———. 2000. "Joint Memorandum Circular: Establishing a Monitoring Framework and Disclosure System for Local Government Bond Flotations." Manila. Third draft, November.

Pigey, Julianna. 1999. "Fiscal Decentralization and Local Government Finance in Hungary 1989-1999." U. S. Agency for International Development, Washington, D.C.

Pinto, Brian, Vladimir Drebenstov, and Alexander Morozov. 2000. *Dismantling Russia's Nonpayments System and Creating Conditions for Growth.* Technical Paper. World Bank, Washington D.C.

Polackova Brixi, Hana, Allen Schick, and Leila Zlaoui. 2000. "The Challenge of Fiscal Risks in Transition: The Case of the Czech Republic, Bulgaria and Hungary." World Bank, European and Central Asia Region, Washington, D.C.

Pradhan, H. K. 2002. "Local Government Finance and Bond Market Financing: India." Xavier Labour Relations Institute, Jamshedpur, India.

Prud'homme, R. 1999. "Subsovereign Bond Issues: The Experience of Zimbabwe." Prepared for World Bank Joint Program on Subsovereign Capital Markets, Harare.

Rajivan, K. 1999. "The Tamil Nadu Urban Development Fund (TNUDF): A Case Study." World Bank Institute, Urban and City Management Program, Washington, D.C.

———. 2003. "Strengthening Urban Management: India, Unlocking the Potential of Cities." Presentation for the World Bank Institute, Urban and City Management Program, January, Hyderabad, India.

Rao, M. Govinda. 2000. "Fiscal Decentralization in Indian Federalism." Paper presented at the International Monetary Fund Conference on Fiscal Decentralization, 20–21 November, Washington, D.C. Institute for Social and Economic Change, Bangalore.

Rao, M. Govinda, and Nirvikar Singh. 2000. "The Political Economy of Center-State Fiscal Transfers in India." Working paper. Stanford University, Center for Research on Economic Development and Policy Reform, Stanford, Calif.

Reed, John. 2003. "World Report: Poland—Koldko Fights to See His Plan." *Financial Times,* 15 April.

Reserve Bank of Zimbabwe. 1997. *Quarterly Economic Statistical Bulletin* (September–December). Harare.

———. 1999. Quarterly Economic and Statistical Review 21 (1, 2). Harare.

Rekhviashvili, Irakli. 1998. "Decentralization Experience and Reforms: Case Study on Hungary." World Bank, Washington, D.C.

Rekhviashvili, Irakli. 2001. "Decentralization Experience and Reforms: Case Study on Hungary." Report prepared for the World Bank Institute Intergovernmental Fiscal Relations and Local Financial Management Program, Washington, D.C.

Republic of South Africa. 1998 *White Paper on Local Government*. Pretoria

———. 2000. Policy Framework for Municipal Borrowing and Financial Emergencies: Pretoria.

Rodrik, Dani. 2003. "Growth Strategies." Paper prepared for *Handbook of Economic Growth* (Forthcoming) Harvard University. Cambridge, Massachusetts.

Rosen, David. 2002. *An Investor's Perspective on Subnational Borrowing*. Subnational Credit Market Project. World Bank. Washington, D.C.

Schiffer, Jonathan R, Joan Feldbaum-Vidra, and David H. Levey. 2002. "Opinion Update: Poland." Moody's Investors Service, New York.

Schuler, K., D. Sheets, and D. Weig. 1998. *Money Markets in Selected Southern African Countries* CAER Discussion Paper No. 20. U.S. Agency for International Development, Washington, D.C.

Serrano Castro, Julio. 2002. Presentation at "Primer Seminario de Financiamiento Estatal y Municipal," Asociación Mexicana de Intermediarios Bursátiles. [http://www.amib.com.mx/seminarioFinEstMun/11.AMIBJSC.ppt].

Shiria, Sayuri. 2002. *Is the Equity Market Really Developed in the People's Republic of China?* Research Paper 41, Asian Development Bank Institute, Tokyo.

Smith, Richard. 1998. "1999 May Prove to Be Pivotal Year." *Standard and Poor's Bond Insurance Book 1998*. New York: Standard & Poor's.

Smoke, Paul. 1999. "Improving Local Infrastructure Finance in Developing Countries through Grant-Loan Linkages: Ideas from Indonesia's Water Sector." *International Journal of Public Administration*: 1561–85.

Spahn, Paul Bernd. 1997. "Decentralized Government and Macroeconomic Control." *Infrastructure Notes Newsletter*. Urban No. FM-12. Washington, D.C.: World Bank.

Sprio, Nicholas. 2003. "World Report: Poland—The Big Credit Squeeze Is On." *Financial Times*, 15 April.

Stalebrink, Odd. 2002. "Government Accounting and Financial Reporting in Transition: 'Earnings Management' under the Accrual and Consolidation Model." Unpublished doctoral dissertation, George Mason University, School of Public Policy, Fairfax, Virginia.

Standard & Poor's. 2002. Various issues. *Local and Regional Government Ratings*. New York.

Steffenson, J., and S. Trollegaard. 2000. Fiscal Decentralization and Sub-National Finance in Relation to Infrastructure and Service Provision: Synthesis Report of 6 Sub-Saharan African Country Studies. Study directed by the World Bank and financed by the Danish International Development Agency with support from the U.S. Agency for International Development, Washington, D.C.

Stiglitz, Joseph. 2002. *Globalization and Its Discontents.* New York: W. W. Norton.

Szepesi, Gabor, and Gyorgy Szmetana. 2000. "Municipal Debt Management and Bankruptcy Intervention in Hungary: Case Studies and Lessons Learned (1996-2000)." World Bank, Washington, D.C.

Tamil Nadu, Finance Department. 1996. *State Finance Commission Report.* Chennai, India.

————. 2000. Report of Second State Finance Commission: Summary of Findings and Recommendations. Chennai, India.

Tchepournykh, Maria, and William Simonsen. 1999. "The Development of a Municipal Bond Market in Russia: The Good, the Bad, and the Ugly." *Municipal Finance Journal* 20:1 (spring).

Ter-Minassian, Teresa, and Jon Craig. 1997. *Fiscal Federalism in Theory and Practice.* International Monetary Fund, Washington, D.C.

Ter-Minassian, Teresa, and Jon Craig. 1997. Control of Subnational Government Borrowing. In Ter-Minassian, Teresa (ed). *Fiscal Federalism in Theory and Practice.* Chapter 7. Washington, D.C.: International Monetary Fund.

Tirona, Jesus. 2001. Remarks of the president of the Local Government Unit Guarantee Corporation at the Asian Development Bank's Credit Assessment and Access Seminar, Manila, 30 January.

Tirona, Jesus. 2003. MAPping the Future: Philippine LGU Debt Market. *Manila Bulletin* June 11.

USAID (U.S. Agency for International Development). 1997. "Financial Institutions Reform and Expansion Project: Debt Component." USAID/India, Washington, D.C.

Varley, Robert. 2001. *Indonesia: Financing Small Scale Urban Infrastructure in the Era of Decentralization.* Manila: Asian Development Bank.

Veno, David, and Richard Smith. "Bond Insurers International Exposure; Opportunity Reward and Manageable Risk." Standard & Poor's Corporation, *Credit Week Municipal* (September 28, 1998), p. 21.

Wei, Feng. (2000) *China's Financial Sector Reform in the Transition to a Market Economy: Key issues and Policy Options.* Transaction Publishers, Rutgers University, New Brunswick.

Weitz, Ahmed. 2001. *Options for Municipal Finance in Indonesia.* Manila: Asian Development Bank.

Wong, Christine. 1999.. "Extra-budgetary Funds." Presentation at Intergovernmental Fiscal Relations and Local Financial Management Seminar, Economic Development Institute and the Learning and Leadership Center, World Bank, Chiang Mai, Thailand (March 3).

World Bank. 1995. "TNUDP Supervision Mission Note." International Development Association, Washington, D.C.

———. 1996. *Russian Federation: Toward Medium-Term Viability.* Washington, D.C.

———. 1998. "Zimbabwe: Financial Sector Review," Washington, D.C.

———. 1999a. "East-Asia Cross-Regional Study on Capital Markets Development at the Sub-National Level," Washington, D.C.

———. 1999b. "Project Appraisal: US$100 Million Loan to the Republic of the Philippines for a Local Government Finance and Development Project." Report 18971-PH, Washington, D.C.

———. 2000a. *World Development Report 1999/2000: Entering the 21st Century.* New York: Oxford University Press.

———. 2000b. "Municipal Finance in Brazil: Main Issues," Washington, D.C.

———. 2000c. Mainstreaming CDS: Experience of Tamil Nadu Urban Development Project, India, Presentation, February 2000, Washington, D.C.

———. 2001a. "Brazil: Financing Municipal Investment," Washington, D.C.

———. 2001b. "Options for Urban Local Governance Development Program (ULGRP) Proposed Support Facilities." Project Concept Document, East Asia and Pacific Region, Washington, D.C.

———. 2001c. "Decentralization in the Transition Economies: Challenges and the Road Ahead." Europe and Central Asia Region, Poverty Reduction and Economic Management Unit, Washington, D.C.

———. 2002a. *Global Development Finance 2002.* Washington, D.C.

———. 2002b. "Indonesia: Urban Local Governance Reform Project." Project Concept Document, Washington, D.C.

———. 2002c. *World Development Report 2002: Building Institutions for Markets.* New York: Oxford University Press.

———. 2002d. "China: National Development and Sub-National Finance." East Asia and Pacific Region Report No. 22951-China (April), Washington, D.C.

———. 2002e. Project Appraisal Document, Tamil Nadu Urban Development Fund, Washington, D.C.

World Bank Institute. 2000. *Building Subnational Debt Markets in Developing and Transitioning Economies.* Washington, D.C.

———. 2003a. " Project Appraisal Document: China, Shanghai Urban Environment Project, East Asia and Pacific Region: (May) Washington, D.C.

———. 2003b. "Subnational Government Access to the Credit Markets in Four Southeast Asian Countries A Reconnaissance: China Annex Materials, East Asia and Pacific Region (June), Washington D.C.

Xu, Xiaoping. 1998. *China's Financial System under Transition.* New York: St. Martin's Press, Inc.

Yergin, Daniel, and Joseph Stanislaw. 1999. *The Commanding Height.* New York: Simon and Shuster.

Zimbabwe, Central Statistical Office. 1999. *Quarterly Digest of Statistics* (June). Harare.

———. 2000. *National Accounts 1985–1999.* Harare. November.

Index

Note: italics used as follows:
f for figures, *n* for notes, *t*
for tables, *b* for boxes